GOTHIC
WRITERS

GOTHIC WRITERS

A Critical and Bibliographical Guide

Edited by
Douglass H. Thomson, Jack G. Voller,
and Frederick S. Frank

Greenwood Press
Westport, Connecticut • London

Library of Congress Cataloging-in-Publication Data

Gothic writers : a critical and bibliographical guide / edited by Douglass H. Thomson,
Jack G. Voller, and Frederick S. Frank.
    p. cm.
  Includes bibliographical references and indexes.
  ISBN 0–313–30500–5 (alk. paper)
    1. Gothic revival (Literature)—History and criticism.   2. Gothic revival
(Literature)—Bio-bibliography.   3. Horror tales—History and criticism.   4. Horror
tales—Bio-bibliography.   5. Fantasy fiction—History and criticism.   6. Fantasy
fiction—Bio-bibliography.   I. Thomson, Douglass H.   II. Voller, Jack G.   III. Frank,
Frederick S.
  PN3435.G68   2002
  809'.91—dc21   2001023325

British Library Cataloguing in Publication Data is available.

Library of Congress Catalog Card Number: 2001023325
ISBN: 0–313–30500–5

First published in 2002

Greenwood Press, 88 Post Road West, Westport, CT 06881
An imprint of Greenwood Publishing Group, Inc.
www.greenwood.com

Printed in the United States of America

∞

The paper used in this book complies with the
Permanent Paper Standard issued by the National
Information Standards Organization (Z39.48–1984).

10 9 8 7 6 5 4 3 2 1

CONTENTS

Preface   ix

Acknowledgments   xiii

Introduction   xv

John Aikin and Anna Laetitia Aikin Barbauld
Douglass H. Thomson   1

William Harrison Ainsworth
Jack G. Voller   7

Ueda Akinari
Frederick S. Frank   12

Gertrude Atherton
Jack G. Voller   20

Margaret Atwood
Carol Margaret Davison   24

Jane Austen and the *Northanger* Novelists (Lawrence Flammenberg
[Karl Friedrich Kahlert], Carl Grosse, Francis Lathom, Eliza Parsons,
Regina Maria Roche, and Eleanor Sleath)
Douglass H. Thomson and Frederick S. Frank   33

François Thomas Marie de Baculard d'Arnaud
Frederick S. Frank   48

William Beckford
Jack G. Voller   53

Ambrose Gwinett Bierce
Douglass H. Thomson   60

Charlotte Brontë and Emily Brontë
Douglass H. Thomson   69

Charles Brockden Brown
Douglass H. Thomson   76

Edward Bulwer-Lytton
Marie Mulvey-Roberts   83

Wilkie Collins
Frederick S. Frank   90

Charlotte Dacre [Rosa Matilda]
Douglass H. Thomson   99

Charles Dickens
Douglass H. Thomson   104

François Guillaume Ducray-Duminil
Frederick S. Frank   116

Mary Wilkins Freeman
Jack G. Voller   120

William Godwin
Douglass H. Thomson   125

Gothic Chapbooks, Bluebooks, and Short Stories in the Magazines
Frederick S. Frank   133

Gothic Drama
Frederick S. Frank   147

Nathaniel Hawthorne
Frederick S. Frank   165

E[rnst] T[heodor] A[madeus] Hoffmann
Douglass H. Thomson   177

James Hogg
Douglass H. Thomson   185

Washington Irving
Jack G. Voller   195

Henry James
Douglass H. Thomson   202

Stephen King
Tony Magistrale   212

Contents

Izumi Kyoka
Frederick S. Frank   225

D. H. Lawrence
John Humma   233

Sophia Lee
Douglass H. Thomson   241

Joseph Sheridan Le Fanu
Jack G. Voller   248

Matthew Gregory "Monk" Lewis
Jack G. Voller   254

George Lippard
Frederick S. Frank   261

H[oward] P[hillips] Lovecraft
S.T. Joshi   270

Arthur Machen
Jack G. Voller   278

Charles Robert Maturin
Jack G. Voller   283

Herman Melville
Douglass H. Thomson   290

Toni Morrison
David Dudley   295

Joyce Carol Oates
Susan Allen Ford   303

Flannery O'Connor
Douglass H. Thomson   315

Vladimir Fyodorovich Odoevsky
Frederick S. Frank   321

Edgar Allan Poe
Frederick S. Frank   330

John Polidori
Douglass H. Thomson   344

Ann Radcliffe
Frederick S. Frank   349

Clara Reeve
Jack G. Voller   361

Count Donatien Alphonse François Sade [the Marquis de Sade]
   Douglass H. Thomson   365

Friedrich von Schiller
   Tom Lloyd   372

Sir Walter Scott
   Michael Gamer   380

Mary Wollstonecraft Shelley
   Marie Mulvey-Roberts   389

Percy Bysshe Shelley
   Jack G. Voller and Douglass H. Thomson   399

Charlotte Turner Smith
   Jack G. Voller   408

Robert Louis Stevenson
   Douglass H. Thomson   412

Bram Stoker
   Jack G. Voller   420

Ludwig Tieck
   Tom Lloyd   429

Horace Walpole
   Frederick S. Frank   437

Timeline of Gothic Authors and Works (1762–1999)   449

General Bibliography of Critical Sources and Resources   457

Index of Authors and Titles   469

Index of Critics, Editors, and Translators   501

About the Editors and Contributors   515

PREFACE

Gothic Writers: A Critical and Bibliographical Guide is designed to accommodate the critical and bibliographical requirements of a broad spectrum of users from scholarly researchers in need of critical assistance to general readers seeking an introduction to the literature of the Gothic and its abundant criticism. Although it is primarily a reference work, the book is also an atlas of criticism and may be consulted selectively or perused chapter by chapter. Whether the user is an undergraduate seeking a promising topic for a term paper, a well-published academic seeking to stay abreast of contemporary developments in Gothic studies, or simply a curious reader perhaps delving into the Gothic for the first time, *Gothic Writers* will serve the diverse needs of these different categories of users.

No lengthy case needs to be made for a reference work of this type. The growth of both popular interest in the classical Gothic texts of the eighteenth century and academic research and writing about the Gothic during the last three decades of the twentieth century has made reliable reference works and current primary and secondary bibliographies not just necessary for students of the Gothic, but crucial because the database of Gothic fiction and criticism has proliferated almost exponentially since the great revival in Gothic studies commenced in the late 1950s. A glance at the "General Bibliography of Critical Sources and Resources" at the end of the volume will quickly reveal how extremely busy the production of Gothic criticism has been over the last three decades as well as the acceleration of writing about Gothic in the 1990s. Confronted with so much material, compilers of reference works and bibliographies have not been able to keep up with the flood tide of publications, although several admirable attempts have been made. In the 1990s, the field saw the publication of Neil Barron's *Horror Literature: A Reader's Guide*, first published in 1990 and reissued in expanded form in 1999 as *Fantasy and Horror: A Critical and Historical Guide to Literature, Illustration, Film, TV, Radio, and the Internet*. In 1998 alone, three outstanding reference works appeared: Marie Mulvey-Roberts's *The Handbook to Gothic Literature*, a dictionary-style handbook of authors, themes, and "Gothic specialisms"; David Pringle's *St. James Guide to Horror, Ghost, and Gothic Writers*, containing over 400 Anglo-American-author entries and 90 foreign-language-writer entries; and Clive Bloom's *Gothic Horror: A Reader's Guide from Poe to King and Beyond*, a collection of critical extracts. *Gothic Writers* does not presume to replace these recent reference works, but it does seek to go beyond them by offering several unique features that both professional researchers and informal users should find valuable.

In its coverage, *Gothic Writers* strives to reflect the repercussions of the broader application of the adjective "Gothic" currently used to describe many works and writers not previously associated with horror literature.[1] A decade ago, D.H. Lawrence and Friedrich Schiller would not have been included in a book of this type, and non-Western writers, such as the two Japanese Gothicists Ueda Akinari and Izumi Kyoka, would have been overlooked or omitted. By acknowledging the evolving critical expansion of the Gothic label and by including writers outside the canon or unknown to Western readers, *Gothic Writers* is designed to widen the scope of Gothic studies in general and to redelineate the parameters of the term. The very dynamism of the adjective "Gothic" and the ongoing debate over its meaning and application, then, have governed the selection of writers included in *Gothic Writers*. The user will find coverage of all of the major Gothic writers in Great Britain and the United States together with many Gothic authors once considered minor figures in both countries who have now risen to major status. Charlotte Dacre [Rosa Matilda] among the English Gothics and George Lippard among the American Gothics are prominent examples of the shift from obscurity to centrality that numerous forgotten Goths are now undergoing. Once regarded by literary historians as an almost exclusively Anglo-American literary movement, the Gothic today is widely accepted as a global genre free of restrictive chronological or national boundaries. This fact, along with the realization that the Gothic can no longer be consigned to a single time period as it was once assigned to the late eighteenth century, has dictated the choice of authors from Horace Walpole in the eighteenth century to Joyce Carol Oates and Stephen King in the twentieth. Even the purists are beginning to concede that Gothicism is less a genre frozen in time than an impulse spanning cultures, nations, and historical periods; *Gothic Writers* endeavors to register this shift.

Gothic Writers is organized into fifty-four entries arranged alphabetically rather than chronologically. Hence the atemporality of the Gothic form itself is reflected in the nonchronological structure of *Gothic Writers*. For users who are uncomfortable with a lack of sequential dating of the authors and their works a chronological listing of writers and titles is provided in the backmatter, creating a timeline from Walpole's *Castle of Otranto* (1764) to the present day. Three of the entries, "Gothic Chapbooks," "Gothic Drama," and "Jane Austen and the *Northanger* Novelists," involve groups of writers. All of the other entries are author-specific discussions of approximately fifty writers from around the world. Each entry consists of a listing of "Principal Gothic Works" and "Modern Reprints and Editions" followed by a critical commentary and analytic evaluation of the author's Gothic status. Annotated bibliographies of "Selected Criticism" embracing current and historical opinion are appended to all entries and are intended to serve as topical bibliographies that might prompt further investigation. With close to 1,000 annotated entries in the "Selected Criticism" sections of *Gothic Writers*, the bibliographies provide access to an enormous body of scholarship and testify to the past and present range of Gothic criticism; the entries identify the key issues in various critical debates about the nature and worth of Gothic fiction, including significant shifts in the meaning of the term and the emergent debate over the success or failure of the Gothic as a form. Consulted in tandem with the critical titles listed in the "General Bibliography of Critical Sources and Resources," the author-specific listings under "Selected Criticism" will equip the user of *Gothic Writers* to grasp both the texts and the contexts of the Gothic movement. One subsection of the "General Bibliography," "Web Sites and Internet Resources," merits special comment. Web sites dedicated to various aspects of the Gothic and to individual authors (many of these of no relevance whatsoever to the Gothic researcher) can be found across the Internet. The sites listed in this subsection of the "General Bibliography" contain information about links for accessing those sites on the Internet that are most germane to the serious scholar. Titles in the "General Bibliography" are usually not repeated in the "Selected Criticism" sections and vice versa.

The two indexes, an Authors/Titles Index and a Critics/Editors/Translators Index, are self-explanatory and allow multiple points of entry for the researcher. The critics index also shows the names of all editors, compilers, and translators. The author title/index shows primary works and authors' names mentioned in the entries.

The editors invite comments and suggestions on any aspect of the book's format or content. Our constant goal has been to produce a reliable and current guide to and through the expanding Gothic universe.

NOTE

1. For an eloquent defense of the conservative or historically restrictive use of the term "Gothic," see Maurice Lévy, " 'Gothic' and the Critical Idiom," in *Gothick Origins and Innovations* (Amsterdam and Atlanta, GA: Rodopi, 1994); Costerus New Series edition 91, 1–15. For a very broad and nontraditional application of the term "Gothic," see Mark Edmundson, *Nightmare on Main Street: Angels, Sadomasochism, and the Culture of the Gothic* (Cambridge; MA: Harvard University Press, 1997). To observe the term "Gothic" in transition, see Henry J. Hughes, "Familiarity of the Strange: Japan's Gothic Tradition," *Criticism* 42 (2000): 59–89. "Japanese Gothic shares with the West its subversion of religious and social norms, an obsession with sex and death, and a fear of the supernatural or unknown. These are human qualities, not the province of one culture. 'Gothic' is a translation term." (60).

ACKNOWLEDGMENTS

The editors of *Gothic Writers* would like to express their fullest appreciation to our contributors from Canada, the United Kingdom, and the United States whose knowledge of and enthusiasm for various Gothic writers they have so willingly shared. Our own views of the Gothic have been challenged, sharpened, and enriched by the energetic scholarship of all those who helped to build this book. Deepest thanks to Michael Gamer of the University of Pennsylvania; David Dudley, John Humma, and Tom Lloyd of Georgia Southern University; S.T. Joshi of New York City; Carol Davison of the University of Windsor; Marie Mulvey-Roberts of the University of the West of England; Susan Allen Ford of Delta State University; and Tony Magistrale of the University of Vermont. Their specific contributions to *Gothic Writers* may be found in "About the Authors and Contributors." The intellectual dedication of all of these students of the Gothic enhances the book throughout and demonstrates anew the value of co-operative scholarship as a creative venture.

Frederick S. Frank
Douglass H. Thomson
Jack G. Voller

INTRODUCTION

THE CHANGING CRITICAL FORTUNES OF THE GOTHIC; OR, VICE REWORDED

> The vicious taste of our modern Ratcliffe, Monk Lewis, German Romances—Take as a specimen the last, I have read, the Bravo of Venice/in the combination of the highest sensation, wonder of effects produced by supernatural power, without the means—thus gratifying our instinct of free-will that would fain be emancipated from the thraldom of ordinary nature—& would indeed annihilate both space & time—with the lowest of all human scarce-human faculties—viz—Cunning—low thieves' Cunning—Trap door—picklocks—low confederacies &c/Can these things be admired without a bad effect on the mind.
>
> Samuel Taylor Coleridge (*Notebooks*. V.3. Ed. Kathleen Coburn. 3449)

Coleridge's musing in his *Notebook* entry from 1808 bears the candid testimony of an earnestly moral critic attempting to come to terms with the disturbing power of Gothic literature. His ambivalence also typifies the varied range of responses that have characterized critical reaction to the Gothic from the earliest reviews of Walpole down to present times. The problem for Coleridge and many subsequent commentators is that while this literature ostensibly panders to the "lowest of all human scarce-human faculties," with its reliance on stock conventions to do so, it still comes uncomfortably close to eliciting from the reader the kind of response associated with high visionary (and profoundly Coleridgean) literature: a thrilling sense of the mind emancipated from the ordinary restraints of nature, time, and space. How can such a "vicious" literature gratify instincts the Romantic imagination equates with our greatest capacity for creativity and even divinity? A brief history of critical reaction to Gothic literature provides a rich variety of answers to Coleridge's final, unanswered, and endlessly provocative question, ranging from philosophical elaborations upon his moral and aesthetic premises to psychoanalytic subversions of them. More recent critical studies that analyze the power of the Gothic achievement take a different direction by grounding it very specifically in time and space, by reading it as a reflection of historical change and of the always-contested region where cultural values are formed. These new studies have stimulated an invigoration of Gothic studies, as we witness a dismantling of Coleridge's implied distinction between high and low literary cultures and a rewording of his alarm about imaginative virtue assailed by popular vice. But the best of these studies still address his disturbing question of why the Gothic should exert such a powerful hold upon its readers, and perhaps especially upon those readers who would otherwise reject or disparage it.

EARLY REACTIONS AND THEIR CRITICAL DESCENDANTS

The earliest critics of the Gothic in the English press establish the double plot of its reception, as their vehement reaction against "the trashy fantasies and cheap excitements of the Terror school" betrays anxiety about this fiction's great popular appeal.[1] Wordsworth's withering contempt for these "frantic novels" that cater to a "degrading thirst after outrageous stimulation" (600) represents a culmination of anti-Gothic commentary, reaching back to the first notices of *The Castle of Otranto*—"composed of such rotten materials, [it] is a phenomenon we cannot account for"[2]—and finding its most spectacular demonstration in the controversy engendered by Matthew Gregory Lewis's *Monk*. Most of these negative reviews build a moral argument upon an aesthetic premise: because Gothic fiction does not appeal to our more refined perceptions but instead panders to such low impulses as mere "curiosity," "a craving for extraordinary incident," and an overheated sensibility, it "blunt[s] the discriminating powers of the mind" (600) and impairs active sympathy and serious moral reflection. Given "the magnitude of the general evil" (600)—and perhaps here Wordsworth refers to the flood of shilling shockers and pulp Gothics that were all the rage in the 1790s—one can understand the fiercely negative reaction, certainly from an Enlightenment perspective, reaching back to Samuel Johnson's warnings in *The Rambler* about the deleterious effects of fiction, but also from the emerging aesthetics of Romanticism and its emphasis on a lyrical (or less "incident"-driven) imagination.[3]

Yet many subplots complicate this main assault on the Gothic as the literature of vice, not the least of which is the Romantic poets' frequent appropriation of Gothic materials in their writings.[4] One enduring strand of critical reaction finds writers offering philosophical defenses of the Gothic that challenge its denigration on moral and aesthetic terms. Early on we find an attempt, based on Edmund Burke's analysis of the sublime, to discover a redemptive value in the literature of terror. John Aikin and Anna Laetitia Aikin make this bold argument in favor of "The Pleasure Derived from Objects of Terror": "Where the agency of invisible beings is introduced, of 'forms unseen, and mightier far than we,' our imagination, darting forth, explores with rapture the new world which is laid open to its view, and rejoices in the expansion of its powers. Passion and fancy cooperating elevate the soul to its highest pitch; and the pain of terror is lost in amazement" (Skarda and Jaffe's *The Evil Image*, 13). The Aikins also insist that "the more wild, fanciful and extraordinary are the circumstances of a scene of horror, the more pleasure we receive from it" (124); where the scene is "too near common nature" (124), we will be disgusted by it. Although Ann Radcliffe in her fiction preferred only the illusion of the "extraordinary" (later called the "explained supernatural"), she echoes the Aikins' distinction between the high and low Gothic, insisting on a difference between mere "horror," a vulgar and debased response, and a higher mode of "terror" that leads to an apprehension of the sublime ("On the Supernatural in Poetry," 1826). Yet the terms of these distinctions have proved highly malleable. In the charged aesthetics of the 1790s, for example, at a time when literary forms of terror become entangled with the real Terror abroad, the distinction between "natural" (read "domestic") and "extraordinary" (read "foreign") was used by many critics in an exact inversion of the Aikins' terms. Coleridge, for example, indicts the Gothic for its "attempt to please by what is unnatural . . . by a departure from the observance of real life" (*The Critical Review* 23 [1798]: 167)—arguably the Aikins' primary criterion for the sublime in terror.

Despite the fluidity of such distinctions, one continues to find a fondness for dialectical ordering of the Gothic experience in the more philosophical approaches of today. S.L. Varnado defends the Gothic as a "numinous" literature whose primary value is the way it unsettles our complacent assumptions about the phenomenal world; he argues against those who would dismiss the Gothic as too unreal or removed from human experience or "morally neutral" by insisting that it has much "to say about man's ethical condition" (132). Tzvetan Todorov's influential distinction between the "marvelous" and the "uncanny" advances Radcliffe's contrast between "real" horror and imaginable terror by focusing on what may be called "the uncertainty principle" of Gothic fiction, the way it challenges a reader to choose between accepting its premises (the "marvelous") or prosecuting them (the "uncanny"). These and other dialectical approaches, ably demonstrated by Jack Voller's *The Supernatural Sublime*, attest to the serious philosophical interest in what many early detractors considered the least intellectually respectable of all literary genres.

Another strand that powerfully complicates the moral argument against Gothic literature is attention to its political dimensions. Thanks to the efforts of such critics as Ronald Paulson, Maurice Lévy, and E.J. Clery (to name only a very few), we now read the moral strictures against the Gothic in the late eighteenth century as reflections of the anxiety occasioned by this revolutionary period of political and economic change. Some of the earliest reactions to the Gothic phenomenon recognize the politically volatile nature of the genre: an anonymous critic in the *Monthly Magazine* of 1797 memorably terms the genre the "terrorist system of novel-writing," and the Marquis de Sade in his essay "Idée sur les romans" perceives the English Gothic novel as "the inevitable product of the revolutionary shocks with which the whole of Europe resounded" (Sage 1990, 120). Whether from an eighteenth-century or a twentieth-century perspective, political readings of the Gothic once again emphasize its dual nature. On the one hand, with its gallery of dissipated aristocrats and long-suffering bourgeoisie heroes and heroines, the Gothic almost too obviously expresses middle-class rage against unchecked aristocratic power. On the other, its often-conservative framework, especially in what critics identify as "the female Gothic," works constantly to undercut or to contain its more anarchic energies, providing a moral proving ground in which virtue and a whole range of domestic values are rewarded.

Perhaps no approach to Gothic literature more sharply complicates the moral arguments against it than a religious reading, the very quarter from which one would most expect it to be considered sacrilegious (one recalls, for example, Coleridge's fervent diatribe against Lewis's blasphemous use of Scripture in *The Monk*). Religious historians of the sectarian age in which the Gothic was conceived have revealed a host of ironies regarding its frequent condemnation from the pulpit. For one thing, many critics pointed to the too-enlightened and rational religion of the late eighteenth century, with its dismissal of "superstition," as giving rise to the Gothic penchant for the miraculous and the irrational: what conventional religious belief failed to satisfy, the Gothic novelists did.[5] Once again, we encounter an opposing thread of argument. Victor Sage enlarges upon the oft-noted anti-Catholic strain of Gothic fiction to argue that it is fundamentally a product of the Protestant imagination; other critics, such as James Rieger and Joel Porte, suggest that the power of much Gothic horror draws upon the return of traditional Christian teachings to haunt the freethinkers and radicals of the day. Consider the dark destiny awaiting that thrilling figure of the Gothic and Romantic imagination, the Promethean overreacher, from William Godwin's St. Leon to Mary Shelley's Frankenstein or from Charles Brockden Brown's Carwin to Herman Melville's Ahab. Consider the overreacher's terrifyingly orthodox and archetypally Gothic double: the Wandering Jew, the being who denies and mocks Christ only to be tormented throughout eternity for his blasphemy. Although Gothic literature has frequently been attacked from religious quarters, its critical history reveals how profoundly its tales of the supernatural draw from and powerfully rework traditional religious materials.

One can see, then, that from its inception, critical reaction to the Gothic has been characterized by a wonderful maze of cross-purposes that reflect the divided nature of the genre itself. The very term has generated two quite different critical narratives in the twentieth century: one of the strict constructionists who speak of the Gothic as a European literary phenomenon ranging from 1765 to 1820; the other of critics who treat the Gothic not so much as a genre as a literary "impulse" or mode of perception with broad dissemination abroad and beyond any defined period. *Gothic Writers* contains entries on just about all of the important early Gothic novelists as well as representative examples of later and non-Western storytellers writing in the Gothic spirit. Let us first turn to the story of the recovery of the traditional Gothic canon in the twentieth century before studying its recent dispersal across a range of genres and critical discourses.

ESTABLISHING A CANON OF THE FIRST GOTHICS IN THE TWENTIETH CENTURY

Edith Birkhead's *The Tale of Terror* (1921) inaugurates a new regard, both scholarly and popular, for the first Gothics, offering various categories of the British Gothic (for example, "Scott and the Novel of Terror," "Godwin and the Rosicrucian Novel") and an anticipatory consideration of American Gothicism. Eino Railo's *The Haunted Castle* (1927) and J.M.S. Tompkins's still-worthy *The Popular Novel in England, 1770–1800* (1932) provide early, requisite taxonomies, Railo through a catalog of favorite Gothic conventions and formulas (an enduring procedure for Gothic enthusiasts),[6] Tompkins through attention to the way the genre's often-labyrinthine plots opened up formal possibilities for the novel. With his ambitious *The Gothic Quest: A History of the Gothic Novel* (1938) and his frustrating but still-useful *A Gothic Bibliography* (1941), Montague Summers sought to recover, catalog, and interpret the many minor Gothic titles once lost to literary history. Although some of the enthusiasm and eccentricities of his method and that of his fellow pioneer in primary bibliography, Devendra Varma, incurred criticism from scholarly quarters concerning early Gothic studies (at this stage, hardly a respectable literary enterprise anyway), it is to the work of Summers and Varma that we owe the establishment of a canon for the first Gothic revival of 1764–1820. Various other scholars have followed their lead in exhuming and offering critical summaries of these "first Gothics."[7] Varma's thirty facsimile editions for Arno Press made available for the first time many Gothic titles that had fallen into oblivion. The original search for lost Gothic titles had been launched by Michael Sadleir in his persistent pursuit of the seven "horrid" novels mentioned in chapter 6 of Jane Austen's *Northanger Abbey*, a fascinating detective story told in the *Gothic Writers* entry on the subject. Today, the Sadleir-Black Collection in the Alderman Library of the University of Virginia remains the foremost research facility for the Gothic novel in its several mutations.

These pioneering critics performed a valuable service in recovering and fixing a canon of Gothic fiction in the 1764–1820 period. They further offered three historically sound explanations for placing its terminus at 1820 or thereabouts: the appearance around that date of three great, late novels that in their masterful reworking of earlier materials represent a culmination of the Gothic achievement, Mary Shelley's *Frankenstein* (1818), Charles Robert Maturin's *Melmoth the Wanderer* (1820), and James Hogg's *Confessions of a Justified Sinner*

(1824); the decisive parodies of *Northanger Abbey* (1818) and Thomas Love Peacock's grand spoofs, *Headlong Hall* (1816) and *Nightmare Abbey* (1818), which actually continue a long line of counter-Gothic satires reaching back into the 1790s; and Sir Walter Scott's naturalizing of Gothic themes in terms of the historical romance, a genre more congenial to later, Victorian tastes.[8] In establishing this historical niche for Gothic literature, these early scholars tended to regard the *genre noir* as a rebellion against tidily defined Enlightenment norms and to follow Mario Praz's influential *The Romantic Agony* (1933) in his conception of the Gothic as a dark, agonized anticipation of later forms of Romanticism. The effect, probably unintended, was to marginalize the Gothic by locating it within a larger literary movement as some minor aspect or aberration of that movement or its genres, such as the novel. This historical pedigree did little to advance serious critical study of the Gothic from the 1940s to the 1960s: the reigning formalist approach, with its emphasis on economy of expression, irony, and artful paradox, saw little commendable in the rambling plots and strident pieties of the Gothic novel;[9] scholars of American literature seeking to define a national grain under such banners as realism and naturalism also saw little value in this exotic import. Robert Hume's debate-stirring article "Gothic versus Romantic: A Reevaluation of the Gothic Novel" (1969) promised a new treatment of the Gothic as a "serious subject" for criticism, but in seeing the genre as "mired in the temporal [world] . . . and unresolvable ambiguities" as opposed to a Coleridgean "Romanticism" that "transcend[s] the flux of the purely temporal to find joy and security in a higher beauty" (290), Hume really just reiterates the idea of the Gothic as an unfinished or imperfect form of the Romantic. Characteristic of this approach is G.R. Thompson's collection *The Gothic Imagination: Essays in Dark Romanticism* (1974), which, despite its emphasis on treating the Gothic within the larger parameters of the Romantic, contains actually a number of still very valuable cross-disciplinary studies of its subject. Although by the 1960s and early 1970s the Gothic was becoming a subject fit for study and research, Thompson's preface to the volume still bears testimony to the precarious nature of the critical enterprise at this stage, as he offers an apologia for his fellow contributors bravely risking their professional reputations in addressing what was then such an academically suspect topic.

Today, with the enormous growth in Gothic studies, Thompson's defense has all the poignant charm of bygone days. Marilyn Gaull, editor of the journal *The Wordsworth Circle*, has expressed a mixture of chagrin and amazement about the burgeoning Gothic enterprise in her article "The Profession of Romanticism: Caverns Measureless and the Sunless Sea," noting that "[t]here were so many people engaged in producing works about the Gothic that we couldn't find anyone to write a review" (51). Her concern is understandable. In any given recent year, we can find an average of ten books on the subject and a spate of handbooks and bibliographies; dozens of articles plus a new academic society, the International Gothic Association, and its new journal, *Gothic Studies* (1999), an academic periodical to be dedicated entirely to Gothic matters; a plethora of

Web sites, some valuable, others less so; and an expanding number of courses in Gothic literature at all academic levels. What accounts for this second, belated Gothic revival? A cynic might answer that given the well-traveled critical terrain of the major authors and movements, a detour into the dark corridor of Gothic studies was professionally inevitable; an enthusiast might point to eerie parallels between today and those heady fin de siècle times of 200 years ago. One thing is clear: the very nature of the Gothic and its critical narrative up to this stage make it a perfect vehicle for the concerns of recent critical methodologies, especially their scrutiny of canon formation and reformation.

CRITICAL APPROACHES TO THE GOTHIC

One of these methodologies actually has a long and storied connection with the Gothic: the psychoanalytic approach. Today invigorated by Lacanian and feminist perspectives, psychologically oriented critics continue to find ever more sophisticated pathologies in its various languages of forbidden, thwarted, and perversely fulfilled desire.[10] Freud's famous essay on "The Uncanny" (see especially the entry in *Gothic Writers* on E.T.A. Hoffmann) seems in retrospect an inevitable meeting of method and subject matter, as he easily demonstrates the convention of the "explained supernatural" and other normative impulses of the early Gothics as mechanisms of repression that only fitfully shield or sublimate the genre's darker, instinctual drives. Employed in a broader cultural sense, the Freudian method sees the entire emergence of the Gothic obsession with forbidden realms of desire not as a reaction against the strictures of Right Reason and other such late-eighteenth-century superegos but as an inescapable consequence of the age's allegedly reductive pieties. While many critics have elaborated on this theory concerning the historical genesis of the Gothic, another effect of Freudian readings has been to move the very idea of the Gothic beyond its 1764–1820 context: now seen not so much as a discrete historical phenomenon but as an enduring instance of libidinal intrusion into the waking world, the idea of the Gothic becomes far more malleable and wide-ranging as an impulse always ready to articulate those dark secrets about ourselves we wish to deny. André Breton in his "Limites non Frontières du Surréalisme" (1937) championed the first Gothic novelists (and especially what he considered Walpole's "automatic writing") as a powerful model for the Surrealist attack on academic art. Leslie Fiedler with his *Love and Death in the American Novel* (1960) noisily marked an end to the sober neglect of the Gothic in American literature. In recanonizing Charles Brockden Brown as a seminal figure in the development of American literature, he stressed how the Gothic has always played a spoiler's role, in writings from Poe to the present, operating as a dark counternarrative to our reassuring national myths of progress and security. The "Selected Criticism" sections of *Gothic Writers* reveal the enormous influence of Freudian interpretation: countless Gothic bogeys and ghosts have been interpreted as sublimated expressions of various social and personal psychoses. One finds in these repetitious (almost compulsive from a Freudian perspective) acts of "discovery" a weird irony: these studies repeatedly advance the thesis that later Gothic writers, for example, from Poe to Oates, move the genre beyond a crude, otherwordly sense of evil to a psychological understanding of it, although the first Gothic writers themselves first provide the clue and material for such an understanding.

Although psychoanalytic interpretation was the earliest methodology to do so, it has been only one of many critical approaches to complicate Gothic literature's elemental presentation of good versus evil and its generic and historical parameters. With the advent of deconstructive reading, what once was considered the main flaw of the Gothic—its contradictions and irresolutions—quickly became something like its greatest virtue. Critics questioned traditional dialectical constructions (like Hume's) that subordinated Gothicism to Romanticism, finding instead that the two shared many epistemological uncertainties and complexities.[11] Jerold E. Hogle, with his many essays on the idea of a "Gothic Counterfeit," very deconstructively reads such typical conventions of the genre as false narrators and fake texts as tropes of its inherent textual instability and indeterminacy.[12] Typical of this new direction in Gothic studies is William Veeder's and Gordon Hirsh's *Dr. Jekyll and Mr. Hyde after One Hundred Years*, a collection of essays that productively complicate the novel's allegory of good versus evil through attention to its subversive syntax and its curious elision of the female.

The deconstruction of familiar ethical and aesthetic definitions of the Gothic opened the crypt for a whole range of new historical and cultural studies. Following the lead of Maurice Lévy, the first modern scholar to read the Gothic in the context of the French Revolution, many critics returned to the historical context of the first Gothics with fresh insight, finding in the novels both a contesting and a reflection of domestic ideology, a secret identification with the anarchic energies of revolution and an anxious desire to contain them.[13] In a final strange twist in the winding narrative of critical reactions to the Gothic, the genre now came to be regarded as a more telling register of social change and upheaval than Romantic literature and its familiar pattern of transcending the particular and the historical. Wordsworth, we remember, had attributed the public's taste for "frantic novels" to, in part, "the great national events daily taking place" (600): many materialist critics read Gothic novels as providing a more authentic commentary on those events than "natural piety" and other historical sublimations of the major poets.

Accompanying this energetic revisioning of the first Gothic revival came a number of studies that extend an understanding of Gothicism beyond historical and national boundaries. Louis Gross's *Redefining the American Gothic: From Wieland to Day of the Dead* (1989) boldly argues that "there is a more central position for the Gothic in American literature than in any other national literature"; he sees the mode as presenting "an alternative vision of American experience" that gives voice to those groups marginalized by the mainstream: women, gays, colonials, and, above all, African Americans as "the most wholly Other voice" in our fiction (2–3). Mark Edmundson's ambitious *Nightmare on Main Street: Angels, Sadomasochism, and the Culture of Gothic* (1997) examines how the libidinal energies of the Gothic have permeated the mainstream of American thought. In the contemporary world of O.J., the *Jerry Springer Show*, and slasher films, Edmunson finds "a culture at large that has become suffused with Gothic assumptions, with Gothic characters and plots" (12). In her *Gothic America: Narrative, History, and Nation* (1997), Teresa Goddu assails interior and psychological readings of the Gothic to demonstrate how "the Gothic disrupts the dream world of national myth with the nightmare of history" (4). These and other studies, some finding Gothic traits in writers as diverse as Gabriel García Marquez and Toni Morrison, have rewritten the idea of the Gothic as a distinct genre in favor of it as an "impulse" ranging across a range of literature. At times in the polemical discourse of postmodernism, the term almost figures as a metaphor for the abject and the marginalized, as we witness the revenge of popular culture upon the high literary culture that stigmatized it.

Because of the climactic role it has played in the chronicles of Gothic criticism, we have reserved the feminist approach to Gothic literature for last since it richly anticipates, includes, and offers variations on the other methodologies that are currently rewriting the history of Gothic studies. Feminist scholars share with the earlier bibliographers such as Summers and Lévy the quest to recover and edit Gothic titles by women authors who had been consigned to oblivion by literary history.[14] Under the potent term "female Gothic" they have defined a remarkably coherent and developing canon, reaching back to Clara Reeve and Ann Radcliffe, carrying on through such seemingly diverse nineteenth-century novelists as the Brontës, Charlotte Perkins Gilman, and E.D.E.N. Southworth, and continuing today with the popular Harlequin romances or, on the other hand, with the great achievements of Shirley Jackson, Joyce Carol Oates, and Angela Carter. Feminist critical approaches to the Gothic have opened a number of important new lines of inquiry. One line, developed in studies by Elaine Showalter, Juliann Fleenor, and Michelle Massé, among others, emphasizes the victimization of women in Gothic fiction, finding in the entrapped heroine and her sexual persecution powerful reflections and, sometimes, indictments of restrictive patriarchal social and filial structures. Another line, ably represented by Kay Mussell's *Fantasy and Reconciliation: Contemporary Formulas of Women's Romance Fiction* (1984), stresses how the female Gothic socializes its female audience, thrilling its readership with sexual terror and intrigue but safely returning them to the reassurance of a bourgeoisie closure. A third and relatively newer line of criticism follows Ellen Moer's in reusing her term "female Gothic" to reveal the ways that the Gothic enables expression of female rage and rebellion at the same time that it provides for women a viable and lucrative niche in the literary marketplace. Few critical theories of the Gothic better understand the social and historical reasons for its marginalization, and feminist reading of the Gothic romance remains a productive area of interpretation that typifies the vitality of current Gothic studies.[15]

Gothic Writers bears rich testimony to the past and present range of Gothic scholarship and documents that Gothic studies is a still-developing field. Reference to any of the book's entries will show that one of the Gothic's most enduring aspects is its capacity to call forth a broad and contestable range of critical reaction. We hope that in our presentation of a variety of Gothic writers and the lively critical commentary they have elicited readers will discover, once again, that Coleridgean sense of "wonder" occasioned by this most magical and protean of literary genres.

NOTES

1. The quotation comes from that famous twentieth-century descendant of earnest eighteenth- and nineteenth-century moral critics, F.R. Leavis in his *Revaluation* (1947) (New York: Norton, 1963). 227.

2. *The Critical Review* 19 (1765): 50–51. Wordsworth's attack on the Gothic is contained in his "Preface" to *Lyrical Ballads* (1802), *William Wordsworth: The Oxford Authors*. Ed. Stephen Gill. Oxford, New York: Oxford UP, 1984. See Robert Spector's *The English Gothic: A Bibliographic Guide to Writers from Horace Walpole to Mary Shelley* for sources of and commentaries on the early reviews. Victor Sage's *The Gothick Novel: A Casebook* contains reviews and reactions from the earliest critics up to the present day. Sage points out the obvious: many of the "overt critics" of the Gothic were also "covert readers" of the literature. See also the chapter on "Readers' Responses" in Rictor Norton's *Gothic Readings: The First Wave, 1764–1840*.

3. Stephen Gill suggests that much of Wordsworth's and Coleridge's case against the literature of "situations" and their quarrel with public tastes stem from their somewhat envious reaction to two Gothic success stories: Gottfried Bürger's poetry and Monk Lewis's *Castle Spectre*. See *William Wordsworth: A Life* (Oxford and New York: Oxford University Press, 1990).

4. For the Romantic poets' Gothic usages, see Michael Gamer, *Romanticism and the Gothic: Genre, Reception, and Canon Formation*, Cambridge Studies in Romanticism 40 (Cambridge, Cambridge University Press, 2000). For another useful study of the Romantic poets' Gothicism, see Steven Jones, " 'Supernatural, or at Least Romantic': The Ancient Mariner and Parody," *Romanticism on the Net* 15 (August 1999): <http://users.ox.ac.uk/~scat0385/sejstc.html>. Also see Douglass H. Thomson's "Gothic Literature: What the Romantic Writers Read" at <http://www2.gasov.edu:80/facstaff/dougt/gothic.htm>.

5. In *English Romanticism: The Human Context*, Marilyn Gaull suggests that "on the public level, [the] recurrent pattern of primitive thinking, appearing during the period from 1760 to 1830, is symptomatic of sudden dislocation, challenge to, or loss of faith in the theological interpretation of nature before there was a scientific one to replace it." (233) See also Victor Sage, *Horror Fiction in the Protestant Tradition*.

6. See, for example, Eve Kosofsky Sedgwick, *The Coherence of Gothic Conventions*.

Also see Thomas Meade Harwell, "Toward a Gothic Metaphysic: Gothic Parts," *Publications of the Arkansas Philological Association* 12:2 (1986): 33–43.

7. For plot summaries and critical synopses of the early Gothic novels, see the titles listed under "Primary Bibliographies of the Gothic" in the "General Bibliography." Montague Summers's *A Gothic Bibliography*, Ann Tracy's *The Gothic Novel, 1790–1830: Plot Summaries and Index to Motifs*, and Frederick Frank's *The First Gothics: A Critical Guide to the English Gothic Novel* contain vital data for establishing a canon of first Gothics.

8. Despite this terminus, Sage and Sedgwick, among other critics, have pointed out the "Victorian survival" of Gothic conventions in ghost stories, penny dreadfuls, and the major novels (such as those of the Brontës and Dickens) of the period.

9. For a more recent and well-argued example of formalist doubts about the Gothic novel, see Elizabeth Napier's *The Failure of the Gothic: Problems of Disjunction in an Eighteenth-Century Literary Form* (New York: Oxford University Press, 1986).

10. For a particularly daunting example of the newer Lacanian method, which also employs Julia Kristeva's theory of abjection, see Anne Williams's *Art of Darkness: A Poetics of Gothic* (Chicago: University of Chicago Press, 1995). For Kristeva see *Desire in Language: A Semiotic Approach to Literature and Art*, Ed. Leon S. Roudiez; translated by Thomas Gora, Alice Jardine, and Leon S. Roudiez. (New York: Columbia University Press, 1980).

11. A deeply theorized example of this kind of reevaluation is Marshall Brown, "A Philosophical View of the Gothic Novel," *Studies in Romanticism* 26 (1987): 275–301.

12. See Hogle's "The Gothic Ghost of the Counterfeit and the Progress of Abjection" in *A Companion to the Gothic*, 293–304.

13. Among many recent titles in this vein are E.J. Clery, *The Rise of Supernatural Fiction, 1762–1800* (1995), and Robert Miles, *Gothic Writing, 1750–1820: A Genealogy* (1993). Chris Baldick and Robert Mighall in their provocative essay "Gothic Criticism" take sharp issue with recent new historicist readings of the political dimension of Gothic fiction. *A Companion to the Gothic*, 209–228.

14. See, for example, Adriana Craciun's edition of Charlotte Dacre's *Zofloya; or, The Moor: A Romance of the Fifteenth Century* and April Alliston's edition of Sophia Lee's *The Recess*.

15. For an idea of the range and vitality of these new responses, see the following titles in the "General Bibliography" under "General Histories and Studies" in Definition and Theory": Susanne Becker's *Gothic Forms of Feminine Fictions*; E.J. Clery's *Women's Gothic: From Clara Reeve to Mary Shelley*; Eugenia De La Motte's *Perils of the Night: A Feminist Study of Nineteenth-Century Gothic*; Kate Ferguson Ellis's *The Contested Castle: Gothic Novels and the Subversion of Domestic Ideology*; Diane Hoeveler's *Gothic Feminism: The Professionalization of Gender from Charlotte Smith to the Brontës*; Michelle A. Massé's *In the Name of Love: Women, Masochism, and the Gothic;* Paulina Palmer's *Lesbian Gothic: Transgressive Fictions*; Bette Roberts's *The Gothic Romance: Its Appeal to Women Writers and Readers in Late Eighteenth-Century England*; and Susan Wolstenholme's *Gothic (Re)visions: Writing Women as Readers*; as well as Juliann Fleenor's edited collection *The Female Gothic*, listed under "Essay Collections Dedicated to the Gothic."

JOHN AIKIN
(1747–1822)
ANNA LAETITIA AIKIN
BARBAULD
(1743–1825)

Douglass H. Thomson

PRINCIPAL GOTHIC WORKS

"On the Pleasure Derived from Objects of Terror; with Sir Bertrand, a Fragment." In *Miscellaneous Pieces in Prose*. London: J. Johnson, 1773; 2nd ed., 1775; 3rd ed., 1792. (The essay was extensively reprinted in eighteenth-century periodicals.)

Gothic Stories: Sir Bertrand by Mrs. Barbauld. Manchester: G. Nicholson, 1797.

Gothic Stories: Sir Bertrand's Adventures in a Ruinous Castle. London: S. Fisher, 1799. (Plagiarized reduction of the "Sir Bertrand" fragment in chapbook format.)

MODERN REPRINTS AND EDITIONS

The Candle and the Tower. Ed. Robert D. Spector. New York: Warner Paperback Books, 1974. (Contains "Sir Bertrand, a Fragment.")

The Evil Image: Two Centuries of Gothic Short Fiction and Poetry. Ed. Patricia Skarda and Nora Crow Jaffe. New York: New American Library, 1981. (Contains "On the Pleasure Derived from Objects of Terror" and "Sir Bertrand, a Fragment.")

Gothic Readings: The First Wave, 1764–1840. Ed. Rictor Norton. London and New York: Leicester University Press, 2000. (Contains "Sir Bertrand, a Fragment" and "On the Pleasure Derived from Objects of Terror.")

Gothic Tales of Terror. Ed. Peter Haining. Baltimore: Penguin, 1973. (Contains "Sir Bertrand, a Fragment.")

The Oxford Book of Gothic Tales. Ed. Chris Baldick. Oxford: Oxford University Press, 1992. (Contains "Sir Bertrand, a Fragment.")

The "Sir Bertrand" fragment and its prefatory essay offer an early, important defense of the imaginative power of the Gothic romance, but not without some expression of concern for the potential abuse of that power. As Unitarian educators, the Aikins wished to distinguish a high, literarily acceptable form of terror from a troubling "deception," its equally alluring presentation in the "poorest and most insipid narrative" (Skarda and Jaffe 12). To do so, the Aikins offered not only their exemplary "Fragment," which dramatizes in miniature an archetypal arrangement of Gothic motifs, but a spirited argument for "the plea-sure derived from objects of terror" that engages even as it extends Edmund Burke's comments on the sublime in his 1757 treatise *A Philosophical Enquiry into the Origin of Our Ideas of the Sublime and Beautiful*. In making distinctions between terror high and low, authentic and "deceptive," marvelous and natural, the Aikins introduced dichotomies that shaped the debate about the literary value of the Gothic for years to come.

Many modern bibliographers have followed the tendency of eighteenth-century reprinters of the tale to attribute it to Anna Laetitia Aikin, who went on to become the famous poet, educator, and essayist Mrs. Barbauld. But it seems clear from her niece Lucy Aikin's 1825 edition of her aunt's works "with a Memoir" that primary authorship of the tale belongs to Anna's brother Dr. John Aikin. Given the collaborative nature of the volume in which the tale and its essay first appeared, the *Miscellaneous Pieces in Prose* of 1773, one cannot be sure of the exact degree of each author's contribution, although critics strongly suspect the hand of Anna Laetitia in the prefatory piece at least. The work dates from a period that was crucially formative in the Aikins' life: their residence at the Dissenting Warrington Academy, that cradle of Unitarian thought presided over by such luminaries as the Aikins' father (John, Sr.) and Joseph Priestley. At first glance it may seem odd that such a tale, with its haunted castle, sar-cophagal *la belle dame*, and supernatural machinery, would stem from an in-tellectual environment at war with the old superstitions and religious enthusiasms. But actually the Unitarian context, with its own unsteady blend of the material and the spiritual (Priestley could, for example, deny the divinity of Christ but allow for miracles), proved a congenial background for this early investigation of tensions within the Gothic ethos. John Aikin went on to write imitations of Gottfried Bürger in his *Poems* of 1781, and we have a record of how Anna Laetitia (by then Barbauld) thrilled an Edinburgh literary society with her reading of William Taylor's translation of Bürger's famously Gothic "Le-nore." As educators, poets, editors, and Unitarians, the Aikins were in a partic-ularly compelling position to study the complex ways in which the Gothic negotiated between Enlightenment and "Romantic" values, between the phe-nomenal and the noumenal, the empirical and the otherworldly, the pragmatic and the fantastic.

Such varying intellectual commitments inform the procedure of this work, which affirms the "pleasure derived from objects of terror" yet seeks to find a redemptive value for that terror. The prefatory essay directly addresses Burke's remarks on the subject in his *Philosophical Enquiry into the Origin of Our Ideas of the Sublime and Beautiful* and plays off Burke's postulates regarding the connections between supernatural fear and danger and sublime delight and grat-ification. Because for Burke the "sublime is an idea belonging to self-preservation," he insists that "no pleasure from a positive cause belongs to it"

(*Enquiry* 38). Instead he reserves (somewhat at odds with common usage, he admits) the word "delight" for our aesthetic experience of the sublime, delight being "a negative pleasure" expressing "the sensation which accompanies the removal of pain or danger" (36). The Aikins' title and entire procedure appear to argue against Burke in the way they supply that "positive cause" of the "pleasure derived from objects of terror" denied by him. Their first strategy is to offer, as Walpole earlier did in his preface to the second edition of *The Castle of Otranto*, a distinguished pedigree for the literature of terror. Greek, Roman, and Jacobean tragedy, the poet William Collins (Barbauld later edited a volume of his poems, which includes his influential "Ode to Fear"), Milton, and, above all, Shakespeare are adduced to dignify the line of terror, which leads to the "very spirited modern attempt" of Walpole (12). But how do we distinguish between the "real pleasure" derived from the high tradition of literary terror and a troubling "deception," its often equally alluring presentation in "tedious and disgusting pages" that merely pander to "the uneasy craving of an unsatisfied desire" and keep poor children in an unpleasurable state of "pale and mute attention" (12)?

The Aikins offer two distinctions. The first concerns a mix of literary craft and expressive theory that recalls the ancient author Longinus's widely read treatise *On the Sublime*. "Well-wrought" scenes of terror "which are formed by a sublime and vigorous imagination" (13) qualify. Second, that terror should be "artificial," and the more marvelous, the better: "Hence, the more wild, fanciful, and extraordinary are the circumstances of a scene of horror, the more pleasure we receive from it; and where they are too near common nature, though violently borne by curiosity through the adventure, we cannot repeat it or reflect on it, without an overbalance of pain" (13). Although the Aikins perhaps echo another of Burke's criteria for the sublime, that of "distance," in their exclusion of circumstances "too near common nature," they clearly go beyond his insistence that our fascination with terror stems solely from our instinct for self-preservation. Theirs is an imaginative "pleasure constantly attached to the excitement of surprise from new and wonderful objects" (13).

The "Fragment," in which both natural and artificial "manners are attempted" (13), provides a striking demonstration of the principles the Aikins set forth in their preface. Sir Bertrand wanders lost on "a desolate waste," his courage near exhaustion as his inability to find his way on an ominously dark evening includes such natural "fears" as "unknown pits and bogs" (14). The Aikins furnish a clear dividing line between "natural" and "marvelous" terror as the moon sinks beneath a dark cloud and the knight-errant beholds a gloomy, derelict castle; now the reader is ushered into a world of pure fantasy. A will-o'-the-wispish "blue flame" leads the hero into the castle as a deep tolling bell sounds, and the massive entry door mysteriously slams behind him, trapping him in a chamber of horrors. These include a "dead cold hand" (15) thrust at him from the shadows that Sir Bertrand furiously lops off, a frightening ascent of a winding staircase that grows "narrower and narrower" (15), and battles with spectral antagonists, including "gigantic statues of black marble" (15) that spring to life to fight him. The reward of all Sir Bertrand's efforts comes from the kiss of a half-shrouded, cadaverous lady who magically transforms the dark world into a bright and resplendent feast in which the erstwhile sleeping beauty and "a troop of nymphs far more fair than the Graces" (16) welcome Sir Bertrand as their hero. Here the narrative breaks off, inviting readers to furnish their own speculations. Sir Bertrand's adventures may begin in the natural world, but the Aikins clearly steer us into the world where for them the true pleasure of terror resides: "the wild, the fanciful, and extraordinary" (13). In doing so, they provide the outline of a quest story and its harrowing details that will find numerous imitations and variations in the Gothic explosion to come.

What is just as important, the Aikins provide the vocabulary for an aesthetic justification of the dark genre, one that will inform the direction of critical debate about the merits of the Gothic during its greatest period of popularity. In her essay "On the Supernatural in Poetry" (1826), Ann Radcliffe elaborates upon the Aikins' distinction between pleasurable and disgusting forms of the Gothic by differentiating between mere "horror" and a higher mode of "terror" related to the sublime. The Aikins' closely related distinction between "natural" and "artificial" horror also paves the way for that favorite and heavily debated plot device of Clara Reeve and Radcliffe, the summoning of supernatural terror only to explain away the seemingly otherworldly by assigning it a natural cause. In the charged aesthetic of the 1790s, at a time when literary forms of terror became entangled with the real Terror stalking the streets of revolutionary Paris, the distinction between "natural" (read "domestic") and "extraordinary" (read "foreign") was used by many critics in an exact inversion of the Aikins' terms. Ironically, the Gothic was now taken to task for its "attempt to please by what is unnatural . . . by a departure from the observance of real life" (Coleridge, *The Critical Review* 23 [1798]: 167), arguably the Aikins' primary criterion for the sublime in terror. Thus begins high Romantic argument with its competitor in the literary marketplace. But the Aikins' final, most important justification of the Gothic accords perfectly with the high Romantic understanding of the sublime: "Where the agency of invisible beings is introduced, of 'forms unseen, and mightier far than we,' our imagination, darting forth, explores with rapture the new world which is laid open to its view, and rejoices in the expansion of its powers. Passion and fancy cooperating elevate the soul to its highest pitch; and the pain of terror is lost in amazement" (13). With this bold argument, the Aikins closely anticipate a more famous treatment of the sublime, in which Immanuel Kant insists that the great power of the mode lies in "a satisfaction in the extension of the imagination by itself" ("Of the Mathematically Sublime," section 25). From the pens of late Enlightenment educators actually comes an argument justifying the terrific and the marvelous in terms with which most of high Romanticism would later agree.

SELECTED CRITICISM

Aikin, Lucy. *The Works of Anna Laetitia Barbauld, with a Memoir*. London: Longman, 1825. Aikin disclaims her aunt's hand in the tale, finding it "alien from the character of that brilliant and airy imagination [of hers] which was never conversant with terror," but the niece's comments may be an attempt to distance such a dark tale from Barbauld, whom the record does reveal was conversant with the literature of terror.

Birkhead, Edith. "The Beginnings of Gothic Romance." In *The Tale of Terror: A Study of the Gothic Romance*. New York: Russell & Russell, 1963: 28–31. Gives a plot summary of "Sir Bertrand," mentions connections with Ann Radcliffe's notions of terror, and points out that "Sir Bertrand" is not included in *The Works of Anna Letitia Barbauld* edited by Miss Lucy Aikin in 1825."

Burke, Edmund. *A Philosophical Enquiry into the Origin of Our Ideas of the Sublime and Beautiful*. Ed. James T. Boulton. Notre Dame, IN: University of Notre Dame Press, 1968. Burke's treatise is a key document in the theory of Gothic pleasure. The Aikins' essay and fragment extend and refine Burke's comments on "the pleasure derived from objects of terror."

Grove, Allen W. "To Make a Long Story Short: Gothic Fragments and the Gender Politics of Incompleteness." *Studies in Short Fiction* 34 (1997): 1–9. Includes the Aikins' fragment along with those of Mary Hays and Harriet Lee to demonstrate how fragmentation is often used to "expose the restrictive gender politics characteristic of the ancient romance." Rather than considering such works as merely "incomplete," one should view them as providing "an invaluable paradigm for conceptualizing and understanding late eighteenth-century fiction as a whole."

Kant, Immanuel. "Of the Mathematically Sublime," Section 25 of the *Critique* of *Judgment, The Critical Tradition*. Ed. David H. Richter. 2nd Edition. New York: Bedford, 1998, 272. Although more philosophically complex than the Aikins, Kant offers a definition of the sublime similar to theirs.

Moorman, Mary. *William Wordsworth: The Early Years*. Oxford: Clarendon Press, 1957. Traces the young Wordsworth's borrowings from "Sir Bertrand" in his "Vale of Esthwaite," although Moorman wrongly attributes the tale to Lucy Aikin, Barbauld's niece.

Perry, Ruth. "Incest as the Meaning of the Gothic Novel." *The Eighteenth Century: Theory and Interpretation* 39 (1998): 261–278. Examines the primary role of "eroticized danger" in "Sir Bertrand" and other works. Argues that "the Gothic novel expresses the latitude and the longitude of a particular kind of 'evil,' namely the fear and desire for intrafamilial sex."

Pitcher, E.W. "Eighteenth-Century Gothic Fragments and the Paradigm of Violation and Repair." *Studies in Short Fiction* 33 (1996): 35–42. Examines several Gothic fragments, including the Aikins' "Sir Bertrand," in light of Steven Cohan's thesis of "regressive drive" and "progressive drive" as developed in *Violation and Repair in the English Novel* (1986).

Thacker, Christopher. "That Long Labyrinth of Darkness." In *The Wildness Pleases: The Origins of Romanticism*. New York: St. Martin's Press, 1983: 111–128. Comments on the Aikins' contribution to Gothic atmospherics and aesthetic theory.

Thomson, Douglass H. "Terror High and Low: The Aikins' 'On the Pleasure Derived from Objects of Terror; with Sir Bertrand, a Fragment.' " *Wordsworth Circle* 29 (1998): 72–75. 'Sir Bertrand' and its accompanying essay offer a theory of "The Pleasure Derived from Objects of Terror" that goes well beyond Burke's analysis of the sublime and paves the way for later Gothic variations upon Walpole's Gothicism. Their essay "attempts to legitimize that pleasure by making a distinction between high and low terror, between the marvelous and the natural."

Tracy, Ann B. "Sir Bertrand, a Fragment." In *The Gothic Novel, 1790–1830: Plot Summaries and Index to Motifs*. Lexington: University Press of Kentucky, 1981: 17–18. A brief synopsis of the "Fragment."

WILLIAM HARRISON AINSWORTH
(1805–1882)

Jack G. Voller

PRINCIPAL GOTHIC WORKS

Sir John Chiverton: A Romance. London: John Ebers, 1826. (Written in collaboration
with John Partington Aston; London: private printing, 1827.)

Rookwood. London: Richard Bentley, 1834. 3 vols. London: John Macrone, 1835.

Jack Sheppard: A Romance. London: Bentley, 1834.

Turpin's Ride to York. London: Glover, 1839. (Extract from the second half of *Rookwood*.)

Rookwood: A Romantic Drama, in Two Acts. London: John Dicks, 1845. (A dramatization
by George Dibdin Pitt.)

The Tower of London: A Historical Romance. Illus. George Cruikshank. London: Richard
Bentley, 1840.

The Tower of London: or, Queen Mary, an Historical Drama in Three Acts by Tom
Taylor. London: J. Dicks, 1840.

*The Tower of London; or, The Death Omen and the Fate of Lady Jane Grey, a Drama
in Three Acts* by Thomas H. Higgie and Thomas H. Lacy. London: Lacy, 1840.

Guy Fawkes; or, The Gunpowder Treason: A Historical Romance, Bentley's Miscellany,
1840–1841. Serial publication. Illus. George Cruikshank; London: Richard Bentley, 1841; London: Routledge, 1841; New York: A.L. Burt, 1841; New York:
N.C. Nafis, 1841; Paris: Baudry's European Library, 1841; *Ainsworth's Magazine*,
1849–1850; Serial publication; London: Routledge, 1857; London: Routledge,
1878.

Windsor Castle. Ainsworth's Magazine, 1842–1843. Illus. George Cruikshank. Paris:
Baudry's European Library, 1843; London: Colburn, 1843. 3 vols. 1st ed. London:
Colburn, 1843; London: Colburn, 1843–1844. Illus. by George Cruikshank; New
York: New World Extra Series, 1843; London: Colburn, 1844; Leipzig: B.
Tauchnitz, 1844; London: Parry, Blenkarn, 1847; London: Chapman & Hall,
1850; London: Routledge, 1853; London: Routledge, Warnes [Warne] and Rou-
tledge, 1859.

Herne the Hunter: A Romantic Drama in Three Acts by Tom Taylor. London: J. Dicks,
1843. (A dramatization of episodes from *Windsor Castle*.)

Auriol; or, The Elixir of Life. Colburn's New Monthly Magazine and Humorist, nos. 295,

296, and 301 (1845–1846); London: Chapman & Hall, 1850; Vol. 12 of His
    Works series; London: Routledge, 1865.
The Lancashire Witches: A Romance of Pendle Forest. Sunday Times, January–December
    1848; London: Colburn, 1849.
*The Flitch of Bacon; or, The Custom of Dunmow: A Tale of English Home. New Monthly
    Magazine*, 1853; Serial publication. London: Routledge, 1854. Illus. by John Gil-
    bert. London: Routledge, 1855; London: Routledge, 1856; Leipzig: B. Tauchnitz,
    1854; Collection of British Authors, vol. 302.
Myddleton Pomfret. Bentley's Miscellany, 1867–1868; Serial publication in nine parts;
    London: Chapman & Hall, 1868; Leipzig: B. Tauchnitz, 1868; London: Chapman
    & Hall, 1878; London: Routledge, 1881. Illus. Frederick Gilbert.
Chetwynd Calverlly: A Tale. London: Tinsley, 1876.
Stanley Brereton. Bolton Weekly Journal, 1881. Serial publication; London: Routledge,
    1881; Leipzig: B. Tauchnitz, 1881; London and New York: Routledge, Dutton,
    1882.

MODERN REPRINTS AND EDITIONS

Auriol: or, The Elixir of Life. New York: Arno Press, 1976.
The Elixer of Life (Auriol). London: New English Library, 1966.
Gothic Readings: The First Wave, 1764–1840. Ed. Rictor Norton. London and New
    York: Leicester University Press, 2000. (Contains the preface to *Rookwood*.)
Guy Fawkes. London: F. Warne, 1924.
The Lancashire Witches: A Romance of Pendle Forest. London and New York: F. Warne,
    1924; Veevers & Hensman, 1964. (The Veevers & Hensman edition, based on
    the privately published edition of 1849, was "condensed and translated from the
    Lancashire dialect by Irene Pollitt." London and New York: Granada, 1983.)
Rookwood. London, Toronto, and New York: J.M. Dent, E.P. Dutton, 1931; New York:
    W. Foulsham, 1946; London: Routledge, 1968; New York: AMS Press, 1979;
    Philadelphia: G. Barrie, 1985.
Stanley Brereton. London and New York: Routledge/Dutton, 1983.
The Tower of London: A Historical Romance. London and New York: J.M. Dent, E.P.
    Dutton, 1931; London: Collins, 1953; Bath: Chivers, 1974.
Windsor Castle. Bath: Chivers, 1974.

With a lifetime that spanned the majority of both the Romantic and the Victorian
periods, William Harrison Ainsworth is in many respects the representative
"transitional" artist. Not that Ainsworth's corpus fully represents the evolution
of Gothic literature into its representative Victorian modes; Ainsworth in fact
never moved much beyond a late Gothic style that only hinted at post-Gothic
modes to come.

    Since the Gothic is a "popular" literary genre, the simple popularity of Ains-
worth's work provides ample insight into the sociohistorical significance of his
work. Ainsworth struck literary gold with one of his earliest productions, *Rookwood*, published in 1834, and spent the remainder of his long literary career (his
last novel was published less than a year before he died) reworking the same

literary ground. Much of his work contains a substantial degree of supernaturalism of the Gothic sort. Yet the cultural tide had turned in a way Ainsworth never fully recognized, and never again did he achieve the fame that followed the publication of the egregiously Gothic *Rookwood* and the two or three novels that followed it. It is not too much to say that Ainsworth was a Romantic-era Gothic writer who was born too late and outlived the vogue of the only literary type he mastered.

Yet Ainsworth was more than a hack. Born into a prominent and well-to-do Manchester family, Ainsworth not only received a superior education but acquired from his lawyer father a passionate love of criminal history; a deep friendship with one of his father's clerks, James Crossley, provided further impetus to Ainsworth's literary development. While Gothic melodrama remained an essential element of Ainsworth's writing, his fascination with criminals helped create the "Newgate novel" popular in the early and mid-Victorian periods.

Himself a lawyer, albeit a reluctant one, Ainsworth readily seized on the modest success of his early publications—the youthful production *Sir John Chiverton* was noticed favorably by Sir Walter Scott—as an indication that literature should be his principal pursuit; he practiced law in London for only four years before devoting himself entirely to literature. Prolific as both an author and editor, and indeed often an owner of literary magazines, Ainsworth remained active in letters until the last months of his life.

The Gothic was arguably Ainsworth's greatest love, although it competed in him with the lore of criminal exploit. *Rookwood*, the novel that made Ainsworth's fame and that he never succeeded in bettering, is perhaps the most representative example of his contributions to the genre, contributions too numerous and extensive to be considered in detail here. *Rookwood* is a novel that in one sense cannot decide between the two objects of Ainsworth's literary affection: half of the work is set in and around the Gothic hall of Rookwood, while the other half focuses on the exploits of the legendary and real highwayman Dick Turpin, who has little to do with the novel's main plot, a fairly standard Gothic inheritance drama. Yet Turpin, whose story is told with engaging energy and verve, is not the "hook" that Ainsworth dangles before his readers; it is the Gothic that opens the novel and dominates its first half, and *Rookwood*'s opening chapters are as Gothic as it gets: "Within a sepulchral vault, and at midnight, two persons were seated" (1931, 11). With that opening sentence Ainsworth leads us into a nightmare world in which the young protagonist, Luke Rookwood, quickly finds his mother's corpse at his feet; he accidentally yanks her decaying hand from her body, secures her wedding ring, and sets out to establish his true identity as the legitimate heir to the vast estate of Rookwood, a quest that involves his mysterious grandfather, a missing will, two love affairs, a wicked stepmother, and a displaced brother. Along the way are scenes in caves, crypts, ruins, and mountains; we meet murderers and Gypsies and deviants; extremes of passion are commonplace; love is lost and won in an instant, once even with the aid of a love potion; and hints of the supernatural are everywhere. Ainsworth is so committed to the Gothic mode of his work that continuity of character and structural integrity are both willingly sacrificed to the pursuit—the rather successful pursuit, it should be noted—of emotional extremes and exuberance; such authorial lapses are common in Ainsworth's novels. While *Rookwood* is not as blatantly supernaturalist as many of Ainsworth's other novels, it nonetheless fully earns its reputation as an over-the-top Gothic thriller. It was a huge financial success for Ainsworth, going through five editions in three years, and allowed Ainsworth to abandon law and set himself up as the literary dandy he clearly enjoyed being, attending fashionable parties and serving as an early mentor to writers such as Dickens, Thackeray, and Disraeli.

Ainsworth's next novel, *Crichton*, eschewed the Gothic and criminal elements for a more historical focus, in this case on the sixteenth-century French court. While it also sold well, it did not have the power of his previous novel, and so Ainsworth returned to Gothic with the hugely popular *Jack Sheppard*, a crime novel that inspired numerous imitations and dramatic adaptations. For the next few years, Ainsworth was one of the best-known writers in England.

But in the 1840s the cultural tides shifted, and the domestic realism of writers such as Gaskell, Thackeray, and Dickens found the wide audience that was losing interest in the fading Gothic and historical traditions and the "rogue" fiction to which Ainsworth was powerfully drawn. Although he published and edited constantly, continuing to champion the use of Gothic and supernaturalist elements, the later years of his life were spent in relative obscurity and diminished financial circumstances.

SELECTED CRITICISM

Ellis, S.M. *William Harrison Ainsworth and His Friends*. London and New York: J. Lane, 1911. On Ainsworth's prominence as a novelist. Contains occasional remarks on Ainsworth's conscious reuse and revision of the Gothic romance.

Ligocki, Llewellyn. "The Imitators and the Imitated: Scott, Ainsworth, and the Critics." *Papers of the Bibliographical Society of America* 67 (1973): 443–446. Brief consideration of Ainsworth's debt to Scott, particularly as regards the historical novel. Ligocki speculates that "it may be that [Ainsworth] saw fundamental differences between his and Scott's views of the supernatural." It is clear from Scott's own practice and his theoretical pronouncements that his preference for a very restrained supernaturalism is the polar opposite of Ainsworth's aggressive and melodramatic supernaturalism.

Massé, Michelle. "Gothic Repetition: Husbands, Horrors, and Things That Go Bump in the Night." *Signs: Journal of Women in Culture and Society* 15 (1990): 679–709. Discusses the story "The Spectre Bride."

Sanders, Andrew. "A Gothic Revival: William Harrison Ainsworth's *The Tower of London*." In *The Victorian Historical Novel, 1840–1880*. New York: St. Martin's Press, 1979: 32–46. Ainsworth's novels attempt to return to popularity those elements of the Gothic that Ainsworth, unlike his audience, never outgrew. "Ainsworth was committed to the idea of a novel which would resurrect the style and technique of Gothic fiction."

Schroeder, Natalie. "William Harrison Ainsworth." In *Supernatural Fiction Writers: Fantasy and Horror*. Ed. E.F. Bleiler. New York: Scribner's, 1985: 187–193. A biographical overview and helpful discussion of the supernatural elements in many of Ainsworth's novels.

Worth, George J. *William Harrison Ainsworth*. Twayne's English Authors Series 138. New York: Twayne, 1972. An effective general introduction to Ainsworth's work, but the plot synopses are too brief to be of much value. Describes Ainsworth's debt to the Gothic tradition and is admirably objective in assessing his position in the canon.

UEDA AKINARI
(1734–1809)
Frederick S. Frank

PRINCIPAL GOTHIC WORKS

Kinko Kidan Ugetsu monogatari [Tales of Moonlight and Rain]. Kyoto and Osaka: Nomura Chobei, 1776. (Contains "Shiramine" [White Peak], "Kikuka no chigiri" [Chrysanthemum Tryst], "Asaji ga yado" [The House amid the Thickets], "Muo no rigyo" [The Carp That Came to My Dream], "Bupposo" [Bird of Paradise], "Kibitsu no kama" [The Cauldron of Kibitsu], "Jasie no in" [The Lust of the White Serpent], "Aozukin" [The Blue Hood], and "Himpukuron" [Wealth and Poverty].)

Harusame monogatari [Tales of the Spring Rain]. Story collection in manuscript. (Contains "Chi katabira" [The Bloodstained Robe], "Shikubi no egao" [The Smiling Death's-Head], and "Miyagi ga tsuka" [The Grave of Miyagi].)

MODERN REPRINTS AND EDITIONS

A Japanese Miscellany: The Writings of Lafcadio Hearn. Boston: Houghton, Mifflin, 1901. (Includes the dream fantasy "The Carp That Came In from My Dream" and the tale of the ghostly warrior "Chrysanthemum Tryst.")

Tales of Moonlight and Rain: A Complete English Version of the Eighteenth-Century Japanese Collection of Tales of the Supernatural, Based on the First Woodblock Edition of 1776 with Illustrations and an Introduction for Western Readers. Ed. and trans. Leon M. Zolbrod. Vancouver: University of British Columbia Press, 1974.

Tales of the Spring Rain. Ed., trans., and intro. Barry Jackman. Tokyo: University of Tokyo Press, 1975.

The writings of the eighteenth-century Japanese Gothicist Ueda Akinari confirm the presence of the Gothic spirit in oriental literature. All of the traditional features of the genre are firmly embedded in Akinari's tales of terror, with a special place given to the psychological monstrosities of the dream life and the intrusion of the malicious supernatural into human lives at their most vulnerable moments. The residue of feudalism and bushido codes of Japanese culture in the eighteenth century provide that sense of enclosure and entrapment crucial to the evocation of Gothic fear. The superiority of evil to goodness in Akinari's Gothic work links him with Western Gothicism at its most pessimistic extremes. According to Akinari's modern translator Leon Zolbrod, "The form that Akinari helped to perfect led to a species of historical romance similar to the Gothic novel in the West. Although Akinari's ghosts and otherworldly creatures show an animal nature that defied control and mastery, they have neither the bleeding skulls nor luminous hands of the spirits of Gothic novels; nor are they headless apparitions clad in armour or eerie forms extending phosphorescent claws toward the victim's throat. Rather, they are at once more primitive and more modern" (*Tales of Moonlight and Rain* 53–54). While his characters are often menaced by supernatural forces, it is their psychological and spiritual peril that links Akinari's Gothicism to primitive and modern monstrosity.

Early in the twentieth century, Akinari's place in the Gothic tradition was recognized by the orientalist Lafcadio Hearn (Koizumi Yakumo, 1850–1904), who included two Akinari tales in *A Japanese Miscellany* (1901). More recently, his Gothic virtuosity has been admired and praised by Yukio Mishima (1925–1970), whose sensational ritual suicide in 1970 might have been borrowed from one of Akinari's lurid plots. Currently gaining in popularity with general readers as well as students of Gothic fiction, his works remained almost unknown and untranslated in the West until the appearance of a monographic assessment by Pierre Humbertclaude in 1940.

Akinari's life was filled with mystery, misery, rejection, and physical affliction. He was born in Osaka in 1734, possibly in a bordello, to a woman who may have been a prostitute. The stigma of illegitimacy would mar him for life. Rejected by his mother, he was adopted by Ueda Masuke, a former samurai who had become a paper dealer. He contracted smallpox, which left him marked for life by a crippling deformity of the middle finger of the right hand. The digital deformity accounts for Akinari's occasional use of the pen name "Senshi Kijin" (Mr. Oddfinger). Never having known his real father, Akinari thought of himself as a pariah stigmatized by disease and doomed to misfortune. Such a stance accounts for the pathological tone of many of the narrators as well as the recurrence of mutilation and youthful failure in the tales. As a young man, he developed an interest in *haiku* poetry, signing his own compositions with the pseudonym "Mucho." The muted quality of the three-line *haiku* verse form was later reflected in the style of the Gothic pieces, particularly in the understated horror of the climaxes. In 1760, he married Ueyama Tama and in 1766 published his first book, a collection of "naughty" character profiles, *Shodo kikimimi seken-zaru* [Worldly Apes with a Smattering of Various Arts]. This was followed in 1768 by the first Gothic work, nine stories collected under the title *Ugetsu monogatari* [Tales of Moonlight and Rain]. An elegant volume complete with woodcuts was later published in 1776. After his home and paper business in

Osaka were destroyed by fire, Akinari moved to Kashima, where he began the study of medicine under the tutelage of Tsuga Teisho, a physician and writer of sophisticated, belletristic literature called *yomihon*. He returned to Osaka, practiced medicine, and there became preoccupied with classical literary study and serious writing in his determination to transcend his marked life by achieving artistic success. By 1788, he had abandoned his medical practice to devote himself wholly to literature, most especially *tanka* poetry (a thirty-one-syllable verse form also called *waka*). Total loss of sight in his left eye and visual problems hampered his work but deepened his Gothic vision of self and society. Impoverished and facing permanent blindness, he moved to Kyoto, where he contemplated suicide after the death of his wife in 1797. Possibly to forestall suicidal desires, Akinari began writing another Gothic short-story set, *Harusame monogatari* [Tales of the Spring Rain], finishing the manuscript in 1802. After a period of physical distress and intellectual inertia, he attempted to destroy all of his writings in 1807. He died two years later in Kyoto at the age of seventy-five, unaware of the fact that *Tales of Moonlight and Rain* would soon be regarded in Japan as one of the most important prose works of the eighteenth century.

Each of the nine tales in *Tales of Moonlight and Rain* displays immediately identifiable Gothic occurrences, situations, conflicts, and characterization. Their settings are historical, with action placed in tenth- to seventeenth-century Japan, a medieval period of samurai warfare, social disorder, and imperial intrigue. Akinari's management of malign supernatural forces etched against the blood-stained canvas of feudal history was influenced to some extent by the Chinese supernatural tales in *Ch'ien tang hsin hua* [New Tales for Lamplight], in which the cultural and historical horrors of violent social transition figure prominently. The severe and simple style of the tales also demonstrates the influence of the *setsuwa*, a Japanese story form rooted in fable, parable, and supernatural incident. Akinari was also familiar with the *kusazoshi*, the Japanese literary equivalent of the Gothic chapbook or rapid tale of terror.

Functioning as a symbol of the desire for permanence, peace, and stability, rain signifies throughout the tales that form of innocense that precedes any deep contact with evil, while moonlight signifies the sinister illumination of experience, a knowledge often accompanied by death, madness, or psychic torment. In many of the tales, the precarious balance of good and evil is often tipped in evil's favor as Akinari depicts moments of dark enlightenment when rain yields to moonlight. Within this general symbolic context, three characteristic Gothic motifs empower the stories and link them to one another in a chain of supernatural cause and effect. The perilous or fatal journey during which the characters undergo an unexplainable supernatural experience is a story pattern found in several of the nine tales. A pestilential or pathological atmosphere fraught with spectral depictions of disease is common to many of the pieces. Confining spaces charged with phantasmic energy "where demons might appear and consort with men, and humans fear not to mingle with spirits" (114) are deployed throughout Akinari's closed Gothic world. Within the framework of the dark journey, the terrible place, and palsied universe are to be found most of the horrific objects and conditions of mainstream Western Gothicism, including cadaverous confrontation, psychotic retrospection, imminent mutilation by architectural forces, torture, ghostly assaults, gruesome prophecies, peripatetic corpses, haunted abodes presided over by restless spirits, madness, murder, erotic sadism, satanic transformation, demonic dominance and possession, necrophagia or corpse eating, and psychotic pleasure in pain. Several of the nocturnal climaxes in Akinari's tales have close psychological and stylistic parallels with the night scenes in Poe's homicidal and suicidal fantasies.

"White Peak," the opening story in *Tales of Moonlight and Rain*, is a tale of demonic encounter, dark prophecy, and an awakening to the power of evil. Out of a kind of Faustian curiosity and desire for contact with the demonic world, the poet-narrator conjures up the phantom of the emperor Sutoku (reigned 1123–1141) by chanting a cabalistic verse. The imperial ghost delivers a hideous account of his potency, informing the narrator that it is "I who have recently caused all of the trouble in the world" (100) and accusing him of a selfish ignorance of the ways of the world. Centuries ago, the emperor had written an oath in blood, thrown the sutras or scriptural precepts into the sea, and denounced humankind to become "a king of Evil." "I finally became a great king of Evil, head of the more than 300 kinds of demons. Every time my band sees happiness, they turn it into misery. Whenever they see the country at peace, they cause war" (100). His satanic revelation climaxes in his gruesome metamorphosis into a hawklike being. Now realizing his peril of soul, the narrator dispels the king of evil with another charm, but recollecting the bloody history of the realm, the narrator has to admit the power of the demon emperor and, by extension, his own and every man's involvement with the evil of the world. Now wiser, the poet-narrator knows and will build on the knowledge that "what he related was as terrifying as it was mysterious" (108).

"The Cauldron of Kibitsu" is a story of appalling spectral revenge taken by a dead wife upon her unfaithful husband. Akinari uses the familiar Gothic situation of the ghost vigil along with some precisely installed Gothic acoustics in the form of a single "scream of bloodcurdling intensity" (159) to dramatize a dark truth about the human heart. The dissolute and unfaithful Shotaro has a posthumous rendezvous with Isora, whose spirit has been lurking about his house for forty-one nights. The dire consequences of his adultery and the supernatural power of the phantom spouse have been ominously foreshadowed by the silent boiling of the cauldron at the shrine of Kibitsu. On the forty-second night of his vigil, his friend Hikoroku hears Shotaro shout in agony (the tale's single scream), then vanish. As a grisly memento of her return and revenge, Isora has left on display atop the house eaves "nothing else than a bleeding head torn and mangled. This was the only trace of Shotaro that remained" (160). Like the formalized violence of a *No* theater scene, the bloody head illuminated by Hikoroku's raised torch highlights the tale's moral by showing "the power of the supernatural. Thus, the story has been handed down" (160). Such abrupt, unrelieved horror has led some commentators to point out the closeness in method between Akinari's horror tableaux and the formalized violence of the *No* drama.

The longest tale in the set, "The Lust of the White Serpent," should remind Western readers of the legend of the snake that inhabits a human body, a "bosom serpent" as in Hawthorne's gruesome fantasy "Egotism; or, The Bosom Serpent." Akinari gives another snake figure shared by many folklores, the Lamia or serpent lady, an especially grotesque vitality in his descriptions of the tale's fatal woman, Manago. Encountering her in a storm and giving her his umbrella, the naïve young man, Toyoo, finds himself entangled in her guileful coils. Giving him an antique sword, Manago proposes to the young man, pledging "a thousand years of love with you" (166). Invading Toyoo's life in a ghostly manner, she works her will upon him until he is tormented to the point of obsession by the beautiful demon and begs for release from an old Buddhist priest. He marries Tomiko, thinking that taking a natural mate might expel the evil spirit of the snake-woman, but the effect is the opposite when Tomiko's voice and appearance change to "unmistakably that of Manago" (179). When a priest tries to seize and destroy her, she asserts her power over men by transforming herself into an enormous serpent.

No sooner did he open the door of the sleeping chamber, than a demon thrust its head out at the priest. The projecting extremity was so huge that it filled the doorway, gleaming even whiter than newly fallen snow, with eyes like mirrors and horns like the bare bows of a tree. The creature opened its mouth more than three feet wide; its crimson tongue darted, as if to swallow the priest in a single gulp. (180)

In a final effort to free himself from his snake-bride, Toyoo throws a monk's robe over Manago to smother her, but upon removing the robe "there lay Tomiko, unconscious, with a white serpent more than three feet in length coiled motionlessly on her breast" (183). The Lamia's victory over human love is complete. Like the "Horla" in Maupassant's tale of demonic possession by a deadly creature or like the invasion of the Lady Rowena's body by Ligeia, the strength of the vampiric woman or "conqueror worm" in beautiful disguise is reaffirmed by the remorseless climax.

The story in the set that most resembles the monastic horrors of many eighteenth-century Gothic novels is "The Blue Hood," a parable of dark enlightenment. When the Zen Buddhist priest Kaian Zenji pauses at the mountain hamlet of Tomita, he is mistaken by the frightened residents for the mountain demon, a mad Buddhist abbot who fell in love with a boy, then devoured his corpse after the boy's death. Akinari's description of the abbot's corpse feast is a loathsome horror photograph. "Then, refusing to allow the body to rot and decay, he sucked the flesh and licked the bones until he utterly devoured it. 'The abbot has turned into a devil,' the people in the temple said, and they all

fled" (188). After his bestialization by the taste of human flesh, the abbot becomes a ghoul who raids and cannibalizes the villagers. Like Matthew Gregory
Lewis's Ambrosio in *The Monk*, he is changed by sexual lust into a monster.
"Once he descended into the sinful path of lust and covetousness, he was
changed into a demon, and he fell victim to the flames of the fires in the hell
of delusion. This probably came to pass because of his self-righteous and ar-
rogant nature" (192). Deciding to rid the mountain of the monster, Kaian Zenji
goes alone to the ruined temple where the abbot lurks in mad solitude. Giving
him his blue-dyed hood, Kaian Zenji recites a gnostic verse for the reclamation
of the abbot's soul. After a year, Kaian revisits the ruined temple, there to
encounter the abbot's wraith, now a living ghost that continually chants the
salvational stanzas. When Kaian strikes him with his Zen rod, the figure vanishes, "leaving only the blue hood and a skeleton lying in the weeds. At this
instant the monk probably overcame his stubborn attachment to evil. Surely a
divine principle was in operation" (193). Allegorically, the tale deals with the
salvational power of art over the savagery of human nature and is rare among
Akinari's stories in its moralized depiction of the triumph of goodness over evil
and the human over the inhuman.

Two stories in the collection *Tales of the Spring Rain*, "The Smiling Death's-
Head" and "The Grave of Miyagi," are tales of passion with strong Gothic
overtones in atmosphere and characterization. In contrast to the gruesome supernatural content of most of the pieces in *Tales of Moonlight and Rain*, these
tales achieve their effect by a concentration on the morbid beauty of death. In
fact, several of the tales may be read as extended epitaphs with minimal supernatural action but a great deal of supernatural reverie. The narrator of "The
Grave of Miyagi," a poet, has come to Kanzaki near Osaka to trace the legend
and locate the grave of the prostitute Miyagi. Her lover, Jutabei, had been poisoned, and she had been made the sexual slave of his murderer, Fujidayu. She
ended her tragic life with a prayer to Buddha and a leap into the sea. Now her
soul is elegized by the poet, whose quest after her memory finally brings him
to a "stone monument scarcely the width of an outspread fan. Thus I wrote,
paying homage to the soul of Miyagi. I have heard that now not a trace remains
of her grave, for it was thirty years ago that I wrote the poem" (*Tales of the
Spring Rain* 154). As may be seen, Akinari's Gothicism in this tale is lyric and
not episodic, its mood celebrating the joy that resides in sorrow itself.

In the almost naturalistic story "The Smiling Death's-Head," a father's avarice
destroys his son's happiness, and a brother murders his sister to prevent his
family honor from being tainted. The saki brewer Gosoji is determined to block
the love match between his son, Gozo, and the beautiful Mune simply because
"she hasn't any money" (102). Complicating the conflict between father and son
is Motosuke, Mune's honor-driven brother. When Gozo brings Mune into Gosoji's house as his bride, the stage is set for the tale's Gothic resolution. Abruptly
and without warning, Motosuke intervenes. " 'She is your wife. She must die
in your house.' With these words, he drew his sword and struck off his sister's

head. Gozo lifted up Mune's severed head and wrapped it in his kimono sleeve. Not letting fall a single tear, he started to walk out of the gate" (109). Following a trial for murder, the three men are banished and dispossessed of all wealth, while the legend of the severed head of Mune, a head that "retains even in death its brave smile and courageous expression" (112), is absorbed into the legends of the district. Although Akinari's use of the living head lacks the horrific impact of the screaming skull of a Western Gothic writer like F. Marion Crawford, he nevertheless succeeds in inspiring the fear, awe, and wonder that lie at the heart of Gothic beauty.

The dramatic and episodic Gothicism of *Tales of Moonlight and Rain* is counterpointed by the lyric and reflective Gothicism of *Tales of the Spring Rain*. Both sets of stories establish Ueda Akinari as a Gothic innovator worthy of the attention of all modern readers who are interested in the persistence of the Gothic in non-Western cultures. Akinari's influence on the development of a Japanese Gothic tradition is registered in the work of Izumi Kyoka (1873–1939), whose masterful short stories of the Meiji period (1868–1912) have been compared with Poe's tales. Four recently translated Kyoka stories, "The Surgery Room," "The Holy Man of Mount Koya," "One Day in Spring," and "Osen and Sokichi," clearly show the influence of Ueda Akinari on his Gothic successors as an inspirational model.

In the two prefaces to the first Gothic novel, *The Castle of Otranto*, Horace Walpole advised his readers to expect to find the characters in "extraordinary positions" and further indicated that his Gothic tale would provide "a constant vicissitude of interesting passions." Walpole's criteria for Gothic liminality are repeatedly applied with astonishing force in the demonized universe of Japan's Ueda Akinari.

SELECTED CRITICISM

Araki, James T. "A Critical Approach to the *Ugetsu Monogatari*." *Monumenta Nipponica* 22:1–2 (1967): 49–64. Comments on the mythic, mystic, and Gothic properties of the tales as well as Akinari's conviction of the reality and immediacy of the supernatural.

Carpenter, Juliet. "Izumi Kyoka: Meije-Era Gothic." *Japan Quarterly* 31 (1984): 154–158. Introduces Western readers to the Gothicism of Kyoka and comments on the universal aspects of Meiji-era Gothic.

Hughes, Henry J. "Familiarity of the Strange: Japan's Gothic Tradition." *Criticism* 42 (2000): 59–89. The section of the article titled "Ueda Akinari: Edo Gothic Innovator" comments on the tales and refers to Akinari as "a great scholar of his culture's medieval past and a believer in ghosts and demons" as well as "the forces of sorcery and sex that disturb social and religious norms."

Humbertclaude, Pierre. "Essai sur la vie et l'oeuvre de Ueda Akinari." *Monumenta Nipponica* 3 (1940): 98–119; 4 (1941): 102–123; 5 (1942): 52–85. A three-part monograph on the life and works of Ueda Akinari.

Inouye, Charles Shiro. Introduction to *Japanese Gothic Tales* by Izumi Kyoka. Honolulu:

University of Hawaii Press, 1996:1–10. Maintains that "great Gothic writers such as Poe and Kyoka are understandable across differences of time and space because, though they might speak eloquently of their particular cultures, their concerns transcend national circumstance." Similarly, Akinari's Gothic is rooted in Japanese culture and history but is also not limited to nationality or historical period.

Jackman, Barry. Introduction to *Tales of the Spring Rain*. Tokyo: University of Tokyo Press, 1975:vii–xviii. Provides a biography of Akinari and comments briefly on the Gothic qualities of the nine pieces in *Tales of Moonlight and Rain*. "Ghosts and evil spirits frequently appear, and many of the most effective stories depend on a supernatural twist of the plot at the conclusion."

Takada, Mamoru. "Ugetsu Monogatari: A Critical Interpretation." In *Tales of Moonlight and Rain: Japanese Gothic Tales*. Tokyo: University of Tokyo Press, 1971:xxi–xxix. Places the tales in a Gothic context and connects them with the horror motifs of Western Gothicism.

Zolbrod, Leon M. Introduction to *Tales of Moonlight and Rain*. Vancouver: University of British Columbia Press, 1974:19–94. Gives a biographical sketch and discusses Akinari's style, influence, philosophy, and attitude toward the supernatural.

GERTRUDE ATHERTON
(1857–1948)
Jack G. Voller

PRINCIPAL GOTHIC WORKS

"Death and the Woman." *Vanity Fair* 49 (1892): 25–26.
"A Christmas Witch." *Godey's Magazine* 126 (January 1893): 9–40.
"The Twins." *Speaker* [London], 20 June 1896: 664–665. (Original title of "The Striding Place.")
"The Dead and the Countess." *Smart Set* 7 (1902): 55–61.
The Bell in the Fog and Other Stories. New York and London: Harper & Brothers, 1905; London and New York: Macmillan, 1905.
"The Foghorn." *Good Housekeeping*, 97 (1933): 16–17, 129–132.
The Foghorn Stories. Boston: Houghton Mifflin, 1934; (Contains "The Eternal Now," "The Striding Place," "The Foghorn," "The Greatest Good of the Greatest Number" [First published in *The Bell in the Fog*].)
Contemporary California Short Stories. [San Francisco]: Book Club of California, 1937. (Vol. 4 contains "The Foghorn.")
The Haunted Omnibus. Ed. Alexander Lang and Lynd Ward New York: Farrar & Rinehart, 1937. (Contains "The Foghorn.")

MODERN REPRINTS AND EDITIONS

The Bell in the Fog and Other Stories. New York: MSS Information Corp., 1968. (The American Short Story series, vol. 1. Rpt. of the 1905 edition.)
The Foghorn. Freeport, NY: Books for Libraries Press, 1970.
Haunted Women: The Best Supernatural Tales by American Women Writers. Ed. Alfred Bendixen. New York: Ungar, 1985, 1986; New York: Continuum, 1985, 1987. (An excellent collection that contains "The Bell in the Fog.")

Born on the day before Halloween in 1857, Gertrude Horn Atherton became and remains best known for those works that have led many critics to label her a "regionalist" in her novels and stories of California. Such a label is, in Atherton's case, reductive, not only because her strong and enduring interest in issues of class, gender, and social displacement gives her work a power belied by her simple surfaces and favored settings, but also because her range was in fact considerable. Atherton also produced historical novels, novels set in various states and countries, a highly regarded biographical novel of Alexander Hamilton as well as an edition of his letters, film scripts, and mystery tales as well as stories of psychological and supernaturalist interest.

Atherton was a prolific author, and her output of supernaturalist tales represents a tiny fraction of her total work. Given this, it is hardly surprising that Atherton's "Gothic" works have been almost completely ignored by critics and scholars, as the scant list of selected criticism makes clear. What is most striking about such neglence is that Atherton is clearly working quite adeptly in the psychological strain of the supernaturalist tale. Her most famous such piece, "The Bell in the Fog," is an avowedly Jamesian work and a critique of James that should have pointed the way to more study of Atherton's supernaturalism. In this long short story, Atherton eschews obvious supernaturalism; the "fantastic" element in the work, the appearance of a young Blanche Root who appears to be a reincarnation of the long-dead Blanche, is important not for any horror or dread it raises but for its ability to open a window into the psyche of the story's true subject, the Jamesian author Ralph Ort, whose emotional remoteness and cultural prominence are both his most effective weapons and his true weaknesses. Although Atherton had considerable regard for James—she dedicated the volume to him and wrote in her autobiography *Adventures of a Novelist* that "surely *The Turn of the Screw* is the most horrifying ghost story ever written"— she also remarks that James is the "hero" of her story. She clearly rejects the emotional "aridity" and cultural aloofness of the Ort/James character, which she, according to Bruce R. McElderry, sees as the cause of James's loss of much of his audience in the middle of his career (272).

Atherton's virtually ignored supernaturalist tale "A Christmas Witch" is a striking counterpart to "The Bell in the Fog," for it both mirrors and inverts "Bell," which it predates by some eleven years. It explores in more detail, and with more melodrama, the reincarnation theme suggested in "The Bell in the Fog." In "A Christmas Witch," the young Heloise quite firmly believes herself to be the reincarnation of her murderous ancestor Noel, and when her doting father takes the eldritch Heloise, repeatedly identified as a "witch," "elf," "ghost," or even "incarnated impulse," to the family's ancestral mansion in France, Heloise doggedly pursues her long-dead ancestress. In a family mansion that meets all of the Gothic requirements and then some (the "wehr-wolf" being the most dramatic addition), Atherton even invokes the Gothic atmospherics of Jane Austen's *Northanger Abbey* when Heloise finally dreams that her long-dead ancestress visits her. Upon awakening, she finds that, as in her dream, she did in fact descend to a long-hidden crypt, dig Noel's coffin out of the hard ground, and reunite her skull with the rest of her skeleton. This is the Gothic climax of the story, which then focuses on Heloise's return to California and her continued inability, one that discomfits her not in the least, to accommodate herself to the demands of society. The story feels pronouncedly metaphoric in a way that adds to the social critique of "The Bell in the Fog." Whereas the later story focuses on the emotionally remote Jamesian author and critiques his assumptions of superiority and ownership, "A Christmas Witch" is an exuberant study of a young girl who is "owned" by nobody, who in contrast to the passive Blanche Root refuses to be ordered, controlled, or disciplined by anyone, and who at age nine thinks nothing of riding alone into the California forests to shoot a bear for her father's Christmas present. Heloise refuses to subordinate herself to any man, even her doting, compliant father; only when he dies is she able to demonstrate any filial affection or piety, and her rejection of suitors and social mores further confirms her essential independence. There may not be a place for a woman such as her, Atherton suggests, as a young adult, unable to tolerate the presence of her conformist half sisters. Heloise has her own house built deep in the forest and twenty feet off the ground. The relative ease with which Atherton abandons the dense supernaturalism of the story's first half confirms that issues of female power and socialization, not Gothic mansions and floating skulls, are her true concern. Although Atherton, following the lead of Ambrose Bierce, felt that "A Christmas Witch" was an inferior production, and although it is a bit heavy-handed at times, Atherton was right to move toward a subtler, more psychological Gothic. It has an engaging and a thematic correlation to other Atherton works that should lead it to be more fully examined.

When Atherton returned to "Gothic" themes a dozen years further into her career, her works showed the restrained energies of "The Bell in the Fog." From "The Striding Place," which Atherton called "the best short story I have ever written," to "The Eternal Now" to "The Dead and the Countess," Atherton is concerned not with horror, but with the mind in crisis, with psychology, with the operations of mental processes under various forms of pressure. In this she is much like Poe, the influence of whom on Atherton is in need of much study, and who like her rarely wrote blatantly "supernatural" tales. In her most "supernatural" work, "Death and the Woman," Atherton most resembles the Poe of "The Masque of the Red Death," yet she exercises considerably more restraint. The protagonist hears the approach of Death, yet never actually sees him. "The Dead and the Countess" is a reworking of Poe's "Premature Burial," and in her nonsupernaturalist but decidedly post-Gothic works "The Foghorn" and "The Greatest Good of the Greatest Number," Atherton mines a psychological vein first discovered by Poe. Both of these stories are studies of psychological extremes: "The Foghorn" concerns an elderly woman who, on her deathbed, lives more in the past than the present, and Atherton draws us in so deftly that the story is nearly complete before the situation is fully revealed; "The Greatest Good of the Greatest Number" examines one man's grasp of the power of life and death, and of the moral and social currents that swirl around that power and its exercise.

SELECTED CRITICISM

Holt, Marilyn J. "Gertrude Atherton." In *Supernatural Fiction Writers: Fantasy and Horror*. Ed. E.F. Bleiler. New York: Scribner's, 1985: 777–781. The only study to date focusing on Atherton's supernaturalism, Holt's analysis argues that her supernaturalist works "derive in part from a belief in the harmony between the individual and the spiritual and natural worlds." While occasionally insightful, Holt's entry ignores Atherton's psychological Gothic, overlooks "A Christmas Witch," and fundamentally errs in identifying "The Dead and the Countess" as "a straightforward supernatural tale of the dead speaking to the living." The countess is accidentally buried alive and is rescued.

Leider, Emily Wortis. *California's Daughter: Gertrude Atherton and Her Times*. Stanford, CA: Stanford University Press, 1991. Although this is a detailed and intelligent study of Atherton's life and major works, it gives scant attention to Atherton's Gothic works, briefly dismissing all except "A Christmas Witch," which Leider finds "has remarkable wit and energy," as "short on nuance or insight."

McClure, Charlotte S. "Gertrude Atherton (1857–1948)." *American Literary Realism, 1870–1910* 9 (1976): 95–101. A brief bibliographical essay.

———. "A Checklist of the Writings of and about Gertrude Atherton." *American Literary Realism, 1870–1910* 9 (1976): 103–162. Still a valuable checklist, although the omission of "A Christmas Witch" and a few other minor errors somewhat compromise its value.

———. *Gertrude Atherton*. Twayne's United States Authors Series 324. Boston: Twayne, 1979. A very useful introduction to the life and works of Atherton, although, like most studies of Atherton, it focuses on her novels and has practically nothing to say on the subject of Atherton's Gothic works.

McElderry, Bruce R., Jr. "Gertrude Atherton and Henry James." *Colby Library Quarterly* 3 (1954): 269–272. Considers the "cryptic fashion" in which "The Bell in the Fog" records Atherton's impressions of and attitude toward James, and how the story constitutes "a warning to James of his isolation from his old reading public."

Pennell, Melissa McFarland. "Through the Golden Gate: Madness and the Persephone Myth in Gertrude Atherton's 'The Foghorn.' " In *Images of Persephone: Feminist Readings in Western Literature*. Ed. Elizabeth Hayes. Gainesville: University Press of Florida, 1994: 84–98. Arguing that Atherton's tale is "a tightly constructed, highly effective Gothic tale of madness and deception," Pennell focuses her attention on Atherton's adaptation of the Persephone myth in this story, which "explores a woman's need to create her own story and self-image."

MARGARET ATWOOD
(1939–   )
Carol Margaret Davison

PRINCIPAL GOTHIC WORKS

"Speeches for Dr. Frankenstein." In *The Animals in That Country*. Boston: Atlantic–
Little, Brown, 1968: 42–47.
The Journals of Susanna Moodie. Toronto: Oxford University Press, 1970.
Surfacing. Toronto: McClelland & Stewart, 1972.
Survival: A Thematic Guide to Canadian Literature. Toronto: Anansi, 1972. (Criticism.)
Lady Oracle. Toronto: McClelland & Stewart, 1976.

In both her critical and creative work, Margaret Atwood, one of Canada's most
celebrated contemporary writers, has long exhibited a fascination with the
Gothic. On at least two occasions in the mid-1980s, she taught a course on the
subject of Southern Ontario Gothic, and in an interview with Joyce Carol Oates
in 1978, she made reference to her long-standing interest in supernatural fantasy
and the Gothic and to her related unfinished Harvard dissertation. Tentatively
titled "The English Metaphysical Romance," Atwood's doctoral project focused
on H. Rider Haggard and other late Victorian writers. One critic, Eli Mandel,
has claimed that Atwood's graduate work was not abandoned but was, rather,
distilled along more creative lines into such works as *Surfacing*.

In her Gothic-related critical work, Atwood's *Survival: A Thematic Guide to
Canadian Literature* (1972) took its cue from Northrop Frye's description of
Canadian poetry as marked by "incubus and *cauchemar* [nightmare]" (*The Bush
Garden: Essays on the Canadian Imagination*, 1971). Examining a broad spectrum of Canadian fiction and poetry, *Survival* was instrumental in bringing the
"darker side" of Canadian literature to light. Atwood argues that the single
unifying symbol at the core of the Canadian literary tradition is survival. Physical survival dominates the early literature, while spiritual survival dominates
the later works in which death in its varied but connected forms—death by

nature, by Indian assault, and by "bushing," where "a character isolated in Nature goes crazy"—is the central Canadian experience, an ever-present threat that happens "with startling frequency." Atwood never mentions the term "Gothic" in *Survival* and misunderstands the nature of the Burkean sublime in her second chapter, "Nature the Monster," but she nonetheless articulates a dynamic between physical landscapes and psychic states in the Canadian canon that was and still is at the forefront of the established European Gothic tradition.

It fell to another literary critic to tease out the implications of Atwood's observations in *Survival* and thus to better establish the nature, parameters, and development of the Gothic tradition in Canadian literature. In her 1976 study *The Haunted Wilderness: The Gothic and Grotesque in Canadian Fiction*, Margot Northey advances a corrective both to the bias she perceives toward realist fiction in Canadian literary criticism and to the common misperception that the Gothic is a rarity in Canadian literature. Albeit in a somewhat sketchy and elementary manner (due to the then-prevalent view of the Gothic as an illegitimate form and the dearth of specialized studies devoted to it), *The Haunted Wilderness* illustrates, in works ranging from John Richardson's *Wacousta; or, The Prophecy: A Tale of the Canadas* (1832) and William Kirby's *The Golden Dog* (1877) to Leonard Cohen's *Beautiful Losers* (1966) and Mordecai Richler's *Cocksure* (1968), that "there is a dark band of Gothicism which stretches from earliest to recent times" (14). Northey rightly takes Atwood's criticism to task for "repeatedly head[ing] towards the subject [of Gothic] only to veer off," but she includes an examination of Atwood's *Surfacing* (1972)—a novel she describes as a didactic and prescriptive fictional counterpart to Atwood's critical work, *Survival*—as a prime example of "sociological Gothic," a category Northey coins to describe Gothic fiction whose principal agenda is social critique.

Atwood's 1977 essay "Canadian Monsters: Some Aspects of the Supernatural in Canadian Fiction" extends her central thesis in *Survival*. Describing herself as a "mere collector of Canadian monsters" whose job is not necessarily to interpret them, Atwood counters Earle Birney's assertion in his poem "Can. Lit" that Canada is haunted only by its lack of ghosts. Given the role of the North in Canadian literature as "a symbol for the unexplored, the unconscious, the romantic, the mysterious, and the magical," Atwood declares that it is "not surprising that a large number of Canadian monsters have their origin in native Indian and Eskimo myths" (98). She cites the legendary figures of the cannibalistic Wendigo and the trickster Coyote as supportive examples. Examining recurrent "image-clusters" in the literature, Atwood returns to a more detailed analysis of the ambivalent role of the North in the Canadian cultural imagination in her 1991 Clarendon Lectures in English Literature, later published as the volume *Strange Things: The Malevolent North in Canadian Literature*. Although Atwood does not consider the established Gothic tradition and its conventions, her discussion about the allure and terror of becoming the Other by "going native" in her chapter on "The Grey Owl Syndrome" provides some interesting raw material for a reassessment of the Gothic literary tradition in Canada.

It may be argued that while most of Atwood's novels and stories invoke a Gothic mood or incorporate Gothic elements such as an ambivalent hero-villain or the figure of the double, few may be described as fully sustained Gothic works. If Atwood may be said to have a Gothic period, however, it falls between the late 1960s and the mid-1970s. Published in Atwood's 1968 poetry collection *The Animals in That Country*, "Speeches for Dr. Frankenstein" attests to Atwood's early interest in the genre. While she exploits Mary Shelley's use of the double motif in her rendition of the relationship between Victor Frankenstein and his creature (her monster also gets the last word), "Speeches" diverges from its parent text when Atwood's monster ultimately deserts its maker.

Atwood's earliest experiment in sustained Gothic comes in *The Journals of Susanna Moodie*, a series of unsettling poems arranged into three sections inspired by the life and writings of the author of *Roughing It in the Bush*. Notably, *Roughing It* is one of the texts Atwood cites in *Survival* as best exemplifying the ambivalent attitude toward nature in early Canadian literature. Like several classic Gothic works, *Journals* is an oneiric production that features dream sequences and repeatedly explores the permeable boundary between conscious reality and unconscious dream. As Atwood relates in the afterword, this volume took a year and a half to complete and was engendered by a strange dream in which she envisioned a solitary white figure singing in an opera she had written about Susanna Moodie. According to Atwood, Moodie is the prototypical Canadian because she is marked by a "violent duality"—"She claims to be an ardent Canadian patriot while all the time she is standing back from the country and criticizing it as though she were a detached observer, a stranger" (216). Intriguingly, Moodie's double voices in *Journals* are more complex and work on more levels than Atwood's brief description suggests. *Journals* serves as a template for Atwood's later manipulation of the Gothic (particularly in *Surfacing*) to probe various connected and complex aspects of identity, especially gender and national identity.

Journals is arranged into three sections: the first, 1832–1840, chronicles the seven years Moodie spent in the Canadian bush; the second, 1840–1871, recounts Moodie's reflections about that time; the final section, 1871–1969, relays her later years in Belleville, followed by her death and "resurrection" in the twentieth century when Atwood transforms her into the irrepressible voice of the Canadian wilderness. The popular female Gothic image of a woman traveling into unknown territory, which represents both her unconscious self and her heretofore-repressed desires and fears about the institution of marriage, opens Journal 1. Atwood transfers the traditional motif of terra incognita that usually applies to the tenebrous, labyrinthine Gothic castle in a foreign, generally Roman Catholic setting, to the Canadian bush, which she enters, fittingly, via Quebec. Here Moodie is a representative Canadian immigrant, an invading alien who believes, mistakenly, that order may be created out of chaos. As she illustrates in "The Planters" and its sister poem "The Immigrants" (Journal 2), immigrants to Canada are necessarily delusional: the past, represented by the old country in the appropriately Gothic form of "perfect thumbnail castles preserved / like gallstones in a glass bottle," (43) feeds their belief in a future civilization. To embrace the possibility of order, Moodie suggests, the settlers must deny their present-day reality and the true nature of the bush.

As Moodie discovers in the second set of journals, the dark wilderness calls forth the darker forces within the human psyche. In the poem "Charivari," a black man who marries a white woman is brutally murdered by several European settlers. As Atwood also suggests later in *Surfacing*, the Canadian bush brings out the heart of darkness that exists at the core of so-called civilization. A fascinating counterdynamic is also at work along gender lines, however, as Moodie not only enters her "own ignorance" like the other immigrants when she arrives in the bush, but eventually comes face-to-face with her own repressed female nature that is reflected within it. "Looking in the Mirror," a poem written just prior to Moodie's departure from the bush, best conveys this association. During her seven years there, Moodie has been irreversibly altered. A physical interfacing even seems to have occurred as her skin has become "thickened / with bark and the white hairs of roots" (112). The poem's concluding lines, however, confirm her awareness that she has not developed in any way alien to her nature. As she articulates it, "you find only / the shape you already are / but what / if you have forgotten that / or discover you / have never known." Intriguingly, Atwood's invocation of the classic female Gothic anxiety regarding the usually prospective husband's potentially terrifying secret identity is more consciously brought to bear on Moodie's own lack of self-knowledge. The predominant focus in the poem "Wereman," for example, may be on her "shadowy husband," who is perceived as "an X, a concept / defined against a blank," but Moodie concludes by suggesting that she mirrors him and is equally impenetrable to both him and herself. Toward the poem's end, the tables are turned when she wonders what he sees when he looks at her.

In Journal 2, Atwood takes Moodie's connection to the bush to a deeper, more macabre level. Here the wilderness is a type of cannibal that ritualistically devours its victims, such as Moodie's son, who is figuratively consumed by a lake. Here too, Moodie's voice assumes a calmer, more matter-of-fact tone. Without a trace of hysteria, and increasingly like a prophetess who articulates a series of truths about the wilderness, Moodie dispels the illusions of the settlers with definitive claims. The immigrants ride in railway cars "across an ocean of unknown / land to an unknown land." There is no safe or known place. In the third dream poem, "Night Bear Which Frightened Cattle" (146), it is Moodie's voice of reason, in keeping with the Gothic tradition, that utters the most chilling truth; she reminds the settlers that while they may laugh at their fears from within their houses, real terrors do actually lurk without. Attempts to repress this knowledge, to shelter oneself from the wilderness and the associated wild side of one's nature, are entirely in vain. The bush will overcome everything. In "The Deaths of the Other Children," bush life is a slow-but-sure process of disintegration. This new insight radically alters her assessment of her seven years in the bush. Reconsidering them, she wonders, "Did I spend all those years / building up this edifice / my composite / self, this crumbling hovel?" Ultimately, all so-called order, civilization, and individuality will return to the void.

The third and final set of journal poems covers Moodie's postbush life in Belleville, when, among other things, she becomes fascinated by criminals and the insane. As she deteriorates physically, the question of her own mental health is also raised. In "Alternate Thoughts from Underground," Moodie relates her deep hatred of this new country after her bush experience. She cannot simply begin to love it once her husband has become successful. While this piece seems to be conveyed from the perspective of Moodie's ostensibly genteel and civilized self, "Alternate Thoughts from Underground" taps into her more nature-affiliated voice. In fact, the belief system embraced in "Alternate Thoughts" is indisputably pagan as Moodie becomes one with the land. Speaking from beyond the grave to the surrounding "babylons" populated by their "glib superstructures," Moodie is now fervently anticivilization. She decisively subverts the Christian sense of Apocalypse when she declares at the poem's end that "at the last / judgement we will all be trees" (212). In the volume's final poem, "A Bus along St. Clair: December," not only is the boundary between Moodie and the wilderness eradicated, but so is that between past and present. Portraying herself as an old woman seated across from a complete stranger on a Toronto bus in 1969, Moodie enunciates her most Gothic message, namely, that repressed truths will invariably return to plague those who try to deny them, as she becomes the haunting voice of a repressed and abused natural world. She reminds the deluded city dweller that "though they buried me in monuments / of concrete slabs, of cables . . . I have my ways of getting through / there is no city; / this is the centre of a forest / your place is empty."

In its focus on a female protagonist whose repressed nature and emotions are released and healed by a profound experience in the wilderness, *Surfacing* is a modern Canadian example of the female Gothic. Relayed from the perspective of an unnamed female narrator, *Surfacing* chronicles a journey she, her lover, and another couple make into the forests of Quebec after her father has been reported missing from his cabin there. While the trip is initially treated as casual, it soon becomes an intense exploration of the narrator's long-repressed feelings regarding her family (particularly her father) and her emotionally wrenching experiences in various love relationships. An abortion during a relationship with a married man is a particularly burdensome and painful memory that left her both emotionally dead and haunted. The "surfacing" and allaying of such heretofore-buried memories constitute the novel's focus.

As elsewhere in Atwood's fiction, the Canadian wilderness replaces the European castle as the site of the protagonist's exploration of her psychic closets. In its role as a foreign, Roman Catholic, and "uncanny" locale where the foreign and the familiar, the conscious and the unconscious, intermingle, Quebec is the equivalent of Italy in Ann Radcliffe's classic Gothic works. Atwood puts a more feminist spin on this, however, as Quebec functions as a patriarchal space where women are socially repressed. As the narrator relates in the early chapters, the Church plays a special role in this regard. Women have no access to birth control or divorce, and even their attire is regulated: "Many of them lived all their lives beside the lake without learning to swim because they were ashamed to put on bathing suits" (231). Given these associations, Quebec functions as a particularly appropriate locale in which the narrator wrestles with her earlier, generally negative experiences with men. Her healing/purification process is ritualistic in nature and involves, among other things, swimming naked in the lake, an especially significant act given the traditional constraints placed upon Quebecois women.

In keeping with Gothic conventions, the narrator must unearth, examine, and resolve fundamental questions of inheritance before this final cleansing ritual occurs, although in her case spiritual/emotional inheritance is key while material inheritance is virtually neglected. She considers and ultimately rejects her rationalist father's unbalanced worldview because it denies the emotions. Only then does she reconcile the two halves of what she describes as her divided self and realize that she is more than just "a head." While she is in this wilderness, she also considers her past before making a decision regarding her current lover, Joe. Although she gives no definitive response to his marriage proposal, the narrator ultimately chooses to remain with him and move into a new stage of their relationship. Her suggestion that she is pregnant at the novel's end signals both the fertility of their union and a certain regeneration after her traumatic abortion experience.

The Gothic is manipulated in *Surfacing* to address pressing gender and nationalist issues. Here again, the ambivalent wilderness is key. While it may be the site of healing and reconciliation, it may also engender violent regression and discord, but in that it may annihilate barriers and hierarchies and return people to an earlier state of equality, it is positive. The lake water, for example, is described as "multilingual," a site where the English-French language barrier is eradicated. The narrator intimates the so-called Western civilization has a darker side that may emerge after prolonged contact with the wilderness. We all possess the innate ability to return to a savage state. Her representation of Americans is inextricably bound up with this threat and provides what is, perhaps, this novel's most telling Gothic image. Drawing on the genre of American horror cinema, the narrator proffers a disturbing future vision of Americans as machinelike body snatchers who are increasingly moving north, where they threaten to control Canadians. A resolution is offered, however, in the final two chapters regarding the narrator's views on Canada's relationship to the United States. Although this "pervasive enemy" may be advancing, she assuages her fears with the thought that perhaps it is possible to avoid emulating them.

The 1976 publication *Lady Oracle* has garnered the most critical attention as an explicitly Gothic production within the Atwood canon. Sybil Vincent has characterized it as "the most Gothic of Gothic novels, a Gothic novel about Gothic novels" (153). Originally subtitled *A Gothic Romance, Lady Oracle* is clearly Atwood's most consciously Gothic production. In several interviews about this work, she labels the Gothic an explicitly female form that "centers on [the idea that] *My husband is trying to kill me.*" *Lady Oracle* belongs, as Atwood and others have pointed out, in the tradition of Jane Austen's *Northanger Abbey*. Although the power of Atwood's Gothic parody, especially as a daughter text to Austen's, has been greatly misrepresented, *Lady Oracle* does work within this tradition because it also foregrounds and plays on the disjunction between "the real world" and the romantic expectations generated by such genres as Gothic/romance literature.

Atwood's novel relates the story of Joan Foster, an author of costume Gothics who stages her own death and flees to Italy when her "past lives" and various identities begin to catch up with her. Joan is a mistress of escape, a female Houdini whose life is bound up in denial, specifically the denial of complex gender identities. In this, she is portrayed as a true product of her monstrous society. *Lady Oracle* should be classified as a "feminist Gothic" novel, as Atwood exposes how established late-twentieth-century sexual norms and feminine ideals are truly Gothic in nature. In advancing this message, Joan Foster anticipates Angela Carter's statement in the afterword to her collected short stories, *Burning Your Boats* (1996), that "we live in Gothic times."

Drawing on *Frankenstein*, Joan's principal bogey is her monstrous mother, an obsessive-compulsive housewife who upholds, at the cost of her own happiness, her society's ideals regarding femininity. Tyrannized by her triple-mirrored vanity table, Joan's "triple-headed monster [mother]" is extremely ashamed of her young, overweight daughter. Significantly, this mother's emotional distance persists even after Joan successfully loses weight and, for all intents and purposes, conforms to those ideals. In keeping with such traditionally Gothic works as Radcliffe's *Mysteries of Udolpho*, Atwood portrays Joan as plagued by the question of her true parentage and "the sins of the fathers" (although, in this instance, the emphasis is on the sins of the mothers). Although Joan is occasionally at odds with her society's gender ideology, she also eventually evolves into "a duplicitous monster." Her escape into and production of costume Gothics exhibits a concerted effort to uphold a dangerous worldview. In the final analysis, Joan's efforts fail.

Writing in retrospect from the vantage point of Italy, Joan recounts her life's highlights, interspersing them with highly melodramatic segments from her latest escapist novel. The climax of the novel, which relates Joan's revelation regarding her essentially schizophrenic society, involves a subversion of the costume Gothic's gender conventions and a blurring of the boundary between her own life story and that of her novel's two principal female characters, Charlotte and Felicia. It is implied that the reconciliation of the disparate fragments of Joan's identity will follow. Convinced that the future is, in general, better for people,

Joan determines at the novel's end to abandon writing costume Gothics in favor of science fiction.

Atwood's neo-Gothic texts, with their subjective appeal and willingness to confront problems of Canadian identity as well as female wholeness, are striking examples of the Gothic spirit nationalized and personalized in modern literature. Surely Atwood was referring to her own work when she remarked in her thematic study of Canadian horror fiction, *Strange Things*, that "there is indeed a mass of dark intimations in the Canadian soul" (121).

SELECTED CRITICISM

Atwood, Margaret. "Canadian Monsters: Some Aspects of the Supernatural in Canadian Fiction." In *The Canadian Imagination: Dimensions of a Literary Culture*. Ed. David Staines. Cambridge, MA: Harvard University Press, 1977: 97–122. By commenting on the Canadian Gothic tradition, Atwood reveals her own foundations in the wilderness and its monsters. "The North is a symbol for the world of the unexplored, the unconscious, the Romantic, the mysterious, and the magical."

———. *Strange Things: The Malevolent North in Canadian Literature*. Oxford and New York: Oxford University Press, 1995. Thematic study of the wilderness environment as a determining force for the Canadian Gothic impulse.

Becker, Susanne. "Exceeding Even Gothic Texture: Margaret Atwood and *Lady Oracle*." In *Gothic Forms of Feminine Fictions*. Manchester and New York: Manchester University Press, 1999: 151–198. *Lady Oracle* is described as a "reverential parody" that "rewrites the conventions and repeats the experience of feminine Gothicism to explore its possibilities in contemporary female literary culture, not just to ridicule it."

Gillespie, Tracey. "Elements of the Gothic in the Novels of Margaret Atwood." M.A. thesis, University of Alberta, 1990. Focuses on what Gillespie claims are Atwood's three Gothic novels to 1990: *Lady Oracle, Bodily Harm*, and *The Handmaid's Tale*. While earlier female Gothic is essentially conservative, Atwood's use of the genre has "a wider public, political emphasis."

Grace, Sherrill. *Violent Duality: A Study of Margaret Atwood*. Montreal: Véhicule Press, 1980. Chapter 7, "More Than a Very Double Life," provides an illuminating close reading of *Lady Oracle*. "It is an amusing parody of Gothic romance and realist conventions, a satiric commentary upon Atwood's own experiences as a writer and upon aspects of contemporary society, and a portrayal of 'the perils of Gothic thinking.'"

Howells, Coral Ann. *Margaret Atwood*. Basingstoke: Macmillan, 1996. Chapter 4, "Atwoodian Gothic: From *Lady Oracle* to *The Robber Bride*," argues that the Gothic is pervasive in Atwood's works and dates back to her early watercolors of sinister knights and unconscious damsels from the late 1960s.

Ingersoll, Earl G., ed. *Margaret Atwood: Conversations*. Princeton: Ontario Review Press, 1990. Features a wide variety of intriguing and informative interviews (two with Joyce Carol Oates in 1978) that shed light on Atwood's interest in and attitudes toward the Gothic, a genre she describes in a 1978 interview with Karla Hammond as "very much a woman's form."

Mandel, Eli. "Atwood Gothic." *Malahat Review* 41 (1977): 165–174. Mentions the
    Gothic elements in *Surfacing* and *Survival*, "a ghost story disguised as politics
    and criticism." The ghosts that haunt *Surfacing* extend beyond "sexual fears,
    repressed contents of the imagination, [and] social rigidity" to include "perhaps
    even the unwritten thesis Atwood proposed for her Ph.D. on Gothic romance."

McCombs, Judith. "Atwood's Haunted Sequences: *The Circle Game, The Journals of
    Susanna Moodie*, and *Power Politics*." In *The Art of Margaret Atwood: Essays
    in Criticism*. Ed. Arnold E. Davidson and Cathy N. Davidson. Toronto: Anansi,
    1981: 35–54. The Gothic, "the neglected and long outcast stepchild of literature,"
    is revived in Margaret Atwood's three long poetry sequences, *The Circle Game*
    (1966), *The Journals of Susanna Moodie* (1970), and *Power Politics* (1971). *The
    Circle Game* is dominated by the "internal Gothic"; *The Journals of Susanna
    Moodie* focuses on "wilderness Gothic"; *Power Politics* centers on "the Franken-
    steinian mirrored and remirrored Other."

McMillan, Ann. "The Transforming Eye: *Lady Oracle* and Gothic Tradition." In *Mar-
    garet Atwood: Vision and Forms*. Ed. Kathryn VanSpanckeren and Jan Garden
    Castro. Carbondale: Southern Illinois University Press, 1988: 48–64. Argues that
    there are two Gothic traditions: Gothic naturalism and Gothic fantasy. *Northanger
    Abbey* and *Lady Oracle* combine both, creating stories "that refuse the simpler
    resolutions of both Gothic traditions."

Northey, Margot. "Sociological Gothic: *Wild Geese* and *Surfacing*." In *The Haunted Wil-
    derness: The Gothic and Grotesque in Canadian Fiction*. Toronto and Buffalo:
    University of Toronto Press, 1976: 62–69. The predominant "dark spirit" prevalent
    in *Surfacing* is the threat posed to Canada of becoming American, which is a syn-
    ecdoche for "a repressive, technological imperialism which is the legacy of a com-
    bined liberalism and Calvinism."

Rao, Eleonora. "A Fascination with Romance: *Lady Oracle*." In *Strategies for Identity:
    The Fiction of Margaret Atwood*. New York: Peter Lang, 1993: 28–39. Provides
    a detailed comparison of *Lady Oracle* and Jane Austen's *Northanger Abbey*. At-
    wood's novel is, like Austen's, an anti-Gothic work.

Rosowski, Susan J. "Margaret Atwood's *Lady Oracle*: Fantasy and the Modern Gothic
    Novel." In *Critical Essays on Margaret Atwood*. Ed. Judith McCombs. Boston:
    G.K. Hall, 1988: 197–208. "Gothic horrors exist not 'beyond social patterns,
    rational decisions, and institutionally approved emotions,' but within them."

Vincent, Sybil Korff. "The Mirror and the Cameo: Margaret Atwood's Comic/Gothic
    Novel, *Lady Oracle*." In *The Female Gothic*. Ed. Juliann E. Fleenor. Montreal:
    Eden Press, 1983: 153–163. A generically aware analysis of *Lady Oracle* as a
    traditional female Gothic work that "expresses conflicts within the female re-
    garding her own sexuality and identity, and uses a highly stylized form and elab-
    orate detail to effect psychic catharsis."

JANE AUSTEN AND THE *NORTHANGER* NOVELISTS

(Lawrence Flammenberg [Karl Friedrich Kahlert], Carl Grosse, Francis Lathom, Eliza Parsons, Regina Maria Roche, and Eleanor Sleath)

Douglass H. Thomson and Frederick S. Frank

PRINCIPAL GOTHIC WORKS

Jane Austen (1775–1817)

Northanger Abbey. London: John Murray, 1818. (Written in 1798 at the zenith of the Gothic craze, but not published until 1818.)

Lawrence Flammenberg [pseud. of Karl Friedrich Kahlert] (1765–1813)

The Necromancer; or, The Tale of the Black Forest: Founded on Facts. London: Minerva-Press for William Lane, 1794. (Translated by Peter Teuthold from a German romance, *Der Geisterbanner: Eine Wundergeschichte aus mündlichen und schriftlichen Traditionen gesammelt* [The Spectral Banner: A Wondrous Tale Collected from Oral and Written Traditions].)

Carl Grosse (1768–1847)

Horrid Mysteries. London: Minerva-Press for William Lane, 1796. (Translated from the German by Peter Will.)

Francis Lathom (1777–1832)

The Midnight Bell: A German Story Founded on Incidents of Real Life. London: H.D. Symonds, 1798.

Eliza Parsons (1748–1811)

Castle of Wolfenbach: A German Story. London: Minerva-Press for William Lane, 1793.
The Mysterious Warning: A German Tale. London: Minerva-Press for William Lane, 1796.

Regina Maria Roche (1764–1845)

Clermont: A Tale. London: Minerva-Press for William Lane, 1798.

Eleanor Sleath (dates unknown)

The Orphan of the Rhine. London: Minerva-Press for William Lane, 1798.

MODERN REPRINTS AND EDITIONS

Austen, Jane. *Northanger Abbey*. Ed. Anne Henry Ehrenpreis. Baltimore: Penguin, 1972.
   (This edition is cited in the text.)
———. *Northanger Abbey*. Ed. Claire Grogan. Peterborough, Ontario: Broadview Press,
   1996.
Flammenberg, Lawrence [pseud. of Karl Friedrich Kahlert]. *The Necromancer; or, The
   Tale of the Black Forest*. Ed. Montague Summers. London: Robert Holden, 1927.
———. *The Necromancer; or, The Tale of the Black Forest*. Ed. Devendra P. Varma.
   London: Folio Press, 1968.
Gothic Readings: The First Wave. 1764–1840. Ed. Rictor Norton. London and New
   York: Leicester University Press, 2000. (Contains excerpts from the seven
   Northanger novels and the complete text of "The Terrorist System of Novel-
   Writing.")
Grosse, Carl. *Horrid Mysteries*. Ed. Devendra P. Varma. London: Folio Press, 1968.
Lathom, Francis. *The Midnight Bell: A German Story Founded on Incidents in Real Life*.
   Ed. Devendra P. Varma. London: Folio Press, 1968.
Parsons, Eliza. *Castle of Wolfenbach: A German Story*. Ed. Devendra P. Varma. London:
   Folio Press, 1968.
———. *The Mysterious Warning: A German Tale*. Ed. Devendra P. Varma. London:
   Folio Press, 1968.
Roche, Regina Maria. *Clermont: A Tale*. Ed. Devendra P. Varma. London: Folio Press,
   1968.
Sleath, Eleanor. *The Orphan of the Rhine*. Ed. Devendra P. Varma. London: Folio Press,
   1968.

Jane Austen's gentle parody of Gothic novels and sensibility in *Northanger
Abbey* occupies an illuminating place in the culture wars of the late 1790s. By
this time the Gothic had reached its peak of popularity, outstripping the claims
of more domestic and didactic fiction and prompting a rash of alarmed reviewers
and satirists to take it upon themselves to excoriate this "degrading thirst after
outrageous stimulation," to quote from Wordsworth's withering estimate of these
"frantic novels" in the preface to *The Lyrical Ballads*. One of Austen's serious
aims in *Northanger Abbey*, completed in 1798, was to defend the novel as a
genre, and she must have felt compelled to distinguish her understanding of the
novel from that of the Gothic craze flooding the literary marketplace. Austen
seems most prominently concerned with the achievement of Ann Radcliffe, but
the famous inclusion of Isabella Thorpe's seven "horrid" novels—for years

thought to be of Austen's parodic invention until they were proved by twentieth-century scholarship to be the real things—shows that she knew well a broad range of the literary competition in the Gothic marketplace. Yet while the literary stakes may have been high, Austen's parody of the Gothic differs markedly from the corrosive satires and shrill moral reviews found everywhere in the late 1790s. Through the career and education of a new kind of heroine, Catherine Morland, Austen aims not so much to denigrate but to rehabilitate the Gothic sensibility, as she acknowledges its imaginative power but gently and delightfully succeeds in tempering its more uncritical enthusiasms.

Many cultural forces informed the sharp turn against the Gothic at the end of the century, not the least its own tendency toward self-parody as its plots grew all the more extravagant and mannered and as a spate of less skilled imitators, like some of the names on Isabella Thorpe's list, glutted the bookstalls with "shilling shockers" and the like. From religious quarters, one finds constant complaining about the Gothic's impious use of the preternatural and the occult; from the still-dominant neoclassical aesthetic, a sharp disdain for its wayward design, morally ambiguous characters, and departure from scenes of common life. Defenders of the domestic sphere expressed alarm about the message this fiction was sending to its principal readership of women. It seemed to "teach" young women to abandon the hearth, develop an exquisite quasi-poetic sensibility, and expect the reward of an appreciative husband above one's station in life. We should also not forget that during this time of war and economic turmoil, reviewers and satirists took aim at what they considered the foreign and insurgent elements of Gothic fiction. One anonymous reviewer went so far as to term the genre "The Terrorist System of Novel-Writing." Writing in the form of a letter to the editor of the *Monthly Magazine* for August 1797 and signing his work "A Jacobin Novelist," the anonymous correspondent complained that "so prone are we to imitation, that we have exactly and faithfully copied the SYSTEM OF TERROR, if not in our streets, at least in our circulating libraries and in our closets" (Norton, *Gothic Readings* 299). Clearly, any number of cultural forces, including counterrevolutionary and francophobic feelings, stood poised to belittle the Gothic, and Austen's *Northanger Abbey* was only one, if far and away the best, of the many parodies aimed at the distressing popularity of Gothic literature.

In 1798, the same year in which Jane Austen completed the writing of *Northanger Abbey*, an author signing himself with the initials "R.S." deployed his pen as a lance upon which he impaled *The Monk* in a line-by-line dismantling of Matthew Gregory Lewis's work in the flagellating burlesque *The New Monk*. Far sharper than Austen's stylish lampoon of the Gothic heroine and her self-induced crises, *The New Monk* was terminal satire, perhaps intended as the revenge of a disgruntled former reader or writer of Gothic romances on the false muse. R.S.'s savage mockery of Lewis's best-seller pivots on one simple but devastatingly effective strategy: place the sordid and supernatural details of Lewis's medieval Spanish Gothic on domestic English soil (for example, Ambrosio becomes a ranting Methodist minister and the convent and catacombs of St. Clare an English boarding school), and let the resulting dislocation indict both Gothic absurdity and the English taste for it. Although R.S. shares with Austen a keen knowledge of his target and a domestication of Gothic themes, his is a virulent, no-holds-barred attack, intended to debunk and destroy a single book. The satirist's response to pernicious fiction was to sneer the errant audience back into its senses. If, as Alexander Pope said, "Art is nature to advantage dressed," then it followed for the Gothic satirist that bad art is nature to disadvantage overdressed.

Jane Austen's Horatian objective was not to eliminate the Gothic novel from the literary scene or to prohibit its reading. As Austen mounted her assault on the misuse and abuse of Gothic fiction, she gradually unveiled an educable heroine and reader who resumes control and cures herself of the Gothic fever. There is nothing wrong with reading Gothic novels unless the mind of the reader fails to discipline "an imagination resolved on alarm" or succumbs to a "craving to be frightened" (38), as Austen's narrator cautions. Catherine's infatuation with "horrid novels," delightfully teased by Henry Tilney on the coach ride, fuels her fantasies about what Northanger Abbey may hold in the way of mysterious entanglements and dark secrets in General Tilney's past. But a grave setback for these expectations occurs—and who can forget that wonderful moment of deflation of the awful and awesome?—when Catherine discovers that the contents of the "hidden" manuscript turn out to be a laundry list. Her mortification is complete when Henry Tilney, the voice of reason and common sense, reveals to her the ridiculous depravity of her "craving for extraordinary incident." While earlier critics often aligned Catherine's restored composure with the clarity of her moral understanding—the emergence of a susceptible young woman from her Gothic delusions, tutored by a sensible young man—more recent critics have tended to see her imaginative qualities as positive forces in the novel. Henry Tilney himself admits to a partiality for *The Mysteries of Udolpho* and like books. It is not that Gothic novels in themselves are instruments of depravity, for the pleasures and pitfalls of Gothic fiction lie in how one reads it and what one looks for in its fantastic content. As Austen's wonderful understatement concludes: "Charming as were all Mrs. Radcliffe's works, and charming even as were the works of all her imitators, it was not in them perhaps that human nature, at least in the midland counties of England, was to be looked for" (202).

Catherine's emergence from her Gothic misreading of events coincides with her final understanding of the gold-digging ways of Isabella Thorpe, with Austen's laying bare the economic reality too conveniently sublimated by many Gothic plots. When Isabella supplies Catherine with the seven "all horrid" titles, she clearly understands better than her companion the true object of a Gothic heroine's career: a wealthy husband. Throughout the nineteenth century, the spooky and gory titles on Isabella Thorpe's reading list were thought to be fictitious, the inspired products of Jane Austen's comic imagination. When the possibility was raised that the seven *Northanger* Gothics were authentic, a leading Victorian critic, George Saintsbury, dismissed the claim with disparaging finality. "I should like some better authority than Miss Isabella Thorpe's to assure me of their existence" (19), Saintsbury erroneously pontificated. Rumors of the existence of the "lost" *Northanger* novels continued to circulate until two dedicated Gothophiles and amateur collectors of Gothic fiction, dissatisfied with Saintsbury's pronouncement, began a quest to locate the titles in hopes of verifying both their authenticity and their special relevance to the themes of *Northanger Abbey*.

The search was initiated in earnest by Montague Summers in 1916 with a letter-query to the readers of *Notes and Queries* concerning the whereabouts of the "horrid romances" recommended to Catherine Morland by Isabella Thorpe. Summers's appeal for information provoked several responses, most notably from the Trollope scholar and Victorian bibliographer Michael Sadleir and the eighteenth-century specialist Alan D. McKillop. Fascinated by the challenge of finding these apocryphal Gothics, Sadleir began his search as a casual aside to his central book-collecting passion for realistic Victorian fiction. His first acquisition came in 1922 when he found one of the rarest of the seven, Carl Grosse's *Horrid Mysteries*, almost by accident. Discoveries of the remaining six titles followed, enabling Sadleir to refute Saintsbury and provide future Gothic questers with a useful historical perspective on the role played by Radcliffe's "charming imitators" in shaping late-eighteenth-century reading habits and public taste. Sadleir's monograph, written for the English Association in 1927, narrates his adventure in Gothic-novel archeology and includes a postscript on the finding of the rarest and most elusive title among the seven, Eleanor Sleath's *Orphan of the Rhine*. Sadleir was also the first scholar to make the case for Jane Austen's strategic and deliberate selection of Gothic titles to fit her themes and character interplay in *Northanger Abbey*. Issues such as why no romance by Radcliffe appears on Isabella Thorpe's list or why the list includes two titles by Eliza Parsons begin with the bibliophiliac probings of Michael Sadleir. Sadleir's validation of the *Northanger* septet also encouraged readers to wonder how many of the seven titles Jane Austen herself had read or at least skimmed for ideas to enliven the burlesque. Had Jane Austen herself, like her heroine Catherine Morland, ever been seduced and victimized by this lurid reading fare, or had she or her sister Cassandra ever "meditated, by turns, on broken promises and broken arches, phaetons and false hangings, Tilneys and trap-doors" (103)?

The seven horrid titles comprising Catherine Morland's Gothic reading list are considered here according to the order recommended by Isabella Thorpe. As Bette B. Roberts notes in her chapter "The Horrid Novels: *The Mysteries of Udolpho* and *Northanger Abbey*," "Austen does not arrange these books in chronological order; nor does she group together the two written by one author, Eliza Parsons. . . . Austen does not list these particular works as representatives of the history of Gothic fiction; rather, she regards them in all likelihood as typical of the very worst of the genre. . . . Austen's omission of Radcliffe from the list is no accident" (90). Giving no order whatsoever to Isabella Thorpe's list making seems to have been Austen's game in an effort to expose the typical Gothic-novel reader's utter lack of discrimination. But her playful selection is not without its purpose. Thorpe's book list contains every species of Gothic fiction being rapidly written and avidly read in the 1790s from the palpitations of Radcliffean terror to the fleshly nauseousness of Lewisite Gothic. The natural, unnatural, and supernatural degrees of both terror and horror are represented in the seven titles, as is the Gothic audience's preference for translations of the German *Schauerroman* (or shudder novel). Sadleir's eye caught the satiric distinction between Isabella's choices and Austen's intentions. His estimate of Jane Austen's seven choices from among the plethora of horrid titles available to her stresses her purposefulness and her familiarity with the entire spectrum of spectral-novel fashions and types, and the final word on her choices belongs to him: "Jane Austen's pick of Gothic novels was rather deliberate than random, was made for the stories' rather than their titles' sake. Chance alone could hardly have achieved so representative a choice" (9).

Eliza Parsons. One can only guess why Eliza Parsons alone of the *Northanger* novelists has the honor of having two of her novels placed on Isabella Thorpe's list: *Castle of Wolfenbach* and *The Mysterious Warning*. Oddly, Thorpe pluralized one of the Parsons titles when she added an "s" to "Warning," perhaps to create a more enticing confection for the eager Catherine. Parsons's "German tales" remain valuable today as specimens of pulp Gothics, but the novels are highly derivative variations on Radcliffean themes, as mechanical in plotting as they are stilted in dialogue. Parsons was a widow who churned out some sixty novels and romances as a means of providing her struggling family with a living. Her prefaces advertise the author as an unfortunate and invite the reader's sympathy for both her plight and "her deficiency in talents."

Castle of Wolfenbach follows the meandering career of the intricately persecuted and terrorized Matilda, who, fleeing from her lustful Uncle Weimar, spends some requisite time in the gloomy castle of the title, the scene, she later learns, "of murder and atrocious crimes." The novel rushes breathlessly through a number of other disjointed adventures and poorly interwoven subplots until the necessary but clumsy repentance of the uncle and the happy ending of a safe and virtuous marriage for Matilda. Does Henry Tilney have this novel's Matilda in mind when he teases Catherine with the "memoirs of the wretched Matilda" she could expect to find secreted away in Northanger Abbey? It is hard to tell because "Matilda" is a modular name almost ubiquitous in Gothic lore, but Henry's reference is both clever and titillating.

The voice of *The Mysterious Warning*, first appearing as supernatural, then, following the precedent of Clara Reeve and Radcliffe, explained away as natural, warns the innocent and remarkably obtuse hero, Count Ferdinand, to flee from his new wife Claudina, who, we eventually learn after a series of most improbable adventures, is his half sister. The oracle of this information is the Turkish concubine Fatima, as Parsons manages to spice her German tale with some of the current taste for Orientalism as well. Here again, evil too-conveniently self-destructs, and all ends happily for the virtuous characters. Parsons's world is one of moral absolutes. The caveat "Vice to be hated / Needs but to be seen" ends *The Mysterious Warning*, a book in which Providence ultimately foils the designs of the wicked, and young men and women learn to honor their elders. Her shrill presentation of unspeakable evil and trendy exoticism, awkwardly counterbalanced by her voices of reason and piety, makes Parsons's fiction a paradigm of the kind of unconscious moral schizophrenia highly characteristic of the first English Gothics. One assumes that Catherine, like other readers of her generation, read them more for the exquisite horrors they offer than for the education they numbingly inculcate.

Regina Maria Roche. A gentler, more poetic, and clearly more skilled compatriot of Eliza Parsons, Regina Maria Roche arguably occupies with good reason the second place on Isabella's list, for her story of the long-suffering heroine Madeline in *Clermont* provides a pattern of wish fulfillment for Austen's eager heroine—and all the mysterious and maddeningly protracted "horrors" needed to occupy her leisure hours at Bath. Roche was a deeply religious woman who wrote some sixteen novels, many dabbling in sentimental and Gothic themes, all governed by a firm moral purpose to show how "the ways of Providence are justified to man." Critics consider *Clermont* her most Gothic and obviously Radcliffean novel. In this story, we find such Radcliffean staples as the central plight of a virtuous and delicately beautiful heroine reared among and poetically appreciative of Alpine scenery; her mournful father, a strict moralist nursing some mysterious wound from the past; an ideal love match for Madeline in the virtuous (and oboe-playing) Henri de Sevignie, who, also mysteriously, seems prevented from marrying her; then, the egress of the vulnerable heroine from her pastoral world into one of social and familial intrigue, where she is subjected to numerous inexplicable persecutions, is forced to make her way through various subterranean passages, and, finally, is menaced by a libidinous villain, the dissipated D'Alembert. Roche also includes the requisite appearance of the seemingly supernatural, the haunted cry of a murdered count and a spectral, accusing finger thrust forth from a rich tapestry, which are later revealed as the machinations of one Lafroy, the evil henchman of D'Alembert.

Clermont's plot is much too involved to summarize here. Roche herself seems to struggle to pull the various threads together in the final volume 4, in which all the virtuous are rewarded and all the wicked are foiled. The long-suffering and sleepless Madeline eventually wins her beloved Henri, mainly by strictly adhering to the Gothic heroine's code of moral rectitude and unswerving loyalty to her father, even though for a long period of the novel, Clermont is suspected of fratricide. Indeed, her passivity and her refusal to question the mysterious familial intrigues that constantly threaten her allow the plot to achieve its riddling complexity. Reading Roche allows one to appreciate better Radcliffe's superior artistry and the greater daring of her heroines. Yet to "earn" her Henry, Catherine Morland must move beyond the models of both Radcliffe and Roche to gain a crucial understanding about herself. It is *Northanger Abbey*'s strength as a bildungsroman or novel of education that marks Austen's most important accomplishment in her revision of the maiden-centered Gothic.

Lawrence Flammenberg [pseud. of Karl Friedrich Kahlert]. Regarded by Michael Sadleir as having the most incoherent and baffling plot of the seven horrid novels, *The Necromancer* is "a conglomerate of violent episodes thrown loosely together and not always achieving even a semblance of logical sequence" (Sadleir 17). The amorphousness of the novel may be the result of the translator's incompetent management of his German sources. What might have been an anthology of separate legends and supernatural tales about the Black Forest was hastily amalgamated into a nearly incomprehensible Germanic Gothic meant to allure the Minerva-Press readers. The site of action is the Schwarzwald or Black Forest of Germany, primal Gothic territory abounding in midnight rides and riders, demons' dens, warlocks' conclaves, blood-trailing shadows, driverless carriages speeding through the night, spook-crowded cottages, silhouetted ruins, and horizons studded with gibbets; and nearly every page is packed with the grim and gruesome flora and fauna of the Gothic landscape that the Minerva clientele had come to demand. The main story of the necromancer Volkert is buried deep in the interior of the novel's layers of oblique narratives and wild subplots. Penetrating to this central story is an ordeal even for the experienced Gothic reader. Volkert, it seems, had dictated his memoirs as he awaited execution for the crime of necromancy or the raising of the dead. In line with the Gothic's mandatory prop of the mysterious manuscript, Volkert's memoirs reside within a tomb that in turn resides within "the Gothic remains of a half-decayed castle." The repellent contents of Volkert's papers, contorted, disconnected, and frequently unintelligible, form a Gothic novel within several other Gothic novels. Volkert's narration of his sensational crimes and punishments abruptly breaks off when a bolt of retributive lightning "hiss[es] suddenly through the dreary vault licking the damp walls with a hollow clap of thunder" (3.432), silencing the necromancer as he gloats over his evil career. Obviously, Austen wanted to include the most outrageous specimen of Germanic Gothic excess that she could find. With its *schauerromantik* prodigality, Kahlert's *Necromancer* perfectly suited her design.

Francis Lathom. Francis Lathom's *Midnight Bell* is the only Gothic not published by the Minerva Press chosen by Jane Austen. Published by H.D. Symonds in 1798, it was the second Gothic novel (his first Gothic, *The Castle of Ollada*, was published by the Minerva Press in 1795) by a writer who established himself in the public eye over the next two decades as a professional supplier of Gothic goods manufactured according to formula. *The Midnight Bell* probably earned its place on the reading list because it was a fake translation from a nonexistent German source, another new category of authorial chicanery coming into vogue in the late 1790s. A special feature of Lathom's sham Germanic shocker was its staging of several horrific scenes in revolutionary Paris during the height of the Terror, a fillip that contemporized the Gothic spirit for English readers and hinted at the Revolution's darker aspects. The novel's titling—it is named for one of the Gothic's standard sinister acoustics—had become routine for Gothic authors and is gently mocked by Austen, who knew that the solemn sound effect proclaimed in the title had little or no relevance to the story and tolled far too late in the romance to warn the hero, Adolphus, that the killer of his mother was his father. Sworn to avenge this family crime, Adolphus undergoes a series of stereotypical adventures, one of which brings him to Paris just as the Revolution is turning on its own and dissolving in a sea of blood. But Lathom's scenes from the Reign of Terror have no bearing on the hero's fate or the decisions he makes. Their cheaply sensational inclusion was quite properly criticized in Sadleir's negative estimate of the dubious Gothic worth of *The Midnight Bell*, a book that even Catherine Morland might have found "queerly disappointing, clumsy in construction, humourless, and mechanical" (Sadleir 15).

Eleanor Sleath. *The Orphan of the Rhine* was the last *Northanger* novel unearthed by Sadleir and is usually considered to be the rarest of these seven rare books. Stylistically, the novel is at an opposite pole from the voluptuous supernaturalism of Grosse's *Horrid Mysteries* and the *schauerromantik* superfluity of *The Necromancer* and might therefore have been selected by Jane Austen as a counterpoise to these exaggerated Gothic examples. The novel's grandly gloomy poetic landscapes bring it closer than any other work on the reading list to the topographical finesse of Radcliffe. Since we know of Austen's regard for Radcliffe, Sleath may then occupy a place in the *Northanger* set that is somewhat less satiric in nature than those of the other six titles. By including *The Orphan of the Rhine*, Austen may have been allowing that a long Gothic need not be dull or dismally stereotypical or confusingly plotted. The descriptions of the sublime scenery between the Rhine and Salzburg are done with a gloomy magnificence on a par with Radcliffe's own painterly eye. Sleath's treatment of the heroine's genealogical predicaments and attraction to ruins compares favorably to Radcliffe's skill in these matters. Although the romance is lengthy, the triadic plot is plain and unencumbered by that obstacle of many incompetent Gothic novelists, a ganglion of inset tales. One passage from a standard Gothic scene, the first sighting of the castle by the heroine, will show Sleath's stylistic capabilities. As Laurette gazes upon the castle, the awesome sublime builds slowly to a pinnacle of terrifying beauty:

The castle, which was seated upon an eminence, about a quarter of a league from the bed of the river, seemed to have been separated by nature from the habitable world by deep and impenetrable woods. Two of the towers, which were all that remained entire, were half secreted in a forest; the others which were mouldering into ruins, opened into a narrow cultivated plain terminating in a rocky declivity at the bottom of which flowed the Rhine, wide, deep, and silent. (1.83).

Landscape poems like this one adorn the heroine's journey down the Rhine as she makes slow but steady genealogical progress toward her destiny. Sadleir's final discovery among the *Northanger* novels also turned out to be his favorite, earning his praise as "a strangely attractive absurdity which excites a sort of sugary fascination over the reader" (Sadleir 22), and, he might have added, over Jane Austen as well.

Carl Grosse. Resisting any synopsis, *Horrid Mysteries* makes use of the basic Gothic plot of flight and pursuit in the haunted underground, but this melodramatic floorplan is internationally enlarged by Grosse. Instead of moving through the subterranean labyrinth of a haunted castle, the victims are pursued through a sinister political underworld and enmeshed in a labyrinth of conspiracy, betrayal, and ritual death perpetrated by a secret brotherhood whose purposes remain darkly obscure. Secret societies such as the Freemasons and the Illuminati had become a subject for Gothic fiction, and Grosse no doubt wished to concoct a complexly plotted novel that would appeal to this vogue. Austen again shows her shrewd awareness of Gothic fads in her placement of Grosse's crime novel on Isabella Thorpe's reading list. The main character in *Horrid Mysteries* has sworn the blood oath and become the society's murderous automaton. His attempts to escape the web spun around his life by the society take him from country to country in his flight from the evil machinations of the brotherhood. His flight through the sinister corridors of power alternates with the appearances of an archvillain called Genius Amanuel, whose driving passion is the manipulation of young men in the brotherhood's criminal service and murderous schemes. The flight of the main character from the brotherhood's clutches also shares the stage with the voluptuous victimization of several heroines as Grosse injects scenes of sadistic fleshliness at many points. One heroine, Elmira, suffers at least three deaths by sexual assault and awakens after one of them while she is being transported in a coffin. Incidents such as this prompted Sadleir to rate the four volumes of *Horrid Mysteries* to have been composed with "a lurid, if inconsequent power. The reader seems to assist at a series of apocalyptic visions, which by their sheer opulence of language crush him into gibbering acquiescence" (Sadleir 18).

SELECTED CRITICISM

The Seven "All Horrid" Titles and Austen's *Northanger Abbey*

Anderson, Walter E. "From Northanger to Woodston: Catherine's Education to Common Life." *Philological Quarterly* 63 (1985): 493–509. Finds the Gothic material intrinsically related to the novel's unity. The satire on Gothic romances "produce[s] no serious conflict between the Bath and Northanger sections or the love and education plots."

Auerbach, Nina. "Jane Austen and Romantic Imprisonment." In *Jane Austen in a Social Context*. Ed. David Monaghan. Totowa, NJ: Barnes & Noble, 1981: 9–27. Views the satire of *Northanger Abbey* as not entirely anti-Gothic and disapproving.

Black, Robert Kerr. *The Sadleir-Black Gothic Collection: An Address before the Bibli-*

ographical Society of the University of Virginia. Charlottesville: Alderman Library of the University of Virginia, 1949. This pamphlet contains Sadleir's account of his quest to retrieve the "lost" *Northanger* novels. Black eventually purchased Sadleir's collection of Gothic fiction and donated it to the Rare Book Department of the Alderman Library.

Blakey, Dorothy. *The Minerva Press, 1790–1820.* London: Printed for the Bibliographical Society at the University Press, Oxford, 1939. Gives bibliographical descriptions of the six of the seven *Northanger* novels that were published by William Lane's Minerva-Press, the major supplier of Gothic fiction throughout the 1790s.

Ehrenpreis, Anne Henry. Introduction to *Northanger Abbey.* Baltimore: Penguin, 1972: 7–24. Austen's lampoon is directed more at the inane habits and tastes of Gothic readers of the 1790s than at Gothic novelists themselves. "What is significant in the characters is not so much their choice of books as the way they read them."

Emden, Cecil S. "The Composition of *Northanger Abbey.*" *Review of English Studies* 19 (1968): 279–287. Proposes that "the main body of *Northanger Abbey* was written in about 1794, and that the sections burlesquing horror novels, and Mrs. Radcliffe's *Mysteries of Udolpho* in particular, were added some four years later."

Frank, Frederick S. "Gothic Gold: The Sadleir-Black Gothic Collection." *Studies in Eighteenth-Century Culture* 26 (1998): 287–312. Discusses Sadleir's persistent search for the missing *Northanger* novels and their central importance to the Sadleir-Black Collection.

Glock, Waldo S. "Catherine Morland's Gothic Delusions: A Defense of *Northanger Abbey.*" *Rocky Mountain Review of Language and Literature* 32 (1978): 33–46. Argues for the structural integrity of the Gothic satire with other sections of *Northanger Abbey.* "The meaning of Catherine's adventures, including her Gothic aberrations at Northanger, is indissolubly a part of the formal structure of the novel."

Hoeveler, Diane Long. "Vindicating *Northanger Abbey*: Mary Wollstonecraft, Jane Austen, and Gothic Feminism." In *Jane Austen and Discourses of Feminism.* Ed. Devoney Looser. New York: St. Martin's Press, 1995: 117–135. "*Northanger Abbey* reads as a critique of both the Gothic and sentimental sensibilities that were being foisted on women at the time."

Jerinic, Maria. "In Defense of the Gothic: Rereading *Northanger Abbey.*" In *Jane Austen and Discourses of Feminism.* Ed. Devoney Looser. New York: St. Martin's Press, 1995: 137–149. Jane Austen's satire does not condemn the genre of the Gothic.

Lamont, Claire. "Jane Austen's Gothic Architecture." In *Exhibited by Candlelight: Sources and Developments in the Gothic Tradition.* Ed. Valeria Tinkler-Villani, Peter Davidson, and Jane Stevenson. Amsterdam: Rodopi, 1995: 107–115. In *Northanger Abbey,* Jane Austen "uses architecture as a way of exploring unacknowledged areas of human psychology." In particular, "there is sexual tension" in Catherine Morland's reactions to the abbey.

Lau, Beth. "Madeline at Northanger Abbey: Keats's Anti-Romances and Gothic Satire." *Journal of English and Germanic Philology* 84 (1985): 30–50. Although Austen made fun of the Gothic, she also "reflects appreciation of Mrs. Radcliffe's works."

Levine, George. "Translating the Monstrous: *Northanger Abbey.*" *Nineteenth-Century Fiction* 30 (1975): 335–350. The novel simultaneously celebrates and denigrates Gothic fiction even as it "demystifies personal and social relations."

Loveridge, Mark. "*Northanger Abbey*; or, Nature and Probability." *Nineteenth-Century*

Literature 56 (1991): 1–29. "The Gothic world temporarily acts as a comic sublime for the natural heroine."

McKinney, David D. *The Imprints of Gloomth: The Gothic Novel in England, 1765–1830*. Charlottesville: Alderman Library, University of Virginia, 1988. A twenty-five-page pamphlet that discusses various titles in the Sadleir-Black Gothic Collection.

Mudrick, Marvin. "The Literary Pretext Continued: Irony versus Gothicism: *Northanger Abbey*." In *Jane Austen: Irony as Defense and Discovery*. Princeton: Princeton University Press, 1952: 37–49. Austen relies on ironic techniques to solve the problem of how to write "simultaneously a Gothic novel and a realistic novel and gain and keep the reader's acceptance of the latter while proving that the former is false and absurd."

Roberts, Bette B. "The Horrid Novels: *The Mysteries of Udolpho* and *Northanger Abbey*." In *Gothic Fictions: Prohibition/Transgression*. Ed. Kenneth W. Graham. New York: AMS Press, 1989: 89–111. Discusses all seven *Northanger* novels and speculates on Austen's motives for choosing these titles. "The horrids on the list, even as Gothic novels, represent extreme cases of unnecessarily complicated plotting."

Roberts, Marilyn. "Catherine Morland: Gothic Heroine after All?" *Topic: A Journal of the Liberal Arts* 48 (1997): 22–30. An antiparodic reading of the novel and the heroine's character.

Saintsbury, George. *Tales of Mystery: Mrs. Radcliffe, Lewis, Maturin*. New York: Macmillan, 1891.

"The Terrorist System of Novel-Writing." Letter to the editor, *Monthly Magazine*, 41: 21 (August 1797): 102–104; Rpt. in *Gothic Readings: The First Wave, 1764–1840*. Ed. Rictor Norton. London and New York: Leicester University Press, 2000: 299–303. The anonymous critic signed himself "A Jacobin Novelist" and ended his letter: "Mr. Editor, if thy soul is not harrowed up, I am glad to escape from this scene of horror."

Wallace, Tara Ghoshal. "*Northanger Abbey* and the Limits of Parody." *Studies in the Novel* 20 (1988): 262–273. Austen's technique "mocks and undermines her own chosen method—parodic discourse" to position the reader as "an opponent who struggles with the narrator for control over the text."

The Discovery and Content of the Seven *Northanger* Titles

Sadleir, Michael. *The Northanger Novels: A Footnote to Jane Austen*. English Association Pamphlet No. 68. November 1927. A twenty-three-page monograph discussing both the search for and the content of all seven *Northanger* novels. "The *Northanger* novels fall into three divisions of which one is itself subdivisible. *Clermont* is the rhapsodic sensibility romance in its finest form. *The Castle of Wolfenbach, The Mysterious Warning, The Orphan of the Rhine*, and *Midnight Bell* are terror-novels that pretend for fashion's sake to be translations from the German. *The Necromancer* is of this same class but with a difference. *Horrid Mysteries* not only remains a book quite distinct in nature and origins from its fellows but on a different and higher plane of intrinsic importance and interest."

Sadleir's pamphlet is the necessary starting point for all students of the *Northanger* seven.

————. " 'All Horrid?': Jane Austen and the Gothic Romance." In *Things Past*. London: Constable, 1944: 167–200. Maintains that Jane Austen's selection of horrid titles via Isabella Thorpe was "rather deliberate than random and made for their stories' rather than their titles' sake."

Summers, Montague. " 'Northanger Abbey': 'Horrid Romances.' " *Notes and Queries* 2 (1 July 1916): 9. In an author's query, Summers initiated the quest for, first, the existence, then the location of the seven *Northanger* titles later verified by Sadleir. See also Summers's " 'Northanger Abbey': 'Horrid Romances,' " *Notes and Queries* 2 (29 July 1916): 97–98; " 'Northanger Abbey': 'Horrid Romances,' " *Times Literary Supplement* 27 December 1917: 649.

Tracy, Ann B. *The Gothic Novel, 1790–1830: Plot Summaries and Index to Motifs*. Lexington: University Press of Kentucky, 1981. Offers excellent plot summaries that clarify the complex multiple plots of the *Northanger* novels.

Lawrence Flammenberg [pseud. of Karl Friedrich Kahlert]

Conger, Syndy M. "A German Ancestor for Mary Shelley's Monster: Kahlert, Schiller, and the Buried Treasure of *Northanger Abbey*." *Philological Quarterly* 59 (1980): 216–232. A source study showing the influence of Kahlert's/Flammenberg's *Necromancer* on *Frankenstein*.

McKillop, Alan D. "Jane Austen's Gothic Titles." *Notes and Queries* 9 (1921): 361–362. Verifies the authenticity and discusses the authorship of *The Necromancer of the Black Forest*.

Varma, Devendra P. Introduction to *The Necromancer; or, The Tale of the Black Forest*. London: Folio Press, 1968: iii–xv. Mentions the skeptical review of the novel in *Monthly Review* for April 1795 that challenged the title's claim of a novel "founded on facts."

Carl Grosse

Christensen, Merten A. "*Udolpho, Horrid Mysteries*, and Coleridge's Machinery of the Imagination." *Wordsworth Circle* 2 (1971): 153–159. Analyzes and explains the role of Grosse's Gothic and others in the formation of Coleridge's supernaturalism in *The Rime of the Ancient Mariner* and other poems.

Le Tellier, Robert Ignatius. *Kindred Spirits: Interrelations and Affinities between the Romantic Novels of England and Germany (1790–1820), with Special Reference to the Work of Carl Grosse (1768–1847), Forgotten Gothic Novelist and Theorist of the Sublime*. Salzburg, Austria: Institut für Anglistik und Amerikanistik, 1982. With the exception of the work of Michael Sadleir and Montague Summers, the sole critical study of Grosse in the twentieth century.

Varma, Devendra P. Introduction to *Horrid Mysteries*. London: Folio Press, 1968: iii–xii. Grosse styled himself the "Marquis of Pharnusa" and wrote several Gothic romances, including *Der Dolch* [The Dagger].

Francis Lathom

Grove, Allen Whitlock. "Coming out of the Castle: Renegotiating Gender and Sexuality in Eighteenth-Century Gothic Fiction." Doctoral dissertation, University of Pennsylvania, 1996. [*DAI* 57:2491A]. Cites Lewis's *Monk*, Francis Lathom's *Midnight Bell*, and other Gothics to show "that Gothic fictions reveal a politics of complexity that undermines romance convention and explodes limiting definitions of gender and sexuality."

McConnochie, Arthur. "Francis Lathom, Forgotten Goth." Doctoral dissertation, University of Virginia, 1949.

Varma, Devendra P. Introduction to *The Midnight Bell*. London: Folio Press, 1968: iii–xiv. Discusses Lathom's long and successful career as a writer of Gothic thrillers.

Eliza Parsons

Roberts, Bette B. "Marital Fears and Polygamous Fantasies in Eliza Parsons' *Mysterious Warning*." *Journal of Popular Culture* 12 (1978): 42–51. A psychocultural reading. "What women writers find in the Gothic romance is a perfectly acceptable opportunity for the expression of unspoken fantasies based upon their subordinate roles in a patriarchal society."

Varma, Devendra P. Introduction to *The Castle of Wolfenbach*. London: Folio Press, 1968: iii–xiii. Outlines Parson's literary life as Gothifier and writer of sharp social satires.

———. Introduction to *The Mysterious Warning*. London: Folio Press, 1968: iii–xi. Discusses Parsons's ability to work in the dual modes of horror and terror.

Regina Maria Roche

Howells, Coral Ann. "Minerva Press Fiction, 1764–1819: Regina Marie Roche, *The Children of the Abbey*, and Mary-Ann Radcliffe, *Manfroné; or, The One-handed Monk*." In *Love, Mystery, and Misery: Feeling in Gothic Fiction*. Atlantic Highlands, NJ: Humanities Press, 1978: 82–100. Roche's novels share with many other Minerva Press Gothics a fear of "the personal and social consequences of any release of passion or instinctual drives. *The Children of the Abbey* is unmistakably Gothic in feeling with characteristic strains of morbid anxiety and repressed hysteria."

Schroeder, Natalie E. "Regina Maria Roche: Popular Novelist." Doctoral dissertation, Northwestern University, 1979. [*DAI* 39:4962A–4963A]. Surveys Roche's sixteen novels written over a forty-five-year period. "Mrs. Roche's romances usually include Gothic scenes, but apart from *Clermont* she is not properly described as a Gothic novelist."

———. "Regina Maria Roche, Popular Novelist, 1789–1834: The Rochean Canon." *Papers of the Bibliographical Society of America* 73 (1979): 462–468. Bibliographical descriptions and categorizations of Roche's sixteen novels. Roche is "one of the minor luminaries of the generation of Charlotte Smith and Ann Radcliffe."

———. "*The Mysteries of Udolpho* and *Clermont*: The Radcliffean Encroachment on

the Art of Regina Maria Roche." *Studies in the Novel* 12 (1980): 131–143. Finds
  that *Clermont* shows a potency for horror that exceeds the Radcliffean encroachment on Roche's art.
————. "The Anti-Feminist Reception of Regina Maria Roche." *Essays in Literature* 9
  (1982): 55–65. What the readership thought of her work.
Varma, Devendra P. Introduction to *Clermont*. London: Folio Press, 1968: iii–xiv. Discusses Roche's achievement of a Gothic midway between the leisurely terrors of
  Radcliffe and the headlong horrors of Monk Lewis.

Eleanor Sleath

Sadleir, Michael. "Postscript" to *The Northanger Novels: A Footnote to Jane Austen*.
  London: English Association, 1927. On the finding of *The Orphan of the Rhine*
  during the preparation of the pamphlet.
Varma, Devendra P. Introduction to *The Orphan of the Rhine*. London: Folio Press, 1968:
  iii–ix. The novel abounds in the grandly gloomy topographies of Ann Radcliffe.

FRANÇOIS THOMAS MARIE de BACULARD d'ARNAUD (1718–1805)

Frederick S. Frank

PRINCIPAL GOTHIC WORKS

Coligny; ou, La Saint Barthelemi. Amsterdam: Du Sauzet, 1750; Berlin: n.p., 1751. (Tragic drama based on the murder of the Huguenot leader Admiral Coligny and the Catholic massacre of the Protestants on 24 August 1572.)

Les Amans malheureux; ou, Les Comte de Comminge [The Unfortunate Lovers; or, The Count of Comminge]. Paris: L'Esclapart, 1764. (A dramatic adaptation of Claudine Alexandrine Guérin, Madame de Tencin's, novel *Mémoires du comte de Comminge*; Amants used in later editions.)

Clary; ou, Le retour a la vertu récompensé [Clary; or, The Return to Virtue Rewarded]. Paris: Chez l'Esclapart, libraire, quai de Gévres, 1767. (Based on Richardson's *Clarissa* [1749]).

Fanni, ou, La nouvelle Paméla [Fanny, or the New Pamela]. Paris: Chez l'Esclapart, libraire, quai de Gêvres, 1767. (A heavily sentimentalized version of Samuel Richardson's *Pamela; or, Virtue Rewarded* [1740].)

Euphémie; ou, Le Triomphe de la réligion [Euphémie; or, The Triumph of Religion]. Paris: Le Jay, 1768. (The drama has the dismal scenery and lugubrious apparatus of the English Gothic's monastic shockers. *Euphémie* was never acted but was avidly read by the English Gothicists.)

Batilde; ou, L'Héroisme de l'amour, anecdote historique [Batilde; or, The Heroism of Love, Historical Anecdote]. Paris: Le Jay, 1770.

Fayel. Paris: Le Jay, 1770. (Tragic drama with abundant Gothic stage business and amorous cannibalism. The *châtelaine* or lady of the castle, de Coucy, eats the heart of her husband offstage.)

Les Époux malheureux; ou, Histoire de Monsieur et Madame de la Bédoyère [The Wicked Husband; or, History of Mr. and Mrs. Bédoyère]. Paris: Chez la veuve Ballard & Fils, imprimeurs du roi, rue des Mathurins; et chez Laporte, libraire, rue des Noyers, 1783. (The novel anticipates the familial ruthlessness of later domestic Gothic fiction.)

MODERN REPRINTS AND EDITIONS

Les Amants malheureux; ou, Les Comte de Comminge [The Unfortunate Lovers; or, The
    Count of Comminge]. Preface by Michel Delon. Paris: Desjonquères, 1985. (The
    novel by Madame de Tencin).

Montague Summers was the first historian of Gothicism to call attention to the
important role of François Baculard d'Arnaud in shaping the course of English
Gothic fiction in the 1790s, referring to this master of the *genre sombre* in a
headnote to Baculard d'Arnaud in *A Gothic Bibliography* as "a great influence
on the development of the Gothic romance" (4).[1] The *roman noir*, or French
Gothic novel, reached the English audience by way of many translations during
the 1780s and found an enthusiastic reception in the pages of popular periodicals such as *The Lady's Magazine and Museum of the Belles-Lettres*, where
d'Arnaud's lugubrious tales of monastic victimization in underground surroundings caught the eye of Ann Radcliffe and Sophia Lee, whose *The Recess* is filled
with the places, moods, and trappings of d'Arnaudesque Gothicism. Clara
Reeve, author of *The Old English Baron*, based her novel *Exiles; or, The Memoirs of the Count de Cronstadt* (1788) on d'Arnaud's novella *D'Alamanzi, anecdote française* (1776). Perhaps his works more than any other continental
source presented a collage of terror and melancholy and a concentration on the
pleasures of pain that would become the substance of many Radcliffean Gothics
throughout the 1790s.

    Funereal decor, tangible corpses, monastic villainy, extravagant victimization
at the hands of close relatives, slimy catacombs, caverns, labyrinths, and an exquisitely cadaverous mise-en-scène were the leading features of his murky melodramas and dark novels of pain and death that professed to be didactic but actually
reveled in algolagnic ecstasies. Only the presence of genuine specters and unambiguously supernatural events that would later characterize the "high" Gothic was
lacking from d'Arnaud's otherwise fully developed Gothic array of characters,
settings, and effects. Lovers consigned to graveyards, mausoleums, or tenebrous
buildings located amid sinister landscapes are the leitmotifs of a Gothic style of
romancing that came to be widely known in the 1780s as *darnauderie*. To attain
the macabre beauty and morbid sensationalism he sought, d'Arnaud's Gothic
muse drew deeply upon the poets of the English Graveyard school, especially the
grandiose descriptions of mortality and the raptures on dying he found in Edward
Young's *Night Thoughts* (1742–1746) (the work's full title is *The Complaint; or,
Night Thoughts on Life, Death, and Immortality*; it was translated into French by
Pierre Prime Félicien Le Tourneur in 1769 as *Les nuits d'Young*). D'Arnaud
shared Young's vision of the world as "a melancholy vault / The vale funereal, the
sad cypress gloom; / The land of apparitions, empty shades!" (*Night Thoughts*
116–118). *Darnaudèrie* Gothic also owes much to the lyric celebrations of death
intoned throughout James Hervey's (1714–1758) series of epitaphic prose mus-

ings, *Meditations among the Tombs* (1746) and *Contemplations on the Night* (1747). Spearheaded by d'Arnaud, the early *roman noir* blended the morbid grandeurs of the Graveyard poets with the erotic intensity of such ur-Gothic writers as the Abbé Prévost, Madame de Tencin, and Madame de Genlis. The momentum of d'Arnaud's plots with their climactic fusion of sex and death later surfaced in the perverse sexual Gothic of the Marquis de Sade and such English Gothic writers as Charlotte Dacre [Rosa Matilda], whose satanic novel *Zofloya* resonates with the spirit of *darnauderie* Gothic.

D'Arnaud's biography reveals a life almost wholly devoted to literature, especially the creation of lurid dramatic spectacles of strange and destructive passion. His dramas and novels were praised by Rousseau ("Monsieur Arnaud écrit avec son coeur") and sponsored by Voltaire, who secured a place for him at the famous theater of Frederick the Great at Potsdam before falling out with d'Arnaud, perhaps out of jealousy over the young dramatist's success.

D'Arnaud alternated his writing activities between the novella and the stage, making a strong impression on future Gothicists with the horror plays *Les Amants malheureux; ou, Le Comte de Comminge* and *Euphémie; ou, Le Triomphe de la réligion*. He launched his dramatic career with *Fayel*, a tragedy in a medieval setting based on the Châtelain de Coucy, the lady of the castle, whose perverted devotion drives her to eat the heart of the master of Coucy, albeit offstage. Some accounts report that cordials were served by the management to revive spectators overcome by this repulsive *coup de théâtre*. In his next play, the Gothified anti-Catholic tragedy *Coligny*, d'Arnaud anticipated the fiendish Catholicism of the English horror novel of the late 1790s by mounting a morbid pageant of Catholic maliciousness and Protestant suffering that featured malignant Trappist fathers, "Corridors, labyrinthes, et caveaux de châteaux," and other prime examples of Gothic scenery and atmosphere. The play was set during the Massacre of St. Bartholomew, an apt historical choice that evoked the kind of atmosphere of religious terror later common in the pages of the Gothic from Matthew Gregory Lewis's *Monk* to "The Spaniard's Tale" in Charles Robert Maturin's *Melmoth the Wanderer*. The virulent anticlericalism of *Coligny* would leave its mark on future French Gothic drama, as seen in the theme and structure of Jacques-Marie Boutet de Monvel's Gothic extravaganza of monkish cruelty, *Les Victimes de cloîtrées* (1792).

The twenty-four novellas or tales in the collection *Les Epreuves du sentiment* [The Trials of Feeling] overflow with Gothic matter and sentiment of every sort, but it was in his plays that his Gothicism left an indelible mark on the English Gothicists. D'Arnaud's last two plays were masterworks of cadaverous subterranean nightmare, offering the sorts of cryptic thrills, hideous shudders, and charnel incarcerations later to become almost mandatory in the English Gothic novels of the 1790s and the shilling shockers of the early 1800s. Dantean gloom and underground entrapment are the main characteristics of his *drame monacal* (monastic drama) *Euphémie; ou, Le Triomphe de la réligion*. Among her other Gothic predicaments, the heroine falls headlong into a tomb as she gropes about in an infernally dark crypt in a scene that looks directly ahead to Agnes's ordeal in the slimy cellars of the Abbey of St. Clare in *The Monk*. In *Les Amants malheureux*, the Count of Comminge's father separates the lovers by imprisoning his son in the fetid cells of the Abbey de la Trappe, his anguish enhanced by the innovative sadism of the monks. James R. Foster's synopsis of *Les Amants malheureux* suggests just how closely d'Arnaud comes to producing a bonafide Gothic shocker in 1764, the same year as Walpole's *Castle of Otranto* and just as the English Gothic genre was getting under way:

Adélaide [the heroine] has become a member of the Trappist brotherhood to be near her lover. But she does not reveal her identity to him until the hour of her death. When this is imminent, the Count of Comminge has a prophetic dream. He hears groans arising from the tombs and discerns in the semi-darkness the silhouette of a woman in mourning. It is Adélaide, but when he tries to embrace her, his arms encircle a tombstone and a menacing specter cries, "Arrête! Tu vois Adélaide," and with a sinister "je t'attends" vanishes amid a thunderclap and a roar from the Inferno. On awakening, Comminge hears the passing bell. A "monk" is dying. It is Adélaide. After a heartbreaking colloquy with him, she expires, and he throws himself into her grave. (198)

Obviously, this scene requires only the element of spectral aggression to achieve full Gothic status. Here and elsewhere in his dramas and novels, d'Arnaud treads a fine line between tears and terror, often crossing into the effluvial territory of the latter. Any accurate historical genealogy of terror and horror fiction must recognize the contributions of d'Arnaud to the emergence and proliferation of the *roman noir* during the 1790s. No doubt there would have been some type of Gothic eruption during the last decade of the eighteenth century without the example of *darnauderie* Gothic, but its nature and direction might have been far less pronounced without his stimulus to the English Gothic imagination's need for morbid melancholy and delectable death.

NOTE

1. The author's surname is listed in the *National Union Catalogue* under "d'Arnaud," but his name is frequently given in French and English sources as "Baculard d'Arnaud," Either form is acceptable.

SELECTED CRITICISM

Abensour, Liliane, and Françoise Charras, eds. *Romantisme noir*. Paris: Herne, 1978. Offers representative selections from Baculard d'Arnaud's novels and dramas under the topical category of "Prisons."

Dawson, Robert L. "Baculard d'Arnaud (1718–1805): Life and Prose Fiction." Doctoral dissertation, Yale University, 1972. [*DAI* 33:2367A]. Gives careful literary analyses of *Les Époux malheureux* and notes that this work was avidly read by the

English Gothicists, especially the Lee sisters and Radcliffe. Investigates "the relationship of the concept of terror to sentiment."

————. *Baculard d'Arnaud, Life and Prose Fiction*. Banbury, Oxfordshire, UK: Voltaire Foundation, Thorpe Mandeville House, 1976. An assessment of the novellas that link Baculard d'Arnaud to the creation of the *roman noir*.

Delon, Michel. *Histoires anglaises/Baculard d'Arnaud, Florian, Sade*. Cadeilhan: Zulma, 1993. A comparative study that examines Baculard d'Arnaud's influence on Sade's spectacles of suffering and his philosophy of natural vice.

Foster, James R. "d'Arnaud, Clara Reeve, and the Lees." In *History of the Pre-Romantic Novel in England*. Modern Language Association of America, 1949: 186–284. Traces d'Arnaud's popularity and influence. The extravagant melancholia of the English Gothic novel derives from his influence. "Not without cause has he been called a good undertaker's man. He gives his reader a bad case of the dismals under pretense of driving home a moral lesson."

Goard, Robert R. "Baculard d'Arnaud (1718–1805): A Novelist of the Middle Way." Doctoral dissertation, University of Wisconsin, 1970. [*DAI* 31:5362A]. A survey of the novels and dramas. Maintains that the key to Baculard d'Arnaud's "popularity lies in his conscious effort to keep the *juste milieu, inter utrumque tene*."

Grieder, Josephine. "The Prose Fiction of Baculard d'Arnaud in Late Eighteenth-Century England." *French Studies* 24 (1970): 113–126. Refers to Baculard d'Arnaud's considerable influence on the Gothic fiction of Ann Radcliffe and his association of terror with sentiment.

Hale, Terry. "Roman Noir." In *The Handbook to Gothic Literature*. Ed. Marie Mulvey-Roberts. New York: New York University Press, 1998: 189–195. Briefly mentions d'Arnaud's "substantial" influence on English Gothic fiction.

Inklaar, D. *François-Thomas de Baculard d'Arnaud, ses imitateurs en Hollande et dans d'autres pays*. Paris and Gravenhage, 1925. Discusses d'Arnaud's extensive influence outside France.

Lévy, Maurice. "Une nouvelle source d'Anne Radcliffe: *Les memoires du comte de Comminge*." *Caliban* 1 (1964): 149–156. Ann Radcliffe's *Sicilian Romance* has many roots in Baculard d'Arnaud's drama and its source, Madame de Tencin's novel.

Martin, Angus. "Baculard d'Arnaud et la vogue des series de nouvelles en France au XVIIIe siècle." *Revue d'Histoire Littéraire de la France* 73 (1973): 982–992. Discusses d'Arnaud's role in establishing the vogue of short periodical fiction and gives a bibliographical summary of his work in English translation.

Price, L.M. "The Relation of Baculard d'Arnaud to German Literature." *Monatshefte für deutschen Unterricht* 37 (1945): 151–160. D'Arnaud's influence on the morbid, the passionate, and Sturm und Drang German writers of the eighteenth century is traced. Also presents a bibliography, "[Baculard d']Arnaud and German Drama."

Summers, Montague. *A Gothic Bibliography*. New York: Russell & Russell, 1964:4–5. Lists those works that "had a great influence on the development of the Gothic romance."

Touitou, Béatrice. *Baculard d'Arnaud*. Paris: Memini: Diffusion Presses universitaires de France, 1997. The best modern study.

WILLIAM BECKFORD
(1760–1844)
Jack G. Voller

PRINCIPAL GOTHIC WORKS

An Arabian Tale, from an Unpublished Manuscript, with Notes Critical and Explanatory. London: J. Johnson, 1786. (Translated from the French by the Reverend Samuel Henley and not titled *Vathek* until later editions.)

Vathek. Lausanne: Isaac Hignou, 1787. (The French version.)

Azemia [pseud. Jacquetta Jenks]. London: Sampson Low, 1797; 2nd ed. London: Sampson Low, 1798.

Vathek. London: Clarke, 1816.

The History of the Caliph Vathek. London: Sampson Low, 1868.

MODERN REPRINTS AND EDITIONS

The Episodes of Vathek. Trans. Frank Marzials. London: Swift, 1912. (First publication of several oriental tales or "Episodes.")

Gothic Readings: The First Wave, 1764–1840. Ed. Rictor Norton. London and New York: Leicester University Press, 2000. (Contains excerpts from *Azemia: A Novel*.)

Modern Novel Writing (1796) and *Azemia* (1797). Intro. Herman Mittle Levy, Jr. Gainesville: Scholars' Facsimiles & Reprints, 1970.

Vathek. Ed. Guy Chapman. Cambridge, UK: Constable, 1929. (Includes the *Episodes of Vathek*.)

Vathek. In *Three Gothic Novels*, Ed. E.F. Bleiler. New York: Dover Books, 1966.

Vathek. Ed. Roger Lonsdale. New York: Oxford University Press, 1970. (Includes an introduction arguing against the "Gothic" label due to the novel's ironic, comic dimension.)

Vathek and Other Stories. Ed. Malcolm Jack. London: Pickering & Chatto, 1993; London: Penguin, 1995. (Includes an introduction as well as the full text of *Vathek* and excerpts from "The Long Story"; *Biographical Memoirs; Modern Novel Writing; Azemia; Dreams, Waking Thoughts, and Incidents; The Journal of William*

*Beckford in Portugal and Spain, 1787–88; Italy, with Sketches of Spain and
Portugal; and Recollections of an Excursion to the Monasteries of Alcobaca and
Batalha.*)

William Beckford is not alone in being a "one-Gothic" writer, but he is in many
ways one of the most important among those authors whose fame rests on a
single Gothic novel. Published before most of the well-known English Gothics
of the late 1780s and 1790s, and thus published early enough to cast a shadow
across the entire Romantic period, *Vathek* is a work that helped mark the end
of one era and the emergence of another. In its neoclassicism, evident in Beckford's clarity, satire, and attention to detail, the novel seems a crowning point
of the late Augustan tradition. In its traumatic and flamboyant supernaturalism,
its hints of "perverse" sexuality, and its valorization of unnamable desire and
the quest it compels, the novel presages key elements of Romanticism.

In another foreshadowing of Romantic practice, Beckford's personal life and
the psychological and social conflicts that were often a part of it frequently and
even consistently found their way in very thinly veiled form into his works.
Born into vast wealth thanks to Jamaican sugar plantations (a source of income
also for the author of *The Monk*, Matthew Lewis) and the benefactor of political
prestige (Beckford's father was twice lord mayor of London), Beckford knew a
childhood world that was pampered and privileged, inculcating in him the self-
indulgence and sybaritic tendencies that characterized much of his early adult
life.

With a loving but distant father, a strictly religious mother from a noble
family, and tutors who often indulged the precocious youth, Beckford grew
uncomfortable with restraint, and much of his literary output is characterized by
some combination of egotistical quest, fantasy, and escape. He found a perfect
outlet for all three in the oriental literature he first encountered in his father's
ample library, especially in the early-eighteenth-century translation of *Thousand
and One Arabian Nights* by Antoine Galland. So taken was Beckford by the
world of the Middle East that he later learned Arabic and in fact came to know
more of Middle Eastern culture than most other Westerners of his time who
wrote of it.

Beckford's real-life escapes from the restraint and decorum of upper-class
eighteenth-century life were both of the customary sort—he traveled extensively
in Europe—and of a problematic sort as well. Some of his travels, including a
nearly twelve-year stay abroad, were necessitated by the scandals that repeatedly
attached themselves to Beckford during his life. An early affair with a cousin's
wife (she provided the model for Nouronihar in *Vathek*) proved only a precursor
to the more scandalous homosexual intrigues in which Beckford indulged, intrigues that hounded him out of England and prevented him from receiving the
peerage he ardently sought. A marriage to Lady Margaret Gordon in 1783 appeared to provide some measure of stability, but her death just three years later
shortly after giving birth to their second daughter helped push Beckford into the
relatively solitary life he lived in his later decades.

The year of his wife's death, 1786, was one of the most momentous of Beckford's life. He and his family had again been forced to leave England by accusations, quite likely with some basis in fact, although exacerbated by political enmity, of sodomy involving the young William "Kitty" Courtenay, later the ninth earl of Devon, whose politically connected family had long-standing disagreements with the Beckfords. Later in 1786, *Vathek* was published, much to Beckford's outrage. Originally written in French, *Vathek* had been given to the Reverend Samuel Henley, a family friend, to translate and annotate. Beckford, then at work on additional material for the novel, the "Episodes of Vathek," which are steeped in necrophilia, homosexuality, and incest, ordered Henley to refrain from submitting the translation for publication, but Henley not only ignored Beckford's order, he had the work printed with a preface suggesting that it was an anonymous translation from the Arabic. Beckford quickly published a French version in 1787 and then a more polished version (the manuscript and publishing history of *Vathek* is quite complex) the following year. Various aspects of the complicated textual history of Vathek are unraveled in Kenneth Graham's article "*Vathek* in English and French."

While *Vathek* was Beckford's main literary claim to fame during his life, he was perhaps just as well known or just as infamous for his building of Fonthill Abbey in Wiltshire, the site of scandalous sexual intrigues. Fonthill was a vast pseudo-Gothic structure on extensive grounds with landscape designed by Beckford himself that became something of a national landmark and architectural curiosity. With a central tower nearly 300 feet high and vaulted galleries and corridors filled with the books and works of art Beckford avidly collected, Fonthill became a monument to Beckford's own excesses, a private space that gave Beckford a refuge from a world where his fullest self-expression was met with alarm and outrage. An avid student of monasteries, he later in his life published *Recollections of an Excursion to the Monasteries of Alcobaça and Batalha* (1835), based on visits in 1794 during which he was taken by both the buildings and the young novices. In constructing Fonthill Abbey, Beckford created his own secular shrine to culture, art, and self, a shrine that, fittingly, kept falling down, and that finally consumed so much of Beckford's substance that he was forced to sell it. A few years later, the central tower collapsed fully and finally, never to be rebuilt.

Beckford's other writings—most of them either travel works or satires—were fairly well received, although his early *Dreams, Waking Thoughts, and Visions*, later revised and published in 1834 as *Italy; with Sketches of Spain and Portugal*, was suppressed by his family out of concerns both with Beckford's emerging propensity for getting into trouble and with the book's air of self-indulgence. His satire on novel writing, *Azemia*, is remarkable for its wit, much of it directed at political enemies such as William Pitt, his former childhood friend, but for a convincing demonstration of Beckford's ability to write a Gothic thriller, one must turn to *Vathek*.

Finally, it is *Vathek* for which Beckford will be most remembered, a work that reflects the life that is Beckford's next claim to lasting fame. *Vathek* is the tale of a sybaritic Middle Eastern potentate whose "insatiable curiosity" leads him to a vague but damningly binding involvement with the forces of evil. Its power and lasting resonance come not from its quest narrative but from Beckford's oddly harmonious blending of the grotesque and the comic, the satiric and the perverse. With a sardonic detachment Beckford details with Augustan clarity the illicit lusts and murderous outrages of his sensuous caliph and concludes the novel with a compelling scene of damnation, its vagueness matching the ambiguity of Vathek's nebulous desire for ever-greater wisdom, wealth, and indulgence.

Vathek's proto-Romantic quest, like much of Beckford's work in general, is a journey into subterranean spaces, with grottoes, caves, valleys, gulfs, and halls described in terms that acknowledge both the emergence of the sublime as a culturally resonant aesthetic and the psychological symbolism of such topographic features. Vathek is equally at home and equally discontent in both towers and underground chambers; his sexual ambiguity (mirroring Beckford's own) is readily recognizable in the novel's topographic range, in the unnamable desire that sends Vathek on his journey, and in the comparison of Beckford's outré Gothic tower at Fonthill and the neoclassical Lansdown Tower at Bath. Driven on his quest by the vague promise of the Giaour's tantalizing suggestions of power and occult wisdom, Vathek surrenders all considerations of moral and social responsibility as he journeys toward Eblis, a Beckfordian, sybaritic hell. That Vathek's quest ends with a form of eternal damnation largely void of Christian metaphysics in a subterranean space is arguably one of the most Gothic resonances in what is superficially not very Gothic at all. An Augustan might never have left the city, and a Romantic would have scaled some remote mountainous height, but Beckford's protagonist, located midway between Milton's Satan and Byron's Manfred, eagerly follows the Giaour, a creature of the underworld, on a journey that requires him to sacrifice children, wives, and even his own mother, finally to reach a solipsistic hell the very nature of whose torments both validates the unnameable desire and its associated hubris and affirms the impossibility of its attainment as well as "the appeal of evil" (Gemmett 17). The vagueness attending the conclusion of Beckford's earlier "The Long Story," alternately also known as "The Vision," which also ends in a cave after an arduous journey, confirms the pattern of the futile quest in Beckford's writings.

There is, finally, only self-longing and suffering in Beckford's world, a solipsism become a hellish isolation, and *Vathek*'s own place in English literature, removed enough from oriental tale and Gothic novel and Romantic quest to be fully none of them, thus becomes a fitting image of the isolating horrific emptiness that no amount of sardonic grotesquerie or deep irony can alleviate or hide. With its relatively sure command of Eastern lore and its ironic comedy, *Vathek* is distinctly unlike the conventional Gothic novel of the Romantic period, yet the work has long been recognized by many critics as having close affinities with Gothicism through its depiction not of stock atmospherics or character types but through its recognition of the damning potential inherent in a titanic self-focus. In some ways, *Vathek* both presages the Romantic period and foretells its demise, for the consuming desire of Vathek ostensibly for the occult wisdom and the treasures of the pre-Adamite sultans he expects to find in the cavernous hell of Eblis leads to his damnation, a personal tragedy that will be reenacted on the stage of Romanticism many times. The caliph's abandonment of moral and communal considerations, and his hellish fate, could well serve as a critique of Romantic solipsism long before Byron and Shelley exposed the dangerous side of the ego.

SELECTED CRITICISM

Alexander, Boyd. *England's Wealthiest Son: A Study of William Beckford*. London: Centaur, 1962. One of the major modern studies of Beckford's life and work.

Benrahhal-Serghini, El-Habib. "The Road to Istakhar: A Critical Study of the Text and Context of William Beckford's 'Vathek' and the 'Episodes', 1760–1844." Doctoral dissertation, Universitaire Instelling Antwerpen, 1995. [*DAI* 55:2839A]. Focuses on the "ideology of power" in *Vathek* and the *Episodes*. Also examines "the affiliations that *Vathek* and the *Episodes* may have with the Gothic tradition." Beckford emphasizes the relationship between the creative imagination and the ideology of power in these works.

Chapman, Guy. *Beckford*. London: Rupert Hart-Davis, 1952. A biography still worth consulting that seeks to correct errors and inaccuracies in earlier biographical efforts.

Claésson, Dick. *William Beckford av Fonthill, Wilts., 1760–1844: En forskningsöversikt, Litteraturvetenskapliga institutionen*. Göteborgs, Sweden: Göteborgs Universitet, Meddelanden No. 17, 1995. An introductory bibliographical essay, discussing Beckford research, listing and discussing some eighty books and articles on Beckford, and introducing the author to a Swedish audience. Divided in two parts: (1) a life and (2) a survey of research. Intended as an introduction to Beckfordiana.

———. "A Survey of William Beckford's Unpublished Romance *L'Esplendente*." *Studies on Voltaire and the Eighteenth Century* 358 (1997): 189–201. Summarizes this unfinished and unpublished youthful romance of Beckford's, noting its similarities to the extant eighteenth-century oriental tradition in England, to Beckford's satiric *Biographical Memoirs of Extraordinary Painters*, and—perhaps least of all—to the Gothic. Claésson rejects an autobiographical reading of the fragment for one that recognizes a "deep irony" presaging *Vathek*.

Fothergill, Brian. *Beckford of Fonthill*. London: Faber and Faber, 1979. One of the best biographies of Beckford.

Frank, Frederick S. "William Beckford's Vathek: An Arabian Tale." In *Survey of Modern Fantasy Literature*. Ed. Frank N. Magill. Englewood Cliffs, NJ: Salem, 1983: 2023–2027. Argues persuasively for an essential Romantic/Gothic nature to *Vathek*, which is much more sophisticated in its sense of cynicism and anxiety than conventional oriental tales or pre-Romantic Gothics.

Franklin, Michael. "William Beckford (1760–1844)." In *The Handbook to Gothic Lit-*

erature. Ed. Marie Mulvey-Roberts. New York: New York University Press, 1998: 20–23. A sharp-edged assessment of Beckford's spoiled life, a "Beckfordism . . . [that] anticipated Byronism," a "recreating his own Orient out of authentic materials to accommodate Gothic extremes of sensibility."

Garrett, John. "Ending in Infinity: William Beckford's Arabian Tale." *Eighteenth-Century Fiction* 5 (1992): 15–34. Argues that for Beckford "the East" functions symbolically as the infinite, and thus *Vathek*'s trek to Eblis becomes a type of the unending Romantic quest.

Gemmett, Robert James. *William Beckford.* Boston: Twayne, 1977. As is usual with the Twayne author-series volumes, this is a sound overview of Beckford's life and works by a foremost Beckford bibliographer and scholar. It includes a review of the oriental-tale tradition as well as a detailed consideration of all of Beckford's works and how, for a "Romantic escapist" like Beckford, "the world of fiction [proved] more tolerable than that of reality." Gemmett argues convincingly that Beckford's work of the 1770s and 1780s is fundamentally autobiographical.

Graham, Kenneth W. "*Vathek* in English and French." *Studies in Bibliography* 28 (1975): 153–166. Corrects some of the errors and assumptions about Henley's translation of *Vathek* into English and discusses other features of the complicated publication history.

———, ed. *Vathek and the Escape from Time: Bicentenary Revaluations.* New York: AMS Press, 1990. Contains a dozen essays on Beckford's novel, including Michel Baridon's "Vathek—Megalomaniac Caliph or Pundit of the Avant-Garde?" which furthers the discussions of contrasting extremes in *Vathek*; Brian Fothergill's "The Influence of Landscape and Architecture on the Composition of *Vathek*," a source study; Frederick S. Frank's "The Gothic *Vathek*: The Problem of Genre Resolved," which argues convincingly for the presence of fundamentally Gothic elements in the novel; R.B. Gill's "The Enlightened Occultist: Beckford's Presence in *Vathek*," which argues for an essentially autobiographical understanding of Beckford's novel; Kenneth W. Graham's " 'Inconnue dans les Annales de la Terre': Beckford's Benign and Demonic Influence on Poe," which discusses Beckford's influence on Poe; Peter Hyland's "*Vathek*, Heaven, and Hell," which focuses on the value of the landscape and *Vathek*'s relationship to it; Jürgen Klein's "*Vathek* and Decadence," which discusses Beckford's use of Orientalism as a means of enhancing the novel's sense of decadence; Temple Maynard's "The Movement Underground and the Escape From Time in Beckford's Fiction," which analyzes the novel's prominent use of subterranean imagery and its psychological value as escape and evasion for Beckford himself; Maria Laura Bettencourt Pires's "*Vathek* and Portugal," which discusses the reception and influence of *Vathek* in Portuguese arts and letters; J.E. Svilpis's "Orientalism, Fantasy, and *Vathek*," which treats Beckford's use of Orientalism as a cultural positioning that enables Beckford's critique of "occidental" thought and restriction; and Devendra Varma's "Beckford Treasures Rediscovered: Mystic Glow of Persian Sufism in *Vathek*," which studies the influence of Sufi thought on Beckford.

Haggerty, George E. "Literature and Homosexuality in the Late Eighteenth Century: Walpole, Beckford, and Lewis." In *Homosexual Themes in Literary Studies.* Ed. Wayne R. Dynes and Stephen Donaldson. New York: Garland, 1992: 167–178. Analyzing the role played by the sociocultural psychodynamics of homosexual desire in late-eighteenth-century England, Haggerty argues that for Beckford, *Vathek* served as "a testimony to the horror with which he contemplated his own internal paradox of innocent love and damning desire or reacted to the social repulsion that greeted publication of his sexual self."

Mahmoud, Fatma Moussa, ed. *William Beckford of Fonthill, 1760–1844*. Cairo: C. Tsoumas, 1960. Rpt. Port Washington, NY: Kennikat Press, 1972. This essay collection contains André Parreaux's "The Caliph and the Swinish Multitude," which argues that *Azemia* and *Modern Novel Writing* are primarily political, rather than literary, attacks; Boyd Alexander's "The Decay of Beckford's Genius," which attempts to explain Beckford's relatively small literary output—his "literary sterility"—by reference to his homosexuality and the psychosocial turmoil it occasioned him; Geoffrey Bullough's "Beckford's Early Travels and His 'Dream of Delusion,' " which examines the "marred mind" of Beckford as it is revealed in the various forms of travel narrative he produced; Magdi Wahba's "Beckford, Portugal, and 'Childish Error,' " which examines Beckford's homosexual activities in Portugal as a form of "narcissistic pederasty"; Fatma Moussa Mahmoud's "Beckford, *Vathek*, and the Oriental Tale," which surveys prior works in the oriental-tale tradition as well as the novel's reception and influences; and Mahmoud Manzalaoui's "Pseudo-Orientalism in Transition: The Age of *Vathek*," which finds that *Vathek* moves well beyond its predecessors in its grasp and understanding of Middle Eastern culture. Mahmoud's "Catalogue of William Beckford Bicentenary Exhibition at Yale: A Review" completes the collection.

Roberts, Adam, and Eric Robertson. "The Giaour's Sabre: A Reading of Beckford's *Vathek*." *Studies in Romanticism* 35:2 (1996): 199–212. Foregrounding recent theoretical work on the nature of textuality and translation, the authors find that the Giaour's sword, with its shifting text, "offers a *mise en abyme* of the novel's own narrative strategy: it promises access to a transcendental signifier, but this is an empty promise."

Shaffer, E.S. "Milton's Hell: William Beckford's Place in the Graphic and the Literary Tradition." In *Milton, the Metaphysicals, and Romanticism*. Ed. Lisa Low and Anthony Harding. Cambridge: Cambridge University Press, 1994: 65–83. Another contribution to the ongoing reassessment of Beckford's role as a mediatory figure strategically positioned between neoclassicism and Romanticism, this essay argues that Beckford, with his considerable knowledge of art and in particular of the "graphic tradition" that surrounds Milton's work, employed Miltonic imagery in a way "that shows the movement towards the revision of a conventional cultic hell into a personal hell which characterizes Romantic poetry."

Stableford, Brian. "Beckford, William." In *St. James Guide to Horror, Ghost, and Gothic Writers*. Ed. David Pringle. Detroit: St. James Press, 1998: 39–40. A concise look at *Vathek* in the context of Beckford's life. Stableford's brief entry examines both the roots of *Vathek* in the *Arabian Nights* and in the satiric writings of Voltaire and its highly idiosyncratic nature. Summing up the Romantic aspect of the work, Stableford finds that "Vathek can only be self-condemned to a Hell of his own: the realization that his boundless desires must remain forever unsatisfied."

Varma, Devendra P. "William Beckford." In *Supernatural Fiction Writers*. Ed. E.F. Bleiler. New York: Scribner's, 1985: 139–144. An overview of Beckford's work and life, stressing the autobiographical dimension of Beckford's work. "Vathek is a projection of his own personality, of a man caught in the web of his own temperament, rushing headlong into destruction."

AMBROSE GWINETT BIERCE
(1842–1914?)

Douglass H. Thomson

PRINCIPAL GOTHIC WORKS

Tales of Soldiers and Civilians. San Francisco: E.L.G. Steele, 1891.
In the Midst of Life: Tales of Soldiers and Civilians. London: Chatto, 1892.
Can Such Things Be? New York: Cassell, 1893.
Fantastic Fables. New York: G.P. Putnam's Sons, 1899.
The Collected Works of Ambrose Bierce. 12 vols. New York and Washington, DC: Neale, 1909–1912.

MODERN REPRINTS AND EDITIONS

The Collected Fables of Ambrose Bierce. Ed. S.T. Joshi. Columbus: Ohio State University Press, 2000.
The Complete Short Stories of Ambrose Bierce. Ed. Ernest Jerome Hopkins. Garden City, NY: Doubleday, 1970.
Ghost and Horror Stories of Ambrose Bierce. Ed. E.F. Bleiler. New York: Dover, 1964. (This edition is cited in the text.)
In the Midst of Life and Other Tales. Ed. Marcus Cunliffe. New York: New American Library, 1961.
The Moonlit Road, and Other Ghost and Horror Stories of Ambrose Bierce. Mineola, NY: Dover Publications, 1998.
The Stories and Fables of Ambrose Bierce. Ed. Edward Wagenknecht. Owings Mills, MD: Stemmer House, 1977.
Tales of Horror and Fantasy. Ed. E.F. Bleiler. Mattituck, NY: Amereon House, 1987.

Does anyone quite forget his or her first reading of "An Occurrence at Owl Creek Bridge"? At the time I was a seventh-grade Civil War aficionado, a proud owner of a square foot of the Gettysburg Battlefield—a fund-raising promotion I couldn't quite fathom. I felt that I owned that square foot of history and became an ardent believer in the heroic romance of that great conflict. But then came this "stunning blow upon the back of the neck" (58) of Peyton Farquhar, just as his miraculous escape from the hangman's noose and his dream of returning from the war to his beautiful wife look within inches of fulfillment. Why would anyone play this dark joke upon the reader? I remember going back with a kind of grim determination to see where I had been fooled: yes, the improbable escape and almost happy ending now became understood as the hypnotically and horribly frozen milliseconds of a dying man's delusions. I did not want to read this tale again, and I didn't, not until many years later as I prepared this entry on Bierce and became convinced that he is worth reading and rereading, although one can understand why some may demur. His is not a reassuring picture of the human condition. Still, one finds something bracing in Bierce's unflinching vision: he is a detonator of both romantic illusion and realist sobriety whose tightly woven tales helped purge the Gothic of some of its excesses and sentimentality. His fellow cynic H.L. Mencken was on the mark when he commented that "death to Bierce was not something repulsive, but a sort of low-comedy—the last act of a squalid and rib-rocking buffoonery" ("The Ambrose Bierce Mystery," *American Mercury* 18 September 1929, 124).

The classic English Gothic has long, convoluted plots, extended and painstaking reflection on the proprieties of behavior when one is faced with dark temptations, and some kind of redemptive moral norm or lesson. Bierce's ghost and horror stories have none of these things. When Bierce is considered in the context of a developing Gothic tradition, he often figures as a turning point in the development of a modern, grimmer version of American horror fiction. The most unsentimental of all Gothic writers, Bierce brings a fierce irony and Poe-like economy to his tales of terror, displacing the sublime with the sordid and the expansive with the tautly wrought. Gary Hoppenstand has demonstrated how Bierce's economy of style stems in great part from his journalistic background and from the growing commercial influence of periodicals and credits him with offering an important transformation of the Gothic tale. Hoppenstand's work, along with some groundbreaking primary scholarship led by the efforts of S.T. Joshi, promises to rescue Bierce from his relatively marginal status in the canons of both American and Gothic literature. Often treated merely as a transitional figure whose tumultuous biography of mysterious doings and misanthropy eclipses his literary achievement, Bierce stands ready today to be appreciated as one of the Gothic tale's fine craftsmen.

Not that the enigmas of Bierce's life do not still command attention: in addition to Roy Morris' fine recent biography, *Ambrose Bierce: Alone in Bad Company,* and Joshi's and Schultz's *Bits of Autobiography* (Bierce in his own words), two fascinating novels, Carlos Fuentes's *Old Gringo* and Oakley Hall's *Ambrose Bierce and the Queen of Spades*, feature the famous iconoclast as their main character. Generations have been fascinated by his legendary misanthropy, fierce independence, and larger-than-life presence. Many disagree about the character of that misanthropy, some seeing it as a calculated and profitable pose, others as the real and vitriolic essence of his character; all agree that his fighting in

the Civil War, in which he received a serious head wound at the Battle of
Kennesaw Mountain, had much to do with his no-nonsense vision of American
culture and politics; and all also agree that his utterly unromanticized Civil War
stories, with their brutal twists and cruel climaxes, are the finest to have been
written by a survivor. Many admire his subsequent career as a wickedly funny
satirist and muckraking journalist for William Randolph Hearst's *San Francisco
Examiner*, who fearlessly took on the robber barons and their sycophants at a
time of real violence in the newspaper wars. Yet just about anybody who has
read his journalistic invective or his witty *Devil's Dictionary* must wince at his
ferociously sardonic attacks on just about everyone and everything. Finally, and
most infamously, there is the mystery of his death, which has called forth the
kind of biographical detective work long associated with Gothic mystery: early
theories favored some kind of entanglement with Villa—all that Bierce left us
with was the cryptic "going to Mexico with a definite purpose . . . not at present
disclosable" (Pope 196)—and recent research, finally laying to rest the fantastic
theory that he committed suicide by leaping into the Grand Canyon, suggests
that the old soldier was killed in the Battle of Ojinaga in January 1914. One
can only surmise that Bierce would take a grim delight in baffling those who
long sought to dispel this uncertainty surrounding his death.

For, from the first of his horror stories to the last, death provides the center
of consciousness, the theme that pervades all, the reality that none of his characters can avoid coming to grips with, no matter how desperately and understandably they try to do so. Chatto, the English publisher of *Tales of Soldiers
and Civilians*, recognized this master theme in adding a phrase from the funeral
service of *The Book of Common Prayer* to the title of its edition ("in the midst
of life we are in death"). Very near-to-death or postmortem consciousness is
Bierce's special domain, from the grim irony of such Civil War stories as "Owl
Creek" and "One of the Missing" to the ghost who "steps out of the darkness"
(189) and elegizes himself in "The Stranger" and on to the strangely Lovecraftian "Inhabitant of Carcosa" and the murdered wife's narrative in "The Moonlit
Road," both of which must rely on that rather awkward plot device, mediums,
to communicate their dark visions from the other side. Listen as death stealthily,
inexorably closes in on the main character in "The Death of Halpin Frayser":

A strange sensation began slowly to take possession of his body and his mind. He could
not say which, if any, of his senses was affected; he felt it rather as a consciousness—
a mysterious mental assurance of some overpowering presence—some supernatural malevolence different in kind from the invisible existences that swarmed about him, and
superior to them in power. He knew that it had uttered that hideous laugh. And now it
seemed to be approaching him; from what direction he did not know—dared not con-
jecture. All his former fears were forgotten or merged in that gigantic terror that now
held him in thrall. (4)

This is Gothic terror of a special kind: as horrifying as Poe but somehow,
strangely, more dispassionate, intriguing in terms of its special context, the Oed-

ipal horror of a devouring mother-ghost, but ultimately powerful and haunting in its fundamental encounter with death itself. Frayser's experience bears remarkable similarities to one of Bierce's own "Visions of the Night," in which he recalls encountering his dead self, and it is tempting to see that dream as providing a kind of master plot or governing theme in his fiction. No other writer looks as steadily and as unflinchingly at death.

Later, as the woodsmen discover Halpin's corpse, we are treated to another of Bierce's specialties: a coroner's-eye view of what death leaves behind (in Frayser's case, no less than five paragraphs of close description with such nice details of the strangling as a head at an impossible angle; fists tightly clenched; purple-black neck and protruding tongue; and "expanded eyes staring blankly backward in a direction opposite to that of the feet" [12]). One also recalls the corpse mangled by "The Damned Thing" and its wicked subtitle ("A Man Though Naked May Be in Rags") and the six-year-old deaf-mute child of "Chickamauga," who wanders through a Civil War battlefield of mutilated men only to find his own mother in splinters, her head "a frothy mass of gray crowned with clusters of crimson bubbles" (*In the Midst of Life*, ed. Cunliffe, 33). This kind of moribund detail and morbid humor has understandably repelled many readers and has even invited some critics, like E.F. Bleiler, to question Bierce's sanity. But this grotesque detail points to one of the enabling paradoxes in Bierce's artistic achievement: although he disdained the realist school, once defining realism as "the art of depicting nature as it is seen by toads" (*The Devil's Dictionary*), he brings a reporter's eye and precision reminiscent of Matthew Brady's Civil War photos to his ghost and horror stories. And although in another passage from the *Dictionary* he exalts romance as "fiction that owes no allegiance to the God of Things as They Are," his romances everywhere draw power from their closely detailed California and western settings, often of middle- or lower-class life. He is actually the most gritty and realistic of romance writers.

Freud once remarked that an artist can overcome our "feeling of repulsion" about a story's subject matter by "bribing" us with "the purely formal—that is, aesthetic—yield of pleasure which he offers us in the presentation of his fantasies" ("Creative Writers and Daydreaming"), and one can find many such pleasures in Bierce's innovatively designed tales. One of his favorite devices is to offer, even within the limited range of his short tales, a number of incomplete or contradictory points of view in regard to a central mystery that almost always revolves around a death or a murder. These are frequently organized into little subsections with teasing titles ("One Does Not Always Marry When Insane," "Who Drives Sane Oxen Should Himself Be Tame," "An Explanation from the Tomb") that offer fractured perspectives from before, during, and after the central enigma, but rarely in sequence. The reader is left to do some careful detective work reconstructing the sequence of events and weighing the credibility of each point of view. Often the sum of the fragmentary views argues for the presence of the supernatural, usually the return of a murdered wife to haunt the scene of her death. In "The Secret of Macarger's Gulch," a man finds confirmation years later that the strange dream he had in a Nevada cabin of a murdered woman and her evil, scar-faced husband points to actual events. In "The Moonlit Road," the story of the murdered wife is told three times, with a novel twist—neither son nor wife (who speaks posthumously through a medium) is aware that the father and husband is the murderer. In "The Middle Toe of the Right Foot," we find, through the anatomical clue of the title, that the ghost of a murdered wife has returned to exact her revenge on her husband as he duels with her lover. If Poe felt that the death of a beautiful woman is the most poetical topic in the world, Bierce, it seems, finds her uncertain demise the most convenient of plot devices.

These and many others of Bierce's tales arguably fall into that old Gothic category of tales of horror (or the new Todorovan category of the "marvelous"), in which the supernatural figures as real or the reader finds that "new laws of nature must be entertained to account for the phenomena." (*The Fantastic* 41). In addition to the tales of ghostly wives, one finds the ghost of a rejected woman returning to haunt her erstwhile lover to death in "Beyond the Wall" and an invisible monster in "The Damned Thing," whose "reality" is asserted not just by its savage murder of Hugh Morgan but by the novel "scientific" theory that there are colors that exist outside of the known spectrum: "And, God help me! The Damned Thing is of such a color!" (39). The most perfect and allegorical of these horror stories may be "The Night-Doings at 'Deadman's,' " in which the figure of Death himself comes to free a persecuted Chinaman denied a proper burial, and the figure of Satan, appearing as "a swarthy little gentleman from San Francisco" (173), comes to snatch the soul of the persecutor. Yet where most Gothic presentations of "real" horrors (in scare quotations, at least) suggest on the part of the writer some commitment to the otherworldly, some mythopoetics of the godly and the godless, some familiar logic of salvation and damnation, Bierce's tales stubbornly do not. One finds a recurrent and peculiarly modernist sense that his characters live in a random universe, where horror and death can visit bad people as well as the good or, even more likely, the unwitting. Apache Indians trap some cowboys in a cave, and they sensibly, given the alternative, defer on futile heroics and decide that suicide is the best way out. A pregnant mother watches as a panther rips to pieces her one child only to have the one she is bearing metamorphose into a panther and become hunted down. A man terrified of snakes dies of a fit occasioned by a stuffed snake: "its eyes were two shoe buttons" (97). Few of Bierce's victims necessarily deserve their fate; all seem involved in some dark cosmic joke. Even his ghosts and messengers from the other side of the grave are often clueless; far from being emissaries of divine retribution and justice in the typically Gothic manner, some actually appear confused about the manner of their departure from life. In sum, the reader will be frustrated in finding an organizing worldview or metaphysics in these tales—Bierce indeed seems intent on such a frustration—but they do yield a consistent strategy: a grim delight in denying the reader a satisfying or even philosophical consolation for the existence of death—not evil, just death. This is why Bierce's horror stories, in which real ghosts return to baffle and shatter the lives of the living, stand in a secondary position to the tales in which he offers us no final answers, no recourse, even, to the malleable fiction of the supernatural. For in these endlessly puzzling tales he is most characteristically Biercian, working artfully to baffle his readers and to shatter any one interpretation, working, finally, to show that his readers have no better answer to the enigma of death than his characters do.

These enigmatic tales include "The Death of Halpin Frayser," which has encouraged many critics to complete or to explain the fragmentary elegy—written in his own blood—left by the deceased; "A Watcher by the Dead," which leaves one utterly bewildered whether the man haunting the gamblers at the end is the watcher of the dead or the man who had pretended to be dead; and "An Adventure at Brownville," in which a handsome fellow given to singing the Duke's aria from *Rigoletto* unaccountably accounts for the death of two completely unresisting young women in his company. Quintessentially Biercian in structure and riddling irony is "The Suitable Surroundings." The tale begins with a young frontier lad braving a haunted house, only to discover a dead man within in the posture of reading; we then flash back to "The Day Before" to learn that the man, Willard Marsh, had been dared by a writer of ghost stories, James Colston, to read a particularly hideous story of his in "suitable surroundings," meaning the haunted house. Then we move forward to "The Day After," where an inquiry is conducted into the cause of Marsh's death and a manuscript of Colston's is presented that contains the too-horrible tale and the news that Colston intends to commit suicide after Marsh has kept his compact. But we never get to know the details of this death-inducing tale. Nor is Colston permitted to commit suicide, as a concluding dispatch "From the 'Times' " tells us: instead he has been intercepted and placed in an insane asylum, while, the story acidly ends, "most of our esteemed contemporary's other writers are still at large" (104). Arguably in this tale we have something like a Gothic writer's defense of the power of his storytelling, his ability, quite literally, to scare us to death. But we never get to hear that story, because the son-in-law of the original inhabitant of the haunted house burns the manuscript, and it turns out that Colston is a loony anyway. Did Colston sneak up on Marsh and play a role in his own story's killing of the reader? Or did the brave lad's unexpected appearance frighten Marsh to death? Just why does the son-in-law burn the malevolent manuscript? We just will never know, as dark joke follows dark mystery, and we find that "the deep truth is imageless," or that we, like Marsh, have been implicated in a diabolical hoax, perpetrated by Bierce himself.

In his *Philosophical Enquiry into the Origins of Our Ideas of the Sublime and the Beautiful*, Edmund Burke argued that "the sublime is an idea belonging to self-preservation," (33) and that literary presentations of awesome and life-imperiling scenes, if properly distanced, "if not noxious and not carried to violence, are capable of producing delight" (36) and imaginative reverie in a reader. Perhaps Bierce is finally best understood as the writer of the antisublime, one who never allows us that reassuring distance. Death for Bierce was hardly the occasion for high tragic or sublime musings; nor, as Mencken noted, was it particularly "repulsive" but instead "a sort of low-comedy," in which, one might add, the joke is often played upon the reader. Who is, after all, that mysterious baritone airily singing "La donna è mobile" in the wake of a young woman's senseless death? Many might see him as Satan, but I prefer Bierce himself, writer of *The Devil's Dictionary*—and of some devilishly clever ghost stories.

SELECTED CRITICISM

Bleiler, E.F. Introduction to *Ghost and Horror Stories of Ambrose Bierce*. New York: Dover, 1964. (v–xx). "For Bierce the ultimate source of horror was the human mind; the foulest disgust emerged from conventional human relations; and the Gothic apparatus was simply a symbolization of this festering and decay." There is a real emphasis on "Bitter Bierce" in this biocritical essay.

Fry, Carrol L., and Wayne A. Chandler. "An Epiphany at Owl Creek Bridge: Intimations of Immortalities in Ambrose Bierce's Fiction." *Studies in Weird Fiction* 24 (1999): 8–14. Offers a novel interpretation of Bierce's most visited tale as a story of "psychic abduction rather than psychological process," leading "readers to interpret the story as a contact with the supernatural" (and thus placing the tale more in the company of the "fantastic" genre of *Can Such Things Be?*). In complicating the idea of Bierce as a realist, this article intelligently stresses Bierce's purposeful "indeterminacy," at least one element of which is his playful "Gothic sensationalism."

Gale, Robert L. *An Ambrose Bierce Companion*. Westport, CT: Greenwood Press, 2000. Contains materials helpful for an understanding of both the Gothic and non-Gothic elements in Bierce's writings.

Grenander, Mary Elizabeth. *Ambrose Bierce*. New York: Twayne, 1971. In such stories as "An Occurrence at Owl Creek Bridge" and "The Man and the Snake," Bierce "has given the terror tale an ironical turn of the screw."

Hoppenstand, Gary. "Ambrose Bierce and the Transformation of the Gothic Tale in the Nineteenth-Century American Periodical." In *Periodical Literature in Nineteenth-Century America*. Ed. Kenneth M. Price and Susan Belasco Smith. Charlottesville: University Press of Virginia, 1995: 220–238. Easily the most important study on Bierce and the Gothic tradition, arguing that "the best of his Gothic stories compare favorably to the best of his Civil War stories." Breaks Bierce's Gothic into four categories: (1) ghost stories; (2) stories of family violence; (3) satiric pieces; and (4) scientific; and sees the latter, especially "Moxon's Master," as providing a rich vein of influence in the American merging of the Gothic with science fiction.

Joshi, S.T. "Ambrose Bierce: Horror as Satire." In *The Weird Tale*. Austin: University of Texas Press, 1990. Elaborates on Mencken's comment that "death to Bierce was not something repulsive, but a sort of low-comedy."

———. "The Fiction of Ambrose Bierce: A Bibliographical Survey." *Studies in Weird*

Fiction 23 (1998): 31–37. Provides information on the first printings and editions of Bierce's tales of the uncanny, many but not all of which appeared in the *San Francisco Examiner*.

Joshi, S.T., and David Schultz, eds. *A Sole Survivor: Bits of Autobiography*: Knoxville: University of Tennessee Press, 1998. An important primary source of information.

———. *Ambrose Bierce: An Annotated Bibliography of Primary Sources*. Westport, CT: Greenwood Press, 1999. Important source study.

McLean, Robert C. "The Deaths in Ambrose Bierce's 'Halpin Frayser.' " *Papers on Language and Literature* 10 (1974): 394–402. Sees the tale as a "distinctly American or ambiguous Gothic" in which Bierce provides enough clues for a psychological explanation of Frayser's death yet still preserves a supernatural aura to the work.

Morris, Roy. *Ambrose Bierce: Alone in Bad Company*. Oxford: Oxford University Press, 1999. An entertaining new biography that revisits and clarifies many of the mysteries surrounding Bierce's life.

Pope, Bertha Clark, ed. "Letter to Josephine McCrackin, 13 September 1913." In *The Letters of Ambrose Bierce*, San Francisco: Book Club of California, 1922. An important document concerning the mystery of his disappearance. Also see Leon Day, "Ambrose Bierce Has the Last Word—Again," *Studies in Weird Fiction* 24 (1999): 1–5.

Rubens, Philip M. "The Gothic Foundations of Ambrose Bierce's Fiction." *Nyctalops* 2 (1978): 29–31. Discusses how Bierce inherits and complicates formal techniques of the Gothic, including multiple narratives and time manipulations, to help create a sense of enigma and the provisional supernatural.

Rubens, Philip M. and Robert Jones. "Ambrose Bierce: A Bibliographic Essay and Bibliography." *American Literary Realism* 16 (1983): 73–91. Supplements George E. Fortenberry's "Ambrose Bierce (1842–1914?): A Critical Bibliography of Secondary Comment." *American Literary Realism* 4 (1971): 11–56.

Stark, Cruce. "The Color of 'The Damned Thing': The Occult as The Suprasensational." In *The Haunted Dusk: American Supernatural Fiction, 1820–1920*. Ed. Howard Kerr, John W. Crowley, and Charles L. Crow. Athens: University of Georgia Press, 1983: 211–227. Notes in this "Explanation from the Tomb" the relatively rare use of the genuinely supernatural force in Bierce's fiction (wrongly, I think); Bierce's ghost stories more often focus on "the uncontrollable terrors from within."

Stein, William B. "Bierce's 'The Death of Halpin Frayser: The Poetics of Gothic Consciousness." *ESQ: A Journal of the American Renaissance* 18 (1972): 115–122. Examines Bierce's recurrent theme, "the pitiless indifference of the creator," in terms of how his internalized Puritanism returns to disrupt American ideals of self-reliance and freedom.

Wiggins, Robert A. "Ambrose Bierce: A Romantic in an Age of Realism." *American Literary Realism* 4 (1971): 1–10. Places Bierce in a "dark tradition" opposed to realism, one that stresses "abnormal psychological states," "grotesque personalities," and preference for "the violent, the perverse, and the shocking" (6). Has trouble naming what such a countertradition might be called, but sounds an awful lot like something being called the "American Gothic" today. (Wiggins does note, as others have, Bierce's affinities with the "Southern Gothic.")

Wymer, Thomas L. "Ambrose Bierce." In *Supernatural Fiction Writers: Fantasy and Horror*. Ed. E.F. Bleiler. New York: Scribner's, 1985: 731–737. Bierce helps Americanize the Gothic through his regional settings and psychological version of terror.

CHARLOTTE BRONTË
(1816–1855)
EMILY BRONTË
(1818–1848)

Douglass H. Thomson

PRINCIPAL GOTHIC WORKS

Brontë, Charlotte [pseud. Currer Bell]. *Jane Eyre*. London: Smith, Elder, 1847.
———. *Villette*. London: Smith, Elder & Co., 1853.
Brontë, Emily [pseud. Ellis Bell]. *Wuthering Heights*. London: Newby, 1847.

MODERN REPRINTS AND EDITIONS

Brontë, Charlotte. *Jane Eyre*. Ed. Richard J. Dunn. New York: W.W. Norton, 1971. (This edition is cited in the text.)
———. *Jane Eyre*. Ed. Beth Newman. Case Studies in Contemporary Criticism. Boston: Bedford Books of St. Martin's Press, 1996.
———. *Villette*. Ed. Herbert Rosengarten and Margaret Smith. Oxford: Clarendon University Press, 1984.
Brontë, Emily. *Wuthering Heights*. Ed. William R. Sale, Jr., and Richard J. Dunn. New York: W.W. Norton, 1990.
———. *Wuthering Heights*. Ed. Linda H. Peterson. Case Studies in Contemporary Criticism. Boston: Bedford Books of St. Martin's Press, 1992.
———. *Wuthering Heights*. Ed. Ian Jack, intro. Patsy Stoneman. Oxford: Oxford University Press, 1998.

Virginia Woolf once complained that the sudden intrusion of Grace Poole and her strange attic world into *Jane Eyre* constitutes an "awkward break" that disturbs the "continuity" of the novel: "One might say . . . that the woman who wrote these pages had more genius than Austen; but if one reads them over and marks that jerk in them, that indignation, one sees that she will never get her genius expressed whole and entire. Her books will be deformed and twisted. She will write in rage where she should write calmly" (555). One finds something poignant about the irony of Woolf, in her pioneering feminist study *A*

Room of One's Own, criticizing Charlotte Brontë for this breach, this apparent discontinuity. For as recent criticism has almost ubiquitously argued, the attic world of Grace Poole and the madwoman she attends upon serve not as an interruption of feminist concerns but as a powerful metaphor for them: Bertha Mason, the mad wife hidden in the attic, is the demonic counterpoint to the "angel-in-the-house" image under which Jane chafes, the very embodiment of the rage and passion that women must repress in Victorian society. We have now come to reassess in similar terms another "deformed and twisted" characteristic of the Brontëan achievement that had bothered critics: the sisters' pervasive invocation of the Gothic spirit. Like Woolf's uneasiness with that abrupt reminder of madness, critics had long been uneasy with or apologetic about the so-called Gothic trappings of the novels (for example, Heathcliff's vampiric obsessions with Catherine Earnshaw or the telepathic voices that summon Jane to Rochester). Yet we now understand the Brontës' Gothicism as a fundamental aspect of their exploration of the female psyche in a world that denies waking expression of a woman's sexual and intellectual being.

There has always seemed something Gothic about the Brontës' early years: their life amid the gorgeously gloomy world of moors and cemetery at Haworth Parsonage; their upbringing by the alternately encouraging and despondent Reverend Patrick Brontë after the early death of their mother; their nightmarish sojourn at the Cowan Bridge Clergy Daughters' School (bitterly recalled by Charlotte in her depiction of the Calvinistic Lowood School in *Jane Eyre*); the career and early death of their favorite but dissipated brother Branwell—the list could go on. From this isolated and often-bleak existence, the sisters retreated into a richly imaginative one of their own making, creating closely knit romantic legends, interspersed with poems, of the never-never lands of Gondal, Angria, and Zamorna. As Christine Alexander has shown, part of the inspiration for this childhood literature and for their mature fiction came from the sisters' readings in literary annuals loaded with Gothic tales and images, including the visionary landscapes of John Martin. Also influential were the novels of Charlotte Smith, Ann Radcliffe, Mary Shelley, and possibly Charlotte Dacre and the poetry and figure of Byron and his virtuosic re-creation of the Gothic villain-hero, the lineaments of which can be clearly seen in the figures of Heathcliff and Rochester and even, according to Sandra Gilbert, in *Jane Eyre* as a kind of "Byronic heroine."

Early criticism of the Brontës' fiction treated the sisters as a kind of *lusus naturae*, with praise for their native genius and imaginative power but with censure for their unruly passions, invocation of the supernatural, and indecorous tampering with social hierarchy. In recent scholarship, the Brontës, along with Mary Shelley and Ann Radcliffe, have been pivotal in definition of the "female Gothic," and their so-called irregularities have been reinterpreted as expressions of dissatisfaction with the patriarchy. At first glance, it would appear that the Gothic is a tricky genre for the expression of feminist concerns. The Brontës' novels share with earlier Gothics a fascination with dark, secretive, and moody

Byronic heroes, and each includes the fairy-tale ending of a heroine engaged to be married, hardly a convincing indication of a break from "patriarchal" convention. Yet working within these conventions, the Brontës transform Gothic plotting in some significant ways. First, as Syndy Conger and many other critics have asserted, the Brontëan heroine moves beyond her Gothic (especially her Radcliffean) counterpart in terms of moral complexity, desire for freedom, and passion. Jane resists Rochester not only because of the obvious sexual threat that he—like all Gothic villain-heroes—poses but because her love for him threatens to compromise her being, her integrity, her hard-earned moral independence. Catherine's "wailing for her demon lover" in *Wuthering Heights* is immeasurably more complex than that of earlier Gothic romances: Heathcliff is at once her soul mate, tormentor, true love, and infernal conscience. Together they wreck the staid gentility of Victorian society even as their thwarted passion falls victim to and thus indicts those class restrictions. Lucy Snowe's love for M. Paul in *Villette* represents an almost direct inversion of Gothic plotting: she must move beyond the usual Gothic heroine's suspicious mythologizing of the dark continental male to realize that he will actually allow her freedom and intellectual equality, and she does just this. *Jane Eyre* and *Wuthering Heights* also contain a central reversal of traditional Gothic plotting: both Jane and Catherine reject the virtuous, socially acceptable hero (St. John Rivers, Edgar Linton) typically reserved for the Gothic heroine after her dalliances with the mysterious dark hero. The Brontëan heroines' relationships with their men afford them not merely the context in which to affirm their "virtue" or to define their economic condition, but to test their independence and strong wills.

The Brontës' pervasive use of the supernatural has struck many critics as too Gothic, but surely they succeed in creating a new and distinctly female psychology for the conventions of terror and the otherworldly. Not many feminist critics have been happy with the telepathic voices that summon Jane back to a conveniently chastised Rochester. But there's the rub: the voices are fantastic and Gothic, and they do indicate Jane's love for Rochester. Perhaps these voices have proved disappointing to critics with little appreciation for the Gothic because other moments of the supernatural in the novels invite such rich psychological interpretation. Both Jane and Catherine encounter ghosts, Jane during the memorable scene of rebellion in the red room and Catherine during her final illness, that are obvious but powerful mirror images of their own passions denied by the restrictive social order. Catherine's haunting recalls the appearance of her child-ghost that had earlier terrified the priggish Lockwood; hovering between the nightmare world and the other world—why else does Lockwood use her married name of Linton?—the visitation is at once a desperate image of woman denied her true home and an indictment of the narrow range of Victorian feeling and imagination personified in Lockwood. Significantly, his nightmare takes its origin from his reading in an ultra-Calvinist text by the Reverend James Branderham crammed with marginalia ("faded hieroglyphics") of the young and rebellious Cathy. Here certainly is a metaphor for the Gothic: a darkly religious text that marginalizes the female, forcing her passions outside the domestic sphere, making her a ghost of her own desire. Heathcliff is every bit as haunted and haunting as Catherine, and his final morbid reverie about their corpses dissolving into one another provides a particularly Gothic twist to the novel's central *liebestod* motif.

Unlike the tempestuous atmosphere and landscape that pervade Emily's novel and help build its eerie quality, Charlotte's use of the Gothic is occasional and counterbalanced by a sobering degree of realism in her novels. We experience in her fiction the terribly unromantic reality of poverty, the boredom and isolation of the governess's life, and the Wollstonecraftian insistence on education, rational self-control, and self-vindication. These make the moments when something weird breaks through—such as Jane's thrice-dreamed vision of a "baby phantom" and Lucy Snowe's remarkably vivid opium reverie—all the more telling in psychological terms. What we encounter are the passionate energies no longer held in check by the societal superego, the fire, quite literally in *Jane Eyre*, lashing out at the "snowe." So much has been written on Bertha Mason Rochester as an emblem of Jane's libido or feminine rage or pent-up passion that I will simply refer the reader to the many interpretations cited in the "Selected Criticism" section. But it is worth remembering that part of Bertha's power stems from her Gothic lineage: when Jane first hears that "preternatural laugh," she thinks of the entrapped women in "Bluebeard's castle" (114). Later she likens the castle specter of Bertha to that "foul German spectre—the Vampire" (281). Brontë's later variation on a stereotypical Gothic episode in *Villette*, Lucy Snowe's repeated encounters with a ghostly nun, will never achieve the renown of mad Bertha but best indicates the range and pliability of her reworking of that tradition. On one level, the nun haunting the *pensionnat* is an obvious double of Lucy, an indictment of her renunciation of the passions and her cloistered existence. But as the nun's legend in good Gothic fashion involves a tale of fatal, forbidden love, and as her reality involves a pretext for allowing two lovers who are very much alive to carry out their tryst, the nun also functions as a lesser Bertha Mason, an emblem of the passions Lucy denies herself. Yet as these two lovers are the foppish de Hamal (in drag as the nun) and the coquettish Ginevra Hanshawe, the entire Gothic scene functions as well as a parody of aristocratic intrigue and hypocrisy.

Lucy's unveiling of that most familiar of Gothic specters can be seen as a fitting conclusion to the Brontës' lifelong fascination with the *genre noir*. From thrilling one another as children with the ghostly tale to discovering in its idiom a powerful new means of voicing the buried life of women, the Brontës explored the full range of the Gothic imagination, and Charlotte's playful rendering of the nun suggests that she also understood the rich potential of the Gothic for parody as well.

SELECTED CRITICISM

Alexander, Christine. " 'That Kingdom of Gloom': Charlotte Brontë, the Annuals, and the Gothic." *Nineteenth-Century Literature* 47 (1993): 409–436. From the very

Gothic engravings and romances of the literary annuals, Brontë learned "a set of conventions that could be used first as raw material, then as the chief ingredient of parody, and finally, . . . as a means to explore the riddles of our thought and feeling."

Aspects of Jane Eyre. London: BBC Educational Publishing, 1998. A seventy-one-minute videocassette narrated by Libby Fawbert. Covers the background of Charlotte Brontë, education, religion, *Jane Eyre* as a Gothic novel, and feminist approaches to the characters of Jane Eyre and Mr. Rochester and romantic love. Includes clips from three BBC dramatizations of *Jane Eyre* and reading of selected passages by Miriam Margolyes.

Brennan, Matthew C. "Emily Brontë's *Wuthering Heights*." In *The Gothic Psyche: Disintegration and Growth in Nineteenth-Century English Literature*. Columbia, SC: Camden House, 1997: 77–96. Jungian reading that sees "the roles of Catherine as [Lockwood's] anima and Heathcliff as his shadow. This plot encoded in Lockwood's dream enacts the Gothic paradigm of unity, division, and disintegration."

Conger, Syndy McMillen. "The Reconstruction of the Gothic Feminine Ideal in Emily Brontë's *Wuthering Heights*." In *The Female Gothic*. Ed. Juliann Fleenor. Montreal: Eden Press, 1983: 91–106. A study of Emily Brontë's transformation of the Gothic heroine. The depiction of Catherine Earnshaw, with her passion, moral complexities, and strong will, moves beyond the essentially passive, long-suffering heroines of earlier Gothic novels.

Crosby, Christina. "Charlotte Brontë's Haunted Text." *Studies in English Literature, 1500–1900* 24 (1984): 701–715. Studies the various levels of meaning involved in Lucy Snowe's encounter with the veiled ghostly nun.

Dickerson, Vanessa. "Spells and Dreams, Hollows and Moors: Supernaturalism in *Jane Eyre* and *Wuthering Heights*." In *Victorian Ghosts in the Noontide*. Columbia: University of Missouri Press, 1996: 48–79. "The supernatural enabled the sisters to explore with transcendent force women's ambivalent position in a world that denies or frustrates her need for autonomy."

Gilbert, Sandra M. "A Dialogue of Self and Soul: Plain Jane's Progress." In *The Madwoman in the Attic*. New Haven: Yale University Press, 1979. Famous reading of Rochester's wife, Bertha Mason, as Jane Eyre's "truest and darkest double" and the pent-up embodiment of female creativity and passion (336–371).

Gordon, Jan B. "Gossip, Diary, Letter, Text: Anne Brontë's Narrative Tenant and the Problematic of the Gothic Sequel." *ELH* 51 (1984): 719–745. As a "Gothic sequel," *The Tenant of Wildfell Hall* attempts to domesticate the damage done by the publication of *Wuthering Heights*, here seen as a betrayal of the Brontë's private imaginative life.

Haggerty, George. "The Gothic Form of *Wuthering Heights*." *Victorian Newsletter* 74 (1988): 1–6. Refers to *Wuthering Heights* as "the first truly successful Gothic novel with an idiom capable of animating the social form with the private fantasy."

Heilman, Robert. "Charlotte Brontë's 'New Gothic.' " In *From Jane Austen to Joseph Conrad: Essays Collected in Memory of James T. Hillhouse*. Ed. Robert C. Rathburn and Martin Steinmann, Jr. Minneapolis: University of Minnesota Press, 1958: 118–32. In using and transforming stale Gothic conventions, Charlotte Brontë opens up the novel form to "an original and intense exploration of feeling that increases the range and depth of fiction."

Heller, Tamar. "Jane Eyre, Bertha, and the Female Gothic." In *Approaches to Teaching*

Brontë's Jane Eyre. Ed. Diane Hoeveler and Beth Lau. New York: Modern Language Association, 1993: 49–55. Examines ways in which the "female Gothic is a dark mirror of the courtship plot" and suggests that Charlotte Brontë feels "ambivalence about the qualities in Jane—passion, anger, and sexuality—that Bertha supposedly embodies."

Hoeveler, Diane. "The Brontës and Romantic Feminism." In *Gothic Feminism: The Professionalization of Gender from Charlotte Smith to the Brontës*. University Park: Pennsylvania State University Press, 1998: 185–241. Discusses the appropriate use of the Gothic in *Wuthering Heights, Jane Eyre*, and *Villette*. Lucy Snowe, the heroine of *Villette*, "embodies Charlotte Brontë's supreme psychological achievement because Lucy is finally pure psychic energy set free from the trammels of that most Gothic of nightmares, the female body."

Homans, Margaret. "Dreaming of Children: Literalization in *Jane Eyre* and *Wuthering Heights*." In *The Female Gothic*. Ed. Juliann Fleenor. Montreal: Eden Press, 1983: 257–279. Equates the "Gothic literalization of subjective states," itself a feminine reaction against male Romantic ideation, and the dynamics of "childbearing, in which what was once internal acquires its own objective reality." Jane ultimately refuses "to transfer the self from subject to object"; Cathy, in doing so in bearing a child, "necessarily" dies.

Milbank, Alison. " 'Handling the Veil': Charlotte Brontë." In *Daughters of the House: Modes of the Gothic in Victorian Fiction*. New York: St. Martin's Press, 1992: 140–157. This challenge to accepted definitions of the "female Gothic" includes a section on *Villette*.

Nichols, Nina da Vinci. "Place and Eros in Radcliffe, Lewis, and Brontë." In *The Female Gothic*. Ed. Juliann Fleenor. Montreal: Eden Press, 1983: 187–206. A study of how imagery of place and dream reflects the hidden desire of the Gothic heroine for independence and sexual fulfillment, things denied them by prevailing patriarchal codes. Brontë's melancholy ending describes a "sombre Utopia precisely because moral equity found no room at the inns of Victorian society."

Pykett, Lyn. "Gender and Genre in *Wuthering Heights*: Gothic Plot and Domestic Fiction." In *Wuthering Heights*. Ed. Patsy Stoneman. New Casebooks. London: Macmillan, 1993: 86–99. Traces the beginnings of Gothic feminism back to the novel.

Ronald, Ann. "Terror-Gothic: Nightmare and Dream in Ann Radcliffe and Charlotte Brontë." In *The Female Gothic*. Ed. Juliann Fleenor. Montreal: Eden Press, 1983: 176–186. Studies the journey and fairy-tale motifs common to Radcliffe and Brontë to explain how their "inherent ambiguity" about "virile men, sexuality, and marriage" accounts for their hold on female readers.

Showalter, Elaine. "Feminine Heroes: Charlotte Brontë and George Eliot." In *A Literature of Their Own*. Princeton: Princeton University Press, 1977: 100–152. Memorable discussion of Jane Eyre and Bertha Mason Rochester in the context of that now-familiar Victorian schizophrenia, the angel in the house and the devil in the flesh.

Tofanelli, John. "The Gothic Confessional: Language and Subjectivity in the Gothic Novel, *Villette*, and *Bleak House*." Doctoral dissertation, Stanford University, 1988. [*DAI* 48:1780A–1781A]. Analyzes the Gothicism of *Villette* in terms of earlier Gothic treatments of order and culture.

Tournebize, Cassilde. "Complexité et ambivalence de l'espace 'gothique' dans *Jane Eyre*." *Caliban* 33 (1996): 83–91. Examines the thematic role played by various Gothic spaces in the novel.

Twitchell, James. "Heathcliff as Vampire." *Southern Humanities Review* 11 (1971): 355–362. Both the physical and mental traits of the vampire are to be found in Heathcliff.

Wein, Toni. "Gothic Desire in Charlotte Brontë's *Villette*." *Studies in English Literature, 1500–1900* 39 (1999): 733–746. Considers the significance of Matthew Lewis's *Monk* for Charlotte Brontë's *Villette*. *Villette* redefines subliminal desire by drawing on *The Monk* for its analysis of substitution's dangers and delights and attacks a practice that makes women counters in a system of barter. Brontë makes the spectral nun stand for a desire that has become disembodied and endlessly deferred.

Woolf, Virginia. *A Room of One's Own*. New York: Harcourt, Brace, 1929. Rpt. in *The Critical Tradition*. 2nd ed. Ed. David H. Richter. New York: Bedford, 1998: 554–560. Contains a memorable contrast of Jane Austen and Charlotte Brontë.

CHARLES BROCKDEN BROWN
(1771–1810)

Douglass H. Thomson

PRINCIPAL GOTHIC WORKS

Wieland; or, The Transformation: An American Tale. New York: T. & J. Swords for H. Caritat, 1798.
"Insanity: A Fragment." *Weekly Magazine,* 19 May 1798.
Arthur Mervyn; or, Memoirs of the Year 1793. Philadelphia: H. Maxwell, 1799.
Edgar Huntly; or, Memoirs of a Sleepwalker. Philadelphia: H. Maxwell, 1799.
Ormond; or, The Secret Witness. New York: G. Forman, 1799; London: Minerva Press, 1800.
Arthur Mervyn; or, Memoirs of the Year 1793: Second Part. New York: George F. Hopkins, 1800.

MODERN REPRINTS AND EDITIONS

Arthur Mervyn; or, Memoirs of the Year 1793. Ed. Warner Berthoff. New York: Holt, Rinehart, & Winston, 1962.
Edgar Huntly, or, Memoirs of a Sleep-Walker. Ed. Norman S. Grabo. New York: Penguin Books, 1988.
The Novels and Related Works of Charles Brockden Brown. Ed. Sydney J. Krause, Alexander Cowie, and S.W. Reid. 6 vols. Kent, OH: Kent State University Press, 1977–1987.
Ormond; or, The Secret Witness. Ed. Ernest Marchand. New York: Hafner, 1937.
Ormond; or, The Secret Witness. Ed. Mary Chapman. Peterborough, Ontario: Broadview Press, 1999.
Three Gothic Novels: Wieland, Arthur Mervyn, Edgar Huntly. Notes by Sydney J. Krause. New York: Library of America, 1998.
Wieland; or, The Transformation. Intro. by Fred Lewis Pattee. New York: Harcourt, Brace, 1926; New York: Hafner, 1960.
Wieland; and Memoirs of Carwin the Biloquist. Ed. Jay Fliegelman. New York: Penguin Books, 1991. (This edition is cited in the text.)

Wieland; or, The Transformation and Memoirs of Carwin the Biloquist. Ed. Emory
    Elliott. Oxford: Oxford University Press, 1994.

If one had to choose a single motto for the Gothic and its intricate weavings of
deferral and revelation, it would be hard to find a better one than Clara Wieland's summation of what she has learned through her terrifying ordeals: "Those
sentiments which we ought not to disclose, it is criminal to harbor" (91). At
first, the statement does not seem to make sense, or, to put it another way, it
seems to resist sense. If harboring or repressing certain sentiments, for example,
the kind that Clara harbors for Pleyel, is a criminal thing, the argument should
urge revelation and more frank communication of these feelings. But something
apparently forbids at the outset disclosure of these sentiments, perhaps in Clara's
case modesty and "rectitude," that favorite moral noun of Charles Brockden
Brown's heroines. It seems that there is no way out. Disclosure incurs societal
censure; deferral or repression of feeling borders on the criminal and, for Brown,
frequently leads to disease, madness, and ultimately death. Yet try as many
critics have to make Brown an opponent of such various superegos as rationalism and Puritanism, it is hard to see him as a "Romantic" defender of the
imagination and full disclosure of feeling. After all, Edgar Huntly's decision to
communicate thoughts that ought not to be disclosed, thoughts that Sarsefield
emphatically tells him he should not disclose, leads directly to the death of both
Clitheroe Edny and Sarsefield's child and precipitates the general calamity that
ends Brown's last Gothic novel.

This vicious circle might be called the catch-22 of the Gothic: a strong compulsion toward order and closure that cannot contain, and indeed seems at times
to breed, a fascination with the forbidden and the libidinous; a revolutionary
exploration of the darker regions of consciousness that yet appears haunted by
the moral systems it threatens to violate. Such paradoxes epitomize Brown's
fiction and his critical legacy. He has been read repeatedly as a critic of the
Enlightenment and Lockean epistemology, as a demystifier of Rousseauistic idealism, as an opponent of religious fanaticism, and as a tester of Godwinian ideals
(see, for example, the criticism of Pattee and Voloshin). Yet from opposing
quarters come arguments that his fiction is haunted by a Calvinist, darkly religious vision, one that even expresses profound misgivings about the value of
the literary imagination itself, as the critics Paul Levine and Michael Bell have
pointed out. Some early critics simply dismissed such incongruities as the inevitable loose ends of Brown's almost manic method of composition. He wrote
his four major works within the space of two years, working on several books
simultaneously. Others see him as a deliberate ironist using notoriously unreliable narrators, artfully plotted doppelgängers, and protean points of view that
produce an almost postmodernist resistance to closure. Patrick Brancaccio and
Norman Grabo are but two of many commentators who find the central intel-
ligences in Brown's novels circumspect and unreliable. Perhaps the most productive approach is to see the irresolutions in Brown as reflecting the larger

tensions of a developing American vision, one that wrestles with the European intellectual legacy but that betrays some anxiety over its influence. Brown's fiction subjects new ideals of the Revolution and the frontier and private property and the self-determining individual to a dark scrutiny, one that acknowledges political, economic, and religious uncertainty in its search for an American identity.

Many of these reassessments have somewhat curiously led critics to question whether Brown should be considered a Gothic novelist at all. The usual logic of such an argument goes as follows: because Brown delves so deeply into areas of the American consciousness and unconsciousness and so alters the setting of his scenes of horror, he offers a more profound or psychologically complex or politically canny vision than one finds in the usual Gothic novel. But one is left to wonder just what constitutes this too-conveniently monolithic and naïve genre against which Brown is measured. Gauged in terms of the catch-22 mentioned earlier, Brown emerges as quintessentially Gothic. It is true that Brown insists in his preface to *Edgar Huntly* that he will move beyond "puerile superstition and exploded manners; Gothic castles and chimeras" to engage "the sympathy of the reader" (Grabo, 3). But his alternative choices and substitutions for the Gothic castle—isolated residences at the edge of the "western wilderness" and cities in plague—allow him, if anything, a greater range in creating an American landscape of terror. Such plot devices as ventriloquism and sleepwalking become powerful metaphors for exploring the id and allow Brown endless variations on the natural-versus-marvelous dichotomy of terror introduced by Clara Reeve and Ann Radcliffe. Murderous voices whisper from closets; mysterious manuscripts are buried, exhumed, stolen, or repressed; a plague observer dreams of his own interment while he is still alive; compellingly enigmatic Europeans appear and disappear, carrying with them signs of angst, supernatural power, and impenetrable secrets that enthrall the narrators' imaginations; bodies spontaneously combust; will-o'-the-wisps beckon nighttime walkers to destruction. Indeed, the most important action in a Brown novel usually occurs at night. He is the novelist of the night, with virtually all of his most relentless Gothic narrative, *Edgar Huntly*, taking place in the pitch dark. Darkling, his characters hover in exquisitely prolonged states of uncertainty amid nocturnal gloom, unsure as to whether their fears proceed from some otherworldly and irreversible fatality or from some real and palpable source of evil, or, almost unthinkably, from their own delusions and madness.

These characters offer telling variations on significant Gothic themes and conventions. Theodore Wieland provides a spectacular realization of that sense of religious terror that haunts many Gothics. It may be right to say that through him Brown wishes to expose the dangers of religious fanaticism, but Wieland's murderous power does border on the supernatural, as no prison can hold him. Also cutting across the idea of Brown's fiction as simply anti-Calvinist is the remarkable and very typically Gothic ineffectuality of his exemplars of right reason. Henry Pleyel in *Wieland*, Sarsefield in *Edgar Huntly*, and Dr. Stephens in *Arthur Mervyn* are given to homilies warning about the dangers of superstition, religious zeal, and an overactive imagination, but blinded by their rational perspective, they repeatedly miss or misinterpret crucial events unfolding before them. The same error of intellectual pride attends another Enlightenment ideal central to the Gothic sensibility: the Adam Smithian capacity of the sympathetic imagination to identify with and to alleviate the suffering of others. Brown's earnest moral vision frequently seems to endorse this power of sympathy (it distinguishes Clara Wieland and Dr. Stephens), but it can, as with Edgar Huntly and Clara as well, become obsessive, until it appears, in Sydney Krause's phrase, "an inordinate sensitivity on behalf of unmerited suffering" (Introduction xxvii). So resistless is Edgar Huntly's identification with Clitheroe Edny that he becomes his double, following his descent into sleepwalking and, arguably, madness. Perhaps Clara Wieland best represents the complexity of Brown's moral vision: caught between Henry Pleyel's rationalism and her brother's religious fanaticism, uncertain of the dividing line between the phenomenal and the noumenal, alternately self-reliant and desperate for domestic harmony, desiring but fearful of desire, living the American dream only to find it turning into a nightmare, she may represent a new kind of Gothic heroine, as does Constantia Dudley of *Ormond*, a bit more independent, wary, in short, American, but her considerable virtues prove no match for the dark forces arrayed against her.

Given these conflicting moral perspectives, Brown's villain-heroes assume a power quintessentially Gothic in its expansiveness and ambiguity. Carwin's voices, denied by reason and too readily embraced by religion, gain a weird omnipresence and assume a power that not even their manipulator can control. Edny, an erstwhile "hero" of his own rags-to-riches narrative, mistakenly thinks that he has become a villain. Welbeck, the proto-Byronic forger and cynic, teaches his student Arthur Mervyn so well that he finds himself hounded by the young man's demonic pursuit. Ormond epitomizes Brown's recurrent fascination with the dark, Radcliffean seducer. We cannot omit Theodore Wieland, the infanticidal religious maniac who murders his family in the name of divine will. All deserve their place in any Gothic roll call of monomaniacal villain-heroes.

Yet it is finally not in his diabolical characters or in his new landscape of terror that the true importance of Brown's Gothic achievement lies. That significance lies rather in the complexity of his vision as a "moral painter," as Brown himself described the novelist in the preface to *Wieland*. All English Gothics up to this stage (1798), no matter how at cross-purposes they at times seem, had been governed by a strong, normative moral code wherein, as Napier has noted, "the vicious are punished, the virtuous are rewarded, and social and ethical imbalances are tidily corrected" (10). Brown's broken points of view, fictions within fictions, and uncertain narrators resist such didactic impulses and provide an arresting, new complexity to the Gothic exploration of good and evil. Therein lies the true historical value of Brown's fiction for such later American writers as Irving, Poe, Hawthorne, and Melville and for such devotees of his novels as the Shelleys. With such complex characters as Victor Frankenstein,

Beatrice Cenci, and Ahab on the horizon, Brown's Gothic fiction paved the way for a much more complex moral vision, one in which the process of discovering the potential for evil within an individual became more terrifying than any threat from without.

SELECTED CRITICISM

Bell, Michael. " 'The Double-tongued Deceiver': Sincerity and Duplicity in the Novels of Charles Brockden Brown." *Early American Literature* 9 (1974): 143–163. While many critics designate a specific philosophical position opposed by Brown, Bell sees him as expressing misgivings about the literary imagination itself. Bell concentrates on the volatile imaginations of narrators such as Clara Wieland and Edgar Huntly.

Berthold, Dennis. "Desacralizing the American Gothic: An Iconographic Approach to *Edgar Huntly.*" *Studies in American Fiction* 14 (1986): 127–138. Maintains that *Edgar Huntly* cannot be classified as a pure Gothic novel because the book is an amalgam of forms "enlisting other genres in the service of translating the Gothic for American needs and purposes."

Brancaccio, Patrick. "Studied Ambiguities: *Arthur Mervyn* and the Problem of the Unreliable Narrator." *American Literature* 42 (1970): 18–27. Inaugurates a series of articles by critics that stress the notorious trickiness of Brown's narrators. Brown experimented with "techniques of multiple perspective and the device of the unreliable narrator."

Christophersen, Bill. *The Apparition in the Glass: Charles Brockden Brown's American Gothic.* Athens: University of Georgia Press, 1994. Important study of the novels that bridges the gap between "Gothic" and historicist interpretations. "Those qualities in Brown's romances that seem to me most profound and American are the Gothic qualities." Stresses Brown's transformation of Gothic materials to enable his explorations of the new nation's hopes and doubts and argues that only eight of the nine voices heard in *Wieland* can be assigned to Carwin.

Fliegelman, Jay. "Ventriloquists, Counterfeiters, and the Seduction of the Mind." In *Prodigals and Pilgrims: The American Revolution against Patriarchal Authority, 1750–1800.* Cambridge, MA: Harvard University Press, 1984: 68–96. Reads Brown's novels in terms of the late-eighteenth-century rebellion against European paternalism and treats Brown's use of terror simply as an expression of his ambiguity regarding the promise and perils of liberty. See also Fliegelman's introduction to the Penguin edition of *Wieland.*

Goddu, Teresa A. "Diseased Discourse: Charles Brockden Brown's *Arthur Mervyn.*" In *Gothic America: Narrative, History, and Nation.* New York: Columbia University Press, 1997: 31–50. In assailing "interior, psychological readings" of the Gothic, Goddu regards Brown's dark mimesis of economic and political anxieties as foundational for the formation of Gothic America.

Grabo, Norman S. *The Coincidental Art of Charles Brockden Brown.* Chapel Hill: University of North Carolina Press, 1981. A formalist approach that defends Brown's conscious artistry against some early critical detractors. Focuses on how doubling and coincidence enable Brown to depict American cultural deformity.

Hazlitt, William. "American Literature." *Edinburgh Review*, October 1829. Rpt. in *The*

Complete Works of William Hazlitt. Ed. P.P. Howe. New York: AMS Press, 1967: 16:319–320. "[Brown's] strength and his efforts are convulsive throes—his works are a banquet of horrors." The result: his novels "are full (to disease) of imagination—but it is forced, violent, and shocking." Also draws parallels with William Godwin's *Caleb Williams* and Mary Shelley's *Frankenstein.*

Heller, Terry. "Charles Brockden Brown." In *Critical Survey of Long Fiction*, vol. 1. Ed. Frank Magill. Englewood Cliffs, NJ: Salem Press, 1983: 2:312–324. Refers to Brown as "the Americanizer of the Gothic," whose work applied Gothic conventions to the "exploring of the human mind in moments of ethically significant decision."

Hinds, Elizabeth Jane Wall. "Charles Brockden Brown and the Frontiers of Discourse." In *Frontier Gothic: Terror and Wonder at the Frontier in American Literature.* Ed. David Mogen, Scott P. Sanders, and Joanne B. Karpinski. Rutherford, NJ: Fairleigh Dickinson University Press, 1993: 109–125. "Brown's Gothicism does not reside in a hidden evil of character to be exposed and exorcised, as in M.G. Lewis's *The Monk*, but grows out of a landscape already exposed yet forever impenetrable."

Krause, Sydney J. Introduction to *Edgar Huntly: or, Memoirs of a Sleep-Walker.* Kent, OH: Kent State University Press, 1984: vii–li. Probably the single best critical study of the novel. Combines detailed background material with an acute psychological reading of the doublings in the novel and analyzes the novel's treatment of Indians.

———. "Penn's Elm and *Edgar Huntly*: 'Dark Instruction to the Heart.' " *American Literature* 66 (1994): 463–484. A new historicist exegesis from one of Brown's most distinguished scholars. Waldegrave's "Elm is appropriately Gothicized" as it presents a darkly ironic counterpoint to Penn's elm and his hoped-for peace with the Delawares.

Levine, Paul. "The American Novel Begins." *American Scholar* 35 (1966): 134–148. Helpful in reviewing the most important of Brown's early critical defenders, D.H. Lawrence, Richard Chase, Leslie Fiedler, and Vernon Parrington. All treat seriously Brown's Gothicism and link his Gothic tendencies to the residual Calvinism in his novels.

Martin, John. "Charles Brockden Brown's Gothic Enlightenment." *Transactions of the Samuel, Johnson Society of the Northwest* 16 (1985): 63–72. Discusses the ending of *Wieland* as illustrative of the "psychic cost" of rationalism. Reason alone is no adequate defense against the Gothic perils of the innermost self.

Parker, Patricia. *Charles Brockden Brown: A Reference Guide.* Boston: G.K. Hall, 1980. Contains annotated references from the earliest reviews up to 1980.

Pattee, Fred Lewis. Introduction to *Wieland; or, The Transformation.* New York: Hafner, 1960: ix–xlvi. One of the first pro-Gothic assessments of Brown. Sees *Wieland* as combining the Godwinian novel of social commentary, the Richardsonian novel of seduction, and the Radcliffean Gothic novel with features distinctly Brown's own.

Ringe, Donald A. *Charles Brockden Brown.* Boston: Twayne, G.K. Hall, 1991. A revised edition of Ringe's 1966 study that incorporates helpful new material in addition to providing solid chapters on biography, critical reception, and interpretation of Brown's novels and other writings.

Rombes, Nicholas, Jr. " 'All Was Lonely, Darksome, and Waste': *Wieland* and the Construction of the New Republic." *Studies in American Fiction* 22 (1994): 37–46. Political doubts and fears are embedded in the novel's Gothic imagery.

Rosenthal, Bernard, ed. *Critical Essays on Charles Brockden Brown.* Boston: G.K. Hall, 1981. Contains ten essays exploring various aspects of Brown's fiction. Includes Nina Baym's important essay "A Minority Reading of *Wieland*" (87–103), which sees the novel as unevenly working to transcend the Gothic to the tragic and which calls into question Brown as a novelist of ideas.

Voloshin, Beverly R. "*Edgar Huntly* and the Coherence of the Self." *Early American Literature* 23 (1988): 262–280. Studies how the nightmare world of the novel subverts Lockean epistemology and other eighteenth-century theories concerning the harmony of mind and nature.

Warfel, Harry R. *Charles Brockden Brown: American Gothic Novelist.* Gainesville: University of Florida Press, 1949. Unapologetically treats Brown as first and foremost a Gothic novelist. Studies Brown's Americanization of the eighteenth-century Gothic and how he anticipates Poe and Hawthorne.

Watts, Steven. *The Romance of Real Life: Charles Brockden Brown and the Origins of American Culture.* Baltimore: Johns Hopkins University Press, 1994. Examines Brown's fictional and nonfictional prose in "the socioeconomic and political transformation of post-Revolutionary America." Contains a bibliographical essay from a trenchantly new historical perspective.

Witherington, Paul. "Charles Brockden Brown: A Bibliographical Essay." *Early American Literature* 9 (1974): 164–187. A review of scholarship divided into three historical periods.

EDWARD BULWER-LYTTON
(1803–1873)
Marie Mulvey-Roberts

PRINCIPAL GOTHIC WORKS

Falkland. London: Colburn, 1827. Rpt. in *The Works of Edward Bulwer Lytton (Lord Lytton)*. Vol. 8. New York: P.F. Collier, 1850.

Pelham, or The Adventures of a Gentleman. London: Colburn, 1828.

"A Manuscript Found in a Mad-House." *The Literary Souvenir*, 1829. Rpt. in *The Gift Book*. London: J. Dillon, G. Holland, and F. Herbert, 1847: 220–228.

"Monos and Daimonos—A Legend." *New Monthly Magazine*. (1830): 28–112; 387–392.

"Arasmanes, The Seeker." *The Amulet* (1834); reprinted in *The Student*; reprinted in *Miscellaneous Prose Works*, 3 vols. London: Richard Bentley, 1868: 2. 112–145.

The Last Days of Pompeii. London: Bentley, 1834.

Pilgrims of the Rhine. London: Saunders and Otley, 1834.

Zicci. Monthly Chronicle, March–August 1838.

Zanoni. London: Saunders and Otley, 1842.

Lucretia; or, The Children of Night. London: Saunders and Otley, 1846.

"The Haunted and the Haunters." *Blackwood's*, 86 (1859): 224–244.

A Strange Story. London: Sampson Low, 1861–1862.

"The Tale of Kosem Kesamin the Magician." In *Miscellaneous Prose Works*. 3 vols. London: Richard Bentley, 1868: 2:211–228.

The Coming Race. Edinburgh and London: Blackwood, 1871.

The New Knebworth Edition of the Novels and Romances of the Right Hon. Lord Lytton. 28 vols. London: George Routledge & Sons, 1895–1898.

MODERN REPRINTS AND EDITIONS

The Coming Race. Intro. Julian Wolfreys, Stroud, Gloucestershire: Alan Sutton, 1995.

Falkland. Ed. Herbert Van Thal, intro. Park Honan. London: Cassell, 1967.

The Haunted and the Haunters: The House and the Brain. London: Simpson, Marshall, & Hamilton, 1925.

The Haunted and the Haunters and other Gothic Tales. Ed. William Lawrence. Knebworth, Herts.: Knebworth House Education and Preservation Trust, 2000.

The Last Days of Pompeii. London: Heron Books, 1968.
The Last Days of Pompeii. Geneva: Edito-Service, 1974.
Pelham; or, The Adventures of a Gentleman. Ed. and intro. Jerome J. McGann. Lincoln:
    University of Nebraska Press, 1972.
A Strange Story: An Alchemical Novel. London: Shambala, 1973.
Zanoni: A Rosicrucian Tale. Preface Paul M. Allen. Blauvelt, NY: Rudolph Steiner
    Publications, 1971.

A novelist and politician who became the secretary for the colonies (1858–1859), Edward Bulwer-Lytton was a figure of national and international importance whose novels were as widely read as those of his close friend Charles Dickens. He was rewarded for his contribution to literature with a peerage in 1838, with the result that his full name was augmented to Sir Edward George Earle Lytton Bulwer-Lytton. (Here he will be referred to simply as Bulwer).

His family home, Knebworth House, was a nineteenth-century equivalent of Horace Walpole's Strawberry Hill. After his mother's death in 1843, he inherited the house, which he Gothicized by turning it into a petrified menagerie of griffins, gargoyles, and mythological creatures known as "the beasties." For him, as Lord Cobbhold, his great-grandson, recalls, they were the guardians of his home, "Where haunted floors dear footsteps back can give, / And in our Lares all our fathers live" (Kent 353). Inside the house, the ghostly spinning wheel of the resident ghost Jenny Spinner had on occasion been heard whirling from the east wing of the house. It was here, according to a family legend, that she had been confined against her will. The pattern repeated itself when in 1858 Bulwer became the butt of stern public criticism for committing his wife, Rosina, to a private lunatic asylum. Here was an episode of Gothic terror that could easily have stepped out of the pages of his terror fiction. In doing so, it exemplified the observation made in his first novel *Falkland* (1827) that "life is our real night" (707).

Bulwer's initial literary impulse had been toward the Gothic. *Falkland* is a potpourri of an overheated melodrama with a dash of Goethe's *Faust* and Mary Shelley's *Frankenstein*. The names of the hero and heroine are likely to be a tribute to William Godwin, whom he admired. Because it was considered to be "turbid, heating and unwholesome" (see the preface to *Falkland*, qtd. in Kent 353), the novel was not reprinted in England during Bulwer's lifetime. It tells the story of Erasmus Falkland, who, while reading Charles Maturin's *Melmoth the Wanderer* (1820), indulges his passion for the married Lady Emily Mandeville. Besotted by his affections, she recklessly offers to assist him in his desire to prove that there is life after death by declaring, "I would gladly die that I might return to you!" (*Falkland* 1827, 699). After being persuaded to commit adultery, she is confronted by her husband, who discovers her plan to elope with her lover. The shock of the disclosure causes her literally to drop dead. Bulwer's Gothic debut culminates in Falkland's reaction to an apparition of Emily, who has kept her promise to him as a revenant: "His eyelids trembled, and the balls reeled and glazed, like those of a dying man; a deadly fear gathered over him, so that his flesh quivered, and every hair in his head seemed instinct with a separate life, the very marrow of his bones crept, and his blood waxed thick and thick, as if stagnating into an ebbless and frozen substance. He started in a wild and unutterable terror" (707).

For his second novel, the silver-fork or fashionable novel *Pelham: or, The Adventures of a Gentleman*, Bulwer relegated the Gothic interest to a subplot about a mistress who had been placed in a lunatic asylum after having been raped by her lover's enemy. Bulwer's brand of domestic Gothic had shifted from the gloomy castles of Walpole and Radcliffe to the interior of the madhouse. In his short story "A Manuscript Found in a Madhouse" (1829), the deformed and hideously ugly hero, who has similarities to the monster in Mary Shelley's *Frankenstein*, is a lunatic who tells the story of his alienated life. Most of Bulwer's interest in madness centers on women, as in *Pelham* and *Godolphin*, in which the daughter of an astrologer goes mad after being abandoned by the title hero. The heroine of *Lucretia; or, The Children of Night* is a homicidal mother who after killing her son degenerates into a raving maniac who is confined within a madhouse. Her incarceration may be seen as a dress rehearsal for the time when Bulwer would confine his wife, from whom he had been separated since 1836. Due to public outrage, Rosina, unlike Lucretia, was released after just over three weeks. Through scurrilous writings and public demonstrations, she resumed her revenge on her husband for multiple grievances, disrupting his life at every turn.

It is possible that Rosina may have been responsible for a description of Bulwer that was published in her memoirs *A Blighted Life* (1880) in the form of an extract from an anonymous diary entry for 15 June 1864. The portrait would do justice to the most horrifying of one of his own Gothic characters: "His hair is wild and like tow; his voice is harsh and slimy, and slobbering; he presents an appearance foul and horrid. . . . I do not know that I ever saw so odious a wretch, and I would not sit near or talk to him for a thousand pounds, poor as I am. I cannot describe his putrid corpse-like loathsomeness" (93).

Possibly because of the anxiety of never knowing when or where Rosina would appear next, it is not surprising that themes of haunting and persecution recur in some of Bulwer's shorter Gothic fiction. A year after Rosina's release, he published anonymously in *Blackwood's Magazine* the disturbing ghost story "The Haunted and the Haunters" (1859). It was based on an actual account of the haunting of a mill in Willington inhabited by the Proctor family, which had been harrowed by mysterious noises and apparitions. Bulwer's tale departs from ghost-story conventions since it is set in the center of the metropolis at Oxford Street in London. The reputation of the house attracts the attention of a man keen to sleep in a haunted house. Once ensconced for the night, he experiences a number of poltergeist phenomena and unpleasant sensations: "I felt as if some strange and ghastly exhalation were rising up from the chinks of that rugged floor, and filling the atmosphere with a venomous influence hostile to human life" (Lawrence 2000). Within a secret room from which the malevolent energy has been emanating, he unearths a hidden crime and evidence of ritual magic. In the longer of the two versions of the story (first published in Blackwood's in 1859), the narrator elaborates on his hypothesis that human agency working through a mesmeric influence was at the bottom of the spectral mysteries being investigated.

"Monos and Daimonos" is about a haunting with a manifestly human face. As the title suggests (the Greek word "monos" meaning "one" accompanied with "daim" denoting deity and the suggestion of a demon in the word "daimonos"), the tale records a parable of the psyche. The narrator, whose greatest luxury is solitude, meets his *doppelgänger*, who refuses to leave him alone: "It was impossible to awe, to silence, or to shun him" (*The Haunted and The Haunters* 27). Haunted by thoughts of murder, he is disappointed when his persistent companion narrowly escapes drowning only to declaim, "We will not part even here!" (28). Driven to desperation by his "despicable persecutor" (28), the narrator kills him, but to no avail, for "six feet from me, and no more, was that ghastly and dead thing" (31). Edgar Allan Poe's reaction to the story in a letter to T.H. White was that it embodied "the ludicrous heightened into the grotesque; the fearful coloured into the horrible; the witty exaggerated into the burlesque; the singular wrought out into the strange and mystical." He went on to comment: "You may say this is bad taste. I have my doubts about it" (qtd. in the introduction to *The Haunted and the Haunters* 2000, 11).

Ghosts held a particular fascination for Bulwer. He invited a number of mediums to his Knebworth home, including the celebrated Daniel Dunglas Home. Seances were held there, which Bulwer was unable to authenticate or discredit. To a certain extent he must have been convinced, or else he would not have tried to get in touch with his daughter Emily after her death in 1848. His researches were part of a concerted effort to understand the supernatural, an endeavor that was reflected in his Gothic writings. Bulwer was the progenitor of metaphysical Gothic that was characterized by an intellectual approach to his magical, mystical, or spiritual subject, which sometimes included learned footnotes or philosophical disquisitions. He was steeped in mesmerism, spiritualism, psychical research, and the paranormal, and his pursuit of a rational explanation to the occult through scientific empiricism was a Victorian version of Ann Radcliffe's ratiocination of the supernatural. The most famous examples of this subgenre are "The Haunted and the Haunters," *Zanoni*, and *A Strange Story*.

In 1835, Bulwer dreamed of a magus who produced the *elixir vitae* (elixir of life) that could banish old age, disease, and death. He was inspired to write *Zicci* (1838), which he claimed was the shorter version of a hieroglyphic manuscript passed to the narrator by someone suspected of being a Rosicrucian. Out of this fragment emerged the full-length novel *Zanoni*, which is set during the French Revolution and has been seen as an inspiration for Dickens's *Tale of Two Cities* (1859). Bulwer's metaphysical focus is in dramatizing the opposition between the actual and the ideal through two Rosicrucian characters, Zanoni and Mejnour, both of whom have obtained the secret of perpetual life. As an embodiment of the ideal, Zanoni forfeits his immortality through his love for a mortal woman, Viola, for whom he sacrifices his life on the guillotine during the Reign of Terror. One of Bulwer's intentions is to distinguish the true seeker of occult wisdom from the false. Zanoni and Mejnour are true adepts, while the apprentice magus Glyndon is motivated by his own sensual pleasures in his desire to obtain the elixir of life. As a punishment, he encounters the sinister supernatural entity the Dweller of the Threshold, which is a fiendish manifestation of his own fears.

Another suspect occultist is Margrave in *A Strange Story*. Dickens had persuaded Bulwer to write this novel in serial form for his magazine *All the Year Round*. Margrave has abused the gift of eternal life for his own ends. For instance, he uses his beauty and mesmeric personality to try and overwhelm the innocent Lilian. Dr. Allen Fenwick, who is in love with Lilian, sets out to expose Marwick as a ruthless magician who murdered the Rosicrucian sage Haroun of Aleppo for the elixir of life. Margrave is eventually destroyed by the fiends he had invoked while attempting to complete the alchemical *opus magnum*. As Bulwer points out in his preface to *Night and Morning* (1841), "He who would arrive at the Fairy Land, must face the phantoms." The *Athenaeum* dismissed the novel as a concoction of "magic and science, poetry and prose" that "meet here in a sort of witch-dance. The tale will be a torment for any bystander who has not eaten of the insane root" (220). As a kind of literary mandrake, *A Strange Story* is a variation of the Faustian legend, which in turn is a reworking of the story of the forbidden fruit told in Genesis. As the hostile reviewer intuits, only the transgressors who have tasted such occult wisdom can truly appreciate this metaphysical Gothic.

Prohibited esoteric knowledge attracted Bulwer from his earliest Rosicrucian story "Narenor" (1823–1824) to *The Coming Race*, where he describes a magical energy called "Vril." A number of cryptic comments extrapolated from his writings have led to speculation that he was actually involved in ritual magic after having been initiated into a brotherhood of an occult order. In the introduction to *Zanoni*, for instance, it is tempting to apply the tantalizing statement made by the elderly Glyndon to the author himself: "Who but a Rosicrucian could explain the Rosicrucian mysteries?" From such statements have sprung a number of bogus claims. It has been alleged, for example, that Bulwer as a supreme hierophant presided over the initiation of Eliphas Lévi, the French occultist, into a high degree of the Supreme Grand Dome in Paris sometime between 1856 and 1858. Furthermore, they were reputed to have developed a magical partnership for the purpose of conjuring up Apollonius of Tyana in three ceremonies. The last of these was said to have taken place on the rooftop of a shop in Regent Street, London. There is no evidence that Bulwer ever met Eliphas Lévi or that he engaged in any such activities. In 1871, on the strength of an unsubstantiated reputation for operative occultism, he was made the honorary grand patron of the Societas Rosicruciana in Anglia, an honor that was bestowed upon him without his knowledge or consent.

More convincingly does Dr. Wynn Westcott, a prominent member of the society, make the suggestion that Bulwer was initiated into a Rosicrucian lodge in Frankfurt, as it was corroborated by the author himself in 1842. However, in the absence of any evidence of the existence of the lodge or record of his membership, the claim has been dismissed as apocryphal. It is possible that Bulwer was initiated by a maverick society of Rosicrucians whose existence, like the original Brotherhood of the Rosy Cross or Invisibles, was so secretive and elusive that it evaded all attempts to verify its existence.

In the study of his fantasy Gothicized home, Bulwer kept his opium pipe and Gothic relic of the actual skull of the ancient Egyptian high priest Arbaces, who is portrayed as the licentious and malevolent magician in his most popular novel, *The Last Days of Pompeii* (1834). These were appropriate accoutrements for the doyen of Gothic writers. Bulwer is unjustly neglected nowadays, not only for his novels but also as the originator of many literary subgenres. For instance, he is not widely recognized for inspiring Poe or for being a precursor of the sensation fiction of Wilkie Collins, Charles Dickens, and Mary Elizabeth Braddon. Neither is he acknowledged for founding the first detective novel, *Eugene Aram* (1832). For the grisly plot, Bulwer had drawn on Thomas Hood's *Dream of Eugene Aram*, which tells the true story of a Norfolk teacher who had been hanged for murder. Bulwer ranges across the spectrum of Gothic writing from real-life horror to the romanticized Germanic tradition of *Pilgrims of the Rhine*. In a letter to Dickens dated around 1861, Bulwer expressed his belief that the supernatural furnished a legitimate province of fiction (Wolff 292). He certainly proved himself to be a master of ghostly terror. A variation on life after death is that of the bodily immortality, which he explored through his Rosicrucian fiction. Bulwer's domestic Gothic was part of what he regarded as the absorbing tyranny of everyday life, while his more transcendent metaphysical Gothic looked forward to a time when the paranormal becomes explainable. "Whether, in so doing, tables walk of their own accord, or fiend-like shapes appear in a magic circle, or bodiless hands rise and remove material objects, or a thing of Darkness, such as presented itself to me, freeze our blood—still am I persuaded that these are but agencies conveyed, as by electric wires, to my own brain from the brain of another" ("The Haunted and the Haunters," 1925 edition, 57). This explanation, claiming that supernatural phenomena are caused by telepathic hypnotic or mesmeric influences, could just as well apply to the way in which terror is transmitted from the brain of the writer to the brain of the reader of Gothic fiction across the centuries. This textual necromancy is another manifestation of the dynamic interchange between life and death raised by Bulwer's spine-tingling question: "Are the dead too near?" *See also* **Wilkie Collins** and **Charles Dickens**.

SELECTED CRITICISM

Bulwer-Lytton, Rosina. *A Blighted Life*. Ed. Marie Mulvey-Roberts. Bristol: Thoemmes Press, 1994. Contains memorable attacks on the character of Edward from the wife he tried to have committed.

Christensen, Allan Conrad. *Edward Bulwer-Lytton: The Fiction of New Regions*. Athens: University of Georgia Press, 1976. Bulwer's Gothic writings are put into context in this overview of his literary output, which is the first complete critical analysis of his novels and prose romances.

Dahl, Curtis. "Bulwer-Lytton and the School of Catastrophe." *Philological Quarterly* 32 (1953): 428–442. Studies the Gothic influence on *The Last Days of Pompeii*.

Eigner, Edwin M. *The Metaphysical Novel in England and America: Dickens, Bulwer, Melville, and Hawthorne*. Berkeley: University of California Press, 1978. An important contribution to Bulwer studies that claims that he was responsible for transporting German idealism into English literature.

Fradin, Joseph. " 'The Absorbing Tyranny of Every-day Life': Bulwer-Lytton's *A Strange Story*." *Nineteenth-Century Fiction* 16 (1961): 1–16. In this useful analysis of *A Strange Story*, there are helpful insights into the impact of Darwinism on Bulwer's fiction even though it is unnecessarily disparaging of his work.

Kelly, Richard. "The Haunted House of Bulwer-Lytton." *Studies in Short Fiction* 8 (1971): 581–587. A persuasive argument is made that Bulwer's ghost story is a fictional rationalization of the phenomena experienced by the author at the seances of Daniel Home.

Kent, Charles. *Wit and Wisdom of E. Bulwer, Lord Lytton*. London: Routledge, 1883. Appreciative selections with commentaries.

Liljegren, S.B. *Bulwer-Lytton's Novels and Isis Unveiled*. Cambridge, MA: Harvard University Press, 1957. Explores the influence of Bulwer's Rosicrucian characters on Madame Blavatsky's "Masters."

Mulvey-Roberts, Marie. "*Zanoni*: A Novel of Initiation." In *Gothic Immortals: The Fiction of the Brotherhood of the Rosy Cross*. London: Routledge, 1990. Bulwer's *Zanoni, A Strange Story*, and selected short stories are examined within the context of the Rosicrucian-novel as a subcategory of the Gothic.

Pollin, Burton R. "Bulwer-Lytton and 'The Tell-Tale Heart.' " *American Notes and Queries* 4 (1965): 7–8. A convincing argument is advanced that Bulwer's short story "Monos and Daimonos" made a substantial contribution to Poe's "The Tell-Tale Heart."

Poston, Lawrence. "Beyond the Occult: The Godwinian Nexus of Bulwer's *Zanoni*." *Studies in Romanticism* 37 (1998): 131–161. Like Godwin, Bulwer manipulates the devices and atmosphere of the Gothic to intensify his political message. *Zanoni* "draws on Gothic motifs to move beyond the occult to a revised definition of the spiritual life."

Small, Helen. "Edward Bulwer-Lytton." In *The Handbook to Gothic Literature*. Ed. Marie Mulvey-Roberts. New York: New York University Press 1998: 33–35. Some key points are made, such as the observation that Bulwer helped lead the Gothic away from the Radcliffean sublime toward the darker aspects of ordinary life.

Wescott, W. W. *The Rosacrucians, Past and Present, at Home and Abroad*. London: SRAA (Societas Rosicrucians in Anglia). Provides information on Bulwer's association with the brotherhood.

Wolff, Robert Lee. *Strange Stories, and Other Explorations in Victorian Fiction*. Boston: Gambit, 1971. An important text in making inroads into the discussions regarding the relationship between mesmerism and nineteenth-century fiction, taking Bulwer as seriously as he deserves.

WILKIE COLLINS
(1824–1889)
Frederick S. Frank

PRINCIPAL GOTHIC WORKS

After Dark. London: Smith, Elder, 1856. (Contains the following stories: "A Terribly Strange Bed," "The Yellow Mask," and "The Lady of Glenwith Grange.")

The Dead Secret. London: Bradbury & Evans, 1857.

The Queen of Hearts. London: Hurst & Blackett, 1859. (Contains the following stories: "Mad Monkton," "The Dead Hand," "The Dream-Woman," and "The Biter Bit.")

The Woman in White. London: Sampson Low, 1860.

Armadale. London: Smith, Elder, 1866. (Originally serialized in *Cornhill Magazine*, 1864–1866.)

The Moonstone. London: Tinsley, 1868. (Originally serialized in *All the Year Round*, 1867–1868.)

The Haunted Hotel: A Mystery of Modern Venice, to Which Is Added My Lady's Money. London: Chatto & Windus, 1878.

"The Devil's Spectacles." *Spirit of the Times*, 20 December 1879.

Little Novels. London: Chatto & Windus, 1887. (Contains the following stories: "Miss Jéromette and the Clergyman" and "Mrs. Zant and the Ghost.")

MODERN REPRINTS AND EDITIONS

Armadale. Ed. Catherine Peters. New York: Oxford University Press, 1999.

The Dead Secret. Ed. Ira B. Nadel. New York: Oxford University Press, 1997. (A critical edition of the novel that includes Collins's preface.)

The Haunted Hotel. In *Three Supernatural Novels of the Victorian Period*. Ed. E.F. Bleiler. New York: Dover Books, 1975.

Mad Monkton and Other Stories. Ed. Norman Page. New York: Oxford University Press, 1998. (Contents: "A Terribly Strange Bed"; "A Stolen Letter"; "Mad Monkton"; "The Ostler"; "The Diary of Anne Rodway"; "The Lady of Glenwith Grange"; "The Dead Hand"; "The Biter Bit"; "John Jago's Ghost"; "The Clergyman's Confession"; "The Captain's Last Love"; "Who Killed Zebedee?")

The Moonstone. Ed. Dorothy L. Sayers. New York: Dutton, 1967.

The Moonstone. Ed. Steve Farmer. Toronto: Broadview Press, 1999.

Tales of Terror and the Supernatural. Ed. Herbert van Thal. New York: Dover Publications, 1972. (Contains twelve tales: "The Dream-Woman," "A Terribly Strange Bed," "The Dead Hand," " 'Blow Up the Brig!' " "Mr. Lepel and the Housekeeper," "Miss Bertha and the Yankee," "Mr. Policeman and the Cook," "Fauntleroy," "A Stolen Letter," "The Lady of Glenwith Grange," "Mad Monkton," and "The Biter Bit"). (This edition is cited in the text.)

The Woman in White. Ed. Harvey Sucksmith. Oxford and New York: Oxford University Press, 1980.

The 1860s witnessed a resurgence of Gothic fiction in the form of the "sensation" novel, a hybrid genre that combined many of the features of the Gothic nightside with the daylight realism typical of the Victorian novel at midcentury. The Gothic had not been defunct in the four intervening decades since the publication of Charles Robert Maturin's *Robert Melmoth the Wanderer* (1820). Crime and "Newgate" fiction, vampire pulps, Gothified history novels, penny dreadfuls, serialized ghost stories, tales of mystery, suspense, detection, and revenge in the periodicals, and straightforward revivals of the Gothic short story gave evidence for the survival of Gothicism prior to the work of the "sensation" novelists. Mary Elizabeth Braddon's *Black Band* (1861) and *Lady Audley's Secret* (1862), Edward Bulwer-Lytton's *A Strange Story* (1861), Mrs. Henry Wood's *Shadow of Ashlydyat* (1863), Joseph Sheridan Le Fanu's *Uncle Silas* (1864), and the American writer Mrs. Harriet Elizabeth Spofford's *Sir Rohan's Ghost* (1860) offered readers in quest of lurid jolts a plethora of weird, ghostly, macabre, mysterious, and sinister sensations, locating these in the midst of everyday life and the familiar surroundings of the drawing room, the parlor, the attic, the cellar, the lonely country house, and the busy city streets. These writers revived the Gothic by remystifying the ordinary and the normal. Sensation fiction often reversed the norms of Victorian sincerity to expose the sometimes-monstrous abnormalities lurking behind the age's decorous deportment, "stripping the veils from Victorian respectability and prudery, exposing bigamists and adulterers, vampires and murderesses" (Brantlinger 3) and other things of the night not hidden away in haunted castles but inhabiting the house next door. Sensation fiction was a domesticated extension of the earlier Gothic, particularly the Radcliffean mode in which the authenticity of the supernatural is in abeyance for most of the narrative. Even so sturdy a realist as George Eliot could occasionally put aside her allegiance to everyday life to indulge the urge for sensation, as she did in the miniature parlor thriller "The Lifted Veil" (1867), while the young Henry James displayed a flair for the ghastly and ghostly in his spooky story "The Romance of Certain Old Clothes" (*Atlantic Monthly*, February 1868).

Patrick Brantlinger has provided a serviceable definition for this updating of the Gothic in which Wilkie Collins would excel. The sensation novel is a "unique mixture of contemporary domestic realism with elements of the Gothic romance" (1). Moving from the haunted castle to the middle-class household, the sensation novelists sought to blur the distinction between social and psychic realities. By creating an atmosphere that was at once both familiar and strange, the typical sensation novel sought to arouse, excite, and shock its readers by countering Victorian certitude with anxiety, mystery, and uncertainty about self and society that hard-line social realism had failed to address. Even Charles Dickens, a close friend of Wilkie Collins, conceded the special power of sensation fiction when he tapped into its usages in his two final novels, *Our Mutual Friend* and *The Mystery of Edwin Drood*, both books drawing heavily on the style and strategies of sensation fiction. Earlier Dickens books with their figures of comic evil such as the dwarf Daniel Quilp in *The Old Curiosity Shop*, the murderer Bill Sykes in *Oliver Twist*, the scheming clerk Uriah Heep in *David Copperfield*, the brutal husband Jonas Chuzzlewit in *Martin Chuzzlewit*, and the heartless lawyers Tulkinghorn and Vholes in *Bleak House* inspired Collins with a cast of grotesque and criminal character models. Dickens's own version of the detective, Mr. Datchery in *The Mystery of Edwin Drood*, is clearly an offshoot of Collins's professional sleuths.

Gaining the forefront of the sensational school of fiction, Wilkie Collins produced an immense body of highly saleable popular fiction. He was a writer of and for the marketplace, and his twenty-three novels and novellas and many short stories catered to the appetite for the mysterious, the gory, and the paranormal fulfilled by sensation fiction. Most of his work is a subtle and satisfying blend of Gothic fantasy and domestic realism that allows readers to experience and enjoy the nightside of things without abandoning the security of hearth and home. Terror arises for readers of sensation fiction when ordinary people much like themselves are caught in extraordinary or supernatural circumstances. In both the novels and the short stories, the sensation of eeriness arises when the familiar and the ordinary suddenly become strange, bizarre, and menacing. Horrific suspense in the older Gothic vein is replaced by emotional anxiety, psychological tension, and just plain jitters as Collins saturates his atmosphere with hints, clues, and innuendoes that precede the jolt or shock that occurs when the natural and the supernatural collide.

Some readers might want to argue that the Gothic is present in Collins's novels not as pure subject matter but as fancy upholstery or stylistic frippery designed to give a decorative cover to tales of family crime, domestic mystery, social violence, and supernatural eruption. But an equally strong case can be made for the enriching presence of Gothic elements in *The Woman in White, Armadale, The Moonstone*, and *The Haunted Hotel*. Each of these novels and many others by Collins offer a confluence of traditional Gothic settings and moods incorporated with a solid sense of Victorian middle-class values. The result is a brilliant fusion of Gothic frisson with the realistic novel of manners, or "novels with a secret," as Collins himself often described them in casual conversation.

His first great public success, *The Woman in White* (first published serially in Dickens's magazine *All the Year Round*) integrates a Gothic plot involving a series of confinements in country houses with the grim business of masculine marital tyranny. An added Gothic dimension is seen in Collins's use of multiple narrators who relate the same dark tale in oppositional sequence. The menaced maiden and baronial villain of the Gothic of Walpole and Radcliffe are reincarnated in the personages of Anne Catherick, the half-mad woman in white who has been imprisoned in a madhouse by the villainous Sir Perceval Glyde, whose baleful mansion at Blackwater Park in Hampshire is a renovated Victorian version of Walpole's castle or Radcliffe's abbeys. Glyde also schemes against Laura Fairlie, the novel's second endangered maiden, to obtain her legacy. Instead of a detective or police inspector, Collins introduces the resourceful, clever, and compassionate woman, Marian Holcombe, as rescuer and resolver, a stroke that certainly must have attracted first readers to Collins's daring portrayal of dauntless feminine potency. Gothic justice is brought up-to-date when Collins arranges to have the illegitimate Sir Perceval Glyde burn to death while forging his false identity in the parish register. Commenting on the Gothicism of *The Woman in White* in his book *Gothic*, Fred Botting has credited Collins with the renovation of the Radcliffean romance of unbearable suspense and domestic evil: "In *The Woman in White* the transgressions of individual desire threaten family and society from within. Sensational effects, however, owe much to Gothic, particularly Radcliffean, styles of evoking terror, mystery, and superstitious expectation. The plot, figures, and narrative form of *The Woman in White* also structurally resemble Radcliffe's Gothic, though transposed into shapes more appropriate to the nineteenth century" (131).

Armadale also abounds in refurbished hardcore Gothic detail, but is more sensational than suggestive (or Radcliffean) in its "transposition" of Gothic figures and events. The story line reverts back to James Hogg's psychological thriller of the stalking twin bent on the mental destruction of the main character, *The Private Memoirs and Confessions of a Justified Sinner*. The diabolic other in the novel is the brilliantly named Ozias Midwinter, an evil double who drives young Allan Armadale to near insanity for some lurid motive of dark satisfaction. His shadowy and sinister presence in Armadale's life is preternatural rather than supernatural, as Collins prefers to present ghostly beings as ectoplasmic shadows rather than as clear-cut specters, thus leaving their authenticity in limbo. Perhaps as a counterforce to the strong, good woman Marian Holcombe of the previous novel, Collins introduced one of Victorian literature's most malevolent women in Lydia Gwilt, a talented demon on a par with Monk Lewis's Matilda but clad in the dress and mannerisms of the Victorian middle-class lady. The undertow of frustrated sexuality in Lydia Gwilt's personality also hearkens back to the dark ladies of Gothic fiction.

In *The Moonstone*, Collins anticipated the formula of Kipling by bringing the mysterious East into fatal collision with the aggrandizing West. The curse placed on the stolen Moonstone diamond by its Hindu owners as they seek to recover the jewel carries through several generations. When Rachel Verinder inherits the Moonstone on her eighteenth birthday, then loses it on the same night, a chain of strange and awful coincidences begins to work its way through her life. Her salvation and the solution to the mystery come by way of a human agency in the person of Sergeant Cuff, the detective who assumes the function of the older deus ex machina figures of early Gothic fiction. Other members of the novel's cast, Franklin Blake, Rachel's lover who has stolen the gem while under the influence of opium, the odiously hypocritical Godfrey Ablewhite, and the drug addict Ezra Jennings, are striking specimens of the Victorian underworld, realistic Gothic grotesques on a par with Collins's friend Dickens's memorable London street-and-alley spooky characters.

While the novels exploit the Gothic to heighten and enhance suspense, gloominess, and the sinister, Collins's many shorter tales of suspense, paranormal behavior, and spectral surprise frequently achieve pure or high Gothic status. The household spooks and other spiritual beings who frequently appear in the tales usually occupy the gray zone between the real thing and what Victorian parascience might call spiritual manifestations. In nearly every single short tale of terror, the abnormal encroaches on normal life and threatens to assume full supernatural dimensions.

In the *After Dark* story "A Terribly Strange Bed," Collins allows the narrator to perform a preternatural transposition of the homely household object into a fantastic and phantasmic infernal screwlike machine that takes on a life of its own and threatens to crush the narrator to death. Whether hallucinated or real, the strange plight of the victim is fully supernaturalized by the victim himself in this household thriller.

Another story in *After Dark*, "The Yellow Mask," has scenic and dramatic qualities that connect it directly to the extravagantly evil monks of the shilling shocker. Collins inclines toward natural terror in this Victorianized version of the monastic shocker without ruling out the possibility of the supernatural. The maliciously cunning priest Father Rocco plots against his niece and persecutes and pursues her even beyond death. The yellow mask that conceals the dead countenance of the niece is taken as real by Father Rocco's other victim, Fabio d'Ascoli, when he removes the mask of his partner at a ball and is driven mad by the sight of the dead beloved. Just as the infernal machine of Poe's "The Pit and the Pendulum" seems to have been transferred to "A Terribly Strange Bed," so Poe's unmasking climax of "The Masque of the Red Death" informs the startling and hideous climax of "The Yellow Mask."

The ten tales in the collection *The Queen of Hearts* are interlocking and interdependent in their mysterious crises and enigmatic conflicts of will. Collins invites and encourages the reader to detect parallels between the characters from tale to tale and to formulate links between the genuinely supernatural and the apparently supernatural experienced by the various narrators. Two stories, "Mad Monkton" and "The Dead Hand," eschew all rational resolution of the irrational and use what we would call today an indecisive or unreliable narrator to maintain the possibility, if not quite the probability, of the existence of an alien zone within the most normal of selves resisting understanding or control. In "Mad

Monkton," Collins employs hereditary family madness, joining this standard Gothic fare to the motif of the restless and unburied corpse. The grisly but necessary duty of retrieving the corpse from Italy and returning it to the family vault at Wincot Abbey falls to Monkton. The Gothic rhetoric of Monkton's anguish would be familiar to any reader of Radcliffe, Ainsworth, Poe, or Mary Shelley.

"Mark what I say! The spirit that appeared to me in the Abbey, that has never left me since, that stands there now by your side, warns me to escape from the fatality which hangs over our race, and commands me, if I would avoid it, to bury the unburied dead. The spectre-presence will never leave me till I have sheltered the corpse that cries to the earth to cover it! I dare not return—I dare not marry till I have filled the place that is empty in Wincot vault." His eyes flashed and dilated; his voice deepened; a fanatic ecstasy shone in his expression as he uttered these words. (235)

Similar moments of high Gothic sensation occur in "The Dead Hand," a fine story that makes use of the Gothic theme of a night spent with a peripatetic corpse, "the trial of watching out the long night in the same chamber with the dead" (46). Installed repeatedly by the chapbookers, the chamber containing a cadaverous fellow lodger goes all the way back to Edmund Twyford's nocturnal ordeal inside the haunted apartment in Clara Reeve's *Old English Baron*. Recognizing the sensational appeal of the situation, Dickens included the story in *Household Words* in the October 1857 number under a less alluring title, "The Double-bedded Room." Told at the inn where he has stopped that he will be sharing a room with "the quietest man I ever came across," Arthur Holliday gropes his way toward the truth of his situation during an evening of mounting horror when he discovers that "the man had moved. One of his arms was outside the clothes; his face was turned a little on the pillow; the eyelids were wide open" (51). Readers acquainted with Poe's bedtime story, "The Tell-Tale Heart," must have noted Collins's redoing of one of the central jolts of Poe's tale: "It was open—wide, wide open." Jolts of this sort arouse a skeptical character to a hysterical acceptance of supernatural fact. Although a plausible explanation is provided for Arthur Holliday's weird experience, the possibility that the body did indeed come alive is left open at the conclusion, to the delight of Collins's readers.

"The Dream-Woman" (titled "The Ostler" when it was first published in the Christmas 1855 number of *Household Words*) redeploys the figure of the revenant or ghostly being who "returns" to life to achieve its sensational effects. The Dream-Woman is a knife-wielding succubus whose horrid appearance at her victim's bedside is one of Collins's best night shades and jolting moments:

Between the foot of his bed and the closed door there stood a woman with a knife in her hand, looking at him. He was stricken speechless with terror, but he did not lose the preternatural clearness of his faculties, and he never took his eyes off the woman. She said not a word as they stared each other in the face, but she began to move slowly towards the left-hand side of the bed. Speechless, with no expression in her face, with no noise following her footfall, she came closer and closer—stopped—and slowly raised the knife. He laid his right arm over his throat to save it; but, as he saw the knife coming down, threw his hand across the bed to the right side, and jerked his body over that way just as the knife descended on the mattress within an inch of his shoulder. (7)

The vividness of this nightmare—if it is indeed a nightmare—with its garish overtones of sexual aggression must have gratified the Victorian sensation seeker as fully as the jolt delivered by the appearance of the bleeding nun at Raymond's bedside in Matthew Lewis's *The Monk*. The story recounts the returns and invasions of the Dream-Woman while keeping in abeyance her subjective or her objective existence. Her final and most horrifying manifestation is her return to her victim's life in the shape of his wife. The bedside climax again carries reverberations of Poe's "Ligeia" in a ghastly reunion of the living and the dead: "His eyes opened toward the left-hand side of the bed and there stood—The Dream-Woman again? No! His wife; the living reality, with the dream-spectre's face, in the dream-spectre's attitude; the fair arm up, the knife clasped in the delicate white hand" (21). With sensational summits of this sort, it is small wonder that Wilkie Collins preferred the piece for public readings.

Perhaps not quite as jolting but equally worth reading for their enjoyable macabre content and morbid melodrama are the stories " 'Blow Up the Brig!' " "The Devil's Spectacles," and "Mrs. Zant and the Ghost." In each, the terror is tinctured by touches of Biercian humor and the type of black comedy found in Poe's burlesques and drolleries. The apparition that troubles the narrator in " 'Blow Up the Brig' " is the ghost of a bedroom candlestick. In the Hoffmannesque tour de force "The Devil's Spectacles," another piece written specifically for a Christmas annual, the devilish glasses "reveal all of the faults and none of the merits" (Donaldson 237) of the people the narrator scrutinizes. In "Mrs. Zant and the Ghost," a widow is rescued from seduction by the ghostly intercession of her departed husband.

Within the limits of what he attempted to accomplish with an inherited Gothic tradition, Collins was preeminently successful and seldom disappointed his readers. Sensation fiction by its very nature was concocted to please via the shudder and the shiver while demanding minimal serious reflection over its bizarre, melodramatic, and mysterious characters and their spooky trials. Collins was not unconcerned with the glaring social ills of his time, but seldom allowed the reformer's vision to supersede the showman's urge to spectacle and exhibition. By never forgetting that the business of the thriller was to thrill, Collins extended the Gothic heritage to new ends and propelled the popular fiction of anxiety into new vistas of creepiness.

SELECTED CRITICISM

Andrew, R.V. *Wilkie Collins: A Critical Survey of His Prose Fiction with a Bibliography*. New York: Garland, 1979. An excellent guide to the Collins canon.

Bernstein, Stephen. "Reading Blackwater Park: Gothicism, Narrative, and Ideology in *The Woman in White*." *Studies in the Novel* 25 (1993): 291–305. Discusses the function of the ancestral seat of the Glyde family to demonstrate its "status as a Gothic setting."

Booth, Bradford A. "Wilkie Collins and the Art of Fiction." *Nineteenth-Century Fiction* 6 (1951): 131–143. Collins creates suspense and horror by depicting abnormal forces at work in normal lives.

Botting, Fred. "Homely Gothic." In *Gothic*. New Critical Idiom Series. London and New York: Routledge, 1996: 131–134. Collins's Gothic is a highly successful updating of Radcliffean terror. "A rational explanation of criminal mysteries by means of detection and law rather than the hand of providence situates Gothic patterns in a thoroughly Victorian context."

Brantlinger, Patrick. "What Is 'Sensational' about the 'Sensation Novel'?" *Nineteenth-Century Fiction* 37 (1982): 1–28. "Multiple narration, an air of preternatural significance, astonishing coincidences, stereotypic villainy" characterize the sensation novels of the 1860s. A prominent trait of sensation fiction was "an apparent disintegration of narrative authority, caused by the introduction of secular mystery as a main ingredient of plots."

Donaldson, Norman "Wilkie Collins." In *Supernatural Fiction Writers*, Ed. E. F. Bleiler. New York: Charles Scribner's Sons, 1985: 233–238.

Eliot, T.S. "Wilkie Collins and Dickens." In *Selected Essays*. New York: Harcourt, Brace, & World, 1960: 409–418. Originally published in *Times Literary Supplement* 4 August 1927: 525–526. An appreciation of Collins's superlative achievement in the field of detective fiction. In this area of horror, he outranks Poe.

Ellis, S.M. *Wilkie Collins, Le Fanu, and Others*. London: Constable, 1931. A valuable discussion of Collins's career as Victorian Gothicist and its relationship to Le Fanu and other writers of the sensation school.

Gasson, Andrew. *Wilkie Collins: An Illustrated Guide*. Oxford: Oxford University Press, 1998. Pictorial guide to Collins and his contemporaries.

Heller, Wendy Tamar. *Dead Secrets: Wilkie Collins and the Female Gothic*. New Haven: Yale University Press, 1992. A feminist reading of Collins's novels and short fiction showing how social commentary is embedded in their Gothic horrors. "Collins uses the Gothic not only to tell a story about female victimization, but also to encode a plot of feminine subversion that resembles a narrative pattern feminist critics have identified in nineteenth-century women's writing."

Hendershot, Cyndy. "A Sensation Novel's Appropriation of the Terror-Gothic: Wilkie Collins' *The Woman in White*." *Clues: A Journal of Detection* 13 (1992): 127–133. Collins's adept reintroduction of Gothic motifs, sites, and characters results in a novel that belongs to the mainstream Gothic tradition.

Kendrick, Walter M. "The Sensationalism of *The Woman in White*." *Nineteenth-Century Fiction* 32 (1977): 18–35. Shows how the novel, like many of its Gothic predecessors in the craft of sensation, subordinates character to a sensational plot.

Milbank, Alison. "From the Sublime to the Uncanny: Victorian Gothic and Sensation Fiction." In *Gothick Origins and Innovations*. Ed. Allan Lloyd Smith and Victor Sage. Costerus New Series 91. Amsterdam and Atlanta, GA: Rodopi, 1994: 169–179. On the influence of early Gothic fiction on Collins's *Woman in White* and other Victorian sensation novels. Suggests that the female Gothic "has a Utopian project, one based on an awareness of the sublime as an empowering aesthetic."

Muller, C.H. "Victorian Sensationalism: The Short Stories of Wilkie Collins." *Unisa English Studies* 11:1 (1973): 12–24. Establishes Collins's Gothic model for several stories to be "the conventional Gothic ghost story in which a traveller is obliged to spend the night in a haunted chamber," as in "The Dead Hand."

Pykett, Lyn, ed. *Wilkie Collins*. New Casebooks. New York: St. Martin's Press, 1998. A collection of essays and other material to permit the student to arrive at his or her own assessment of Collins's achievement. Contents: General Editor's Preface; Introduction by Lyn Pykett; 1. Patrick Brantlinger, "What Is 'Sensational' about the 'Sensation Novel'?" 2. U.C. Knoepflmacher, "The Counterworld of Victorian Fiction and *The Woman in White*"; 3. Walter M. Kendrick, "The Sensationalism of *The Woman in White*"; 4. Mark M. Hennelly, Jr., "Reading Detection in *The Woman in White*"; 5. Ann Cvetkovich, "Ghostlier Determinations: The Economy of Sensation and *The Woman in White*"; 6. Deirdre David, "Rewriting the Male Plot in Wilkie Collins's *No Name*"; 7. Jenny Bourne Taylor, "*Armadale*: The Sensitive Subject as Palimpsest"; 8. A.D. Hutter, "Dreams, Transformations, and Literature: The Implications of Detective Fiction"; 9. D.A. Miller, "From Roman Policier to Roman-Police: Wilkie Collins's *The Moonstone*"; 10. Elisabeth Rose Gruner, "Family Secrets and the Mysteries of *The Moonstone*"; 11. Wendy Tamar Heller, "Blank Spaces: Ideological Tensions and the Detective Work of *The Moonstone*"; Further Reading; Notes on Contributors; Index.

Rance, Nick. " 'A Terribly Strange Bed': Self-subverting Gothic." *Wilkie Collins Society Journal* 7 (1987): 5–12. The story's high Gothicism lies in Collins's skillful use of the animated and malicious object, the bed that moves by its own will.

———. *Wilkie Collins and Other Sensation Novelists*. Rutherford, NJ: Fairleigh Dickinson University Press, 1991. A critical and evaluative survey of Collins and his sensation contemporaries. Also stands as a history of the "sensation" novel as a discrete form.

Reierstad, Keith Brown. "The Demon in the House; or, The Domestication of Gothic in the Novels of Wilkie Collins." Doctoral dissertation, University of Pennsylvania, 1976. [*DAI* 37:2204A]. "The sensation novels of Wilkie Collins are descendants of the Gothic novel in both techniques and themes." Radcliffe's *Mysteries of Udolpho* is a constant model for Collins.

Thoms, Peter. *The Windings of the Labyrinth: Quest and Structure in the Major Novels of Wilkie Collins*. Athens: Ohio University Press, 1992. Demonstrates Collins's strong reliance on previous Gothic examples for the structuring of his mysteries.

CHARLOTTE DACRE
[ROSA MATILDA]
(1771/1772?–1825)

Douglass H. Thomson

PRINCIPAL GOTHIC WORKS

Confessions of the Nun of St. Omer: A Tale, in Three Volumes. London: Printed by D.N. Shury for J.F. Hughes, 1805.

Hours of Solitude: A Collection of Original Poems Now First Published by Charlotte Dacre. London: Printed by D.N. Shury, for Hughes & Ridgeway, 1805. (Most of Dacre's writings were published under her pseudonym, "Rosa Matilda.")

Zofloya; or, The Moor: A Romance of the Fifteenth Century. London: Printed for Longman, Hurst, Rees, & Orme, 1806.

The Libertine. London: Printed for T. Cadell & W. Davies, 1807.

The Passions. London: Printed for T. Cadell & W. Davies, 1811.

MODERN REPRINTS AND EDITIONS

Confessions of the Nun of St. Omer: A Tale. Ed. Devendra P. Varma. New York: Arno Press, 1972.

Hours of Solitude. Ed. Donald H. Reiman. New York: Garland, 1978.

The Libertine. Ed. Devendra P. Varma. New York: Arno Press, 1974.

The Passions. Ed. Devendra P. Varma. New York: Arno Press, 1974.

Zofloya; or, The Moor: A Romance of the Fifteenth Century. Ed. Devendra P. Varma, with a new foreword by G. Wilson Knight. New York: Arno Press, 1974.

Zofloya; or, The Moor: A Romance of the Fifteenth Century. Ed. Adriana Craciun. Peterborough, Ontario: Broadview Press, 1997. (This edition is cited in the text. Also contains *The Demon of Venice*, an 1810 pirated abridgement of Dacre's novel.)

Zofloya; or, The Moor. Ed. Kim Ian Michasiw. New York: Oxford University Press, 1997.

One can find no better evidence of the current Gothic revival than the recent publication of two fine new editions of Charlotte Dacre's *Zofloya*—and these from an author whose works were once so obscure that the ardent Gothic bibliophile Montague Summers lamented that they were among the most difficult to discover in English fiction. Although we have had to wait this long for scholarly editions of Dacre's novel, *Zofloya* has long occupied a place in the canon of first Gothics, mainly for two reasons: first, for Dacre's creation, in the figure of the stunningly libidinous and cruel Victoria di Loredani, of a female version of Matthew Lewis's infamous monk, Ambrosio; and second, for the powerful impact this novel had on the youthful Percy Shelley, evident in his two early and very Gothic novels *Zastrozzi* (1810) and *St. Irvyne; or, The Rosicrucian* (1811). Historical reasons for Dacre's lapse into obscurity are not hard to find. Byron delivered an early blow in dismissively linking her with the fleshly school of the Della Cruscan poets, and one can see how her frankly sexual femmes fatales would not endear her to most Victorian publishing houses. The still relatively few modern critics to read *Zofloya* (her other three novels still await sustained critical attention) have tended to find fault with its seeming cross-purposes, especially in regard to the premises of Victoria's villainous career. The novel begins with the promising Wollstonecraftian suggestion that Victoria's villainy stems from a corrupt upbringing, only to lose sight of that premise as the satanic Zofloya enters as both corrupter and emblem of corruption. Yet today's new approach to Dacre's Gothic achievement, led by Adriana Craciun, sees in the uncertainties of her novels a powerful medium to explore a range of gender and genre issues.

The tantalizingly little we know of Dacre's life locates her in several significant crosscurrents of early-nineteenth-century culture. She was the daughter of the controversial Jonathan King (dubbed the "Jew King" by Byron), a Jewish banker and political radical along Godwinian lines, and his first wife Deborah, whom he divorced when Dacre was fourteen to marry into the nobility. All four of Dacre's novels seem to reflect this heritage as outsider and radical, and one with a sympathy for the abandoned woman, in their pervasive engagement with the ideas of Wollstonecraft and Godwin. Indeed, the philosopher-seducer Fribourg of the early *Confessions of the Nun of St. Omer* seems to have conned his arguments against social convention and the sanctity of marriage directly from Godwin's *Political Justice*. But one also finds a strongly conservative backlash to these radical promptings in Dacre's fiction and poems, one of which canonizes William Pitt, perhaps reflecting her marriage to the Tory editor of the *Morning Post*, Nicholas Byrne. Fribourg, after all, is the villain of the novel, as are all "sophists" (her favorite term for them) who argue against the traditional obligations of wife and mother. And no matter how sympathetically drawn her adulteresses may be, from the long-hesitating Cazire of *The Nun of St. Omer* to the impulsive Victoria, all await an emphatic moral reckoning: Cazire becomes the nun who writes memoirs of her profligacy to warn her son; Julia, the heroine of *The Passions*, who succumbs to the insidious arguments of the avenging Appollonia, perishes, bloodied, "half-naked," and thus frozen to death outside the door of the husband she has betrayed; the twice-seduced Gabrielle of *The*

Libertine labors mightily the length of the novel to rescue her stubbornly dissolute lover, the libertine and gambler Angelo, and mercifully dies before the twin suicides of her children, who have gone on to pursue the same path of sin as their father; and, of course, we have the spectacular destruction of Victoria, obviously indebted to *The Monk*, as the satanic Zofloya "whirl[s] her headlong down the dreadful abyss!" (254). The moral appears gratingly obvious: "Beware how you even cursorily infringe on the sacred duties of a Father and a Husband" (*Confessions of the Nun of St. Omer.* 2, 201.)

This central cross-purpose, a long and sustained flirtation with the dark and libidinous side of human nature only to be checked by a strident moral closure, is anything but unique to the tradition of first Gothic novels, especially first female Gothics. Indeed, it may be said to typify them. Still, as Craciun argues, Dacre's achievement is noteworthy in the way its fissures and seeming contradictions call into question a whole range of gender and genre issues: "[Dacre's] *femmes fatales* subvert the persistent category of the proper woman . . . not only by embodying its antithesis, but by demonstrating the instability of these [culturally constructed] categories themselves" (Introduction 23). In this reading of the novels, the very shrillness of the moralistic closure points to and indeed indicates a certain residual anarchism, as the persistent tendency of the Gothic to offer opposing gender stereotypes runs the risk of exposing the arbitrary nature of such distinctions. For in Dacre, for once and for all, we have not the usual villain-hero but women, strong-willed and with minds, ransacking these gender types. Take, for example, Appollonia's brilliant and sustained seduction of Julia (and there are lesbian elements in it, to further complicate things) in Dacre's final and only epistolary novel, *The Passions.* Here is a virtuosic argument indeed: in her letters to Julia, Appollonia begins in eloquent feminist fashion extolling the virtues of female friendship and its capacities for sympathy and understanding in an often-indifferent and callous male world; she continues along, on an only slightly lesser Sadean register, to reveal the arbitrariness of religious scruples and to obliterate the numbingly familiar argument of Enlightenment thinkers that "virtue is happiness" (2.97); next, abetted by "the glowing sophisms of [her] voluptuous imagery (2.31)—mainly drawn from Rousseau and Helvétius—Appollonia convincingly demonstrates the ineffectuality of reason and the sweetness of temptation; add to these a classic *carpe diem* and then some fast metaphysical conjuring (e.g., we are unwitting participants in a grand destiny we cannot resist), and the poor Julia does not stand a chance. She gives in to Count Darlowitz and betrays her proud husband, the Baron Rotzendorf. What, Dacre seems to ask, keeps a Julia from becoming an Appollonia or Victoria, especially when the traditional moral and gender arguments against her becoming so can be used to seduce her?

Readers should consult the introduction to Adriana Craciun's edition of *Zofloya* for a more sustained discussion of the gender- and genre-shattering nature of Dacre's female libertines and how "her [novels] reveal the violent disorder of female subjectivity, and its violent repression by demonic masculinity" (23).

What is equally striking in terms of the Gothic tradition is Dacre's deconstruction of the opposing masculine type, the virtuous, oft-betrayed, long-suffering,
and, to many modern tastes, insufferably bland male hero. Cazire immediately
pinpoints the problem with the impossibly virtuous (and English) St. Elmer,
who loves her from a distance but does nothing to alleviate her poverty, who
lectures her via letters to resist temptation but who only succeeds in making the
forbidden fruit sweeter: "Oh, St. Elmer, had you but one error, it should be
dearer to my heart than all your virtues" (*The Nun* 2.190). As Julia wonders
why she feels such "inexplicable disquietude" (2.72) while she is living in a
perfect family surrounded with models of virtue, we might ask if that very
numbing perfection leads to her downfall, especially as her husband and another
exemplar of right reason, the Count Weimar, keep thrusting before Julia the
impossibly angelic Amelia as her only role model. The daring, culminating blow
against these exemplars of male virtue is Victoria's rape of the drugged and
spellbound Henriquez. Long hemmed in by the dictates of right reason and
proper conduct, the woman will finally have her way. In tentatively exposing
the models of male virtue as fraudulent and in quietly suggesting that they may
unwittingly contribute to the heroine's downfall, Dacre leaves open a space for
interpretation that surely qualifies the nature of her and the Gothic genre's typical moral closure.

Too long read as a merely feminine re-creation of Lewis's villainous monk,
Victoria di Loredani, as well as Dacre's other characters, needs to be considered
in the wider intellectual climate of Dacre's other contemporaries who were challenging traditional definitions of gender, among them Mary Robinson, to whom
she wrote an admiring poem, Mary Wollstonecraft, Godwin, Rousseau, Byron,
and Sade himself. Her achievement also deserves greater attention in the continuing debate about the genders of Romanticism, for her willful heroines un-
settle the often accepted division between an egotistically male sublime and a
female ethos of care and nurture. As Cracium points out, we still do not really
know what to make of a Victoria or the neglected "countertradition" of femmes
fatales she so potently inaugurates. Perhaps Dacre did not, either, but she has
left us a kind of heroine who complicates the typical gender associations of the
Gothic and who continues to challenge critics to define her place in the woman's
tradition of the female Gothic.

SELECTED CRITICISM

Craciun, Adriana. " 'I Hasten to Be Disembodied': Charlotte Dacre, the Demon Lover,
and Representations of the Body." *European Romantic Review* 6 (1995): 75–97.
Studies the volatile gender features of *Zofloya*, especially the growing masculin-
ization of Victoria, to demonstrate how the novel displays an assertion of the
bodily self against its culturally determined identity.
———. Introduction to *Zofloya; or, The Moor: A Romance of the Fifteenth Century*.
Peterborough, Ontario: Broadview Press, 1997: 9–32. Provides both the scholarly

context and theoretical framework for a major reassessment of Dacre's literary achievement. The edition includes early reviews of the novel.

Dunn, James A. "Charlotte Dacre and the Feminization of Violence." *Nineteenth-Century Literature* 53 (1998): 307–327. On Dacre's use of irony. Also differentiates her work from Matthew Lewis's *Monk*. "Her novels completely reverse the gender stereotypes so rampant in traditional Gothic formulas. Let us have our sex and violence but let us see what it looks like beyond the stock feminine props of persecution and victimization; let us make women the subject rather than the object of toxic erotic agony."

Hoeveler, Diane Long. "Charlotte Dacre's *Zofloya*: A Case Study in Miscegenation as Sexual and Racial Nausea." *European Romantic Review* 8 (1997): 185–199. On Charlotte Dacre's use of feminist themes and thought.

Jones, Ann H. "Charlotte Dacre." In *Ideas and Innovations: Best Sellers of Jane Austen's Age*. New York: AMS Press, 1986: 224–249. On *Zofloya* as a new Gothic in its own right rather than simply a feminist imitation of Lewis's *Monk*.

Michasiw, Kim Ian. Introduction to *Zofloya; or, The Moor*. New York: Oxford University Press, 1997. Solid in placing the novel within the revolutionary contexts of Dacre's life, the period in which she lived, and the Gothic tradition.

Miles, Robert. "Avatars of Matthew Lewis' *The Monk*: Ann Radcliffe's *The Italian* and Charlotte Dacre's *Zofloya, or The Moor*." In *Gothic Writing, 1750–1820: A Genealogy*. London: Routledge, 1993: 160–188. Discusses how Dacre's novel, while obviously indebted to Lewis's *Monk*, transgresses many boundaries of the genre, especially in its various explanations for the nature of Victoria's evil nature.

Napier, Elizabeth. *The Failure of Gothic: Problems of Disjunction in an Eighteenth-Century Literary Form*. New York: Oxford University Press, 1987. *Zofloya* fails because of the novel's fascination with an expansive evil that loses sight of its promising Wollstonecraftian premise that Victoria's evil stems from a lack of education and intelligent role models.

Peck, Walter E. "Appendix A: Shelley's Indebtedness in *Zastrozzi* to Previous Romances." In *Shelley: His Life and Work*. Boston: Houghton, Mifflin, 1927: 1:305–309. An old but still valid source study of Shelley's debt to Dacre's *Zofloya* in the writing of his own two Gothic novels, *Zastrozzi* and *St. Irvyne*.

Summers, Montague. "Byron's 'Lovely Rosa.'" In *Essays in Petto*. Freeport, NY: Books for Libraries Press, 1967: 55–73. Concerns Summers's interesting search to exhume this obscure figure and to restore her to the Gothic pantheon.

Swinburne, Algernon Charles. "Letter to H.B. Forman, 22 November 1886." In *The Swinburne Letters*. Ed. Cecil Y. Lang. New Haven: Yale University Press, 1959–1962: 6:174–175. Perceptively likens *Zofloya*'s long-suffering Lilla and ruthless Victoria to, respectively, Sade's *Justine* and *Juliette*. Also see Craciun's "Introduction" for the Sadean characteristics of the novel.

CHARLES DICKENS
(1812–1870)
Douglass H. Thomson

PRINCIPAL GOTHIC WORKS

Virtually all of Dickens's novels have received some attention for their Gothic elements; listed here are those covered in this entry and the "Selected Criticism" section. The citation refers to the first publication of the work in book form and does not include earlier publication as a serial.

Interpolated Tales in *The Pickwick Papers*. London: Chapman & Hall, 1837. "A Madman's Manuscript," "The Bagman's Story," "The Story of the Goblins Who Stole a Sexton," and "The Story of the Bagman's Uncle."

"The Baron of Grogzwig." Chapter 6 of *The Life and Adventures of Nicholas Nickleby*, London: Chapman & Hall, 1839.

Oliver Twist: or, The Parish Boy's Progress. London: R. Bentley, 1839.

Barnaby Rudge: A Tale of the Riots of 'Eighty. London: Chapman & Hall, 1841.

The Old Curiosity Shop. London: Chapman & Hall, 1841.

Dombey and Son. London: Bradbury & Evans, 1846–1848.

The Haunted Man and the Ghost's Bargain: A Fancy for Christmas-time. London: Bradbury & Evans, 1848.

"Ghosts and Ghost-seers." Essay-review of *The Nightside of Nature; or, Ghosts and Ghost-Seers* by Catherine Crowe. *Examiner*, 26 February 1848.

The Life and Adventures of Martin Chuzzlewit. London: Chapman & Hall, 1850.

"To Be Read at Dusk." *The Keepsake*, 1852.

Bleak House. London: Bradbury & Evans, 1853.

"The Ghost in the Bride's Chamber." In *The Lazy Tour of Two Idle Apprentices*. *Household Words*, 1857.

Little Dorrit. London: Bradbury & Evans, 1857.

"The Rapping Spirits." *Household Words*, 1858.

"The Haunted House," "The Mortals in the House," and "The Ghost in Master B's Room." *All the Year Round*, Christmas Number, 1859.

Great Expectations. London: Chapman & Hall, 1861.

Our Mutual Friend. London: Chapman & Hall, 1865.
"The Trial for Murder: To Be Taken with a Grain of Salt." *All the Year Round*, Christmas
    Number, 1865.
"No. 1 Branch Line: The Signalman." *All the Year Round*, Christmas Number, 1866.
The Mystery of Edwin Drood. London: Chapman & Hall, 1870.

MODERN REPRINTS AND EDITIONS

Listed here are editions referred to in the text.

Barnaby Rudge. Ed. and intro. G.W. Spence. Baltimore: Penguin, 1973.
Best Ghost Stories. Ed. Christine Baker. Ware, Hertfordshire, UK: Wordsworth Editions,
    1997.
Bleak House. Ed. Norman Page, intro. J. Hillis Miller. London and New York: Penguin
    Books, 1985.
The Complete Ghost Stories of Charles Dickens. Ed. Peter Haining. New York: Wash-
    ington Square Press, 1982.
Dombey and Son. Ed. Peter Fairclough, and intro. Raymond Williams. Harmondsworth:
    Penguin Books, 1970.
Great Expectations. Ed. Angus Calder. Baltimore: Penguin Books, 1972.
The Letters of Charles Dickens. Ed. Margaret Brown, Kathleen Tillotson, and Graham
    Storey. London: Pilgrim Edition, 1999.
The Life and Adventures of Martin Chuzzlewit. Ed. and intro. P.N. Furbank. London:
    Penguin, 1968.
Little Dorrit. Ed. John Holloway. London and New York: Penguin Books, 1994.
The Mystery of Edwin Drood. Ed. Arthur J. Cox, intro. Angus Wilson. New York:
    Penguin Books, 1974.
Nicholas Nickleby. Ed. and intro. Michael Slater. New York: Penguin Books, 1978.
The Old Curiosity Shop. Ed. Angus Easson, intro. Malcolm Andrews. Harmondsworth,
    Middlesex: Penguin Books, 1972.
Oliver Twist. Ed. Peter Fairclough, intro. Angus Wilson. New York: Penguin Books,
    1966.
Our Mutual Friend. Ed. and intro. Stephen Gill. New York: Penguin Books, 1971.
The Posthumous Papers of the Pickwick Club. Ed. and intro. Robert L. Patten. Har-
    mondsworth: Penguin, 1972.

Arguably the greatest of all popular novelists and the most popular of great
novelists, Charles Dickens throughout his career easily and ably made great use
of the Gothic and ghost-story-telling materials beloved by his public. From the
"interpolated tales" in *The Pickwick Papers* to the numerous Gothic resonances
in his major novels, ghost stories, and Christmas tales and ending with the many
mysteries surrounding *The Mystery of Edwin Drood*, Dickens's fiction repeatedly attests his fascination with "changing what was real and familiar . . . to what
was wild and magical" ("The Haunted Man" in *Best Ghost Stories* 200). Along
with Victorian "sensation" writers like Wilkie Collins and Joseph Sheridan Le
Fanu and the writers who contributed to the enormously popular Christmas

issues of the magazines he edited, Dickens succeeded in domesticating and urbanizing the Gothic experience, voicing its sense of the uncanny (*unheimlich*) in household (*heimisch*) words. Sometimes the effect is a comforting one, a fireside tale that conveys a satisfying shudder but whose end, as in the famous "Christmas Carol" and many others of his ghost stories, is genial and therapeutic; at other times, the effect is disturbing as Dickens marshals Gothic imagery of terror, disease, and stagnation to characterize truly haunted men and women and to convey the real horrors of poverty and suffering in industrialized London. Numerous critical studies trace Dickens's borrowing or reworking of this or that Gothic convention (e.g., Satis House in *Great Expectations* or Chesny Wold in *Bleak House*—or London itself in several novels—as variations on the Gothic haunted castle; Quilp, Tulkinghorn, and Jasper as Gothic villains; the many daughters of his households as descendants of the Radcliffean heroine), but it is a harder thing to get at (and perhaps easy to exaggerate) the impact of the Gothic tradition upon his fiction—and of his fiction upon that tradition. As no previous study of the "Gothic Dickens" has addressed the relation of his ghost stories to the more obviously Gothic elements in his novels, this entry will focus on a relatively neglected short novel or long ghost story, "The Haunted Man and the Ghost's Bargain" (in *Best Ghost Stories*), analyzing in the story Dickens's wonderfully skillful evocation of many Gothic motifs and discussing how these motifs also find important places and various uses in his novels.

Twilight in the haunted room of the Haunted Man "everywhere release[s] the shadows prisoned up all day . . . to gather like mustering swarms of ghosts" as Dickens depicts how "they fantastically mocked the shapes of household objects, making the nurse an ogress, the rocking-horse a monster, the wondering child, half-scared and half-amused, a stranger to itself" (127). This is the bewitching hour when "little readers of storybooks, by the firelight, trembled to think of Cassim Baba cut into quarters" and other such delightfully frightful things culled from the *Arabian Nights* and related sources of exotic terror. The opening scene sets the stage for the Haunted Man's encounter with a far more fearsome specter, the "Phantom" of his own blasted hopes from the past. But this wonderful twilight evocation of ghosts and goblins also bears testimony to Dickens's fond familiarity with the popular literatures of terror. When he was a child, his nurse, Mary Weller, delighted in playing the role of ogress, terrifying the young Dickens with tales of bloody vengeance and supernatural hauntings. Modern scholars have established and continue to interpret the direct impact of such first Gothic writers as Walpole, Radcliffe, Lewis, and Maturin upon Dickens's fiction; other shaping influences—themselves descendants of the Gothic tradition—include such media as the "penny dreadfuls" (especially the *Terrific Register* and *Mysteries of London*); the supernatural tales from *Blackwood's Magazine*, which bear a strong resemblance to the interpolated tales of *Pickwick*; the popular Gothic melodramas of the stage; and the "sensation novelists" Charles Reade, Edward Bulwer-Lytton, and Wilkie Collins, the latter a good friend and occasional collaborator of Dickens. Add to these literary sources Dickens's keen, but very skeptical interest in the spiritualism that was all the rage and his own practicing of mesmerism, and the picture is one of an author well versed in Gothic literature and its near descendants, who understood its great popular appeal and who could draw purposefully upon its resonant conventions. Dickens satirizes spiritualism in such tales as "The Rapping Spirits" and "The Mortals in the House." In an extensive review of Catherine Crowe's *Nightside of Nature; or, Ghosts and Ghost-Seers*, he systematically debunks her arguments for belief in "presentiments, warnings, wraiths, witches, doubles, apparitions, troubled spirits, haunted houses [and] spectral lights." He explains our fascination for ghosts as "that attraction of repulsion to the awful veil that hangs so heavily and inexorably over the grave," in other words, our uneasy consciousness of death. Although the review offers persistent demystification of the spirit world, it shows Dickens's extensive knowledge of the subject.

The Haunted Man and the Ghost's Bargain (1848) occupies a middle place in Dickens's ghost stories, being the last of his "fancies" for Christmastime and anticipating the more serious treatment of the supernatural found in such tales as "The Ghost in the Bride's Chamber" (1857) and "No. 1 Branch Line: The Signalman" (1866). It concerns the story of a man of science, the chemist Redlaw, who is so plagued by memories of a blighted past that he agrees to let a grisly phantom erase all sensation emanating from that source. But the ghost includes an unanticipated bargain: not only will Redlaw lose his memory of the past but he will spread, like a contagious disease, the loss to all those he meets. That loss also contains an even more sinister bargain: the relinquishing of one's understanding of the past kills the infected person's sense of compassion and, indeed, his or her very humanity. The use of a supernatural device thus allows Dickens to underscore a major theme of all his fiction, the need to fathom and accept responsibility for the past, but this is a Christmas tale, and through the agency of a ministering angel of the house, Milly, all memories are restored, as Redlaw and those he infects eventually regain their humanity and learn the spiritual value of forgiveness. This therapeutic value of confrontation with the supernatural underpins many of Dickens's early ghost stories. In one of the Bagman's tales from *The Pickwick Papers*, a queer, talking chair alerts the tipsy Tom Smart to the dubious moral character of the man engaged to his landlady, and Tom reveals the secret to the lady, wins her love, and lives happily ever after. In "The Story of the Goblins Who Stole a Sexton" (also from *Pickwick*), a horrific goblin, very Gothically depicted by Phiz, frightens the gallows humors out of the hard-hearted grave digger Gabriel Grub and makes him, in a Scrooge-like conversion, a better man. In "The Baron of Grogzwig" (chapter 6 of *Nicholas Nickleby*), an equally terrific "Genius of Despair and Suicide" appears in answer to the gloomy Baron's decision to kill himself but has the opposite effect of giving him a reason to live. We also have the happy penitential pattern of the beloved "A Christmas Carol," which numbers among its Gothic effects the chilling figures of Want and Ignorance enwrapped by the Ghost of Christmas Present's robe. Perhaps the genial, essentially comic spirit of these early tales is best captured in another set piece from *Pickwick* (chapter 21), in which a tenant sensibly suggests to a ghost haunting his dilapidated room at the Inns that as "space is nothing to [him]" (129), there are far fairer places all over the earth for him to visit in his nocturnal wanderings. The ghost happily agrees, promises the tenant that he will spread the word to other such misguided haunters of houses, and embarks upon a much needed vacation from the spot.

While one might argue that the lighthearted presentation of these spooks—usually encountered after bouts of heavy drinking by those they visit—disqualifies these tales as Gothic, later ghost stories of Dickens treat the realm of the paranormal more seriously. "The Haunted Man" (in *Best Ghost Stories*), for example (and despite its happy ending), certainly has its chilling moments; witness, for example, the first appearance of the phantom: "Ghastly and cold, colorless in its leaden face and hands, but with his features, and his bright eyes, and his grizzled hair, and dressed in the gloomy shadow of his dress, it came into his terrible appearance of existence, motionless, without a sound. . . . This, then, was the Something that had passed and gone already. This was the dread companion of the haunted man!" (137). One finds several such instances of a more genuinely Gothic horror in Dickens's short stories. The early "A Madman's Manuscript" (from *Pickwick*) reads very much like a tale from Poe, with its manic narrator dubiously justifying the murder of his wife as, pursued by demons of his own making, he slips into insanity. The spectral narrator of "The Ghost in the Bride's Chamber" dryly relates the really horrible story of his engineering, for money, his young wife's death through privation and starvation and his murder of the man who loved her; holding one of a pair of listeners in thrall through a "thread of fire" stretching from his eyes to his listener's (a metaphor of mesmeric power), the ghost explains how he pays for his crimes nightly by reenacting his hanging twelve times over at midnight. He can escape this horrid retribution only if he can get two people to listen to his story at the same time, but alas, the listener's companion, Mr. Idle (a pseudonym for Collins), has slipped into a spell and has not heard the ghost's confession. Dickens called this "bit of Diablerie" a "very odd story, with a wild picturesque fancy in it" (*Letters*, 4 October 1857). So too, in a lesser register, is "The Trial for Murder," in which the foreman of a jury repeatedly sees the ghost of a murdered victim haunting the killer during his trial, although we are asked to take the narrator's account "with a grain of salt." Perhaps Dickens's finest achievement in these taut, utterly unsentimental ghost stories is the riddling "No. 1 Branch Line: The Signalman," in which a dedicated railroad signalman is troubled by an apparition of his profession whose appearance signals forthcoming accidents along the line, the last of which is his own death. Unlike his Christmas tales, these stories are very much in the line of sensation fiction, presenting ghostly invasions of both domestic and public spheres as their complex points of view suggest some dark secret haunting Victorian notions of progress and normalcy.

Indeed, the major focus of recent critics addressing Dickens in relation to the Gothic tradition has been his use of Gothic imagery to characterize the real horrors of industrial, urban England. Hoping that he can use his dubious gift of erasing the past for some social good, Redlaw, the now-not-so-haunted man, journeys to the poorest section of town at night in hopes of providing the down-trodden inhabitants with the meager consolation of forgetfulness. This "waste piece of ground" upon which a "ruinous collection of houses . . . stood, or rather did not altogether tumble down, unfenced, undrained, unlighted, and bordered by a sluggish ditch" (169), typifies Dickens's use of infernal imagery to create an "urban Gothic" in his depictions of human squalor: these include the brutal city scenes of *Oliver Twist, The Old Curiosity Shop* with its hellish descent to Birmingham, and scenes in other novels such as the dark apotheosis of Tom-All-Alone's in *Bleak House* or the wasteland of Stagg's Gardens in *Dombey and Son*. Directing Redlaw on his hellish journey and anticipating the figure of L'il Jo is a nameless "Baby Savage," a child so immured to the dehumanizing effects of poverty that he is less human than animal. A great source of this scene's horror, a horror at once Gothic, profoundly political, and tellingly psy-chological, is Redlaw's stunned realization that, deprived of memory and com-passion, his expression matches exactly the dead stare of the slum rat-child. He first encounters in this slum underground the spectral figure of an abused woman who desperately insists that her husband never laid a hand on her, although it is unclear whether this dubious amnesia is her own sad denial or a product of Redlaw's infection. In demanding that his readers remember the poor of En-gland, Dickens repeatedly and strategically uses Gothic and nightmare imagery to attack Victorian complacency. Larry Kirkpatrick sums up recent critical per-ception by concluding that as a "social critic," Dickens "converts the Gothic lesson of horror into telling criticism of social abuses" (24).

Infernos of urban poverty comprise just one aspect of Dickens's Gothicized cityscape. Haunted houses dominate many of his novels. The critics Allan Prit-chard and Robert Mighall find clear Gothic echoes in the labyrinth of the Courts of Chancery in *Bleak House*. Outside London, but significantly infected by the city, stands that edifice of power secretly rotting from within, Chesney Wold with its Ghost's Walk. David Jarrett sees a reworking of "the sinister old castle that harbors mystery, gloom, and guilty secrets" (161) in the description of the creaking Clennam household. Pat Hodgell discovers an "archetypal Gothic im-age" in Dickens's presentation of the innocent Nell surrounded by the sinister and strange shapes of the Old Curiosity Shop. No list would be complete without that crypt writ large, Satis House, with its time-plagued inhabitant, Miss Hav-isham in *Great Expectations*. The dwelling of "The Haunted Man" (in *Best Ghost Stories*) shares many of the features of these other haunted houses. It is "solitary and vaultlike—an old retired part of an ancient endowment for stu-dents, once a brave edifice, but now the obsolete whim of forgotten architects; smoke-age-and-weather-darkened, squeezed on every side by the overgrowing of the city" (125). It "thunder[ed] with echoes when a distant voice was raised or a door was shut—echoes, not confined to the many low passages and empty rooms, but rumbling and grumbling till they were stifled in the heavy air of the forgotten crypt where the Norman arches were half-buried in the earth" (125–126). It demonically withers the Christmas holly that the sentimentalist Swidgers bring in their futile attempt to exorcise its ghosts. Many of these Gothic houses, such as Redlaw's crypt, symbolically depict the haunted minds of their inhabitants. Others, like Chesney World and Tulkinghorn's grim chambers, comprise part of Dickens's criticism of an economic and legal system that thrives on secrets and dark obscurity. Indeed, in Ann Ronald's view, industrialized and labyrinthine "London becomes Dickens's ultimate Gothic castle" (75).

A similar division between political and psychological interests characterizes Dickens's remarkable gallery of villains, many of whom in their secrecy and insatiability resemble their Gothic forerunners. Some of them in their exploitation of the system personify the kinds of social abuses Dickens finds horrifying: the villainous figures of Monks, Fagin, and Sikes in *Oliver Twist* serve not just to indict the obvious, the cruel exploitation of children, but to incriminate the entire economic and political system that has spawned and tolerates them. The vampiric Tulkinghorn, whose very "calling is the acquisition of secrets, and the holding possession of such power as they give him" (*Bleak House* 567), symbolizes the frighteningly impenetrable power of the legal system. But Dickens has a more purely psychological fascination with some of his other memorable villains, such as the maniacally weird dwarf Quilp who torments Little Nell. Of his last and most consummately Gothic villain, John Jasper, in the unfinished *Mystery of Edwin Drood* he writes that experts "perpetually misread" the criminal mind "because they persist in trying to reconcile it with the average intellect of average man, instead of identifying it as a wonder apart" (182), and his interest in exploring that dark "wonder," fueled by contemporary accounts of real murders, includes his creation of such killers as Bill Sikes in *Oliver Twist* Barnaby Rudge, Jonas Chuzzlewit, and Bradley Headstone in *Our Mutual Friend*. Place in the hands of these and other fearsome villains the kinds of innocents found in Dickens's fiction, from Oliver to Little Nell, from Florence Dombey to Pip, and one has the recipe for high melodrama of the kind that more than one critic has traced to Radcliffe's powerful formula of the maiden hounded and haunted by some dark figure.

Of these villains, Jasper bears the richest affinities with such compulsive and schizoid Gothic villains as Robert Wringhim in James Hogg's *Confessions of a Justified Sinner* or even Matthew Gregory Lewis's Ambrosio in *The Monk*. He is at once a man of the church and a murderer; a choirmaster who sings his best when he is excited by anticipation of his crime and an opium addict who vainly tries to relive in his reveries the thrill of the murder; a coldhearted, lustful pursuer of the delicate Rosa; and, many critics argue, a homosexual tormented by his attraction to the man he eventually kills. Although George Bernard Shaw and some critics find fault with *The Mystery of Edwin Drood* as being too much in the line of the serialized Victorian blood, tale, other readers have praised Dickens's masterfully Gothic interweaving of light and dark imagery in the unfinished novel, especially the way the contradictions inherent in Jasper's char-

acter find equivalents in the Cloisterham church grounds: a place of light overseen by that ghoulish connoisseur of "old graves and ruins," Durdles; the home
of a cathedral that many sleuths of the mystery believe contains the murdered
body of Drood. Considered within the context of Dickens's careerlong fascination with the criminal mind, *The Mystery of Edwin Drood* represents a fittingly
mysterious coda to his exploration of Gothic psychology.

The villain haunting "The Haunted Man" (in *Best Ghost Stories*) is, like Com-
peyson of *Great Expectations*, a shadowy figure who does not really emerge
from obscurity to reveal his secrets until late in the story. Longford holds the
key to the despair that has long plagued Redlaw. Betrothed to Redlaw's beloved
sister, Longford instead eloped with the woman Redlaw loved, thus ruining in
his mind forevermore his family's prospects for happiness. But as Dickens
makes clear, the real demon haunting Redlaw is himself in his refusal to make
peace with his past: "the Ghost," the narrator too knowingly speculates at the
end, may just be "but an embodiment of [Redlaw's] gloomy thoughts" (200).
Yet another, relatively neglected aspect of Dickens's relation to the Gothic involves this use of its language of terror to characterize the mental life of haunted
men and women, and in this movement toward a more interior, psychological
treatment of the Gothic, he joins many other nineteenth-century writers. Listen
to the tormented thoughts of Jonas Chuzzlewit, racked with guilt from his murder of Tigg:

Dread and fear haunted him, to an extent he had never counted on, and could not manage
in the least degree. He was so horribly afraid of that infernal room at home. This made
him, in a gloomy, murderous, mad way, not only fearful *for* himself, but *of* himself; for
being, as it were, a part of the room: a something supposed to be there, yet missing from
it: he invested himself with its mysterious terrors; and when he pictured in his mind the
ugly chamber, false and quiet, through the dark hours of two nights; the tumbled bed,
and he not in it, though believed to be; he became in a manner his own ghost and
phantom, and was at once the haunting spirit and the haunted man. (804)

This description, with all of its Gothic echoes, perfectly fits Redlaw as well,
who certainly becomes "in a manner his own ghost and phantom." One finds
several such powerful psychological specters haunting Dickens's characters.
Glimpses of shadows and "ghostly" appearances haunt Pip's meetings with Estella and Molly until he finally realizes that what had haunted him, at the time
hidden below the level of consciousness, was his vague perception of Estella's
resemblance to her parents. At the very end of the novel, having fathomed the
secret, he no longer sees this shadow of a ghostly "another" or other parting or
passing from her. Lady Dedlock, plagued by her earlier love affair, becomes so
obsessed with keeping it a secret that she becomes something very much like
the legendary figure haunting the "Ghost's Walk." Finally, we have that infamous figure who is entombed in her past, Miss Havisham, as Dickens uses that

old Gothic horror device, the prospect of live burial, to characterize her morbid state of mind.

Redlaw is finally able, with the aid of Milly, the angel of the house, to exorcise his demon and to make peace with his past and with those characters in the present who care for him. Some critics, as is well known, take Dickens to task for such happy endings. Rosemary Jackson argues that although Dickens uses Gothic conventions to depict "the kind of psychological dislocations and social deprivations which he perceived as the effects of a capitalist economy," he finally reveals "a reluctance to examine too closely the economic and ideological causes of his characters' discontent" (102). Indeed, she sees those early "pockets of darkness," the interpolated tales effaced or left behind by Pickwick's genial optimism, as paradigmatic of Dickens's sublimation of this discontent. One could answer that such contradictions, especially of the kind found in implausibly happy endings, are anything but foreign to the Gothic tradition, but the reader himself must decide if the Gothic elements in Dickens's fiction are essential to his vision or merely strategic means for some larger purpose. Perhaps too exclusive a focus on the Gothic side of this great novelist risks scaring the dickens out of Dickens. But even this short survey of the topic reveals that Dickens could skillfully draw on a wide range of Gothic conventions for a wide range of literary, psychological, and political effects. A final, touching example comes from "The Ghost in Master B's Room" (1859), in which Dickens uses Gothic imagery lyrically to depict his work as a writer as he searches for the ghostly presences of his own past selves:

Ah me, ah me! No other ghost has haunted the boy's room, my friends, since I have occupied it, than the ghost of my own childhood, the ghost of my own innocence, the ghost of my own airy belief. Many a time I have pursued the phantom: never with this man's stride of mine to come up with it, never with these man's hands of mine to touch it, never more to this man's heart of mine to hold it in its purity. And here you see me working out, as cheerfully and thankfully as I may, my doom of [conjuring] a constant change of customers, and of lying down and rising up with the skeleton allotted to me for my mortal companion. (251)

See also **Wilkie Collins**.

SELECTED CRITICISM

Coolidge, Archibald. "Charles Dickens and Mrs. Radcliffe: A Farewell to Wilkie Collins." *Dickensian* 58 (1962): 112–116. Argues for the central place of Radcliffe's influence upon Dickens's heroines and how this "Romantic" strain helps explain his divergence from Collins.

Cordery, Gareth. "The Gothic and the Sentimental in Charles Dickens." Doctoral dissertation, University of Wisconsin, 1975. [*DAI* 36:6697A]. The best treatment of Dickens's Gothicism, as Cordery traces "the Gothic spirit which informs Dickens's novels."

Greenman, David J. "Dickens's Ultimate Achievements in the Ghost Story: 'To Be Taken with a Grain of Salt' and 'The Signalman.' " *Dickensian* 85 (1989): 40–48. In these stories whose "final words provide an amazing Gothic surprise," Dickens grounds the supernatural "in the real, everyday world, characterized by fascination with *and* incredulity about the reality of [the] uncanny."

Hodgell, Pat. "Charles Dickens's *Old Curiosity Shop*: The Gothic Novel in Transition." *Riverside Quarterly* 8 (1990): 152–169. Valuably extends beyond a placing of the novel within the Gothic tradition to discuss the overall issue of Dickens's Gothicism.

Jackson, Rosemary. "The Silenced Text: Shades of Gothic in Victorian Fiction." *Minnesota Review* 13 (1979): 98–112. An early and trenchant New Historicist interpretation of Gothic elements in Dickens's fiction.

Jarrett, David. "The Fall of the House of Clennam: Gothic Conventions in *Little Dorrit*." *Dickensian* 73 (1977): 155–161. Studies various Gothic conventions in the novel: "the sinister old castle that harbors mystery, gloom, and guilty secrets [that creaking Clennam household]; the hero's search for the secret of his birth [Arthur's discovery of his true parentage]; the setting right of wrongs passed from one generation to another; the use of dreams [Mrs. Flintwinch's dream of multiple Mr. Flintwinches]; the ancestral portrait motif; the old manuscript; and the climactic destruction of the castle."

Kirkpatrick, Larry. "The Gothic Flame of Charles Dickens." *Victorian Newsletter* 31 (1967): 20–24. One of the best and most balanced discussions of Dickens's various uses of the Gothic. As an artist, he retools Gothic materials "to define symbolically the moral stature of his Victorian world." He "converts the Gothic lesson of horror into telling criticism of social abuses."

Loe, Thomas. "Gothic Plot in *Great Expectations*." *Dickens Quarterly* 6 (1989): 102–110. The Gothic plot underpins and connects its two other "plots" (the bildungsroman and the novel of manners) to create "the authentic drama of nightmarish quality of an individual's life when others have manipulated it, and the consequent need for moral self-determination." Draws strong parallels between this Gothic plot and Radcliffe's plotting in *The Italian*.

Maxwell, Richard. "Crowds and Creativity in *The Old Curiosity Shop*." *Journal of English and Germanic Philology* 78 (1979): 49–71. Compares the opening scenario of the novel with Victorian Gothics such as *Varney the Vampyre* and Edward Howard's *Rattlin the Reefer*. In its grotesqueries and persecutions, the novel also contains other overt parallels with Gothic fiction.

McMaster, R.D. "Dickens and the Horrific." *Dalhousie Review* 38 (1958): 18–28. Quotes Carlyle's opinion of Dickens's mastery of horror. "Lurking under Dickens's sparkling, clear and sunny utterance [are] deeper than all, if one has the eye to see deep enough, dark fateful silent elements, tragical to look upon, and hiding among the dazzling radiances as of the sun, the elements of death itself."

Mighall, Robert. *A Geography of Victorian Gothic Fiction: Mapping History's Nightmares*. Oxford: Oxford University Press, 1999. Includes discussion of Dickens's important role in helping to create a modern Gothic. Studies specifically the urban horror of *Oliver Twist*, the mutually contaminating exchanges among the haunted houses of *Bleak House*, and Dickens's reworking of earlier curse narratives in *Little Dorrit* and other novels.

Milbank, Alison. *Daughters of the House: Modes of the Gothic in Victorian Fiction*.

New York: St. Martin's Press, 1992. Attention to the Gothic treatment accorded to his heroines, and also to the houses with which they are associated, illumines "both his choice of woman as the subjective focus . . . and the seemingly contradictory mixture of social critique and pessimism about change" found in Dickens's middle novels. Questions the idea of a female Gothic, regarding, for example, in the story of Esther Summerson the way Dickens uses the "Gothic trope of the heroine's emancipation from the house" as a model for potential social change.

Phillips, Walter. *Dickens, Reade, and Collins, Sensation Novelists: A Study in the Conditions and Theories of Novel Writing in Victorian England*. New York: Columbia University Press, 1919. A seminal and still-valuable study of Dickens's participation in the "sensation" school that examines both his magazine tales and the novels in arguing that this tradition helped democratize Gothic terror.

Pritchard, Allan. "The Urban Gothic of *Bleak House*." *Nineteenth-Century Literature* 45 (1991): 432–452. "A major part of Dickens's solution to the problem of depicting the modern city was to turn to the conventions devised from Gothic horror fiction," including the labyrinth, ruins, garrets and the subterranean cellars, and fog (evoking Burkean obscurity).

Punter, David. "Gothic and the Sensation Novel." In *The Literature of Terror*. London: Longman, 1980: 214–238. A solid chapter on Dickens's reworking of Gothic materials (e.g., the innocent victimized by an expansive evil, London as a haunted castle, melodramatic polarization of good and evil) from such sources as Radcliffe, Reynolds, and tales from *Blackwood's*. A key point: Dickens combines "the genre of Gothic nightmare with that of social denunciation."

Ronald, Ann. "Dickens's Gloomiest Gothic Castle." *Dickens Studies Newsletter* 6 (1975): 71–75. By studying the Gothic features of the Jarndyce residence, Chesney Wold, Vholes's office, and other Gothic spaces in *Bleak House*, contends that "obscured by fog and portrayed in terms of ruin, London becomes Dickens's [ultimate] Gothic castle."

Sage, Victor. "Gothic Laughter: Farce and Horror in Five Texts." In *Gothick Origins and Innovations*. Ed. Allan Lloyd Smith and Victor Sage. Costerus New Series 91. Amsterdam and Atlanta, GA: Rodopi, 1994: 190–203. One of the five horror texts is Dickens's *Dombey and Son*. The christening of Paul Dombey is one of many moments "using the mingled farce and the undertow of unease of the Gothic register as a kind of shorthand."

Stone, Harry. *The Night Side of Dickens: Cannibalism, Passion, Necessity*. Columbus: Ohio State University Press, 1994. A rich source study of the darker elements in Dickens's fiction; returns repeatedly to "The Ghost in the Bride's Chamber" as Dickens's most seminal Gothic achievement, which draws from Lewis's spectral "White Women" and paves the way for such characters as Miss Havisham.

Sucksmith, Harvey P. "The Secret of Immediacy: Dickens's Debt to the Tale of Terror in *Blackwood's*." *Nineteenth-Century Fiction* 26 (1971): 145–157. The *Blackwood's* tales point the way for Dickens's diablerie in being "fundamentally different from the traditional Gothic tale" in their creation of a "realistic terror through precision of descriptive detail." In place of a "purely romantic terror through vague suggestion," Dickens follows the magazine writers in the "scientific accuracy" of his descriptions and "the methodical thoroughness" of his analysis.

Tracy, Robert, " 'The Old Story' and Inside Stories: Modish Fiction and Fictional Modes in *Oliver Twist*." *Dickens Studies Annual* 17 (1988): 1–33. Argues that many characters in the novel, the workhouse doctor, Bumble, and Fagin, seek to narrate Oliver's story in various idioms and genres, including the Gothic. Also discusses the novel's relation to Gothic fiction, particularly in the presentation of Monks.

FRANÇOIS GUILLAUME DUCRAY-DUMINIL
(1761–1819)

Frederick S. Frank

PRINCIPAL GOTHIC WORKS

Alexis; ou, La Maisonnette dans les bois [Alexis; or, The Cottage in the Woods]. Paris: Maradan, 1789. (The novel is often mentioned as one of Ann Radcliffe's principal models for *The Romance of the Forest*. The publisher Maridan also printed many translations of English Gothics into French.)

Victor; ou, L'Enfant de la forĕt [Victor; or, The Child of the Forest]. Paris: Le Prieur, 1796.

Coelina; ou, L'Enfant du mystère [Coelina; or, The Child of Mystery]. Paris: Le Prieur, 1798. (This popular four-volume *roman noir* was republished by the Minerva-Press in 1803 as *A Tale of Mystery, or Celina: A Novel* altered from the French of Ducray-Duminil, in a translation by the Gothic novelist Mary Meeke.)

Paul; ou, La Ferme abandonée [Paul; or, The Abandoned Farmhouse]. Paris: Le Prieur, 1799.

Slighted and seldom mentioned in literary histories of France, François Guillaume Ducray-Duminil has routinely been reduced to a footnote as "an imitator of Walpole" when critics bother to mention him at all. P.E. Charvat's *Literary History of France* (Barnes & Noble, 1967) passes over Ducray-Duminil, while Denis Hollier's *New History of French Literature* (Harvard University Press, 1989) is completely silent on his work and on the pre-Gothic accomplishments of Ducray-Duminil's countryman Baculard d'Arnaud, the two most important writers of the *roman noir* at the end of the eighteenth century. Two early-twentieth-century scholars of the Gothic, Alice Killen and Montague Summers, recognized the importance of the Gothic's French connection and commented on the influential role played by Ducray-Duminil in furnishing both an inspirational and a literal source for the Gothic scenes of Radcliffe's *Romance of the Forest* and in helping the Gothic romance to find its voice in the 1790s. In *A Gothic Bibliography*, Summers lists eleven novels by Ducray-Duminil appearing between 1788 and 1813 and notes eight English translations appearing between 1802 and 1817. He further comments on dramatic adaptations of *Alexis, Victor,* and *Coelina,* the three most purely Gothic books among Ducray-Duminil's romances, into comedies and melodramas by one of the leading French playwrights of the day, René-Charles Guilbert de Pixérécourt (1773–1844), whose 1799 dramatic adaptation of *The Mysteries of Udolpho* as *La Château des Apenans; ou, Le Fantôme vivant* transformed Radcliffe's novel into a gloomy *roman noir dramatique* in the manner of Ducray-Duminil. Some of Ducray-Duminil's English translators were themselves Gothic novelists and terror-writer stringers affiliated with the Minerva Press, a leading manufacturer of Gothic fiction.

The omission of Ducray-Duminil from the roster of French writers who influenced the course of English Gothicism in the 1790s is puzzling and critically unjustified. In the appendix to her *Popular Novel in England,* J.M.S. Tompkins alluded briefly to the strong French influence when she observed that "there was a steady trickle of French translations during the last half of the Eighteenth Century, and French novels were widely known and often reviewed in the original" (367). She mentions Rousseau, Prévost, Voltaire, Baculard d'Arnaud, Madame Riccoboni, Marmontel, Madame de Genlis, and Claris de Florian among those whose works were translated but makes no mention of Ducray-Duminil, whose books were at least as popular with English audiences as those of the other French romancers of the 1790s. A new awareness of Ducray-Duminil's proper place in the lexicon of terror was introduced by Robert D. Mayo's identification of the French Gothicist as the principal model for the gloomy sublimity first of Radcliffe and then of her legion of followers. Mayo's lead was not pursued by the new critics of the Gothic, however, and Ducray-Duminil remains the obscurest of all the French dark romance writers of the revolutionary era who helped to determine the tone and direction of the Gothic romance in the 1790s.

A few modern critics such as Maurice Lévy have begun to show how the Gothics of Ducray-Duminil made available the violently contradictory motifs of the French Revolution to the English Gothic imagination of the mid-1790s. But to date, except for a single study in Italian by Giorgio De Piaggi, there is no comprehensive analysis of the significant impact of this "forgotten father of the *roman noir*" (117) on the development of the English Gothic novel during its most formative decade. In *The Handbook to Gothic Literature,* Terry Hale severely understates the strange omission of Ducray-Duminil from accounts of the rise of the Gothic in his generalized conclusion that "a great deal of detailed research remains to be done with regard to the *roman noir*" (195).

Despite its bucolic title, *Alexis; or, The Cottage in the Woods* is far more Gothic than pastoral in both setting and action, a fact that explains Radcliffe's deep attraction to the work. The characters' complicated adventures in the underground and the blending of sublime melancholy with moments of terror suggest the preferences and procedures of Radcliffe before the fact. The plot of *Alexis* reappears in only slightly altered form in numerous English Gothics that adhere to the Radcliffean methodology of extracting pleasure from terror amid darkly sublime landscapes. Deep inside the robber-ridden forest of Chamboran stands the cottage of Candor, his daughter Clairette, and their servant, Germain. A brooding and guilt-ridden father plagued by some secret crime and a daughter in love with nature in its darker forms look ahead to the Gothic families of later wilderness Gothics. Candor has banished himself from society, his self-exile caused by his having been deceived into murdering his wife and child. The infanticide theme raises the possibility that the American Gothic novelist Charles Brockden Brown had read *Alexis* or at least knew about Ducray-Duminil's use of child murder and applied the crime of Candor to the child-killing episode of *Wieland* (1798). Directly beneath the cottage lies a subterranean sepulcher surrounded by a network of passages and containing the remains of Candor's victims. Tempted by the heroine's curiosity for the forbidden subterranean, Clairette eventually explores her father's private underworld, the secret hell upon which his idyllic hermitage is built, when she discovers a hidden staircase and descends into the catacombs. Here, within Walpole's "long labyrinth of darkness," she has her rendezvous with the mysterious young wanderer, Alexis, who has taken refuge with Candor and his family during a terrible storm. The genealogical outcome of this meeting in the underground is as predictable as the liaison of Theodore and Isabella in *The Castle of Otranto* with the revelation of Alexis's relationship with Candor and Clairette. Chilling episodes, loss of way in the burial chambers beneath the cottage, and a maiden groping about in the dark explain the relevance of Ducray-Duminil's first Gothic to his English successors.

   Victor; or, The Child of the Forest and *Coelina; or, The Child of Mystery* repeat the plot and reproduce the bizarre subterranean ambience of *Alexis*, but since both of these novels were written after the Revolution had turned upon its own and dissolved in a sea of blood, they have the grim pessimism of the fin de siècle Gothic antivision seen in Matthew Gregory Lewis's *Monk*. Characters in these Gothics are not always able to return to the surface or to recover domestic bliss as a result of their contact with the Gothic world where they find themselves damned to the darkness. Ducray-Duminil's legacy to the English Gothic novel is considerable. His work not only enriched Radcliffe's preoccupation with wilderness landscape as a generator of the terrific sublime, but also suggested to her and her followers how to make the oppressed situation of the maiden within the confines of the Gothic family the focal point of fearful pleasure.

SELECTED CRITICISM

De Piaggi, Giorgio. "Un padre dimenticato del 'roman noir': François Guillaume Ducray-Duminil." In *La narrazione: Temi e techniche dal medioevo ai Nostri giorni.* Abano Terme, Italy: Piovan, 1987: 117–136. Refers to Ducray-Duminil as the "forgotten father of the *roman noir*." His novels contain nearly every element of

Radcliffean terror Gothic before the fact, including the gambit of the explained supernatural.

Gaspard, Claire. "*Coelina*, de Ducray-Duminil à Pixérécourt à l'aube de la 'littérature industrielle." In *Mélodrames et romans noirs 1750–1890*. Ed. Simone Bernard-Griffiths and Jean Sgard. Toulouse: Presses Universitaires du Mirail 2000: 127–144. *Coelina; or, The Child of Mystery* inspired Pixérécourt, who in turn inspired later theatrical versions of the *roman noir*.

Gillet, Jean. "Ducray-Duminil, le gothique, et la révolution." *Europe: Revue Littéraire Mensuelle* 659 (1984): 63–72. Ducray-Duminil's novels reflect in detail the terrors and excesses of the French Revolution. The Gothic transforms itself into a metaphor of revolutionary conflicts.

Hale, Terry. "*Roman Noir*." In *The Handbook to Gothic Literature*. Ed. Marie Mulvey-Roberts. New York: New York University Press, 1998: 189–195. Brief mention of Ducray-Duminil, but no titles by Ducray-Duminil are appraised in the survey.

Humphrey, George. "*Victor; ou, L'Enfant de la forêt* et la roman terrifiant." *French Review* 33 (1959): 137–145. Relates the themes and characters of the novel to Radcliffe's Gothics, especially *The Romance of the Forest*. "Dans *Victor*, Ducray-Duminil employes des mêmes procédés dont se sert Mrs. Radcliffe pour inspirer la terreur."

Lévy, Maurice. "Anne Radcliffe et ses demeures." In *Le Roman "gothique" anglais, 1764–1824*. Toulouse: Association des Publications de la Faculté des Lettres et Sciences Humaines de Toulouse, 1968: 213–303. Discusses Radcliffe's transpositions and substitutions from Ducray-Duminil's *Alexis* to her *Romance of the Forest*. "Radcliffe ait substitué à la maisonnette un cadre *gothique*, n'est pas fait pour nous surprendre." Identifies specific parallels between passages in *Alexis* and passages in *The Romance of the Forest*, particularly Adeline's nightmare of the haunted chamber. Also compares Ducray-Duminil's Candor with Radcliffe's La Motte.

Mayo, Robert D. "Ann Radcliffe and Ducray-Duminil." *Modern Language Review* 36 (1941): 501–505. This source study demonstrates Radcliffe's extensive debt to Ducray-Duminil in her *Romance of the Forest*. Because *Alexis* contains "more horrors in the Gothic vein than any single work of its predecessors in France, it must be regarded as an additional link between the French and the English traditions of terror."

Summers, Montague. "Ducray-Duminil, François Guillaume." In *A Gothic Bibliography*. New York: Russell & Russell, 1964: 38–39. Lists the novels, translations, and dramatic adaptations. *Romans noirs* "were frequently translated into English by our native novelists [and] directly influenced the development of the Gothic novel in England."

Tilby, Michael. "Ducray-Duminil's *Victor, ou l'enfant de la forêt* in the Context of the Revolution." *Studies on Voltaire and the Eighteenth Century* 249 (1987): 407–438. Ducray-Duminil's political naïveté was radically altered by the Revolution. He Gothified his fiction accordingly, making the horrors of *Victor* reflect the horrors of the Reign of Terror.

Tompkins, J.M.S. "Appendix I: Foreign Novels in England." In *The Popular Novel in England, 1770–1800*. London: Constable, 1932. Rpt. London: Methuen, 1969: 367–369. Briefly outlines the influence of the *roman noir* on the work of Ann Radcliffe, Sophia Lee, and others.

MARY WILKINS FREEMAN
(1852–1930)
Jack G. Voller

PRINCIPAL GOTHIC WORKS

"A Symphony in Lavender." *Harper's Bazaar*, August 1883. (Also published in *A Humble Romance and Other Stories*.)

"A Far-away Melody." *Harper's Bazaar*, September 1883. (Also published in *A Humble Romance and Other Stories*.)

A Humble Romance and Other Stories. New York: Harper, 1887.

"A Gentle Ghost." *Harper's*, August 1889. (Also published in *A New England Nun and Other Stories*.)

"The Twelfth Guest." *Harper's*, December 1889.

A New England Nun and Other Stories. New York: Harper, 1891.

"The Little Maid at the Door." *Harper's*, February 1892. (Also published in *Silence and Other Stories*.)

"The School-Teacher's Story." *Romance*, February 1894.

Silence and Other Stories. London and New York: Harper, 1898.

"The Wind in the Rose-Bush." *Everybody's Magazine*, February 1902. (Also published in *The Wind in the Rose-Bush and Other Stories of the Supernatural*.)

"The Lost Ghost." *Everybody's Magazine*, May 1902. (Also published in *The Wind in the Rose-Bush and Other Stories of the Supernatural*.)

"The Vacant Lot." *Everybody's Magazine*, September 1902.

"Luella Miller." *Everybody's Magazine*, December 1902.

"The Southwest Chamber." In *The Wind in the Rose-Bush and Other Stories of the Supernatural*, 1903.

The Wind in the Rose-Bush and Other Stories of the Supernatural. New York: Doubleday, Page, 1903; London: John Murray, 1903.

"The Hall Bedroom." In *Short Story Classics*. (*American*). Ed. William Patton. New York: P.F. Collier, 1905.

"The Witch's Daughter." *Harper's Weekly*, 10 December 1910.

"The Jade Bracelet." *Forum*, April 1918.

MODERN REPRINTS AND EDITIONS

In addition to the titles listed here, a handful of Freeman's supernaturalist tales appear with some regularity in various horror anthologies; "Luella Miller" seems to be the most popular choice of anthologists.

The Best Short Stories of Mary E. Wilkins Ed. Henry W. Lanier. Saint Clair Shores, MI: Scholarly Publications, 1971.
Collected Ghost Stories by Mary E. Wilkins Freeman. Ed. Edward Wagenknecht. Sauk City, WI: Arkham House, 1974.
A Humble Romance, and Other Stories. New York: AMS Press, 1970. (Contains "A Symphony in Lavender" and "A Far-away Melody.")
A Mary Wilkins Freeman Reader. Ed. Mary R. Reichardt. Lincoln: University of Nebraska, 1997. (Contains "Luella Miller," and "The Lost Ghost.")
The Uncollected Stories of Mary Wilkins Freeman. Ed. Mary R. Reichardt. Jackson: University Press of Mississippi, 1992. (Contains "The Hall Bedroom" and "The Witch's Daughter.")
The Wind in the Rose-Bush and Other Stories of the Supernatural. Ed. Alfred Bendixen. Chicago: Academy Chicago, 1986.

Born on Halloween in 1852, Mary Wilkins Freeman spent much of her life in the New England about which she wrote with such detail and authority. While the vast majority of her work, including drama, poetry, and children's literature, is in the realist mode, Freeman wrote a number of supernatural tales, most of which were published in popular magazines before being reprinted in various short-story collections. Many early critics reacted negatively to her supernaturalist fiction, seeing it as vastly inferior to the realist work with which Freeman established her reputation; this, combined with a decreasing interest, in the decades that saw the two world wars and the Great Depression, in the "feminine" subject matter of many of her works, caused Freeman's ghostly fiction to languish.

In recent decades, prompted largely by the perspectives and insights of feminist critics, Freeman's ghostly and other works have begun to receive appreciative scholarly attention. It is appropriate that such critics would be in the forefront of a renewed interest in Freeman's work, for in her ghostly tales Freeman often features "spinstered" or otherwise-marginalized women or girls whose encounters with the ghostly are a symbolic engagement with their own familial and emotional anxieties. Indeed, dysfunctional families and repressed emotional and libidinal energies are the motive engines driving most of Freeman's supernaturalist work. Her own anxieties about authorship, marriage, and sexuality combine in these works to make them quite compelling for critics able to see beyond the surface of these tales, with their domestic settings and concerns, and into the psychological complexities that such surfaces mask. As was common for women writers in the nineteenth and early twentieth centuries, Freeman's use of the supernatural was a means of giving voice to and examining psychological, emotional, and social issues that the constraints of realism simply did not permit. The "lapse" that for many critics (often male) Freeman's ghost stories represent is in fact a deliberate shift on her part, an engagement with what she referred to as a "symbolism" and "mysticism" that even she recognized might not sell as well as her realist work but that nonetheless allowed her, as Leah Glasser has noted, "to give oblique expression to disturbing personal issues without fear of exposure" (220). As many critics have noted, much of Freeman's supernaturalist fiction was written around the time of her marriage, pleasant at first but eventually destroyed by his alcoholism, to Dr. Charles Freeman, a fact that gives credence to the claim that these tales are deeply involved in the complex psychodynamics of love, sexuality, autonomy, emotional fulfillment, and social expectation.

One of Freeman's most famous tales is the frequently reprinted "Luella Miller," a brief work that gives compact and powerful expression to most of the issues that absorbed her. The phenomenally helpless Luella Miller is essentially a vampire of the domestic, a woman so unable, despite the lack of any physical disability, to care for herself that her helplessness, an exaggerated expression of the cult of feminine fragility, destroys the lives of those who are drawn to her. Husbands, lovers, neighbor widows, and hired maidens all become drained of vitality, utterly decimated and finally destroyed by the ideal of feminine helplessness that Luella represents. She is, in one sense, the apotheosis of Mary Wollstonecraft's female in her *Vindication of the Rights of Woman*, for she embodies the cultivated helplessness and incapacity that Wollstonecraft identified as a burden not just for women but for all of human society. Freeman's tale literalizes that parasitic relationship, and as we watch all who help Luella die, we see the working out, to its most destructive and ultimate end, of the flawed logic of gender inequality that Wollstonecraft assailed. Only when the narrator of the tale, a no-nonsense, pragmatic older woman, finally resists the powerful draw of Luella, refusing to cater to her every need, does Luella finally die. Just as Virginia Woolf kills off Patmore's Angel in the House, Freeman kills off The Helpless Woman, and once the ghost of Luella leads a parade of her victims' spirits out of her house, that house stands empty and shunned, a haunting reminder of the angel-less domestic space slowly coming into being in the new century.

Over and over again Freeman engages the themes of gender and duty and love and family, seeking to map the treacherous pathways through a tangle of often conflicting needs and demands that, then as now, make simple formulas impossible. Spinsters may be perverse or compassionate, as they are in "The Southwest Chamber" and "A Far-away Melody"; children may be lost ghosts or merely unhappy neighbors, as in "The Lost Ghost" or "The Twelfth Guest"; love may redeem and console, though more often it is a daunting prospect best held at arm's length and avoided, as in "A Symphony in Lavender." Freeman's ghosts are, in the final analysis, not the denizens of some malefic otherworld but (dis)embodied projections of the human psyche and the complex sociocultural cross-currents in which it is caught. While her ghosts have much of the "reality" or sense of presence of those found in more traditional, antiquarian ghost stories, their symbolic and thematic weight owes much more to the nascent "psychological" ghost story as practiced more deftly and less accessibly by Henry James. Freeman stands then at a cultural crossroads, at the watershed moment of the turn of the previous century when "the New Woman" and the new science of psychoanalysis were together revealing and providing a language for discussing the tangled intersection of society, gender, and being.

SELECTED CRITICISM

Bendixen, Alfred. "Afterword." In *The Wind in the Rose-Bush and Other Stories of the Supernatural*. Ed. Alfred Bendixen. Chicago: Academy Chicago, 1986. A brief survey of critical responses to Freeman's supernaturalist fiction and an insightful discussion of the tales in this volume, which Bendixen sees, in their concern with "frustrated ambition, stifled desire and denied love," as a "logical extension" of Freeman's earlier work.

Fisher, Benjamin F. "Transitions from Victorian to Modern: The Supernatural Stories of Mary Wilkins Freeman and Edith Wharton." In *American Supernatural Fiction: From Edith Wharton to the Weird Tales Writers*. Ed. Douglas Robillard. New York: Garland, 1996: 3–42. Surveying all of Freeman's ghostly tales, Fisher analyzes Freeman's "domestication" of the Gothic and her use of its tropes to explore "thwarted, failed human relationships." Useful bibliographic information and some reception history.

Fisken, Beth Wynne. "The 'Faces of Children That Had Never Been': Ghost Stories by Mary Wilkins Freeman." In *Haunting the House of Fiction: Feminist Perspectives on Ghost Stories by American Women*. Ed. Lynette Carpenter and Wendy K. Kolmar. Knoxville: University of Tennessee Press, 1991: 41–63. Argues that Freeman's repeated examination of "orphaned and neglected" children in her ghostly fiction may have its source in the death, at age seventeen, of Wilkins's sister Anna and in her own ambivalence toward motherhood.

Foster, Edward. *Mary E. Wilkins Freeman*. New York: Hendricks House, 1956. An early overview of Freeman's work, with valuable biographical insights.

Glasser, Leah Blatt. *In a Closet Hidden: The Life and Work of Mary E. Wilkins Freeman*. Amherst: University of Massachusetts Press, 1996. One of the best full-length studies of Freeman, Glasser's book is a complex and revealing look at Freeman's corpus and the influences that shaped her thinking and her art. Especially insightful regarding the extent to which Freeman's fiction reflects her life events, Glasser sees in the ghostly fiction a study of Freeman's anxieties regarding marriage, work, sexuality, and the social assessment of a woman's involvement in these areas of human experience.

Hirsch, David H. "Subdued Meaning in 'A New England Nun.' " *Studies in Short Fiction* 2 (1965): 124–136. Notes the residual Gothic tone of the story.

Oaks, Susan. "The Haunting Will: The Ghost Stories of Mary Wilkins Freeman." *Colby Library Quarterly* 21 (1985): 208–220. Argues that Freeman's supernaturalist works continue "to explore the theme that is basic to all of her fiction—the operation of the individual will"; these tales depart from Freeman's earlier work,

Oaks claims, in that they examine "the will's negative side," manifested in the moral failings of the protagonists.

Patrick, Barbara. "Lady Terrorists: Nineteenth-Century American Women Writers and the Ghost Story." In *American Women Short Story Writers: A Collection of Critical Essays*. Ed. Julie Brown. New York: Garland, 1995: 73–84. Noting that women's supernaturalist fiction of the late nineteenth and early twentieth centuries addressed "the immorality of the treatment of women in America," Patrick analyzes "Luella Miller" as a work that "depicts the mortifying effects of women's domestication," figured in the helplessness of Luella that is vampiric in its intensity and dependence.

Pattee, Fred Lewis. "On the Terminal Moraine of New England Puritanism." In *Side-Lights on American Literature*. New York: Century, 1922: 175–209. An important early study of Freeman that begins to elucidate the interior psychological complexity of many of Freeman's characters.

Reichardt, Mary R. "Mary Wilkins Freeman: One Hundred Years of Criticism." *Legacy: A Journal of American Women Writers* 4:2 (1987): 31–44. A reception history of Freeman's work and solid overview of important critical developments in Freeman scholarship.

———. *Mary Wilkins Freeman: A Study of the Short Fiction*. New York: Twayne, 1997. Arguing that Freeman's supernaturalist stories are of a piece with her other work, Reichardt finds that Freeman's ghost stories, which often employ various "doubling" strategies, have as their focus "troubled hearts, those burdened by unfulfilled desires, family tensions, suppressed jealousy or anger, or despair."

Shaw, S. Bradley. "New England Gothic by the Light of Common Day: Lizzie Borden and Mary E. Wilkins Freeman's 'The Long Arm.' " *New England Quarterly* 70 (1997): 211–236. Sources for the story are found in the Lizzie Borden axe murders.

Westbrook, Perry. *Mary Wilkins Freeman*, rev. ed. TUSAS 122. Boston: Twayne, 1988. Examines Freeman's views of social conditions and the operation of the human will. Finds that "among American writers Freeman is the supreme analyst of the Puritan will in its constructive strengths, in its aberrations, and in its decadence into mere whim and stubbornness."

WILLIAM GODWIN
(1756–1836)

Douglass H. Thomson

PRINCIPAL GOTHIC WORKS

Imogen: A Pastoral Romance. London: William Lane, 1784.

Things As They Are; or, The Adventures of Caleb Williams. London: B. Crosby, 1794. (There were six reprintings in the 1790s and twenty-five in the 1800s, most noticeably *Caleb Williams; with a Life of the Author by Mrs. Shelley* [Paris: Galignani, 1831]. Godwin's novel also spawned a popular play, *The Iron Chest*, written by George Colman the younger. [London: Printed by T. Woodfall, for Messrs. Cadell & Davies, 1798].)

Things As They Are; or The Adventures of Caleb Williams, Philadelphia: Rice, 1795.

Les Choses comme elles sont; ou, Les Aventures de Caleb Williams. Traduit de l'Anglais, par des gens de la campagne. Paris: Dufart, 1797.

St. Leon: A Tale of the Sixteenth Century. London: G.G. and J. Robinson, 1799. (The novel inspired two dramatic works: John Burk, *Bethlem Gabor, Lord of Transylvania; or, The Man Hating Palatine: An Historical Drama in Three Acts*. Petersburg, VA: [J. Dickson for Somervell & Conrad, 1807]; John Hobart Caunter, *St. Leon: A Drama, in Three Acts* [London: Edward Churton, 1835].)

Lives of the Necromancers; or, An Account of the Most Eminent Persons in Successive Ages, Who Have Claimed for Themselves, or to Whom Has Been Imputed by Others, the Exercise of Magical Power. London: F.J. Mason, 1834.

MODERN REPRINTS AND EDITIONS

The Adventures of Caleb Williams; or, Things As They Are. Ed. George Sherburn. New York: Holt, Rinehart & Winston, 1965.

Caleb Williams; or, Things As They Are. Moscow: Foreign Languages Publishing House, 1959.

Caleb Williams; or, Things As They Are. Intro. Ernest A. Baker. London: New English Library, 1966.

Caleb Williams. Ed. and intro. David McCracken. New York: Norton, 1977.

Caleb Williams. Ed. Gary Handwerk and Arnold A. Markley. Toronto: Broadview Press, 2000.

The Collected Novels and Memoirs of William Godwin. Ed. Mark Philp. 8 vols. London: Pickering & Chatto, 1992. (Vol. 3 is *Caleb Williams.* Vol. 4 is *St. Leon*).

Damon and Delia; Italian Letters; Imogen. Ed. Pamela Clemit. London: W. Pickering, 1992.

Imogen: A Pastoral Romance. Intro. Jack W. Marken. New York: New York Public Library, 1963.

The Iron Chest, by George Colman the younger. Oxford: Woodstock Books, 1989.

Lives of the Necromancers. Cincinnati: Art Guild Reprints, 1968.

St. Leon: A Tale of the Sixteenth Century. Foreword by Devendra P. Varma, intro. Juliet Beckett. New York: Arno Press, 1972.

St. Leon: A Tale of the Sixteenth Century. New York: AMS Press, 1975.

St. Leon: A Tale of the Sixteenth Century. Ed. Pamela Clemit. Oxford and New York: Oxford University Press, 1994. (This edition is cited in the text.)

Things As They Are; or, The Adventures of Caleb Williams. Ed. and intro. Maurice Hindle. Harmondsworth, UK: Penguin, 1988. (This edition is cited in the text.)

A onetime Sandemanian minister, writing of his early studies that "all my enquiries terminated in Calvinism" (Marshall 41), who came to be regarded as one of the most notorious "Jacobinical" atheists of his age; author of *An Enquiry Concerning Political Justice* (1793) and one of the most profoundly influential political radicals of his day, who yet expressed profound ambivalence in his fiction about the possibility and even desirability of sweeping social change; at one level an ultrarationalist and meliorist who yet wrote as his final work *Lives of the Necromancers,* which congenially explores the alchemists and other seekers of knowledge "in forbidden paths" (6); a novelist whose political aim to expose "things as they are" led to a more profoundly Gothic psychology in *Caleb Williams* than in his later and more obviously supernatural *St. Leon*—such are the striking contradictions one encounters in the career of William Godwin. Although Godwin was an enthusiastic reader of Walpole, Schiller, and Radcliffe, few critics are satisfied with the idea of him as a Gothic novelist per se, and this despite many recent studies of Gothic elements in his fiction. The more fruitful and crucial question to ask is why these Gothic elements emerge in a writer who renounced religious superstition and old customs as impediments to his belief in the perfectibility of mankind. Just what haunts those two of the most haunted and hounded heroes of the 1790s, Caleb Williams and Reginald St. Leon? Why would Godwin, a rationalist, radical, and atheist, turn to the Gothic and reinvest it with a power that would render his work influential to later writers in the genre such as Charles Brockden Brown, Percy Shelley, Charles Robert Maturin, and his daughter, Mary Shelley? In exploring these seeming paradoxes, one finally comes to understand that Godwin, no matter how marginally "Gothic" he may on some counts appear, is central to a political and religious understanding of Gothicism in the 1790s and beyond.

Following his somewhat reluctant apostasy from the Presbyterian church in

1783, Godwin determined to make his living by writing, and he entered a literary marketplace increasingly dominated by the Gothic story and its variants. Two of his earliest novels, *Damon and Delia* and *Italian Letters* (both 1783), involve sentimental plots, the first ending with the triumph of the young lovers over recalcitrant parents, the latter, an epistolary novel, ending in a deadly duel; neither is particularly Gothic. However, a neglected work from this period, *Imogen: A Pastoral Romance*, does provide clear indications of Godwin's familiarity with Walpole's Gothic conventions and a distinctive treatment of them at this early stage. Its highly contrived idyllic valley of Clwyd, a Welsh pastoral world overseen by benevolent Druidic bards and featuring the perfectly virtuous Imogen and her faithful shepherd Edwin, is invaded by the evil magician Roderic, who employs a terrific tempest generated by a "dreadful" goblin to enable him to abduct the fair Imogen and spirit her away to his evil castle. The abduction scene, the atmospherics of the castle, Roderic's repeated temptations of Imogen, many of these accompanied by supernatural machinery conned from Godwin's main source, Milton's *Comus*, and the attractive but self-destructive villainy of the magician all place the short novel in the context of the Gothic tradition. Indeed, five of the six chapters of this so-called pastoral romance actually take place in the castle, thus anticipating the central peril of Gothic fiction, especially in Radcliffe's novels of the 1790s. Another weird anticipation of a famous Gothic occurrence takes place during the thunderstorm when a lightning bolt strikes an oak tree, "monarch of the plain" and to the Druids, leaving in "the very trunk a gaping and tremendous rift" (40), a portent that closely resembles a similar lightning strike in Godwin's daughter's *Frankenstein*. But Godwin's twin theses, first, that "it is not in the power of events to undermine the felicity of virtue" (45), and second, that virtue becomes purer as it meets adversity, strangely drain this fantastic setting of much of its potential Gothic drama and suspense: Imogen is simply impervious to all temptation, even when the magician uses his wand to assume the guise of her beloved swain, and Roderic's increasingly petulant evil makes him no match for Imogen's and Edwin's sweet and simple virtue. Even the most promising Gothic special effect of the novel, the sudden vanishing of the castle as Roderic meets his final defeat (recalling the collapse of the Castle of Otranto and which some critics identify as a possible source for "The Fall of the House of Usher") is thoroughly expected, having been prophesied four or five times earlier in the novel. Already in *Imogen* we witness Godwin the writer of popular fiction meeting Godwin the philosopher of ideas. In this pastoral romance with strong Gothic features, virtue triumphs over property and corrupt power, themes that emerge again powerfully in the treatise *Political Justice* and are tested in his next and most famous novel.

Published during the advent of revolutionary horrors in France, *Caleb Williams* purports to provide a compelling narrative demonstration of Godwin's political agenda. In criticizing "Things as They Are" at every level of society, Godwin emphasizes the debilitating political helplessness of the lower classes in the figure of the encyclopedically persecuted Williams and his conflicted

relationship with his superior and master, Falkland. Alternately venerating, serving, fearing, and hating his master, Williams represents an England betrayed by
its ruling classes, punished for its pursuit of a liberating knowledge, persecuted
by its attempt to redefine relationships of power, and confused by its inability
to do so. Obviously unlike Imogen, Caleb does not find that virtue emerges
purer and triumphant through its meeting with adversity. The ending Godwin
originally wrote for the novel finds Falkland vindicated by a hopelessly predis-
posed legal system and Williams locked in confinement and slowly being poisoned into madness and death.

But as James Rieger and Joel Porte have convincingly demonstrated, the
strong "framework of secularized Calvinism" that underpins the novel qualifies
its political agenda and introduces an unmistakably Gothic sense of foreboding,
dread, and victimization. Caleb's sense of guilt in discovering Falkland's secret
crime is never expiated, and his "conviction of merited and universal persecution" (Rieger 37) transcends its assigned and often effective function as an expression of political oppression and inequity. For Caleb does not just rail against
economic tyranny and "prejudice of birth" (293); he becomes infected with an
unshakable understanding of how his "mistaken thirst of knowledge" (139) reveals his own depravity, which "no penitence, no anguish can expiate" (331),
which "was to admit neither of forgiveness nor remission" (139). Falkland's
persecution of the sinner quickly assumes mythic proportions. Caleb twice refers
to Falkland as divinity (150, 331). Like the shrinking Adam, Caleb seeks oblivion: "Let me go and hide myself where may never see you more" (126) as
Falkland returns with all the fury of an indignant deity: "I shall crush you in
the end with the same indifference that I would any other little insect that disturbed my serenity. . . . You shall never quit [my service] with life. If you attempt it, you shall never cease to rue your folly as long as you exist. That is
my will; and I will not have it resisted" (159–160). Also like the angered Father,
Falkland is everywhere, all-knowing and all-powerful. Caleb laments: "Could
no human ingenuity and exertion effect [my freedom]? Did his power reach
through all space, and his eye penetrate every concealment? Was he like that
mysterious being, to protect us from whose fierce revenge mountains and hills,
we are told [see Hosea 10:8 and Luke 23:30], might fall on us in vain?" (249).
Falkland appears inscrutable to the sinner unable to comprehend the origins of
evil: "Unacquainted with the source of the evil, observing its perpetual increase,
and finding it so far as I could perceive entirely arbitrary in nature, I was unable
to ascertain its limits, or the degree in which it would finally overwhelm me"
(306). In sum, Caleb's guilt and persecution are rendered in unmistakably Calvinist terms, offering a frightening depiction of what Joel Porte likens to "sinners
in the hands of an angry God."

The purpose of this framework is open to debate. Godwin's revised ending
(the published one) makes his political message more oblique and his religious
irony more pronounced. After finally confronting and exposing his persecutor,
Caleb only feels a greater sense of his own depravity and that of all mankind's.

He has become a Calvinist to rival the fanaticism of Hawthorne's Young Good-man Brown: "But what use are talents and sentiments in the corrupt wilderness of human society? It is a rank and rotten soil from which every finer shrub draws poison as it grows" (336). Has Godwin's political meliorism encountered the dark teachings of his early age, in Rieger's formulation, a "hangover of religious paranoia" (39) that returns to haunt the erstwhile ultrarationalist and atheist? Or is it merely, as Porte contends, "an internalized Calvinism which Godwin . . . pressed naturally [and strategically] into the service of a common Gothic fable of total decay" (54)? Whatever the answers to these questions it is undeniable that this undercurrent of religious terror shapes the most distinctly Gothic features of the novel: the extreme suffering Caleb undergoes for his curiosity, which had led to his discovery of Falkland's hidden manuscript of guilt; the strange doubling between pursuer and pursued; the claustrophobic rendering of England, not just realized in several Gothicky dungeon scenes but in Caleb's utter inability to find freedom anywhere; and, of course, the figure of Gines, the diabolic agent of Falkland who relentlessly stalks Caleb. When Caleb resorts to the disguise of an old Jew in one of his many fruitless attempts to escape from persecution by Falkland, Godwin summons up the figure who crystallizes the Gothic pattern of transgression and retribution and who will reemerge in many Gothic novels, from Matthew Lewis's *Monk* to Percy Shelley's *St. Irvyne* to Maturin's *Melmoth the Wanderer*.

Godwin's Reginald St. Leon not only receives the damning gifts of eternal life and the philosopher's stone from a Wandering Jew figure but, in his lonely, blasted excursions, becomes a figure of the Wandering Jew himself. A cursory overview of the novel's plot would seem to place its conventions even more in the world of the Gothic than *Caleb Williams*. We have the typically questionable Promethean hero whose overreaching brings terrible destruction to all about him and who suffers many moments of torment himself. These include a thirteen-year imprisonment by the Inquisition, the gruesome murder of his faithful Negro servant, an auto-da-fé, and confinement in a subterranean vault by the gigantic Hungarian misanthrope Bethlem Gabor, the most Gothic character in the book and an inspiration for a later melodrama by John Burk. Yet despite the sixteenth-century context and the overt introduction of the supernatural, the novel actually appears less Gothic than its forerunner; the brooding sense of religious terror that pervades *Caleb Williams* has been displaced by a deliberate philosophical agenda through which Godwin revises some of his earlier, more radical or heretical stands.

The radical Godwin of *Political Justice* had argued, as part of his case for the innate dignity of each individual set against the corrupting influences of society, that "we ought to be able to do without one another. He is the most perfect man to whom society is not a necessary of life, but a luxury." These words can well serve as an ironic indictment of St. Leon, who finds that he longs desperately for the social and domestic relationships denied to him by his great secret knowledge. Godwin himself notes in his preface to the novel that he has "modified" some of his earlier beliefs, chiefly regarding a new emphasis on "the domestic and private affections" (xxxiv). This new promotion of the "culture of the heart" bears the unmistakable influence of Mary Wollstonecraft's thinking, which is eloquently rendered in the figure of the noble Marguerite, one of fiction's most perfect mothers and wives, who repeatedly warns St. Leon of the destructive consequences of his pursuing personal fame. Thus St. Leon's transgressions, first gaming, then, more alienating, his alchemical pursuits, are not attended in the usual Gothic manner with infernal machinery or thunderings of an offended deity. St. Leon's isolation and repeatedly failed philanthropy simply serve to underscore Godwin's surprisingly conservative moral: "Live in the midst of your family; cultivate domestic affection; be the solace and joy of your wife; watch for the present and future welfare of your children; and be assured that you will then be found no contemptible or unbeneficial member of the community at large" (48).

One could say that such a philosophical agenda of domestic virtues hardly seems congenial to the spirit of the Gothic. But Godwin's depiction of the solipsistic quester and breaker of taboos in opposition to the domestic sphere has great resonance in the tradition of the female Gothic, and in many important ways, *St. Leon*, with its tribute to the ideas of Mary Wollstonecraft, can be seen as a transitional piece between Radcliffe's novels and Mary Shelley's *Frankenstein*. Indeed, the divided allegiances within Godwin's vision help underscore and pinpoint some important dynamics of the larger Gothic vision: a strange return to traditional religious understandings of fate to chastise the freethinker or intellectual overreacher by the sense of entrapment or persecution; a criticism of chivalric and aristocratic and Burkean values set against a growing suspicion of revolutionary change or disquietude about "the way things might become"; a fascination with the solitary seeker qualified by a strong emphasis on the virtues of the domestic sphere. Therein rests the final paradox and great value of Godwin for an understanding of the Gothic: although he was perhaps only a marginal or partial Goth himself, his writing powerfully articulates political and religious tensions within the Gothic scene as a whole.

SELECTED CRITICISM

Butler, Marilyn. "Godwin, Burke, and *Caleb Williams*." *Essays in Criticism* 32 (1982): 237–257. A seminal article on the full political import of the novel. By arguing against more psychoanalytic and "Calvinistic" readings of the Falkland/Caleb relationship, Butler provides an important counterbalance to the more "Gothic" interpretations of the novel.

Clemit, Pamela. *The Godwinian Novel: The Rational Fictions of Godwin, Brockden Brown, Mary Shelley*. Oxford: Clarendon Press, 1993. Godwin draws upon "the non-realistic techniques of the Gothic . . . to provide a mode of indirect commentary on the inner lives of individuals oppressed by institutions." Probably the best single study of new elements brought to the novelistic tradition by Godwin.

Flanders, Wallace. "Godwin and Gothicism: *St. Leon*." *Texas Studies in Literature and Language* 8 (1967): 533–545. The novel adapts a "serious metaphorical use of the supernatural" to deepen its depiction of St. Leon's crime of moral isolation.

Graham, Kenneth. "The Gothic Unity of Godwin's *Caleb Williams*." *Papers on Language and Literature* 20 (1984): 47–59. "To exemplify the universal conflict between tyranny and liberty, Godwin chose a narrator who perceives the world in Gothic polarities."

———. *The Politics of Narrative: Ideology and Social Change in William Godwin's Caleb Williams*. New York: AMS Press, 1990. Graham offers the most detailed study of the novel in Gothic terms, tracing its reworking of materials from Walpole, Beckford, and Radcliffe.

Handwerk, Gary. "Of Caleb's Guilt and Godwin's Truth: Ideology and Ethics in *Caleb Williams*." *ELH* 60 (1993): 939–960. Discusses how the novel both extends and calls into question the program for "political amelioration" advocated by *Political Justice*.

Lévy, Ellen. "The Philosophical Gothic of *St. Leon*." *Caliban* 33 (1996): 51–62. "Godwin harnesses to his didactic cart a pair of imaginative steeds in the form of a re-imagined historical context and the heightening Gothic mode." Discusses the interplay of political, philosophical, and Gothic elements in the novel, especially Godwin's treatment of prisons, which figure both as an indictment of "coercive authority" and a "metaphor" for the isolation caused by St. Leon's breaking of domestic trust.

Maertz, Gregory. "Family Resemblances: Intertextual Dialogue between Father and Daughter Novelists in Godwin's *St. Leon* and Shelley's *Frankenstein*." *University of Mississippi Studies in English* 11–12 (1993): 303–320. Reads *Frankenstein* as a response to Godwin's ideas in *St. Leon*.

Marshall, Peter H. *William Godwin*. New Haven: Yale University Press, 1984. Definitive biography. Argues convincingly that Godwin never quite left behind the influence of his early Calvinist training.

Myers, Mitzi. "Godwin's Changing Conception of *Caleb Williams*." *Studies in English Literature, 1500–1900* 12 (1972): 591–628. Studies how Godwin's desire to "realize fully the psychologically intricate and morally ambivalent" nature of his characters moved him beyond both stock Gothic characterization and straightforward exposition of his political agenda.

Pollin, Burton R. *Godwin Criticism: A Synoptic Bibliography*. Toronto: University of Toronto Press, 1967. In need of updating but still a useful bibliographic guide.

Porte, Joel. "In the Hands of an Angry God: Religious Terror in Gothic Fiction." In *The Gothic Imagination: Essays in Dark Romanticism*. Ed. G.R. Thompson. Pullman: Washington State University Press, 1974: 42–64. An important essay that offers insights about the "Prometheus as Protestant" syndrome in *Caleb Williams* and a number of other famous texts with strong Gothic inclinations.

Rieger, James. *The Mutiny Within: The Heresies of Percy Bysshe Shelley*. New York: George Braziller, 1967. Includes a perceptive discussion of the heresies of William Godwin and their paradoxical legacy in his fiction. Important for Gothic studies in that it locates a new source of terror: the return of traditional religious guilt to haunt the freethinkers of the day.

Rizzo, Betty. "The Gothic *Caleb Williams*." *Studies on Voltaire and the Eighteenth Cen-*

tury 305 (1992): 1387–1389. Argues that Godwin uses Gothic conventions to depict "the conditions of the victims of patriarchy."

Sullivan, Garrett A., Jr. " 'A Story to Be Hastily Gobbled Up': *Caleb Williams* and Print Culture." *Studies in Romanticism* 32 (1993): 323–337. Referencing Gines's spurious pamphlet and Caleb's own industry as a writer, charts Godwin's ambiguous attitude toward the burgeoning print culture: it promises a means of genuine political scrutiny and work but might succumb to popular entertainment, that is, "a story to be hastily gobbled up."

Thompson, James. "Surveillance in William Godwin's *Caleb Williams*." In *Gothic Fictions: Prohibition/Transgression*. Ed. Kenneth W. Graham. New York: AMS Press, 1989: 173–198. Locates another interesting source of Gothic terror in the paranoia occasioned by state surveillance: "the penetration of state apparatus into the everyday life of individuals."

Watt, James. "The Loyalist Gothic Romance." In *Contesting the Gothic: Fiction, Genre, and Cultural Conflict, 1764–1832*. Cambridge: Cambridge University Press, 1999: 42–69. Reads *Imogen* in the context of *The Castle of Otranto* as a "loyalist Gothic," a celebration in the Welsh arcadia of native literary values against continental influences.

GOTHIC CHAPBOOKS, BLUEBOOKS, AND SHORT STORIES IN THE MAGAZINES
(1790–1820)

Frederick S. Frank

PRINCIPAL GOTHIC WORKS

Here follows a highly selective listing of bluebooks, chapbooks, shilling shockers, and periodical Gothics. See also all of the titles mentioned under "Modern Reprints and Editions" and "Selected Criticism." Titles listed constitute only a minute but representative sampling of shorter Gothic fiction published in the period.

Selected Signed Chapbooks and Bluebooks

Barrington, George. *Eliza; or, The Unhappy Nun*, London: Tegg & Castleman, 1803. 72 pages. (Horrifying accounts of convent incarceration derive from Denis Diderot's *La Religieuse* [The Nun, 1796] and the ordeal of Agnes in Matthew Lewis's *Monk.*)

Chamberlain, Frederic. *Lucretia; or, The Robbers of the Hyrcanean Forest*. London: J. Lee, undated. 36 pages. (A typical *Räuberroman* or robber romance. This type of Gothic derives originally from Friedrich Schiller's 1781 drama *Die Räuber* [The Robbers].)

Chapman, M. *Marleton Abbey; or, The Mystic Tomb of St. Angelo. Tell-Tale; Or, Universal Museum, Consisting of a Series of Interesting Adventures, Voyages, Histories, Lives, Tales, and Romances* 5 (1805): 912–1106. (A sample of the Gothic short tale in the magazines.)

Crookenden, Isaac. *The Story of Morella De Alto; or, The Crimes of Scorpino Developed*, London: S. Fisher, 1804. 24 pages. (Morella's story is the sexual saga of legions of menaced maidens. Scorpino kidnaps, rapes, and murders for twenty-three pages until he is stopped by the fires of the Inquisition.)

———. *Fatal Secrets; or, Etherlinda de Salmoni: A Sicilian Story*. London: J. Lee, 1806. 36 pages. (A plagiarized reduction of incidents and scenes taken from Ann Radcliffe's *Sicilian Romance* and *The Italian.*)

———. *The Mysterious Murder; or, The Usurper of Naples: An Original Romance, to*

Which Is Prefixed The Nocturnal Assassin, or Spanish Jealousy. London: J. Lee, 1806. 36 pages. (Two stories each involving incest and monastic persecution. In *The Mysterious Murder*, the heroine narrowly avoids marriage to her own father.)

————. *Horrible Revenge; or, The Monster of Italy!!* London: R. Harrild, 1808. (Extrapolates situations and characters from Lewis, Radcliffe, and Dacre and adds the brother-sister incest motif and Italianate villainy to bring the chapbook up to the publisher's thirty-six-page quota.)

————. *Romantic Tales: "The Revengeful Turk; or, Mystic Cavern"; "The Distressed Nun; or, Sufferings of Herselia di Brindoli of Florence"; "The Vindictive Monk; or, The Fatal Ring."* London: S. Fisher, undated. 46 pages. (A specimen of a Gothic sampler or anthology.)

Giberne, Charles. *Haunted Tower; or, The Adventures of Sir Egbert Rothsay*. London: R. Hunter, 1822. 72 pages. (Listed in Peter Haining's "Brief Bibliography" of bluebooks and chapbooks in *The Shilling Shockers*.)

Grosett, Emilia. *The Monastery of St. Mary; or, The White Maid of Avenel*, London: J. Bailey, undated. 36 pages. (Appears to be a plagiarized condensation of episodes from two of Sir Walter Scott's novels, *The Monastery* [1820] and *The Abbot* [1819].)

Legge, F. *The Spectre Chief; or, The Blood-stained Banner: An Ancient Romance*. London: J. Bailey, 1800. 24 pages. (*The Spectre Chief* appears in the title only, not in the tale itself. A second Gothic tale, *Baron Fitzallan*, is attached to the first story to fulfill the quota of twenty-four pages.)

Whalley, Thomas Sedgwick. *Edwy and Edilda: A Gothic Tale in Five Parts*. Dublin: S. Colbert, 1783. 174 pages. (A rare example of a short Gothic in verse. There are 174 pages of stanzaic chapters or "fitts," each containing about 200 quatrains in balladic meter.)

Wilkinson, Sarah. *The Subterraneous Passage; or, Gothic Cell*. London: Ann Lemoine, 1803. 36 pages. (The victim Antoinette and her monastic tormentor Father Anselmo are transcriptions of Antonia and Father Ambrosio in Matthew Lewis's *Monk*.)

————. *The Knights of Calatrava; or, The Days of Chivalry*, London: B. Mace, 1804. 36 pages. (Deadly fraternal rivalry interlaced with monastic fiendishness yield a run-of-the-mill chapbook.)

————. *The Sorcerer's Palace; or, The Princess of Sinadone. Tell-Tale; or, Universal Museum, Consisting of a Series of Interesting Adventures, Voyages, Histories, Lives, Tales, and Romances* 6 (1805): 43–98. (A magazine Gothic.)

————. *The Water Spectre; or, An Bratach*. London: Ann Lemoine, 1805. 36 pages. (The villain Muchardus is a crude copy of Macbeth stripped of everything save the bloodthirstiness of Shakespeare's character.)

————. *Torbolton Abbey; A Gothic Tale. New Gleaner, or Entertainment for the Fire-Side* 2 (1810): 30–41. (A magazine Gothic.)

————. *The Ruffian Boy; or, Castle of Waldemar: A Venetian Tale, on Which Is Founded the Interesting Popular Melodrama Now Performing at the Surrey Theatre Taken from Mrs. Opie's Celebrated Tale of That Name*. London: J. Bailey, undated. 36 pages. (An abridgement of Amelia Opie's Gothic melodrama with woodcuts.)

————. *The Spectres; or, Lord Oswald and Lady Rosa. Including an Account of the Marchioness of Civetti Who Was Basely Consigned to a Dungeon beneath Her Castle by Her Eldest Son, Whose Cruel Avarice Plunged Him into the Commis-*

sion of the Worst of Crimes. That Stain the Annals of the Human Race: An Original Romantic Tale. London: Langley, undated. 31 pages. (The Gothic's sub-title advertises one startling event to allure the reader.)

Unsigned and Pseudonymous Chapbooks and Bluebooks

The Abbess of St. Hilda: A Dismal, Dreadful, Horrid Story! London: J. Ker, 1800. 38 pages. (A typical monastic shocker.)

The Affecting History of Louisa, the Wandering Maniac; or, "The Lady of the Hay-Stack." London: A. Neil, 1804. 38 pages. (The chapbooker obtained the details of the wanderings of the royal exile, supposed to be the natural daughter of the German emperor, Francis I, from the correspondence of Hannah More.)

Almagro and Claude; or, Monastic Murder, Exemplified in the Dreadful Doom of an Unfortunate Nun. London: Dean & Munday, 1803. 44 pages. (A crude condensation of the Raymond and Agnes story from *The Monk*.)

The Avenger; or, The Sicilian Vespers: a Romance of the Thirteenth Century, Not Inapplicable to the Nineteenth. London: J.J. Stockdale, 1810. 72 pages. ("The demand for ghosts, necromancy, and murders," writes the anonymous chapbooker in the preface, "enables me to maintain myself, my wife, and four children.")

The Banditti of the Forest: or, The Mysterious Dagger. [signed "C."] *Lady's Monthly Museum, or Polite Repository of Amusement and Instruction* 9–10, July 1811–February 1812, (Aug. 1811): 248–267; (Sep. 1811): 311–326; (Oct. 1811): 415–434; (Nov. 1811): 563–588; (Dec. 1811): 640–661; (Jan. 1812): 697–722; (Feb. 1812): 31–50; 102–142. (A robber romance designed for the magazine trade.)

The Black Castle; or, The Spectre of the Forest. London: Dean & Munday, 1808. 72 pages. (Composite plagiarism with numerous sources, including Ann Radcliffe's *Romance of the Forest*.)

The Black Forest: or, The Cavern of Horrors. London: Ann Lemoine, 1802. 38 pages. (Several of Ann Radcliffe's novels melted down to twenty-four pages.)

The Bloody Hand; or, The Fatal Cup: A Tale of Horror! London: Stevens Circulating Library, undated. 24 pages. (A typical lurid specimen of the chapbook Gothics of the period and a plagiarized amalgamation of best-selling Gothics.)

The Castle of Lydenberg; or, The History of Raymond and Agnes, with the Story of the Bleeding Nun; and the Method by Which the Wandering Jew Quieted the Nun's Troubled Spirit. London: S. Fisher, 1798. 72 pages. (Based upon several episodes taken from *The Monk*, especially Agnes's anguish in the monastic underground.)

The Castle of Montreuil and Barre; or, The Histories of the Marquis La Brun and the Baron La Marche, the Late Inhabitants and Proprietors of the Two Castles: A Gothic Story. London: S. Fisher, 1799. 50 pages. (Appears to be a plagiarized reduction of Radcliffe's first novel, *The Castles of Athlin and Dunbayne*.)

The Castle of St. Gerald. London: J. Ker, undated. 34 pages. (Walpole's *Castle of Otranto* in thirty-four pages with embellishments taken from other Gothics.)

The Cavern of Horrors; or, Miseries of Miranda: a Neapolitan Tale. London: T. Hurst, 1802. 72 pages. (The chapbook heroine is the Radcliffean maiden writ large. A census of Miranda's miseries reveals that "she successfully negotiates eleven swoons" inside and outside the cavern.)

Clairville Castle; or, The History of Albert and Emma. London: J. Ker, undated. 38

pages. (A plagiarized imitation of Clara Reeve's *Old English Baron* mixed with Radcliffean elements. A four-page oriental tale, "Ogus and Cara Khan; or, The Force of Love," is appended to the main narrative to fill the page quota.)

The Convent of St. Ursula; or, Incidents at Ottagro. London: John Arliss, 1809. 40 pages. (Counterfeit Radcliffean romance. As the heroine approaches Count Ottagro's castle, "She had a fair view of that Gothic fabric. Up the ponderous buttresses that supported the pile, the ivy twined its fond embrace, and half-shaded the arched casements, whose heavy framework seemed of itself to half exclude the cheering light of day.")

The Convent Spectre; or, Unfortunate Daughter. London: T. & R. Hughes, 1808. 36 pages. (One of the best-preserved chapbooks in the Sadleir-Black Gothic Collection. A well-crafted imitation of Radcliffe's eerie atmosphere and effects.)

Cronstadt Castle; or, The Mysterious Visitor. London: J. Ker, 1803. 33 pages. (One story in a four-part anthology entitled *The Entertainer.* The other tales are *The Magician; or, The Mystical Adventures of Seraphina, Domestic Misery; or, The Victim of Seduction,* and *Oswick, the Bold Outlaw.*)

De La Mark and Constantia; or, Ancient Heroism: A Gothick Tale. London: Tegg & Castleman, 1803. 72 pages. (The word "Gothic" in the subtitle refers to twelfth-century England.)

Don Algonah; or, The Sorceress of Montillo. London: T. Hurst, 1802. 72 pages. (The Sadleir-Black Gothic Collection contains three variant versions of the chapbook, all seemingly by different hands.)

Edmund and Albina; or, Gothic Times. London: J. Ker, 1801. 36 pages. (A Gothified history of the sham Middle Ages.)

Fatal Vows; or, The False Monk: A Romance. London: Thomas Tegg, 1810. 28 pages. (An imitation of Lewis loosely based on *The Monk.*)

Gothic Stories: "Sir Bertrand's Adventures in a Ruinous Castle." London: S. Fisher, 1799. 72 pages. (Plagiarized reduction of the "Sir Bertrand" fragment of Anna Laetitia Aikin Barbauld.)

The Gothic Story of Courville Castle; or, The Illegitimate Son, a Victim of Prejudice and Passion. London: S. Fisher, 1804. 46 pages. (The appendage to the subtitle reads: "Owing to the early impressions inculcated with unremitting assiduity by an implacable mother, whose resentment to her husband excited her son to envy, usurpation and murder; but retributive justice at length restores the right heir to his lawful possessions to which is added 'The English Earl; or, The History of Fitzwalter.' ")

Horatio and Camilla; or, The Nuns of St. Mary. London: Ann Lemoine, 1804. 36 pages. (A monastic shocker.)

The Horrible Revenge; or, The Assassin of the Solitary Castle. London: J. Fairburn, 1828. 24 pages. (A lurid frontispiece and a garish title precede the chapbook that takes the form of a revenger's memoir.)

The Horrors of the Secluded Castle; or, Virtue Triumphant. London: T. & R. Hughes, 1807. 38 pages. (A complex imitation of Clara Reeve's *Old English Baron.*)

Lovel Castle; or, The Rightful Heir Restored: A Gothic Tale. London: Dean & Munday, 1818. 72 pages. (A plagiarized imitation of Clara Reeve's *Old English Baron.*)

Manfredi; or, The Mysterious Hermit. London: G. Stevens, 1820. 36 pages. (A sort of sequel to the fate of Walpole's Manfred after the fall of the Castle of Otranto.)

The Midnight Groan; or, The Spectre of the Chapel. London: T. & R. Hughes, 1808. 36

pages. (Based on events taken from those Gothics dealing with secret societies such as Carl Grosse's *Horrid Mysteries*.)

Midnight Horrors; or, The Bandit's Daughter. London: Dean & Munday, 1807. (A 36 page robber romance.)

The Midnight Monitor; or, Solemn Warnings from the Invisible World. London: Champante & Whitrow, undated. 40 pages. (Sold for six pence and purported to be a true account "of horrid apparitions, tall and ghastly.")

The Monk: A Romance: In Which Is Depicted the Wonderful Adventures of Ambrosio, Friar of the Order of Capuchins, Who Was Diverted from the Track of Virtue by the Artifices of a Female Demon. London: W. Mason, 1820. (Toned-down plagiarism of Lewis's novel.)

The Monk; or, Father Innocent, Abbot of Capuchins. London: Tegg & Castleman, 1803. 72 pages. (Plagiarized condensation of sensational incidents taken from *The Monk*.)

The Monks of Cluny; or, Castle-Acre Monastery. London: Ann Lemoine & J. Row, 1807. 60 pages. (Gothic only in title; otherwise, a moralizing medieval tale.)

The Mysterious Bride; or, The Statue Spectre. London: T. Hughes, 1800. (Cleverly constructed 72 page bluebook bordering on Gothic satire.)

The Mysterious Omen; or, Awful Retribution. London: J.R. Harrild, 1812. 24 pages. (Appears to be a plagiarism of Francis Lathom's *Midnight Bell*.)

The Mystery of the Black Convent: An Interesting Spanish Tale of the Eleventh Century. London: A. Neil, undated. 36 pages. (Plagiarized composite of salacious scenes from *The Monk*.)

The Mystic Tower, or, Villainy Punished. London: Kaygill, 1800. 42 pages. (Revives the terror apparatus of Walpole's *Castle of Otranto* and books like it.)

Parental Murder; or, The Brothers: An Interesting Romance in Which Virtue and Villainy Are Contrasted, and Followed by Reward and Retribution. London: T. & R. Hughes, 1807. 40 pages. (According to the bluebook's preface, the purpose is "to draw two characters who were as essentially different in principle as they were in practice.")

The Prophetic Warning; or, The Castle of Lindendorff. London: J. Ker, 1800. 38 pages. (A four-page filler story, *Rinaldo and Adeline; or, The Ghost of St. Cyril*, follows the main tale, which is a patchwork of plagiarized Gothic names and events.)

The Recluse of the Woods; or, The Generous Warrior: a Gothic Romance. London: Ann Lemoine, 1809. 36 pages. (A thinly disguised imitation of Clara Reeve's *Old English Baron* priced at four pence.)

The Secret Oath; or, The Blood-stained Dagger. London: T. Hurst, 1802. 72 pages. (Typical shilling shocker dealing with secret societies.)

Shrewtzer Castle; or, The Perfidious Brother: a German Romance, Including the Pathetic Tale of Edmund's Ghost. London: A. Neil, 1802. 72 pages. (Sham translation from the German.)

A Tale of Mystery; or, The Castle of Solitude. Containing the Dreadful Imprisonment of Count L. and the Countess Harmina, His Lady. London: Thomas Tegg, 1803. 72 pages. (Except for the epigraph from *Hamlet*, "I could a tale unfold whose lightest word would harrow up thy soul," an almost incoherent chapbook.)

Theodore and Emma; or, The Italian Bandit, in Which the Fatal Effects of Revenge Are Portrayed in the Character of Marquis De Rovigno, Who, Disappointed at the Preference Given to the Count De Valenza by the Daughter of the Duke of Parma,

Enrolls Himself in the Company of Daring Banditti, in Order to Accomplish His Diabolical Scheme of Assassinating the Count, Waldemar, Who, in the Engagement with Theodore, Accidentally Kills His Own Father! Also, the Melancholy Catastrophe Which Attends the Counts De Valenza and Ravenna, in the Deaths of Theodore and Emma. London: J. Bailey, 1800. 72 pages. (The anonymous chapbooker signed the work as "an Etonian.")

The Three Ghosts of the Forest, a Tale of Horror: An Original Romance. London: J. Ker, 1803. 36 pages. (Routine Radcliffean Gothic. The use of the word "original" in the subtitle was not to be taken seriously.)

The Tomb of Aurora; or, The Mysterious Summons. London: Ann Lemoine, 1807. 48 pages. (The name of the main character, Marquis de Verezzi, was later used by Percy Shelley in *Zastrozzi*. Attached to the main story is "The Prisoner; or, The Fortress of Howlitz: A German Tale.")

The Wandering Spirit; or, Memoirs of the House of Morno. London; T. Hurst, 1802. 72 pages. (The Sadleir-Black Collection contains two variant versions of the chapbook, one a possible plagiarism of the other.)

Wolfstein; or, The Mysterious Bandit: a Terrific Romance; To Which Is Added, The Bronze Statue: A Pathetic Tale. London: J. Bailey, undated. 38 pages. (Both Percy and Mary Shelley were well acquainted with the chapbook and bluebook aspects of Gothicism. The name of the young hero in one of Percy Shelley's earliest works, *St. Irvyne; or, The Rosicrucian*, is Wolfstein. Shelley launched his writing career by authoring two Gothic novels, *St. Irvyne* and *Zastrozzi*, both clearly of bluebook quality and content.)

MODERN REPRINTS AND EDITIONS

The Candle and the Tower. Ed. Robert D. Spector. New York: Warner, 1974. (This anthology of Gothic tales, short stories, fragments, romances, and novellas offers thirteen typical selections extracted from periodicals and annuals. Reprinted are *Edeliza: A Gothic Tale*, signed "E.W." and first published in *Lady's Magazine* 33 [1802]: 476–484; *The Clock Has Struck!!!* by William Farrow, first published in *Lady's Magazine* 40 [1809]: 402–407; *The Castle of Constanzo*, unsigned and first published in *Universal Magazine of Knowledge and Pleasure* 75 [1784]: 74–77; *The Friar's Tale* by Anna Seward, first published in *Variety: a Collection of Essays, Written in the Year 1787*, then republished in *Hibernian* [1788]: 396–399, 475–476; *Rodriguez and Isabella; or, The Terrors of Conscience: A Tale*, unsigned and published in *Lady's Magazine* 39 [1808]: 51–53; *Retribution: A Tale Founded on Facts* by Thomas Bellamy, first published in The *Monthly Mirror*, 2 [1796]: 340–343, 407–410, 465–473; *Sir Bertrand: A Fragment* by Anna Laetitia Barbauld, first published in *Miscellaneous Pieces in Prose by J. and A.L. Aiken* [1773]: 119–137; *Henry Fitzowen* by Nathan Drake, first published in The *Speculator* 1 [1790]: 119–148 under the title *Sir Gawen*, then retitled and reprinted as *Henry Fitzowen* in Drake's *Literary Hours* [1798]; *Raymond; A Fragment*, signed "Juvenis" and first published in *Lady's Magazine* 30 [1799]: 57–59; *The Nun*, signed "S.P." and first published in *European Magazine* 25 [1794]: 337–342, 425–429; *The Cave of St. Sidwell: a Romance*, signed "E.F." and first published in two installments in *Lady's Monthly Museum* 2 [1807]: 26, 31, 80–

88, 171–176, 218–222; 3 [1807]: 34–39, 55–57; *Schrabraco, A Romance*, unsigned and first published in *Lady's Monthly Museum* 1 [1798]: 85–93, 179–185,
263–274, 362–372; and *The Castle De Warrenne: A Romance*, unsigned and first
published in *Lady's Monthly Museum* 5 [1800]: 17–34, 97–116, 181–197, 265–
285, 349–359, 433–443. Of these various Gothic types, Spector observes: "By
far the most satisfying form of Gothic in the magazines is the romance or novella.
Like the novel itself, this form uses fictional rhythm to build gradually an em-
pathetic response to the Gothic world.")

The Demon of Venice: An Original Romance, by a Lady. "Appendix D" to *Zofloya; or,
The Moor: A Romance of the Fifteenth Century* by Charlotte Dacre. Ed. Adriana
Craciun. Peterborough Ontario: Broadview Press, 1997. (A reprint of the anon-
ymous chapbook version of *Zofloya* published by Thomas Tegg in 1810.)

Gothic Readings: The First Wave, 1764–1840. Ed. Rictor Norton. London and New
York: Leicester University Press, 2000. (Contains excerpts from the following
chapbooks: Victor Jules Sarret, *Koenigsmark the Robber; or, The Terror of
Bohemia* [London: Tegg & Castleman, n.d.]; unsigned, *The Midnight Groan; or,
The Spectre of the Chapel, Involving an Exposure of the Horrible Secrets of the
Nocturnal Assembly: A Gothic Romance* [London: T. & R. Hughes, 1808]).

*Gothic Tales of Terror: Classic Stories from Great Britain, Europe, and the United
States, 1765–1840*. Ed. Peter Haining. New York: Taplinger, 1972. (Contains
"The Monk of Horror; or, The Conclave of Corpses" taken from *Tales of the
Crypt—in the Style of The Monk* [1798] and "The Black Spider" [London, 1798],
two anonymous short Gothics with eye-catching titles.)

The Oxford Book of Gothic Tales. Ed. Chris Baldick. Oxford and New York: Oxford
University Press, 1992. (Contains the following anonymous Gothic tales: "The
Friar's Tale"; "Raymond: A Fragment"; "The Parricide Punished"; "The Ruins
of the Abbey of Fitzmartin"; and "The Astrologer's Prediction; or, The Maniac's
Fate"; and one signed short Gothic, "The Vindictive Monk; or, The Fatal Ring"
by Isaac Crookenden.)

The Shilling Shockers: Stories of Terror from the Gothic Bluebooks. Ed. Peter Haining.
New York: St. Martin's Press, 1979. (The anthology contains four signed and six
unsigned shilling-shocker titles: "The Vindictive Monk; or, The Fatal Ring" by
Isaac Crookenden; "The Mysterious Novice; or, The Convent of the Grey Penitents" by Sarah Wilkinson; "Captive of the Banditti: A Terrific Tale Concluded"
by Dr. Nathan Drake and "Others," A.N. These unsigned Tales: "The Spectre
Mother; or, The Haunted Tower"; "The Life and Horrid Adventures of the Cel-
ebrated Dr. Faustus"; "The Old Tower of Frankenstein"; "The Bride of the Isles:
A Tale Founded on the Popular Legend of the Vampire"; "The Lunatic and His
Turkey: A Tale of Witchcraft"; "The Severed Arm; or, The Wehr-wolf of Lim-
ousin"; and "Five Hundred Years Hence!" by "D." Also has selected engravings.
Reprinted as *Tales from the Gothic Bluebooks* [Chislehurst, Kent, UK: Gothic
Society at the Gargoyle's Head Press, 1995].)

In the late 1790s, hordes of short Gothics, mainly plagiarized abridgements,
reductions, and condensations of the leading Gothic authors, inundated the bookstalls and cheap printing shops. These chapbooks and bluebooks generally sold
for a shilling or less and were designed to be read just once, then thrown away

or handed on to the next impoverished reader. Since plagiarism was rampant, most of the titles were pseudonymous or anonymous, although a few of the shilling shockers are signed or initialed. Almost invariably, each shilling shocker proved to contain a recycled plot pilfered with little or no alteration except for character names from episodes taken from *The Monk* and Ann Radcliffe's romances, then reduced to sensational or gory essentials to satisfy the twenty-four-, thirty-six-, or seventy-two-page quota of horror prescribed by the publisher. Of the ephemeral shelf life and death of these diminutive Gothics, Montague Summers has written: "The Gothic chapbook passed from hand to hand and was literally read to pieces. Even if a virgin copy or two by some chance survived, they would not have been for a moment deemed worthy of the bookshelf, or even of a cardboard cover. They were thrown out contemptuously. So what were thought rubbish by our grandmothers have become unique treasures today, a thing which is no new phenomenon in the annals of bibliography" (*The Gothic Quest* 85).

After the marketplace successes of Matthew Lewis's *Monk* and Radcliffe's *Mysteries of Udolpho* and *The Italian*, the mass production of cheap Gothic imitations became a full-time profitable industry aimed at gratifying a growing and changing Gothic readership. The handsomely bound and relatively expensive Gothic novels published by William Lane's Minerva Press, the leading distributor of double- and triple-volume Gothics, continued to maintain a wide audience, but a new kind of Gothic reader with little patience for serpentine plots and sluggish terrors created a huge market for the short shocker. Nor were most of these new readers even aware of the achievements of Walpole, Beckford, Reeve, Radcliffe, and Lewis in the Gothic field, and thus they were oblivious to the fact that what was being bought for sixpence and read for an hour was probably a pirated distillation of a longer Gothic. When Wordsworth complained in the Preface to the *Lyrical Ballads* (1798) about swarms of "frantic novels" that crudely pandered to the "degrading thirst after outrageous stimulation," his disgust was clearly meant as a critique of the debasement of taste caused by the proliferation of the little Gothics.

Small London publishing houses such as S. Fisher of St. John Lane, John Arliss of Bartholomew Close, and Ann Lemoine of White Rose Court, book dealers that were often little more than printing shops, churned out these primitive paperbacks in bulk quantities, a fact that tells us a great deal about the minimal needs and insatiable demands of a new proletarian readership for things horrid at the close of the eighteenth century. Certainly the most enterprising entrepreneur of shilling shockers was the publisher Thomas Tegg of Cheapside, known in publishing circles as "the lord of the remainder trade." Shilling shockers by Tegg could be expected to feature a macabre and stentorian two-part title (e.g., *A Tale of Mystery; or, The Castle of Solitude, Containing the Dreadful Imprisonment of Count L. and the Countess Harmina, His Lady*) accompanied by a lurid frontispiece woodcut or engraving, de rigueur in the chapbook trade. However, a fearsome woodcut on a frontispiece or a bloodcurdling engraving on a title page did not necessarily guarantee that the event depicted would occur in the chapbook's text. It was the engraver's task to select the most crepuscular or sensational supernatural scene or episode from the chapbook's text, then pictorialize it to entice the prospective consumer. If no suitable horrific event could be located, the artist then fabricated his own without regard to plot.

The physical appearance of the chapbooks and bluebooks is itself of interest to those drawn to the popular and pulpish underside of the Gothic movement. According to William Whyte Watt, one of the few modern scholars who have bothered to study and catalog this neglected phenomenon of popular Gothicism, these pocket-size Gothics "were about four by seven inches in size, and their closely printed pages were poorly stitched into a cover of flimsy blue paper" (11). Their cheap production explains why the Gothic chapbooks and bluebooks are so rare even in special collections today. The bluebooks tend to be somewhat longer than the chapbooks and perhaps a bit more substantially glued together. Both types of short Gothic always lack board bindings and are given to falling apart because of flimsiness and the low quality of the paper. As the disposable rubbish of a subliterate body of literature, the shilling shockers came to be regarded as the toxic literary waste of the Gothic period. Unwanted by collectors and uncollected in their prime, shilling-shocker chapbooks remain the most un-collectible and elusive of all Gothic artifacts. No autonomous collection of the shorter Gothic exists, but the most extensive array of short Gothics in any library collection is to be found in the archives of the Sadleir-Black Gothic Collection in the Alderman Library at the University of Virginia. The number and variety of short Gothics in the collection indicate acute shifts in the tastes and expec-tations of the large and quirkish Gothic readership at the midpoint of high Goth-icism (circa 1800). With their phantasmic engravings, they reflect the crassly promotional group style of this branch of Gothicism, but their crudity does not diminish their historical value for serious students of the Gothic period. As Lord Ernle urged in *The Light Reading of Our Ancestors*, the best means of knowing the history of a literary period as thoroughly as possible is to probe beneath the surviving or official classics of that period to what people were actually reading, a theory of taste demonstrated ad nauseam by the chapbook segment of the Sadleir-Black Collection.

Watt also identified certain subtypes of shilling shocker, referring to the many chapbook versions of Lewis's *The Monk* as "monastic shockers" and suggesting that many chapbookers specialized in this kind of Gothic because of its ease of forged reproduction and sales appeal. Watt summarizes the contents of the typ-ical monastic shocker as follows:

The setting of the "monastic shocker" generally included a convent for the imprisonment of a disobedient heroine, which should have: one cell for solitary confinement; one underground vault for slow starvation; one large nave for taking the veil and for funerals, with a window through which the melancholy hero could view the sad procedure; one "dismal" bell to ring upon such occasions to inform approaching relatives of the nun's fate; a congregation of nuns to stand about looking pale and chanting "Nunc Dimittis" and "De Profundis"; and a generous assortment of Madonnas, crucifixes, coarse food, and human skulls and bones, preferably female. (22)

Similar in length, episodic brevity, and literary quality to the chapbooks were the many Gothic tales appearing in annuals, keepsakes, and monthlies where the same formula that had rendered the monastic shocker a favorite with the chapbook audience was applied to periodical Gothics. Although periodical Gothics could occasionally demonstrate originality and artistic craftsmanship, for the most part they were counterfeit versions of the work of Radcliffe and Lewis, sometimes reworked from the chapbook versions of these romances, making forgeries of forgeries a relatively common feature of magazine Gothics. Upon inspection, the 30,000-word Gothic story *The Midnight Assassin; or, Confessions of the Monk Rinaldi* that appeared in *Marvellous Magazine and Compendium of Prodigies* for May 1802 is a bare-bones version of Radcliffe's *Italian* refurbished from several possible chapbook reductions of that work. Because Gothic climaxes and melodramatic horrors suited the abortive conditions of serialization, the horror story in the periodicals often crept along through several numbers until the characters, as Watt observes, "were brought to the altar or the grave" within the prescribed page limits. The pseudonymous "E.F." 's Gothic novelette *The Cave of St. Sidwell* filled six installments of *Lady's Monthly Museum* in 1807 following the pattern of the unsigned novella *The Castle De Warrenne*, which had appeared in the same periodical in serialized form in 1800. The appeal of the Gothic tale in the periodicals, as Robert D. Spector points out, rests in part on magazine Gothicism's advantage of brevity over the "prohibitively lengthy" (Introduction, *The Candle and the Tower*, 10) Gothic novels that frequently served as sources for these short works. The bulk of periodical Gothics were "clumsy and amateurish, but all of it attested to a reader delight in material that critical taste abhorred" (10).

Chapbookers, bluebookers, and periodical Gothicists preferred not to sign their work to avoid justifiable charges of plagiarism. While anonymity and unscrupulous imitation were the standards, a few authors did use signatures, and a handful of chapbookers actually achieved originality and artistic merit. The names of Isaac Crookenden and Sarah Wilkinson, appearing frequently as they do on chapbook title pages, suggest that these authors pursued lucrative careers of Gothic counterfeiting and were household names that the Gothic public sought out for their special aptitude at thrills and chills. Wilkinson is a fascinating example of a Gothic author who excelled in both the tawdry chapbook arena and the writing of full-length Gothic romances. Her prolific pen oozed every shade of blood from the subtle and muted terror of the Radcliffean school to the unremitting gore and supernatural extravagance of Lewisite horror. In his *Gothic Bibliography*, Montague Summers itemizes eighteen titles by Sarah Wilkinson, including bluebooks and chapbooks, sentimental and historical Gothics, and a conversion of Lewis's Gothic drama *The Castle Spectre* into a successful Gothic novelette.

Even an approximate number of bluebooks and chapbooks published between 1795 and 1820 cannot be confidently conjectured because of the transitory nature of these little Gothics, but if the Gothic activity of Crookenden and Wilkinson may be cited as typical, then an educated guess would place the figure in the 10,000s. Their availability today is due to the searches and researches of a few zealous anthologists such as Peter Haining who have managed to cast some light into one of Gothicism's darkest scholarly closets. Two of Peter Haining's anthologies are dedicated exclusively to this type of Gothic fiction. His pursuit of the Gothic chapbooks has persuaded Haining of their special role as a body of surviving evidence for understanding the Gothic phenomenon at its popular apex:

My research has not only unearthed some important and clearly original material in these publications, but increased a long-held conviction that they are the seeds from which the modern horror short story flowered. Certainly during my study of the "golden years" of the "shilling shockers" I have been able to locate a number of items which considerably extend our knowledge and our appreciation of the genre. One of these discoveries, the recovery of one of the innumerable Thomas Tegg chapbooks, is the anonymous tale of terror "The Old Tower of Frankenstein," the probable source for the naming in Mary Shelley's *Frankenstein*. (*The Shilling Shockers* 123)

The first great collector of chapbooks and bluebooks, Michael Sadleir, located and identified many of these disposable Gothics while assembling the collection that would bear his name. While Sadleir was sorting and classifying his collection, he had the good sense not to "purify" it by jettisoning the many bluebooks and chapbooks he had acquired. Of the 1,135 titles in the Sadleir-Black Gothic Collection, approximately 200 titles definitely fall into the bluebook/chapbook category. As one of the first proponents of Gothic studies and defenders of the historical importance of the genre, Sadleir realized the central role that such short and shabby Gothic fiction had played in the rise of Romanticism and the extension of Gothicism into the Victorian age. Modern Gothic scholarship is indebted to the scholarly ardor of Haining and Sadleir in providing the database for further discoveries in the unique influence of chapbook Gothicism on the Gothic movement as a whole.

SELECTED CRITICISM

Baldick, Chris. "The End of the Line: The Family Curse in Shorter Gothic Fiction." In *Exhibited by Candlelight: Sources and Developments in the Gothic Tradition*. Ed. Valeria Tinkler-Villani, Peter Davidson, and Jane Stevenson. Amsterdam and Atlanta, GA: Rodopi, 1995: 147–157. "The shilling shocker, which flourished in the popular market in the first two decades of the nineteenth century, was parasitic upon the Gothic novel in the more obvious mode of plagiarism."

Frank, Frederick S. "The Gothic Romance, 1762–1820." In *Horror Literature: A Core Collection and Reference Guide*. Ed. Marshall B. Tymn. New York: R.R. Bowker, 1981: 3–175. Includes commentaries on the following bluebooks and chapbooks: *Almagro and Claude; or, Monastic Murder, Exemplified in the Dreadful Doom of an Unfortunate Nun* (1803); C.F. Barrett, *Douglas Castle; or, The Cell of Mystery: A Scottish Tale* (1803); C.F. Barrett, *The Round Tower; or, The Mysterious Witness: An Irish Legendary Tale of the Sixth Century* (1803); *The Black Valley; or, The Castle of Rosenberg* (1803); *The Bloody Hand; or, The Fatal Cup: A Tale of Horror!* (undated); Isaac Crookenden, *The Skeleton; or, Mysterious Discovery* (1805); Isaac Crookenden, *Horrible Revenge; or, The Monster of Italy!!* (1808); Isaac Crookenden, *The Spectre of the Turret; or, Guolto Castle* (undated); *De La Mark and Constantia; or, Ancient Heroism: A Gothick Tale* (1803); *Durston Castle; or, The Ghost of Eleonora: A Gothic Story; Gothic Stories: "The Enchanted Castle; A Fragment"; "Ethelbert; or, The Phantom of the Castle"; "The Mysterious Vision; or, Perfidy Punished"* (1801); F. Legge, *The Spectre Chief; or, The Blood-stained Banner: An Ancient Romance* (1800); *Lovel Castle; or, The Rightful Heir Restored: A Gothic Tale* (1818); *The Midnight Groan; or, The Spectre of the Chapel, Involving an Exposure of the Horrible Secrets of the Nocturnal Assembly: A Gothic Romance* (1808); *The Midnight Monitor; or, Solemn Warnings from the Invisible World* (undated); *The Mystic Tower; or, Villainy Punished* (undated); *The Prophetic Warning; or, The Castle of Lindendorff* (1800); *The Recluse of the Woods; or, The Generous Warrior: A Gothic Romance* (1809); *Shrewtzer Castle; or, The Perfidious Brother: A German Romance, Including the Pathetic Tale of Edmund's Ghost* (1802); *The Spectre Mother; or, The Haunted Tower* (1800); Alexander Thompson, *The Three Ghosts of the Forest: A Tale of Horror* (1803); *The Wandering Spirit; or, The Memoirs of the House of Morno* (1802); Lucy Watkins, *Romano Castle; or, The Horrors of the Forest* (undated); Thomas Sedgwick Whalley, *Edwy and Edilda: A Gothic Tale in Five Parts* (1783); Sarah Wilkinson, *The Castle Spectre; or, Family Horrors: A Gothic Story* (1807); Sarah Wilkinson, *The Castle of Montabino; or, The Orphan Sisters* (1810); and *Wolfstein; or, The Mysterious Bandit: A Terrific Romance; To Which Is Added, The Bronze Statue: A Pathetic Tale* (n.d.). Most of these titles and others are also critically summarized in *The First Gothics*.

————. *The First Gothics: A Critical Guide to the English Gothic Novel*. New York: Garland, 1987. Includes critical synopses of many shilling shockers and Gothic bluebooks among the 500 annotated books, most of these titles reposing in the Sadleir-Black Gothic Collection at the University of Virginia. See the section "Principal Gothic Works" for a representative inventory of titles in the Sadleir-Black Gothic Collection. See also the chapbook and bluebook titles listed under Frederick S. Frank, "The Gothic Romance, 1762–1820," *Horror Literature: A Core Collection and Reference Guide*.

————. "Illustrations from the Early Gothic Novels." In *Gothic Fictions: Prohibition/ Transgression*. Ed. Kenneth W. Graham. New York: AMS Press, 1989: 270–287. Presents nine engravings from the Gothic chapbooks with commentaries on each. Anonymous chapbooks: *Somerset Castle; or, The Father and Daughter* (1804); *The Southern Tower; or, Conjugal Sacrifice and Retribution* (1802); *The Gothic Story of Courville Castle; or, The Illegitimate Son* (1804); and *Lewis Tyrell; or, The Depraved Count* (1804); and these signed chapbooks: *Douglas Castle; or,*

> *The Cell of Mystery* (1803) by C.F. Barrett; *The Round Tower; or, The Mysterious Witness: An Irish Legendary Tale of the Sixth Century* (1803) by C.F. Barrett; *Romano Castle; or, The Horrors of the Forest* (undated) by Lucy Watkins; *The Spectre of the Turret; or, Guolto Castle* (undated) by Isaac Crookenden; and *Monkcliffe Abbey: A Tale of the Fifteenth Century* (1805) by Sarah Wilkinson.

————. "Gothic Gold: The Sadleir-Black Gothic Collection." *Studies in Eighteenth-Century Culture* 26 (1998): 287–312. Comments on the chapbook and bluebook holdings in the premier collection of early Gothic literature in the world. Has nine engravings and woodcuts with commentaries taken from the following chapbooks: *The Round Tower; or, The Mysterious Witness: an Irish Legendary Tale of the Sixth Century* (1803) by C.F. Barrett; *The Skeleton; or, Mysterious Discovery: A Gothic Romance* (1805) by Isaac Crookenden; *Romano Castle; or, The Horrors of the Forest* (undated) by Lucy Watkins; *The Castle of Montabino; or, The Orphan Sisters* (1810) by Sarah Wilkinson; *Zittaw the Cruel; or, The Woodsman's Daughter: A Polish Romance* (undated) and unsigned; *Ildefonzo and Alberoni; or, Tales of Horror* (1803), unsigned; *Maximilian and Selina; or, The Mysterious Abbot: A Flemish Tale* (1804), unsigned; *The Midnight Assassin; or, The Confession of the Monk Rinaldi* (1802), unsigned; and *The Secret Tribunal; or, The Court of Winceslaus* (1803), unsigned.

Haining, Peter. Introduction to *The Shilling Shockers: Stories of Terror from the Gothic Bluebooks*, New York: St. Martin's Press, 1979: 13–19. Sees the thirty-six- and seventy-two-page little Gothics as "the seeds from which the modern horror story flowered." The ten shilling shockers anthologized by Haining also demonstrate their literary value as "a bridge between the lengthy Gothic novels and the short story of terror." Presents a brief bibliography of shilling shockers containing fifty-two titles.

Hall, Daniel. "The Gothic Tide: Schauerroman and Gothic Novel in the Late Eighteenth Century: Papers from the Conference Held at the University of Leeds from 15 to 17 September, 1997." In *The Novel in Anglo-German Context: Cultural Cross-Currents and Affinities*. Ed. Susanne Stark. Amsterdam: Rodopi, 2000; 51–60. Comments on the importation of German horrid titles and shudder novels.

Jacobs, Edward. "Anonymous Signatures: Circulating Libraries, Conventionality, and the Production of Gothic Romances." *ELH* 62 (1995): 603–629. Drawing evidence from the book catalogs of the publishers Thomas Lowndes and Heavisides, shows statistically how and how many "definitive texts of the gothic genre were published almost exclusively by circulating library publishers. By supporting the novelistic construction of female writing as reproductive, yet at the same time developing new, alternative kinds of fiction such as Gothic romances, circulating-library publishers demonstrated that reproductivity could both perpetuate hegemonic 'models' and turn singular 'departures' from hegemonic values into full-fledged sub-cultures."

Mayo, Robert D. "The Gothic Story in the Magazines." *Modern Language Review* 37 (1942): 448–454. Chronicles the phenomenon of the short Gothics in such periodicals as *Blackwood's Magazine*. "By 1810 the Gothic story was a well defined and familiar species of fiction. One scene dissolves swiftly into another in a sequence where the only law is suspense, wonder, strangeness, and fear."

————. "Gothic Romance in the Magazines." *Publications of the Modern Language Association*, 65 (1950): 762–789. An exhaustive inventory of Gothic short-story writing in the magazines from 1770 to 1820. "Although plagiarism was rampant and although this is a definite feature of Gothic romance in the magazines, it is not the most interesting one."

Pitcher, E.W. "Changes in Short Fiction in Britain, 1785–1810: Philosophic Tales, Gothic Tales, and Fragments and Visions." *Studies in Short Fiction* 13 (1976): 331–354. Discusses innovations in the abridged Gothic tale in the period and cites typical shilling-shocker examples such as *The Three Ghosts of the Forest: A Tale of Horror* (London: J. Ker & Hughes, 1803).

———. "*Frankenstein* as Short Fiction: A Unique Adaptation of Mary Shelley's Novel." *Studies in Short Fiction* 20 (1983): 49–52. Comments on a periodical condensation of the novel, *The Monster Made by Man; or, The Punishment of Presumption*, appearing anonymously in *Endless Entertainments; or, Comic, Terrific, and Legendary Tales* (1826).

———. "Eighteenth-Century Gothic Fragments and the Paradigm of Violation and Repair." *Studies in Short Fiction* 33 (1996): 35–42. Comments on "Raymond: A Fragment" (1799).

Redden, Sister Mary Maurita. *The Gothic Fiction in the American Magazines (1765–1800)*. Washington, DC: Catholic University of America Press, 1939. Surveys the addiction of American readers to the periodical Gothics and provides a chronological record.

Summers, Montague. "The Publishers and the Circulating Libraries." In *The Gothic Quest: A History of the Gothic Novel* (1938). New York: Russell & Russell, 1964: 60–105. In the chapter, Summers describes the physical appearance, pricing, and marketing of the bluebooks and chapbooks, accompanying his commentary with dozens of titles.

———. *A Gothic Bibliography* (1941). New York: Russell & Russell, 1964. Buried in Summers's unsegregated and uncategorized lists of Gothics are many chapbooks and bluebooks.

Tracy, Ann B. *The Gothic Novel, 1790–1830: Plot Summaries and Index to Motifs*. Lexington: University Press of Kentucky, 1981. Summarizes the contents of several chapbooks and bluebooks in the Sadleir-Black Gothic Collection. "I have included a few chapbooks, especially a selection from Isaac Crookenden and Sarah Wilkinson. These outrageous little stories are part of the Gothic phenomenon and may be useful to someone wishing to acquire an overall view."

Watt, William Whyte. *Shilling Shockers of the Gothic School: A Study of Chapbook Gothic Romances* (1932). New York: Russell & Russell, 1967. Watt's fifty-four-page monograph remains the best scholarly study of the Gothic chapbooks. Deals wittily and sympathetically with these miniature Gothics and plagiarized condensations of long Gothic novels. "In their brevity alone the shilling shockers form an important step between the long Gothic novels and the more plausible short stories of terror."

GOTHIC DRAMA
(1768–1830)
Frederick S. Frank

PRINCIPAL GOTHIC WORKS

Additional Gothic dramas of the period in their surviving original scripts and actors' copies may be found in the Larpent Collection of Eighteenth Century Drama, Huntington Library, San Marino, California.

Signed Gothic Plays

Andrews, Miles Peter. *The Enchanted Castle*. 1786. (First acted at Covent Garden, December 1786. Larpent Collection 752.)

————. *The Mysteries of the Castle*. London: T.N. Longman, 1795. (First acted at Covent Garden, January 1795). Larpent Collection 1054. Drama based on incidents adapted loosely from Radcliffe's *Mysteries of Udolpho*. According to Bertrand Evans, "His combination of comedy and terror pointed out a new direction for Gothic drama, a direction which would widen the distance between it and the Gothic novel" (114).

Baillie, Joanna. *De Monfort*. 1800. (First acted at Drury Lane, April 1800. Larpent Collection 1287. Gothic drama important for its revised portrayal of the menaced maiden of Gothic fiction.)

Barnett, C.Z. *The Phantom Bride; or, The Castilian Bandit*. 1820. (First acted at the Royal Pavilion, 1820.)

Birch, Samuel. *The Black Forest*. 1798. (First acted at Covent Garden, December 1798. Larpent Collection 1236. Makes use of German Gothic motifs such as the Schwarzwald or Black Forest of the title.)

Boaden, James. *Fontainville Forest*. London: Hookham & Carpenter, 1794. (First acted at Covent Garden, March 1794. Larpent Collection 1014. Dramatic condensation of Ann Radcliffe's *Romance of the Forest*. The play's success encouraged Boaden to adapt other Radcliffe novels to the stage.)

————. *The Secret Tribunal*. 1795. (First acted at Covent Garden, June 1795. Larpent Collection 1085. Derives its terror from the popular Gothic subject of the Vehmgericht or secret Fehmic court.)

————. *The Italian Monk*. London: G.G. & J. Robinson, 1797. (First acted at the Haymarket, August 1797. A moralized dramatic version of Radcliffe's *Italian*. Father Schedoni repents on stage.)

Byron, George Gordon, Lord. *Manfred: A Dramatic Poem*. 1817. (Byron's dramatic poem features a version of the Gothic hero-villain whose character is "an awful chaos—light and darkness, and mind and dust, and passions and pure thoughts, mix'd and contending without end or order.")

Carr, George Charles. *St. Margaret's Cave*. 1804. (Larpent Collection 1432.)

————. *The Towers of Urbandine*. 1805. (Larpent Collection 1467. A stupendous Gothic melodrama featuring four villains and six interlocking victimization plots set in a devastated abbey, a haunted castle, a menacing convent, a slimy cavern, and a "bosky" forest.)

Cobb, James. *The Haunted Tower*. 1789. (First acted at Drury Lane, November 1789. Larpent Collection 850. Operatic spoof of one of the Gothic's central sites, the forbidden chamber within a haunted tower.)

Colman, George, the younger. *The Iron Chest*. 1796. (First acted at Drury Lane, March 1796. Larpent Collection 1116. A dramatic adaptation of William Godwin's *Caleb Williams*. One of the novel's Gothic objects, Falkland's secret box, furnishes the play's title.)

Crowley, Hannah. *Albina, Countess of Raimond*. 1779. (First acted at the Haymarket, July 1779. Larpent Collection 486.)

Cumberland, Richard. *The Carmelite*. 1784. (First acted at Covent Garden, December 1784. Larpent Collection 674. Early Gothic play combining mystery with a spectacular dénouement. Cumberland devised a highly spectacular scene for the final unveiling of all secrets.)

Dibdin, Thomas John. *The Forest of Hermanstadt; or, A Princess and No Princess*. 1808. (First acted at Covent Garden, October 1808. Larpent Collection 1556.)

Goldsmith, Mary. *Angelina; or, Wolcot Castle*, 1804. (Larpent Collection 1431.)

Grosette, Henry William. *Raymond and Agnes; or, The Bleeding Nun of Lindenberg*. 1797. (First acted at Covent Garden, June 1797. Larpent Collection 1597. Stages one of the more gruesome episodes of *The Monk*, the bleeding nun's visit to Raymond's bedside.)

Hartson, Hall. *The Countess of Salisbury*. London: J. Bell, 1763. (A dramatic adaptation of Thomas Leland's *Longsword, Earl of Salisbury*. Act 1 features "An Avenue Leading to a Gothic Castle" where much of the action occurs.)

Hiffernan, Paul. *The Heroine of the Cave*. 1775. (First acted at Drury Lane, March 1775. Larpent Collection 368. Early Gothic play that mixes tears with terror in a familiar Gothic setting.)

Holcroft, Thomas. *The Inquisitor*. 1798. (First acted at the Haymarket, June 1798. Larpent Collection 1220. A theatrical exposé of the dreadful doings of the Inquisition. The Inquisitor's character is modeled on Radcliffe's Father Schedoni in *The Italian*.)

————. *A Tale of Mystery*. 1802. Larpent Collection 1246. (First acted at Covent Garden, November 1802. Stentorian melodrama based on René Charles Guilbert de Pixérécourt's *Coelina; ou, L'Enfant du mystère*.)

Home, John. *The Fatal Discovery*. London: T. Becket & P.A. De Hondt, 1769. (Has cavern scenes and other Gothic environments.)

Hull, Thomas. *Henry II or, The Fall of Rosamond: A Tragedy*. London: C. G. May, 1773. (Larpent Collection 352).

Jephson, Robert. *The Count of Narbonne*. 1781. (First acted at Covent Garden, November 1781. Larpent Collection 575. Commercially successful dramatization of Walpole's *Castle of Otranto*. The play received Walpole's imprimatur and assistance in production. Jephson eliminated most of the supernatural apparatus.)

Kemble, Stephen. *The Castle of Otranto*. 1793. (Larpent Collection 995. Gadget-driven stage version of various supernatural scenes in Walpole's *Castle of Otranto*.)

Kerr, John Atkinson. *The Wandering Boys; or, The Castle of Olival*. 1814. (First acted at Covent Garden, February 1814. Larpent Collection 1801.)

———. *The Monster and Magician; or, The Fate of Frankenstein*. 1826.

Lawler, Dennis. *The Earls of Hammersmith; or, The Cellar Spectre*. 1814. (First acted at the Olympic, January 1814. Larpent Collection 1799. Gothic burlesque and spoof on the resident specter character.)

Lewis, Matthew Gregory. *The Castle Spectre*. London: J. Bell, 1798. (First acted at Drury Lane, December 1797. Larpent Collection 1187. Described by Jeffrey Cox as "the quintessential Gothic drama. . . . It demonstrated that the Gothic could draw vast audiences, that it could touch upon revolutionary themes, and that it could bridge the gap between popular dramatic fare and 'high' literature." Introduction *Seven Gothic Dramas* 40.)

———. *Adelmorn, the Outlaw*. 1801. (First acted at Drury Lane, May 1801. Larpent Collection 1319. Described by Bertrand Evans as "a link—and a particularly valuable one—between the crude and monstrous elements of the Gothic school and the finer Romantic ones of Shelley's *Prometheus Unbound* and Byron's *Manfred*.") (146)

———. *The Captive: A Monodrama or Tragic Scene*. 1803. (Larpent Collection 1374.)

———. *Rugantino; or, The Bravo of Venice*. 1805. (First acted at Covent Garden, 1805. Larpent Collection 1459.)

———. *The Wood Daemon; or, The Clock Has Struck*. 1807. (First acted at Drury Lane, April 1807. Larpent Collection 1514. Flashes of brilliance earned Lewis's Gothic melodrama a permanent place in the annals of Gothic theater. Frequently performed throughout the nineteenth century.)

———. *Venoni; or, The Novice of St. Mark's*. 1808. (First acted at Drury Lane, December 1808. Larpent Collection 1561.)

———. *Timour the Tartar*. 1811. (First acted at Covent Garden, April 1811. Larpent Collection 1670.)

Manners, George. *Edgar; or, Northern Feuds*. 1806. (First acted at Covent Garden, May 1806. Larpent Collection 1484.)

Maturin, Charles Robert. *Bertram; or, The Castle of St. Aldobrand*. London: John Murray, 1816. (First acted at Drury Lane, May 1816. Larpent Collection 1922. Maturin's Gothic tragedy consolidated the Byronic hero and Gothic villain into a single character.)

———. *Manuel*. New York: David Longworth at the Dramatic Repository Shakespeare Gallery, 1817. (First acted at Drury Lane, March 1817. Larpent Collection 1957. Unsuccessful Gothic tragedy.)

———. *Fredolfo*. Philadelphia: M. Carey, 1819. (First acted at Covent Garden, May 1819. Larpent Collection 2088. Unsuccessful Gothic tragedy.)

McDonald, Andrew. *Vimonda: A Tragedy*. 1787. (First acted at the Haymarket, Septem-

ber 1787. Larpent Collection 785. High Gothic melodrama involving ghostly mas-
querades and casual slaughters. The heroine, Vimonda, perishes of shock at the
end.)

Milner, Henry M. *Frankenstein; or, The Man and the Monster! or, The Fate of Frankenstein: A Peculiar Romantic Melo-Dramatic Pantomimic Spectacle, in Two Acts,
Founded Principally on Mrs. Shelley's Singular Work, in Two Acts*. 1826 (Pre-
miered at the Royal Coburg Theatre on 3 July 1826).

More, Hannah. *Percy*. 1777. (First acted at Covent Garden, December 1777. Larpent
Collection 440. This Scottish historical tragedy has balladic as well as Gothic
properties. Elwina, the persecuted heroine, is definitely a Gothic type.)

Murphy, Arthur. *The Grecian Daughter*. 1771. (First acted at Drury Lane, February 1771.
Larpent Collection 331. Although the play is set in ancient Syracuse, it manages
to include "a melange of Gothic motifs.") (Evans 42)

North, Francis. *The Kentish Barons*. 1791. (First acted at the Haymarket, June 1791.
Larpent Collection 875. Stylish Gothic-historical melodrama that enjoyed a respectable run at the Haymarket Theatre. The action "oscillates between castles
and various natural settings.")

O'Keefe, John. *Banditti; or, Love in a Labyrinth*. 1781. (First acted at Covent Garden,
November 1781. A comic opera and theatrical parody of grotto and cavern Gothics. Offers amorous specters, displaced lovers, and fierce banditti. Larpent Collection 577.

Peake, Richard Brinsley. *Presumption; or, The Fate of Frankenstein*. 1823. (First acted
at the Lyceum, July 1823. Larpent Collection 2359.)

Sheil, R.L. *Evadne; or, The Statue*. 1819. (First acted at Covent Garden, 1819. Larpent
Collection 2072.)

————. *The Phantom; or, Montoni*. 1820. (First acted at Covent Garden, May 1820.
Larpent Collection 2147. Melodrama based on Radcliffe's villain in *The Mysteries
of Udolpho*.)

Shelley, Percy Bysshe. *The Cenci*. London: Charles & James Ollier, 1820. (The play was
written in Rome and Leghorn, Italy, and finished in August 1819 and published
in 1820. Rejected by directors when Shelley submitted it, *The Cenci* remained
"closet" drama until it was finally produced privately in 1886 by the Shelley
Society.)

Siddons, Henry. *The Sicilian Romance; or, The Apparition of the Cliffs*. 1794. (First
acted at Covent Garden, May 1794. Larpent Collection 1027. Scenes adapted from
Radcliffe's second novel.)

————. *A Tale of Terror*. 1803. (First acted at Covent Garden, May 1803. Larpent
Collection 1811.)

Walker, C.E. *The Warlock of the Glen*. 1820. (First acted at Covent Garden, December
1820. Larpent Collection 2182.)

Walpole, Horace. *The Mysterious Mother*. Twickenham: "Printed Privately" Strawberry
Hill Press, 1768. (The first Gothic drama. The play was never staged because
Walpole thought its subject matter to be too repulsive for an audience.)

West, Benjamin. *Melmoth the Wanderer*. 1823. (First acted at the Royal Coburg, July
1823. Melodrama based on Charles Robert Maturin's Gothic novel of 1820.)

Anonymous Gothic Plays

Don Raymond; or, The Castle of Lindenburgh. 1797. (Acted at Covent Garden, March
    1797. Larpent Collection 1157. A pantomime and ballet based on the Raymond
    and Agnes episodes in Lewis's *Monk.*)
Lord of the Castle. 1817. (Acted at the Strand Theatre, 13 October 1817. Larpent Col-
    lection 1989.)
The Mystic Cavern. 1803. (Acted at Norwich, May 1803. Larpent Collection 1373.)
Raymond and Agnes; or, The Bleeding Nun. 1808. (Larpent Collection 1597.)
Right and Might; or, The Castle of Ellangowan. 1816. (First acted at Covent Garden,
    February 1816. Larpent Collection 1912.)
The Secret Castle; or, Henry and Edwy. 1799. (Acted at Manchester, 1799. Larpent
    Collection 1274.)

MODERN REPRINTS AND EDITIONS

The Castle of Otranto and The Mysterious Mother, written by Horace Walpole, edited
    with introduction and notes by Montague Summers. Printed at Chiswick Press
    for Houghton Mifflin Company and Constable and Company Limited, 1925.
The Castle Spectre: A Drama by Matthew Gregory Lewis. Ed. Jonathan Wordsworth.
    Oxford: Woodstock Books, 1990.
The Cenci by Percy Bysshe Shelley. Ed. Roland A. Duerksen. Indianapolis: Bobbs-
    Merrill, 1970.
Five Romantic Plays, 1768–1821. Ed. Paul Baines, Edward Burns, Michael Cordner,
    Peter Holland, Martin Wiggins. Oxford and New York: Oxford University Press,
    2000. Contains Horace Walpole's *The Mysterious Mother* and Joanna Baillie's
    De Monfort.
Gothic Readings: The First Wave, 1764–1840. Ed. Rictor Norton. London and New
    York: Leicester University Press, 2000. (Contains scenic excerpts from Walpole's
    Mysterious Mother, Lewis's *Castle Spectre*, Baillie's *De Monfort*, Maturin's *Ber-
    tram*, and James Robinson Planché's *Vampire.*)
Hideous Progenies. Dramatizations of Frankenstein from Mary Shelley to the Present.
    Steven Earl Forry. Philadelphia: University of Pennsylvania Press, 1990. (Reprints
    the complete scripts of Richard Brinsley Peake's *Presumption; or, The Fate of
    Frankenstein* [1823]), Henry M. Milner's *Frankenstein; or, the Man and the
    Monster* [1826], and John Atkinson Kerr's *The Monster and Magician; or, The
    Fate of Frankenstein* [1826].)
The Hour of One: Six Gothic Melodramas. Ed. Stephen Wischhusen. London: Gordon
    Fraser, 1975. (Facsimiles of the scripts of M.G. Lewis's *Castle Spectre*, Thomas
    Holcroft's *Tale of Mystery*, J.R. Planché's *Vampire*, H.M. Milner's *Frankenstein;
    or, The Man and the Monster*, and two melodramas by Edward Fitzball, *The
    Devil's Elixir* and *The Flying Dutchman.*)
The Plays of James Boaden. Ed. Steven Cohan. New York: Garland Publishing, 1980.
    (The sole modern edition of Boaden's dramatic works.)
The Plays of Robert Jephson. Ed. Temple James Maynard. New York: Garland Publish-

ing, 1980. (Contains the full script of *The Count of Narbonne*, first performed on 17 November 1781 at Covent Garden.)

Seven Gothic Dramas, 1789–1825. Ed. Jeffrey Cox. Athens: Ohio University Press, 1992. (Contains Francis North's *Kentish Barons*, M.G. Lewis's *Castle Spectre*, John Cartwright Cross's *Julia of Louvain; or Monkish Cruelty*, Joanna Baillie's *De Monfort*, M.G. Lewis's *Captive*, Charles Robert Maturin's *Bertram; or, The Castle of St. Aldobrand*, and Richard Brinsley Peake's *Presumption; or, The Fate of Frankenstein.*)

Sisters of Gore: Seven Gothic Melodramas by British Women, 1790–1843. Ed. John Franceschina. New York and London: Routledge, 1997. (Contents: *The Ward of the Castle* by Miss Burke; *The Mysterious Marriage* by Harriet Lee; *The Old Oak Chest* by Jane Scott; *Raymond de Percy* by Margaret Harvey; *St. Clair of the Isles* by Elizabeth Polack; *The Bond* by Catherine Gore; and *Dacre of the South* by Catherine Gore.)

The thirty years between the publication of Horace Walpole's *Castle of Otranto* and Ann Radcliffe's *Mysteries of Udolpho* marked a period of stagnation and regression for the Gothic novel, which faltered after the appearance of Walpole's provocative prototype. With the notable exception of the Gothic drama, the spectral energies released by Walpole temporarily deserted the literary scene, their ambience to be found almost solely in the dramatic productions. The plays of this strange interlude in the development of the Gothic indicate that there was no hiatus in horror, but that the drama rather than the novel now became the preferred mode of Gothicism for nearly three decades after the initial Gothic explosion. A perusal of the approximately 2,650 play titles contained in the catalog of the Larpent Collection of Eighteenth Century Drama at the Huntington Library in San Marino, California, verifies the popularity of the Gothic drama for the remainder of the eighteenth century and confirms the importance of the Gothic's dramatic phase to the acceleration and proliferation of the Gothic tradition as a whole.

Despite its key role in the shaping of the Gothic in its earliest stages, literary historians of the Gothic have been reluctant to acknowledge the Gothic drama as the vital link between Walpole's highly dramatic first Gothic novel, with its multitude of props and special effects, and the gloomy scenery and spectacular *coups de théâtre* of his successors. As Walpole's two prefaces to *Otranto* underscore, much of the narrative strategy underlying the horrors and terrors of the first Gothic novel was theatrically inspired by the novel's subterranean settings and shadowy interiors, lunar menace and solar absence, lurid acoustics, peregrinating armor, mobile paintings and statues, and other audiovisual contraptions assigned a major role in his notion of the Gothic. Given the audacious theatricality of *Otranto*, it is small wonder that the Gothic quickly found a home on the stage instead of on the page as it struggled to survive in the decorous climate of the arts of the 1770s.

Modern Gothic studies have perpetuated a distorted view of the development of the Gothic as a whole by generally overlooking the role played by Gothic drama. Except for Bertrand Evans's indispensable appendix of Gothic plays in *Gothic Drama from Walpole to Shelley*, no primary bibliographies of Gothic theatrical activity have been compiled. Nor are the titles of Gothic plays segregated from the novel titles in the Sadleir-Black Gothic Collection or Montague Summers's seminal bibliography of Gothic fiction, *A Gothic Bibliography*. Secondary bibliographies of the Gothic drama reflect a similar state of avoidance. R.D. Spector's *The English Gothic: A Bibliographic Guide to Writers from Horace Walpole to Mary Shelley* (1983) contains random references to Gothic drama but does not propose the subject as an independent area of inquiry. Even Montague Summers and Devendra P. Varma, the founders of modern Gothic studies, omit Gothic theater almost entirely from their general histories of Gothic fiction, *The Gothic Quest* and *The Gothic Flame*. Except for a handful of scholarly articles and dissertations, the only books to venture into the stage adventures of the Gothic are Bertrand Evans's landmark monograph *Gothic Drama from Walpole to Shelley* and the long introduction to Jeffrey N. Cox's anthology *Seven Gothic Dramas, 1789–1825*. The political relevance of Gothic plays to the revolutionary and reactionary decade of the 1790s has been addressed by Paula R. Backscheider in *Spectacular Politics: Theatrical Power and Mass Culture in Early Modern England*. Jeffrey Cox's introduction to his anthology of Gothic drama criticizes the obscure position of Gothic drama in the field of Gothic studies:

Immense popularity and little critical respect—this might be the epitaph for the Gothic drama that filled the London stages in the decades around the turn from the eighteenth to the nineteenth century. We almost completely ignore these plays that found such favor with audiences of the day, not yet finding in them the interest we have discovered in the Gothic romances which also sit at the margins of the "great tradition." It is ironic, given the obscurity of the Gothic drama, that the Gothic romance provides a key example of the new processes of canon reformation within the academy. (2)

Another irony of indifference to the Gothic drama lies in the fact that three of the five major Gothic novelists were also highly active Gothic dramatists and two of these three became professional Gothic playwrights. William Beckford and Ann Radcliffe wrote no plays, but Walpole, Matthew Lewis, and Charles Robert Maturin extended their Gothicizing to the stage. Just as he had broken new ground with the first Gothic novel, so Walpole was in the vanguard of the Gothic drama with his 1768 play of incest and horrific mystery, *The Mysterious Mother*. Both Lewis and Maturin wrote extensively for the theater. Their works held the boards at Covent Garden and Drury Lane and were enhanced by successful runs and public acclaim. Lewis enjoyed a second career as a Gothic dramatist after the controversy aroused by the immorality of *The Monk* had subsided, while Maturin's public reputation in the nineteenth century rested as much on his fame as a Gothic dramatist as on his notoriety as a Gothic novelist. The finest of his six Gothic novels, *Melmoth the Wanderer*, was published in

1820 after his career in the theater had ended. Bertrand Evans has stressed the role of Gothic theater as a shaping force in his pioneering monograph *Gothic Drama from Walpole to Shelley*, noting that the Gothic drama was instrumental both in sustaining the Gothic mood after *The Castle of Otranto* and in disseminating the ideas of the Gothic revival in the arts after Walpole had demonstrated their power and appeal:

Scholarship has led everyone to suppose that the Gothic school was composed of novelists only. Dramatists, however, participated as actively as novelists in the Gothic Revival. The plays as much as the novels deserve study. Among them are several specimens of the Gothic mode as remarkable as *The Castle of Otranto, The Mysteries of Udolpho*, and *Melmoth*. The Gothic drama expresses the *Zeitgeist* as revealingly as the Gothic novel and also reflects equally well the transition from the Age of Johnson to the Age of Byron. (2)

The Elizabethan and Jacobean antecedents of the Gothic drama have been thoroughly traced by Clara McIntyre, Paul Lewis, and other commentators to show that the plays of Shakespeare and his contemporaries were a primary source of the Gothic drama. A full array of Gothic sound effects, gloomy scenery, frenzied characters, sanguinary events, gruesome stage business, and supernatural contraptions is the stock-in-trade of Elizabethan and Jacobean blood tragedies. Thomas Kyd's *Spanish Tragedy* (1592), Cyril Tourneur's *Revenger's Tragedy* (1607), John Webster's *Duchess of Malfi* (1614), and John Ford's *'Tis Pity She's a Whore* (1633) are crowded with Gothic incidents and atmosphere. A rhetorical precedent for the heroic evil of numerous Gothic villains reverberates in the "mighty lines" and demonic soliloquies spoken by Christopher Marlowe's criminal overreachers in *Doctor Faustus* (1588), *Tamburlaine* (1590), and *The Jew of Malta* (1592), Shakespeare's donations to the Gothic theatrical idiom can scarcely be overstated. He launched his theatrical career with the Gothic crowd pleaser and horror show *Titus Andronicus* (1594), a sadistic farrago of relentless horror that offered the audience infanticide, cannibalism, mutilation, rape, death by live burial, satanic villainy, pursuit and sexual violation of a maiden, and an entourage of wicked characters who are themselves savage Goths. The great tragedies are filled with preternatural and supernatural places, people, and events to the extent that *Othello, King Lear*, and, most especially, *Macbeth* furnish the Gothic dramatists with literally everything needed to attain their goals. Iago's love of evil and demonic ingenuity, Goneril's antipaternal ferocity, and Macbeth's "black and deep desires" are later to be integral in helping the Gothic drama to find its voice. The formula for horror in *Hamlet*, a dark perplex of unspeakable deeds and intrafamilial sexual crimes committed inside a haunted castle, becomes the quintessential Gothic plot.

In the tragedies of the Restoration, the Gothic mood sometimes overshadows all other dramatic ends, as in the mortuarial gloom and terror of several scenes in William Congreve's *Mourning Bride* (1697), a tragedy dominated by the horror motif of an unidentified headless corpse. The tragedies of Thomas Otway, Thomas Southerne, and Nathaniel Lee exhibit strong Gothic properties and transmit to the Gothic novelists and dramatists of the eighteenth century a treasury of morbid and sensational material. Lines and passages from Otway's *Venice Preserved* (1682), Southerne's *Fatal Marriage* (1694), and Lee's *Sophonisba* (1676) and *The Rival Queens* (1677) often appear as epigraphs in Gothic novels. Beginning with Walpole, Gothic plays almost without exception reflect an implicit or explicit indebtedness to the previous theaters of blood and cruelty active during the Restoration and Elizabethan eras. An aesthetic commitment to horror for horror's sake became the heritage of these earlier periods of theater to the Gothic playwrights.

Immediately prior to Walpole's first Gothic drama, John Home's historical tragedy *Douglas* (1756) anticipated the attitudes of the Gothic playwrights toward their materials "in a singular devotion to the ends of mystery, gloom, and terror" (Evans 26). The proto-Gothicism of *Douglas* was followed in 1763 by the Irish playwright Hall Hartson's *Countess of Salisbury*, another dark historical pageant that introduced audiences to the pleasures of Gothic spectacle and passion. Hartson's play was a transcription of Thomas Leland's ur-Gothic novel *Longsword, Earl of Salisbury* (1762), a work sometimes cited by literary historians as the beginning of Gothic fiction. With its brooding medievalism and placement of the menaced maiden within an ancient castle, *The Countess of Salisbury* struck the same chords of Gothic excitement that would arouse readers of Walpole's first Gothic novel. Lacking only an emphasis upon "terror as the principal engine" (first preface to *The Castle of Otranto*), the plays of Home and Hartson capitalized on the changing aesthetic climate to lay the foundations for a new Gothic theater.

Never performed and regarded by Walpole himself as too repulsive in its subject matter for public viewing, *The Mysterious Mother* is an instructive specimen of the Gothic drama's early stage qualities. The repulsive theme is the mother's crime of incest committed deliberately and vindictively by the Countess of Narbonne to punish her son Edmund for an assignation. The mother's deliberate act of incest (she sleeps with Edmund) brings terrible consequences for herself and her children, with the deed's horrible nature rendered almost unbearable by her concealment of the crime. To prolong and intensify the sexual suspense, Walpole withholds information about the mother's guilt until the play's final scene, when the full horror is unveiled. At the play's Oedipal climax, both the characters and the audience learn that the daughter of the incest, the young woman Adeliza, is Edmund's sister, daughter, and wife. Walpole restricted the supernatural to an atmospheric role in *The Mysterious Mother*, allowing the ominous potency of the weather and the sinister aliveness of the Castle of Narbonne to supplement the mounting horror of the incest theme. In the monastic cunning of Father Benedict, the Countess's confessor, Walpole created a superlative portrait of Catholic villainy. By placing natural characters in unnatural circumstances, Walpole generated psychological tension through familial victimization and created the paradigmatic Gothic drama of internecine filial conflict and sexual depravity.

Throughout the 1770s, the Gothic drama proliferated even as the Gothic novel languished or retreated into dull didacticism, as it had in Clara Reeve's *Old English Baron*. It was Gothic theater and not Gothic narrative that impelled Gothicism from 1768 to 1789, the year of Ann Radcliffe's first novel. Bertrand Evans's view that "Gothic drama had an earlier, somewhat swifter growth" than Gothic fiction is borne out by the performance statistics. "Dramatic exploitation of Gothic elements began in earnest within ten years after *The Mysterious Mother*" (18). John Home's *Fatal Discovery* (1769), Arthur Murphy's *Grecian Daughter* (1771), Henry Hull's *Henry Second; or, The Fall of Rosamond* (1773), and Hannah More's *Percy* (1777) contain Gothic scenes and equipment calculated to appeal to the new taste for the dark sublime on the stage. In 1779, a play by Hannah Crowley achieved a total convergence of Gothic moods and machinery in a landmark piece of theater whose every detail renders it a genuinely Gothic drama in all aspects. *Albina, Countess of Raimond* opens in "a magnificent Gothic hall" and moves its Gothic paraphernalia to stage center in allowing grottoes, hidden trapdoors, and other architectural props to play a role in the fates of the characters. Albina herself advances female villainy from where the mysterious mother had left it upon her suicide and produces the conditions in which satanic women such as Lewis's Matilda and Charlotte Dacre's Victoria di Loredani would later thrive. The aggressive horror of Crowley's *Albina* lends more authority to Evans's claim that the Gothic drama achieved "full development" on the literary scene prior to 1792, that the Gothic novel would follow the drama's lead and example, and that the renaissance in Gothic fiction in the 1790s would not have occurred without the impetus to the Gothic administered by the writing of Gothic plays.

While such dramatists as Crowley were moving toward horror for horror's sake on stage, one playwright, Robert Jephson, urged restraint and attempted a reversion to propriety in his dramatic adaptation of *The Castle of Otranto, The Count of Narbonne*. Sanctioned by Walpole himself, Jephson's play dismantled all of the stupendous hardware of horror of *The Castle of Otranto*, the Brobdingnagian helmet of Alfonso, the walking portrait of Ricardo, the gigantic *disjecta membra* or body parts living within the castle walls, the bleeding statue, and all of the other supernatural titillations. The result was heavily moralized melodrama that saw Jephson substitute the rhetoric of suffering for spectral excitation. But placed beside the other Gothic plays of the 1780s and 1790s, Jephson's *Count of Narbonne* seems a dissonant exception to the major tendencies of Gothic theater toward supernatural spectacle.

Andrew McDonald's *Vimonda* and James Cobb's *Haunted Tower* were full dramatic expressions of the Gothic drama's revolutionary and radical spirit unfettered by any concessions to the didactic. McDonald's single-minded purpose in *Vimonda* was to terrify, horrify, and mystify his audience beyond rational recall. By opting for spectacle and avoiding completely any vindication of virtue,

McDonald's *Vimonda* countered the retrogression in Gothic theater of Jephson's *Count of Narbonne*. In the carnage of characters at the end of *Vimonda*, the good expire with the wicked without the slightest regard for poetic justice or the moral stasis of traditional melodrama. By blending the serious with the silly, Cobb's *Haunted Tower* gave the audience raucous entertainment by mixing mock-Gothic with high Gothic elements. That most Gothic of sites, the dark tower, dominated the set and served as the focal point for mystery, mayhem, and moonshine that pointed the way toward future parodies and lampoons of Gothic nonsense.

Perhaps the most innovative Gothic playwright of the early 1790s was James Boaden. Boaden skillfully arranged several of Radcliffe's Gothic romances for the Gothic stage and in the process divested the Radcliffean Gothic of its rationalized and explained supernatural characteristics. "His decision," Evans observes, "was to omit not Radcliffe's excesses, but her natural explanations of the supernatural. For the first time, a playwright undertook to out-Gothicize a novelist" (93). Boaden's *Fontainville Forest* not only condensed and accelerated the plot of Radcliffe's *Romance of the Forest*, it also brought a new level of stimulus to Gothic theater by way of an authentic and unexplained supernatural. Two of his later plays, *The Secret Tribunal* and *The Italian Monk*, are dramatic improvements over the sluggish terrors of Radcliffe. His revision of Radcliffe's *Italian* has been called by Boaden's modern editor, Steven Cohan, "his most ambitious dramatic undertaking, and, given his desire to move his audience to tears as well as screams, it would turn out to be his most imaginatively coherent rendering of Gothic fiction on stage" (v). The influence of Boaden's alteration of the Radcliffean terror plot into the Lewisite horror plot moved the Gothic drama closer to an ideal of absolute atrocity that would in turn have an impact on the first theatrical undertaking of a Gothic novelist-turned-dramatist, Monk Lewis.

Probably the *opus classicum* of Gothic theater of the 1790s was Lewis's highly successful *Castle Spectre*. The *Castle Spectre* opened at the Theatre Royal in Drury Lane on 14 December 1797 and went through forty-seven performances, its impressive run signaling both an unabated craving for Gothic theater and a salacious curiosity about the notorious author of *The Monk*. Lewis knew that he could trade on his scandalous reputation. He knew as well as what audiences wanted above all was a specter equal or superior in horrific potency to the bleeding nun of *The Monk*, and such is precisely what Lewis provides, but not until the second scene of act 4 at which point, according to the stage direction,

the folding doors unclose, and the oratory is seen illuminated. In its centre, stands a tall female figure, her white and flowing garments spotted with blood; her veil is thrown back, and discovers a pale and melancholy countenance; her eyes are lifted upwards, her arms extended toward heaven, and a large wound appears on her bosom. At length the

spectre advances slowly to a soft and plaintive strain; she stops opposite Reginald's
picture, and gazes upon it in silence. (*Castle Spectre* IV.ii)

According to Lewis's biographer, Louis Peck, the return of the bleeding nun
in this Gothic scene was the main cause of the play's extraordinary reception.
Although it was completely extraneous to the plot and was given no lines, the
castle specter easily upstaged both the heroine, Angela, and the villain, Osmond.

Managers, actors, and friends had urged Lewis to forego the apparition, but he had
persisted and his judgement did not err. The figure of the bleeding nun, popularized in
The Monk, is here again exploited, this time as a benign instead of an evil apparition.
That she accomplished nothing for the plot mattered not a whit to Lewis or the public.
Many contemporary accounts attest to the moving power of the scene. (73)

Hereafter, the electricity of Gothic drama would depend not on trite plots or
refabricated characters transposed from the Gothic novels of Radcliffe and Walpole but on riveting moments of audiovisual frisson thrust upon the audience in
phantasmagoric settings that "fitted the taste of the audience like a glove"
(Wordsworth's view of *The Castle Spectre* as expressed to William Hazlitt).
With Lewis's bleeding nun leading the way, the Gothic drama now strode boldly
into the nineteenth century. (*William Hazlitt* 17: 118).

Joanna Baillie's *De Monfort*, produced at Drury Lane in April 1800, is a
prime example of the appearance of a distinctively female Gothic impulse in
the rise of the Gothic drama. In his introduction to *Seven Gothic Dramas*, Jeffrey
Cox credits Baillie with going beyond the usual thrills of maidenly peril in her
presentation of alternative images of women. Feminist Gothic theater originates
with Baillie's "close investigation of the passion of hatred" (54) in the distresses
of Jane De Monfort, the sister of the protagonist. While the male characters are
villainous stereotypes, "her role is far less conventional, and Baillie's treatment
of her reveals the play's revisionary stance toward its Gothic tradition. Baillie's
plays embody a sustained meditation upon the roles and plots that constrict
women, a meditation not matched in her period by other dramatists or for that
matter by the better known Gothic novelists" (57). In her refusal to repeat the
character cliché of hysterical maiden or shrieking, weeping, virginal victim in
the character of Jane De Monfort, Baillie endowed Gothic theater with a new
and emotionally valid female character. Rejecting conventional passivity, Jane
De Monfort's calm self-control opposed all of the accepted formulas of how
victimized women were supposed to sob and shriek when they were locked
inside the Gothic world.

Between 1800 and 1816, when Maturin's *Bertram; or, The Castle of St. Aldobrand* made its debut, the Gothic drama maintained its public popularity with
operatic and burlesque extravaganzas as well as straight dramatic productions.
Thomas Holcroft's *A Tale of Mystery*, Mary Goldsmith's *Angelina; or, Wolcot
Castle*, Lewis's *Wood Daemon; or, The Clock Has Struck*, and the anonymous

The Bleeding Nun; or, Raymond and Agnes demonstrated both the commercial resiliency and stagnant conventionality of Gothic theater. Like the Gothic blue-books and chapbooks of the first decade of the nineteenth century, these plays' repetitive plots, modular characters, and interchangeable settings continued to elate an uncritical audience whose tastes were much like those of the Gothic chapbook readers. The seemingly endless reproduction of Gothic horror encouraged a few dramatists to upbraid both the craft and its clientele by resorting to broad farce and rough satire. Dennis Lawler's *Earls of Hammersmith; or, The Cellar Spectre*, a clever one-act farce performed at the Olympic Theater in January 1814, was one of several attempts to rid the Gothic drama of its ludicrous excesses. Lawler's point-by-point burlesque of various Gothic predicaments reduces the horrid to the hilarious at every turn. To prove his worthiness to Lady Margaret Marrowbones, Sir Walter Wisehead volunteers to spend one night within a forbidden chamber. Midway through the vigil, a phantom footman delivers a direful warning to Wisehead: "Wed not Lady Margaret Marrowbones! She is your grandmother!" a wonderful one-line undercutting of the usual genealogical enigma of the Gothic tale. Having neatly ridiculed the ghastly stage business of numerous Gothic novels and dramas, Lawler finishes off the lampoon by an absurd shift of scene to a mock robber drama in the forest depths. Sir Walter joins the banditti apparently for the purpose of mastering the rhetoric spoken in plays such as Schiller's *Robbers* by nobly articulate outlaws. But the polished parody of *The Earls of Hammersmith* failed to deliver the *coup de grâce* to the inanities of Gothic theater. Instead, Gothic drama now entered a decadent phase, somewhat delayed and offset by the dramatic success of Maturin's *Bertram* and the originality of the literary or "closet" Gothic dramas of the major Romantic poets. Rather than simply dying out, Gothic drama lingered on until it was subsumed by plays, operas, and farces based on Mary Shelley's *Frankenstein* throughout the 1820s.

The Gothic dramas composed by Maturin, Byron, and Percy Shelley near the close of the Gothic movement merit special consideration. Maturin's *Bertram; or, The Castle of St. Aldobrand* was dedicated to Sir Walter Scott and starred the great tragedian Edmund Kean in the title role. Maturin's exploration of the virtues and dangers of the Napoleonic personality in the rebellious outcast Bertram bears some resemblance to the metaphysical and ethical contradictions prominent in Manfred in Byron's Gothic drama of that name. Both Maturin's *Bertram* and Byron's *Manfred* sought ways of fusing the Gothic with the tragic in their portraits of the heroic criminal or satanic/angelic sinner. The Gothic hero-villain, always a morally oxymoronic personage, retained his mixed moral nature while acquiring tragic stature in the hands of Maturin and Byron. Byron's Manfred "represents the high Romantic expression, in dramatic form, of the Gothic spirit. Byron's tragedy might be described as a consummation of Gothic evolution on the stage. The crude Gothic protagonists of nearly fifty years passed into this most striking portrait of the Byronic hero" (Evans 232).

Although it was never acted in Shelley's lifetime, *The Cenci* (1819) assumes a unique place in the history of the Gothic drama as a transformational work of high dramatic art in its refinement of Gothic crudities into deeply moving poetic tragedy. The play revives the forbidden theme of incest first introduced by Walpole in *The Mysterious Mother* but relates this theme to Shelley's philosophic interests in the conflict between the ideal and the real, a struggle often won by the brutish and carnal forces of human nature. Saturated with domestic violence and filial brutality, *The Cenci* explores paternal incest, the most heinous of Gothic passions, finally realizing the bond between Gothic and tragic modes that earlier Gothic dramatists had been groping toward. Paternal hatred expressed as incestuous lust leads directly to parricide in Shelley's plot, which is drawn from the real history of a real Florentine family. "The theme of persecution aligns it with Gothic tradition in both fiction and drama. The principal characters are Gothic types idealized" (Evans 232). The victim of incest, Beatrice Cenci, and its vicious perpetrator, her father, Count Francesco Cenci, are Shelley's transmuted versions of the Gothic maiden and villain now relocated to historical context rather than being distanced by remote nightmare fantasy.

No sudden decline in Gothic theater followed the work of Maturin, Byron, and Shelley. Rather, Gothic theater remained a continuum flourishing well into the 1830s, then transferring its energies to Victorian melodrama. Much of the later history of the Gothic drama between 1820 and 1830 can be described in terms of the emergence of the *Frankenstein* play in melodramatic, operatic, and comic formats. Dramatized *Frankenstein*s began in 1823 with Richard Brinsley Peake's *Presumption; or, The Fate of Frankenstein*. The transition from novel to drama excised all of the philosophical subtleties of Mary Shelley's text while highlighting the bizarre and macabre aspects of the story and taking advantage of the creature's monstrous stage potential. "Wild action, alchemical rituals, and Gothic settings replaced the novel's epistolary format, scientific background, and internalized landscape. Pithy maxims, divine intercession, and human repentance for hubristic transgression replaced the ambiguous moral stance of Mary Shelley" (Forry, *Hideous Progenies* 91). Other stage versions of *Frankenstein* such as Henry M. Milner's *Frankenstein; or, The Man and the Monster* vulgarized the novel into a Gothic costume drama replete with oversimplified moral themes and sentimental dialogue. John Atkinson Kerr's *Monster and Magician; or, The Fate of Frankenstein* eliminated all of the novel's moral ambiguities by degrading Shelley's epic story of miscreation into puerile pantomime. By 1830, the Gothic drama had degenerated into a "raree show" exhibition.

Jeffrey Cox has suggested that the Gothic drama exhibits "two key historical moments, one during the 1790s and one around 1815," linking these high points to the fall of the Bastille, the Reign of Terror, and the fall of Napoleon and contending that "it is only during the period organized around these events that the Gothic drama achieved its full power" (8). The Gothic on stage from 1768, the writing of Walpole's *Mysterious Mother*, to 1816, the production of Maturin's *Bertram*, remains an overlooked chapter in the history of the Gothic movement as a whole. Immensely popular for more than half a century, Gothic theater was at least as influential as the Gothic novel in determining the course of Romanticism and at certain moments was a vital and transforming force. Once dismissed by historians of theater and treated as superfluous in scholarly accounts of Gothicism, the Gothic drama deserves recognition as a major tributary in the gallery of horror. *See also* **Matthew Gregory Lewis, Charles Robert Maturin**, and **Horace Walpole**.

SELECTED CRITICISM

Adelsperger, Walter Charles. "Aspects of Staging of Plays of the Gothic Revival in England." Doctoral dissertation, Ohio State University, 1960. [*DAI* 20:4212–4213]. Onstage mechanics, dramaturgy, and special effects created for Gothic plays. Offers a useful glossary of Gothic drama.

Anthony, M. Susan. " 'Some Deed of Dreadful Note': Productions of Gothic Dramas in the United States, 1790 to 1830." Doctoral dissertation, University of Maryland, 1997. [*DAI* 58:3366A]. A theater-history survey that examines forty years of Gothic drama on the American stage, studies staging, production, and critical reception of Gothic plays given "in the four major theatrical centers: Philadelphia, New York, Charleston, and Boston, and identifies the most popular plays in those cities over time to reveal possible implications about the audiences in each city." Concludes that the Gothic dramas "embodied the accepted values in American society between 1790 and 1830."

Backscheider, Paula R. "Gothic Drama and National Crisis." In *Spectacular Politics: Theatrical Power and Mass Culture in Early Modern England.* Baltimore: Johns Hopkins University Press, 1993: 149–233. Assesses the popularity and appeal of Gothic drama in the revolutionary decade of the 1790s. "Inscribed in the Gothic drama are two major concerns: sex as political allegory and public opinion."

Brandenberg, Alice S. "The Theme of *The Mysterious Mother.*" *Modern Language Quarterly* 10 (1949): 464–474. Walpole's Gothic play presents "incest as a tragic subject and not merely as a device for achieving cheap sensation."

Cameron, Kenneth Neill, and Horst Frenz. "The Stage History of Shelley's *The Cenci.*" *PMLA* 60 (1945): 1080–1105. A survey of productions with comments on staging and acting of Shelley's Gothic drama.

Carpi, Daniela. "Il soprannaturale nel teatro elisabettiano-giacobiano e nel romanzo gotico: Tra metafisico e sociale." *Quaderni di Filologia Germanica della Facoltà di Lettere e Filosofia dell' Università di Bologna* 1 (1980): 41–54. Traces the theatrical origins of the Gothic drama back to the lurid blood tragedies of Kyd, Webster, Shakespeare, and Ford.

Cohan, Steven. Introduction to *The Plays of James Boaden.* New York: Garland, 1980: iii–xxxvii. Comments extensively on *The Italian Monk.* "By revising Radcliffe's ending, Boaden allowed spectators a range of emotions from terror to pathos within a conservative and sentimental moral framework. By the end Schedoni's figure draws tears rather than shudders from the audience."

The Complete Works of William Hazlitt, Ed. P. P. Howe after the edition of A.R. Waller and Arnold Glover, London and Toronto: J.M. Dent, 1930–34, vol. 17, p. 118.

Cox, Jeffrey N. Introduction to *Seven Gothic Dramas, 1789–1825*. Athens: Ohio University Press, 1992: 1–77. Because the Gothic in its dramatic form was concurrent with the Gothic in narrative form, it merits both historicizing and serious critical attention. "The Gothic drama provides one central set of texts that challenge the controlling preconceptions about nineteenth-century drama."

Doe, Donald Bartlett. "The Sublime as an Aesthetic Correlative: A Study of Late Eighteenth-Century English Aesthetic Theory, Landscape Painting, and Gothic Drama." Doctoral dissertation, Ohio University, 1978. [*DAI* 39:516A]. Chapter 4 deals with Andrew McDonald's *Vimonda*. "Gothic drama often functions as a relevant predicate for the notion of sublimity."

Evans, Bertrand. *Gothic Drama from Walpole to Shelley*. Berkeley and Los Angeles: University of California Press, 1947. The first book-length study of Gothic theater. The ten chapters cover such topics as "The First Gothic Plays," "Full Development of Gothic Drama before 1762," "Ann Radcliffe and Gothic Drama," and "Lewis and Gothic Drama." Remains the premier study of the dramatic aspect of Gothicism. Evans advises that "the plays, as much as the novels, deserve study. Among them are several specimens of the Gothic mode as remarkable as *The Castle of Otranto*, *The Mysteries of Udolpho*, and *Melmoth*." Has a chronological roster of 131 plays with dates and theaters of first performance.

Forry, Steven. "Dramatizations of *Frankenstein* 1821–1986 A Comprehensive List." *English Language Notes* 25:2 (1987): 63–79. Annotated chronology of dramatic adaptations of *Frankenstein*. There are 96 citations.

————. *Hideous Progenies Dramatizations of Frankenstein from Mary Shelley to the Present*. Philadelphia: University of Pennsylvania Press, 1990. Theatrical history of the novel in dramatic and cinematic form. "Wild action, alchemical rituals, and Gothic settings replace the novel's epistolary format."

Gamer, Michael. "National Supernaturalism: Joanna Baillie, Germany, and the Gothic Drama." *Theatre Survey* 38:2 (1997): 49–88. Discusses the use by the Gothic dramatist Joanna Baillie of the supernatural and spectacular conventions of Gothic drama. Notes that Baillie wrote at a time when both the costs and the benefits of representing the supernatural on stage were very high and in a cultural moment when Gothic drama had become strongly stigmatized as "German" and therefore as Jacobin and aesthetic.

Hayter, Alethea. "Coleridge, Maturin's *Bertram*, and Drury Lane." In *New Approaches to Coleridge: Biographical and Critical Essays*. Ed. Donald Sultana. New York: Barnes & Noble, 1981: 17–37. Coleridge's reactions to Maturin's 1816 Gothic play.

Hitchens, Gordon. " 'A Breathless Eagerness in the Audience': Historical Notes on Dr. Frankenstein and His Monster." *Film Comment* 6 (1970): 49–51. On melodramatic versions of *Frankenstein*.

Holzknecht, Karl J. "Horace Walpole as Dramatist." *South Atlantic Quarterly* 28 (1929): 174–189. In Walpole's Gothic tragedy *The Mysterious Mother*, "all of the Gothic machinery of *Otranto* is present."

Inverso, Mary Beth. *The Gothic Impulse in Contemporary Drama*. Theatre and Dramatic Studies 63. Ann Arbor: UMI Research Press, 1989. The first chapter, "Gothic Narration and Gothic Melodrama: Some Crucial Distinctions," deals with Lewis's *Castle Spectre* and the beginnings of Gothic drama. The remainder of the study deals with the Gothic element in modern plays.

Kaufman, Pamela J. "Oedipus and the Gothic Drama: A Psychologic Study of Gothic Drama in Eighteenth-Century England." Doctoral dissertation, University of California at Los Angeles, 1970. [*DAI* 31:2348A]. Surveys more than seventy plays, including the Gothic of the major Romantic poets. "Incest appears to have a positive value for the Gothicists, becoming a love religion."

Lewis, Paul. "*The Atheist's Tragedy* and *The Castle of Otranto*: Expressions of the Gothic Vision," *Notes and Queries* 25 (1978): 52–54. Draws parallels between the Elizabethan blood tragedy and the first Gothic novel.

Loomis, Emerson R. "Gothic Drama as a Source for Gothic Fiction in the Magazines." *Notes and Queries* 15 (1968): 28–29. Shows how popular Gothic plays such as Lewis's *Wood Daemon* were often the sources for tales of terror in the periodicals.

MacMillan, Dougald, comp. *Catalogue of the Larpent Plays in the Huntington Library*. San Marino, CA: Henry Huntington Library, 1939. A rich source for Gothic forms of the drama in the period 1768–1800. Of the approximately 2,600 plays indexed in the collection, approximately 150 are classifiable as Gothic dramas or exhibit Gothic traits.

"Masters of the Melodrama—The Centenary of Thomas Dibdin—from Gothic to the Crime Play." *Times Literary Supplement* 20 September 1944: 470. While Dibdin's plays were a reaction against the extremes of Gothic melodrama, such stage spectacles as *The Ruffian Boy* exhibited Gothic elements and influence.

Maynard, Temple James. Introduction to *The Plays of Robert Jephson*. New York: Garland, 1980: xiv–xvii. Jephson desupernaturalized and de-Gothified Walpole's *Castle of Otranto*. Walpole was involved in the production, "remained loyal to the play and continued to commend it."

McIntyre, Clara F. "Were the Gothic Novels Gothic?" *PMLA* 36 (1921): 644–667. Gothic characterization and atmosphere derive from Renaissance dramatic forms.

———. "The Later Career of the Elizabethan Villain-Hero." *PMLA* 40 (1925): 874–880. The Gothic hero-villain in both the novels and dramas is a close copy of figures of "great power stained with crime" that appeared in Elizabethan and Jacobean tragedies of blood.

Neufeld, Mary Diana. "The Adaptation of the Gothic Novel to the English Stage, 1765–1826." Doctoral dissertation, Cornell University, 1977. [*DAI* 38:6407A]. "Gothic playwrights substituted more acceptable thrills from the pool of Gothic effects and sometimes changed the characterizations in the novels to suit the requirements of poetic justice."

Nitchie, Elizabeth. "The Stage History of *Frankenstein*." *South Atlantic Quarterly* 41 (1942): 384–398. Surveys the success or failure of various dramatic adaptations of *Frankenstein* such as H.M. Milner's *Frankenstein; or, The Man and the Monster* (1823).

Partin, Bruce Lynn. "The Horror Play: Its Transition from the Epic to the Dramatic Mode." Doctoral dissertation, Ohio State University, 1977. [*DAI* 37:4714A]. Provides an overview of *The Castle of Otranto*, *The Monk*, *Frankenstein*, and other works of Gothic fiction on stage. Includes material on the vampire play in the nineteenth and twentieth centuries.

Peck, Louis. *A Life of Matthew G. Lewis, Author of the Monk*. Cambridge, MA: Harvard University Press, 1961. Chapter Four, "Dramas," surveys Lewis's career as a Gothic playwright.

Ranger, Paul. *Terror and Pity Reign in Every Breast: Gothic Drama in the London Patent*

Theatres, 1750–1820. London: Society for Theatre Research, 1991: 61–62. Discusses the stage design, scenery, and direction of the Drury Lane 1800 production of Joanna Baillie's *De Monfort*. The designer was William Capon, who introduced the architectural features of the Gothic revival to the London stage.

Robertson, Fiona. "Castle Spectres: Scott, Gothic Drama, and the Search for the Narrator." In *Scott in Carnival*. Ed. J.H. Alexander and David Hewitt. Aberdeen: Association for Scottish Literary Studies, 1993: 444–458. On the Scott–Monk Lewis connection and Scott's use of the Gothic's dramatic elements in his novels.

Thorp, Willard. "The Stage Adventures of Some Gothic Novels." *PMLA* 43 (1928): 476–486. Comments on dramatic adaptations of Walpole and Radcliffe, including Robert Jephson's *Count of Narbonne*, Miles Peter Andrews's *Enchanted Castle*, Andrew McDonald's *Vimonda*, and James Boaden's *Italian Monk*. Concludes that the Gothic playwrights "seem to have taken pains to minimize the horrors of their originals rather than to utilize them for dramatic effect."

Verhoeven, W.M. "Opening the Text: The Locked-Trunk Motif in Late Eighteenth-Century British and American Gothic Fiction." In *Exhibited by Candlelight: Sources and Developments in the Gothic Tradition*. Ed. Valeria Tinkler-Villani, Peter Davidson, and Jane Stevenson. Amsterdam: Rodopi, 1995: 205–219. Discusses the Gothic prop of the secret box in George Colman the younger's *Iron Chest*. "Colman's use of the locked-trunk motif is in line with the conventional Gothic practice of associating the dark, the unknown, and the hidden with feelings of guilt."

Worrall, David. "The Political Culture of Gothic Drama." In *A Companion to the Gothic*. Ed. David Punter. Oxford and Malden, MA: Blackwell, 2000: 94–106. Argues that "our knowledge of romantic-period Gothic drama can be informed by the politics of an increasingly plebeian theatre." Discusses plays by Robert Jephson, James Boaden, Miles Peter Andrews, John Cartwright Cross, and others.

NATHANIEL HAWTHORNE
(1804–1864)

Frederick S. Frank

PRINCIPAL GOTHIC WORKS

Fanshawe. Boston: Marsh & Capen, 1828.

Twice-told Tales. Boston: American Stationers, John B. Russell, 1837. (The collection contains thirty-six stories, most of which contain Gothic themes, events, characters, and settings. One cluster of stories, "Legends of the Province House," has these four pieces: "Howe's Masquerade," "Edward Randolph's Portrait," "Lady Eleanor's Mantle," and "Old Esther Dudley." Particularly noteworthy for their Gothicism are "The Gray Champion," "The Wedding Knell," "The Minister's Black Veil," "Wakefield," "The Prophetic Pictures," "The Hollow of the Three Hills," "The Haunted Mind," and "The White Old Maid.")

Mosses from an Old Manse. New York and London: Wiley & Putnam, 1846. (The collection contains twenty-six pieces. Gothic themes, events, characters, and settings are especially evident in the following stories: "The Birthmark," "Young Goodman Brown," "Rappaccini's Daughter," "Fire Worship," "Monsieur du Miroir," "Egotism; or, The Bosom Serpent," "Roger Malvin's Burial," and "Earth's Holocaust.")

The Scarlet Letter. Boston: Ticknor, Reed & Fields, 1850.

The House of the Seven Gables. Boston: Ticknor, Reed & Fields, 1851.

The Snow-Image, and Other Tales. London: Henry G. Bohn, 1851; Boston: Ticknor, Reed & Fields, 1852. (The collection contains fourteen pieces, with the Gothic especially evident in the following tales: "Ethan Brand," "The Man of Adamant: An Apologue," "The Devil in Manuscript," "The Wives of the Dead," and "My Kinsman, Major Molineux.")

The Marble Faun; or, The Romance of Monte Beni. Boston: Ticknor & Fields, 1860.

Appendix: The Ancestral Footstep; Outlines of an English Romance, in *Old Manse Edition, The Complete Writings of Nathaniel Hawthorne*, in 22 volumes. Boston and New York: Houghton Mifflin, 1900, Vol. 14, 329–433. (An unfinished Gothic romance, highly disjointed and fragmentary.)

The Dolliver Romance, in *Old Manse Edition, The Complete Works of Nathaniel Hawthorne*, in 22 volumes. Boston and New York: Houghton Mifflin, 1900, Vol. 14, 1–67. (This fragment remained incomplete at Hawthorne's death in 1864.)

MODERN REPRINTS AND EDITIONS

The Centenary Edition of the Works of Nathaniel Hawthorne. Ed. William Charvat.
    Columbus: Ohio State University Press, 1962. (The authoritative edition in 23
    volumes.)
The Complete Novels and Selected Tales of Nathaniel Hawthorne. Ed. Norman Holmes
    Pearson. New York: Modern Library/Random House, 1937. (This edition is cited
    in the text.)
Hawthorne's Tales and Sketches. Ed. Roy H. Pearce. New York: Library of America,
    1996.
The House of the Seven Gables. Ed. Seymour L. Gross. New York: W.W. Norton, 1967.
The Marble Faun; or, The Romance of Monte Beni. Intro. Maxwell Geismar. New York:
    Pocket Books, 1958.
The Scarlet Letter. Ed. Sculley Bradley. New York: W.W. Norton, 1978. (This edition
    is cited in the text.)

Solitary by temperament, bedeviled by an ancestral misdeed that tainted his
family name in the persecution and public murder of the 1692 Salem witchcraft
trials, and plagued with a guilty ambivalence over the very act of becoming a
writer, Nathaniel Hawthorne found in the ways and means of the Gothic tradition
a ready-made vocabulary of isolation, guilt, social fear, and spiritual skepticism
that accomodated his moral doubts about both himself and his young nation.
Hawthorne's biographers (see especially Randall Stewart's biography) all comment on his contact with English Gothic fiction as a young man struggling with
the decision of whether or not to become a writer of fiction. He admired the
romances of Ann Radcliffe and would later drape one of his most withdrawn
and mysterious characters in a black veil transferred from *The Mysteries of
Udolpho* to the face of the minister in "The Minister's Black Veil," thereby
deepening the symbolic possibilities of the Gothic object and expanding it into
a multiple symbol of both guilt and mourning.

  The process of subjectifying the objective devices of terror and horror that
he extracted from the Gothic tradition remained Hawthorne's lifelong approach
as he sought a Gothic style that would intensify but not overwhelm his somber
themes. The transformation of horrific objects and events into psychic symbols
of a terror that struck deeper than mere physical fright was not an original
method with Hawthorne. Reading William Godwin as an aspiring young writer,
he immediately noticed his modifications of Gothic machinery to expose social
horrors. Godwin's polemical handling of the psychology of guilt in *Caleb Williams* as well as the novel's close study of how a concealed crime might engender guilt in both the criminal and the victim fascinated Hawthorne. He took
note as well of just how Godwinian Gothic had socialized and mentalized horror
and terror in its nightmarish depiction of a haunted and unsafe society in order
to promote a grim moral message about "Things As They Are" without any
direct moralizing. Young Hawthorne also read Matthew Lewis's *Romantic Tales*
and *The Monk* together with the novels of Sir Walter Scott and Charles Maturin.

Scott's Gothification of history left a permanent impression on Hawthorne's vision of the past, while Maturin's successful fusion of the Gothic with the tragic in *Melmoth the Wanderer* suggested to Hawthorne the value the Gothic might hold for a Gothic writer in search of a tragic voice. Maturin's elevation of the Gothic to pinnacles of moral horror and mental terror and his presentation of heroic evil in the wanderer's egotistical quest showed Hawthorne how the Gothic might be turned to serious purposes.

Hawthorne's first attempt at short-story writing was the lost collection titled *Seven Tales of My Native Land*, which he suppressed, just as he attempted to destroy all copies of his first heavily Gothic novel, *Fanshawe*. (The young Hawthorne had it published at his own expense.) These juvenilia no doubt contained trial-and-error efforts to work out viable ways of incorporating the Gothic's "power of blackness" (the phrase comes from Melville's review of Hawthorne's *Mosses from an Old Manse*) into three grand tragic themes: the impenetrable darkness of the human heart; the horrifying refusal of human beings to be human or accept human limits; and sequestration by memory, both personal and cultural, that provoked an overwhelming sense of entrapment in a corrupt and inescapable past. Hawthorne's cautious appropriation of the Gothic was a major aspect of his artistic makeup from his beginnings as a writer and enabled him to enter into that "neutral territory," as he called it in the prologue to *The Scarlet Letter*, "somewhere between the real world and fairy-land, where the Actual and the Imaginary may meet, and each imbue itself with the nature of the other" (31). For Hawthorne, "neutral territory" usually meant Gothic landscapes and the tenebrous scenery of a fallen world looming in the midst of a new Eden.

Although the Gothic is but a single strand of Hawthorne's dark tapestry, it is a persistent and necessary strand, for without its energies the allegories would be flat and the austere historical texture of the novels and tales far less compelling. Never an end in itself, Hawthorne's imposition of Gothicism on his materials is a vital means of gaining access to what he calls in the preface to *Mosses from an Old Manse* "the inner passages of my being." Only in a single story, "The White Old Maid," is there any regression to the gruesomeness of horror for horror's sake. Only in the final writings, *The Ancestral Footstep* and *The Dolliver Romance*, is there anything resembling straightforward and unadulterated Gothicism, and these posthumously published works, precisely because of their absolute Gothic conventionality, are written off as failures.

Hawthorne resorts to everything useful to his own ends as he selects judiciously from the large catalog of Gothic effects, manipulating the Gothic without succumbing to its sensational extremes. The Gothic constantly enriches, but never dominates his narratives, even in the awkward first attempts to link the Gothic to American materials. Throughout his career, Hawthorne preferred to use its preternatural and supernatural properties as well as its special capacity of rendering the dead past as a living force to probe the depths of human experience and to articulate the unspoken truths about the human heart. For Hawthorne, the Gothic's greatest asset lay in its adaptability to the dilemmas of

conscience, moral reckoning, and egotistical motive that drive his characters to
the very limits of their humanness and beyond while testing their resiliency to
remain human in soul-threatening circumstances. Hawthorne's preoccupation
with what Henry James calls in his classic study of Hawthorne "the deeper
psychology" (51) resulted in a version of the American Gothic that was sharply
distinct from Poe's linear adaptations of the tradition. Subordinated to his tragic
themes, the Gothic assumed its place as one of Hawthorne's most reliable techniques of moral clarification that allowed him to concentrate on the intransigence
of evil and the fragility of innocence in a vibrant and expanding society that set
no apparent limits on the aspiration for profit or power. "He is usually careful,"
observes Neal Doubleday, "not to allow the interest of the Gothic element to
obscure the theme. What is Gothic is merely a vehicle for the theme" (252).

Almost systematically, Hawthorne tested the workability of Gothic ideas in
the many short stories that precede the writing of his major novels. The majority
of the tales in the two short-story collections *Twice-told Tales* and *Mosses from
an Old Manse* are saturated with Gothic effects and devices superimposed upon
Puritan and New England history. Their concreteness of place and time stands
in marked contrast to Poe's ahistorical and indefinite Gothic environments. By
their titles alone, many of the tales immediately suggest some Gothic act, place,
person, atmosphere, or plot pattern. Demonic or satanic encounters, mirrors that
hold images of the dark past, decaying families locked up in decayed houses,
haunted minds pursued by fiends within, eerie landscapes alive with evil, ghostly
music and macabre pageants, shadowy vistas of unnameable horror in the deep
woods, restless corpses demanding burial, inscrutable villains and diabolical scientists who treat their own flesh and blood as mere material in their experiments,
Faustian wanderers, menaced maidens, dark and tangled genealogies, living,
breathing, bleeding portraits and statues, funereal weddings, intense and pyrotechnic night scenes, intricately sinister victimization, and regular intrusions of
the supernatural into the natural world are among the routine Gothic materials
that Hawthorne refashions and refines to higher ends during his short-story-
writing phase.

Unlike Poe, who launches his Gothic narratives with a "preconceived effect"
in view, Hawthorne usually begins his Gothification of American history by
starting with a moral abstraction, for example, the necessary coexistent tension
of good and evil within the self, then applies Gothic formulas in a distanced
and subdued fashion to see if the abstraction can be made dramatically true and
psychologically vivid, always refusing to simplify what is morally complex and
mysterious. Hawthorne discovered an additional dimension of the Gothic crucial
to his interest in the dream state. Earlier Gothic writers had shown Hawthorne
how reality and the dream state could be blurred to the point where the nightmare assumed a materiality of its own more "real" than waking reality itself
and where the darkest recesses of consciousness became luridly incandescent.
Two tales in particular, "My Kinsman, Major Molineux" and "Young Goodman
Brown," make use of the night journey that culminates in a moment of dark

enlightenment for the young Americans who venture away from home. Both tales present a black pilgrimage into the "neutral territory" between consciousness and unconsciousness where nothing less than the young voyagers' salvation or damnation hangs in the balance. Satan himself appears in both stories, as he had appeared often in the pages of Gothic fiction, as a dark, fatherly intercessor who offers the young American the precious wisdom of self. How young Robin Molineux and Young Goodman Brown choose to respond to their moment of truth is staged in Gothic terms as a reunion with the fiendish father within. Robin Molineux's night journey is positive even though his delusion of self-innocence is permanently shattered; but for Young Goodman Brown, the same night journey into the heart of darkness and the same rendezvous with self result in a rejection of his humanness at the climactic moment when the devil prepares to grant him membership in the sinful race by a bloody baptismal touch. Robin Molineux finds his kinsman and returns from his night journey with new communal ties, but Young Goodman Brown rejects the moral value of the night experience by refusing to rejoin family and community. The terror of both tales turns on misanthropic pride, a moral horror that is deeply human but hardly uniquely American.

The variegated Gothicism of many stories in *Twice-told Tales* registers Hawthorne's effort to determine what was and was not essential to him for the enhancement of his tragic art. "The Gray Champion," a story based on a real incident in seventeenth-century New England history, shows his inclination to import a well-worn Gothic prop, in this case, the potent or deadly glance, then reset the lethal optic that normally appears as a facial weapon of the Gothic villain to create a political ghost story with a democratic moral. The "hoary apparition" of the Gray Champion materializes at those moments of history whenever and wherever European tyranny threatens American liberty. When the despotic colonial governor, Sir Edmund Andros, tries to crush all opposition in the streets of Boston, the spectral figure in gray emerges from the crowd to repel Andros and his men with a lethal stare, gesture, and curse. With the despot immobilized, the Gray Champion "melt[s] slowly into the hues of twilight" (866) to reappear whenever freedom is threatened. The tale shows perfectly Hawthorne's practice of refurbishing a standard Gothic object, in this case, the eye that maims or slays, then altering its horrific potential to evoke something deeper than mere surface alarm or maidenly panic. The Gothic castle's residential avenging specter of a wronged or murdered relative becomes the fable's phantom of liberty, while the supernatural optical power that had once been one of the perverse strengths of William Beckford's Vathek is transmuted into the omnipotent glare of American freedom.

Similar successful transmutations of melodramatic devices and stock characters of the Gothic occur throughout the early stories. "The Wedding Knell" is built around a familiar Gothic acoustic, the midnight bell that tolls by supernatural touch, and the specter bridegroom or demon lover who extends a grisly invitation to the horrified bride. " 'Come, my bride!' said those pale lips. 'The hearse is ready. The sexton stands waiting for us at the door of the tomb; let us be married; and then to our coffins!' " (871). Similarly, in "The Minister's Black Veil," the darkly draped portrait in Udolpho Castle that frightened Emily St. Aubert half to death is transported to the eternally hidden face of the Reverend Mr. Hooper. In *The Mysteries of Udolpho*, the black veil functions merely to heighten suspense and to build a terror of the unknown to a breaking point, but Hawthorne transforms it into a symbol of either a heartless act of isolation from humanity or a compassionate gesture by a conscience in perpetual mourning for all of sinful humanity—the reader cannot say which, since Hawthorne never resolves the ambiguity of the remade Gothic symbol.

The shudder originally induced by the animated portrait of early Gothic fiction is endowed with ambiguous qualities in two stories in which Hawthorne rehangs the magic portrait in his own gallery of effects, "The Prophetic Pictures" and "Edward Randolph's Portrait." In "The Prophetic Pictures," the human beings who sit for their portraits begin to take on the malicious qualities deliberately painted into the works of art by the artist. "Edward Randolph's Portrait" is set during the year of the Boston Massacre, 1770, and involves the terrible ravages of ancestral guilt. The contorted features of Governor Hutchinson's guilty ancestor, Edward Randolph, are transmitted point by point to the dead face of Hutchinson after he repeats his ancestor's crime by violating the liberty of the people. Hawthorne's animated portraits are called upon to perform much more than the previous uses of the prop in Gothic fiction, and typical of Hawthorne's Gothic, they advance the theme without displacing it.

Demonic encounter and an apparent victory for evil over innocence mark "The Hollow of the Three Hills," one of the earliest of Hawthorne's witchcraft stories. The unnamed young lady's rendezvous with a witch and the placing of her head in the hag's lap with the accompanying ghostly chuckle produce an eerie feeling of terror that makes the tale one of Hawthorne's best early Gothic pieces. "The White Old Maid" is in a category of its own by virtue of its nearly Poe-like construction and climax. Here Hawthorne uncharacteristically ventures into the charnel and emetic Gothic of Monk Lewis and the Schauerromancers, an unusual departure from his customarily subdued and subtle Gothicism. The tale commences with a corpse kiss and culminates in a cadaverous embrace celebrating a necrophiliac liaison of lovers in the foul-smelling bedchamber of a moldering mansion. For once, no moral is implied or intended as Hawthorne revels in a sickening climax worthy of Poe, Lewis, or any one of the cheap chapbookers.

One story in *Twice-told Tales* is not a story at all but a sort of Gothic nocturne or oneiric fugue narrated by a troubled dreamer who describes that moment of pleasing terror when "things of the mind become dim spectres to the eye" (235). Entitled "The Haunted Mind," this night piece contains several statements that might stand as prescriptions for the American way of Gothicism. Made to behold a pageant of ghastly shadows while asleep, the narrator becomes aware that the mind is a dungeon that "holds its hell within itself," recalling the inner hells of

Marlowe's *Doctor Faustus* and Milton's *Paradise Lost*. For the narrator, there is no exit from the self's black hole or release from "the nightmare of the soul; this heavy, heavy sinking of the spirits; this wintry gloom about the heart; this indistinct horror of the mind, blending itself with the darkness of the chamber" (236). Note again the curious process whereby the psychological and spiritual become material and tangible as the haunted mind finds itself helplessly suspended in the neutral zone.

If "The Haunted Mind" holds one key to Hawthorne's Gothic, the overlooked sketch "Monsieur du Miroir" [Mr. Mirror] has a similar significance in the second collection of short fiction, *Mosses from an Old Manse*. As the narrator peers at his reflection, he is startled to see a creature both familiar and alien, the stranger in the mirror. The revelation of a sinister twin lurking in the mirror opens a line of Gothicism developed by Hawthorne into full-fledged terror of the unknown self in many of the finest stories in *Mosses from an Old Manse*. The mysterious stranger facing the narrator in the mirror is, of course, a version of the *doppelgänger* or secret self, a figure sometimes angelic but often diabolic in the Romantic period. Almost playfully, Hawthorne raises the disturbing possibility of a lower self hiding in the shadows of every human being and poised to take control over any one of us without warning. Mr. Mirror possesses the power to displace his human counterpart at any point, although Hawthorne stops the sketch far short of reaching any such occult outcome. The sketch ends with the narrator in a perplexed mood of uneasy awareness over his unanticipated confrontation with the "other" in his life. In "The Haunted Mind," Hawthorne had linked the mirror to the dangerous faculty of imagination when he mused that "the imagination is a mirror, imparting vividness to all ideas, without the power of selecting or controlling them" (235).

The finest of the Gothic tales in *Mosses from an Old Manse* and *The Snow Image* harbor Hawthorne's deepest fears of the unchecked intellect and fancy. He uses various Gothic motifs as a means of clarifying such spiritual crises as the dehumanization that can occur during the act of artistic creation and the moral horror that can arise when the cold and probing intellect decides to violate "the sanctity of the human heart" when it is driven by a pitiless curiosity or Faustian need to know. These tales scrutinize the catastrophic consequences of intellectual arrogance that find Hawthorne consciously readjusting psychologies of several of the traditional Gothic hero-villains to enforce his moral point. In "Rappaccini's Daughter," the gaunt and black-clad botanist Doctor Rappaccini exemplifies the influence that the villains of Ann Radcliffe—in this case, Father Schedoni in *The Italian*—could have on Hawthorne's conception of domestic malice. Inexplicable patriarchal evil in the form of a father's indifference toward his daughter's humanity through his fiendish toxic experimentation on her reveals Hawthorne's fascination with the familial insularity of Gothic evil. How the search for a worthwhile truth can sometimes dehumanize and diabolize the searcher, a theme brought to its tragic limits in Maturin's *Melmoth the Wanderer*, appears in "Ethan Brand," a pyrotechnic tale of nocturnal meetings climaxing in a fiery mountaintop suicide with the hero-villain's defiant leap into the hell mouth of a blazing lime kiln. Ethan Brand's selfish search for the unpardonable sin repeats the selfish quest of Maturin's Melmoth, who would find his salvation at the expense of others' sufferings. The egotistical heroism of the Gothic villain surfaces again in the character of Aylmer in "The Birthmark," a recasting of Mary Shelley's *Frankenstein* and, more specifically, of Victor Frankenstein's urge to improve upon nature by making flawless what God had left flawed, the removal of a birthmark on the body of Aylmer's wife, Georgiana. Here the attempt to perfect instead destroys, as Hawthorne brings to bear his fear and distrust of theoretical science, especially as it might operate within a democratic culture hell-bent on expansion and invention. In these stories, Hawthorne developed American equivalents for European Gothic characters and locales and evolved his version of an American Satan to counter the popular notion of an American Adam that the transcendental writers were promoting.

Many other stories in *Mosses from an Old Manse* and the later collection *The Snow Image* are exacting exercises in the refinement of Hawthorne's Gothic art. "Fire Worship" is less a story than a comic meditation that turns one of the Gothic's lurid lighting scenes into a droll night piece on the infernal nature of modern technology, "the cheerless and ungenial stove" (729). "Egotism; or, The Bosom Serpent" capitalizes on the self-horror and revulsion inherent in the ancient belief that a snake might reside within a human body and inflict its venomous will on the helpless host. Allured by the horrific prospect of a bosom serpent, an idea that requires no further Gothification, Hawthorne lingers over the moment before the mirror when Roderick Elliston, whose egotism has metamorphosed into a bodily viper, "catch[es] a glimpse of the snake's head far down within his throat" (1113). There is an equally powerful reuse of the Gothic body in the form of the restless corpse that demands interment in "Roger Malvin's Burial." Here Hawthorne converts the straightforward revenge on the living sought by the unburied body into a strange tale of guilt and terrible redemption. "The Man of Adamant" is a gruesome parable of misanthropy set in a natural American Gothic locale, a cavern in the forest depths, that becomes the perverted sanctuary of the tale's marble-hearted egomaniac, Richard Digby. The story even restages a favorite subterranean climax of the Schauerromancers when a group of children uncover the petrified corpse of Digby within its gloomy recess when they pull down a wall and push aside a slab of rock to reveal the stalactite man. In "The Wives of the Dead," Hawthorne builds the suspense of the tale around the motif of the corpse vigil as the two wives await the ghostly returns of their dead husbands, one lost at sea and the other killed in battle. The story is an example of how the Gothic element in Hawthorne's art is brought under masterly control and directed at the illumination of a moral dilemma or problem of conscience. Each wife receives a visit from her dead husband while the other sleeps; each wife keeps her secret of the miraculous return from the other out of compassion for the other's loss.

The apprenticeship to the Gothic in all its facets in the short fiction equipped

Hawthorne to apply the Gothic intelligently to achieve the moral focus he desired in *The Scarlet Letter, The House of the Seven Gables*, and to a lesser extent in the international novel *The Marble Faun*. His first novel, *The Scarlet Letter*, relies extensively upon Gothic paraphernalia and atmosphere to provide a perspective for exploring the terrors, mysteries, and perplexing tensions of the moral life. Like many Gothic novelists, Hawthorne gives historical distance to his subject by setting the psychodrama in the merciless and repressive social prison of seventeenth-century New England Calvinism. From the Catholic horrors of his English Gothic models, Hawthorne extrapolated those conditions of fear, guilt, and desire that entrap the characters in countless monastic shockers. The Puritan zeal that demonizes both the villain, Roger Chillingworth, and the society he represents closes in on the novel's victims, Hester Prynne and Arthur Dimmesdale. The novel's powerful night scenes, its heightening of the natural into the supernatural, and its substitution of a Puritan equivalent for the Catholic matrix of terror contribute to making *The Scarlet Letter* an American Gothic novel of the serious and introspective type initially attempted by Charles Brockden Brown in *Wieland, Arthur Mervyn*, and *Edgar Huntly*. "Hawthorne's Gothic prisons in *The Scarlet Letter* are, as he says in one of the forest chapters, 'dungeons of the heart.' His enigmas, like the 'mysterious horror' of the letter on Dimmesdale's chest, pose questions about theology and psychology" (Lewis 281).

Many critics of the American Gothic classify *The House of the Seven Gables* as a technical achievement in transcribing the European Gothic to American artistic requirements and cultural conditions. The novel is certainly the most formally Gothic of Hawthorne's novels when its contents are compared against prototypes such as Walpole's novel of a doomed house, *The Castle of Otranto*. An ancestral crime and curse and a haunted interior crammed with supernatural appliances such as portraits that stare back and music that floats from ghostly instruments attest to the purity and orthodoxy of the novel's formal Gothic features. But although *The House of the Seven Gables* makes use of nearly every trapping and prop appearing on Jane Lundblad's checklist of Gothic essentials (see Lundblad, *Nathaniel Hawthorne and the Tradition of the Gothic Romance*), what emerges is not a repetition of Walpole's pseudomedieval fantasy but a new strain of Gothic romance suitable to a new democracy and aptly designated "Yankee Gothic" by the critic Ronald T. Curran. By the time of the novel's writing, Hawthorne had mastered the tendency to allow the Gothic business in his fiction to become thematic instead by regulating it and incorporating it stylistically to make it serve as a vehicle for his themes. As a result, the Gothic constantly enriches both style and theme in *The House of the Seven Gables*. To the subjective prisons the characters build around themselves Hawthorne adds the terrible burden of history, national as well as familial, to observe how moral regeneration might arise from ethical failure. The disinheritance and death of the wizard, Matthew Maule, the legacy of guilt of Colonel Pyncheon and his blood-drinking ancestor, Judge Jaffrey Pyncheon, the pathetic victimization and incarceration of Clifford and Hepzibah Pyncheon by the dark past symbolized by their immurement in time within their seven-gabled house of pain—these elements demonstrate how closely Hawthorne adhered to earlier blueprints for Gothic success in the construction of the novel. The plot conforms to European Gothic novels in that it involves the supernatural working out of the ancestral curse down through history that ends in the purification of the family name by an acknowledgment of sinful participation in the family crime. What is uniquely neo-Gothic in Hawthorne's rendering of a standard Gothic myth is his affirmation of the democratic ideal that when goodness sometimes does arise from the evil in human nature, it sometimes can choose to triumph over the malign legacy imposed by the past. The curse is broken when Holgrave, a descendant of Matthew Maule, marries Phoebe Pyncheon, the daughter of darkness and Pyncheon depravity. Hawthorne's close formal observance of the Gothic modus operandi in *The House of the Seven Gables* never detracts from his Americanization of Gothic. Every spectral event and supernatural object that the house contains bear reminders of the pervasive presentness of a past whose historical and psychological primacy cannot be denied. Perhaps this is why at the conclusion of the novel, Hawthorne's haunted house, unlike Walpole's haunted castle, remains intact and inhabited by living Americans.

With the writing of *The House of the Seven Gables*, Hawthorne had accomplished what Charles Brockden Brown, John Neal, and other writers of the early Republic had only approximated in their search for an American Gothic. Hawthorne's qualified and carefully controlled use of the Gothic enabled him to come to terms with those moral enigmas that concerned him most and to dramatize their importance to an American readership. In the Gothic's repository of dark images Hawthorne found a vision compatible with his pessimistic suspicions about human nature that he could employ to throw light upon these doubts and fears. Without always being conscious of its presence as a catalyst to his imagination, Hawthorne reverted to the Gothic in nearly everything that he wrote because he came to realize that certain aspects of human evil could be given fullest expression only through its dark conceits. Like Poe in Hawthorne's own time and Henry James, Mark Twain, and Ambrose Bierce later in the century, Hawthorne's recourse to the Gothic was almost predetermined, given the emergencies of conscience and ironies of culture that he faced. As Donald Ringe concludes:

As long as Americans turn their backs on the total experience of mankind, fail to perceive the significance of the past, and refuse to accept the reality of those ghosts and devils that emerge from its gloomy depths or lurk in the human heart, they will not achieve the insight that can only come from a full awareness of the dark underside of life. The Gothic world of Hawthorne's fiction serves as an appropriate vehicle for expressing those somber truths which Hawthorne believed Americans of his generation needed to know most. (176)

SELECTED CRITICISM

Allen, M.L. "The Black Veil: Three Versions of a Symbol." *English Studies* 47 (1966): 286–289. Discusses the process of transformation from Radcliffean Gothic object in *The Mysteries of Udolpho* to Hawthornesque Gothic symbol in "The Minister's Black Veil."

Baym, Nina. "Hawthorne's Gothic Discards: *Fanshawe* and 'Alice Doane['s Appeal].' " *Nathaniel Hawthorne Journal* (1974): 105–115. Examples of early failures of Hawthorne's attempts to "combine the basic elements of the Gothic with the American environment."

Calhoun, Thomas O. "Hawthorne's Gothic: An Approach to the Four Last Fragments." *Genre* 3 (1970): 229–241. On *The Ancestral Footstep* and *The Dolliver Romance*, fragmentary and unfinished works in which the Gothic occupies the foreground rather than the background of the narratives.

Chisholm, Richard M. "The Use of Gothic Materials in Hawthorne's Mature Romances." Doctoral dissertation, Columbia University, 1970. [*DAI* 31:382A]. "Hawthorne uses Gothic material to suggest qualities of inner experience."

Curran, Ronald T. " 'Yankee Gothic': Hawthorne's Castle of Pyncheon." *Studies in the Novel* 8 (1976): 69–80. Reads *The House of the Seven Gables* as "a democratic version of the standard Gothic romance." Yankee Gothic is a conscious reversal of European Gothic models, as Hawthorne's Gothic reflects "his own ambivalent faith in American democracy."

Doubleday, Neal Frank. "Hawthorne's Use of Three Gothic Patterns." *College English* 7 (1946): 250–262. The three patterns are mysterious portraits, witchcraft, and esoteric researches that transgress mortal limits.

Goddu, Teresa A. "(Un)veiling the Marketplace: Nathaniel Hawthorne, Louisa May Alcott, and the Female Gothic." In *Gothic America: Narrative, History, and Nation*. New York: Columbia University Press, 1997: 105–116. Studies "the Gothic metaphor of mesmerism" in placing *The Blithedale Romance* in the American Gothic tradition. Hawthorne himself is just as guilty of cheap "market manipulation" as any of the female scribblers he denounced.

Graham, Wendy. *Gothic Elements and Religion in Nathaniel Hawthorne's Fiction*. Marburg: Tectum Verlag, 1999. Investigates Hawthorne's modifications of traditional Gothic material to accommodate his moral themes.

Hull, Raymona E. "Hawthorne and the Magic Elixir of Life: The Failure of a Gothic Theme." *ESQ: A Journal of the American Renaissance* 18 (1972): 97–107. Studies Hawthorne's demon-driven scientists and their involvement with "the elixir of life, the aqua vitae, or philosopher's stone, that archetypal symbol dating from the earliest records of alchemy that was a plot device in many a Gothic romance."

James, Henry. *Hawthorne*. Ithaca: Cornell University Press, 1956.

Lewis, Paul. " 'Mournful Mysteries': Gothic Speculation in *The Scarlet Letter*." *American Transcendental Quarterly* 44 (1979): 279–293. Evaluates the success of Hawthorne's Gothic practices by drawing many explicit connections between Lewis's *Monk* and *The Scarlet Letter*.

Lloyd Smith, Allan. "Hawthorne's Gothic Tales." In *Critical Essays on Hawthorne's Short Stories*. Ed. Albert von Frank. Boston: G.K. Hall, 1991: 232–243. Views the characters, places, and events of Hawthorne's short fiction from a psycho-

sexual angle. In Hawthorne's hands, "the Gothic is 'performed'; it is not allowed
to direct the form of the narrative."

Lundblad, Jane. *Nathaniel Hawthorne and the Tradition of The Gothic Romance*. New
York: Haskell House, 1964. Originally published as *Nathaniel Hawthorne and
European Literary Tradition* (Cambridge, MA: Harvard University Press, 1947),
the study identifies these traditional elements in Hawthorne's writings: the manuscript; the castle; the crime; religion; Italians; deformity; ghosts; magic; nature;
armored knights; works of art; and blood. "The scenery and whole machinery of
Gothic romance became, just like Puritanism or spiritualism, one of Hawthorne's
media of artistic expression."

Martin, Robert K. "Haunted by Jim Crow: Gothic Fictions by Hawthorne and Faulkner."
In *American Gothic: New Interventions in a National Narrative*. Ed. R.K. Martin
and Eric Savoy. Iowa City: University of Iowa Press, 1998: 129–142. Examines
Faulkner's *Absalom, Absalom!* and Hawthorne's *House of the Seven Gables* to
discover how conflicts and tensions of race and gender are "expressed through
Gothic elements. The emphasis on stolen land and bartered bodies joins the two
texts of Hawthorne and Faulkner as national narratives and original myths that
locate the Gothic as a national repression, a series of crimes that are not incidental
to but rather constitutive of the nation."

Newlin, Paul A. " 'Vague Shapes in the Borderland': The Place of the Uncanny in
Hawthorne's Gothic Vision." *ESQ: A Journal of the American Renaissance* 18
(1972): 83–96. Explains Hawthorne's attraction to the Gothic. "Hawthorne's use
was not directed so much at the senses as at the conscience."

Ringe, Donald A. "Nathaniel Hawthorne." In *American Gothic: Imagination and Reason
in Nineteenth-Century Fiction*. Lexington: University Press of Kentucky, 1982:
152–176. "The influence of literary Gothicism is apparent in some of Hawthorne's
best and most important work. He made good use of what might be called the
general ambience of the mode."

St. Armand, Barton Levi. "Hawthorne's 'Haunted Mind': A Subterranean Drama of the
Self." *Criticism* 13 (1971): 1–25. Hawthorne "strikes a psychic balance between
waking and sleeping" in this nocturnal sketch and others.

Stein, William Bysshe. "Faustian Symbolism in the Gothic Romance." In *Hawthorne's
Faust: A Study of the Devil Archetype*. Gainesville: University of Florida, 1953:
35–50. "More perceptive than other Gothic practitioners, Hawthorne realized that
the devices of Gothic machinery were nothing more than immemorial mythic
images whose function had been obscured by rational thought."

Stewart, Randall. *Nathaniel Hawthorne: A Biography*. New Haven: Yale University
Press, 1948. Discusses the influence of Radcliffe, Godwin, Maturin, and Scott on
the young Hawthorne.

Voller, Jack G. "Allegory and Fantasy: The Short Fiction of Hawthorne and Poe." In
*The Supernatural Sublime: The Metaphysics of Terror in Anglo-American Ro-
manticism*. De Kalb: Northern Illinois University Press, 1994: 209–239. Hawthorne contributed to the creation of an American Gothic tradition by "turning
native elements—forests, frontiers, indians—to Gothic purpose and thereby produced a different sort of romance, a different supernatural literature that was both
less supernatural than much British Gothic fiction and, in some hands at least,
more disturbing."

E[RNST] T[HEODOR] A[MADEUS] HOFFMANN
(1776–1822)
Douglass H. Thomson

PRINCIPAL GOTHIC WORKS

"Die Automata" [The Automaton]. *Zeitung für die elegante Welt*, 1814. (Later included in *Die Serapionsbrüder* with "Eine Spukgeschichte" as a transition to it.)

"Der Magnetiseur" [The Magnetizer or Mesmerist]; "Die Abenteuer der Silvester-Nacht" [Adventures of New Year's Eve]. In *Fantasiestücke in Callots Manier aus dem Tagebuche eines reiseder Enthusiasten*, 4 vols. Bamberg: Kunz, 1814–1815.

Die Elixiere des Teufels: Nachgelassene Papiere des Bruders Medarduseines Capuzmers [The Devil's Elixirs: Posthumous Papers of Brother Medardus]. Berlin: Dunder & Humblot, 1815–1816.

"Ignaz Denner"; "Der Sandmann" [The Sandman]; "Das Majorat" [The Entail]. In *Nachtstücke* herausgegeben von dem Verfasser die *Fantasiestücke in Callots Manier*. Berlin: G. Reimer 1816–1817. 2 vols. ("Ignaz Denner" was originally intended for *Fantasiestücke* but was rejected because of its "gruesomeness.")

"Die Bergwerke zu Falun" [The Mines at Falun]; "Eine Spukgeschichte" [A Ghost Story]; "Vampirismus" [Vampirism]. In *Die Serapionsbrüder*. 4 vols. Berlin: G. Reimer, 1819–1821.

MODERN REPRINTS AND EDITIONS

The Best Tales of Hoffmann. Ed. E.F. Bleiler. New York: Dover, 1967.

The Devil's Elixirs. Trans. Ronald Taylor. London: John Calder, 1963.

"The Entail." In *The Penguin Book of Horror Stories*. Ed. J.A. Cuddon. Baltimore: Penguin, 1984.

Sämtliche Werke in fünf Einzelbänden [Collected Works]. 5 vols. Ed. Walter Müller-Seidel, Friedrich Schnapp, Wolfgang Kron, and Wulf Segebrecht. 5 vol. Munich: Winkler, 1960–1965.

Selected Writings of E.T.A. Hoffmann. Trans. Leonard J. Kent and Elizabeth C. Knight. Foreword by Rene Wellek. 2 vols. Chicago: University of Chicago Press, 1969.

Tales of Hoffmann. Trans. R.J. Hollingdale. New York, N.Y.: Penguin, 1982.

The realm of the supernatural operates on many levels, and often at the same time, in the works of E.T.A. Hoffmann. The reader of his mercurial tales will find the most rapturous of high Romantic reveries set right alongside visions of the grotesque or the absurd or, on the other hand, everyday reality, and it takes only a quirk in plot or the smallest shift in perception to send his characters spinning from one realm to the other. A contemporary critic credited Hoffman with "open[ing] up, like a hidden door in one's everyday living room, the new miraculous fairy realm, in which everything can be explained, dissolved, and formed anew, and yet still remain mysterious and independent" (McGlathery 21). Many modern critics see his fantastic stories as prime specimens of the "fertile chaos" celebrated by such German Romantic writers as Friedrich von Schlegel and Novalis; earlier critics, however, such as Scott and Goethe, found something pathological and repulsive in "the author's forcing the reader to follow him through labyrinths of dream and insanity without a saving thread" (McGlathery 23); that apparent lack of a saving thread and higher moral purpose then endeared him to adherents of *l'art pour l'art*, while his explorations of dreams and insanity continue to invite varied psychoanalytic interpretations, most famously evidenced by Freud's Oedipal interpretation of "The Sandman" in his essay "The Uncanny." One can see from his protean literary achievement and reception that Hoffmann cannot simply be considered a "Gothic" writer, but he deserves a place in the tradition for a number of reasons. First, he was an avid reader of many important first Gothics, whose influence can be clearly detected in some of his earliest tales and in the novel *The Devil's Elixirs*. Moreover, many of his mature, more fully "Romantic" tales continue to draw from and refashion Gothic materials. Finally, Hoffmann's psychological and formal complication of Gothic themes influenced Poe and Hawthorne and led, indirectly, to an opening of all kinds of new possibilities for Gothic and weird fiction.

Hoffman's tumultuous life surely informed his quixotic fiction. During his forty-six years he crisscrossed Europe, living in some of its most vibrant artistic and musical centers during the period of Napoleonic unrest. Born in Königsberg, where he attended a university permeated by the teachings of Kant, Hoffmann began a career as a Prussian civil servant and justice that led him to Plock, Warsaw (where he founded an orchestra and immersed himself in the city's rich musical life), Berlin, Bamberg (the medieval town from which the early German Romantic movement emerged), Leipzig, and Dresden, and finally back to Berlin. He proved to be a hardworking magistrate who often found himself at odds with those in power, above all owing to his satirical attitude toward the military authorities in Posen, but his first love, his true passion, was music. After Napoleon's victory over the Prussians ended his civil service career, he turned to professional music and theater management. He was a prolific composer in the Romantic vein, a conductor, and, under the famous pseudonym "Kapellmeister Johannes Kreisler," a critic who championed the new style. His opera *Undine* was his most notable musical achievement. But his professional struggles and the death of an infant daughter contributed to the drinking for which he was famed. Becoming the "Trinkmeister" ('Drinkmaster') of the Rose Tavern in Bamberg, he sold his first collection of tales, the *Fantasiestücke*, to a wine merchant named Kunz for a cellar of his best vintage (Bleiler ix–x). Some critics have traced Hoffmann's near obsession with the dual nature of human identity in his fiction to the split between his public role as magistrate and his private world of fantasy and music, although one can see how his need, as a judge, to interpret the line separating fact from fiction could also have informed his intricate epistemological parables. Surely his chaotic yet rich life—a student of Kant, a struggling bureaucrat, composer, kapellmeister, battlefield observer, perfecter of the *Künstlermärchen* (the literary fairy tale)—placed him in a position to articulate the vibrant crosscurrents of German Romanticism, to distill its essence and energy into his enigmatic tales.

Part of that heady mix of artistic elements was the Gothic. Hoffman was an enthusiastic reader of Carl Grosse's *Horrid Mysteries* and Matthew Lewis's *Monk*. Other powerful influences include Ludwig Tieck's *Märchen* and Goethe's *Sufferings of Young Werther*; stories of obsessive and fantastically idealized and destructive love are everywhere in his tales. Much of his early fiction is strongly in the Gothic vein. One of his earliest tales, generally not held in high critical regard because of its unalloyed gruesomeness, is "Ignaz Denner," a story of familial cannibalism: the gamekeeper Andres discovers to his horror that his wife's father (Denner) and grandfather, both sinister and fully supernatural figures, feast upon children in order to possess eternal youth. Andres is able to save only his eldest son from his literally bloodthirsty in-laws, and the tale ends with the death of his grief-stricken wife. This grim tale contains no redemptive moral of any kind, nor is it leavened by the witty and ironic reversals one usually tends to associate with Hoffmann. Another early tale, "The Magnetizer," is equally dark. In this tale of mesmerism, the young bride Marie falls dead at the altar due in part to the machinations of a mildly villainous hero, the hypnotic physician Alban, who has come to possess her psychically. Also blending weird science with Gothic atmospherics is "The Automaton," in which a young skeptic, dubious of the clairvoyant powers of Professor X's robot, the talking Turk, learns from the Turk, and later finds confirmed, that at the very moment he finds the woman of his dreams, he will lose her. Yet unlike many Gothic heroes deprived of their soul mates, Ferdinand finds ready if strange consolations, partly in his conviction that although she is lost to him physically, she will remain his forever spiritually, and partly in his initiation into the mysterious world of Professor X, where all things marvelous now seem possible, including tapping into the primordial music of the universe. In the tale's mingling of inspiration and madness, rapturous love and Gothic desertion, high idealism and riddling irony, we find the direction of Hoffmann's later tales.

But this direction was not fully pursued until Hoffmann set about completing a truly Gothic novel, *The Devil's Elixirs*, which he began in the spring of 1814 and published in 1815–1816). Directly inspired by *The Monk* and, in some ways, meant to rival it, the novel borrows the central conflict of Lewis's work. A monk tempted by a demonic agency—here a mysterious devil's elixir reaching all the way back to the temptation of St. Anthony—pursues a career of infamy and lustful gratification. But Hoffmann fantastically complicates the plot by introducing a series of seemingly endless and vertiginous doublings. Not only does Brother Medardus pursue and become pursued by his libidinal double, Count Viktorin, but virtually every character he meets in his winding journey away from and then back to the monastery possesses a dual nature: the heavenly Aurelia is counterbalanced by the sensual Euphemia; two mysterious artist figures monitor Medardus's twisting fate, one a majestic and anonymous "Painter" who resembles the Wandering Jew, the other, Belcampo, a hilarious "Tonsorial Artist" (he is a metaphysical barber) who argues for the wisdom of the insane. Then an ancient document turns up at the end detailing the monk's family history and explaining his destiny in a way that only multiplies personalities. As "the analysis of a man who did not know where he began or ended" (7), *The Devil's Elixirs* goes far beyond *The Monk* in depicting the winding repressions and psychic displacements of its main character, but one senses that the novel form itself is too diffuse a medium for Hoffmann and that his tales more effectively explore that fine dividing line between nightmare and reality, madness and sanity characteristic of his fiction as a whole.

Hoffmann's mature tales may seem to leave behind his earlier Gothic experiments in terms of their epistemological absorptions, rich ironies, and, above all, playfulness (hardly a Gothic staple). But a number of his best pieces offer virtuosic variations on Gothic themes. "Adventures of New Year's Eve" zanily complicates the old story of satanic temptation as Hoffmann imports into the center of this triple-decker his friend Adalbert von Chamisso's story of Peter Schlemihl, a man who has bargained away his shadow to the devil. Flanking Schlemihl's story are those of the Traveling Enthusiast, an unreliable narrator if there ever was one, and Erasmus Spikher, both of whom have been tempted and humiliated by the satanic temptress Julia/Giulietta and her devilish companion, Mr. Everywhere. The Enthusiast's fascination with her, fueled by drinking from a mysterious goblet fringed with signature Gothic blue flames, leads to the public unmasking of his infatuation and to his utter mortification and confusion. Spikher fares even worse, as his concluding narrative, relayed to the Enthusiast in a barroom, relates how he was tempted to offer his wife and child to the seductress, but, repenting, loses his reflection as a price for his dealings with the dark side.

Two of Hoffmann's darkest and most Gothic tales appropriately occupy his *Nachtstücke* (Nightpieces) of 1816–1817: "The Sandman" and "The Entail." The famous case of "The Sandman," one of his best-known art fairy tales, involves the lifelong haunting of a hypernervous Nathaniel by the Sandman, who, as his nurse had told him when he was young, would pluck the eyes from children who were restless at bedtime. The shadowy figure of the Sandman appears first as Coppelius, who works with Nathaniel's father behind closed doors on mysterious alchemical experiments, and then later as Coppola, a peddler of optical instruments who engineers Nathaniel's bizarre infatuation with the mechanical doll Olympia. The Sandman's final appearance neatly interrupts Nathaniel's long-deferred marriage plans when, catching sight of Coppola from afar, he plunges to his death from atop a tower. The tale clearly asks its reader to question the sanity of its central character, although Freud's explanation that Nathaniel displays all the classic symptoms of castration anxiety arising from the Oedipal complex might be too tidy an unraveling of its perplexing ambiguities. The influence of Ludwig Tieck's stories is evident in this agent of terror whose manifestations shift (Sandman/Coppelius/Spalanzani) and in the disturbed protagonist who is drawn to Clara, who represents normality, and Olympia, the automaton whose "lifeless eyes" (*Tales of Hoffman* 1982, 118) reflect the alienation of feeling from thought in Nathaniel. Clara offers Nathaniel a psychological explanation of the uncanny sandman who terrorized him as a boy—he was a "mirror-image" of himself—but for Nathaniel the barriers between reality and the uncanny have collapsed, and no convincing "explained supernatural" is possible. Hence the only solution for his inner fragmentation is suicide, soon after he tries to throw Clara off a tower. His inability to reconcile his inner conflicts between passive and active capacities is symbolized by his mad exclamation "Spin, puppet, spin!" (123). This points to his inability to reintegrate his fragmented self and overcome his tormented childhood in acts of free will.

More forthrightly—if that word can ever be used of Hoffmann's tales—supernatural is "The Entail," a complex story of primogeniture that offers not just a haunting of Baron Roderich's family line but, memorably, of his Baltic castle by the ghost of a departed but nasty servant who had murdered a previous master. The present Baron Roderich feels himself the special target of the ghost's latest plans, as his lovely wife Seraphina perishes in a sleighing accident that bears the unmistakable imprint of the ghost's infernal handiwork. Included within this tale framed by two narrators, one a young man who has fallen for the aggrieved and lovely Baroness, are many fine Gothic atmospherics of the type associated with stories of haunted castles, details that directly recall Walpole's *Castle of Otranto* and anticipate Poe's "Fall of the House of Usher," for which it is often cited as a source. "The Entail" straddles a fine line between spectral mystery and the "explained supernatural," dream and reality. It also has elements of the detective story. The narrator never sees the ghost of Daniel, though he hears terrible sounds behind the walled-up door that may be a ghost or a sick animal raised to horrific status through Daniel's reading of Friedrich Schiller's *Geisterseher*. Or it may be the murderous Daniel whom his uncle banishes from behind the walled-up door, since there is "a terrifying scream and a heavy thud" (197), but Hoffmann withholds certitude, and the narrator must rely on others' testimony. It is when the somnambulist Daniel is alive in V.'s narrative that he is most evidently a horrifying specter, scratching away at the walled-up door where years earlier he murdered Wolfgang. Schiller's supernatural tale provides a playful subtext to the tale of Hoffmann. Daniel and Franz the servant are named after two key characters in Schiller's *Die Räuber*, a robber drama Hoffmann alludes to in "The Sandman" as well.

Although almost all of Hoffmann's tales include some kind of reflection on the perils involved in a meeting between the mortal and the supernatural realms, three from his last full collection of tales, *Die Serapionsbrüder* (1819–1821), best exhibit the Gothic spirit. "A Ghost Story" is exactly that: the device of a floating saucer convinces young Adelgune's family that her perceptions of the ghostly "White Woman" are to be taken seriously. Thus they test the ghost by changing the clocks to try to baffle its customary appearance at 9:00 and prove that the visitation is a hoax. Despite the change, the White Woman shows up on cue, leaving the family in shambles as the mother dies of a nervous fit and the father seeks and finds death at the Battle of Waterloo. A title surely deserving mention on the roll call of Hoffmann's more Gothic tales, but somewhat mis-leadingly so because he did not supply that title, is "Vampirismus." The central figure, the Baroness Aurelia, is driven not to suck blood but to eat flesh (an appetite triggered by her physician's discussion of a pregnant woman's unnatural appetite). The tale has some supremely Gothic moments, none more so than her husband Hyppolit's nightmarish vision of Aurelia in a graveyard dancing among female ghouls in a true Walpurgisnacht ritual.

Finally, we have Hoffmann's powerful story "The Mines at Falun." In this chthonic fantasy of love and death, a young sailor, Elis Fröbom, is led through his dreams and the mysterious agency of a ghostly miner named Torbern to come to Falun in quest of the secrets of the Queen of the Mines. On the day of his wedding to his supervisor's lovely daughter Ulla, Elis feels summoned to prove his greater allegiance to the Queen as he descends in quest of a magic jewel. That descent leads to his death, although his body turns up perfectly preserved some fifty years later, only to fall to pieces in the loving embrace of the still-loyal and now-aged Ulla. Influenced by Tieck's story "The Runenberg," the story highlights Elis's inability to mediate the gaps between differing public and private selves. Just as Tieck's hunter surrenders absolutely to the hideous Woodwoman, Elis finally dedicates his "real being" to the Queen of the Mines rather than to Ulla, who represents an "angel of light" in a public sphere who cannot cover an abyss associated with his obsessive subterranean drives. Elis penetrates depths of nature that accelerate his alienation and fixation on Medusan "inconsolable torments." His obsession with the Queen increases his inability to communicate with others; thus he is unable to express love for Ulla, and it is his would-be father-in-law Pehrson who uses drastic means to facilitate their match. As E.F. Bleiler points out, the figure of the miner in the folklore upon which German Romantic writing drew was not some mere toiler underground, but "a quasisupernatural being who knew the secrets of nature and creation" (xxvii). Much of the dark magic of the tale involves Elis's compelling and weirdly compelled quest to plumb the depths of these mysteries. In essence, he experiences the dangerous visions of the artistic mind.

The deadly but beckoning mine shaft of "The Mines at Falun" provides the most elemental of many abysses in Hoffmann's fiction, but there is also the deep cliff over which the tormented double of Brother Medardus plunges and the black hole inviting disaster in one of the unrenovated wings of Baron Roderich's eerie castle. "Abysmal" might just be the word to describe Hoffmann's fiction in the Gothic style, both in the way his tales summon from deep within the psyche our most fantastic fears and in the way they seem to swallow up any one coherent, rational interpretation of the power they hold over us. *See also* **Ludwig Tieck**.

SELECTED CRITICISM

Bleiler, E.F. Introduction to *The Best Tales of Hoffmann*. New York: Dover, 1967: v–xxxiii. Sees Hoffmann's "blending of literalistic fantasy with allegory, symbolism, philosophy and psychology of the day" as "worlds removed" from the "Gothic prototypes" that "stimulated him when he was young." Isolates three key themes in Hoffmann's fiction: "that denial of revelation can be destructive; that there is a connection between madness and suffering; and that art and life do not mingle, but must be separated."

Cobb, Palmer. "Poe and Hoffmann." *South Atlantic Quarterly* 8 (1909): 68–81. A first and still important influence study.

Heinritz, Reinhard, and Silvia Mergenthal. "Hogg, Hoffmann, and Their Diabolical Elixirs." *Studies in Hogg and His World* 7 (1996): 47–58. Compares Hogg's *Confessions of a Justified Sinner* with Hoffmann's *Die Elixiere des Teufels* [The Devil's Elixirs].

Kamla, Thomas A. "E.T.A. Hoffmann's Vampirism Tale: Instinctual Perversion." *American Imago* 42 (1985): 235–253. A good representative of the countless psychoanalytic interpretations that treat Hoffmann's ostensible horror stories as Freudian parables of displaced desire and psychic conflict.

McGlathery, James T. *E.T.A. Hoffmann*. New York: Twayne, 1997. A very helpful overview of Hoffmann's literary achievement, especially in regard to the tricky chronology and publication history of the tales. Relies extensively on psychobiographical interpretation, especially concerning Hoffmann's futile love for his student Julia Marc.

Negus, Kenneth. "The Family Tree in E.T.A. Hoffmann's *Die Elixiere des Teufels*." *PMLA* 73 (1958): 516–520. Likens the never-ending journey of Medardus and his doppelgängers to that of the Gothic prototype, the Wandering Jew, and sees the ever-proliferating and murky family tree as a key feature of the novel's challenge to a linear understanding of narrative.

———. "The Allusions to Schiller's *Der Geisterseher* in E.T.A. Hoffmann's 'Das Majorat.' " *German Quarterly* 32 (1959): 341–355. Discusses how Hoffmann's evocation of Schiller's ghost world works to deepen his depiction of supernatural intrusion into everyday life.

Nehring, Wolfgang. "Gothic Novel und *Schauerroman*: Tradition und Innovation in Hoffmanns *Die Elixiere des Teufels*." *E.T.A. Hoffmann-Jahrbuch: Mitteilungen der E.T.A. Hoffmann-Gesellschaft* 1 (1992–1993): 36–47. Discusses Hoffmann's addition of psychological complexity and depth in the depiction of the subconscious compared to earlier writers in the Gothic tradition.

Romero, Christiane Zehl. "M.G. Lewis' *The Monk* and E.T.A. Hoffmann's *Die Elixiere des Teufels*: Two Versions of the Gothic." *Neophilologus* 63 (1979): 574–582. Studies Hoffmann's complex humanization of Lewis's often sadistic villain.

Tymms, Ralph. "Hoffmann: The Climax of 'Horror Romanticism.'" In *German Romantic Literature*. London: Methuen, 1955: 347–366. Traces the influence of Tieck on Hoffmann. Argues that "the assumption of a demonized nature" is fundamental to an understanding of the universe of the tales.

Von der Lippe, George B. "Beyond the House of Usher: The Figure of E.T.A. Hoffmann in the Works of Poe." *Modern Language Studies* 9 (1978): 33–41. Traces not just the influence of Hoffmann's fiction but his life and character on Poe's fiction, especially their shared fondness for deranged artist-lovers.

Willson, A. Leslie. "Hoffmann's Horrors." In *Literature and the Occult: Essays in Comparative Literature*. Ed. Luanne Frank. Arlington, Texas: University of Texas at Arlington, 1977. Arlington: Texas at Arlington University Press, 1977: 264–271. Another essay placing Hoffmann in a developing Gothic line between Lewis and Poe, with the idea that he is pivotal in transforming the sense of horror from an external to an internal threat.

Wright, Elizabeth. *E.T.A. Hoffmann and the Rhetoric of Terror*. London: University of London, 1978. Discusses and offers a comparative analysis of the English Gothic novel and Hoffmann's tales of terror, finding his profoundly more complex and deliberately ambiguous.

JAMES HOGG
(1770–1835)

Douglass H. Thomson

PRINCIPAL GOTHIC WORKS

The Brownie of Bodsbeck; and Other Tales. Edinburgh: William Blackwood & John Murray, 1818.

The Three Perils of Man; or, War, Women, and Witchcraft: A Border Romance. London: Longman, Hurst, Rees, Orme, & Brown, 1822.

The Three Perils of Woman; or, Love, Leasing, and Jealousy: A Series of Domestic Scottish Tales. London: Longman, Hurst, Rees, Orme, Brown & Green, 1823.

The Private Memoirs and Confessions of a Justified Sinner, Written by Himself; with a Detail of Curious Traditionary Facts, and Other Evidence, by the Editor. London: Printed for Longman, Hurst, Rees, Orme, Brown & Green, 1824.

The Shepherd's Calendar. Edinburgh: W. Blackwood; London: T. Cadell, 1829. (For the original publication dates of these tales, most of which appeared in *Blackwood's Edinburgh Magazine*, see Douglas Mack's edition of *The Shepherd's Calendar*.)

MODERN REPRINTS AND EDITIONS

The Brownie of Bodsbeck. Ed. Douglas S. Mack. Edinburgh and London: Scottish Academic Press, 1976.

Confessions of a Justified Sinner. Intro. Roger Lewis. New York: Knopf, 1992. (This edition is cited in the text.)

The Private Memoirs and Confessions of a Justified Sinner. Intro. André Gide. New York: Grove Press, 1959.

The Private Memoirs and Confessions of a Justified Sinner. Intro. Robert M. Adams. New York: Norton, 1970.

The Private Memoirs and Confessions of a Justified Sinner. Ed. John Carey. Oxford: Oxford University Press, 1981.

The Shepherd's Calendar. Ed. Douglas S. Mack. Edinburgh: Edinburgh University Press, 1995.

The Three Perils of Man: War, Women, and Witchcraft. Ed. Douglas Gifford. Edinburgh: Canongate, 1996.

The Three Perils of Woman; or, Love, Leasing, and Jealousy: A Series of Domestic Scottish Tales. Ed. David Groves, Antony Hasler, and Douglas S. Mack. Edinburgh: Edinburgh University Press, 1995.

In writing of the wondrously dramatic "riot of diablerie and nightmare" in *The Three Perils of Man*, Douglas Gifford insists on a strong distinction between "the traditional and folk treatment of things supernatural and the neo-Gothic treatment" (viii) of such things in *The Castle of Otranto* and *Melmoth the Wanderer*. Gifford only implies what this distinction might entail, mainly by emphasizing repeatedly the zest and freshness of James Hogg's supernaturalism. Apparently, the Gothic by contrast is more self-conscious and more literary or mannered in its presentation of the otherworldly. This distinction needs to be carefully examined even though it carries a certain resonance in the critical tradition, arguably reaching back to Friedrich Schiller's contrast of the "naïve" and the "sentimental" writer, and, of special relevance regarding Hogg, to Sir Walter Scott's two categories of "marvelous" fiction in his review of *Frankenstein*. Such a distinction must be applied with special caution to the works of James Hogg, who as the "Ettrick Shepherd" encourages consideration as a naïve, unlettered, more Romantically authentic voice, a mere custodian and transmitter of oral tales, but who, as recent criticism has shown, works complexly within and against rustic and national stereotypes. Despite this reappraisal of Hogg's artistry, the old distinction between folk and literary modes continues to shape the reception of his fiction. We value *Confessions of a Justified Sinner* for its obvious psychological and formal complexity and more obvious affinities with a Gothic tradition, while very little critical attention has been paid to Hogg's earlier fantastic novels and the wonderful tales of "Fairies, Deils [his word for devils], and Witches" he wrote throughout his career for *Blackwood's Edinburgh Magazine*. (These tales were collected for publication in *The Shepherd's Calendar* of 1829. Douglas Mack's recent edition provides the original *Blackwood's* texts because the 1829 collection presents versions considerably weakened by condescending editorial revision and interference.) An understanding of Hogg in relation to the Gothic tradition should address the full range of his supernatural fiction, not in terms of how it evolved from folk presentations to the sophistication of *Confessions of a Justified Sinner* but in terms of how this fiction strategically employs and realigns distinctions between folk and literary understanding of the otherworld.

As is well known, Sir Walter Scott, the literary lion of the Scottish revival, played a large but uneven role in the life and aspiring career of James Hogg. As Hogg's friend and literary sponsor, Scott introduced the Ettrick Shepherd— who in the tradition of the Romantic autodidact largely taught himself to read and write at the age of twenty-four—to Edinburgh literary society and invited his collaboration on *Minstrelsy of the Scottish Border* (1802–1803). In many ways and with Scott's encouragement, Hogg was intended to follow the legacy of Burns as "Scotch bard," and like Burns he played the role in hopes of financial and artistic gain yet chafed at the inevitable condescension of Edinburgh intellectual circles. In regard to the poetry and fiction of the supernatural kind, a major feature of Scottish literary excavation since James Macpherson's purportedly Ossianic *Fragments of Ancient Poetry Collected in the Highlands of Scotland* (1760) and William Collins's "An Ode on the Popular Superstitions of the Highlands of Scotland" (1784), Scott, in his *Blackwood's* review of *Frankenstein* (1818), draws a strong and very revealing distinction between a naïve or native sense of the marvelous and "a more philosophical and refined use of the supernatural" (304). In the first case, Scott contends that "the marvelous is itself the principal and most important object both to the author and reader"; we easily excuse "the poet or tale-teller" (note the telling uncertainty as to status) for his introduction of supernatural beings because "he himself is a believer" in such things. As the fiction is avowedly fantastic and asks obviously for suspension of disbelief, the reader can "walk the maze of enchantment with undaunted step" (303). In the more philosophical class including *Frankenstein*, Scott sees "the pleasure derived from the marvelous incidents [as] secondary to that which we extract from observing how mortals like ourselves would be affected" (304). In short, this higher mode is more reflective and instructive and can be more equivocal in its treatment of things supernatural.

The terms of this distinction exactly inform a later quarrel between Hogg and Scott concerning the role of the supernatural in fiction. Scott, whose attitude hardened against the supernatural as time went on, complained that in *The Three Perils of Man* Hogg had "ruined one of the best tales of the world" with the diablerie of the second half of the novel. By 1826, in his review for *Blackwood's* of John Galt's *Omen*, Scott condemns any recourse to "the superstition of the olden time, which believed in spectres, fairies, and other supernatural apparitions. These airy squadrons have long been routed, and are banished to the cottage and the nursery" (Gifford xiii). In his introduction to *The Three Perils of Man*, Douglas Gifford offers a fine discussion of Scott versus Hogg on the issue of the supernatural and includes important excerpts on the subject from Hogg's *Domestic Manners of Sir Walter Scott*. For his part, Hogg, in his tale "The Mysterious Bride," accused a "renegade" Scott of a diluted version of the marvelous, "made up of half and half, like Nathaniel Gowdy's toddy" (Gifford xiv), so artfully qualified as to call into question the very existence of things supernatural.

Scott's distinction actually has great resonance within the Gothic tradition, recalling the time-honored, if often-tricky, distinction between the popular tale of horror and the more literary tale of terror. This distinction unfortunately also places Hogg again within the order of the naïve tale teller, a "believer" in the folk tradition of things supernatural who, as contemporary reviewers repeatedly complained, marred his literary efforts with too-frequent recourse to "the superstition of an olden time." Yet while Hogg in his first novels and in many of his tales for *Blackwood's* is willing to assume this folk voice, his use of the supernatural is anything but naïve. Instead, Hogg artfully exploits conventions of the folk treatment of things supernatural to prosecute its more literary and aristocratic versions, especially as these appear in Scott's "school of chivalry." One can perhaps read his lively reworking of folk materials against the more genteel and exotic first Gothics of the English tradition, but Hogg actually deserves a place within the overall Gothic tradition as a writer who came to be keenly aware of the cultural ramifications of the literature of terror and its volatile position in the literary marketplace.

Hogg's contributions to the Tory *Blackwood's Magazine*, his collection of tales from the Scottish oral tradition, would seem most naturally to fall under Scott's first category of marvelous literature. But the tales instead celebrate a tough-minded, hard-earned wisdom in the values of Ettrick and offer, as Douglas Mack argues, "a sophisticated subversion of some of the assumptions of Enlightenment Edinburgh" ("Introduction" to *The Shepherd's Calendar* xii). This clever reversal of expectations is most easily demonstrated in the narration of two deaths by lightning in "Mr. Adamson of Laverhope" (1823). The first death, that of the title character, concerns a highly colorful folk tale of a cruel farmer given to persecutions of his poor neighbors who gets his just deserts, as the Ettrick farmers contend that a strange *gaberlunzie* (a devil in the guise of a Papist beggar) justly carries Adamson's soul to hell. A blandly scientific two-page account of the death of one Adam Copland, Esq., abruptly concludes the tale, as Hogg makes sure that his reader understands which of the two explanations better represents our response to one of nature's more awesome occurrences. A related skepticism about "the elaborate and subtle" theories of philosophers, a sure swipe at the Scottish Enlightenment, appears in a class of folk tales concerning "Dreams and Apparitions": the abstract and misguided conjectures of the philosopher, dismissed as "nonsense" by Hogg in his editorial role, cannot account for the "compost" of mind and matter mingled in dreams; all that really can or need be said is that "to the unlettered and contemplative mind," dreams argue for the "distinct existence of the soul" (118–119). Hogg adroitly pits the homely metaphor (the unconscious as compost heap) and the moral certainty of folk understanding against the dubious sophistication of academic theory, and this kind of opposition, rich with ironic potential, guides many of his narratives.

"George Dobson's Expedition to Hell" is dismissed by an attending doctor as a mere chimera, but George's death, along with that of the Hon. Mr. R** of L***y and two lawyers, argues for the reality of his infernal hackney-coach ride to the other side. In "The Witches of Traquair," two female saints intercede to save Colin Hyslop from a countryside rife with witches by giving him a "Vial of Repentence" and a medal depicting the crucifixion. Ultimately at a witch trial he is exonerated as being a man "of sincerity and simplicity" (238) and becomes something of a celebrity among the aristocracy and churchmen. This "reformer's tale, founded on a Catholic allegory" (240), as Hogg intriguingly terms it, just might also comment on Hogg's own situation, a rustic from the land of superstition and quaint custom brought in to entertain civilized society. A much more politically direct strike against the nobility forms the basis of the tale "The Brownie of the Black Haggs." A brownie in Scottish lore can be a benevolent household spirit or an evil goblin, and this one, Merodach, who has "the form of a boy, but the features of one a hundred years old, save that his eyes had a brilliancy and restlessness" (244), is something of both. He becomes a scourge to the horribly tyrannical Lady Wheelhope, who is given to beating and killing her servants in fits of temper and who becomes obsessed with defeating Merodach. But everything she plots against the brownie redounds upon herself, including the death of her son and finally herself. At the end, the lady's enemies, persecuted Covenanters, find her mangled corpse and bury "her like a dog" (254). Other tales from *The Shepherd's Calendar*, including the fine "Mary Burnet" (about a wronged lass who returns as a revenant), similarly affirm the wisdom of folk traditions, often at the expense of a skeptical and callous upper class. Directing the subtle interplay of supernatural tale and social criticism, Hogg as editor coyly plays the role of mere archivist and secondhand teller, but this perspective often allows him to carry on a subtle argument against Scott's antiquarianism and to turn the tables against the more sophisticated and Tory audience of *Blackwood's*.

Hogg's first sustained prose fiction, *The Brownie of Bodsbeck*, carries on this argument in a number of ways. In its story of the good Border farmer Walter Laidlaw's aiding of brutally persecuted Covenanters, *The Brownie of Bodsbeck* seems to take direct aim at Scott's more sympathetic treatment of the Royalists and their relentless leader Claverhouse in his 1816 novel *Old Mortality* (although Mack in his introduction to Hogg's novel suggests that it may very well have been written before Scott's). At any rate, Walter is actually less concerned with theological conflict—"Deil [Devil] take what side they war on" (163)—than with providing help and food to those who need it, even if this means imperiling his family and farm and becoming a prisoner of the detested "Clavers." In Hogg's historical revisioning of the conflict, the supernatural, as the title suggests, plays a central yet very pliable role. Walter and all of his kin and "fouk" believe absolutely in fairies and the apparently frightening brownie, a misshapen, dwarfish, and hunchbacked "bogle" given to haunting Walter's Chapelhope farm and carrying on midnight meetings with his beloved yet increasingly alienated daughter Kate. Furthermore, the narrative strongly suggests that the brownie and his infernal band, representing the native folk tradition, are responsible for the deaths of five of the Royalists, an event that incurs the wrath of Clavers and his suspicions against Walter. But we eventually find out with Walter, who barely conquers his fears through his love for his daughter, that this "brownie" is actually one John Brown, a persecuted and crippled Covenanter who has gathered his weary followers in a marvelously hidden cave deep in the Ettrick morasses. In a weirdly ironic way, we find Hogg using the old Gothic device of the apparently supernatural to protect the zealous Covenanters and the explained supernatural to reunite Kate with Walter, who now realizes that she has been using this potent fiction as a ruse to fool the folk and to help her persecuted countrymen. Still, the novel's moral center and eloquence reside in these folk—seen especially in Davie Tait's comic, yet moving prayer and exorcism (128–129)—as their heartfelt superstitions and simplicity in Hogg's treatment deftly underscore the purposeful cruelty of the Royalists and the skewed logic of an Edinburgh court that could arraign the "gudeman" Walter for treason.

A similar give-and-take characterizes Hogg's wrongfully neglected *The Three Perils of Man, or, War, Women, and Witchcraft: A Border Romance*, a story that in its medieval setting again recalls some of Scott's fiction but that carries with it another of Hogg's distinctive versions of the supernatural. The first half of the novel records the siege of Roxburgh Castle by Scottish nobles intent on wresting it from English hands and perfectly evokes the bygone world of chivalry in the court of King Robert, his proud daughter Margaret, and the brave Douglas. But the introduction of the coolly pragmatic Sir Ringan Redhough and his border reivers, who are keenly aware of the real human cost underlying the high-flown courtly rhetoric, serves as a counterbalance to the world of romance, and the siege becomes a bloody, messy affair, with some of Hogg's very likable peasant-heroes sacrificed, as they are in *The Brownie of Bodsbeck*, in most unromantic ways. With characteristic cross-purposes, Hogg thus evokes the "romance" of the fabled Scottish past and provides an ironic commentary upon it. The strong swerve to the supernatural in the second half of the novel stems from the reluctance of Sir Ringan to join the battle against the English troops of Musgrave; he sends a motley crew of Scots to Aikwood, the castle of the warlock and wizard Michael Scott of Dantean fame, to find out from the seer the eventual outcome of the battle. The wonderfully vivid and high-spirited tales of the supernatural that follow mainly concern a contest of magic between Scott and a friar in the loyal crew. These include rending two mountains asunder; Michael's Circe-like transformation of the crew into bulls, which the friar restores to human form; a decidedly comic foreshadowing of the *Confessions of a Justified Sinner*'s theme of dual identity in Scott's dividing of the bewildered Charlie, Gibby, and Tim "into twa"; and such things as the lamentable disappearance of a rich sirloin dinner when the friar unwittingly "blesses the beef in the name of Jesus" (174). Ian Duncan reads the contest "in which duelling magicians pit technological illusion against the real thing" as an "allegorical" representation of Hogg's feud with Scott (77).

The character who resonates most directly with the Gothic tradition is the Faustian Michael Scott, who disdains the friar's recourse to such scientific gimmicks as gunpowder and magic lanterns, while the most Gothic moment is the overreaching wizard's climactic challenge to Satan, which results in a really visionary contest of the four elements. But in a fashion typical of Hogg, the telling of this sublime encounter is left to the dim-witted Gibby, whom the friar yet claims "hast the art, in thy simplicity, of extracting more good out of real evil than any expounder of divine truth throughout the land" (454). In its exuberant mix of chivalric sentiment and gritty detail, the magical and the mundane, the visionary and the comic, *The Three Perils of Man* offers many variations on Gothic themes. It is at once a wonderful example of the "folk treatment of things supernatural" and a surprisingly complex tapestry of literary modes that play off against one another.

If a reader comes to Hogg's next novel, *The Three Perils of Woman; or, Love, Leasing, and Jealousy*, from the context of the maiden-centered Gothic, Hogg's effort might strike one as a Radcliffean plot gone mad. But as Antony Hasler has demonstrated in his introduction to the Stirling/South Carolina edition of the novel (the first republication in over 150 years), the nearer kinship and object of ironic scrutiny for Hogg's novel is the "national tale," especially of the kind practiced by one of his frequent detractors, John Wilson. The national tale frequently linked quasi-allegorical narratives of female education and court-ship to the issues of national identity and union with England and bespoke "acceptance of Hanoverian political and historical settlements" (xxi). Hogg's "cloven fiction" (xxiv), with its disturbingly persistent female revenants, barely cloaked references to prostitution and venereal disease, weird prophecies, and plot "circles," completely disrupts any such notion of historical continuity and simplistic national identity. In *A Series of Lay Sermons*, Hogg wrote against "ladies' novels" and "romances" because their stagey plots of "virtue rewarded and vice punished" conveyed "nothing of the reality of life" and tended to corrupt the feelings and imaginations of their readers. As we come to appreciate the subversive power of *The Three Perils of Woman*, a study awaits its disruptive "insertion of Gothic elements into a novel of manners" (Hasler xxxv).

It is hardly surprising to find that these novels incurred universal censure. Evoking again the image of an untutored or undisciplined Hogg, critics repeat-edly complained about his improprieties, glaring supernaturalism, and mixture of discordant elements, although one suspects that the Edinburgh literary estab-lishment might just as well have been disturbed by the subversive tendencies of the novels. Douglas Gifford suggests that Scott's pronouncements against Hogg's too-blatant supernaturalism led the discouraged writer to create the more equivocal and psychological version of horror contained in *The Private Memoirs and Confessions of a Justified Sinner*. Whatever the impetus for its intricate doubling of a religious fanatic and his demonic counterpart, *Confessions of a Justified Sinner* stands as one of the major novels of the British Gothic school, occupying along with Charles Maturin's *Melmoth the Wanderer* an important place marking the end of the first wave of the Gothic revival. Much of the novel's power stems from features it shares with Hogg's other supernatural fiction: the location, amid its formidable epistemological complexities, of a clear-sighted moral vision in folk wisdom—see, for example, Lucky Shaw's "There are many wolves in sheep's claithing" (164)—its utterly unsentimental-ized view of evil; its implicit critique, as Gary Kelly has shown, of the literary appropriation of an oral tradition, this time in the figure of a fussy editor's excavation of the sarcophagal text; and its deconstruction of high Romantic autobiography. On this latter score one might also note the fantastically effective undermining of Romantic nature reverie in George Colwan's startled apprehension of a "carnivorous," satanic apparition emerging from the "wee little ghost of a rainbow" (35–36), a Gothic transgression of Romantic aesthetics that rivals Victor Frankenstein's confrontation with his monster on an Alpine summit.

Confessions of a Justified Sinner lays bare some of the most fundamental aspects of Gothic pathology. Robert Wringhim's fanatic Calvinism—"How delightful to think that a justified man can do no wrong!" (13)—enables Hogg to exploit the full range of this frequent source of religious terror in Gothic fiction. In *Melmoth the Wanderer*, Maturin presents a similar schizophrenic in the person of an "eminent puritanical preacher" who spends his day lashing out at the sinful nonelect and his nights in tortured apprehension of his own damnation, "curs[ing] God for the very decree he has all day been glorifying Him for." At night, Maturin emphasizes, "his creed retaliates on him." So too, of course, does Wringhim's, and the sinner's descent into madness and the emergence of his evil genius allow Hogg, a self-made man, to satirize in a particularly dark way the more extreme tenets of the Reformed church. But the retaliation of the creed upon its advocate also allows Hogg to portray a powerfully Gothic picture of a soul lost in a terrifyingly inscrutable universe as the pursuer, by way of an infernal logic, becomes the pursued. At the end, Wringhim and the editor offer the rather lame hope that the "justified sinner's" suicide is a heroic act intended to end the existence of the insatiable Gil-Martin, Wringham's demonic double. But the final impression left by *Confessions of a Justified Sinner* is that of an expansive evil unleashed by a diseased soul, one that no conventional closure or system of morality can contain.

In his characteristically double-edged fashion, Hogg thus harrowingly creates the Gothic universe of sinners in the hands of an angry God and obviously criticizes the reductive creed upon which its vision of terror and madness is built. As a writer in the Gothic tradition, he is perhaps somewhat akin to that favorite character of Scottish lore, the brownie, at times a guardian of hearth and folk tradition, at other times a mischievous prankster. In "Dedicatory Verses to Lady Anne Scott," his prefatory poem to *The Brownie of Bodsbeck*, Hogg suggests that his true affinities lay with the folk tradition:

> But when it comes, as come it must,
> The time when I, from earth set free,
> Shall run the spark I fain would be;
> If there's land, as grandsires tell,
> Where Brownies, Elves, and Fairies dwell,
> There my first visit shall be sped (176).

Hogg is very adept at creating a sense of the marvelous and the dreadful, especially in terms that reveal the moral wisdom of the storytelling tradition. But he is equally adept at using the literature of terror to castigate intellectual overreachers and transgressors of his native culture. We need more study of his works within and against the Gothic tradition. *See also* **Sir Walter Scott**.

SELECTED CRITICISM

Bloede, Barbara. "The Gothic Antecedents of *The Three Perils of Man*." *Studies in Hogg and His World* 3 (1992): 76–86. Goes beyond Scott in noting source material for *The Three Perils of Man* in various Gothic novelists.

Blondel, Jacques. "Le Double: James Hogg et R.L. Stevenson." In *Le Double dans le romantisme anglo-américain*. Clermont-Ferrand: Faculté des Lettres et Sciences Humaines de l'Université de Clermont-Ferrand II, 1984: 143–154. A fruitful examination of the double in the two countrymen's novels.

Duncan, Ian. "Walter Scott, James Hogg, and Scottish Gothic." In *A Companion to the Gothic*. Ed. David Punter. Oxford: Blackwell, 2000: 70–80. An excellent discussion of Hogg's Gothicism in terms of his contest with Scott to define a Scottish identity.

Hasler, Antony. Introduction to *The Three Perils of Woman; or, Love, Leasing, and Jealousy; A Series of Domestic Scottish Tales*. Edinburgh: Edinburgh University Press, 1995: i–xlii. Studies how Hogg's novel undermines the usual "providential plotting" of the "national tale" through its use of the "farcical, the calamitous, or the weird," including the Gothic.

Heinritz, Reinhard, and Silvia Mergenthal. "Hogg, Hoffmann, and Their Diabolical Elixirs." *Studies in Hogg and His World* 7 (1996): 47–58. Sees Hoffmann's most Gothic novel, *Die Elixiere des Teufels* (a translation of which was available from *Blackwood's*), as influencing Hogg's demonic doubling of characters in *Confessions of a Justified Sinner*.

Jones, Douglas. "Double Jeopardy and the Chameleon Art in James Hogg's *Justified Sinner*." *Studies in Scottish Literature* 23 (1988): 164–185. A valuable "demonic" reading of the novel set against the usual psychological interpretations of Wringhim's madness.

Kelly, Gary. *English Fiction of the Romantic Period 1789–1830*. London: Longman, 1989. Less concerned with the *Confessions* as a Gothic novel than with its wry subversion of English professional letters and the union scheme. Does note its unraveling of Romantic autobiography.

Mack, Douglas S. "Aspects of the Supernatural in the Shorter Fiction of James Hogg." In *Exhibited by Candlelight: Sources and Developments in the Gothic Tradition*. Ed. Valeria Tinkler-Villani, Peter Davidson and Jane Stevenson. Amsterdam: Rodopi, 1995: 129–35. A first consideration of *The Shepherd's Calendar* in the context of the Gothic tradition. "Hogg's short stories are richly complex works which draw on deep wells of tradition in their resonant use of the supernatural."

———. "The Body in the Opened Grave: Robert Burns and Robert Wringhim." *Studies in Hogg and His World* 7 (1996): 70–79. Is the stubbornly preserved body in the open grave a metaphor of Hogg's conflicted relationship with his predecessor as "Scotch bard"?

Pope, Rebecca A. "Hogg, Wordsworth, and Gothic Autobiography." *Studies in Scottish Literature* 27 (1992): 218–240. Follows Gary Kelly in studying Hogg's subversion of Romantic autobiography.

Redekop, Magdalene. "Beyond Closure: Buried Alive with Hogg's *Justified Sinner*." *ELH* 52 (1985): 159–184. Studies the structural intricacies of Hogg's double narrative and its transgressions of generic expectations, especially the dubious desire of the sinner for a happy ending.

Scott, Sir Walter. "Remarks on *Frankenstein.*" *Blackwood's Edinburgh Magazine* 2 (1818). Rpt. in *Frankenstein; or, The Modern Prometheus.* Ed. D.L. MacDonald and Kathleen Scherf. Peterborough, Ontario: Broadview Press, 1994: 303–309.

Sedgwick, Eve Kosofsky. "Murder Incorporated: *Confessions of a Justified Sinner.*" In *Between Men: English Literature and Male Homosexual Desire.* New York: Columbia University Press, 1985: 97–117. Finds in Hogg's text a perfect case study for male paranoia in terms of homosexual desire.

Smith, Nelson C. "James Hogg." In *Supernatural Fiction Writers.* Ed. E.F. Bleiler. New York: Scribner's, 1985: 177–183. Offers a portrait of Hogg as a literary autodidact. Comments on Hogg's tales of apparitions and witchcraft, "The Barber of Duncow," "The Wool-Gatherer," and "The Hunt of Eildon."

WASHINGTON IRVING
(1783–1859)

Jack G. Voller

PRINCIPAL GOTHIC WORKS

The Sketch Book of Geoffrey Crayon, Gent. 7 parts. New York: C.S. Van Winkle, 1819–1820; 2 vols. London: John Miller, 1820. (Includes "The Legend of Sleepy Hollow," "Rip Van Winkle," and "The Spectre Bridegroom.")

Bracebridge Hall; or, The Humorists. New York: C.S. Van Winkle, 1822; 2 vols. London: John Murray, 1822. (Includes "The Student of Salamanca" and "Dolph Heyliger.")

Tales of a Traveller. 2 vols. London: John Murray, 1824; 4 parts. Philadelphia: Carey and Lea, 1824. (Includes the "Strange Stories by a Nervous Gentleman" series: "The Adventure of My Uncle," "The Adventure of My Aunt," "The Bold Dragoon," "The Adventure of the German Student," "The Adventure of the Mysterious Picture," "The Adventure of the Mysterious Stranger," and "The Story of the Young Italian." Includes also "The Money-Diggers," "The Devil and Tom Walker," and "Wolfert Webber.")

The Alhambra: A Series of Tales and Sketches of the Moors and Spaniards. 2 vols. Philadelphia: Carey and Lea, 1832; 2 vols. London: Colburn and Bentley, 1832. Includes "Legend of the Moor's Legacy," "Legend of the Arabian Astrologer," "The Legend of Prince Ahmed al Kamel," "Governor Manco and the Soldier," "Legend of the Two Discreet Statues," "The Legend of the Enchanted Soldier," "The Adventure of the Mason," "Legend of the Rose of the Alhambra," and "Legend of Don Munio Sancho de Hinojosa."

Wolfert's Roost and Other Papers, Now First Collected. New York: G.P. Putnam, 1855. (Includes "Wolfert's Roost.")

The Complete Works of Washington Irving. 40 vols. New York: Putnam's, 1851.

MODERN REPRINTS AND EDITIONS

Irving's works, especially "The Legend of Sleepy Hollow" and "Rip Van Winkle," are frequently republished and anthologized in various formats

including adaptations and children's versions. The editions listed here are
a few of the best-known editions suitable for scholarly investigation.

The Complete Tales of Washington Irving. Ed. Charles Neider. New York: Da Capo,
  1998. (Reprint of the volume published by Doubleday, 1975). (This edition is
  cited in the text.)
The Complete Works of Washington Irving. 30 vols. Ed. Henry A. Pochmann, Herbert
  L. Kleinfeld, and Richard Dilworth Rust. Madison: University of Wisconsin Press,
  1969–1970; Boston: Twayne, 1970–1989.
The Legend of Sleepy Hollow and Other Stories. Ed. Haskell S. Springer. New York:
  Penguin, 1999. (Retitled edition of *The Sketch-Book*, 1978).
The Sketch Book of Geoffrey Crayon, Gent. Ed. Malcolm Bradbury. London: Dent, 1993.
The Sketch-Book of Geoffrey Crayon, Gent. Ed. Susan Manning. New York: Oxford
  University Press, 1998.
Washington Irving's Tales of the Supernatural. Ed. Edward Wagenknecht. Owings Mills,
  MD: Stemmer House, 1982.

Washington Irving's popular fame rests on a couple of Halloween tales, but his
most valuable achievement comes not as the teller of quaint quasi-ghost stories
set in a misty, nostalgic America of never-was. What Irving created in his Knickerbocker legends and recraftings of European folktales was nothing less than a
bridge across the Atlantic, a fabulist's folkway that linked a nascent American
culture with its roots and origins. Irving, always mentioned as the "father of the
American short story" or "the first American writer to earn a living by his pen,"
was in fact something of a cultural archeologist, deeply interested in foundations
and origins while remaining fully committed to the stability of those structures
built upon them. Such a focus places Irving insistently at a point of juncture,
thus earning him repeated recognition as a figure of transition. A distinctly,
almost characteristically American writer who nonetheless managed to spend
some twenty years of his adult life living in Europe, Irving was indeed a man
of two worlds, one whose works looked both back to the European origins of
America—whether in historical fact, as in his biography of Christopher Columbus, or in fiction, as in his reworking of Spanish or northern European folklore—
and forward, as in his writings about the American frontier.

   Yet this strategic position at a point of interplay between old and new was
turned by Irving to another account, one more specifically concerned with his
post-Gothic fiction and his primary achievement in the genre, perhaps the
greatest achievement of his artistry. Fully aware of the classical Gothic's inability to survive transplantation to the New World, Irving was forced by his
awareness of the fundamental differences between Old and New World sensibilities to recast the Gothic, brighten its darker registers—unsuited to the brash
optimism of a young American culture—and tame its turbulent energies. This
he accomplished most obviously by his use of what has been termed a "sportive"
Gothic, a Gothic rendered with humor and an evident, almost self-indulgent, if

kindly, skepticism. In this inheres the charm of many of Irving's "supernatural" works.

Yet the construction of this skepticism is much more than a source of humor in Irving. It is also the means by which Irving, fitting his works to an American mind-set shaped by Scottish Common Sense philosophy and frontier pragmatism, restrained the reach of the supernatural, permitting it to be enjoyed but rarely condoning it, rarely allowing the possibility of spectral existence to endure even until the end of the story. For Irving's works are full of hedging devices, narrative strategies, frames, and rhetorical tropes that fence in the supernatural, restricting its play so dramatically that we finish Irving's stories not thinking so much of spirits as of superstition, not of ghosts but of gullibility. This is the essence of Irving's greatest achievement, for in his insistent desire to adapt the Gothic to American taste, Irving wrote tale after tale in which belief is the enduring issue, in which we as readers are granted the privilege of watching belief grow and flourish in the story, all the while also watching—because Irving very much wants us to watch—the deliberate construction of that ambiguity that will contain and limit, or shape, that belief. These tales become nothing less than exercises in the elaboration of a psychological framework or device that we witness being built even as we know it is being built in order to affect us and shape our reading. In a very real sense, Irving's Gothic tales are about readerly psychology, in a very self-conscious way, more than they are about spirits. In this, Irving again may best be understood as a transitional figure. As Michael Davitt Bell has noted in his perceptive study of Irving, *The Development of American Romance*, his "parodies of Radcliffe, and his phenomenal style, force the reader from the supernatural to the psychological—to the consideration of the irrational or duplicitous motives of characters and narrators. Irving is an important transitional figure in the increasing subjectification of Gothic terror" (81). Irving is poised between the traditional Gothic, with its reliance on atmospherics and suspense generated by external agencies, and an increasingly subtle Gothic of interiority and psychological nuance that will be practiced by Poe, Le Fanu, and James.

Irving's "Adventure of the German Student," one of his oft-anthologized tales, is perhaps the simplest example of this strategy. One of the "Strange Stories by a Nervous Gentleman" series from *Tales of a Traveller*, "The Adventure of the German Student" begins as a classic ghost tale: "On a stormy night, in the tempestuous times of the French revolution, a young German was returning to his lodgings, at a late hour, across the old part of Paris" (223). The atmospherics and the tale's main thread are pure Gothic, pure "Germanism": the young student, Gottfried Wolfgang, finds a beautiful woman weeping by a guillotine, takes her home, falls madly in love with her, and awakes the next morning to discover that she is a corpse, her head having been severed the day before. He goes mad and is confined to a madhouse, where he later dies.

Yet this straightforward and delightfully well told ghost story is deconstructed by Irving in its final lines. One of the auditors of the story asks if it were "really a fact," to which the tale teller replies: "A fact not to be doubted. I had it from the best authority. The student told it me himself. I saw him in a mad-house in Paris" (227). There the tale ends, the puncturing of our suspension of disbelief the final element, hanging in the air, in our consciousness, like an accusation. Reminiscent of Keats's "Eve of St. Agnes" and bringing to mind Thomas De Quincey's "On the Knocking at the Gate in *Macbeth*," Irving's tale ends with a springing of the trap, a slap-in-the-face revelation that we have been fooled, drawn into a tautly told and well-crafted ghost story precisely so we can have our succumbing to superstition held up before us and revealed for the rationalist surrender it is. What remains is not so much a ghost story as a powerful and pointed reminder of our complicity in the ghostly.

Irving's narrative strategies of control and distance are rarely this straightforward, of course. He was capable of masterly execution of the Radcliffean strategy of revealing apparently supernatural events to have quite natural, real-world causes, although the heightened sense of aesthetic self-awareness, to use Michael Davitt Bell's term, makes his works ultimately very different from Radcliffe's. While a rather impish fondness for ambiguity sometimes allowed Irving to hedge his bets even in such tales, the preponderance of evidence in these tales is usually enough to convince most readers that the realm of the real is the true source of mystery. In works such as the classic "Rip Van Winkle," the naïve, straightforward telling of the tale gives way, in its final moments, to hints and suggestions of duplicity: the neighbors doubt either Rip's sanity or his veracity, and the tale Rip tells is, at first, inconsistent; add to this the repeated emphasis on matrimonial conflict, and it becomes clear that Irving is creating the possibility that Rip's tale is a smokescreen. The "Note" and "Postscript" by Diedrich Knickerbocker, attesting to the verity of the tale and the haunted nature of the Catskill Mountains, appear to confirm the supernatural level of the tale, but the ironic undermining of Knickerbocker's involvement in this story is apparent from the tale's opening parenthetical remarks about his "researches." Knickerbocker's delight in listening to tales told by the old Dutch burghers of New York earned him such high regard that "certain biscuit-makers . . . have gone so far as to imprint his likeness on their New-Year cakes" (2). The return to the Knickerbocker frame at the tale's end, then, serves more to emphasize the superstitiousness and gullibility of Knickerbocker and his cronies, a superstitiousness that Rip exploited in skipping out on his "termagant wife."

Irving relies on more overtly Radcliffean revelations in tales such as "Wolfert Webber, or Golden Dreams" and "The Spectre Bridegroom." Both deploy Radcliffean narrative strategies of increasing suspense and uncertainty only to reveal the sources of that suspense as natural in their cause—in the case of "Webber," by the very Radcliffean device of smugglers and buccaneers, capped off by the ironic deflating of Webber's nocturnal escapades and greed-driven despair when his cabbage farm is subdivided for a new street and houses, leading him to find wealth in his own backyard, in the most literal sense, after all of his midnight diggings have come to naught. "The Spectre Bridegroom," which begins with an epigraph from Falstaff and a footnote that classes the forthcoming tale as "good-for-nothing lore," reveals the "ghostly" manifestation of the specter bridegroom to be nothing more than a human imposter, exploiting superstition in the pursuit of love.

Irving's most substantial achievements in controlled supernaturalism, however, come in tales that go "Rip" one better, building a more elaborate apparatus of containment around a compelling ghost tale. "The Legend of Sleepy Hollow" and "Dolph Heyliger" are Irving's greatest accomplishments in this, his most important vein of work.

"The Legend of Sleepy Hollow," another Diedrich Knickerbocker tale from *The Sketch Book*, begins with an epigraph from James Thomson's *The Castle of Indolence*, and its evocation of "A pleasing land of drowsy head. / Of dreams that wave before the half-shut eye" alerts us, if such a word is appropriate in connection with a tale of languid grace and autumnal ease, a tale to be told to lotus-eaters, to the fanciful nature of what is to come. The story of Ichabod Crane and his competition with Brom Bones for the hand of Katrina Van Tassel is too well known to need rehearsal here. What matters most to the immediate purpose is the means by which Irving develops readerly distance from the "supernatural" events of the tale: his gently ironic tone, the frequent mentions of dreaminess in association with Sleepy Hollow (indeed, the very name of the town itself), the superstitiousness of the townsfolk and their predilection for telling ghost stories, and Ichabod's knowledge of Cotton Mather's account of the Salem witch trials, *The Wonders of the Invisible World*. The mounting suspense of the story, culminating in Ichabod's midnight race against the Galloping Hessian, is followed immediately by the "morning-after" scene, much slower in pace and calmer in tone, and the town's quick recovery from the "disappearance" of its schoolteacher. Yet in the final paragraphs we discover that, the "old country wives" and their tale telling notwithstanding, Ichabod Crane went not to the Nether Realm with the Hessian but to law school (write your own lawyer joke here) and became a politician and a judge. Brom Bones, we are pointedly told, "was observed to look exceedingly knowing whenever the story of Ichabod was related, and always burst into a hearty laugh at the mention of the pumpkin; which led some to suspect that he knew more about the matter than he chose to tell" (54). Even Knickerbocker's postscript, which moves to the intermediary narrative layer, that of the teller of the tale and his audience, which in turn comes before that of Knickerbocker, which is contained in the narrative of Geoffrey Crayon, in the book written by Irving, ends with an affirmation of skepticism and disbelief as the storyteller exclaims, "I don't believe half of it myself" (56).

"Dolph Heyliger," one of Irving's longest "supernatural" tales, is a Knickerbocker tale from *Bracebridge Hall*, that collection of tales that presents itself as a series of tales told at the hall; this one also begins with a premonitory epigram, this time from Shakespeare's fantasy-romance *The Winter's Tale*, and is cast as a tale merely read from the papers of Knickerbocker, one of his "several tales of a lighter nature" (140). Yet once the tale of Dolph Heyliger, the mischievous and aimless hero of the tale, gets under way, it becomes as effective a ghost story as "The Adventure of the German Student." Apprenticed to the town's quack doctor, Dolph volunteers to spend a night in the reportedly haunted country house owned by the doctor and there sees the ghost of an old Flemish burgher, apparently pointing out to him the location of long-buried treasure. After a series of misadventures in the neighboring wilderness—and after hearing the relation of the self-contained ghost story "The Storm Ship"—Dolph returns home and indeed finds treasure hidden where the ghost had indicated. Dolph becomes rich and lives the life of a contented burgher thereafter, all thanks to the ghostly revelation of a buried treasure.

Or not: the tale concludes with a characteristically deconstructive gesture by Knickerbocker/Irving. The final paragraph begins by identifying the tale's provenance with the mock-stern statement "The foregoing tale rests on better authority than most tales of the kind, as I have it at second-hand from the lips of Dolph Heyliger himself" (191) in a manner that itself opens to ironic possibility the narrative authority of what we have just heard/read. The final sentence then erases utterly any supernatural possibility: "It may not be amiss, before concluding, to observe that, in addition to his other accomplishments, Dolph Heyliger was noted for being the ablest drawer of the long-bow in the whole province" (191).

While Irving pursued other supernaturalist narrative approaches in his works, most notably in the unambiguously spectral tales of *The Alhambra*—a work whose continental setting itself provides sufficient distance that the supernatural may be freely indulged without further hedging or restriction—it is in his Knickerbocker/Hudson River tales that Irving forges his most lasting contribution to the Gothic. These great tales provide a recognition of the role of readerly psychology that forms a key stepping-stone to, and profound influence on, the more psychologically sophisticated, if less nostalgically charming, tales of Poe, Le Fanu, and James.

SELECTED CRITICISM

Bell, Michael Davitt, "Strange Stories: Irving's Gothic." In *The Development of American Romance: The Sacrifice of Relation*. Chicago: University of Chicago Press, 1980: 77–85. An effective and insightful study of Irving's use of a post-Radcliffean narrative strategy, one in which "Gothic romance becomes aesthetically self-aware." This awareness is part of Irving's larger examination of the "contest between imagination and its appeal."

Bowden, Mary Weatherspoon. *Washington Irving*. Boston: Twayne, 1981. A solid overview of Irving's life and literary accomplishment.

Clendenning, John. "Irving and the Gothic Tradition." *Bucknell Review* 12:2 (1964): 90–98. Recognizes the psychological dimension of Irving's sportive modulation of the Gothic tradition, as well as the conflict within Irving between the creative imagination and pragmatic rationalism.

Fisher, Benjamin Franklin, IV. "Washington Irving." In *Supernatural Fiction Writers*. Ed. E.F. Bleiler. New York: Scribner's, 1985: 685–691. Provides an overview of Irving's works, emphasizing Irving's deft balancing of ghostly and rationalist explanations.

Getz, John R. "Irving's 'Dolph Heyliger': Ghost Story or Tall Tale?" *Studies in Short Fiction* 16 (1979): 67–68. Sees "Dolph Heyliger" as validating "imaginative truth" through its refusal to explain unambiguously the origin of Dolph's wealth, showing reason to be inadequate.

Griffith, Kelley, Jr. "Ambiguity and Gloom in Irving's 'Adventure of the German Student.' " *CEA Critic* 38:(1975): 10–13. Effectively notes Irving's ironic use of Gothic elements and his reliance on ambiguity to achieve his effects.

Lupack, Barbara Tepa. "Irving's German Student." *Studies in Short Fiction* 21 (1984): 398–400. Reads the tale as "a successful parody of the exhausted Gothic tradition."

Ringe, Donald A. "Irving's Use of the Gothic Mode." *Studies in the Literary Imagination* 7:1 (1974): 51–65. Deemphasizes the ambiguousness of Irving's works, favoring instead the "explained supernatural" approach. "Irving's Gothic tales, sportive though most of them may be, are fundamentally concerned with a problem of human perception, the reasons why people fail to perceive the world as it is, but see instead a world of Gothic terror."

Thompson, G.R. "Washington Irving and the American Ghost Story." In *The Haunted Dusk: American Supernatural Fiction, 1820–1920*. Ed. Howard Kerr, John W. Crowley, and Charles L. Crow. Athens University of Georgia Press, 1983: 13–36. Studies Irving's ambiguity, focusing on the way Irving's "Strange Stories by a Nervous Gentleman" play with the dynamic between the tales' tellers and auditors, resolutely refusing to resolve the tension between supernatural and rationalist explanation. Sees Irving as the foremost developer of the psychological ghost story.

Veeder, William. "Form, Psychoanalysis, and Gender in Gothic Fiction: The Instance of 'Rip Van Winkle.' " In *Gothick Origins and Innovations*. Ed. Allan Lloyd Smith and Victor Sage. Costerus New Series 91. Amsterdam and Atlanta, GA: Rodopi, 1994: 79–94. "Explores the extent to which readers' responses to 'Rip Van Winkle' are gendered. Do men and women react differently to the story, and why?"

HENRY JAMES
(1843–1916)
Douglass H. Thomson

PRINCIPAL GOTHIC WORKS

"The Romance of Certain Old Clothes." *Atlantic Monthly*, February 1868.
"De Grey: A Romance." *Atlantic Monthly*, July 1868.
"The Last of the Valerii." *Atlantic Monthly*, January 1874.
"The Ghostly Rental." *Scribner's Monthly*, September 1876.
The Portrait of a Lady. Boston: Houghton, Mifflin, 1882.
"Sir Edmund Orme." *Black and White*, 25 November 1891.
"The Private Life." *Atlantic Monthly*, April 1892.
"Owen Wingrave." *Graphic*, 28 November 1892.
"The Altar of the Dead." In *Terminations*. London: William Heinemann, 1895.
"The Way It Came." *The Chap Book*, 1 May 1896, and *Chapman's Magazine of Fiction*,
　　　May 1896. (Later renamed "The Friends of the Friends.")
"The Turn of the Screw." *Collier's Weekly*, 27 January–16 April 1898.
"The Real Right Thing." *Collier's Weekly*, 16 December 1899.
"The Third Person." In *The Soft Side*. London: Methuen; New York: Macmillan, 1900.
"Maud-Evelyn." *Atlantic Monthly*, April 1900.
The Sacred Fount. New York: Charles Scribner's Sons, 1901.
"The Beast in the Jungle." In *The Better Sort*. New York: Charles Scribner's Sons, 1903.
The Novels and Tales of Henry James, New York Edition. 26 vols., (1907–1917). New
　　　York: Charles Scribner's Sons, 1907. (Contains all the tales except "De Grey: A
　　　Romance," "The Last of the Valerii," "The Ghostly Rental," "Maud-Evelyn," and
　　　"The Third Person.")
"The Jolly Corner." *English Review*, December 1908.

MODERN REPRINTS AND EDITIONS

A Casebook on Henry James's The Turn of the Screw. Ed. Gerald Willen. New York:
　　　Thomas Y. Crowell, 1960.
The Complete Tales of Henry James. Ed. Leon Edel. 12 vols. Philadelphia: Lippincott,
　　　1962–1965.

The Ghostly Tales of Henry James. Ed. and intro. Leon Edel. New Brunswick, NJ: Rutgers University Press, 1949. (Reissued with a new introduction as *Henry James: Stories of the Supernatural*. [New York, Taplinger, 1970]. Includes, in addition to the tales listed in "Principal Gothic Works," "Nona Vincent," "Sir Dominick Ferrand," and "The Great Good Place.")

Henry James: Selected Short Stories. Ed. Quentin Anderson. New York: Rinehart, 1958.

The Portrait of a Lady. New York: Modern Library, 1951.

The Sacred Fount. Ed. Leon Edel. New York: Grove Press, 1953.

The Tales of Henry James. Ed. Maqbool Aziz. 3 vols. Oxford: Clarendon Press, 1973–1984.

Tales of Henry James. Ed. Christof Wegelin. New York: Norton, 1984.

The Turn of the Screw. Ed. Robert Kimbrough. New York: W.W. Norton, 1966.

The Turn of the Screw. Ed. Peter G. Beidler. Boston: Bedford Books of St. Martin's Press, 1995. (This edition is cited in the text.)

No general summary statement of Henry James's ghost tales will do: they range the gamut from the verifiably horrific to the ironically playful, from the tragic to the comic, from the dreadful to the droll. His short fiction dealing with the supernatural adroitly negotiates the space between or beyond the old "heart-shaking ghost-stories" (which to James "appeared all to have been told") and the "modern 'psychical' case," which does not rouse the "dear old sacred terror" (Beidler 117). James was well versed in both poles of the dialectic; his obvious fondness for the "dear old sacred terror" finds expression in many allusions to the Gothic tradition as he deftly borrows and transforms its conventions. On the other hand, he was equally well versed in modern spiritualism through both his father's and his brother's investigations of mediums and ghosts and his own familiarity with the Society for Psychical Research. His brother, William James, a professor at Harvard, was active in psychic research and wrote *The Principles of Psychology* (1890) and *The Varieties of Religious Experience* (1902). Drawing upon these family connections and other paranormal interests, James creates a canon of ghost tales characterized, as he said of them, by "[t]he strange and sinister embroidered on the very type of the normal and easy" (Edel, *Complete Tales* 8.11). In some of them, he domesticates the sinister and the Gothic, yet in others he shows how strange and even marvelous or perilous the normal life of consciousness can be.

There are to be found in the critical commentary two truisms about James's ghost stories that take us only so far in our understanding of them. The first is that Jamesian ghosts are "psychological," frequently *doppelgängers* or subjective correlatives of inner passions or turmoils, rather than the real things. The second truism is that as James's career proceeds, the ghosts evolve away from the ostensibly "real" and too obviously Gothic. One of his first attempts at writing a Gothic tale, "The Romance of Certain Old Clothes," ends "with marks of ten hideous wounds from two ghostly hands" (I.319) upon the throat of the heroine. Compare this orthodox grisly climax to the more psychologically and symbolically complex handling of material in "The Jolly Corner," in which, as

Vaid comments, "The ghost is but a symbolical embodiment of the phantom [that Spencer Brydon] must exorcise" (236). It is true that James rarely aims at terror as an end in itself. It is also true that all of the tales, with the possible exception of "The Romance of Certain Old Clothes," can be read from a modern perspective in psychological terms. But the illusion of horror or terror, the real experience of dread and trepidation, the exquisite and often-harrowing uncertainty experienced by his characters and by his readers as we try to understand the riddles of their lives—these are all fundamental features of the ghostly and recurrent reminders of the Gothic in James's tales. The thesis that the ghosts become less and less obvious or conventional and more and more oblique and complex has its grain of truth and satisfies our desire for narratives of an author's progress. But can we be sure that even James's last, arguably most complex specter, the "alter-ego" (James's term, not his Freudian critics') of Spencer Brydon, does not draw his power from palpable ghostliness? "It gloomed, it loomed, it was something, it was somebody, the prodigy of a personal presence" (12.224).

How real, in any case, are literary ghosts in general? Instead of perpetuating the debates about the "reality" of James's ghosts, a debate that has long since reached its crescendo in the criticism of *The Turn of the Screw*, a more fruitful approach to James's wonderfully inconclusive ghost stories is afforded by Tzvetan Todorov's well-known distinction between the "marvelous" and the "uncanny":

The fantastic . . . oblige[s] the reader . . . to hesitate between a natural and a supernatural explanation of the events described. . . . If he decides that the laws of reality remain intact and permit an explanation of the phenomena described, we say that the work belongs to another genre: the uncanny. If, on the contrary, he decides that new laws of nature must be entertained to account for the phenomena, we enter the genre of the marvelous. (41)

The "certain hesitation" that Todorov finds "common" to all stories of the fantastic is an especially helpful critical concept for understanding James's craftsmanship. Take, for example, the relatively early tale "The Ghostly Rental." Narrated by a Cambridge divinity student who is skeptical of ghosts, the tale concerns the haunting of a cottage by the daughter of the old captain Diamond, who had uttered a deadly curse on his child for pursuing the wrong man. Having forced the poor father out of his home, the ghost, obligingly enough, pays him rent (American coinage: $133) to provide him his only source of income. When the bedridden captain sends the divinity student to collect the rent, we encounter an instance of the "explained supernatural" very familiar to readers of Ann Radcliffe's rationalized Gothic dénouements: the ghost is actually his alive daughter, who uses the fiction to make some kind of peace with her father. The narrator's suspicions are confirmed; the ghost is a hoax; the marvelous, in Todorov's terms, gives way to the uncanny; the reader emerges from hesitancy. But just as this aspect of the supernatural is unraveled, another ghostly possibility emerges. The daughter suddenly, fantastically, sees the ghost of her father, who, as the student finds upon his return, has died while he was on his collection business. Todorov insists that at the end of such tales the reader is forced to make a decision between a "marvelous" or "naturalistic" understanding of the supernatural, but James's artful tale adds a turn of the screw, leaving both the divinity student and the detective in all of us uncertain about the ghostly. And—this is the important point—that uncertain ghostliness has perfect thematic appropriateness for James's artistic design: it speaks to the daughter's longing for her father, to the tragedy that has prevented their communication, and to the ghost of the love that still exists between them but that will now never be realized.

Virginia Woolf's explanation of James's turn to the ghostly in his short fiction remains one of the most satisfactory discussions of Jamesian Gothic:

> The stories in which Henry James uses the supernatural effectively are those where some quality in a character or in a situation can only be given its fullest meaning by being cut free from facts. Its progress in the unseen world must be closely related to what goes on in this. We must be made to feel that the apparition fits the crisis of passion or of conscience which sent it forth so exactly that the ghost story, besides its virtue as a ghost story, has the additional charm of being also symbolical. (52)

The apparitions fit the crisis of passion and of conscience in "The Ghostly Rental" and in all of the more successful of these tales as well, as our hesitancy between the ghostly and the symbolic gives them their "fullest meaning."

Many of these tales deal with a common Gothic motif, a curse from the past, something left unresolved from a bygone era that plays a mysterious role in shaping the lives of the characters in the present. Naturally enough, our hesitancy concerns whether that specter from the past exerts some independent power (the "marvelous" and also the frighteningly deterministic) or really exists as some crisis of passion or conscience in the present consciousness (the "uncanny"). In "Owen Wingrave," a young and principled pacifist must confront the staunchly militaristic legacy of his family and prove his courage by spending the night in a haunted room in which a Wingrave ancestor had killed his child and then later had mysteriously died himself. Owen is found dead the next morning, with the narrator, a sympathetic military instructor, providing the trenchantly ironic last word: "He looked like a young soldier on the battlefield" (9.51). In "De Grey: A Romance," a curse from medieval times hangs over the family, dooming the betrothed of a De Grey male to death shortly after marriage. "The Last of the Valerii" concerns the haunting of a modern Italian by the great Roman past, principally through the unearthing of a statue of Juno in his villa, which threatens his marriage and his sanity until his young American wife has it reburied. "Sir Edmund Orme" witnesses the return of a jilted lover in the person of a most gentlemanly ghost—he even attends church—who makes sure that the lovely Charlotte does not repeat her mother's error in rejecting him and will, instead, accept the narrator's offer of marriage. In "The Real Right Thing," the ghost of a great writer, Ashton Doyle, "Immense. But dim. Dark. Dreadful" (10.485), returns to haunt the writer who has undertaken his biography. At first a "mystic assistant" (10.479) helping the biographer, he turns into an admonitory presence to disrupt the telling of his tale because the writer cannot capture the "real right thing" about his achievement. In the greatest or, at least, quintessential of these tales with ghosts from the past, "The Altar of the Dead," we have George Stransom, a connoisseur of the dead, who has built a shrine to his lost beloved one, Mary Antrim, and others from his past. He comes to form a profound attachment with an unnamed "priestess of his altar" (9.270), but his reveries and their union are shattered when he discovers that the object of her adoration is Acton Hague, her dead lover and George's onetime friend. She begs him to include Acton in his altar; he refuses and is shattered to find their intimate relationship broken. Finally, ill and broken but finding value again in his precious altar, George sees his way, through the heavenly agency of Mary, to include and forgive Acton and movingly communicates this to the priestess, who has forgiven him for not forgiving Acton. In a highly ambiguous and moving ending, the priestess holds the (probably) dying Stransom as he gazes at his altar: has he, in Christian terms, ascended to the truth through his final act of forgiveness, or has he, in ironic terms, become yet one more light in his own obsessive altar? Nowhere else in James's fiction is death a more palpable presence, yet we are left with characteristic uncertainty as to whether or not the main character has made peace with his past or has fallen victim to it.

Another category of James's ghost stories, which in certain places intersects with "the sense of the past" theme, concerns thwarted or repressed passion, with the ghosts figuring as expressions of sublimated desire. So much has been written on this score concerning his most famous ghost story, *The Turn of the Screw*, that the reader need only be referred to Kimbrough's and Beidler's critical editions of the tale and Willen's casebook, which provide full critical and bibliographical information on the enduring debate regarding its ghosts. Todorov's idea of "hesitancy" provides a more fruitful approach than the either-or of "real" versus psychological debate. The tale is as much a "trap for the unwary" as a trap for the too wary. In "The Friend of the Friends" (first titled "The Way It Came"), a tale often mentioned as a forerunner of *The Turn of the Screw*, a narrator offers an unnamed woman's diary account of her broken engagement and spectral musings. She had tried to bring together two of her friends who shared "a notorious, peculiar power" (9.398), an ability to see the dead. Both her fiancé and her female friend had spectral visits from parents at their point of death, and when her female friend dies, the diary writer is convinced that her fiancé now has the power to commune with her departed spirit. He had admitted to her a visit from the friend on the evening of her death but insists that she was then alive. The narrator thinks otherwise, becomes convinced that the ghostly "she" has come between them, and breaks off the engagement. Neither marry, and she is convinced that his death six years hence is suicide, "a response to an irresistible call" (9.401). As with many of James's tales, "The Friend of the Friends" is perfectly poised between the palpably ghostly (there were witnesses to the parental visitations) and the psychological (it provides a masterful study of jealousy, which often imagines the chimerical as real). The same uncertainty with a gently comic twist pervades "The Third Person," a tale of two aging spinsters, Miss Susan and Miss Amy Frush, who inherit a house haunted by an ancestral Frush who had been hanged for smuggling. This information is conveyed to them via that favorite Gothic device, letters hidden in an old secretary that come to light. On one level, the ghost almost too obviously represents their longing for the male presence sadly lacking in their lives, yet the two Frushes find that in competing for intimacy with the ghost they threaten their friendship, so they decide that it must go. In a nicely whimsical ending, Miss Amy breaks out of her backwater and naughtily smuggles some valuables out of France, apparently allaying the ghostly ancestor, who finally disappears. Thanks to the ghostly, the old ladies have had their adventure and find a measure of peace and a sense of kinship with their past.

A third category of ghostly tales, arguably the most complex, deals with the famous Jamesian theme of the too-private or unlived life. These concern characters who, unlike dear Miss Amy, seem unable to act and live, who verge on leading spectral existences themselves. In these tales, the Todorovan idea of "hesitancy" is thematized at the level of character. We may hesitate as to whether we are in the presence of the marvelous or the uncanny; these characters, however, risk the danger of literally hesitating or procrastinating their lives away. The most famous of these hesitant beings is John Marcher of "The Beast in the Jungle," "a haunted man," feeling himself under the power of a mysterious curse (the beast in the jungle), who avoids any passionate involvement in life, especially and centrally with May Bartram, a woman who shares his "secret" for many years. As she dies, he realizes in a cemetery scene that the curse actually is his refusal to become involved in life. The loss of the woman who loved him and whom he could have loved brings the terrible irony home: "He saw the Jungle of his life and saw the lurking Beast; then, while he looked, perceived it, as by a stir of the air, rise, huge and hideous, for the leap that was to settle him. His eyes darkened—it was close; and instinctively turning, in his hallucination, to avoid it, he flung himself, on his face, on the tomb" (11.402). The language has all the extravagance of an effective Gothic climax and all the precision of a masterful psychological and cultural study of the unlived life.

In an earlier, less celebrated tale dealing with a similar theme, "The Private Life," James offers a virtuoso treatment of the *doppelgänger*. This story presents a socially parasitic and appropriately unnamed narrator who records his fascination with high Anglo-American society at a Swiss resort. The social circle includes the impeccably British Lord and Lady Mellifont, the great novelist Clare Vawdrey, and a famous actress, Blanche Adney, a potential love interest of our narrator, yet she seems more interested in Clare. Together they discover some very weird things. Lord Mellifont, the paragon of social decorum, has no existence, no physical existence, apart from his public life. He has no "private life," and when he is not in the presence of others, he simply ceases to be. Clare, on the other hand, has two beings: one a vacuous public persona who disappoints his adoring readership, the other a mysterious being writing secretively in the dark. His private life is literally realized as a separate being, a spectral demiurgos. The trick is that these presentations, which can be easily understood symbolically (one a satire about English punctilio, the other a parable about the writer's life), come across as eerily paranormal, conveyed not just by the narrator but confirmed by Blanche. Or is the actress toying with the frustrated narrator, a bit of the aspiring but unlikely artist himself? At the end of his tale, he is left alone and disconsolate, abandoned by the objects of his fascination. Perhaps his voyeurism has left him the most sadly private and Prufrockian of all the characters—a mere ghost of a man.

"The Jolly Corner," James's last ghost story, satisfyingly provides a perfect coda or summation of the themes and techniques he had evolved over the forty years of his writing them. Again we find the theme of the unlived life, but this time (unlike John Marcher) the main character, Spencer Brydon, is able to move beyond his selfish absorption to "exorcise" the ghost of his "alter-ego" (12.209). To do so, he must leave an idle existence in Europe and come to his ancestral home in New York City in order to fathom the true legacy of his American past, in order to "stalk a creature more subtle, yet at bay perhaps more formidable, than any beast of the forest" (12.195). This beast is nothing less than the spectral self he has become, and it indicates to him what he could have become, what he still could be, if he dares to live life. And dare he does, as he at the end embraces the love of Alice Staverton and moves beyond the limbo of unacted desire and sexual inertia that haunts many of James's characters. Again the clearly symbolic import of this ghost would seem to favor our dismissal of the marvelous in favor of the uncanny. But why, one wonders, does James depict the ghost as missing two fingers? Why is Spencer's nighttime encounter with the maimed beast so genuinely harrowing and frightening? Perhaps making the decision he does to throw off a dead self and embrace life again partakes of the marvelous after all. What could be more appropriate in terms of James's rich artistic diversity and his virtuosic reworking of Gothic themes than finding that his last and in many ways most frightening ghost story has a happy ending?

SELECTED CRITICISM

Akiyama, Masayuki. "James and Nanboku: A Comparative Study of Supernatural Stories in the West and East." *Comparative Literature Studies* 22 (1985):43–52. Explores parallels between the Kabuki dramas of Nanboku and James's short fiction, especially East and West variations on "the revenge-beyond-the-grave" motif.

Ballinger, Leonora M. " 'Apparitions and Night Fears': Psychological Tension in the Ghostly Tales of Henry James." Doctoral dissertation, New York University,

1996. [*DAI* 57:3490A]. Examines James's "heavy use of Gothic motifs" in the early stories to more subtle methods intermingling the supernatural and the psychological in later tales, *The Turn of the Screw*, "The Last of the Valerii," "The Altar of the Dead," "Private Life," and "Nona Vincent."

Banta, Martha. "The House of Seven Ushers and How They Grew: A Look at Jamesian Gothicism." *Yale Review* 57 (1967): 56–65. James's ghosts represent "the inexplicable menace of the negated life which springs forth from the jungle of the mind." Good on the Gothic psychology of *The Portrait of a Lady*.

———. *Henry James and the Occult: The Great Extension*. Bloomington: Indiana University Press, 1972. Investigation of James's psychological modification of the Gothic tradition in his novels and tales.

Beidler, Peter. *Ghosts, Demons, and Henry James: The Turn of the Screw at the Turn of the Century*. Columbia: University of Missouri Press, 1989. Chapter 2, "Some Pre-Jamesian Ghost Narratives," and chapter 3, "Motifs of the Ghost Case Tradition," relate to James's use of the Gothic tradition. Listed are fourteen motifs used by James that derive from the Gothic: ghosts appearing to two children; noises in the night; the face at the window; the upper part of the figure; the fixed stare; precise description of ghosts; identifying the ghost; the sad face; the felt presence of ghosts; ponds, tables, and stairs; a feeling of cold; cold winds; extinguished lights; and selective seeing of ghosts.

Cady, Edwin H. *The Light of Common Day: Realism in American Fiction*. Bloomington: Indiana University Press, 1971. Observes of "The Beast in the Jungle": "Wholly without the traditional impedimenta, the story of May Bartram and John Marcher is a Gothic tale of personal and moral sensibilities betrayed, stifled, and petrified by romantic egotism until Marcher is left facing the horror of the utter nothingness he has made of his life and May Bartram's love."

Lustig, T.J. *Henry James and the Ghostly*. Cambridge: Cambridge University Press, 1994. In James's work, the ghostly is a far more inclusive rubric than the reader might expect. "The relationships established in the ghost story are no less than a synecdoche of those which obtain in James's fiction as a whole. The ghost story involved chaotic and explosive forces, yet to counteract and channel romantic strangeness through brevity, the point of view and the use of commonplace, prosaic accessories was to practice a form of 'economy.' "

Matheson, Neill. "Talking Horrors: James, Euphemism, and the Specter of Wilde." *American Literature* 71 (1999): 709–750. The Gothic plot of Henry James's *The Turn of the Screw* provided its author with an apt language with which to represent the complex significations and charged effects surrounding same-sex sexuality, an issue made particularly salient by the trials of Oscar Wilde. The euphemistic quality of the story's language draws heavily on the tropes of Gothic discourses, so that sexuality is recurrently cast in the mode of fear and horror, implicating both author and reader in its guilty pleasures.

Merivale, Patricia. "The Esthetics of Perversion: Gothic Artifice in Henry James and Witold Gombrowicz." *PMLA* 93 (1978): 992–1002. Likens *The Turn of the Screw* and *The Sacred Fount* to Gombrowicz's "Gothic artist parables" and reads the main characters as ironic commentaries on the manipulative nature of such fictions.

Nettles, Elsa. "*The Portrait of a Lady* and the Gothic Romance. "*South Atlantic Bulletin* 39:4 (1974): 73–82. Studies James's use and transformation of such stock Gothic

types as the virtuous heroine in distress, the villain-hero, and the imprisoning
castle.

Ringe, Donald A. *American Gothic: Imagination and Reason in Nineteenth-Century Fiction*. Lexington: University Press of Kentucky, 1982. As James keeps "the objects
of terror significantly vague and merely suggest[s] the sinister quality they possess, he . . . stimulates the reader to conjure up in his own imagination a greater
sense of horror than could ever be suggested" by a detailed account of the real
thing. James is thus superior to Howells, "who describes too little," and Bierce,
"who describes too much."

Savoy, Eric. "Spectres of Abjection: The Queer Subject of James's 'The Jolly Corner.' "
In *Spectral Readings: Towards a Gothic Geography*. Ed. Glennis Byron and
David Punter. New York: St. Martin's Press, 1999: 161–174. The Gothicism of
this doppelgänger story relates to James's denial of the American self in deference
to his European self. He "seeks out his apparitional double, his spectral other, in
the rhetorical 'figures' of either his youthful self or a hypothetical American self
whose development was foreclosed by his European sojourn."

Shelden, Pamela Jacobs. "Jamesian Gothicism: The Haunted Castle of the Mind." *Studies
in the Literary Imagination* 7:1 (1974): 121–134. One of several studies that
emphasize and read James's Gothicism in psychological terms; focuses on the
theme of the Gothic double in "The Jolly Corner."

Sklepowich, E.A. "Gossip and Gothicism in *The Sacred Fount*." *Henry James Review* 2
(1981): 112–115. Shows how expertly James used Gothic properties and places
in the urbane Gothicism of the novel and its dynamics of social stigmatization.

Sweeney, Gerard M. "Henry James's 'De Grey': The Gothic as Camouflage of the Medical." *Modern Language Studies* 21:2 (1991): 36–44. A medical explanation for
James's supernatural: the male line of the De Greys is infected with syphilis.

Thorberg, Raymond. "Terror Made Relevant: James's Ghost Stories." *Dalhousie Review*
47 (1967): 185–191. One of the better psychological readings of the ghost stories.

Todorov, Tzvetan. *The Fantastic: A Structural Approach to a Literary Genre*. Trans.
Richard Howard. Cleveland: Press of Case Western Reserve University, 1973.
Famous for its dialectic of the "uncanny" and the "marvelous." The emphasis on
the reader's "hesitancy" seems made for an analysis of James.

Vaid, Krishna B. *Technique in the Tales of Henry James*. Cambridge, MA: Harvard
University Press, 1964. Offers close and careful readings of the symbolic dimensions of James' tales.

Veeder, William. "The Nurturance of the Gothic: *The Turn of the Screw*." *Gothic Studies*
1 (1999): 47–85. Propounds a theory of the Gothic, then applies it to an analysis
of James's novella to develop the thesis that "the death of Miles as he is 'held'
by the governess implicates all of late-Victorian culture." The theory of nurturance
is based on the fact that "societies inflict terrible wounds upon themselves and at
the same time develop mechanisms to help heal these wounds. Gothic fiction
from the later eighteenth century to the present is one such mechanism."

Woolf, Virginia. "Henry James's Ghost Stories." In *Henry James: A Collection of Critical Essays*. Ed. Leon Edel. Englewood Cliffs, NJ: Prentice-Hall, 1963: 48–54:
Woolf's witty critique chides James's ghosts for being "too worldly" and having
"nothing in common with the violent old ghosts—the blood-stained sea captains,

the white horses, the headless ladies of dark lanes and windy commons." Even so, Woolf admits to being scared half to death by *The Turn of the Screw*.

Zablotny, Elaine. "Henry James and the Demonic Vampire and Madonna." *Psychocultural Review* 3 (1979): 203–224. Focuses on James's exploration of psychic vampirism in several of his ghost stories.

STEPHEN KING
(1947–   )

Tony Magistrale

PRINCIPAL GOTHIC WORKS

Carrie. Garden City, NY: Doubleday, 1974.

'Salem's Lot. Garden City, NY: Doubleday, 1975.

Rage. New York: New American Library, 1977. (Under the pseudonym "Richard Bachman.")

The Shining. Garden City, NY: Doubleday, 1977.

Night Shift. Garden City, NY: Doubleday, 1978. (In this short-story collection, the following may be singled out for prominent Gothic content: "The Children of the Corn," "The Ledge," "The Mangler," "Sometimes They Come Back," and "Trucks.")

The Stand. Garden City, NY: Doubleday, 1978. Rev. and unexpurg. New York: Doubleday, 1990.

The Dead Zone. New York: Viking, 1979.

The Long Walk. New York: New American Library, 1979. (Under the pseudonym "Richard Bachman.")

Firestarter. New York: Viking, 1980.

Cujo. New York: Viking, 1981.

Danse Macabre. New York: Everest House, 1981. (Has an introduction, "Nightmares in the Sky." Nonfiction.)

Roadwork. New York: New American Library, 1981. (Under the pseudonym "Richard Bachman.")

Creepshow. New York: New American Library, 1982. (Short-story collection.)

Different Seasons. New York: Viking, 1982. (Short-story collection contains "Apt Pupil").

The Running Man. New York: New American Library, 1982. (Under the pseudonym "Richard Bachman.")

Christine. New York: Viking, 1983.

Cycle of the Werewolf. Westland, MI: Land of Enchantment, 1983.

Pet Sematary. Garden City, NY: Doubleday, 1983.

The Dark Tower: The Gunslinger. West Kingston, RI: Donald M. Grant, 1984.

The Talisman. New York: Viking and G.P. Putnam's Sons, 1984. (With Peter Straub.)

Thinner. New York: New American Library, 1984. (Under the pseudonym "Richard Bachman.")

The Bachman Books: Four Early Novels. New York: New American Library, 1985.

Skeleton Crew. New York: Putnam, 1985. (In this short-story collection, the following may be singled out for prominent Gothic content: "The Raft," "The Monkey," "The Mist," "Survivor Type," and "Uncle Otto's Truck.")

IT. New York: Viking, 1986.

The Dark Tower II: The Drawing of the Three. New York: New American Library, 1987.

The Eyes of the Dragon. New York: Viking, 1987.

Misery. New York: Viking, 1987.

Nightmares in the Sky: Gargoyles and Grotesques. New York: Viking, 1988. (Nonfiction.)

The Tommyknockers. New York: G.P. Putnam's Sons, 1988.

The Dark Half. New York: Viking, 1989.

Four Past Midnight. New York: Viking, 1990. (Short-story collection.)

The Dark Tower III: The Waste Lands. Hampton Falls, NH: Plume, 1991.

Needful Things. New York: Viking, 1991.

Gerald's Game. New York: Viking, 1992.

Dolores Claiborne. New York: Viking, 1993.

Nightmares and Dreamscapes. New York: Viking, 1993. (Short-story collection.)

Insomnia. New York: Viking, 1994.

Rose Madder. New York: Viking, 1995.

Desperation. New York: Viking, 1996.

The Green Mile. New York: Penguin Group, 1996.

The Regulators. New York: Dutton, 1996. (Under the pseudonym "Richard Bachman.")

The Dark Tower IV: Wizard and Glass. New York: Plume, 1997.

Bag of Bones. New York: Scribner's, 1998.

The Girl Who Loved Tom Gordon. New York: Scribner's, 1999.

Hearts in Atlantis. New York: Scribner's, 1999.

Since 1974, the publication year of his first novel, *Carrie*, Stephen King has assembled a prodigious canon of horror fiction. At this writing, he has averaged over a book a year for nearly three decades: thirty-six novels, seven collections of short stories and novellas, and ten screenplays. In his chapter on "Horror Fiction" in *Danse Macabre*, King has psychoanalyzed the cultural roots of horror and recognized his own literary roots in the Gothic's theme of solipsistic imprisonment and "confining narcissism," writing that "the New American Gothic provides a closed loop of character, and in what might be termed a psychological fallacy, the physical surroundings often mimic the inward-turning of the characters themselves" (267).

One consistent element that unifies this broad and eclectic landscape of closed loops and inward-turnings is the Maine setting. King's books and stories have been so strongly shaped by Maine locales that it is impossible to imagine separating landscape from personality, climate from theme. Rather than evoking a chamber-of-commerce, pastoral relationship with the Maine landscape, however, King draws upon a nature that is hostile and savage, an environment where malefic energies reside in secret. In the novel *The Girl Who Loved Tom Gordon*, nine-year-old Trisha McFarland is lost in the Maine woods. For days she wanders deeper into the wilderness in search of human beings or signs of civilized life. Her torment is heightened by her constant struggle against nature's elements from swamp bogs and incessant insect attacks to her feeble efforts to forage food.

In an essay entitled "Beyond the Kittery Bridge: Stephen King's Maine," Burton Hatlen maintains that William Faulkner has remained one of King's favorite novelists from his days as an undergraduate. Modeling much of his canon after Faulkner's convoluted Yoknapatawpha cycle, King's "Maine books also suggest that he is more or less deliberately creating a 'myth of Maine' which is at least loosely analogous to Faulkner's 'myth of the South' " (46). Like Faulkner, the fictional cycle unifying King's Castle Rock microcosm often features families, characters, and events from one book that are referenced again in later books; certain plots are likewise dependent upon events that have transpired in earlier narratives. Even King's fictional towns—Castle Rock, Haven, 'Salem's Lot—share common characteristics peculiar to small Maine communities. To a real extent, these Maine locales are all connecting points on the road to Derry, a city modeled upon Bangor and the epicenter of evil on King's geoliterary map.

Understanding the importance of Maine as a shaping influence on King's fiction is an important starting point to appreciating his art. But his attitude toward Maine, at least in his fiction, is a decidedly bifurcated one. In characters such as Dolores Claiborne, John Smith (*The Dead Zone*), Frannie Goldsmith (*The Stand*), Alan Pangborn (*Needful Things*), and Trisha McFarland, King provides examples of heroism. Common men and women with few pretensions, these Maine natives embody an independent resolve sweetly tempered by a genuine commitment to others. Surrounded by situations that both torment and threaten their psychological stability, these characters, due in no small part to their obstinate streak of Yankee self-reliance, are in possession of unwavering moral centers. They maintain healthy psyches that stand in contrast to the forces of oppression, perversity, and corruption that often characterize their immediate familial and social relationships.

While King clearly admires their independent opposition, he also provides less flattering portraits of small-town Maine life to counterbalance their moral resolve. King seems to understand intuitively that while the small-town Maine environment is capable of producing courageous individuals, it can destroy others because of its pride of isolation, pressures to conform, and lack of compassion. Throughout King's canon, evil manifests itself as a conforming presence, particularly appropriate to the social microcosm of Maine's small-town life. Whether it takes the form of a religious fanatic, the fascistic authority of Randall Flagg (*The Stand, The Eyes of the Dragon, The Dark Tower*), or the social homogeneity dictated by *The Tommyknockers* and *IT*, evil thrives in closed, self-contained worlds. Malefic forces in King are remarkably consistent; they manipulate, restrict, and silence opposition. Usually the narrative itself, while projecting such a consciousness, is appropriately reduced to a single authoritarian voice. In novels such as *IT, The Tommyknockers, Bag of Bones*, and *'Salem's Lot*, the majority exerts a defining will that demands rigid conformity from all the inhabitants of the town—a monological merging in speech, thought, and action. The vampires that eventually take over *'Salem's Lot*, for example, merely reflect the homogeneity of the town itself together with the progressive degradation of individuals into a spiritless mass of hungry undead that completes the moral disintegration of the community. Hatlen views these regional portraits as a kind of "chronic soulsickness prevalent, King implies, throughout post-Vietnam America, but working away with a special insidiousness in the heart of Maine, beguiled by its myth of itself of the Pastoral Paradise" (54).

Generally speaking, Stephen King's early novels are large, ambitious books, encompassing enormous narrative scope and tending to revolve around recognizable genre themes (sometimes conflating two or more in a single text): Gothic horror, dystopian technology, epic fantasy, and the journey quest. King's first fifteen years of work produced novels such as *The Shining, The Stand, Firestarter, The Talisman*, and *IT*. These are fictions that present a macrocosmic view of postmodern America, providing the reader with a journey to the center of a post-Watergate heart of darkness. These books are further linked in that they are rendered from a tremendous narratological range and vision. King's epic propensities are never more strongly evinced than in *The Stand, The Talisman*, and *IT*, texts that weave a vast historical, mythological, and social matrix into a journey quest. Many of the books from this period are also unified by virtue of being road narratives. In each of these tales, King takes us across contemporary America on a system of interstates fraught with danger. The concrete highways that crisscross these books frequently come to symbolize the hard-hearted uniformity of American towns and the personalities populating them that King's young men and women—who often are no more than adolescent boys and girls—must somehow confront and overcome. The influence of the epic-fantasy tradition, particularly J.R.R. Tolkien's *Lord of the Rings*, upon these early King novels cannot be overestimated. Like Tolkien's Frodo, King's young American travelers encounter magical realms and dark challenges that they survive only at the expense of their innocence and by the sharpening of their wits.

In contrast to this macrocosmic examination of America frequently considered from the off-ramps of its interstate highway system, the books that follow *Misery* (as well as *Misery* itself) show evidence of King's ability to produce highly circumscribed, tightly wrought fictions bearing few of his earlier epic tendencies toward narrative and thematic expansiveness. King's work in the 1990s, in addition to being generally shorter and more compact, has also tended to include a more realistic treatment of women. The novels *Gerald's Game, Dolores Claiborne*, and *Rose Madder*, a trio that should be considered together because the narratives share similar themes as well as being written and published consecutively, differ markedly from King's previous fiction. Feminist in orientation, these novels present most of the action from a woman's point of view. If the first half of King's literary canon can be read as an accurate and potent rendition of the American Everyman brooding amid the wastelands of a dystopic America, the second half of his career tends more to focus on representations of the American Everywoman and her disgruntled home life. In his early fiction, individuals move out into a confrontation with a Gothic world; his later work, in contrast, features a domesticized Gothic, where individuals are under assault within their own homes.

As the king of postmodern horror, Stephen King has produced fiction consistently derivative of work that precedes his own. He has, for example, written homages to the classic icons of nineteenth-century horror art: *Frankenstein* in *Pet Sematary*, *Dracula* in *'Salem's Lot*, and *Dr. Jekyll and Mr. Hyde* in *The Dark Half*. In fact, the argument might be made that a vast majority of King's work in the 1970s and 1980s relies heavily upon some variation of the vampire tale. In many of his narratives, malefic forces need a body—hands and legs— to extend their powers and range of mobility into the human world. Thus the ghosts at the Overlook Hotel in *The Shining* as well as the demonic shopkeeper in *Needful Things* first "bite" and then take over their respective victims' psyches and physical entities.

In his most important fiction, however, traditional Gothic tropes, such as the haunted house, revenants, monsters, and other supernatural phenomena, are juxtaposed with contemporary social issues, so that the anxieties that physically manifest themselves in King's novels cannot be easily separated from persistent problems within the American social fabric itself. As King himself asserted in a 1989 interview, "The work underlines again and again that I am not merely dealing with the surreal and the fantastic but, more important, using the surreal and the fantastic to examine the motivations of people and the society and institutions they create" (Magistrale, "Writer" 15).

In the fiction published after and including *Misery*, King has tended more "to examine the motivations of people and society and institutions" than revisit the Gothic tale populated by clearly recognizable personalities, tropes, and plot parallels. In the laudable effort to challenge himself as a writer by composing narratives that are not neatly categorized into the horror-fantasy genre, King has produced a series of books that are dissimilar in subject matter to the narratives that originally established his massive audience and forged his reputation in the 1970s and 1980s as the master of the macabre. Ironically, while the books published during the 1990s have tended to be more mainstream in subject matter, focusing on domestic and gender issues, because of King's established reputation as a popular male horror novelist, his audience base has not enlarged to the point where his work is now included (as it legitimately should be) on the syllabi of women's-studies curricula.

In one of the most important books from King's early period, *The Shining*, we are introduced to a child who embodies both the spirit of endurance and the propensity for goodness that characterize most of King's other youthful protagonists, particularly those from his early period. As Samantha Figliola argues in "The Thousand Faces of Danny Torrance," "Danny epitomizes King's own mythos of childhood. He is the 'marvelous third eye' of childhood perception magnified ten thousand times, a seer who is nonetheless simple and innocent, a psychological sieve for his parents' most deeply buried emotions, a hero forced to enter and escape hell" (56). Danny captivates us with his sweet innocence; his peril at the hands of a psychologically unstable father and agents of an evil design located at the Overlook Hotel only serves to endear him even more to the reader. Danny overcomes these obstacles, in part, because of his supernatural attribute—a precognitive ability to view the past and future called "shining"—and a tremendous capacity for love. Although he undergoes traumatic experiences throughout the better part of the novel, we never doubt his resiliency and place in the future once he is freed from his father and the spirits at the Overlook. Unlike his father, Jack, Danny has a solid support system in his mother and surrogate-father figure, Hallorann, to help him move outside the shadow of his father's dysfunctional behavior.

The conclusion of *The Shining* ultimately embodies Stephen King's profound faith in the resiliency of human nature and the enduring power of love. This novel's ending is often repeated in other King texts. Evil is either vanquished or at least recognized and confronted by the force of human morality, whatever form it happens to assume. As King generally affirms throughout his novels as well as in *Danse Macabre*, the nonfictional treatise on horror art, "If the horror story is our rehearsal for death, then its strict moralities make it also a reaffirmation of life and good will and simple imagination—just one more pipeline to the infinite" (380).

This moral vision or "pipeline to the infinite" is a recurring resource available throughout King's fictional landscape. In *The Shining*, it is the energy of the shining itself that bonds Danny to Dick Hallorann and the latter with his grandmother. In *'Salem's Lot* this force is found in the "inevitable rightness, of whiteness" (413) that Mark Petrie discovers when he assumes the role of the "white knight" by pouring holy water over the blade of an axe in preparing for battle against the vampires. In *The Stand*, this magical property radiates from Mother Abigail, the source of human faith and conduit for divine goodness that counterbalances the evil of Randall Flagg, while in the novel *IT*, it is the circle created by the sexual and emotional union of the Losers Club and their unwavering faith in the turtle and one another that ultimately defeats the monster IT. King may have achieved his reputation by writing about threatening and disconcerting subject matter, but this does not necessarily impose a corollary that his vision is hopeless. As he expressed in a 1981 interview, "I really do believe in the White force. Children are part of that force, which is why I write about them the way I do. There are a lot of horror writers who deal with this struggle, but they tend to concentrate on the Black. But the other force is there, too" (Underwood and Miller 1988, 21). In nearly every one of King's major novels, there exists the presence of goodness, the white force, blind faith, small-group human solidarity, the power of a writer's or child's imagination, or simple love, that essentially breaks the stranglehold of evil, regardless of how its corruption is manifested in human or supernatural form. This unselfish force is always expressed as a highly romantic, antirational impulse.

In most of King's epic fantasies, the forces of "white magic" exist in Manichaean opposition to the powers of supernatural evil. The potential for King's characters to produce acts of good or evil is always dependent upon the individual's ability to control his or her most selfish impulses. In *The Stand*, perhaps more than in any other King novel, free will and moral choice are solidly within the individual's purview; all of the major characters in this book participate directly in determining their own fates. While this determination is never an easy one to make since *The Stand*'s most complicated and engaging characters are pulled in opposing directions simultaneously, personal choices become, nonetheless, a barometer for measuring an individual's capacity for ethical development.

Clearly, a paramount concern in King's early fiction is dramatizing the will of men and women making proactive choices to oppose the dictatorial design of evil. In one of King's largest and most ambitious novels to date, *IT*, the epic scope of *The Stand* is channeled into a single city. The history of Derry, Maine, is carefully documented, and its legacy of corruption must be confronted by the child-adults who are also its principal victims. In preceding works, such as *The Shining* and *'Salem's Lot*, King's portrayal of evil is defined in terms of the "accumulated sum" of its parts: a chronicle of human depravity occurs in one place over an extended period of time. This locale and patterned behavior enable maleficence to emerge as a living organism capable of sustaining itself on renewable instances of violence and corruption. This paradigm is repeated in novels such as *Needful Things* and *IT*, where a town or village assumes core aspects of the Gothic haunted house, including the need for heroes and heroines to do battle against its resident evil force.

Over the past several years, feminist scholars have observed that the roles King has traditionally allotted women in his fiction and specifically female sexuality itself are patronizingly restrictive and frequently negative. Critic Chelsea Quinn Yarbro was the first to lament that "it is disheartening when a writer with so much talent and strength of vision is not able to develop a believable woman character between the ages of seventeen and sixty" (45). Mary Pharr, in a seminal essay that broadens and deepens Yarbro's position, notes that "despite his best efforts, King's women are reflective of American stereotypes. . . . His most convincing female characters are precisely those who are least threatening to men" (21). In a critique devoted to language ideologies in King's novels, Karen Hohne likewise opines that his women characters "are never allowed to speak themselves, to make themselves with words. They get little dialogue, their speech is generally flat and undistinguished or stereotyped, or, worse, their language is distinctive but it is not their own; it is instead that of officiality, a set of languages from whose power they are excluded by their very being" (328).

Sharply aware of criticism similar to what is cited here and generally concurring with it, King has labored to create more human and less stereotypical female personalities, at least since the publication of *Misery*. In *Dolores Claiborne*, for example, the writer completely eschews his traditional third-person narrative form in order to provide Dolores with an autobiographical voice and consciousness. This departure from omniscient point of view to a first-person monologue signals the importance King is willing to invest in legitimizing Dolores's perspective and the domestic issues her narrative explores. Perhaps the truism that middle-aged males begin to explore their "feminine" side is another explanation for King's interest in developing better women characters. It is significant that as King has focused much of his energy on women's issues, his recent fiction has tended to become more circumscribed, centering on one or two individuals almost exclusively.

Misery holds a pivotal position in King's canon; the novel signals a transition that begins to emphasize a new significance for women characters, an intense scrutiny provided to the roles of writer and reader, and a willingness to experiment with a more restricted narratological structure and style. The book takes place almost entirely in the bedroom of a remote Colorado farmhouse. The principal characters—a famous writer named Paul Sheldon, who is held captive by his "number one fan," Annie Wilkes—could easily be figures in a one-act play, where the deliberately oppressive stage backdrop helps to highlight their verbal and physical conflicts. In *Misery*, we encounter one of King's first attempts to create a fiercely independent woman who is neither a madonna nor a whore. Her psychopathology notwithstanding, Annie Wilkes is one of the few women in King's canon who possess real power, even if she ultimately fails to exercise it responsibly. In her systematic torturing of writer Paul Sheldon, Annie appears as a figure who demands to be taken seriously; she is a kind of revenging agent for all past Gothic heroines who have suffered physical and psychological abuse from men. So while *Misery* is not a feminist text, as it remains mired in the destructive, potentially castrating nature of women, its female character is a prototype—at least in terms of her strength, intelligence, and angry resolve—for King's female protagonists who follow her in a series of heroine-centered books published during the 1990s.

Gerald's Game and *Misery* should be viewed as bedroom bookends; both texts are intense psychological explorations of gendered relationships that feature very little physical action, as the protagonists of these narratives are literally tied to their beds. As Linda Badley accurately assesses: "*Misery* blamed a sadistic and all-devouring matriarchy for the protagonist's victimization. *Gerald's Game*, as its title announces, condemns the patriarchy. The latter 'corrects' the misogyny implicit in *Misery*, transporting its situation and setting into female Gothic and taking the woman's point of view" (66). *Gerald's Game* and *Misery* are two of the most complex and ambitious efforts King has yet undertaken. The tales concern nothing less than a wrestling with the destruction and re-creation of selfhood.

The first chapter of *Gerald's Game* is a beautifully orchestrated introduction to all of the major elements that will unfold in the remainder of the text. The major character, Jessie Burlingame, has her hands handcuffed to a bed by her husband, Gerald, during kinky sex play that has gone terribly awry. Far from arousing her sexually, this particular instance of "Gerald's game" revivifies a deeply repressed episode from her childhood that underscores the self-induced psychological bondage she has imposed over her memory of this event. As a young girl, Jessie experienced a single sexual molestation while sitting on her father's lap during a full solar eclipse. But even worse than acting upon his incestual urge was her father's successful effort to cover his involvement by making his daughter into a co-conspirator: " 'I guess we have a bargain,' he said. 'I say nothing, you say nothing. Right? Not to anyone else, not even to each other. Forever and ever, amen. When we walk out of this room, Jess, it never happened' " (185).

For many years, as the girl matures into a woman, the truth is repressed, even as Jessie's relationship with her father deteriorates. Her later involvement with Gerald's bondage fantasy, however, reawakens Jessie's feelings of being powerless and demeaned: "Her response was not so much directed at Gerald as at that hateful feeling that came flooding up from the bottom of her mind" (18). While Gerald interprets her verbal objections as part of a scripted sexual scenario, "She was supposed to protest; after all, that was the game" (3), Jessie is actually beginning to confront the secret she has maintained since adolescence. Her husband's unwillingness to consider her feelings, the undeterred urgency of his arousal, his line of spittle and its nexus to sperm, and even the darkening windows of the late fall afternoon in a secluded cottage by a lake transport Jessie back to her father and the day of the eclipse. As a result, her lethal kick to Gerald's crotch, viewed in this context, is less of an accident than an unconscious urge to castrate her father. Gerald's death occurs in the novel's dramatic first chapter; the remainder of the book centers upon Jessie's self-induced psychotherapy as she struggles to resolve the opposing voices in her head and extricate herself from the bondage that literally and symbolically binds her to Gerald's bed.

In contrast to the singular actions that characterize male behavior in *Gerald's Game, Dolores Claiborne*, and *Rose Madder*, women are defined in each of these narratives by virtue of their relationship with other women. The bond that women form, through their common experience, is so important that King acknowledges it in the dedication to *Gerald's Game* by recognizing various female relatives who have borne his wife's maiden name—Spruce. Presumably, these are the women who have influenced her most profoundly and, at the same time, all the women whom Stephen King understands Tabitha to be.

Over the past three decades, Stephen King has produced a body of literature that is as diverse as it is popular. His work should not be labeled exclusively and, for some, diminutively, as horror fiction, for it draws upon many literary genres and traditions: epic fantasy (*The Stand, The Talisman*, and *IT*), classical tragedy (*The Shining* and *Pet Sematary*), feminism (*Gerald's Game, Dolores Claiborne*, and *Rose Madder*), the romance novel (*Misery*), the American western (*The Dark Tower*), the fairy tale (*The Girl Who Loved Tom Gordon* and *Eyes of the Dragon*), naturalism (*Cujo* and the Bachman books), and political-historical metafiction (*The Dead Zone* and "Apt Pupil"). King is one of those rare artists who has managed to capture the defining spirit of his era at the same time that he has influenced it. Of his contemporaries, perhaps only the Beatles, Steven Spielberg, and maybe Madonna can be said to have accomplished a similar feat. The admonishments of English teachers notwithstanding, Stephen King has already shaped an entire generation of fiction writers, readers, and film students.

Vampiric monsters and supernatural phenomena may be the great popular attractions of King's canon, but at the heart of his fictional universe is a profound sensitivity to the most emotional and deep-seated American anxieties. King himself maintains that his novels, "taken together, form an allegory for a nation that feels it's in a crunch and things are out of control" (Underwood and Miller, *Bare Bones* 94). No less than Hawthorne a century earlier, King is a moralist for our epoch, rendering a vivid portrait of white, middle-class American life in the latter half of the twentieth century. He has tended to celebrate traditional bourgeois values in that family, children, and heterosexual love are central to his work. On the other hand, his critique of American bureaucratic institutions and government itself suggests his continued commitment to the radical politics he first encountered as an undergraduate during the 1960s. The conclusions of his novels are often sentimental and overly optimistic; at the same time, his understanding of patriarchal abuses, particularly as they oppress women, children, and minorities, is uncompromisingly realistic. In the end, it is not just his phenomenal popularity that has made Stephen King America's storyteller, but also his vision of the possibilities and contradictions that are inherent in being American.

SELECTED CRITICISM

Badley, Linda. *Writing Horror, and the Body: The Fiction of Stephen King, Clive Barker, and Anne Rice*. Westport, CT: Greenwood Press, 1996. Looks at the three authors as leading modern Gothicists.

Beahm, George. *Stephen King: America's Best-loved Boogeyman*. Kansas City, MO: Andrews & McMeel, 1998. A biocritical study.

Bleiler, Richard. "Stephen King." In *Supernatural Fiction Writers*. Ed. E.F. Bleiler. New York: Scribner's, 1985: 1037–1044. Assesses King to be one of the most able horror writers of the modern age, with a definite serious purpose behind his "gross outs."

Bloom, Harold, ed. *Stephen King*. Modern Critical Views. Philadelphia: Chelsea House, 1998. A critical study.

Browne, Ray, and Gary Hoppenstand, eds. *The Gothic World of Stephen King: Landscape of Nightmares.* Bowling Green, OH: Bowling Green State University Popular Press, 1988. An anthology of critical essays on the King canon.

Burns, Gail E., and Melinda Kanner. "Women, Danger, and Death: The Perversion of the Female Principle in Stephen King's Fiction." In *Sexual Politics and Popular Culture.* Ed. Diane Raymond. Bowling Green, OH: Bowling Green State University Popular Press, 1990: 158–172. On King and feminism.

Casebeer, Edwin F. "The Art of Balance: Stephen King's Canon." In *A Dark Night's Dreaming: Contemporary American Horror Fiction.* Ed. Tony Magistrale and Michael A. Morrison. Columbia: University of South Carolina Press, 1996: 42–54. "King's early novels demonstrate strong characterizations of preadolescent boys and small children. In the ensuing years, he has added to his palette, and now is taking up the challenge of realistic female protagonists."

Collings, Michael R. *The Annotated Guide to Stephen King: A Primary and Secondary Bibliography of the Works of America's Premier Horror Writer.* Mercer Island, WA: Starmont House, 1986. A comprehensive aid to research.

———. *The Films of Stephen King.* Mercer Island, WA: Starmont House, 1986. A survey of King's work on film.

Davis, Jonathan P. *Stephen King's America.* Bowling Green, OH: Bowling Green State University Popular Press, 1994. On King and U.S. culture.

Egan, James. " 'A Single Powerful Spectacle': Stephen King's Gothic Melodrama." *Extrapolation* 27 (1986): 62–75. "King's treatments of the Gothic and the macabre are the opposite of impulsive meandering—he seeks to create 'a single powerful spectacle,' a strategy which can best be described as melodramatic and formulaic."

Figliola, Samantha. "The Thousand Faces of Danny Torrance." In *Discovering Stephen King's The Shining.* Ed. Tony Magistrale. San Bernardino, CA: Borgo Press, 1998: 54–61. A character analysis of Danny Torrance.

Hanson, Clare. "Stephen King: Powers of Horror." In *American Horror Fiction from Brockden Brown to Stephen King.* Ed. Brian Docherty. New York: St. Martin's Press, 1990: 135–154. Psychoanalytic readings of *Carrie, The Shining*, and *Misery* to demonstrate how "King's fiction is concerned above all with origins, with grounds of being."

Hatlen, Burton. "Beyond the Kittery Bridge: Stephen King's Maine." In *Fear Itself: The Horror Fiction of Stephen King.* Ed. Tim Underwood and Chuck Miller. New York: New American Library, 1984: 45–60. On King's fictive/factual environment in the novels and short stories.

Hicks, James E. "Stephen King's Creation of Horror in 'Salem's Lot: A Prolegomenon towards a New Hermeneutic of the Gothic Novel." In *Consumable Goods: Papers from the North East Popular Culture Association Meeting.* Ed. David K. Vaughan. Orono, ME: University of Maine National Poetry Foundation, 1987: 85–93. In *'Salem's Lot*, King explodes the pastoral/rural ideals of Norman Rockwellian America. "In addition to the levels of malevolence, *'Salem's Lot* is similar in construction to *Frankenstein* and *Dracula*."

Hohne, Karen A. "In Words Not Their Own: Dangerous Women in Stephen King." In *Misogyny in Literature.* Ed. Katherine Anne Ackley. New York: Garland, 1992: 327–345. On King's shift to more realistic, three-dimensional women in his fiction.

Kent, Brian. "Stephen King and His Readers: A Dirty, Compelling Romance." In *A*

Casebook on The Stand. Ed. Tony Magistrale. Mercer Island, WA: Starmont House, 1992: 37–68. Raises issues of reader response to King's novel.

Lant, Kathleen Margaret. "The Rape of Constant Reader: Stephen King's Construction of the Female Reader and Violation of the Female Body in *Misery.*" *Journal of Popular Culture* 30 (1997): 89–114. On King's efforts to adjust to feminist criticism of his depiction of women.

Lant, Kathleen Margaret, and Theresa Thompson, eds. *Imagining the Worst: Stephen King and the Representation of Women.* Westport, CT: Greenwood Press, 1998. Essays dealing with King's changing presentation of women in his fiction.

Magistrale, Tony. "Stephen King's Vietnam Allegory: An Interpretation of 'Children of the Corn.' " *Cuyahoga Review* 2 (1984): 61–66. A provocative reading showing how the gruesome details of the sacrifices correspond with the events of the Vietnam war.

———. *Landscape of Fear: Stephen King's American Gothic.* Bowling Green, OH: Bowling Green State University Popular Press, 1988. A close, careful, and serious reading of King's fiction and a key book for understanding King's sense of the Gothic as a tragic instrument.

———, ed. *The Dark Descent: Essays Defining Stephen King's Horrorscape.* Westport, CT: Greenwood Press, 1992. Sixteen essays on a variety of King works and themes.

———. "The Writer Defines Himself: An Interview with Stephen King." In *Stephen King: The Second Decade, Danse Macabre to The Dark Half.* New York: Twayne, 1992: 1–19. A two-hour interview with King conducted on 2 November 1989. Provides numerous insights into King's reading and favorite authors.

———. "Teaching the Intellectual Merits of Stephen King's Fiction." *Chronicle of Higher Education* 19 June 1998: B7. Makes the case for Stephen King's writings as a serious commentary on the flaws of American culture. Addresses the problem of how to make King as important and intellectually valuable as Melville and Hawthorne in the classroom.

Pharr, Mary. "Partners in the Danse: Women in Stephen King's Fiction." In *The Dark Descent: Essays Defining Stephen King's Horrorscape.* Ed. Tony Magistrale. Westport, CT: Greenwood Press, 1992: 19–32. On the emergence of "real" women in his later work.

Reino, Joseph. *Stephen King: The First Decade, "Carrie" to "Pet Sematary."* Boston: Twayne, 1988. The first of two Twayne studies of the author.

Russell, Sharon A. *Stephen King: A Critical Companion.* Westport, CT: Greenwood Press, 1996. A collection of modern critical views and interpretations.

Underwood, Tim, and Chuck Miller, eds. *Fear Itself: The Horror Fiction of Stephen King.* San Francisco, CA: Underwood-Miller, 1982. A collection of essays considering the King canon up to and including *Cujo* from many angles.

———, eds. *Bare Bones: Conversations on Terror with Stephen King.* New York: McGraw-Hill, 1988. A series of interviews given by King from March 1979 to May 1985.

Winter, Douglas E. *Stephen King: The Art of Darkness: The Life and Fiction of the Master of the Macabre.* New York: New American Library, 1984. A biocritical appreciation of King's achievement. Finds in King's work an "intrinsically subversive" exposé of the Gothic aspects of American life.

Yarbro, Chelsea Quinn. "Cinderella's Revenge—Twists on Fairy Tales and Mythic

Themes in the Work of Stephen King." In *Fear Itself: The Horror Fiction of Stephen King*. Ed. Tim Underwood and Chuck Miller. New York: New American Library, 1984: 45–56. Archetypal analyses of King's ironic manipulation of fairy tales and myths.

IZUMI KYOKA
(1873–1939)
Frederick S. Frank

PRINCIPAL GOTHIC WORKS

Kyoka zenshu [Collected Works]. Tokyo: Iwanami Shoten, 1973–1976. (Most of Kyoka's tales and dramas contain explicit and implicit Gothic effects, machinery, and character relationships. A selection of Gothic pieces includes "Kanmuri Yazaemon" [Crowned Yazaemon] [1895], "Kecho" [Chimera] [1897], and *Tenshu monogatari* [The Castle Tower] [1917].)

MODERN REPRINTS AND EDITIONS

Izumi Kyoka Shusei [Works of Izumi Kyoka]. Tokyo: Chikuma Smoro, 1996. (10 volume reprinting of Kyoka's Fiction in Japanese.)

Japanese Gothic Tales. Ed. and trans. Charles Shiro Inouye. Honolulu: University of Hawaii Press, 1996. (Contains four pieces representative of Kyoka's Gothic work. The two long stories of novella length are "Koya hijiri" [The Holy Man of Mount Koya] and "Shunshu and Shunshu gokoku gokoku" [One day in spring]. The two short Gothic tales are "Gekashitsu" [The Surgery Room] and "Baishoku kamonanban" [Osen and Sokichi]. This edition is cited in the text.)

"A Tale of Three Who Were Blind." In *Modern Japanese Literature.* Ed. Donald Keene, trans. Edward Seidensticker. New York: Grove Press, 1956: 242–253.

Three Tales of Mystery and Imagination: Japanese Gothic by Izumi Kyoka. Ed. and trans. Charles Shiro Inouye. Kanazawa, Japan: Izumi Kyoka Sakuhin Shuppankai, 1992. (Includes "The Surgery Room.")

Parallels with Poe's Gothic life and Gothic art are numerous and inescapable in the life and supernatural fiction of Izumi Kyoka, the finest Japanese Gothic writer of the Meiji period (1868–1912). As Poe is a central presence in an American Gothic tradition, Kyoka is a central figure in a vigorous Gothic tradition that has flourished in Japanese literature beginning with the work of Ueda Akinari in the eighteenth century. Sharing many features of Western Gothicism, both Kyoka and Akinari focus their Gothic visions on assertion of the spectral and spiritual side of life in opposition to the materialism, realism, and martial severity of their Japanese societies. In Kyoka's case, his Gothic can often be understood as a reaction to the oppressive position allotted to women in Japanese life. Other cultural anxieties such as a mounting fear of the aggressive nationalism that would set Japan on the road to imperialism and wars of conquest may be found in Kyoka's later works. He died in 1939, having witnessed the early expansionist resurgence of the samurai code of warrior hegemony over weaker peoples. "When he died in 1939, Kyoka was neglected because his style seemed 'American' in a day when Japanese chauvinism was its most militant" (Inouye 1996, 9).

Much of the fiction is dominated by lovely and deadly mother figures and the fusion of love and death into climactic moments of demonic beauty. "Suffering like Poe," notes Kyoka's English translator, Charles Inouye, "from the untimely death of his mother, Kyoka sought to memorialize her youthful beauty and maternal gentleness through hundreds of literary excursions into the world of the dead" (Inouye 1996, 2). His is the Gothic of maternal obsession guided by his artistic determination to establish a "fictive purgatory" (3) for these heroines who "both seduce and save, tempt and chasten Kyoka's male characters as they wander in mountainous and watery territories of mystery and awe." (3) A glance at the cadaverous properties of one of Kyoka's first Gothic stories, "The Surgery Room," a tale of doomed love culminating in double suicide, will demonstrate the emphasis on sinister beauty of Kyokan Gothic and fix his stylistic and thematic bonds with the female-corpse-filled worlds of Poe and Baudelaire. Baudelaire's concept of the beauty of evil ("esthetique du mal") and Poe's dictum drawn from Sir Francis Bacon that "there is no exquisite beauty without some strangeness in the proportions" are impregnable Gothic truths frequently underscored in Kyoka's narratives of love and death.

In "The Surgery Room," one of Kyoka's earliest Gothic pieces and one of his best, the narrator is an observer in the operating chamber where the beautiful Countess Kifune awaits the descent of the surgeon's scalpel, having refused to receive any anesthetic. To the narrator, she seems already to be a lovely, virginal corpse "wrapped in a spotless, white hospital gown, face drained of color, nose pointed upward, chin narrow and frail" (12). Poe's mother in her funeral shroud or Poe's moribund child-wife Virginia in the diseased beauty of her final hours come immediately to mind. The Countess has refused the anesthetic out of fear of losing consciousness; she is terrified that "she might divulge some secret while in a state of unconsciousness [and] was willing to face death to protect what was in her heart" (14). Held down by the orderlies, she instructs the surgeon, Doctor Takamine, to cut in. "Her dignity weighed heavily upon those in the room" as all observers partake of this moment of fascination, awe, horror, and strange beauty as the doctor's scalpel obeys her command and "found the bone," a chilling sound effect. Seizing the doctor's scalpel, she assists in the completion of the surgery by "plunging it into her body, just below her breast"

(16), a gesture of *seppuku* or fatal self-mutilation on a par with any samurai ritual of disembowelment. Her suicidal declaration of forbidden love might have been conceived by Poe himself, for "at that moment the two of them were absolutely alone, oblivious to earth and heaven and the existence of another soul" (17). The tale's epilogue occurs "nine years earlier" with Doctor Takamine, then a young medical student, and the narrator walking in the Koishikawa Botanical Garden when they see first the Countess Kifune passing by and then two young men whom they overhear discussing their experiences with prostitutes and whores. Having also witnessed the pure beauty of the Countess, the two young gay blades are chastened, causing Doctor Takamine to utter a strange remark: "Did you see how those two men were moved by true beauty? Now that's a subject for your art. That's what you ought to study" (19). This is precisely what the narrator does study in gruesomely ironic terms when he finds himself watching the Countess's self-vivisection, the prelude to the fatal reunion of the Countess and the doctor in the surgery room. The secret that the Countess had preserved at the price of hideous pain involved her adulterous love for the doctor, her heroic devotion to him precipitating his suicide following the fatal operation on his beloved. The tale is a delicate blend of horror and beauty capped by the narrator's ambivalent moral question in the story's final sentence: "Religious thinkers of the world, I pose this question to you. Should these two lovers be found guilty and denied entrance into heaven?" (20) Like the moral interrogatives at the end of a Hawthorne tale, the narrator's rhetorical question repudiates certain values but resolves nothing about the mystery of good and evil in a fallen universe.

Although there is no spectral return or lovers' reunion beyond the grave, the Gothic features of the tale are evident in its structure as well as in its two stylistically opposite parts, the taut drama of sacrifice of the operating room and the pastoral objectivity of the lady in the garden of the first encounter. With the writing of this early story, Kyoka had arrived at his Gothic formula for evoking the beauty that is terrible and the terror that is beautiful. His Gothic stops short of the sort of cadaverous resurrection expected in a Poe tale such as "Ligeia," but Kyoka's location of the action within an enclosed chamber of horrors in the form of the operating room shows his intimate knowledge of the manipulation of Gothic space. Like the dualistic structure of "The Surgery Room," Kyoka's life alternated between trauma and tranquility, between moments of intense aliveness and dark intervals of special deadness that brought him to the edge of suicide. Born in the castle town of Kanazawa, he grew up in one of the gloomiest regions of Japan, inheriting from his actress mother (another strict biographical parallel with Poe) an appreciation for dark fantasy and a dramatic sense of the world as an arena of suffering and violent fatality, both crucial to the development of his Gothic imagination. His attraction to the medieval and the supernatural was conditioned by a childhood spent in the shadow of the Kanazawa Castle whose black moat and beetling towers once tempted him to plunge to his death in the inky depths. In 1889 at the age of sixteen, he left this castle home to devote himself to literature (*bungaku*), moving, as had Poe, to metropolitan surroundings and becoming an itinerant journalist (again, the Poe parallel) as a means of supporting himself while he pursued his private artistic goals. In 1895, the same year as "The Surgery Room," he published the radical essay "Ai to kon'in" ('Love and Marriage') denouncing marriage and similar domestic hells perpetrated by socially coercive roles as "cruel and inhuman punishment." Lovers entrapped by the artificial morality of society would become one of Kyoka's principal Gothic predicaments. Escape from this permutation of the traditional Gothic's haunted castle or closed, bad space is only possible by way of sensational death, as seen in the Countess's lurid sacrifice.

With his major Gothic themes now established by "The Surgery Room," Kyoka extended his mysticism and romanticism to short fiction and dramas that reenact the melodramatic horrors of this first Gothic piece. Stories like "The Surgery Room" won Kyoka a dubious reputation as a writer of grisly potboilers with an added sting of social critique. Like Poe again, he made his readers uncomfortable as he began to explore the more private regions of nostalgia, fear, and fantasy in tales supersaturated with strange moods of thanatoerotic wonder and dread. "His birthplace and his youth provided the raw material," comments Cody Poulton. "While all of Kyoka's works presume some kind of social context, what is stressed is his stance *against* that context. Kyoka's protagonists are typically characters who have become estranged physically and psychologically from society" (327). In choosing his Gothic settings and describing his favorite Gothic places, he repeatedly transforms the dark menace of the Kanazawa Castle of his childhood into modern chambers of horrors such as the surgery room, then reverses this process to create a constant tension between Gothic anxiety in the present tense and Gothic dread in the past tense. Again as in Poe, the factuality of a specific place or the materiality of a specific moment in time could suddenly shift or distort itself to uncontrollable vortices.

The story written soon after "The Surgery Room," "Kecho" [Chimera], vibrates between horror and wonder and is full of pantheistic memories of a boyhood when belief in the gentleness of nature, both human and animal, suddenly collapsed. Half reverie and half fairy tale, the story begins lightly, then becomes a grim parable of loss as the young man Ren's Wordsworthian articles of faith are dashed by corrupt Darwinian realities. Ren has an encounter on a bridge with Doctor Frog, a hideously funny, pompous bureaucrat frog-man or man-frog who combines "low humor and the grotesque, as well as a sense of the absurd and sinister" (Poulton 334). The world of fact is rendered absurd and grotesque in this tale, which climaxes in Ren's rescue from drowning by a brightly colored winged maternal figure, allegorically recognized as the mother of fantasy and angelic guardian of all that is chimerical in life. Saved from the prosaic world of fact by the goddess of the illusory or chimerical, he is lifted out of Gothic nightmare into a purely ethereal world of the sort created by Poe in the poems "Israfel" and "Dreamland" and is granted a purity of vision tantamount to a transcendent state that is "out of space—out of time." The conflict contained in this fairy tale determines the pattern of conflict in the tales that follow in their depiction of a young hero's "psychological regression or mental disintegration, which often takes the form of a metamorphosis into more primitive forms of life and consciousness" (Poulton 332).

The primordial collision between the chimeras of the imagination and the nightmares of reality is given fuller Gothic treatment in the tales and plays that now follow where the fear of losing the chimerical or illusory in the face of hard reality is the paramount Gothic anxiety and where salvation by the chimerical mother is less frequent. In 1900, Kyoka wrote a religious quest story filled with Gothic and Arthurian romance motifs, "Koya hijiri" [The Holy Man of Mount Koya]. The story contains reminders of two Western narrative types, the saint's legend and the adventures of the grail-seeking knight en route to shining wisdom in a dull and dangerous world. Lining the path toward visionary fulfillment for the monk protagonist are macabre occurrences, surreal ordeals, and sinister places of subtle and unsubtle entrapment that the quester must face and master. With this quest story specifically in mind, Kyoka later declared of his nonmimetic art that writing was his means of fulfilling a desire to "pass through reality to reach a still greater power" (Inouye 1996, 174), precisely what the wandering monk accomplishes on his perilous pilgrimage in "The Holy Man of Mount Koya."

The Monk Shucho's legend is told as an inset tale to a curious traveling companion. His adventures begin with his transit of "the notorious Amo pass" where he must cross a sea of snakes "writhing like bridges across my path," a first test of his courage that he fails miserably when a severed serpent spewing yellow fluid throws him into a panic. But a prayer to Buddha revives his courage. Like one of Spenser's knights, he plunges into a deep forest believing that "a dark place like that is better than daylight for strengthening one's faith and pondering the eternal truths, even for a coward such as myself" (35). The tale's first great Gothic episode then commences when something slimy falls on his hat, a huge, bloodsucking slug or leech, the first horrifying drop of a storm of leeches that now rains down on him. The tactility of the imagery here has an ichorish force equal to one of H.P. Lovecraft's creature attacks. "The leeches stuck to my body like beads to a rosary." His passage through a sea of snakes and then a sky of leeches propels him to his next two meetings, first with a man-leech or leech-man, then with a woman-snake or snake-woman, the pair living together at their mountain cottage where the monk seeks shelter. A series of erotic adventures with the serpentine seductress now follows, all of them tests of his "holiness" and all of them calculated to bestialize him, to take away his humanity. Like a Gothic victim tempted by fatal beauty or like Odysseus bewitched by Circe, the monk very nearly abandons his quest and surrenders to carnality. "I realized that my pilgrimage was senseless. To be called a living Buddha by others and to be thronged with crowds of worshippers could only turn my stomach with the stench of humanity" (63). The images of entanglement and bloodletting converge in the tale's climax at the Husband-and-Wife Waterfalls, where the monk imagines that he sees the snake-woman "inside the falling water, now being swept under now rising again, her skin disintegrating and scattering like flower petals amid a thousand unruly streams of water. I gasped at the sight, and immediately she was whole again—the same face, body, breasts, arms, and legs, rising and sinking, suddenly dismembered, then appearing again." About to rescue her (i.e., to embrace sexual passion), he is stopped by an old man who warns him that he will be transformed into a horse, monkey, toad, or bat if he touches *la belle dame sans merci*. The slobbering slug-man he had seen back at the cottage was an example of her hideous work. Inquiring about this daughter of death, he learns that in one of her incarnations she had once been Yakushi, healer of souls, but that in her current avatar she had become the destroyer of souls, an evil beauty whose power over men is on a par with that of such satanic women as Monk Lewis's Matilda and Charlotte Dacre's Victoria di Loredani. "With a puff of her breath she could turn a lost traveler into the animal of her choice." She visits the unholy waterfall in an inverted ritual of purification to replenish her powers of destruction and reinvigorate her evil beauty. Recovering his senses, the monk turns from the woman in the waterfall to resume his pilgrimage, this time not through a lethal shower of leeches but through a shower of real rain. The fall of water, which just previously had connoted danger, violence, gruesome metamorphosis, and loss of self, now regains its natural properties of regeneration and renewal.

Within Kyoka's Gothic canon, "The Holy Man of Mount Koya" has been called "the metastory" (Inouye 1996, 173) with a strange and potent maternal figure of good and evil residing at its epicenter. The tale's uncanny energy, suspenseful pace, and projection of the grotesque in the borderland between natural and supernatural worlds give the story its unremitting Gothic intensity. Many other Kyoka tales reuse the sinister atmosphere and terrifying ambience of this legend of the lost self groping its way to spiritual independence and the sanctuary of art. "Shunchu and Shunchu gokoku" [One Day in Spring] and "Baishoku kamonanban" [Osen and Sokichi] the two other tales in Charles Inouye's anthology *Japanese Gothic Tales*, are dreamlike narratives containing Kyoka's favorite figure of regeneration and destruction, the fatal lady who directs a young man to the higher beauty inherent in death. Other tales with strong Gothic content are "The Night Patrol," "The Maidenhair," "The Night Bell Tolls," "Of a Dragon in the Deep," the Gothically titled "The Grass Labyrinth," and an unfinished piece, "The White Witch's Tale." Along with the influence of Poe, the tangible presences of other Western Gothic writers such as E.T.A. Hoffmann, Guy de Maupassant, and J.K. Huysmans are strongly felt, with the decadent aura of Baudelaire an omnipresent influence.

Japan's most famous contemporary author, Yukio Mishima (1925–1970), held Kyoka to be "a genius who cultivated a garden of peonies amidst the anemic desert of modern Japanese literature. Fervently believing in words and in spirits, he ranks with E.T.A. Hoffmann in the pureness of his Romanticism" (Inouye 1996, 7). Mishima's accolade is fully borne out in Kyoka's Gothic drama *Tenshu monogatari* [The Castle Tower] written in 1917 but not performed until 1951.

In the play, a renegade samurai warrior is seduced and bedeviled by an amorous specter in an upper apartment of Himeji Castle, a classic Gothic love affair. Far below, an army of ghouls besieges the castle and threatens the lovers above. The grisly gift of a severed head is delivered to the lovers and must be licked clean of blood. Here are all of the elements of Gothic crisis embellished by the introduction of *schauerromantik* gore at calculated dramatic intervals. Mishima's view that a successful Gothic tale should be a transgression against the cloying realities is confirmed again and again in the weird transcultural narratives of Japan's most prominent twentieth-century Gothicist, Izumi Kyoka.

SELECTED CRITICISM

Carpenter, Juliet. "Izumi Kyoka: Meiji-Era Gothic." *Japan Quarterly* 31 (1984): 154–158. A survey of the Gothic tales. Maternal obsessions and suicidal climaxes wrought against supernatural backgrounds distinguish Kyoka's work.

Cornyetz, Nina. "Izumi Kyoka's Speculum: Reflections on the Medusa, Thanatos, and Eros." Doctoral dissertation, Columbia University, 1991. [*DAI* 52:3932A]. "Confronts the question of the primacy of woman and mother in Kyoka's work and the symbolic mother in the form of character presentation of women as ambivalent goddess-demon-mothers."

Hughes, Henry J. "Familiarity of the Strange: Japan's Gothic Tradition." *Criticism* 42 (2000): 59–89. "The Japanese Gothic shares with the West its subversion of religious and social norms, an obsession with sex and death and fear of the supernatural or unknown. These are human qualities, not the province of one culture."

Inouye, Charles Shiro. "Water Imagery in the Works of Izumi Kyoka." *Monumenta Nipponica* 46:1(1991): 43–68. Explores the symbolic importance of water in such scenes as the monk's gaze at the waterfall in "The Holy Man of Mount Koya."

———. "Introduction: The Familiarity of Strange Places." In *Japanese Gothic Tales* by Izumi Kyoka. Trans. Charles Shiro Inouye. Honolulu: University of Hawaii Press, 1996: 1–10. Draws parallels between Poe and Kyoka. "Great Gothic writers such as Poe and Kyoka are understandable across differences of time and space, because though they might speak eloquently of their particular cultures, their concerns transcend national circumstance."

———. *The Similitude of Blossoms: A Critical Biography of Izumi Kyoka (1873–1939), Japanese Novelist and Playwright.* Harvard East Asian monographs, 1972. Cambridge: Harvard University Asia Center. Harvard University Press, 1998. Critical Biography by the leading modern Kyoka scholar. Comments extensively on Kyoka's Gothicism.

Jewel, Mark. "Aspects of Narrative Structure in the Work of Izumi Kyoka." Doctoral dissertation, Stanford University, 1984. [*DAI* 46:155A]. Kyoka is the "foremost romanticist of Meiji literature." Vital to an understanding of his Gothicism is his repeated use of two motifs: the image of woman and the uncanny. Both are "linked to specific thematic content in the stories. As the image of woman acquires added depth in the course of a story through association with uncanny events or images, the main character's view of love becomes correspondingly more complex and mature."

Kawakami, Chiyoko. "The Hybrid Narrative World of Izumi Kyoka." Doctoral dissertation, University of Washington, 1996. [*DAI* 57:3924A]. Deals with Kyoka's ghosts by following "[their] evolutional change from the mountain demonness to the urban trickster, and examines the sociocultural implications of this transformation."

Keene, Donald. "Izumi Kyoka." In *Dawn to the West: Japanese Literature of the Modern Era*. New York: Holt, Rinehart & Winston, 1984: 200–219. Discusses Kyoka's important place in twentieth-century Japanese fiction.

Poulton, Cody. "The Grotesque and Gothic: Izumi Kyoka's Japan" *Japan Quarterly* 41 (1994): 324–335. Analyses of various pieces of Kyoka's fiction, including *The Castle Tower* and "Chimera."

D. H. LAWRENCE
(1885–1930)

John Humma

PRINCIPAL GOTHIC WORKS

The Rainbow. London: Methuen, 1915.
Women in Love. New York: Seltzer, 1922.
"The Fox." In *The Ladybird*. London: Martin Secker, 1923.
"The Ladybird." In *The Ladybird*. London: Martin Secker, 1923.
"The Border Line." In *The Woman Who Rode Away and Other Stories*. London: Martin
Secker, 1928.

MODERN REPRINTS AND EDITIONS

The Fox; The Captain's Doll; The Ladybird. Cambridge: Cambridge University Press,
1992.
The Fox; The Captain's Doll; The Ladybird. New York: Viking Penguin, 1994. (This
edition is cited in the text.)
The Rainbow. Cambridge, UK: Cambridge University Press, 1989. (This edition is cited
in the text.)
The Rainbow. New York: Bantam, 1991.
The Rainbow. New York: Everyman's Library, 1993.
The Rainbow. New York: Viking Penguin, 1995.
The Rainbow. Oxford: Oxford University Press, 1998.
The Woman Who Rode Away and Other Stories. Cambridge: Cambridge University Press,
1995.
The Woman Who Rode Away and Other Stories. Ed. Dieter Mehl and Christa Jansohn.
New York: Viking Penguin, 1996. (This edition is cited in the text.)
Women in Love. New York: Everyman's Library, 1992.
Women in Love. New York: Knopf, 1992.
Women in Love. New York: Viking Penguin, 1995.
Women in Love. Cambridge: Cambridge University Press, 1997. (This edition is cited in
the text.)

Women in Love. New York: Bantam, 1996.
Women in Love. Oxford: Oxford University Press, 1998.
Women in Love. New York: Modern Library, 1999.

Gothic features in D.H. Lawrence's writings are always tied into the Lawrencian ethic. This ethic asserts the primacy of the blood, or instincts, while affirming a balance with mind or spirit; a detestation of the mechanistic or instrumental, in whatever form; and a belief in love that does not and must not seek domination over the other. This last aspect finds its best expression in Lawrence's famous "star-equilibrium" concept, as phrased by Birkin to Ursula in *Women in Love*, "of two single equal stars in balanced conjunction" (152). Important, however, is Birkin's seemingly contradictory assertion, essential to Lawrence's later "leadership" idea, that the "highest love impulse" is the desire to "resign your will to the higher being" (141). Lawrence's greatness lies in part in his honesty in dealing with such apparently irreconcilable ideas. As he grapples with these, his fiction comes to embody some of the central Gothic subjects and themes: dread and terror, obsession-compulsion, the attraction of cruelty and violence, the will to power, and forays into the mystical, or paranormal, or supernatural realms. Always, though, these are in service of Lawrence's central ideas.

In *Studies in Classic American Literature*, Lawrence asks, "What then is Moby Dick? He is the deepest blood-being of the white race," "the last phallic being of the white man" (160). Ahab's monomaniacal obsession to destroy the whale contains his dread and horror of his essential self and his compulsion to destroy the blood-sanity of that self. In Lawrence's fiction, we find this dynamic centrally at work. Beginning with his two indisputably great novels. *The Rainbow* and *Women in Love*, and continuing through his writing almost to the end of his life, Lawrence embodies in his fiction significant and compelling Gothic elements.

It is no surprise that the chief symbol in *The Rainbow* is the Roman arch of the iris. Will Brangwen, however, is a church decorator who finds his "consummation" in the Gothic arch of the Lincoln cathedral:

Here the stone leapt up from the plain earth, leapt up in a manifold, clustered desire each time, up, away from the horizontal earth, through twilight and dusk and the whole range of desire, through the swerving, the declination, ah, to the ecstasy, the touch, to the meeting and the consummation, the meeting, the clasp, the close embrace, the neutrality, the perfect swooning consummation, the timeless ecstasy. There his soul remained, at the apex of the arch, clinched in the timeless ecstasy, consummated. (187–188).

His wife, Anna, however, holds back, "mistrusting." To her, the church gargoyles tell another story: "These sly little faces peeped out of the grand tide of the cathedral like something that knew better. They knew quite well, these little imps that retorted on man's own illusion, that the cathedral was not absolute"

(189). For Will, the cathedral, with its pointed Gothic features, represents an escape from the blood self, a substitution of the ecstatic spiritual for the passional or instinctual. Locked in the apex of the arch, the soul is locked out of the "space where stars were wheeling in freedom, with a freedom above them always higher" (188). Anna, though "roused," would "never consent to the knitting of all the leaping stone in a great roof that closed her in . . . , the ultimate confine" (188). In this scene, the division between Anna and Will represents the conflict between high spiritual aspiration and dogged earth-boundedness, an opposition rich with Gothic implications.

This conflict assumes another dimension in the daughter of Will and Anna. Ursula, whose early life the last half of the novel develops, falls in love with her cousin, the soldier Anton Skrebensky, or, rather, perhaps, makes him fall in love with her. Ursula has become locked in her assertion of her female self, the terrible will, as Lawrence would have it, of that devouring vampire self. One night Ursula and Anton go to the Lincolnshire coast, where "in the great flare of [moon]light, she clinched hold of him, hard, as if suddenly she had the strength of destruction . . . till his body was powerless in her grip, his heart melted in fear from the fierce, beaked, harpy's kiss" (445). The moon for Lawrence often becomes the frightening, because domineering, female principle. In its power, or perhaps becoming its priestess, Ursula in the act of love shatters Skrebensky, who afterward in dread and terror "plunged away . . . from the horrible figure that lay stretched in the moonlight on the sands with the tears gathering and travelling on the motionless, eternal face" (445). There are tears, for Ursula responds now with dread to the destroying self she has become—and because she has this night something to expiate.

Her atonement comes when, months later, pregnant with Skrebensky's child, she crosses a field on her way home. "Suddenly she knew there was something else" (451). The something else is the unexpected approach of horses that all at once rampage now around her. This famous scene is written so that neither the reader nor Ursula knows if the horses are literal. But they are real. "In a sort of lightning of knowledge their movement traveled through her, the quiver and strain and thrust of their powerful flanks, as they burst before her and drew on, beyond" (452). The horses constitute a symbol on the order of (for Lawrence) Melville's white whale. Unlike Ahab, however, Ursula will not be destroyed but redeemed (for now, at least) by the blood-being of the horses. The miscarriage that follows hardly matters at this point. Her long recuperation ends appropriately with the symbol of the Roman arch of the rainbow. Having watched, "sick with nausea," the dreary miners, who seemed as if "buried alive," trudge through cold rain to their squalid homes, she saw now the sun miraculously emerge and the rainbow that "stood on the earth." She saw that the rainbow "was arched in [the miners'] blood and would quiver to life in their spirit, that they would cast off their horny covering of disintegration" under the "overarching heaven" (459). In this key moment when she experiences revulsion from herself and her white consciousness and with the aid of the outside world, Ursula finds a necessary hope to begin to build on. In *The Rainbow* and *Women in Love*, the Gothic works as a central dynamic of the action in the way that it grounds the chief conflicts of the relationships. There is also a sense in *The Rainbow* in which the novel works as a sort of reversal of the usual Gothic mode. Ursula suffers a revulsion from her white vampire (in effect) consciousness. The other side of this is the fear and dread of her dark blood-consciousness. The Gothic thus is presented not as what is horrible-bad, undesirable and destructive and to be expunged or destroyed, but rather as what is horrible-good, necessary and vital, to be striven for. But it is terrible and dreadful nonetheless, because it usually means, in Lawrence, the hardly casual ordeal of death and rebirth of the self.

Women in Love is a sequel chiefly as it concerns the further life of Ursula and as it continues a startlingly new narrative mode in which, as Lawrence put it in his famous letter of the time to David Garnett, one must no longer look for "the old stable ego of the self" (*Letters* 2.98–100). What this allows, or in fact encourages, as characters pass through their various "allotropic" states, is a sort of free-ranging portrayal of heightened or expressionistic states of mind. This results, further, in a type of symbolism that, in its extreme affectiveness, might well be called Gothic.

Examples are numerous. An early scene is that in which Hermione Roddice attempts to kill Rupert Birkin in her boudoir. She is writing letters as Birkin enters and takes up a book. In love with Birkin, and chafing under earlier remarks of his about the necessity of maintaining a free self, she cannot concentrate. Hermione is arguably the worst of the blood- and soul-suckers in Lawrence. "Her whole mind was a chaos, darkness breaking in upon it, and herself struggling to gain control with her will, as a swimmer struggles with the swirling water" (104). She thinks that "she must break him down before her, the awful obstruction of him who obstructed her life to the last. It must be done, or she must perish most horribly" (104–105). She manages to strike him only imperfectly with the ball of lapis lazuli so that, while dazed, he manages to extricate himself. He talks to her as if to a ghost of vengeance. " 'No you don't, Hermione,' he said in a low voice, 'I don't let you.' " He observes her "standing tall and attentive, the stone clutched tense in her hand." He tells her to stand away: "As if pressed back by some hand, she stood away, watching him all the time without changing, like a neutralised angel confronting him" (106). Birkin then in the field of bracken strips completely and rolls in the vegetation to get contact with the earth. The element of dread operates on two levels here: first, that of Hermione's dread of Birkin's self-sufficiency and self-containment, which encapsulates her corresponding dread of her own insufficiency; and second, that of Birkin's dread of humanity with its murderously destructive will to power: "What a dread he had of mankind, of other people! It amounted almost to horror, to a sort of dream terror" (108). It is a bizarre episode, but hardly, to be sure, the most bizarre that the novel affords. "Dread" as Lawrence uses it often has an existential aspect à la Heidegger and Jaspers, and it may not be too farfetched to claim that in his treatment of dread he is reconfiguring the emotional dimensions of the Gothic. Certainly he is far from the stock Gothic machinery of chills down the spine, tremblings in the joints, and breathless apprehensions, but this is still a kind of ontological terror that comes from the deepest regions of one's being.

Two fairly early scenes twin to establish the Gothic element of human perversity and cruelty. These are the scene at the train tracks involving Gerald Crich and his horse and the scene involving Gerald and his younger sister's pet rabbit Bismarck. In the first, Ursula and her sister Gudrun stop by the tracks as a train passes. Gerald approaches on his horse, which is frightened of the train. In the attempt to control her, he forces her head to the gate: "The sharp blasts of the chuffing engine broke with more and more force on her. The repeated sharp blows of unknown, terrifying noise struck through her till she was rocking with terror" (111). Ursula shouts, "The fool. Why doesn't he ride her away till it's gone by?" But Gerald only holds her in place, amused: "But he leaned forward, his face shining with fixed amusement, and at last he brought her down, sank her down. . . . But as strong as the pressure of his compulsion was the repulsion of her utter terror" (111). It is indeed a horrifying scene, but perhaps most horrifying is its effect on Gudrun, who looks on with both horror and pleasurable fascination, becoming "faint with poignant dizziness, which seemed to penetrate to her heart" (111). What penetrates chiefly is the compulsive cruelty, the cruelty that achieves its apotheosis in her at the end of the novel. We see the cruelty again in the "Rabbit" chapter. When Gudrun takes Bismarck from his cage, he responds in animal desperation, clawing Gudrun about the wrists. "A heavy rage came over her like a cloud. . . . Her heart was arrested with fury at the mindlessness and bestial stupidity of this struggle, . . . and a heavy cruelty welled up in her" (240). Gerald arrives, however, and takes the situation in hand, subduing the animal with a blow to the back of its neck. It is a small contest of power, with Gerald showing, as with the horse, that he is in control. Bismarck does manage to deliver a lurid scratch to Gerald's arm, however, which Gudrun observes with fascination. "Glancing up at him, into his eyes, she revealed again the mocking, white-cruel recognition. There was a league between them, abhorrent to them both. They were implicated with each other in abhorrent mysteries" (242). These are Gothic mysteries, outside normal human parameters, in which dread and terror coexist with the fascination with power and obsessive cruelty.

The book's last chapters bring Birkin and Ursula together in a happiness that is as complete as it can get in Lawrence. Gudrun and Gerald travel a different course. They find their element in that favorite land of Gothic reckoning, the snowbound mountains of the Swiss Alps. There Gudrun finds Loerke, the homosexual industrial artist, whose instrumentalism far surpasses Gerald's, and whose depths of perversity are bottomless. Since Gudrun's fascination with perversity surpasses Gerald's, she finds herself enthralled by Loerke. His evil genius is no doubt meant to mirror that of the evil spirit Loki of Norse mythology. His "insect-like comprehension" (452) of things repulses Birkin and Ursula. Ursula criticizes his horse statuettes as "stiff" (430), lacking life. Gudrun, naturally (or unnaturally), is fascinated by them. Sensing the spell he has woven over Gudrun, Loerke causes her, both directly and indirectly, to inflict a steady systematic cruelty upon Gerald. When Gerald, having reached his breaking point, cannot complete his attempt to murder her and goes off to die in the snow, Lawrence brings full circle the theme of dread that from its start had propelled the novel. By the half-buried crucifix, Gerald has the realization that "somebody was going to murder him. He had a great dread of being murdered. But it was a dread that stood outside him, like his own ghost" (473). It is his own ghost, so to speak, that murders him, that is, his unreconciled self, which is another way of saying the elemental "sheer slopes and precipices" of snow that he had willed for himself beyond Birkin's help.

Lawrence wrote several short stories in a span of two years in the early 1920s that also are of special interest to the student of the Gothic. The chief of these as Gothic fictions are the novella "The Ladybird" and the story "The Border Line." Interesting also are the ghost stories "The Last Laugh" and "Glad Ghosts" (space exigencies do not permit discussion of them here) and the novella "The Fox," the last the story of Henry, a young soldier recently discharged who returns to the farm his grandfather had owned to find two young women living there trying to eke out a subsistence. With the predatory instincts of a fox, Henry pursues, or rather haunts, in Gothic fashion, the stronger of the young women, March, whose relationship with the neurasthenic and "mental" Banford operates on spiritually lesbian lines. March vigorously resists Henry initially, but at last "she felt the deep, heavy, powerful stroke of his heart, terrible, like something from beyond . . . , like something from outside signaling to her" (52). At the end of the story, Henry allows Banford to be killed in a symbolic accident: a tree he is cutting down crushes her skull. Henry is another of Lawrence's Gothically vital characters who, mysteriously pursuing courses they scarcely comprehend, compel other characters out of their deaths in life.

In "The Ladybird," a Czech prisoner, Count Johann Dionys Psanek, lies in a London hospital with nearly mortal wounds. He has no wish to live. He is visited there by Lady Daphne and her mother, whom he had known before the war. To Daphne he had once given a thimble. He tells Daphne that he cannot die because there is a "devil" (169) in him. He tells her further that he is "a subject of the sun. I belong to the fire-worshippers" (170). His name, Psanek, means "outlaw." We are meant to see him as an outlaw from civilization, which he fears. As he recovers, she knits him shirts. He reveals to her the truth that he lives by, that there is a dark sun, an "invisible fire" (180). Lady Daphne's beauty, he tells her, is merely her "whited sepulchre": "The real you is the wild-cat invisible in the night" (180).

Daphne's husband returns from the war with a disfiguring scar on his cheek. Basil is a well-known Lawrencian type, the mind-conscious individual who lives in dread of physical contact. Dionys, now almost fully recovered, is invited to spend his last days in England at Lady Daphne's. In conversation, Basil tells

Dionys that he believes that mankind will arrive at "a higher state of consciousness, and therefore of life," and ultimately, a "higher plane of love" (198). The central tension of the story comes through Daphne's polite revulsion from the "white passion" (200) of her husband and her increasing attraction to the dark mystery in Count Dionys. He explains to her his family crest, the ladybird, which is also graven onto the thimble. It connects him with the pharaohs and the scarabeus. With the ball of dung between its claws, it embodies the principle of decomposition, corresponding to Dionys's belief that present-day civilization must be destroyed so that a new world can be born out of it. Through Dionys, Lawrence elaborates his notion of a natural aristocracy and the "leadership theme" familiar to Lawrence's readers. Daphne believes that Dionys has "called" her. His "utterly inhuman" (214) singing late at night eventually draws her to his room. She wants to be made love to, but he tells her that there is no place in "the world" for them; yet in the "after-life," of which he is "master," they will come together as "queen" and "master of the underworld" (216). She no longer will be Aphrodite, "the self-conscious one," but the wife of Hades. Thus she loses her earthly dread of life and gains a mystical assurance of life in the "after-death." Dionys assures her that he will be waiting for her on the other side of death. "So don't be afraid in life. Don't be afraid" (220).

Technically, of course, "*The Ladybird*" does not breach that curtain dividing the natural from the supernatural. "The Border Line" does. Katharine Anstruther (modeled on Frieda, Lawrence's wife) marries Philip Farquhar, a celebrated reporter, after her husband, Alan Anstruther, "that red-haired fighting Celt" (78), has been killed in the war. Although she had loved her husband, she finds marriage with Philip, "a little somebody in the world" (588), initially comforting, as she had previously chafed against Alan's "indomitable assumption" that he was "actually first-born, a born lord" (78). She travels by train to be with her Philip, described as "clever and knowing" (never a good thing in Lawrence), whom she has not seen for a time. Although at first she finds it very comforting and pleasant to be married to Philip, a "sense of degradation" (81) begins to set in. She has a layover in Strasbourg; walking the streets of the town, she has a strange mystical feeling as she approaches the cathedral. It is like a "great ghost, a reddish flush in its darkness . . . , standing gigantic, looking down in darkness . . . on the pigmy humanness of the city." Built of "reddish stone," it has "a flush in the darkness like dark flesh" (84). It looms like a "menace . . . out of the upper black heavens, vast . . . demonish" (85). As she ponders this "great blood-creature waiting . . . , blotting out the Cross it was supposed to exalt," she sees a figure ahead of her that she recognizes at once as Alan, "and she knew he had come back to her from the dead" (87) to rescue her from "the supreme modern terror, of a world all ashy and nerve-dead" (87). We are, to be sure, on familiar Lawrencian ground, but the effect is heightened by the extraordinary Gothic presentation of it.

The rest of the story concerns Philip's gradual but certain descent into death caused by the "rupture of a superficial blood-vessel" (95). One night, shortly after he is put to bed, Katharine hears a horrifying cry from his room. He is sitting up in bed, blood all over his face and bed clothes: "He [Anstruther] lay on top of me, and turned my heart cold, and burst my blood-vessels in my chest" (95). Sitting on the opposite bed is Alan: "She knew he had the power over her too" (95). The next night comes another cry. This time Katharine gets into bed with Philip to warm him, but the ghost of Alan pulls her onto the floor. Philip dies before morning, his body in "a pool of blood" (96). In the afternoon, Katharine goes walking. The ghost of Alan joins her, leading her through a wood to a "great pine tree." There he makes love to her, and it is as if "the limbs of the tree [were] enveloping her, crushing her in the last, final ecstasy of submission, squeezing from her the last drop of her passion, like the cold white berries of the mistletoe on the tree of life" (98). Interestingly, in another version of the ending (see the appendix to the Mehl and Jansohn Viking Penguin edition), as Philip lies in his deathbed, his lips unfurled to show "his big teeth in a ghastly grin," Alan takes Katharine to the adjacent bed "in the silent passion for a husband come back from a very long journey" (604). It would almost seem that Lawrence, aware that he was slowly dying from tuberculosis, was preparing his brief for the afterlife in this story and in "The Ladybird," his two most consummate Gothic fictions.

SELECTED CRITICISM

Humma, John. "Lawrence in Another Light: *Women in Love* and Existentialism." *Studies in the Novel* 24 (1992): 392–409. Explores the often-neglected darker elements in Lawrence's novel.

Lawrence, D.H. *Studies in Classic American Literature*. New York: Penguin, 1971. Contains Lawrence's important discussions of Melville, Hawthorne, Poe, and other American writers who share affinities with the Gothic tradition.

———. *The Letters of D.H. Lawrence*. Vol. 2, *June 1913–October 1916*. Ed. George J. Zytaruk and James T. Boulton. Cambridge: Cambridge University Press, 1981.

Lewis, Hanna B. "The Catalytic Child Hero in the Contemporary Gothic Novel." In *The Hero in Transition*. Ed. Ray B. Browne and Marshall W. Fishwick. Bowling Green, OH: Bowling Green University Popular Press, 1983: 151–162. Uses the child Paul in Lawrence's short story "The Rocking Horse Winner" as a model for the catalytic child in modern Gothic fiction.

Stroupe, John H. "Ruskin, Lawrence, and Gothic Naturalism." *Ball State University Forum* 11:2 (1970): 3–9. Draws meaningful comparisons and contrasts between the two authors in their development of a modified Gothic style.

Wilt, Judith. *Ghosts of the Gothic: Austen, Eliot, and Lawrence*. Princeton: Princeton University Press, 1980. Wilt focuses most of her attention upon Lawrence's two great mature novels, *The Rainbow* and *Women in Love*. Her work is groundbreaking in the sense that neither novel until her study had been considered Gothic. She does not treat any of the shorter fictions, where the more traditionally Gothic elements figure.

SOPHIA LEE
(1750–1824)

Douglass H. Thomson

PRINCIPAL GOTHIC WORKS

The Recess; or, A Tale of Other Times. 3 vols. London: T. Cadell, 1783–1785. (By the early 1800s, *The Recess* had gone through five English and two Irish editions, had reached North America, and had been translated into many continental languages. See the "Bibliography" in Alliston's edition [363–364] for detailed information on the popularity and publication history of the novel.)

"The Young Lady's Tale: The Two Emilys." In *Canterbury Tales*. Vol. 2. London: G.G. & J. Robinson, 1798.

"The Clergyman's Tale; or, Pembroke" In *Canterbury Tales*. Vol. 3. London: G.G. & J. Robinson, 1799.

MODERN REPRINTS AND EDITIONS

Canterbury Tales. New York: AMS Press. 1978. (Reprint of 1832 edition published by H. Coburn & R. Bentley as part of the Standard Novels series.)

The Canterbury Tales. Intro. Harriet Gilbert. London: Pandora, 1989. (Selections do not include "The Young Lady's Tale.")

The Recess; or, A Tale of Other Times. Foreword by J.M.S. Tompkins, intro. Devendra P. Varma. New York: Arno Press, 1972.

The Recess; or, A Tale of Other Times. Manchester, NH: Ayer, 1979. (Reprint of the 1972 Arno Press edition.)

The Recess; or, A Tale of Other Times. Ed. April Alliston. Lexington: University Press of Kentucky, 2000. (This edition is cited in the text.)

The Recess. In *Gothic Readings: The First Wave, 1764–1840*. Ed. Rictor Norton. London and New York: Leicester University Press, 2000: 13–17. (Excerpts from the novel.)

Sophia Lee's *The Recess*, "the first English romance that blended interesting fiction with historical events and characters" (Harriet Lee vi), has long been claimed by specialists as a foundational text in the Gothic canon, but a survey of recent criticism reveals it as one of the least read books among the early Gothic novels. April Alliston's excellent new edition of *The Recess* promises to remedy this problem and to encourage reexamination of the place of Lee's fiction in the early development of the female Gothic novel. In addition to presenting a reliable and readable text of a novel that has for too long languished in hard-to-read facsimile editions, Alliston provides an introduction with much-needed information on the life and literary career of Lee, refutes many cursory and misguided estimates of the novel, and places *The Recess* in the contexts necessary for an appreciation of Lee's groundbreaking and influential achievement. She demonstrates that the influence of Baculard d'Arnaud on Lee has been exaggerated due to a wrong attribution to her of a translation of his *Varbeck*. She argues for a much more obvious and decisive set of influences in her family's long theatrical career: Lee was the daughter of two Shakespearean actors, and she could just as well have derived her stagey plot of apparently orphaned royal sisters from *Cymbeline* as from her reading of that important model for historical fiction, Abbé Prévost's *Cleveland*. Perhaps most important, Alliston takes issue with critics who have disparaged Lee's historical knowledge of Elizabethan England, first, by showing how deeply engaged she was with contemporary historical accounts, and second, by showing how her novel constructs its own understanding of just what constitutes history. One might balk at Alliston's enthusiastic claim that "it was *The Recess* that ushered in the great vogue of Gothic fiction in England" (xii), but this fine edition of *The Recess* promises renewed attention to the place of Lee's fiction among the early Gothic novelists and her influence on those writers, especially Ann Radcliffe, to come.

The Recess chronicles the terrible trials of the twin sisters Matilda and Ellinor, long-concealed offspring of a secret marriage between Mary Stuart, the Queen of Scots, and the Duke of Norfolk. Hidden deep within the Recess, a complex of subterranean chambers beneath the remains of St. Vincent's Abbey (recently ruined by the English Reformation), the sisters do not even discover the secret of their birth until their late teens. As Matilda and Ellinor finally and literally see the light of day and leave this Gothic space that is at once womb and prison, the two embark into the dangerous world of courtly intrigue powerfully monitored by Queen Elizabeth, the deadly enemy of their mother. Lee weaves into her "romance" a rich tapestry of historical incidents and persons, taken mainly from her close reading of such contemporary historians as David Hume and William Robertson. Two real-life competitors for Elizabeth's favor, the Lords Leicester and Essex, become the fictional love interests of, respectively, Matilda and Ellinor, as the mainly secret and interior stories of their romances are played out against the grand sweep of late-sixteenth-century history, with a special emphasis on Elizabeth's legendary jealousy and fickleness. Drawing upon a French tradition of historical fiction that "defied both official historiography and the sense of probable female behavior" (Alliston, "Introduction," xv), Lee is credited with writing one of the first such novels in the English tradition, one that exerted an influence on Radcliffe's and Walter Scott's interweaving of real and imagined pasts. Scott's novel *Kenilworth* derives many of its details from Lee's romance. She certainly takes liberties with the chronology of events, but her chief concern is imagining the past as its principal actors might have experienced it. In her relating of history through emphasis on characterization, Lee actually follows the procedure of most eighteenth-century historians. But her sole filters, primarily the always-suffering Matilda and Ellinor, interspersed with some epistles of other women who risk everything to defend them, provide a distinctly female version of history and a narrative line clearly influential in the development of the female Gothic.

That narrative line reveals many similarities to the mother of the female Gothic, Ann Radcliffe, whom historians tantalizingly suggest, but cannot confirm, was a student at the Lee sisters' respected school in Bath. Yet in other important ways, Lee's twin epistolary structure provides a more complex pattern of deferral and revelation than any other of the many first female Gothics. In Lee's novel one finds already full-blown these staples of what has come to be recognized as the Radcliffean Gothic plot: the extreme and prolonged suffering of central female characters, rendered vulnerable by uncertainties concerning their family relations, further hampered by their uneven educations, given to extremes of sensibility, and menaced by sexually predatory males (in Lee's novel directly by the would-be rapist Williams); the exasperatingly ineffectual efforts of the men they love (in this version because of Leicester's and Essex's entanglements with the queen); reveries (briefer in Lee) in which the heroines imagine a freedom and range of expression and happiness denied them by hereditary and economic circumstances; and plots long on mystery and secrecy with a promise of revelation and resolution, usually confirming the durable goodness of domestic virtue despite its terrifying exposure to the dark side of human nature (Lee frequently hints at but finally denies this kind of resolution).

If, as David Punter summarizes, "the world of *The Recess*, even more explicitly than the world of Radcliffe's novels, is one in which women are in constant danger" (59), so, too, is Lee's narrative structure more complex than that of her follower and more equivocal in its points of view. The novel begins with the letters of Matilda, which supply the complex family background of the sisters and the reason for their seclusion in the Recess. The letters also disclose her dangerous passion for Leicester and their secret marriage. Everything that can go wrong does go wrong in this tortured narrative: Leicester, although still professing his love, grows increasingly gloomy at his loss of Elizabeth's favor; Matilda rushes from one hiding place to another (all metonymic recesses) to conceal the secrets of her birth and marriage, barely keeping out of the reach of court spies and menacing banditti; Leicester dies in a duel with one of these; Ellinor becomes estranged from her sister and is left alone and vulnerable at the court of Elizabeth; Mary is executed, and Matilda feels at least partially responsible. She then falls into the hands of vindictive Catholics in France, who should, given her parentage, protect her but who have their own political agenda as Lee, in a narrative otherwise highly critical of the Tudor court, makes clear her alliance with other early Gothic writers' anti-Catholicism. Matilda finally ends up imprisoned for four years as a pauper in Jamaica, gives birth to little Mary, suffers rheumatic fever and becomes thereafter lame, and survives only through the ministrations of the sympathetic black woman, Anana.

Finally returning to England with her child, Matilda receives from Lady Arundel the narrative of her equally beleaguered sister, which recounts her similarly doomed romance with Lord Essex. Ellinor offers a very different version of many of the same events contained in Matilda's story, as she casts doubt upon the integrity of Leicester and the wisdom of Matilda's passion for him. Estranged from Essex, Ellinor eventually goes mad upon hearing of his death in the Tower, and Lee punctuates her later narrative with brief, manic paragraphs to create the effect of her insanity and to further complicate the authority of the narrative as a whole. The novel concludes in Matilda's voice. After further complicating matters by casting doubt upon her poor sister's version of events, Matilda continues with her ardent hope that all might turn out well through a love match that she engineers between Mary and Henry, the next Stuart in line to the throne. But unknown to her mother until the very end, Mary has actually fallen for the unscrupulous Somerset, and both she and Henry are poisoned to death by shadowy court rivals. The novel ends with the utter devastation of Matilda, who has lost all of her loved ones and who turns her eyes toward a heaven that surely promises a brighter existence than the one she has led in this world of intrigue and indecipherable cross-purposes. *The Recess* thus spectacularly denies its women the happy endings reserved for Radcliffe's heroines. More important, the novel's conflicting narrative perspectives suggest that through history women must confront a number of greater challenges, including the problem of their own subjectivity, than those found in the reassuring pattern of romance. Or, to put it another way, Lee's epistemological complexities suggest that official historiography often constructs its narrative of causality and progress at the expense of the interior lives of its characters.

Because the intense dread experienced by Lee's heroines has little to do with even the ostensibly supernatural, Robert Hume has questioned the inclusion of *The Recess* in a canon of Gothic novels. He argues that *The Recess* is "in reality a sentimental-domestic novel transposed into a supposedly historical situation with Gothic trimmings [merely] added for savor" (283). Lee does reserve one of the few clear moments of Gothic terror in the novel for the haughty Elizabeth, when, visited by the deranged Ellinor, the now-guilt-plagued queen mistakes the daughter for the ghost of her departed mother Mary. Yet even this Gothic "trimming" could be called an instance of the "explained-beforehand" supernatural. Beyond such incidents and the important parallels with Radcliffean plotting noted earlier, what really warrants the consideration of Lee's novel within the Gothic tradition is the powerful and multilayered metaphor of its title. The obscure and dark subterranean vaults containing ancestral portraits and deep family secrets become the ubiquitous props and settings of Gothicism and its obsession with the submerged, the secretive, and the libidinal. In Lee's early depiction, the Recess also clearly figures as an image of woman's sequestered existence. It may seem to provide her with protection from the dangerous currents of courtly and patriarchal intrigue, but in cutting her off from knowledge of the world, it makes her only more vulnerable to its troubles and temptations. The Recess is, at once, a womb and a tomb, a refuge and a prison, a promised sanctuary for a female community and a bitter caricature of the domestic sphere. It proves anything but a safe place, as Leicester's early discovery of the Recess sets in motion the tragic events of the novel, and many follow him, especially the villainous Williams, in penetrating its secrets. The metaphor of the Recess extends beyond that specific place hidden beneath the ruins of St. Vincent's Abbey: our heroines must always be recessive, nowhere more so than in the public life of Elizabeth's court, and the novel abounds in related images of their entrapment and isolation. In helping to create one of the Gothic's favorite architectural settings, Lee also uses the Recess as an effective and pliable metaphor for the buried life of women.

Lee's final works of fiction, her even more critically neglected contributions to *Canterbury Tales* (1798–1799), offer some noteworthy variations on other Gothic tropes. "The Young Lady's Tale: The Two Emilys" chronicles the long and intricate sufferings of another Radcliffean heroine, Emily Arden. She struggles to meet the demands of a proud father, Sir Edward Arden, and to rehabilitate a wayward husband, the Marquis of Lenox, while being haunted and persecuted by her evil double, Emily Fitzallen (the bastard child of the Marquis's dissolute father), who swears vengeance on the noble families. Unlike the tragic heroines of *The Recess*, the good Emily eventually triumphs in an ending that strains credulity but provides a feminist fantasy, in which female sensibility and domestic virtue tame dangerous male passion and economic self-interest. The novella deserves greater attention from critics who have called attention to the feminist concerns of *The Recess*. Its one certifiably Gothic moment occurs when the estranged Emily is nightly serenaded by a mysterious flute player, whom her Irish servants believe to be a marble faun come to life. The ghostly musician turns out to be her beloved Marquis come back from the grave alive and well.

"The Clergyman's Tale; or, Pembroke" offers a triple-decker haunting of another fractured and intricately interrelated family occupying the very Gothic Castle St. Hilary in Wales. Again, credibility begins along class lines, with the aristocratic Pembroke skeptical but his Welsh servants all certain that the castle is haunted by the statue of a "gigantic Briton" that springs to life at midnight. Eventually, however, even Pembroke succumbs to a terrifying visitation. We find out at the very end that the ghost is actually the misanthrope Carey (née Hubert Provis), a laudanum addict given to nocturnal wanderings. He is the most interesting character in a novel full again of interwoven Gothic and historical incidents. Hubert's inset narrative of how he has lost his wife and son takes up the second third of the novella, and though he is an avowed human-hater, he takes a weirdly visionary view of human suffering. He has spent time with Hindus and believes that he can communicate with the spirits of his loved ones through two spaniels whom he hints may be their reincarnations. Really!

Not really. In another example of Lee's commitment to the "explained supernatural," it turns out that Hubert's son is really still living, a fact that provides the happy resolution of a plot far too intricate to summarize. With its tightly woven narrative and easy mastery of Gothic conventions, "The Clergyman's Tale" is a little Gothic gem. That mastery might just, as in the case of the two spaniel avatars, include parody, and in her last work of fiction it is tempting to see Lee playfully reflecting upon some of the conventions she fifteen years earlier helped inaugurate in *The Recess*.

SELECTED CRITICISM

Alliston, April. "Secret Communications; or, Faults of Transmission." In *Virtue's Faults: Correspondences in Eighteenth-Century British and French Women's Fiction*. Stanford, CA: Stanford University Press, 1996: 148–187. In making the case for *The Recess* being "the first 'female Gothic' novel," Alliston offers the close and sophisticated reading demanded by the novel's complex narrative structure and doublings. "In *The Recess*, literal frames and related enclosures—tombs, caskets, and letters—constitute Gothic doublings of the maternal precept and example as ambiguous inheritance, at once open and enclosing."

———. "Introduction" to *The Recess*. Lexington: University Press of Kentucky, 2000: ix–xliv. Includes a pro-Gothic revaluation of the novel's Gothic features, especially its enclosures.

Ellis, Kate Ferguson. "*Otranto* Feminized." In *The Contested Castle: Gothic Novels and the Subversion of Domestic Ideology*. Urbana: University of Illinois Press, 1989: 68–75. Discusses Lee's novel to illustrate the thesis that female Gothic writers offer criticism of the terrible misdeeds men commit under the sanction of a ruling domestic ideology, but Ellis's interpretation is marred by some serious misreading of basic elements of the plot.

Foster, James R. "D'Arnaud, Clara Reeve, and the Lees." In *The History of the Pre-Romantic Novel in England*. New York: Modern Language Association, 1949: 186–284. Explores the French connection of the Lee sisters and discusses the fusion of Gothic atmosphere and settings with pseudohistorical plotting.

Hume, Robert. "Gothic versus Romantic: A Revaluation of the Gothic Novel." *PMLA* 84 (1969): 282–290. Opened debate by rejecting the novel's Gothicism. "A novel like *The Recess* (1785), which makes use of historical personages, is in reality a sentimental-domestic novel transposed into a supposedly historical situation with Gothic trimmings added for savor. If wearing a wool tie makes me a sheep, then *The Recess* is a Gothic novel."

Issac, Megan Lynn. "Sophia Lee and the Gothic of Female Community." *Studies in the Novel* 28 (1996): 200–218. "With her emphases on the dangers of secrecy, the ignorance which results from it, the value of female friendship, and the need for female histories as well as male, Lee uses the Gothic novel in an idiosyncratically entertaining and praiseworthy fashion."

Lee, Harriet. Introduction to *Canterbury Tales*. New York: AMS Press, 1978: i–ix. Sophia Lee's sister explains their collaboration on this volume of tales and laments the fact that domestic responsibilities prevented the author of *The Recess* from continuing her literary career.

Lewis, Jayne Elizabeth. " 'Ev'ry Lost Relation': Historical Fictions and Sentimental Incidents in Sophia Lee's *The Recess*." *Eighteenth-Century Fiction* 7 (1995): 165–184. "Lee uses the figure of the injured queen [Mary, Queen of Scots] to investigate the secretly twinned structures of historiography and sensibility," the former grounded in empirical evidence and causality, the latter in interior, transposable descriptions and parataxis. The Gothic elements of the novel function as the latter.

Norton, Rictor. "Portrait of the Artist." In *Mistress of Udolpho: The Life of Ann Radcliffe*. London and New York: Leicester University Press, 1999: 82–91. Finds no evidence to support the claim that Ann Radcliffe was in residence at the Lee sisters' school, but does find many points of contact with Radcliffe's Gothics and Gothicism. "La Motte [in *The Romance of the Forest*] resembles Father Anthony in Sophia Lee's *The Recess*, and the apartment which Adeline discovers connected to her room via a trapdoor is obviously Lee's 'Recess.' "

Punter, David. "The Origins of Gothic Fiction: Sentimentalism, Graveyard Poetry, the Sublime, Smollett, Horace Walpole, Clara Reeve, Sophia Lee." In *The Literature of Terror: A History of Gothic Fictions from 1765 to the Present Day*. London and New York: Longman, 1996: I:22–61. Stresses the innovation of Lee's "modified epistolary technique to give us conflicting viewpoints on events. Above all, *The Recess* is Gothic in being a novel of suspense" and female persecution.

Roberts, Bette B. "Sophia Lee's *The Recess* (1785): The Ambivalence of Female Gothicism." *Massachusetts Studies in English* 6 (1978): 68–82. The ambivalence shows up in the fact that "while the overt portrait of woman's virtuous fortitude and delicacy reinforces her sex role in a patriarchal society, the recurrent pattern of imprisonment and escape, plus a preoccupation with the recess itself, reveals a desire for flight."

Spencer, Jane. "Romance Heroines: The Tradition of Escape; Rewriting History: Sophia Lee's *The Recess*." In *The Rise of the Woman Novelist from Aphra Behn to Jane Austen*. Oxford: Blackwell: 1986: 93–104. Acknowledges the novel's Gothic content in Lee's fictionalization of history.

JOSEPH SHERIDAN LE FANU
(1814–1873)
Jack G. Voller

PRINCIPAL GOTHIC WORKS

"The Ghost and the Bone-Setter." *Dublin University Magazine*, January 1838.
"The Fortunes of Sir Robert Ardagh." *Dublin University Magazine*, March 1838. (Revised as "The Haunted Baronet," *Belgravia*, July–November 1870, and as "Sir Dominick's Bargain," *All the Year Round*, 6 July 1872.)
"The Drunkard's Dream." *Dublin University Magazine*, August 1838. (Revised as "The Vision of Tom Chuff," *All the Year Round*, 8 October 1870.)
"Strange Event in the Life of Schalken the Painter." *Dublin University Magazine*, May 1839.
"A Chapter in the History of a Tyrone Family." *Dublin University Magazine*, October 1839.
"Spalatro, from the Notes of Fra Giacomo." *Dublin University Magazine*, March–April 1843.
"The Mysterious Lodger." *Dublin University Magazine*, January–February 1850.
Ghost Stories and Tales of Mystery. Dublin: McGlashan, 1851; London: Orr, 1851. (Includes "Strange Event in the Life of Schalken the Painter" and "The Watcher.")
"Ghost Stories of the Chapelizod." *Dublin University Magazine*, January 1851.
"Account of Some Strange Disturbances in Aungier Street." *Dublin University Magazine*, December 1853.
"Ultor de Lacy." *Dublin University Magazine*, December 1861.
"Borrhomeo the Astrologer." *Dublin University Magazine*, January 1862.
"An Authentic Narrative of a Haunted House." *Dublin University Magazine*, October 1862.
Uncle Silas: A Tale of Bartram-Haugh. London: Bentley, 1864.
Wylder's Hand: A Novel. London: Bentley, 1864.
"Wicked Captain Walshawe of Wauling." *Dublin University Magazine*, April 1864.
"Squire Toby's Will." *Temple Bar*, January 1868.
The Wyvern Mystery. London: Tinsley, 1869.
"Green Tea." *All the Year Round*, 23 October and 13 November 1869.
"The Child That Went with the Fairies." *All the Year Round*, 5 February 1870.

"The White Cat of Drumgunniol." *All the Year Round*, 2 April 1870.
"Stories of Lough Guir." *All the Year Round*, 23 April 1870.
"Madam Crowl's Ghost." *All the Year Round*, 31 December 1870.
Chronicles of Golden Friars. London: Bentley, 1871. (Includes "The Haunted Baronet.")
"The Dead Sexton." *Once a Week*, December 1871.
"Carmilla." *Dark Blue*, December 1871–March 1872.
In a Glass Darkly. London: Bentley, 1872. (Includes "The Familiar" [a revision of "The
        Watcher"], "Carmilla," "Mr. Justice Harbottle" [a revision of "Account of Some
        Strange Disturbances in Aungier Street"], and "Green Tea.")
"Laura Silver Bell." *Belgravia*, 1872.
"Dickon the Devil." *London Society*, December 1872.
The Purcell Papers. London: Bentley, 1880. (Includes "The Ghost and the Bone-Setter,"
        "The Fortunes of Sir Robert Ardagh," "The Drunkard's Dream," and "Strange
        Event in the Life of Schalken the Painter.")
The Watcher and Other Weird Stories. London: Downey, 1894.

MODERN REPRINTS AND EDITIONS

Best Ghost Stories of J.S. Le Fanu. Ed. E.F. Bleiler. New York: Dover, 1964.
"Carmilla." In *Seven Masterpieces of Gothic Horror*. Ed. Robert D. Spector. New York:
        Bantam, 1963.
Carmilla and 12 Other Classic Tales of Mystery. Ed. Leonard Wolf. New York: Signet,
        1996.
Chronicles of Golden Friars. New York: Arno, 1977. (Includes "The Haunted Baronet.")
The Collected Works of Joseph Sheridan Le Fanu. Ed. Devendra P. Varma. 52 vols.
        New York: Arno Press, 1977.
Ghost Stories and Mysteries. Ed. E.F. Bleiler. New York: Dover, 1975.
Green Tea and Other Ghost Stories. Ed. August Derleth. Sauk City, WI: Arkham House,
        1945.
In a Glass Darkly. Ed. Robert Tracy. New York and Oxford: Oxford University Press,
        1993.
Madam Crowl's Ghost and Other Tales of Mystery. Ed. M.R. James. London: Bell, 1923.
        Rpt. Freeport, NY: Books for Libraries Press, 1971.
The Purcell Papers. Ed. August Derleth. New York: AMS Press, 1975; Sauk City, WI:
        Arkham House, 1975.
Uncle Silas. Ed. Frederick Shroyer. New York: Dover, 1966.
The Wyvern Mystery. New York: Arno Press, 1977.

While the tradition of supernatural literature is replete with authors underappre-
ciated by the academic and literary mainstream, few authors suffer greater injustice in this regard than Joseph Sheridan Le Fanu. Author, editor, lawyer,
magazine publisher, and folklore collector, Le Fanu is one of the masters of the
nineteenth-century supernatural tale, producing works the equal of the best tales
by Wilkie Collins and Charles Dickens. Yet despite such achievement and recent
attempts to popularize his work, and despite being at the forefront of the development of the psychological horror story, Le Fanu remains a slighted figure.

Le Fanu may be understood, in one important sense, as the progressive counterpart to his contemporary William Harrison Ainsworth. While the latter clung to the modes and tropes of the Gothic as he had known them in his youth and so represented a final outpost of the classic Gothic tale in the mid- to late nineteenth century, Le Fanu began the process of turning the Gothic into the modern tale of psychological terror. While he certainly owed a debt to the Gothic, as well as to Irish folklore, his innovation was to shift the primary focus from the machinery of terror to its effect on the mind of its observer/victim. Along with Dickens, Poe, Collins, and Bulwer-Lytton, and arguably foremost among them, Le Fanu orchestrated a midcentury change in the course of the Gothic that forever altered the shape of the tradition.

While Le Fanu certainly produced a number of excellent tales in the more traditional modes of the pure supernatural (e.g., "Madam Crowl's Ghost" and "The Haunted Baronet") and wrote as well a number of works influenced by Irish folklore ("The White Cat of Drumgunniol," "Ultor de Lacy," and "Stories of Lough Guir"), it is his interest in ontological ambiguity and in laying bare the psychological pressures faced by an individual engaged with the possible supernatural that makes Le Fanu a major innovator in the post-Gothic tradition. Tales such as "The Watcher" (revised as "The Familiar"; Le Fanu was an inveterate reviser) and "Green Tea" even more than his popular suspense novels such as *Uncle Silas* and *The Rose and the Key* create a compelling psychological undertow into which the reader is drawn along with the perhaps self-persecuted protagonist. The uncertainty attending the central agent in various stories such as the demonic monkey of "Green Tea" or the mysterious and vengeful stranger(s) in "The Watcher" becomes, through Le Fanu's deft manipulation of tension, suspense, and even Swedenborgian allusion, the consuming and ultimately destabilizing/destabilized narrative center. The horror Le Fanu's protagonists encounter is usually enough to destroy them, yet the finality of their destruction only heightens the essential uncertainty of the apparently supernatural agent's true ontological status. Nor is that issue usually resolved, for the Radcliffean anxiety of ontology and the reassurance sought by the insistent unmasking of the ghostly as human have been trumped in the Victorian post-Gothic ethos by an anxiety of epistemology. It is what we can and cannot know—the boundaries and limitations of knowledge—that shapes the dark dreamworld of much later nineteenth-century horror, thanks to Le Fanu, and in the anxiety generated by the mind's unavailing struggles to resolve ambiguity into certainty lies the core of modern horror. Le Fanu's beleaguered protagonists may indeed succumb because they come to believe that they are hounded by something supernatural, but their deaths truly mark not the triumph of the supernatural, but of the uncertain. His failed heroes surrender not to the ghostly, but to the failure of knowing, and that failure attends the readerly experience of the tale as well—indeed, is Le Fanu's primary concern. This is the Victorian core of Le Fanu's horror, the dramatic failure of rationality combined with the consuming and destructive power of the morally transgressive.

For it is in moral transgression or at least as commonly in their moral lapses that Le Fanu's protagonists open themselves up to the possibility of disruption and annihilation. Whether it is the sexual transgression and vindictive abusiveness of Captain Barton in "The Watcher," the greed and criminality of Toby Crooke in "The Dead Sexton," or the ancestral failure of kinship and compassion in "The Haunted Baronet," Le Fanu's haunted moral universe is predicated soundly upon Victorian virtue and decorum, and even the subtlest and most surreptitious violations of these values bring consuming horror and destruction. From Justice Harbottle to Captain Barton to Sir Bale Mardykes, failure to live up to one's social obligations, to the moral and ethical strictures of class and position and the responsibilities attendant thereon, lead to persecution, perhaps objectively supernatural, perhaps subjective. Often we simply do not know which psychological pressures persecute and ultimately destroy the transgressor. Le Fanu's haunted universe, in short, is insistently characterized by a retributive justice that demands the fullest payment. In this conservative worldview, the established social order is always vindicated, its integrity restored by the elimination of the transgressor, the restoration of true ownership, and the disappearance of the disruptively supernatural—or psychological—menace once the wrong has been righted.

What is perhaps Le Fanu's most famous supernaturalist story perfectly illustrates this quintessentially Victorian stance. "Carmilla," the best vampire story in English before Bram Stoker's *Dracula*, offers a world threatened by subterfuge and inversion, by nightmare and fantasy mingling dangerously and destructively with the world of reason. The very name of the monster, the Countess Mircalla/Millarca/Carmilla, shifts and transforms itself, like the transformation Carmilla herself undergoes, becoming a slinking catlike wraith that insinuates itself into the sleep of its victims. This elusiveness, which involves the mysterious stranger, the unstable name, and nocturnal lesbian sexuality, allows Carmilla to insinuate herself into the Victorian world of Laura and her father, a world displaced and motherless, hence incomplete and a reflection and intensification of Le Fanu's own situation in many respects. In his own life, Le Fanu, with an unhappy marriage to a mentally ill woman who died young, was himself vulnerable to emotional assault. Carmilla is, in fact, the dark double of Laura, an ancient resident of the land in which Laura is an alien, fatherless but "mothered," whereas Laura's father is long a widower, sexually experienced in opposition to Laura's innocence. The inversions and disruptions Carmilla brings to the schloss or castle threaten in the most literal way—a standard threat in Le Fanu—the existence of the young and virginal Laura. Carmilla's seductive energies cause Laura to fall half in love with death: "Dim thoughts of death began to open, and an idea that I was slowly sinking took gentle, and, somehow, not unwelcome possession of me" (*Best Ghost Stories* 307). Only by the timely intervention of male knowledge, energy, and action is Carmilla's consumptive desire thwarted, her predation halted. Men representing science, government, religion, and the military combine their efforts and, by so doing, restore the balance of order in everyday life, reasserting the rule of reason and propriety over the nighttime threats of inversion, seduction, and godlessness.

That such themes repeatedly occur in Le Fanu's tales testifies to the importance that traditional social order held for him. A staunchly Protestant Anglo-Irishman, Le Fanu remained passionately opposed to English reform efforts that would have granted greater rights to Irish Catholics, and the continual reappearance in his fiction of old families faced with decline or disappearance is surely an expression of the anxiety he felt for his own social class. Coupled to the constant presence in his works of supernaturally empowered retributive justice or punishment of social and moral transgression, as well as his interest in ratiocination and epistemology evidenced in his numerous mystery tales (not considered here), the powerful hold traditional Victorian virtues had on Le Fanu's mind becomes self-evident. Yet it is precisely this hold, and its consequence for the transgressive mind, that led to Le Fanu's great achievement and ultimately to the psychological horror story as we have it today.

SELECTED CRITICISM

Achilles, Jochen. "Fantasy as Psychological Necessity: Sheridan Le Fanu's Fiction." In *Gothick Origins and Innovations*. Ed. Allan Lloyd Smith and Victor Sage. Costerus New Series 91. Amsterdam and Atlanta, GA: Rodopi, 1994: 150–168. While not breaking new ground, this chapter provides a valuable assessment of Le Fanu's highly psychologized use of various Gothic tropes.

Ashley, Mike. "Joseph Sheridan Le Fanu." In *St. James Guide to Horror, Ghost, and Gothic Writers*. Ed. David Pringle. Detroit: St. James Press, 1998: 356–358. A brief overview of Le Fanu's major works and his role in creating the psychological ghost story.

Bleiler, E.F. Introduction to *Best Ghost Stories of J.S. Le Fanu*. New York: Dover, 1964: v–xi. An excellent compact introduction to Le Fanu's achievement in the Gothic tradition and his place in Victorian supernaturalist fiction. "Le Fanu seems to have recognized that there must be an aesthetic of supernatural terror."

Browne, Nelson. *Sheridan Le Fanu*. London: Barker, 1951. Despite its age, this book remains an important biography and critical assessment of Le Fanu.

Campbell, James. "Sheridan Le Fanu." In *Supernatural Fiction Writers*. Ed. E.F. Bleiler. New York: Scribner's, 1985: 219–231. A reception history and solid general overview of the supernaturalist achievement of Le Fanu, "the best Victorian writer of the supernatural."

Coughlan, Patricia. "Doubles, Shadows, Sedan-Chairs, and the Past: The Ghost Stories of J.S. Le Fanu." In *Critical Approaches to Anglo-Irish Literature*. Ed. Michael Allen and Angela Wilcox. Totowa, NJ: Barnes & Noble, 1989: 116–130. Le Fanu pioneered a psychological form of the Gothic short story.

Crawford, Gary William. *J. Sheridan Le Fanu: A Bio-bibliography*. Westport, CT: Greenwood Press, 1995. An excellent overview of Le Fanu's life and writings accompanied by a comprehensive bibliography.

Gates, Barbara. "Blue Devils and Green Tea." *Studies in Short Fiction* 24 (1987): 15–23. Notes where suicide occurs in Le Fanu's tales and novels.

Howes, Marjorie. "Misalliance and Anglo-Irish Tradition in Le Fanu's *Uncle Silas*." *Nineteenth-Century Literature* 47 (1992): 164–186. The tradition includes a rich Gothic legacy by way of Charles Robert Maturin and others.

McCormack, W.J. *Sheridan Le Fanu and Victorian Ireland*. Oxford: Clarendon Press, 1980. Solidly locating Le Fanu in his social and historical context, this is one of the most important studies of Le Fanu.

Melada, Ivan. *Sheridan Le Fanu*. Boston: Twayne, 1987. Providing the usual sort of comprehensive biography of the Twayne volumes, this work takes special note of the influence of Swedenborg and of Edmund Burke's sublime on the supernaturalist and mystery works of Le Fanu.

Milbank, Alison. "Doubting Castle: The Gothic Mode of Questioning." In *The Critical Spirit and the Will to Believe: Essays in Nineteenth-Century Literature and Religion*, Ed. David Jasper and T.R. Wright. New York: St. Martin's Press, 1989: 104–119. Although it focuses primarily on *Uncle Silas*, Milbank's chapter offers important insights into the role of doubt and uncertainty in Le Fanu, linking it to Victorian anxiety over religious belief.

Sage, Victor. "Irish Gothic: C.R. Maturin and J.S. Le Fanu." In *A Companion to the Gothic*. Ed. David Punter. Oxford, UK, and Malden, MA: Blackwell, 2000: 81–93. Discusses the interrelationship of "two Huguenot Protestant writers both with family connections in the Irish church, both curiously learned, self-conscious writers, absorbed by their Calvinist heritage, and its relation to aesthetics, psychology, and politics, and both with an irresistible attraction to effects of terror and horror." Also discusses and accounts for the change in Maturin's Gothicism after he began to correspond with Sir Walter Scott.

Stoddart, Helen. " 'The Precautions of Nervous People Are Infectious': Sheridan Le Fanu's Symptomatic Gothic." *Modern Language Review* 86 (1991): 19–34. Comments on the Gothic themes of "Carmilla" and "Green Tea." Their Gothicism is symptomatic "of certain precautionary fears of the late nineteenth century."

Tracy, Robert. Introduction to *In a Glass Darkly* by Sheridan Le Fanu. New York and Oxford: Oxford University Press, 1993: vii–xxviii. An insightful look not only at the stories in this volume, but at Le Fanu's innovations in the tradition of the supernatural tale.

MATTHEW GREGORY "MONK" LEWIS
(1775–1818)
Jack G. Voller

PRINCIPAL GOTHIC WORKS

The Monk. London: J. Bell, 1796; Waterford: J. Saunders, 1796; Dublin: William Porter & N. Kelly, 1797.

The Minister: A Tragedy in Five Acts. London: J. Bell, 1797. (A translation of Schiller's *Kabale und Liebe*, this work was revised by Lewis as *The Harper's Daughter*.)

Ambrosio; or, The Monk: A Romance. London: J. Bell, 1798. (First expurgated edition; Philadelphia: W. Cobbett, 1798. First American edition from the expurgated fourth British edition; London: J. Bell, 1800; London: Wood, Vermon, & Walker, 1815.)

The Castle Spectre: A Drama in Five Acts. London: J. Bell, 1798.

Rolla; or, The Peruvian Hero: A Tragedy in Five Acts. London: J. Bell, 1799. (A translation of August Kotzebue's *Die Spanier in Peru oder Rollas Tod*.)

The Bleeding Nun; or, Raymond and Agnes. London: Kemmish & Son, Stevens and Co., 1800. (Chapbook based on *The Monk*.)

Adelmorn, the Outlaw: A Romantic Drama in Three Acts. London: J. Bell, 1801.

Alfonso, King of Castile. London: J. Bell, 1801.

Tales of Wonder. London: J. Bell, 1801. (Compiled by Lewis, with some poems by him.)

The Bravo of Venice, a Romance: Translated from the German. London: J.F. Hughes, 1805. (A translation of Heinrich Zschokke's *Abellino der grosse Bandit*.)

Rugantino; or, The Bravo of Venice: A Grand Romantic Melo-drama in Two Acts. London: J.F. Hughes, 1805. (A dramatization of Lewis's *The Bravo of Venice*.)

Adelgitha; or, The Fruits of a Single Error: A Tragedy in Five Acts. London: J.F. Hughes, 1806.

The Wood Daemon; or, The Clock Has Struck. London: J. Scales, 1807.

Romantic Tales. London: Longman, Hurst, Rees, & Orme, 1808. (Contains *Mistrust; or, Blanche and Osbright: A Feudal Romance*.)

Venoni; or, The Novice of St. Mark's. London: Longman, Hurst, Rees, and Orme, 1809. (A translation of Boutet de Monvel's *Les Victimes cloîtrées*.)

One O'Clock! or, The Knight and the Wood Daemon: A Grand Musical Romance in

Three Acts. London: Lowndes and Hobbs, 1811. (An adaptation of Lewis's *The Wood Daemon*.)

MODERN REPRINTS AND EDITIONS

The Captive: A Monodrama. In *Seven Gothic Dramas, 1789–1825*. Ed. Jeffrey N. Cox. Athens: Ohio University Press, 1992.

The Castle Spectre. In *The Hour of One: Six Gothic Melodramas*. Ed. Stephen Wischhusen. London: Gordon Fraser, 1975.

Mistrust; or, Blanche and Osbright: A Feudal Romance. In *Seven Masterpieces of Gothic Horror*. Ed. Robert D. Spector. New York: Bantam, 1963.

The Monk. Ed. Louis Peck, intro. John Berryman. New York: Grove Press, 1959.

The Monk. Ed. Howard Anderson. New York: Oxford University Press, 1973. (Added to Oxford World's Classics, 1980. New material added by Emma McEvoy for 1995 edition.)

The Monk. In *Four Gothic Novels*. New York and Oxford: Oxford University Press, 1994.

The Monk: A Romance. Ed. and intro. Christopher MacLachlan. New York and London: Penguin Books, 1998.

The Spectre Bride. Cedar Rapids, IA, and North Hollywood, CA: Nostalgia Broadcasting Corporation, 1977. (A sixty-minute cassette in the Great Moments in Literature series.)

Like Mary Shelley, Matthew Gregory Lewis created with his youthful first novel an enduring Gothic masterpiece, though the correspondences end there. Writing closer to the beginning of the Gothic movement than to its end and remaining firmly within the Gothic arena, Lewis produced what is widely held to be the most notorious Gothic novel of the entire period, a work that both influenced a number of imitators and, by reason of its extreme representations of Gothic tropes and energies, left little room for those who would follow in its wake. *The Monk* was, in many respects, the ne plus ultra of Gothic indulgence, which surely accounts for its continuing popularity. As the critic Joseph Irwin has remarked, *The Monk* is "a culmination of the Gothic movement. [Lewis] originated nothing; he only brought together techniques and materials that had been used before and gave them an almost unmistakable Lewisian touch" (162). That "touch" was the novel's unrestrained libidinal energies and cataclysmic sociosexual upheavals, heavily spiced with a supernaturalism given free rein within a metaphysical framework both recognizable and radical. Lewis's masterwork is populated with demons and religious characters whose moral deformity is unfolded in the language and imagery of both biblical apocalypse and political revolution. The novel's near-breathless pace creates a sense of catastrophe that develops so quickly as to create the impression of an implacable and inevitable fate.

Yet Lewis was himself no brooding revolutionary, no marginalized outcast prophesying doom. He was in fact very much an "establishment" figure in many ways, eagerly cultivating the acquaintance of the nobility and the influential. His father, a lifelong civil servant in the War Department, encouraged his son to pursue government service, and Lewis wrote his novel while serving in the British embassy at The Hague and shortly thereafter served largely ineffectually in Parliament, a fact that so horrified readers and critics when he added "M.P." to the title page of the second edition of his novel that Lewis himself bowdlerized *The Monk* for a subsequent edition in an attempt to silence some of the outcry. No less a figure than Coleridge, who wrote a largely condemnatory review, declared that "yes! the author of the Monk signs himself a LEGISLATOR! We stare and tremble." That Lewis would respond as he did to the public outcry testifies to his desire for public acceptance and approbation.

This same desire may also explain his ability to understand and satisfy public taste. The popularity as well of Lewis's numerous dramas, many of them quite spectacular and egregiously melodramatic, made clear that Lewis was closely in touch with the popular audiences of his day. His conventional social comedies and tragedies were, on the whole, less well received than his Gothic productions, such as *The Castle Spectre* and *Adelmorn, the Outlaw*, suggesting that his talents and instincts lay precisely in that niche of public consciousness that made *The Monk* a cultural phenomenon. Lewis also produced a number of translations, poetic works, and collections, garnering the praise of writers such as Scott, with whom Lewis began a failed editorial collaboration, Byron, and even Coleridge.

But it was *The Monk* that made and sustained Lewis's reputation—so much so that he preferred to be known as "Monk" Lewis—and that attracts attention yet today.

The Monk is the most celebrated novel of Gothic excess, and for good reason. Its main narrative thread is a study of the fate of Ambrosio, the Spanish monk famed for his piety and religious rigor who succumbs to sexual temptation; his fondness for the young novice Rosario (an element of the novel suggestive of Lewis' own repressed homosexuality) turns into lust when Rosario is revealed to be the beautiful and seductive Matilda, who in turn is later to revealed to be a demon. Sated with Matilda, Ambrosio turns his libidinous attention to the beautiful Antonia, whom he rapes (after killing her mother) and imprisons in a catacomb, then murders. With the revelation that Antonia is Ambrosio's sister, that he has murdered his mother, and that the monk has sold his soul to the devil, the novel ends spectacularly with Ambrosio escaping, with Lucifer's help, from the prisons of the Inquisition only to meet a painful, lingering death after being dropped onto a rocky promontory by the exulting fiend. Along the way readers witness a horrific bonding of the dead with the living in the Bleeding Nun's visitations to Raymond—visitations ended only by the intervention of the Wandering Jew—and the gruesome mob murder of the tyrannical abbess of St. Clare. With its underground crypts and chambers; monastic hypocrisy and worldly ambition; lust and love and betrayal; demonic manifestations; ghosts and buried skeletons, Lewis's novel packs as much dark Gothic energy into its three volumes as is possible.

It is precisely this energy which drew readers to this novel. *The Monk*'s success comes from the combined power of an unrestrained supernaturalism, a titillating psychosexual tragedy, and a dark worldview in which mob violence effects the "justice" that evades the best efforts of compassion, pity, reason, the legal system, and common human decency. Ambrosio's fall, engineered by a demon who exploits his false humility and sexual lust, takes the most horrifying of trajectories, for he unwittingly murders his mother in order that he might kidnap, rape, and then murder his own sister. Lewis's own family experience— his mother abandoned the family for another man; his father later took a mistress, much to Lewis's dismay—may have contributed to the making of this novel of familial dysfunction writ large and in blood, but its darkest driving force is something larger and less personal. Lewis's novel taps into the anxieties attendant upon the Terror of mid-1790s France, and these combine with the familial and religious failures in the novel to portray a world in which customary social and moral landmarks have lost their meaning. Petty passions and base desires lead to catastrophes so horrendous as to appall, yet there is no balancing of the novel's metaphysical gloom with redemption for those who manage to retain their goodness. They merely survive, if they are lucky, but Lewis also creates a world in which the innocent and the good meet the foulest of ends. Lewis's many melodramas offer similar, if less salacious, visions of a dark universe. Like *The Monk*, they succeed as popular entertainment if not great literature because they are redolent of power; they sweep us up as fully as their characters, and as their turbulent energies drive relentlessly to the end, we too feel and sense, if only dimly, the vast and consuming void, the "yawning gulph," in Lewis's phrase, that is emerging out of the world of revolution and violent social transformation.

The numerous editions of *The Monk*, as well as its dramatic adaptations (none by Lewis, oddly enough) and chapbook renditions, clearly indicate that Lewis touched a nerve with his novel's dark vision, and while the mid- and late Romantic interest in self would lead to a "psychological" supernaturalist literature more nuanced than anything Lewis could produce, his work remains a touchstone of the Gothic canon, and one that retains today its power to disturb despite its florid melodrama.

Although Lewis was fairly popular as a playwright, he all but abandoned literature when in 1812 he inherited his father's plantations in Jamaica. Devoting himself to the operation of these enterprises, particularly to improving the well-being of his slaves there, Lewis undertook two trips to Jamaica to personally observe conditions and effect improvements. Out of his experiences came the highly regarded *Journal of a West India Proprietor*, mostly concerned with his Jamaican experiences but also including a few poems, among them the Gothic "Isle of the Devils." Returning from his second trip, Lewis took ill, died, and was buried at sea, but the burial took a Gothic twist when the weights attached to the shroud gave way and Lewis's corpse drifted off on the currents, a gruesomely theatrical climax that the creator of the arch-Gothic novel of the eighteenth century might have applauded.

SELECTED CRITICISM

Anderson, Howard. Introduction to *The Monk*. New York and Oxford: Oxford University Press, 1973. Still an insightful consideration of the novel's emotional and psychological power. Also discusses the publication history.

Ashley, Mike. "Matthew Gregory Lewis." In *St. James Guide to Horror, Ghost, and Gothic Writers*. Ed. David Pringle. Detroit: St James Press, 1998: 364–366. Critical plot summaries of several of Lewis's most important works.

Baron-Wilson, Mrs. Cornwall. *The Life and Correspondence of M.G. Lewis, Author of "The Monk, Castle Spectre, etc. with Many Pieces in Prose and Verse Never Before Published."* London: Henry Colburn, 1839. The long-standing basis of much Lewis scholarship, valuable for its reprinting of letters and minor verse pieces.

Blakemore, Steven. "Matthew Lewis's Black Mass: Sexual, Religious Inversion in *The Monk*." *Studies in the Novel* 30 (1998): 521–539. Argues that Lewis "based the novel on the thesis that Catholic monasticism violated nature with its chastity vows, thereby producing deviant sexual practices." The text of *The Monk* "performed the linguistic equivalent of a Black Mass by inverting and subverting the traditional roles of religion and sex."

Brooks, Peter. "Virtue and Terror: *The Monk*." *ELH Journal of English Literary History* 40 (1973): 249–263. An excellent and provocative analysis of the novel's emptying out of the space of the sacred, filling the gap with a sense of terror that undermines a belief in an ordered universe; a very effective historical contextualizing.

Campbell, Ann. "Satire in *The Monk*: Exposure and Reformation." *Romanticism on the Net* 8 (November 1997): ⟨http://users.ox.ac.uk/~scat0385/satire.html⟩. A relatively rare look at a side of Lewis not widely remarked on and his trenchant and frequent use of satire.

Conger, Syndy M. "Confessors and Penitents in M.G. Lewis's *The Monk*." *Romanticism on the Net* 8 (November 1997): ⟨http://users.ox.ac.uk/~scat0385/confessors.html⟩. Taking Michel Foucault's *History of Sexuality* as its point of departure, Conger's article analyzes Lewis's use of the concepts of confession and penitence and how they are informed by and critique Western notions of sexual discourse.

Doyle, Barry. "Freud and the Schizoid in Ambrosio: Determining Desire in *The Monk*." *Gothic Studies* 2 (2000): 61–69. Discusses desire in *The Monk* by way of several "theories of desire," including "Oedipalized desire based on Freud's theory" and later theories such as those of Gilles Deleuze and Felix Guattari in *Anti-Oedipus: Capitalism and Schizophrenia* (1972). "The combining of Oedipus and anti-Oedipus is that 'uneasy relation' which offers a paradigm for reading Gothic identities, Gothic texts, and Gothic aesthetics."

Euridge, Gareth M. "The Company We Keep: Comic Function in M.G. Lewis's *The Monk*." In *Functions of the Fantastic: Selected Essays from the Thirteenth Inter-*

national Conference on the Fantastic in the Arts. Ed. Joe Sanders. Westport, CT: Greenwood Press, 1995: 83–90. The novel not only contains comic and satiric moments but uses such moments to advance its serious themes.

Fogle, Richard. "The Passions of Ambrosio." In *The Classic British Novel.* Ed. Howard M. Harper, Jr., and Charles Edge. Athens: University of Georgia Press, 1972: 36–50. An Aristotelian analysis of the divided character of the hero-villain.

Frank, Frederick S. "*The Monk*: A Bicentenary Bibliography." *Romanticism on the Net* 8 (November 1997): ⟨http://users.ox.ac.uk/~scat0385/monkbiblio.html⟩. The definitive bibliography for Lewis's novel, this annotated work is a comprehensive collection of *Monk*-related criticism and covers various adaptations as well as early reviews and doctoral dissertations. See also Frederick S. Frank, "M.G. Lewis's *The Monk* after Two Hundred Years, 1796–1996: A Bicentenary Bibliography," *Bulletin of Bibliography* 52 (1995): 241–260.

Hennelly, Mark M., Jr. "*The Monk*'s Gothic Bosh and Bosch's Gothic Monks." *Comparative Literature Studies* 24 (1987): 146–164. "Contrary to prevalent criticism, the novel offers an integrated or at least a repeated coordination of its Gothic machinery, especially the sense of place or space, and its Gothic visions."

Hogle, Jerrold E. "The Ghost of the Counterfeit—and the Closet—in *The Monk*." *Romanticism on the Net* 8 (November 1997): ⟨http://users.ox.ac.uk/~scat0385/ghost.html⟩. Examines the role of deception, simulacra, and representation in the novel's consideration of late-eighteenth-century identity construction.

Irwin, Joseph James. *M.G. "Monk" Lewis.* Boston: Twayne, 1976. Overall, a rather perfunctory and not especially sympathetic introduction to Lewis and his work, although the biographical information is sound.

Jones, Wendy. "Stories of Desire in *The Monk*." *ELH: Journal of English Literary History* 57 (1990): 129–150. Narratological analysis of the structuring role of sexual desire.

MacDonald, D.L. "The Erotic Sublime: The Marvellous in *The Monk*." *English Studies in Canada* 18 (1992): 273–285. Applies Burkean aesthetic precepts to the novel's eroticism and emotional intensity.

Meyer, Michael. "Let's Talk about Sex: Confessions and Vows in *The Monk*." *Arbeiten aus Anglistik und Amerikanistik* 20 (1995): 307–316. On the secret sex life of not just Ambrosio but all the characters in the novel.

Mulman, Lisa Naomi. "Sexuality on the Surface: Catholicism and the Erotic Object in Lewis's *The Monk*." *Bucknell Review* 42 (1998): 98–110. "Perched on the precipice of Freud's radical version of self-consciousness, *The Monk* is nonetheless a novel very much engaged with concepts of community and materiality that are not always amenable to the kind of inside/outside dichotomy suggested by Freud's model."

Parreaux, André. *The Publication of "The Monk": A Literary Event, 1796–1798.* Paris: Librairie Marcel Didier, 1960. Reception history that also seeks to establish political and historical context for the novel.

Peck, Louis F. *A Life of Matthew G. Lewis.* Cambridge, MA: Harvard University Press, 1961. A detailed biographical and bibliographical resource, this volume remains an essential guide to Lewis; it also publishes some letters previously unknown.

Punter, David. "1789: The Sex of Revolution." *Criticism* 24 (1982): 201–217. An analysis of a number of important works from the 1790s, including Lewis's novel, which locates the ideological source of *The Monk*'s mob scenes in English anxiety over the French Revolution.

Thomas, William. "They Called Him 'Monk.'" *Personalist* 47 (1966): 81–90. A biographical portrait of the "strange and strange-looking figure, small and goggle-eyed," who wrote the most notorious of Gothic novels.

Tienhooven, Marie-José. "All Roads Lead to England: *The Monk* Constructs the Nation." *Romanticism on the Net* 8 (November 1997): ⟨http://users.ox.ac.uk/~scat0385/nation.html⟩. Historically contextualizing the novel, Tienhooven discusses the way it offers constructions of national identity for a nation struggling with self-identity.

Tracy, Ann B. "M.G. Lewis." In *Supernatural Fiction Writers*. Ed. E.F. Bleiler. New York: Scribner's, 1985: 153–160. A sensitive overview of Lewis's Gothic works that also presents a careful and informed portrait of Lewis.

Tuite, Clara. "Cloistered Closets: Enlightenment Pornography, the Confessional State, Homosexual Persecution, and *The Monk*." *Romanticism on the Net* 8 (November 1997): ⟨http://users.ox.ac.uk/~scat0385/closet.html⟩. Tuite analyzes the role of homoeroticism and its relation to anticlericalism in the novel's sociohistorical critique of both Enlightenment and revolutionary values.

Varma, Devendra P. Introduction to *The Bravo of Venice*. New York: Arno Press, 1972. An excellent introduction to Lewis's powerful drama by one of the foremost Gothic scholars of the century.

———. Introduction to *The Monk*. London: Folio Society, 1984: vii–xvi. Discusses the continuing power and influence of the novel, focusing on its powerful sexual currents as they engage the Romantically charged valorization of the individual.

Watkins, Daniel. "Social Hierarchy in Matthew Lewis' *The Monk*." *Studies in the Novel* 18 (1986): 115–124. Another effective contextualizing of the novel in regard to the turbulent social and cultural energies of the late eighteenth century.

Whitlark, James. "Heresy Hunting: *The Monk* and the French Revolution." *Romanticism on the Net* 8 (November 1997): ⟨http://users.ox.ac.uk/~scat0385/heresy.html⟩. Discusses the anti-Catholicism of the 1790s and its complex relationship to the Revolution, upon which Lewis's novel comments.

Wilson, Lisa M. "'Monk' Lewis as Literary Lion." *Romanticism on the Net* 8 (November 1997): ⟨http://users.ox.ac.uk/~scat0385/literary.html⟩. An adroit consideration of Lewis's popularity in the context of late-eighteenth-century constructions of gender and their relationship to literary production.

GEORGE LIPPARD
(1822–1854)
Frederick S. Frank

PRINCIPAL GOTHIC WORKS

"Legend of the Midnight Death, a Story of the Wissahikon." *Citizen Soldier: A Weekly Newspaper, Devoted to the Interests of the Volunteers and Militia of the United States*, 19 January 1843.

The Ladye Annabel: or, The Doom of the Poisoner: A Romance by an Unknown Author. Philadelphia: R.G. Berford, 1844. (Also published under the title *The Ladye Anabel: A Romance of the Alembic, the Altar, and the Throne.*)

The Quaker City; or, The Monks of Monk Hall: A Romance of Philadelphia Life, Mystery, and Crime. Philadelphia: T.B. Peterson, 1845. (Also serialized in ten installments throughout 1844 and 1845 by G.B. Zieber of Philadelphia and republished in 1849 under the title *The Quaker City: A Romance of the Rich and Poor.*)

The Heart-Broken. Philadelphia: G.B. Zieber, 1848. (Lippard's moving tribute to his fellow Philadelphia, Charles Brockden Brown.)

The Entranced; or, The Wanderer of Eighteen Centuries. Philadelphia: Joseph Severns, 1849. (Also published under the title *Adonai: The Pilgrim of Eternity.*)

Memoirs of a Preacher, a Revelation of the Church and the Home. Philadelphia: Joseph Severns, 1849.

"The Monster with Three Names." *Quaker City*, 17 March 1849. (*Quaker City* was a weekly newspaper founded by Lippard in December 1848.)

The Empire City; or, New York by Night and Day. New York: Stringer & Townsend, 1850.

The Killers: A Narrative of Real Life in Philadelphia . . . by a Member of the Philadelphia Bar. Philadelphia: Hankinson & Bartholomew, 1850.

MODERN REPRINTS AND EDITIONS

The Empire City. Freeport, NY: Books for Libraries Press, 1969.

"From *The Quaker City.*" In *American Gothic: An Anthology, 1787–1916.* Ed. Charles Crow. Malden, MA: Blackwell, 1999. (Acknowledges Lippard's contribution to

the development of a national Gothic by including representative passages from
The Quaker City.)

George Lippard, Prophet of Protest: Writings of an American Radical, 1822–1854. Ed.
David S. Reynolds. New York: Peter Lang, 1986. (Reprints excerpts from Lippard's journal pieces and fiction. Section 5, "Towards Surrealism: The Irrational,
the Erotic, the Nightmarish," has well-chosen samples of his Gothic work. This
edition is cited in the text.)

The Monks of Monk Hall. Ed. Leslie Fiedler. New York: Odyssey Press, 1970.

*The Quaker City; or, The Monks of Monk Hall: A Romance of Philadelphia Life, Mystery,
and Crime.* Ed. David S. Reynolds. Amherst: University of Massachusetts Press,
1995. (This edition is cited in the text.)

Innovative Gothicist, talented pornographer, socialist zealot, crusading journalist, union organizer, pre-Marxian Marxist, fervent feminist, and eccentric Philadelphian, George Lippard deserves to occupy the center stage of the American
Gothic tradition, but until Leslie Fiedler's 1970 edition of Lippard's best-known
novel, *The Quaker City; or, The Monks of Monk Hall,* Lippard was one of
American literature's most disposable writers, an odd hack who wrote obscene
books for the vulgar motive of obtaining money to promote his dangerous socialist schemes and to gain access to the mass audience who theoretically might
rise up to implement his crazy reforms. Until Fiedler's edition recovered his
work, Lippard's important role in the shaping of the American Gothic had been
marginalized and Lippard himself discarded by literary historians as a mercenary
quilldriver who cranked out bales of salacious copy for consumption by the
semiliterate masses. When he was mentioned at all in the literary histories (he
was omitted from Robert E. Spiller and Willard Thorp's *A Literary History of
the United States* 6th printing, 1962), Lippard was categorized as a primitive
muckraker whose pulpish prose negated any artistic or humanitarian value his
writings might contain.

In a life even shorter than that of his friend Edgar Allan Poe (he died at age
thirty-two), Lippard concentrated his literary efforts on the degraded underside
of antebellum democracy, transforming the City of Brotherly Love into a Dantean City of Dis. Lippard's biographer and best modern interpreter, David Reynolds, has located his work within an American Gothic perspective that viewed
the city, one of the society's most visible emblems of progress and democratic
expansion, not as a symbol of the life force of democracy but as the death force
instead, a surreal enclosure more dreadful than the interior of any Gothic castle.
"Lippard is now beginning to be recognized as a leading American precursor
of surrealism because his radical social views were combined with a soaring
imagination that revelled in the irrational, the bizarre, the erotic, and the grotesque" (Reynolds, 1986, 283). He inaugurates an American Gothic idiom that
is characterized by "black humor, eroticism, violence, and demonic energy."

Lippard recognized the city as the place of isolation, loneliness, want, fear,
and predatory struggle, the cosmopolitan equivalent of the sinister spaces of

older Gothic fiction. As a young man, he had wandered the Philadelphia streets hungry and penniless. Like the anguished streetwalker in Blake's poem "London," he beheld "marks of weakness, marks of woe" in the faces that prowled the labyrinthine gloom of Philadelphia's back alleys. He knew firsthand the specters of poverty and the abject loneliness of crowds. "His walks about Philadelphia gave him firsthand knowledge of the terrible effects of the great depression of 1837–44. For a while he lived like a homeless bohemian, roaming the Philadelphian maze "and sleeping in abandoned buildings and artists' studios" (Reynolds, Introduction to *The Quaker City* xi). Later, as a police reporter and investigative journalist for *The Spirit of the Times* and *Citizen Soldier*, two Philadelphia tabloids or penny newspapers, he covered the underworld that later gave him all of the material he needed for his porno-Gothic magnum opus, *The Quaker City; or, The Monks of Monk Hall*. His novels of the doomed city are broadsides of the dismal conditions, rampant criminality, class cruelty, and degenerate self-indulgence that expose the massive corruption of body and spirit festering just barely beneath the veneer of Quaker City respectability. "Because Lippard's overriding goal is to replicate in fiction a society he regards as nightmarish and depraved, he creates an entire nightmare world that is always threatening to destroy ordinary perceptions of objective surroundings" (Reynolds, Introduction to *The Quaker City* xxi).

In portraying the city as hell or nightmare, Lippard felt a strong bond with his Gothic predecessor, Charles Brockden Brown. In a graveside eulogy for Brown, *The Heart-Broken*, Lippard acknowledged his kinship with Brown's apocalyptic fervor in his depiction of the haunted city in his novel *Arthur Mervyn*, a novel in which the yellow-fever epidemic operates as a metaphor for social sickness and moral squalor. "He *did* write novels. It is true that they were extraordinary creations of the kind, lifting a man beyond himself, anatomizing his very soul, laying bare the secret springs of human action, with as much power and truthfulness as though the author were some invisible spirit who looked calmly down from his superior existence upon the loves and hates of poor mortality" (Reynolds, *Prophet of Protest* 138). Brown had transformed Philadelphia into the Gothic city in order to stir and alarm his readership with a darker picture of America's future. Lippard followed Brown's lead by Gothifying the city as plagued by the vices of capitalism, and like Brown, Lippard was deadly serious in his uses of the Gothic to raise the social consciousness of his readership.

Concerning the obligations of the artist, he asserted his duty in language that Thoreau and Emerson would have approved: "Have something to say, and say it with all your might. This is the only rule of literary composition worth minding" (The Journal, *The Quaker City* 12 May 1849: 31). Lippard promoted his utopian social outlook by presenting Philadelphia as the reverse of all that American civilization aspired to become, a benighted place that changed decent people into beasts. His journalistic writings are full of calls to action. "We need unity among our authors; the age pulsates with a great Idea, and that Idea is the right

of Labor to its fruits, coupled with the re-organization of the social system"
(The Journal, *The Quaker City* 10 February 1849: 5). Gothic discourse became
Lippard's method for demonstrating the urgency of his progressive ideals. If the
abhorrent facts of American city life could be made sufficiently horrifying, revolutionary change might follow. Older political forms of Gothicism had often
shown societies entrapped by their pasts, but Lippard's new Gothic appeals
through its pictures of a society in crisis and being consumed by its unchecked
appetites at the present moment in the Republic's history. Lippard's aligning of
his Gothic with the social and moral horrors of contemporary society recalls the
technique of William Godwin, who revised Gothic machinery to precipitate an
outraged awareness of "things as they are." Lippard's contemporization of the
Gothic also has a prophetic quality about it that rejects the optimistic surfaces
of American life. His city fiction reveals a brutal subculture that cannibalizes
and violates itself even as it preaches equality and progress. The redeployment
of the Gothic as an instrument of social critique links Lippard with Hawthorne
and Melville in his own time. These writers and others like them are committed
to the exposure of a darker side of the American self marauding "beneath the
American Renaissance," to use Reynolds's phrase for the oversoul's shadowy
counterpart. Just as Melville and Hawthorne had suggested an obverse destiny
for America, so Lippard said no in thunder to the certainty of the moral and
social progress of democracy under capitalism. What most connects him to later
Gothic apocalypticalists such as Ambrose Bierce, Frank Norris, Theodore Dreiser, and, later, Norman Mailer, Joyce Carol Oates and Stephen King is a sense
of America as failed or fallen civilization barbarized by its own energies and
whose most visible symbol of that failure is the city.

Even in Lippard's first novel, *The Ladye Annabel; or, The Doom of the Poisoner*, orthodox Gothic procedures share the stage with outbursts of social protest, although the book's highly conventional Gothicism overshadows its
revolutionary polemics. The novel also revels in the lugubrious stuff of the
shilling shockers or the grisly stock-in-trade of Victorian proletarian fiction, the
penny dreadfuls and Victorian bloods. Encyclopedic in its horrors, the novel
bombarded its readers (it was first published serially in *Citizen Soldier*) with
lingering descriptions of live burial, necrophilia, and the craft of the torture
chamber, with occasional forays into social commentary about human misery
and the inhumanity of human beings. David Reynolds describes the *The Ladye
Annabel* as a "book . . . full of lip-smacking accounts of decomposing corpses,
spurting blood, and quivering torsos during torture" (*Prophet of Protest* 282).
A typical passage taken from one of many sadistic monologues of the Doomsman, a character who specializes in the aesthetics of agony, illustrates the
novel's ghoulish tone. Approaching the victim, the Doomsman exults:

Hand me the iron—red-hot—and hissing—give me the bowl of melted lead, dipped from
the boiling cauldron. H-i-s-s—it touches the eyeball, the eye is dark forever. H-i-s-s it
licks up the blood, it turns round and round in the socket. Now fill the hollow socket

with the lead, the hissing lead—and, ha, ha, now bring me another iron pointed like this, and heated to a white heat. Let the iron touch the skin to the eyeball, it shrivels like a burnt leaf, deeper sinks the hissing point, turn it round and round, let it lap up the gushing blood. Now the lead, the thick and boiling lead, pour it from the ladle, fill the socket, it hardens, it grows cold—ha, ha, ha, behold the eyes of lead. (Reynolds, *Prophet of Protest* 284)

This sort of "lip-smacking" and tactile Gothic demonstrates Lippard's skill at achieving a degree of abominable shock and repulsive sensation that would earn him a reputation as a depraved and dangerous literary pervert. Similar descriptions of torture embellish the activities of the novel's second villain extraordinaire, the fratricidal wizard Aldarin, whose hideous Red Chamber is a headquarters for dissection and vivisection. Page after page contains graphic accounts of the bodies living and dead that litter Aldarin's Red Chamber, "discoloured faces, green with decay, the rotting relics of what had once enthroned the giant soul." The formula involves the repetitive and ruthless amassing of horror upon horror as Lippard arranges for something horrific or emetic to occur on nearly every page, with the heroine Annabel and all of the other victims reduced to the role of mere props to feed the racks and thumbscrews of the Doomsman and stock the putrid experiments of Aldarin. Such slapdash gore for gore's sake pushed the physical Gothic to its limits and beyond, but made Lippard a best-selling author.

Poe called *The Ladye Annabel* "richly inventive and imaginative" and recognized in Lippard's charnel and mortuarial settings a world of the living dead similar to his own. At his best, Lippard could create scenes of terrifying power, as he did in the masquerade ball of the skeletons attended by the young hero, Adrian:

And with a low bow, each skeleton servitor extended his hand, to receive his fair lord or ladye, his fair young mistress or his gallant young master, as arising from their coffin, they placed their feet on the steps of the hearse, and slowly descended into the courtyard of the ancient castle. Circling and whirling, grouping and clustering, the skeleton band went swaying over the floor, their gay dresses fluttering in the light, while the ruddy lamp-beams fell quivering over each bared brow, tinting the hollow sockets with a crimson glow, and giving a more ghastly grimace to the array of whitened teeth. "Behold thy partner!" cried the master of ceremonies. The maiden turned her face to Adrian, and he stood spell-bound to the spot with sudden horror. Looking from beneath a dropping plume, snow-white in hue, a skull stared him in the face, with the orbless sockets, the cavity of the nose, and the grinning teeth turned to glowing red by the light of the pendent lamps. (Reynolds, *Prophet of Protest* 295)

The loathsome Gothicism of *The Lady-Annabel* remains the dominant structural and stylistic element in Lippard's quintessential porno-Gothic novel, *The Quaker City; or, The Monks of Monk Hall.* The book swarms with "demonic energy" and is as infamous in its shock waves as anything flowing from the imaginations of Monk Lewis or the Marquis de Sade. E.F. Bleiler's judgment that Lippard's novel is "amusing in small doses, disgusting in large" is harsh but accurate, although it should be added that like *The Monk* or *Justine, The Quaker City* is Gothic entertainment at its utmost and is fun to read. The narrative is a Gothic palimpsest "crammed with false identities, disputed inheritances, dubious manuscripts, magical drugs, furtive murder, and living portraits" (Ehrlich 56) abetted by innumerable voyeuristic episodes of cadaverous striptease, incestuous rapes, mesmeric sexual assaults, bleeding bosoms, slimy voluptuousness, and quivering close-ups of naked flesh.

Monk Hall itself is a titanic luxury horror hotel complete with subterranean brothels, torture chambers, secret drug dens, and compartments reserved for sexual assault, with rooms and passageways heavily adorned with erotic and satanic works of art. The patrons of this emporium of hedonism, the "monks" of Monk Hall, are respectable lawyers, bankers, and leading citizens whose degeneracy and hypocrisy Lippard mocks through their unbridled activities inside Monk Hall. The plot moves from compartment to compartment and from seduction to seduction with palpitating maidens such as Devil-Bug's beautiful daughter, Mabel Pyne, and female victims such as Dora Livingstone buffeted about and used as carnal props for the sadistic amusement of Devil-Bug's customers. Livingstone's necrophiliac rape of his wife's cadaver is but one of many raw sex scenes that prompted some readers of the novel to condemn the book as openly obscene. Although Lippard denied that his purpose was lascivious titillation, few readers if any could find any systematic social criticism behind the porno-Gothic episodes. Lippard's strategy of Gothifying and sensationalizing the secret lives of respectable Philadelphians and tearing aside the mask of appearances to reveal the true ugliness and brutishness of "good" people living in a "good" city was sound enough, but social enlightenment was soon pushed aside once Lippard's pen began to drip blood. The result was an American Gothic novel that registered the serious cultural contradictions of Lippard's time and ours, poverty, racial inequality, economic and sexual abjection, environmental horrors, exploitation of workers, female inferiority, plutocratic ruthlessness, and hegemonic class structures all polluting the democratic and republican ideals of the Founding Fathers behind the closed doors of Monk Hall.

The master of ceremonies of Monk Hall is a delightful demon called Devil-Bug, a subhuman superman worthy of a place beside Brown's Carwin, Hawthorne's Roger Chillingworth, Melville's Captain Ahab, and a congregation of later American Satans on the loose in the New World. This spidery brute reigns over the lower world of Monk Hall, conducting the souls of the damned through the perverted rituals of Devil-Bug's private Hades. Homicide is such a routine and commonplace diversion for Devil-Bug that the reader soon loses sympathy for his victims and becomes totally infatuated with the method and manner of the next murder or even what contraption Devil-Bug will employ. First readers of *The Quaker City* probably admired the sadistic mischief of this monster, but a few perceptive readers might also have recognized Devil-Bug as a symbol of democratic entrepreneurship diabolized and the creative impulses of the culture twisted to selfish and vicious ends. "Devil-Bug symbolizes the immorality and amorality seething below the surface of respectable Philadelphia. He embodies the animality and aggressions buried in the heart of civilized man" (Reynolds, 1986, 287). Devil-Bug is democracy's metropolitan id, an American Caliban with no Prospero to control him and a demon of aggressive capitalism who operates Monk Hall as a thriving enterprise of sex and death staffed with slaves and maidens who are forced to cater to his licentious clientele. Lippard introduces Devil-Bug not as a "he" but as an "it," a comic-strip fiend drawn as a caricature of a Jacksonian vigor hideously distorted:

That insect—which it was quite natural to designate by the name of Devil-Bug. It was a strange thickset specimen of flesh and blood, with a short body, marked by immensely broad shoulders, long arms and thin distorted legs. The head of the creature was ludicrously large in proportion to the body. Long masses of stiff black hair fell tangled and matted over a forehead, protuberant to deformity. A flat nose with wide nostrils shooting out into each cheek like the smaller wings of an insect, an immense mouth whose heavy lips disclosed two long rows of bristling teeth, a pointed chin, blackened by a heavy beard, and massive eye-brows meeting over the nose, all furnished the details of a countenance, not exactly calculated to inspire the most pleasant feelings in the world. One eye, small black and shapen like a bead, stared steadily in Byrnewood's face, while the other socket was empty, shrivelled and orbless. His soul was like his body, a mass of hideous and distorted energy. (51)

Equally powerful are Lippard's pictures of the underworld of Monk Hall, a huge cellar that looms just beneath the polite surfaces of Philadelphia life. Like the flaming pit that yawns for sinners in Jonathan Edwards's sermon "Sinners in the Hands of an Angry God," the immediate hells of Monk Hall, and by extensior the hells of "virtuous" America, are not remote but nearby and waiting, more temporal than eternal. One chapter of the novel, "The Dead-Vault of Monk Hall," contains an appalling inventory of what lies just below the surface of this virtuous facade. As Heyward Ehrlich has pointed out, "In Lippard, Calvinism is submerged in Gothicism," (59) and such hellfire is especially evident in the mortuarial descents into Devil-Bug's infernal kingdom:

The beams of the lanthern flashed over a wide cellar, whose arched roof was supported by massive pillars of unplastered brick. Here and there, as the flickering light glanced fitfully along the dark recesses of the place, fragments of wood might be discovered, scattered carelessly around the pillars, or thrown over the floor in crumbling heaps. And now, as a gleam of light shot suddenly into the distant recesses of the cellar, a long row of coffins might be discovered, with the lids broken off and the bones of the dead thrown rudely from their last resting place. The extent of the cellar might not be ascertained by the uncertain light of the lanthern, but whenever the light flared up it disclosed some dark recess, filled with crumbling coffins, or laid bare some obscure nook, where ghastly skulls and fragments of the human skeleton, were thrown together like old lumber in a storehouse. While the broadcloth gentry of the Quaker City guzzle their champaigne two stories above, here, in these cozy cellars of Monk-Hall, old Devil-Bug entertains the thieves and cut-throats of the town. (220).

Lippard's Gothic is sometimes compared to that of William Harrison Ainsworth, Eugène Sue, author of *The Mysteries of Paris* (1843), an exposé of Parisian crime, and G.W.M. Reynolds, author of *Wagner, the Wehr-wolf* (1857), but his novels of crime, debauchery, and sexual violence belong less to an older tradition than to the type of Gothicism later found in the work of naturalists such as Stephen Crane, Frank Norris, and Upton Sinclair. Crane's "The Monster," Norris's *McTeague* and *Vandover and the Brute*, and Sinclair's *Jungle* all show the direct influence of Lippardian Gothic locales and characters. Critics in search of the missing link between the primal Gothicism of Brown, Poe, Hawthorne, and Melville, the transitional Gothicism of James and Bierce, and the biological and environmental Gothicism of the naturalist writers might discover that missing link to be Lippardian Gothic. His reliance on the Gothic as a serious medium for shocking his fellow Americans into an awareness of their shortcomings enabled him to magnify the dark flaws of a less-than-perfect civilization. David Reynolds has commented:

What Lippard shared with Poe, Hawthorne, and Melville was a retrospective, even retrograde use of Gothic tradition. Like Devil-Bug's Monk Hall, the ships of Pym and Ahab and the scaffold of Hester are Gothic castles of another time and place. His work leads to Harriet Beecher Stowe, Frank Norris, Jack London, Theodore Dreiser, John Dos Passos, and Norman Mailer. In his treatment of the city Lippard created a kind of halfway house between "Monk" Lewis and Theodore Dreiser, a place where Gothic terror was politicized and made frighteningly contemporary. (Introduction to *Prophet of Protest* 19)

While certainly "retrograde," Lippard's Gothic is also transitional and anticipatory of modern American Gothic endeavors. Although he cannot be considered a major American writer, his status as a major Gothic writer and pessimistic chronicler of American life is beyond question, notwithstanding his ostracism by literary historians. The inclusion of selections from *The Quaker City* in Charles Crow's recent collection *American Gothic: An Anthology, 1787–1916* is a positive sign of Lippard's resurgence and clear proof that the neglect of one of America's most potent Gothicists is coming to an end.

SELECTED CRITICISM

Butterfield, Roger. "George Lippard and His Secret Brotherhood." *Pennsylvania Magazine of History and Biography* 79 (1955): 285–309. On Lippard's radicalism and involvement with social causes and his journalistic career on the staff of *Citizen Soldier*. Has a valuable appendix, "A Check List of the Separately Published Works of George Lippard."

Curtis, Julia. "Philadelphia in an Uproar: *The Monks of Monk Hall*." *Theatre History*

Studies 5 (1985): 41–47. Vivid account of the mob violence ensuing from a dramatic performance of his "Gothic pot-boiler" *The Quaker City* at the Chestnut Street Theater on 11 November 1844. The play was an adaptation for the stage by Francis C. Wemyss.

De Grazia, Emilio. "Poe's Devoted Democrat, George Lippard." *Poe Studies* 6 (1973): 6–8. On the friendship and exchange of letters between Lippard and Poe. Lippard came to Poe's financial rescue during Poe's desperate final summer of 1849.

Ehrlich, Heyward. "The 'Mysteries' of Philadelphia: Lippard's Quaker City and 'Urban' Gothic." *ESQ: A Journal of the American Renaissance* 60 (1972): 50–65. Perceptive discussion of Lippard's relationship to the Gothic tradition and, more particularly, his adaptation of Gothicism to the American urban scene. "Lippard perceived the Gothic medium as fundamentally a medium for the reformation and exposé of scandal and corruption. To Lippard, such outrages of the day were far more 'Gothic' than the farthest fantasies of the romancers."

Fiedler, Leslie. "The Male Novel." *Partisan Review* 37 (1970): 74–89. Discusses *The Quaker City; or, The Monks of Monk Hall* in terms of horror pornography. "Lippard was near enough culturally to his readers to share their darkest fantasies, but far enough from them to articulate what they could only feel."

Jackson, Joseph. "A Bibliography of the Works of George Lippard." *Pennsylvania Magazine of History and Biography* 54 (1930): 131–54, 381–383 Arranges Lippard's publications by year from 1842 to 1894 and includes an engraving from *The Quaker City; or, The Monks of Monk Hall* that shows Devil-Bug "in his weird chamber seated at a table, while skeletons and ghosts are dimly shown in the background."

Reynolds, David S. *George Lippard*. Boston: Twayne, 1982. A solid biocritical study that shows how Lippard's incessant Gothicizing of America served him well as radical reformer and early muckraker.

———. *George Lippard, Prophet of Protest: Writings of an American Radical, 1822–1854*. New York: Peter Lang, 1986. Contains selections from Lippard's writings and an excellent introduction to Lippard's works. Concerning his Gothic tendencies, Reynolds points out that "apparently his first impulse was to entertain rather than save these masses, for the first product of his pen, *The Ladye Annabel*, was a traditional Gothic romance involving medieval torture, alchemy, social revolution, live burial, and necrophilia."

———. *Beneath The American Renaissance: The Subversive Imagination in the Age of Emerson and Melville*. New York: Alfred A. Knopf, 1988. Discusses Lippard's subversive tactics in *The Quaker City*.

Ridgely, J.V. "George Lippard's *The Quaker City*: The World of the American Porno-Gothic." *Studies in the Literary Imagination* 7:1 (1974): 77–94. Lippard's novel joins social propaganda to pornographic and salacious themes and characters, yielding an effect of "uncontrolled physicality."

Siegel, Adrienne. "Brothels, Bets, and Bars: Popular Literature as Guidebook to the Urban Underground, 1840–1870." *North Dakota Quarterly* 44 (1976): 5–22. Lippard's *Quaker City* is named as one of the principal "guidebooks" to the urban underground.

Stout, Janis. "Urban Gothicists: Brown, Lippard, Poe." In *Sodoms in Eden: The City in American Fiction before 1860*. Westport, CT: Greenwood Press, 1976: 103–129. Places Lippard in a direct line of descent from Charles Brockden Brown's fictions of urban horror and Philadelphia as a site of terror.

H[OWARD] P[HILLIPS]
LOVECRAFT
(1890–1937)

S.T. Joshi

PRINCIPAL GOTHIC WORKS

The Shunned House. Athol, MA: W. Paul Cook/Recluse Press, 1928.
The Shadow over Innsmouth. Everett, PA: Visionary Publishing Co., 1936.
"Notes on Writing Weird Fiction." *Amateur Correspondent* May-June 1937:7–14.
The Outsider and Others. Collected by August Derleth and Donald Wandrei. Sauk City,
    WI: Arkham House, 1939.
The Case of Charles Dexter Ward. London: Gollancz, 1941.

MODERN REPRINTS AND EDITIONS

The Annotated H.P. Lovecraft. Ed. and intro. S.T. Joshi. New York: Dell, 1997.
At the Mountains of Madness and Other Novels. Selected by August Derleth, ed. S.T.
    Joshi. Sauk City, WI: Arkham House, 1985.
The Best of H.P. Lovecraft: Bloodcurdling Tales of Horror and the Macabre. Ed. Robert
    Bloch. New York: Del Rey Books/Ballantine, 1982. (Sixteen Lovecraft tales in-
    troduced by Bloch's essay "Heritage of Horror" This edition cited in text.)
The Call of Cthulhu and Other Weird Stories. Ed. and intro. S.T. Joshi. New York:
    Penguin, 1999.
Dagon and Other Macabre Tales. Selected by August Derleth, ed. S.T. Joshi. Sauk City,
    WI: Arkham House, 1986.
The Dunwich Horror and Others. Selected by August Derleth, ed. S.T. Joshi. Sauk City,
    WI: Arkham House, 1984.
Miscellaneous Writings. Ed. S.T. Joshi. Sauk City, WI: Arkham House, 1995.
Supernatural Horror in Literature. Ed. E.F. Bleiler. New York: Dover, 1973. (Love-
    craft's monograph was originally published in 1927.)
Tales of H.P. Lovecraft. Selected and introduced by Joyce Carol Oates. Hopewell, NJ:
    Ecco Press, 1997.

In *The Supernatural in Fiction* (1952), Peter Penzoldt stated that Lovecraft was
"too well read." By this he meant that on occasion Lovecraft's tales were so

heavily reliant on their literary antecedents that it was sometimes difficult to detect what was genuinely "Lovecraft" and what was some deliberate or unconscious pastiche. Penzoldt's formulation is considerably overstated: most of Lovecraft's borrowings from his predecessors consist in surface details and rarely affect the thematic or philosophical essence of the tales, which remain emphatically "Lovecraftian" even when he is being most derivative.

Those who contend that Lovecraft was too influenced by the literary heritage of Gothic fiction have to contend with the fact that in many instances, he did not read many celebrated authors and works of Gothic literature until a surprisingly late stage in his career. Lovecraft came upon Ambrose Bierce and Lord Dunsany only in 1919; Arthur Machen in 1923; Algernon Blackwood in 1924; and M.R. James in 1925. Many older works of Gothic fiction were somewhat hastily and incompletely absorbed in 1925–1926 while he was doing research for his landmark treatise *Supernatural Horror in Literature* (1927). In one striking instance, Lovecraft devoted several pages of this book to a discussion of Charles Maturin's *Melmoth the Wanderer* (1820), but later admitted that he had never read the whole of this immense novel, but only two extracts of it found in anthologies. The dominant literary influence on Lovecraft's creative work is Edgar Allan Poe, his "God of Fiction," whom he read as early as the age of eight. It could well be said that Lovecraft spent a good part of his career in absorbing—perhaps even overcoming or surmounting—the Poe influence; he may never have fully done so.

Lovecraft was, therefore, among the most diligent Gothic writers in ferreting out the meritorious work of his predecessors. From childhood onward he read all manner of weird writing, from dime novels to the pulp magazines (beginning with the Munsey magazines of the turn of the century and moving on to *Weird Tales, Strange Tales*, and even such crude specimens as *Ghost Stories* and *Terror Tales*) to the loftiest contributions of Poe, Machen, and Dunsany. A variety of little-known works—ranging from Irvin S. Cobb's "Unbroken Chain" (1923) to H. B. Drake's *Shadowy Thing* (1928) to Hans Heinz Bowers's "The Spider" (1931)—demonstrably influenced some of Lovecraft's greatest tales, although again usually in superficial details of plot.

Lovecraft, then, approached the writing of Gothic fiction with the attitude of both an appreciator and a critic. Perhaps he felt that some themes, elements, and plot devices had not been used to full advantage in prior work, although with his habitual modesty he rarely said so explicitly. What he did say, repeatedly, was that many of the conventional staples of Gothic fiction—the ghost, the vampire, the haunted house—had, by his day, become stale and void of imaginative resonance because modern advances in science had shown them to be merely the delusions of ignorance. Some of these elements might still retain a residual power because they drew upon the deepest fears of the human psyche, but they would have to be updated—or, at the very least, expressed more subtly—if they were to be effective in the age of Einstein, Freud, and Bertrand Russell. It was to this kind of updating that Lovecraft devoted the bulk of his career. In so doing, he pushed the envelope of Gothicism so far that it approached the realm of science fiction, but at the same time it remained true to the Gothic impulse that gave it birth. Three dominant themes drawn from Gothic fiction used frequently by Lovecraft, the haunted castle, the Faustian man, and psychic possession, can perhaps most fruitfully be studied here to display Lovecraft's expansion of the form.

The Haunted Castle. The very first tale of Lovecraft's maturity, "The Tomb" (1917), exhibits not one but two haunted dwellings, the tomb itself, which the protagonist, Jervas Dudley, finds insidiously fascinating, and the lavish eighteenth-century mansion that he believes himself to be occupying during his dreams or hallucinations. In the end, this tale proves to be one of psychic possession: Dudley is the virtual twin of an eighteenth-century ancestor, Jervas Hyde, who had perished in the mansion and was therefore denied the chance to be buried in his ancestral tomb.

"The Picture in the House" (1920) finds horror in a lonely house in the remote backwoods of New England, where an ignorant, unkempt individual has prolonged his life unnaturally by means of cannibalism. Perhaps prototypically Gothic is the celebrated "The Outsider" (1921), in which the hapless protagonist strives valiantly to escape from what he fancies to be the dark, dismal, mirrorless castle of his birth and to reach the brilliantly lighted mansion where a lavish party is being held. Although the story borrows heavily from Poe's "Berenice" and "The Masque of the Red Death," it nevertheless plays effectively upon the standard contrast of darkness (ignorance) and light (knowledge): the self-knowledge the outsider gains when he sees his hideous form in a mirror is not the sort he had hoped to obtain. Interesting as these early tales are, they do little to expand the bounds of traditional Gothicism, offering only dim hints of future development.

It is therefore something of a surprise that as early as 1923, Lovecraft wrote one of his most artistically finished tales, "The Rats in the Walls," which might be thought of as a kind of combined homage to Poe's "Fall of the House of Usher" and Hawthorne's *House of the Seven Gables*, which Lovecraft believed to be "New England's greatest contribution to weird literature." Lovecraft still looks to the past, but he does so as much as a scientist as as an antiquarian. The call of ancestry is at the heart of the tale: when Walter de la Poer discovers that his ancestors had been a band of cannibals, he immediately descends the evolutionary scale and becomes a cannibal himself. This climax could not have been conceived by one who did not know of Darwin.

"The Shunned House" (1924) is even more interesting from this perspective. It too, on the surface, seems conventional: the death of a werewolf's descendant in the seventeenth century leads to two centuries of mysterious deaths in a house in Providence, Rhode Island, until the narrator and his uncle eventually put an end to the horror. But consider how Lovecraft makes clear that "the house was never regarded by the solid part of the community as in any real sense 'haunted' "; it was merely thought to be "unlucky." Consider, too, how the entity is dispelled—not by an incantation, but by being doused with acid. But most remarkable is a striking passage in the middle of the tale in which the narrator ponders the true causes of the entity's pervasive influence. "Such a thing was surely not a physical or biochemical impossibility in the light of a newer science which includes the theories of relativity and intra-atomic action." Here is Lovecraft appealing to Einstein and Planck to account for a gelatinous vampire in the cellar of a New England wood-frame house.

The Case of Charles Dexter Ward (Written in 1927, but not published during Lovecraft's lifetime), Lovecraft's greatest homage to the heritage of the Gothic, is considerably more conventional, and in terms of setting—the bungalow where the seventeenth-century wizard Joseph Curwen conducts his nameless experiments—we are not very far from the Gothic castle of tradition. But the novel's interest clearly lies elsewhere. It was shortly after writing this tale that Lovecraft began that exhaustive exploration of the terrors and wonders of his native region—fleetingly hinted at in "The Picture in the House" and "The Festival" (1923)—that would represent his ultimate treatment of the topos of the "haunted locale." In tale after tale, for example, "The Colour out of Space" (1927), "The Dunwich Horror" (1928), "The Whisperer in Darkness" (1930), "The Shadow over Innsmouth" (1931), and "The Thing on the Doorstep" (1933), it is not a single dwelling that is haunted, but an entire city or countryside. Again, the haunting is not the product of mere ghosts or ghouls, but of entities from "outside": the meteorite that lands on a hapless farmer's land in "The Colour out of Space," producing effects strikingly similar to radiation poisoning; the twin offspring of a backwoods farm girl and the cosmic entity Yog-Sothoth, who strew death and madness in "The Dunwich Horror"; the "fungi from Yuggoth," dwelling on the farthest planet in the solar system, who have established an outpost in Vermont in "The Whisperer in Darkness"; and the unholy unions between hybrid fish-frogs and local residents that corrupt the entire town of Innsmouth in "The Shadow over Innsmouth." "The Dreams in the Witch House" (1932) perhaps signalizes Lovecraft's attempt to have his cake and eat it too: in this relatively unsuccessful tale, we see the tug-of-war that was continually waged in the mind of a man who nurtured himself on the historic and aesthetic fruits of the past (colonial architecture, the literature of Greece, Rome, and Augustan England) but who also sought to keep abreast of the newest advances in science and philosophy. In this tale, we seem to be presented with a very conventional haunted house and a very conventional witch; but the witch, it proves, can traverse the fourth dimension by her mastery of mathematics. Lovecraft's depiction of "hyperspace as a bewildering succession of geometrical forms" is a triumph of the imagination, but he lapses into conventionality (particularly curious in an atheist) by having the witch frightened off by a crucifix. Lovecraft cannot decide whether he is writing a typical Gothic tale or a tale of science fiction. As a result, neither facet of the story rings true.

The Faustian Man. The age-old theme of the individual who strives to break the barriers of human limitations was of compelling fascination for Lovecraft, since in many ways this quest echoed his own goals as a writer of weird fiction. In "Notes on Writing Weird Fiction" (1937), he maintained, "I choose weird stories because they suit my inclination best—one of my strongest and most persistent wishes being to achieve, momentarily, the illusion of some strange suspension or violation of the galling limitations of time, space, and natural law, which forever imprison us and frustrate our curiosity about the infinite cosmic spaces beyond the radius of our sight and analysis" (7). It is scarcely to be wondered, then, that Lovecraft reacts with a mixture of horror and fascination to his own depictions of those lonely seekers after unholy knowledge.

Almost a caricature of the mad scientist is Crawford Tillinghast in "From Beyond" (1920), whose histrionic utterances make him a parody of himself. Nevertheless, his quest to harness all space and time by means of a machine that expands the bounds of human sense perception is typical. More subtle is the nebulous figure (whether a figment of the narrator's imagination or not) in "Hypnos" (1923), who appears to have "designs which involved the rulership of the visible universe and more; designs whereby the earth and the stars would move at his command, and the destinies of all living things be his." Such an appalling quest carries its rightful doom.

The Case of Charles Dexter Ward presents two such figures in the baleful seventeenth-century alchemist Joseph Curwen and the hapless twentieth-century student Charles Dexter Ward, Curwen's lineal descendant. Curwen's plan, it transpires, is to capture the "essential saltes" of the great minds of human history, and with this combined knowledge Curwen hopes to gain such power as might endanger "all civilisation, all natural law, perhaps even the fate of the solar system and the universe." Ward, for his part, represents a benign pursuit of knowledge: he has unwittingly been drawn into following Curwen's footsteps to the point of resurrecting Curwen himself from his own essential saltes, but Lovecraft holds him blameless. When Ward writes, "I have brought to light a monstrous abnormality, but I did it for the sake of knowledge" (26), it is Ward's (and Lovecraft's) fully adequate moral justification for his actions. Curwen himself, although he seems cut from the standard Gothic mold, proves to be more a scientist than a wizard: we are led to believe that the perfecting of these "essential saltes" is really more a matter of implementing the proper chemical and biological formulas than of muttering the proper spells.

The kind of unintentional gathering of information engaged in by Ward, what the narrator of "The Call of Cthulhu" (1926) terms "the piecing together of dissociated knowledge," is exhibited by several Lovecraft protagonists, from Henry Akeley in "The Whisperer in Darkness" (who stumbles, to his peril, upon evidences of the fungi from Yuggoth) to Walter Gilman, the student in "The Dreams in the Witch-House," of whom Lovecraft rather wryly states, "Possibly Gilman ought not to have studied so hard" (296). Quite otherwise is the Whateley family in "The Dunwich Horror," who pore through tomes like the *Necronomicon* in search of the formulas that will bring down alien entities from another dimension to plague this earth. Asenath Waite in "The Thing on the

Doorstep" is similarly motivated; incensed at being in a woman's body, she uses some kind of witchcraft to usurp the body of her husband Edward Derby and fulfill her ill-defined but clearly nefarious goals.

To Lovecraft, the perennial student, knowledge is power. Whether it is used for good or ill depends upon the morality of the individual. But in nearly every case, that knowledge is knowledge of the hard sciences—mathematics, physics, chemistry. In his early stories, Lovecraft's protagonists pursue knowledge or other activities in histrionic ways that point to their own mental aberration: the "neurotic virtuosi" who rob graves for aesthetic pleasure in "The Hound" (1922) and the unnamed narrator of "The Lurking Fear" (1922) who seeks out horrors because of a "love of the grotesque and the terrible" are virtual caricatures of this character type. But his later protagonists—all sober, skeptical men of science—augment the horror of the scenario by their very reluctance to accept the implications of their meticulously researched findings. In this sense, Lovecraft's Antarctic novel *At the Mountains of Madness* (1931) is the pinnacle of his achievement.

Psychic Possession. Possession by the devil is something that the unbeliever Lovecraft could scarcely credit, so he had to employ this topos in more ingenious, and more modern, ways. In some ways, this trope fuses with that of the Faust figure in that it is ordinarily a man (or, in rare instances, a woman) of exceptional strength of will who is able to exert his or her psychological dominance over another. Straightforward psychic possession occurs in "The Tomb" and, perhaps, in *The Case of Charles Dexter Ward*, in which Curwen may have exercised some kind of influence that led Ward to follow in his footsteps. But a more interesting kind of possession occurs in two other stories, "The Thing on the Doorstep" and "The Shadow Out of Time" (1934–1935). In the former, Asenath Waite can effect a kind of mind exchange by hypnosis; indeed, she herself is actually the mind of her father, Ephraim Waite, occupying his own daughter's body. Far more interesting is the mind exchange performed by the supremely rational alien entities called the Great Race in "The Shadow out of Time," who spend their entire existence in casting their minds forward and backward in time, temporarily occupying the bodies of a variety of other species throughout the cosmos and thereby learning all they can about the civilizations of their mental captives. In turn, the minds of these individuals are lodged in the bodies of the Great Race, where they write accounts of their own times for the Great Race's immense archives. Although this mental exchange is presented as initially traumatic, it is ultimately seen as benign and even imaginatively liberating. Who would not wish to be able to scan the entire history of the cosmos, written from the vantage point of all the different species that have occupied and will occupy it in the past and future?

Lovecraft may have said, as late as 1930, that "the past is real—it is all there is," but he also looked forward to a time when science had definitively overthrown primitive superstition. As a writer of weird fiction, he knew that he could not entirely jettison the rich heritage of Gothic literature, but he also felt that in the light of modern advances in science, "the time has come when the normal revolt against time, space, and matter must assume a form not overtly incompatible with what is known of reality—when it must be gratified by images forming supplements rather than contradictions of the visible and mensurable universe." Throughout the twenty years of his literary career, he sought as best he could to achieve this difficult goal and in so doing transformed Gothic fiction into something that could be both imaginatively and intellectually satisfying in the modern age.

SELECTED CRITICISM

Burleson, Donald R. *H.P. Lovecraft: A Critical Study.* Westport, CT: Greenwood Press, 1983. Thoroughgoing study of Lovecraft's work, stressing the notion of "ironic impressionism."

———. *Lovecraft: Disturbing the Universe.* Lexington: University Press of Kentucky, 1990. A challenging deconstructionist interpretation of Lovecraft.

Cannon, Peter. *H.P. Lovecraft.* Boston: Twayne, 1989. Competent overview of Lovecraft's work. "Lovecraft is more than a mere horror writer. At the very least he deserves recognition as one of America's greatest literary eccentrics."

Cockcroft, T.G.L. "Some Notes on 'The Shadow over Innsmouth.'" *Lovecraft Studies* 1:3 (1980):3–4. Discusses the work's locales and furnishes a family tree of the story's characters.

De Camp, L. Sprague. *Lovecraft: A Biography.* Garden City, NY: Doubleday, 1975. Uses Lovecraft's letters as a basis and covers his philosophic beliefs.

Emmons, Winfred S., Jr. "A Bibliography of H.P. Lovecraft." *Extrapolation* 3 (1961): 2–25. A checklist of secondary sources.

Indick, Ben. "H.P. Lovecraft and Stephen King: A Pair of New Englanders." *NIEKAS 45: Essays on Dark Fantasy.* Center Harbor, NH: Niekas Publications, 1998:14–17. On Stephen King's admiration for and use of Lovecraft in his own fiction, particularly *The Tommyknockers*, King's "ultimate homage" based on Lovecraft's "Colour out of Space."

Joshi, S. T., ed. *H.P. Lovecraft: Four Decades of Criticism.* Athens: Ohio University Press, 1980. Anthology of previously published criticism on Lovecraft (1944–1978), with a few original items, including J. Vernon Sheals's lengthy discussions of literary influences upon Lovecraft's work. Codifies "the astoundingly ambivalent interpretations imposed upon Lovecraft's work over the last thirty years."

———. *H.P. Lovecraft and Lovecraft Criticism: An Annotated Bibliography.* Kent, OH: Kent State University Press, 1981. Authoritative primary and secondary bibliographies. An updated supplement coedited with Leigh Blackmore appeared in 1985 (West Warwick, RI: Necronomicon Press).

———. *A Subtler Magick: The Writings and Philosophy of H.P. Lovecraft.* San Bernardino, CA: Borgo Press, 1996. Detailed survey of Lovecraft's fiction in light of his philosophical thought.

———. *H.P. Lovecraft: A Life.* West Warwick, RI: Necronomicon Press, 1996.

Leiber, Fritz. "A Literary Copernicus." In *Something about Cats and Other Pieces.* Sauk City, WI: Arkham House, 1949: 290–303; in *H.P. Lovecraft: Four Decades of Criticism* 50–62; In *Lovecraft Remembered.* Ed. Peter Cannon. Sauk City, WI:

Arkham House, 1998: 455–466. A landmark essay discussing how Lovecraft transformed the Gothic tale by transferring the locus of horror to the unknown depths of the cosmos.

Lévy, Maurice. *Lovecraft: A Study in the Fantastic.* Trans. S.T. Joshi. Detroit: Wayne State University Press, 1988. Penetrating thematic study that focuses on Lovecraft's use of landscape, hereditary degeneration, and the dreamworld.

Mariconda, Steven J. *On the Emergence of Cthulhu and Other Observations.* West Warwick, RI: Necronomicon Press, 1995. Wide-ranging collection of essays discussing Lovecraft's prose style, his concept of "background," and several individual tales.

Oakes, David A. *Science and Destabilization in the Modern American Gothic: Lovecraft, Matheson, and King.* Westport, CT: Greenwood Press, 2000. Contributions to the study of science. Like the writings of King and Matheson later, Lovecraft's work reflects the fears of the time in which it was written. "Many of the darkest aspects of society reflected by American Gothic fiction in the twentieth century stem from science and technology."

Pearsall, Anthony B. *The Lovecraft Lexicon: A Dictionary of People and Places in Lovecraft Novels.* Forthcoming. A guide to Lovecraftiana in alphabetized format.

Penzoldt, Peter. *The Supernatural in Fiction.* New York: Humanities Press, 1965. Classic study of the weird tale in English originally published in 1952.

Schultz, David E., and S.T. Joshi, eds. *An Epicure in the Terrible: A Centennial Anthology of Essays in Honor of H.P. Lovecraft.* Rutherford, NJ: Fairleigh Dickinson University Press, 1991. Anthology of original essays by leading Lovecraft scholars, including those by Jacob C. Eckhardt on Lovecraft's New England background, Stefan Dziemianowicz on the "outsider" motif in Lovecraft's work, David E. Schultz on the imaginative development of Lovecraft's fiction, and Robert H. Waugh on the use of landscape in Lovecraft.

St. Armand, Barton L. *The Roots of Horror in the Fiction of H.P. Lovecraft.* Elizabethtown, NY: Dragon Press, 1977. Detailed psychoanalytical study of "The Rats in the Walls."

———. *H.P. Lovecraft: New England Decadent.* Albuquerque, NM: Silver Scarab Press, 1979. Proposes that Lovecraft's work is a distinctive fusion of New England Puritanism and the Decadent movement of the later nineteenth century.

ARTHUR MACHEN
(1863–1947)

Jack G. Voller

PRINCIPAL GOTHIC WORKS

The Chronicle of Clemendy. Carbonnek [Eng.] Society of Pantagruelists, 1888.

The Great God Pan and The Inmost Light. London: John Lane, 1894; Boston: Roberts, 1894.

The Three Impostors. London: John Lane, 1895; Boston: Roberts, 1895. (Contains "The Novel of the Black Seal" and "The Novel of the White Powder.")

The House of Souls. London: E. Grant Richards, 1906; Boston: Dana Estes, 1906. (Contains "The Great God Pan," "The Inmost Light," "The White People," an abridged version of "The Three Impostors," "A Fragment of Life," and "The Red Hand.")

The Hill of Dreams. London: E. Grant Richards, 1907.

The Angels of Mons, The Bowmen, and Other Legends of the War. London: Simpkin, Marshall, Hamilton, Kent and Co., 1915; New York: G. P. Putnam, 1915.

The Terror: A Fantasy. London: Duckworth, 1917.

The Secret Glory. London: Secker, 1922.

The Green Round. London: Benn, 1933.

MODERN REPRINTS AND EDITIONS

Black Crusade. London: Corgi, 1966. (A retitled version of *The Three Impostors*.)

The Children of the Pool and Other Stories. New York: Arno Press, 1976; Salem, NH: Ayer, 1987.

The Great God Pan. Freeport, NY: Books for Libraries Press, 1970; Salem, NH: Ayers Co., 1993.

The Green Round. Sauk City, WI: Arkham House, 1968.

The Hill of Dreams. Horam, UK: Tartarus, 1998.

The House of Souls. Freeport, NY: Books for Libraries Press, 1971; Salem, NH: Ayer, 1989, 1999.

The Strange World of Arthur Machen. New York: Juniper Press, 1960.

Tales of Horror and the Supernatural. Ed. Philip Van Doren Stern. New York: Knopf, 1948; London: Richards Press, 1949.

The Terror: A Fantasy. New York: W.W. Norton, 1965.
The Three Impostors. London: Dent, 1995; Oakland: Chaosium. Forthcoming.

In his pioneering study of the Gothic, *The Gothic Flame*, Devendra Varma argues that the essential impulse of the Gothic is religious, an inquiry into the possibility of the "numinous" and its accessibility from a human world of deceit and desire. As debatable as this thesis may be, it or something very much like it proves substantially true for the works of Arthur Machen, a late Victorian whose interest in the Gothic was fueled by his desire to use popular fiction to investigate the strange and convoluted world of human identity and spiritual, or at least metaphysical, possibility and the horrific limits of that possibility.

Machen's most popular and notorious work, "The Great God Pan," was published in 1890 and both catches the spirit of decadent literature and testifies to the essentially Victorian shape of Machen's important work, a canon that would influence much horror literature to follow. With its portrait of a scientist whose surgical intervention allows a woman to encounter a fundamental reality normally hidden from human perception, "The Great God Pan" flows out of the nineteenth-century "dangerous-science" genre that includes Mary Shelley's *Frankenstein*, Hawthorne's "Rappaccini's Daughter" and "The Birthmark," and Stevenson's *The Strange Case of Dr. Jekyll and Mr. Hyde*. Like these predecessor works, "The Great God Pan" articulates a vision of insidious destruction, in this case sexual. The female child fathered by Pan of a human mother is a consuming seductress, a femme fatale in the dark tradition of the lamia—not in its Keatsian manifestation, but in the horrific version of Stoker's White Worm. In this we may rightly understand Machen's work on one level as a Victorian cautionary tale, a tempering of scientific enthusiasm with the reminder that human moral and psychological capacity is not keeping up with technological achievement. Yet Machen's choice of Pan as the avatar of this underlying reality—an avatar present only indirectly in the story, a frequent characteristic of Machen's tales—points to the deepest concerns of much of Machen's best fiction, for his choice of a pre-Christian deity, elemental in its significance and its consuming, disruptive power, is the token of Machen's interest in exploring a dark world external and prior to the human. Unlike Hawthorne or Stevenson, unlike Le Fanu or Stoker, unlike the Freud-influenced horror writers of the early twentieth century, Machen eschewed the psychological for the myths and parables of destructive power and cosmic mystery.

Yet such an aesthetic and artistic choice was not a rejection of his immediate predecessors' and contemporaries' interest in the psychological as much as it was a complement to it, for it was the mythic, primarily in the garb of Celtic folklore, that gave Machen a symbolic language of dark psychocultural exploration, and pursuing the capabilities of this language was one of Machen's driving compulsions. The techniques of naturalism and the world of scientific inquiry were largely anathema to him. As S.T. Joshi has put it, "The sole goal of Machen's philosophy is to restore the sense of wonder and mystery into our perception of the world" (16). It was through the shadowy imagery of prerational, pre-Christian mythologies that Machen primarily pursued this goal. Pan, fairies, the "Little People"—over and over they appear in Machen's fiction, although only rarely do they actually appear, for Machen's forte is the suggestion, the allusion, the "unutterable" and the "unnameable," and that is precisely the horror. They leave the vaguest of traces that only the most astute may detect, and any attempt to pursue the "Little People" to their hiding places—usually under the hills in some remote corner of Wales—results in unexplained disappearance or unpleasant death. Yet the "Little People," not the leprechauns of St. Patrick's Day or the fairies of Shakespeare and Andrew Lang, but malevolent, troglodytic entities of insidious and sinister power, leave evidence of their existence everywhere: in the streets of London, in newspaper accounts of mysterious disappearances, in "yellow and wizened" changeling babies, in whispered tales of disturbing things that transpire in the night near Roman ruins. Like Machen himself, born in Wales but resident for much of his adult life in London, the "Little People" and their baleful influence have a geographic reach that mirrors their chronological bridging of a vast abyss of time, a theme that Machen explored more deliberately in *The Hill of Dreams*, a quasi-autobiographical novel in which modern London is transformed into an otherworldly vision of "an urban bacchanal of Decadence" (Stableford 384).

The frequent suggestions of a Lovecraftian proto-Cthulhu subterranean race of malefic beings lurking at the margins of human experience and consciousness constitute Machen's laying bare of a Victorian anxiety, a metaphysical version of the psychological anxieties revealed in *Jekyll and Hyde* and *Dracula*, where the acknowledgment of libidinal impulses proves destabilizing and highly threatening. Machen may be seen in this regard as a small and relatively obscure part of the Victorian response to the religious and spiritual decay identified by earlier mainstream writers such as Arthur Hugh Clough and Matthew Arnold and evident at the end of the nineteenth century in the spiritualism that attracted Arthur Conan Doyle and others. What Machen suggests in works such as "The Great God Pan," "The Novel of the Black Seal," *The Hill of Dreams*, "The Red Hand," and the disturbingly powerful "The White People" is that an occult dimension of (super)nature remains vital in the universe; very few humans see or sense it, and still fewer survive their encounters, but it lurks in the remote corners of the kingdom and reaches, as noted earlier, into the cosmopolitan heart of the British Empire, where its energies manifest themselves in mysterious ways rarely amenable to rational inquiry or understanding. Some of Machen's works, with their foregrounding of intuitive insights and "improbability," hollow out the Victorian rationalism championed in fiction by the likes of Doyle's Sherlock Holmes.

Much remains to be studied in Machen's fiction. One need not go too far afield to see these and other such works of Machen's as considerations of Victorian anxieties about imperialism and race, as quasi-ecological parables, and as articulations of a deep unease over the role and capacity of science. Of course they are "spiritual" as well, with the quotation marks most necessary. For although Machen was the son of an Anglican clergyman and himself a devout lifelong Anglican, he clearly felt, at least at times in his life, a need for an alternate or supplemental system of metaphysical investigation, for in 1899 he joined the Hermetic Order of the Golden Dawn, the occult group best known for including William Butler Yeats and Aleister Crowley. But Machen's participation in this group was brief and indeed may have been motivated as much by the recent death of his first wife as by spiritual desire. Yet the fact remains that much of Machen's fiction is given to the examination of the boundaries of human existence, and often in his early fiction especially, the probing of that boundary reveals a far greater universe quietly but pulsingly alive with an elemental, primal power that is, in the most literal sense in a number of Machen's stories, the very undoing of our humanity. Machen's later fiction after his recovery from the near despair brought on by the death of his first wife, and after his devoting considerable time to acting and journalism, often articulated a more benevolent sense of the universe. His famous World War I myth "The Bowmen" took on a life of its own as widely believed evidence of the providential intervention of St. George and the archers of Agincourt on a World War I battlefield. Yet even in his last works Machen registered the dark reverberations of the mythic world whose unseen presence had long shaped his work. *The Green Round* and *The Children of the Pool*, while not among Machen's best work, return to the dark mythic symbolism of the "Little People" and their antipathy to the world of humanity.

Machen's repeated insistence on the powerful penetration of this darkly numinous, mythic world into the realms of everyday humanity constitutes an assault on Victorian complacency that makes Machen a powerfully representative figure of the 1890s Decadent movement, as does his insistence that great literature is identified by the presence of "ecstasy," a sense of deeper truths revealed behind a world of ordinary appearances and "common consciousness." Yet in his repeated narrative engagement with the residues of a primal cosmic energy made manifest and embodied in figures from Greek and Celtic mythologies, Machen also bridges the gap from Victoria to the twentieth century, emerging as "the first British writer of authentically modern horror stories" (Stableford 384).

SELECTED CRITICISM

Briggs, Julia. *Night Visitors: The Rise and Fall of the English Ghost Story*. London: Faber & Faber, 1977. Credits Machen's Gothic with "the release of an alien self, a night-side uninhibited by morality" in his tales.

Goldstone, Adrian, and Wesley D. Sweetser. *A Bibliography of Arthur Machen*. Austin: University of Texas, 1965. Still the definitive bibliography, no mean feat given Machen's prolific output and the complex publishing history of some of his works.

Hurley, Kelly. "Afterword: Narrative Chaos: *The Three Impostors*: Arthur Machen's Urban Chaosmos." In *The Gothic Body: Sexuality, Materialism, and Degeneration at the Fin de Siècle*. New York: Cambridge University Press, 1996: 306–311. Discusses Machen's Gothicism as an expression of "the ruination of the human subject and the ruination of traditional constructs of human identity that accompanied the modeling of new ones at the turn of the century."

Joshi, S.T. "Arthur Machen: The Mystery of the Universe." In *The Weird Tale*. Austin: University of Texas Press, 1990: 12–41. An insightful and perceptive overview of Machen's work, arguing that Machen's "whole work is inspired by one idea and one only: the awesome and utterly unfathomable mystery of the universe."

Reynolds, Aidan, and William Charlton. *Arthur Machen: A Short Account of His Life and Work*. London: Richards, 1963. Full, if at times ponderously detailed, biographical coverage of Machen's life, along with brief considerations of his works and their reception.

Stableford, Brian. "Arthur (Llewellyn) Machen." In *St. James Guide to Horror, Ghost, and Gothic Writers*. Ed. David Pringle. Detroit: St. James Press, 1998: 382–384. Calls "The Great God Pan" "the archetypal decadent horror story. In the ten years between 1890 and 1899, he changed the face of British supernatural fiction, blasting away both the genteel narrative conventions and the ideological foundations of the Victorian ghost story."

Stern, Philip Van Doren. Introduction to *Tales of Horror and the Supernatural* by Arthur Machen. New York: Knopf, 1948: iii–xii. Most useful for its overview of Machen's debt to the Gothic and for its impressionist rendering of Machen's interest in "the inheritance of evil left us from the ancient world." Also contains "A Note on Machen by Robert Hillyer," a personal reminiscence.

Sweetser, Wesley D. *Arthur Machen*. New York: Twayne, 1964. A solid overview of Machen's life and works, if perhaps somewhat dated.

Valentine, Mark. *Arthur Machen*. Mid-Glamorgan, Wales: Seren/Poetry Wales Press, 1995. A biographical study, with close readings (often bordering on lengthy plot summary) of Machen's major works.

CHARLES ROBERT MATURIN
(1782–1824)
Jack G. Voller

PRINCIPAL GOTHIC WORKS

Fatal Revenge: or, The Family of Montorio. London: Longman, Hurst Rees, and Orme, 1807; New York: I. Riley, 1808. (Published under the pseudonym "Dennis Jasper Murphy.")

Bertram; or, The Castle of St. Aldobrand: A Tragedy in Five Acts. London: John Murray, 1816.

Manuel: A Tragedy in Five Acts. London: John Murray, 1817.

Fredolfo: A Tragedy in Five Acts. London: Constable, 1819.

Melmoth the Wanderer: A Tale. 4 vols. London: Hurst & Robinson, 1821.

Melmoth, the Wanderer: A Melo-dramatic Romance, in Three Acts. Adapted by B. West. London: John Lowndes, 1823.

"Leixlip Castle." *The Literary Souvenir; or, Cabinet of Poetry and Romance*, 1825.

MODERN REPRINTS AND EDITIONS

The Fatal Revenge; or, The Family of Montorio. Ed. Maurice Lévy. New York: Arno Press, 1974.

Fatal Revenge; or, The Family of Montorio. Ed. Julian Cowley. Stroud, England: Alan Sutton, 1994.

"Leixlip Castle." In *Gothic Tales of Terror: Classic Horror Stories from Great Britain, Europe, and the United States, 1765–1840*. Ed. Peter Haining. New York: Tap-linger, 1972.

"Leixlip Castle." In *Twelve Gothic Tales*. Ed. Richard Dalby. New York: Oxford University Press, 1998.

Melmoth the Wanderer. Ed. William F. Axton. Lincoln: University of Nebraska Press, 1961.

Melmoth the Wanderer. Ed. Douglas Grant. New York: Oxford University Press, 1968.

Melmoth the Wanderer. Ed. Alethea Hayter. Harmondsworth, England: Penguin, 1977.

It is with Charles Robert Maturin's greatest work, *Melmoth the Wanderer*, published in 1820, that the "classic" Gothic novel is said to end. While this oft-repeated claim is debatable, it clearly connotes the landmark textual and cultural status accorded to this novel. In fact, *Melmoth* may be not so much the last of its kind but among the first of a new kind, for in its disturbing fascination with human suffering and the voyeurizing of that suffering, Maturin's best-known novel declares its primary interest to be in human psychology rather than a supernaturalism real or supposed. There is supernatural incident, to be sure, for John Melmoth has indeed made a Faustian pact with the devil, but neither Melmoth himself nor any other supernatural agency is the cause of the suffering and emotional despair that the Wanderer repeatedly, even greedily, seeks out. The cause of human suffering in this novel is humanity itself: its sectarianism, its greed, and its pride and prejudice.

It is not too much to say that *Melmoth* marks the ne plus ultra of the Gothic, not by being a final participant in its customary tropes and techniques (although it does not eschew them entirely), but by marking the point beyond which no prior "Gothic" work had managed to pass, where to pass meant to become something new, something distinct from the conventional Gothic. By 1820, if not much sooner, the Gothic had become a tradition increasingly unable to come to terms with the shifting sociocultural landscape of the nineteenth-century West. As the poetry of the Romantics had already begun to demonstrate, the conventional Gothic was a limited form, unable to deal effectively or compellingly with the psychological complexities emergent from the Romantic reappraisal of self-construction and personal autonomy. While a few later novelists and playwrights would continue to work the diminished Gothic vein, *Melmoth*, we see in retrospect, signaled the shift to a new and deeper stratum of exploration, a moving away from, if not yet a complete abandonment of, Gothic horror toward a "psychological" horror as it would be developed by Le Fanu and other mid- to late Victorian writers and elevated to a tragic status in the writings of Hawthorne and Melville, two American admirers of *Melmoth the Wanderer*.

Maturin's life was itself something of a study in struggle and despair; early promise in his career as a curate fizzled as the eccentric Maturin's outspoken support of Calvinism, his critiques of established Anglicanism, and the rather outré subjects of his novels and plays combined to leave him branded as an unreliable character, an assessment only encouraged by personal flamboyance and irresponsibility. Financial difficulties were a constant in his life; support from his father dried up when his father was dismissed from his position in the Irish government, and standing security for a relative who defaulted on a loan further exacerbated Maturin's economic straits. His lifelong struggles to support his family—his most successful work, the drama *Bertram*, earned Maturin a considerable sum, much of which was quickly squandered on extravagance— kept Maturin constantly driving his pen, with only a few of his later works generating much in the way of financial rewards.

Encouraged by Byron and Scott, with whom Maturin had corresponded in pursuit of early support and whose work Maturin's novels on Scottish subjects emulate, Maturin persisted in literary efforts to supplement his curate's income even though his early pseudonymous novels, *Fatal Revenge; or, The Family of Montorio, The Wild Irish Boy*, and *The Milesian Chief*, met with only minimal financial or critical success. The endorsement of *Bertram* by Byron and Scott was instrumental in getting it produced at Drury Lane Theatre, where the work met with such success that Maturin vowed to continue as a playwright.

Bertram; or, The Castle of St. Aldobrand is a Gothic revenge thriller of the sort that frequently played on the stages of Romantic-era London. Drawing on Friedrich Schiller's *Die Räuber* and Scott's *Rokeby*, among others (Maturin was an inveterate borrower and was always heavily influenced by earlier works), the play features a dispossessed Byronic villain-hero who, after being rescued from a shipwreck, finds himself in the environs of his enemy, who, after engineering Bertram's exile, had married the woman he loved. Bertram swiftly enacts his revenge, seducing the Lady Imogine and shortly thereafter murdering Lord Aldobrand before killing himself. Overcome with guilt and the sudden death of her child, Imogine goes mad.

As melodramatic as it is, the play as originally conceived was stronger still, for Maturin originally included a supernatural figure, the Dark Knight of the Forest, to encourage Bertram's revenge, although at the instigation of the theater management the scene was removed, only to be published two years later by none other than Sir Walter Scott in his review of Maturin's novel *Women; or, Pour et Contre*. Yet even as it stood, the play was enough to provoke the outrage of some contemporary reviewers. Most notable among them was Coleridge, who harshly attacked the play as "jacobinical," inimical to social order and historical continuity in its radical Gothic recognition of impulse and emotion against the dictates and restraints of morality and civil authority.

Maturin's subsequent dramas were dismal failures, and he refocused his energies upon fiction, producing the work that would assure him a much more visible place in literary history than would otherwise be the case. *Melmoth the Wanderer* remains a landmark of Gothic fiction, despite oddly complex plotting and a somewhat lugubrious style. It invokes Byronic, Faustian, Miltonic, and Wandering Jew themes in its central image of the Wanderer, John Melmoth, whose pursuit of someone to take over his deal with the devil is the motive engine of the entire novel. This quest suits Maturin well, for narrative complexity and plotting are not his literary strong points. *Melmoth* is essentially an episodic narrative, despite the frame of a younger John Melmoth being made privy to the tale of his ancestor's predatory wanderings, which themselves function as a thread of continuity binding the tales. The Wanderer targets individuals in various forms of extreme duress, and thus his quest takes him to prisons, monasteries, and madhouses as he seeks out those whose situations are so dire they might be tempted to change places with him, to bargain away their immortal souls in exchange for earthly relief from anguish. He is never successful, and so the novel ends with his Faustian destruction by the forces of evil.

As such a conclusion would suggest, Gothic machinery and atmospherics are significantly present in this novel, as they are in other works of Maturin such as the demon-lover story "Leixlip Castle," a favorite selection of modern Gothic anthologists. Gothic equipage and atmospherics certainly link *Melmoth* firmly and formally to the dying genre of the Gothic, but in its concern with the depiction of human mental and emotional suffering in extremis the novel looks forward, as many critics have noted, to the work of Poe, Baudelaire, Kafka, and even James Joyce. Like *Bertram, Melmoth* begins with a shipwreck, as a result of which the young John Melmoth, who has already encountered a portrait of his ancestor and an ancient manuscript detailing John Stanton's obsession with the mysterious Wanderer, meets the young Spaniard Monçada. From him the young Melmoth hears "The Tale of the Parricide," in which Monçada relates his escape, with the aid of a parricide monk, from the monastery he had unwillingly joined and, subsequently, from the Inquisition, in whose cell he had been tempted by the Wanderer. Monçada's narrative also includes "The Tale of the Indians," in which Melmoth meets, seduces, and marries (with the aid of a skeleton monk) the innocent Immalee, who ultimately along with her child by Melmoth perishes in the prisons of the Inquisition; "The Tale of Guzman's Family," with its horrific account of poverty-induced suffering; and "The Tale of the Lovers," a story of religious intolerance. The novel concludes, relatively quickly, with the appearance of the Wanderer at the house of the Melmoths; after a restless night, he meets his demonic demise on the seaside cliffs nearby.

Maturin's narrative method has been both praised and excoriated, found to be both tightly controlled and a complete muddle. While the narrative interlayerings (actually even more complex than suggested in the previous paragraph) may well give pause or generate confusion and may not have been fully under Maturin's artistic control, there can be little doubt that their tortuous and interrupted linearities help to create for the reader some sense of the disorientation and lack of control over the circumstances of human existence that much of the novel seeks to chronicle. Several commentators have called attention to the structure of the novel itself as a metaphor of that dark labyrinth called human existence. This is a world, after all, of aberrant psychological mazes, of human minds that strain against the upper limits of knowledge (John Melmoth and his deal with the devil), and that scrape roughly on the shoals of insanity and self-annihilation. While later nineteenth- and twentieth-century writers created superior novels of psychological horror, no one has excelled Maturin's creation of the exemplary Romantic novel, the early nineteenth century's study par excellence of the limits of human selfhood.

SELECTED CRITICISM

Axton, W.F. "Charles Robert Maturin." In *Supernatural Fiction Writers*. Ed. E.F. Bleiler. New York: Scribner's, 1985: 161–168. A detailed consideration of both the context of Maturin's artistic achievement and of the works themselves, particularly *Melmoth*, which Axton finds to be a complex study of "the romantic nightmare of the dissolution of identity."

D'Amico, Diane. "Feeling and Conception of Character in the Novels of Charles Robert Maturin." *Massachusetts Studies in English* 9:3 (1984): 42–54. A psychologically oriented study of Maturin's delineation of hero-villains, focusing especially on Melmoth, and their use as a means of examining human psychological complexities.

Dansky, Richard. "The Wanderer and the Scribbler: Maturin, Scott, and *Melmoth the Wanderer*." *Studies in Weird Fiction* 21 (1997): 2–10. On the Maturin-Scott friendship.

Dawson, Leven M. "*Melmoth the Wanderer*: Paradox and the Gothic Novel." *Studies in English Literature, 1500–1900* 8 (1968): 621–632. Discusses the novel's horror (and its basis in the unnatural) as an early example of psychological inquiry.

Fowler, Kathleen. "Hieroglyphics in Fire: *Melmoth the Wanderer*." *Studies in Romanticism* 25 (1986): 521–539. A study of the convoluted structure of the novel, which Fowler finds to be "a reworking of the Book of Job."

Harris, John Bernhard. *Charles Robert Maturin: The Forgotten Imitator*. New York: Arno Press, 1980. A critical bio-bibliography of Maturin, useful for its synopses of the novels.

Haslam, Richard. "Maturin and the 'Calvinist Sublime.' " In *Gothick Origins and Innovations*. Ed. Allan Lloyd Smith and Victor Sage. Amsterdam: Rodopi, 1994: 44–56. Defining a "Calvinist sublime" ("a theologized aesthetic in which elements of the Calvinist system are sublimated out of a creed and into an artistic programme"), Haslam argues that Maturin's own evolving religious position away from hard-line Calvinism and into an ensuing doubt may be responsible for the increasingly effective use of terror in Maturin's fiction, which was also shaped by a politically informed distrust of Catholicism.

Johnson, Anthony. "Gaps and Gothic Sensibility: Walpole, Lewis, Mary Shelley, and Maturin." In *Exhibited by Candlelight: Sources and Developments in the Gothic Tradition*. Ed. Valeria Tinkler-Villani, Peter Davidson, and Jane Stevenson. Amsterdam: Rodopi, 1995: 7–24. A study of the fragmentary and otherwise "gapped" nature of key Gothic texts, arguing that in *Melmoth the Wanderer* "the convolutedness and incoherence of the whole become a part of the deliberate design."

Jones, Linda B. " 'The Terrors of a Guilty Sleep': Freud's Wolf Man and Dreams of Castration in *Melmoth the Wanderer*." *Gothic Studies* 2 (2000): 50–60. Analyzes several of the dreams in the novel through the psychoanalytic lens of one of Freud's most famous case studies, the Wolf Man. The theme of the fear of the father "express[es] a conflict of castration anxieties which underpins the uncanny sense of loss permeating the text."

Kramer, Dale. *Charles Robert Maturin*. New York: Twayne, 1973. Another solid volume in the Twayne's English Authors Series, this one provides a good overview of Maturin's life and work with special emphasis on his Gothic achievement.

Kullmann, Thomas. "Nature and Psychology in *Melmoth the Wanderer* and *Wuthering Heights*." In *Exhibited by Candlelight: Sources and Developments in the Gothic Tradition*. Ed. Valeria Tinkler-Villani, Peter Davidson, and Jane Stevenson. Amsterdam: Rodopi, 1995: 99–106. Discussion of landscape and weather phenomena in these two late Gothic works, focusing on their symbolic, psychological, and thematic values.

Leerssen, J.Th. "Fiction Poetics and Cultural Stereotype: Local Colour in Scott, Morgan, and Maturin." *Modern Language Review* 86 (1991): 273–284. A consideration of

Maturin's *Wild Irish Boy* and *The Milesian Chief* as "uncomfortably hybrid" works struggling to blend elements of both the romance and the novel; for Irish writers such as Maturin, the romance was associated with "Gaeldom," the novel with "Englishness," and the conflicted presence of both in much nineteenth-century Irish writing bespeaks "the political irreconcilability of Ireland's dividedness."

Lew, Joseph. " 'Unprepared for Sudden Transformations': Identity and Politics in *Melmoth the Wanderer*." *Studies in the Novel* 26 (1994): 173–195. Noting Maturin's frequent attempts to copy the literary successes of Sydney Owenson (Lady Morgan), Lew finds *Melmoth the Wanderer* to be a work freighted with autobiographical significance, speaking to Maturin's own conflicted sense of personal, artistic, and cultural identity.

Lougy, Robert. *Charles Robert Maturin*. Lewisburg, PA: Bucknell University Press, 1974. A biographical-critical study, solid in its research but occasionally given to hints of sensationalism.

Lozes, Jean. "James Joyce dans la tradition 'gothique'?" *Caliban* 33 (1996): 127–136. One of the sources used by Joyce in the writing of *A Portrait of the Artist as a Young Man* was Maturin's *Melmoth the Wanderer*.

McGuire, Karen. "Maturin, Charles Robert." In *Encyclopedia of Romanticism: Culture in Britain, 1780s–1830s*. Ed. Laura Dabundo. New York: Garland, 1992: 364–366. A rather basic overview of Maturin's life and works, with more attention devoted to the former.

Monroe, Judson T. *Tragedy in the Novels of the Reverend Charles Robert Maturin*. New York: Arno Press, 1980. Analyzes Maturin's Gothicism as an aspect of his tragic intentions. Has extensive primary and secondary bibliographies.

Morgan, Chris. "Charles Robert Maturin." In *St. James Guide to Horror, Ghost, and Gothic Writers*. Ed. David Pringle. Detroit: St. James Press, 1998: 396–397. A brief and rather sketchy overview of Maturin's life and Gothic works.

Nikolopoulou, Anastasia. "Medievalism and Historicity in the English Gothic Melodrama: Maturin's *Bertram; or, The Castle of St. Aldobrand*." *Poetica: An International Journal of Linguistic Literary Studies* 39–40 (1994): 139–153. Explores Gothic conventions in Maturin's Gothic play.

Null, Jack. "Structure and Theme in *Melmoth the Wanderer*." *Papers on Language and Literature* 13 (1977): 136–147. Examines the complex and unruly asymmetry of the novel's structure as symbolic of moral and epistemological vacuity.

Oost, Regina B. " 'Servility and Command': Authorship in *Melmoth the Wanderer*." *Papers on Language and Literature* 31 (1995): 291–312. Applies reader-response theory to Maturin's novel.

Scholten, Willem. *Charles Robert Maturin: The Terror-Novelist*. Amsterdam: H.J. Paris, 1933. Rpt. New York: Garland, 1980. A dated work, though still of value for its summaries of Maturin's works and the basics of Maturin's biography.

Smith, Amy Elizabeth. "Experimentation and 'Horrid Curiosity' in Maturin's *Melmoth the Wanderer*." *English Studies* 74 (1993): 524–535. Uncovering the extent to which "The Tale of the Spaniard" draws on Diderot's *La Réligieuse*, Smith argues that Maturin's novel may be most fully understood as "psychological experimentation" with such a strong interest in extreme suffering that not only does it undercut his avowed religious theme, it creates "a level of prurient, voyeuristic interest—for Maturin, his characters, and his audience—that emerges as a central theme in the novel."

Watkins, Daniel. " 'Tenants of a Blasted World': Historical Imagination in Charles Maturin's *Bertram*." *Keats-Shelley Review* 4 (1989): 61–80. Taking Coleridge's scathing attack on the play as its point of departure, this article historically situates the work in the post-Waterloo, nascent industrialist context of eroding class and gender boundaries.

HERMAN MELVILLE
(1819–1891)
Douglass H. Thomson

PRINCIPAL GOTHIC WORKS

Moby-Dick; or, The Whale. New York: Harper, 1851.
Pierre; or, The Ambiguities. New York: Harper, 1852.
"Bartleby the Scrivener: A Story of Wall Street." *Putnam's Monthly Magazine*, November–December 1853.
"The Lightning-Rod Man." *Putnam's Monthly Magazine*, August 1854.
"The Bell Tower." *Putnam's Monthly Magazine*, August 1855.
"Benito Cereno." *Putnam's Monthly Magazine*, October–November–December 1855.
The Piazza Tales. New York: Dix & Edwards, 1856. (Contains "Bartleby the Scrivener: A Tale of Wall Street," "Benito Cereno," "The Bell Tower," and "The Lightning-Rod Man." These tales were originally published anonymously in issues of *Putnam's Monthly Magazine* from 1853 to 1855; their arrangement in *The Piazza Tales* follows the chronology of their appearance.
Billy Budd, Foretopman. In *The Works of Herman Melville.* Vol. 8. London: Bombay and Constable, 1924.

MODERN REPRINTS AND EDITIONS

Billy Budd, Sailor, and Other Stories. New York: Bantam, 1981. (This edition of *Billy Budd* is cited in the text.)
Billy Budd, Sailor, and Selected Tales. Ed. Robert Milder. New York: Oxford University Press, 1997.
Herman Melville: Selected Tales and Poems. Ed. Richard Chase. New York: Holt, Rinehart & Winston, 1960. (This edition of *Billy Budd* is cited in the text.)
Melville's Billy Budd and the Critics. Ed. William T. Stafford. Wadsworth, 1961.
Moby-Dick. Ed. Cyrus R.K. Patell. New York: Oxford University Press, 1999.
The Shorter Novels of Herman Melville. New York: Fawcett, 1964.
The Writings of Herman Melville. Ed. Harrison Hayford and others. 15 vols. Evanston, IL: Northwestern University Press; Chicago: Newberry Library, 1968–1993.

In his introduction to *Herman Melville: Selected Tales and Poems*, the noted American scholar Richard Chase evokes the dark poetics of the Gothic spirit in his description of the eerie world of "Benito Cereno," calling it "a miasma of ancient sin, chaos and decay, an enigmatic world of ruined summerhouses in desolate gardens, of deserted chateaux and rotting balustrades, a savage forest of equivocations, treacheries, and uncommunicated talk among doomed men" (vii). Why does Melville load his maritime saga with persistent evocations of the Gothic tradition, such as likening the slaves on board to Black Friars pacing a gloomy cloister and the "castellated forecastle" to an ancient turret in decay? A simple answer would be that he strategically pressed into service atmospheric details from his reading of Walpole, Beckford, and Radcliffe to help create the nightmare world of the slave ship, the *San Dominick*. But Melville also found in the Gothic something more fundamental to his artistic vision. The first English Gothics provided him with a world of sharp moral contrasts, pitting innocent and vulnerable heroes and heroines against an expansive, yet usually intelligible and confinable evil. While many later writers in the tradition, Melville among them, have been credited with a psychological complication of this sharp Gothic divide between good and evil, he above all offers a profound moral complication of the metaphysical world of the Gothic.

Melville's striking Promethean figures share the most obvious affinity with Gothic literature in the way their devouring egotism and monomania very closely resemble those of that famous Gothic type, the villain-hero. The imaginative allure of these characters has always stemmed from their daring challenge to traditional ethical and Christian teachings. Ahab, of course, stands at the head of the list, as much a pure incarnation of the fearsome will as a trenchant criticism of it. He is a man willing to doom his crew to his fixation, his alleged desire to triumph over what he deems elemental evil, while Melville never lets us forget that Ahab fails to understand the vindictive evil within his own heart. In his mix of sublime thunderings, petty bullying, troubling omnipotence, and superstitious reclusiveness, Ahab could very well stand as the most spectacular and memorable distillation of the Gothic villain-hero, a Promethean to outdo Victor Frankenstein or any of the many prototypes that preceded him. Even more Frankensteinian is the Renaissance overreacher Bannadonna in "The Bell Tower," who not only constructs and secretively occupies a 300-foot-high bell tower as a testimony to his artistic egotism but attempts to usurp the role of God in his creation of an animated "locomotive figure for the belfry" (202). Preoccupied with some last-minute revisions on the bell's engravings before its grand opening, Bannadonna is crushed to death by the weird automaton, and the moral seems quite clear: retribution awaits the ultrahumanist who would make "man the true God" (203). A startlingly swift retribution also meets Melville's last incarnation of the Gothic villain, the Cain-like Claggart of *Billy Budd*, "in whom was the mania of an evil nature . . . born with him and innate, in short, a 'depravity according to nature' " (30). Claggart's obsessive desire to destroy Billy and Billy's accidental killing of him have invited all kinds of critical interpretation, including chiasmic readings in which their roles as good and evil are reversed, but considered in terms of the Gothic tradition, there appears something fundamental in their confrontation: a final unmasking of the terrible allure innocence holds for evil, the fatal attraction that fuels countless Gothic plots.

Herein lies the true irony of Melville's achievement when it is considered in the context of the Gothic tradition. Although he has left us some of literature's most superbly depraved souls in characters who share the most obvious affinities with any number of Gothic villains, the true complexity of his moral and artistic achievement concerns his intricate re-creation of the opposing Gothic stereotype: the innocent. In the usual and especially in Radcliffean Gothic plotting, imperiled innocents invite the reader's identification and moral sympathy as we read on to see if their essential and durable goodness can withstand the intricate and often-spooky persecutions to which they are subjected by the powers of evil. But Melville constantly tests the limits and nature of the reader's sympathetic identification with and understanding of innocence. In "The Lightning-Rod Man," we perhaps witness his and our desired outcome for any confrontation between good and evil as the narrator, with his powerful faith in Providence, sees through the confidence man and his satanic huckstering and throws him out of his house. So too it appears with the "generous" and "benevolent" Captain Delano of "Benito Cereno," who walks into and out of hell unscathed, with no more protection than his astonishingly obtuse faith in the good nature of all men. Yet although Delano is able to rescue Benito Cereno from the horrors of the slave ship, he cannot understand "what has cast such a shadow" (34) over the Spaniard. The "triumph" of the American's innocence is reassuring in terms of the traditional moral formula governing Gothic closure, but surely Melville also suggests that his innocence is a kind of blindness that prevents him from understanding the tragic dimensions of life. Yet possessing moral sympathy for suffering, like the kind the lawyer arguably possesses for Bartleby in "Bartleby the Scrivener," may not solve the enigma of human tragedy. When the enigma of Billy Budd's case is presented to Captain Vere, we become aware that no verdict, no judgment is adequate to the moral dilemma facing both him and the reader. Does Billy die a Christ-like death as a vindication of his innocence against a world of shadowy equivocations and cross-choices? Or does his death indicate the triumph of those dark forces over the good? To what degree can we say that Billy is good and Claggart merely evil when the innocent has killed and the villain dies a victim? Melville takes the central Gothic confrontation of good versus evil and provides a powerful tragic complication of its moral understanding. It is as if the Gothic innocent has emerged from the chamber of horrors only to enter a more bewildering one of moral ambiguities and insoluble cross-purposes.

These are exactly what afflict Pierre Glendinning in the novel subtitled *The Ambiguities*, the book that has proven the enigma of Melville's career. Written during a period of increasing financial difficulties and thus "very much more calculated for popularity than anything" (qtd. in Hayford vol. 10, 367) he had written before, *Pierre* immediately met universally hostile reviews and proved to put Melville in debt to his publisher. Part of Melville's unsuccessful plan to reach a wider audience, especially a female audience, was his determination to write "a regular romance, with a mysterious plot to it, & stirring passions" (qtd. in Hayford 367), an aim recognized but blasted by one of its first reviewers, who classed it among "some of the ancient and most repulsive inventions of the Ann Radcliffe sort—desperate passion at first sight, for a young woman who turns out to be the hero's sister, &c., &c., &c" (qtd. in Hayford 380). But surely *Pierre* would also prove a gigantic disappointment to readers who expected to be entertained by a species of Radcliffean romance. For *Pierre* is in many ways a Gothic novel that has gone metaphysically mad. In the figure of the suicidal Pierre, a man who can do no right because he tries to live as if he could do no wrong, Melville complicates and finally exhausts and deconstructs the figure of the innocent. In order to do what is right by his half sister Isabel, the impossibly gentle and docile and idealistic Pierre abandons his inheritance, deserts a disturbingly doting mother, breaks the heart of his true love Lucy Tartan, and reduces himself to urban poverty, misanthropic fits, imprisonment, and finally suicide by "marrying" Isabel. The scare quotations are apt here, because although Pierre considers the marriage not a real one but instead just an expression of duty to his half sister, hints of incest, that favorite Gothic taboo, abound, not only with Isabel but with his mother. This book tests the limits of not just Gothic fiction but fiction itself; it is at once a romance and an antiromance, another of Melville's tragic evocations of innocence and a disturbingly sardonic view, to quote a distressed contemporary reviewer of the novel, of Melville's picture of "the impracticability of virtue" (qtd. in Hayford 390); a moral complication of the Gothic-sentimental plot read as immoral by the reviewers, yet richly suggestive in the moral issues it raises without ever resolving them. In much of his fiction that shares affinities with the Gothic vision, but nowhere more so than with *Pierre*, Melville took the genre to its illogical conclusion in ways that no other writer has been willing or able to do.

SELECTED CRITICISM

Arvin, Newton. "Melville and the Gothic Novel." *New England Quarterly* 22 (1949): 33–48. Although Arvin considers the presence of the Gothic in Melville's writings a "slight thing," he makes a good case that both his dark metaphysical landscapes and his towering egotists achieve some measure of meaning from the tradition.

Boudreau, Gordon V. "Of Pale Ushers and Gothic Piles: Melville's Architectural Symbology." *ESQ: A Journal of the American Renaissance* 67 (1972): 67–82. Valuably documents Melville's extensive reading in Gothic fiction and suggests a number of influences on his work from that tradition, especially in terms of architectural metaphors and some key archetypes.

Fisher, Benjamin F., IV. "Gothic Possibilities in *Moby-Dick*." In *Gothic Origins and*

Innovations. Ed. Allan Lloyd Smith and Victor Sage. Costerus New Series 91. Amsterdam and Atlanta, GA: Rodopi, 1994: 115–122. "Melville surpasses many of his predecessors in Gothicism by presenting us with what amount to two 'haunted castles,' the Pequod and the sea."

Goldner, Ellen J. "Other(ed) Ghosts: Gothicism and the Bonds of Reason in Melville, Chesnutt, and Morrison." *MELUS* 24:1 (1999): 59–83. The Gothic representations of slavery in Herman Melville's "Benito Cereno" expose the complicity between a Western scientific worldview and slavery. The Gothic elements reveal the distorted way in which the rational discourse views the world, indicating the failures of Western empiricism.

Kosok, Heinz. *Die Bedeutung der Gothic Novel für das Erzählwerk Herman Melvilles* [The Significance of the Gothic Novel for the Narratives of Hermann Melville]. Hamburg: Cram, De Gruyter, 1963. Still the only book-length study of Gothic elements in Melville's writing. Treats ships such as the *Pequod* and the *San Dominick* as floating haunted castles.

Lackey, Kris. " 'More Spiritual Terrors': The Bible and Gothic Imagination in *Moby-Dick*." *South Atlantic Review* 52:2 (1987): 37–50. Examines the interplay between "the popular texts of Gothic romance and holy writ" in the novel as providing a context for its depiction of deep-seated "spiritual fears."

MacPherson, Jay. "Waiting for Shiloh: Transgression and Fall in Melville's 'The Bell-Tower.' " In *Gothic Fictions: Prohibition/Transgression*. Ed. Kenneth W. Graham. New York: AMS Press, 1989: 245–258. Emphasizes a number of Gothic intertexts for Bannadonna, among these the figure of Victor Frankenstein; both are paradigmatic overreachers.

Magistrale, Tony. " 'More Demon than Man': Melville's Ahab as Gothic Villain." In *Spectrum of the Fantastic*. Ed. Donald Palombo. Westport, CT: Greenwood Press, 1988: 81–86. Likens Ahab to the villains and villain-heroes of Walpole, Lewis, Radcliffe, and Maturin. Important in showing how the Gothic supplied Melville with a vehicle to develop his tragic and pessimistic perspectives.

Miles, Robert. " 'Tranced Griefs': Melville's *Pierre* and the Origins of the Gothic." *ELH* 66 (1999): 157–177. Relates the Gothicism of *Pierre* to Melville's classic Gothic sources.

Ryan, Steven T. "The Gothic Formula of 'Bartleby.' " *Arizona Quarterly* 34 (1978): 311–316. Notes Gothic details in Melville's story, most intriguingly the idea of premature burial in Bartleby's spiritual resignation.

Shetty, Nalini V. "Melville's Use of the Gothic Tradition." In *Studies in American Literature: Essays in Honour of William Mulder*. Delhi: Oxford University Press, 1976: 144–53. Explores how Gothic material in the major stories enables Melville to probe the enigma of good versus evil.

Trimpi, Helen P. "Conventions of Romance in *Moby-Dick*." *Southern Review* (Louisiana State University) 7 (1971): 115–129. Studies sources in demon lore, among them the English Gothic, used by Melville in his Faustian tale of Ahab's transgressions.

TONI MORRISON
(1931–   )
David Dudley

PRINCIPAL GOTHIC WORKS

Beloved. New York: Plume, 1987.

With the publication of her novel *Beloved* in 1987, Toni Morrison solidified her position as the preeminent African-American writer of her time. The book received the Pulitzer Prize and quickly became Morrison's most discussed novel, generating a vast number of scholarly articles, finding its way onto the reading list in hundreds of college courses, and helping its creator win the Nobel Prize for Literature in 1993. This widely acclaimed work by the writer whom critic Houston Baker hails as the greatest African-American novelist also happens to be a textbook example of literary Gothic. *Beloved* is filled with the trappings of the Gothic, including an angry, poltergeist-like ghost who shatters mirrors, overturns cook pots, and moves furniture, as well as the later physical manifestation of that same spirit in the girl Beloved, characterized by critics as both succubus and vampire. The novel, however, qualifies as Gothic even more for its themes than for its haunted house and grisly secrets from a past too terrible to remember or discuss. If, as critic Mark Edmundson asserts, it is true that "Gothic shows the dark side, the world of cruelty, lust, perversion, and crime that . . . is hidden beneath established conventions" and "tears through censorship, explodes hypocrisies, to expose the world as the corrupted, reeking place it is" (4), then *Beloved* embodies the Gothic agenda.

Just as the earliest European Gothic reacts to the Enlightenment by darkly illuminating those places in the human heart that rationalism tries to ignore, American Gothic appropriately finds its truest subject in slavery, the "peculiar institution" that exposes the gulf between the ideals upon which the nation was founded and the realities of its history. As a matter of fact, *Beloved* was inspired by an episode in American slavery as Gothic in nature as anyone could imagine: in January 1856, Margaret Garner, a slave, escaped Kentucky to freedom by crossing the icebound Ohio River. But along with several family members, she was apprehended in Cincinnati. Rather than see her children returned to slavery, Garner determined to kill them. She succeeded in cutting the throat of her older daughter but was prevented from slaughtering her other children. Margaret Garner's case became a national cause célèbre, but the outcry did not win the slave mother's freedom. She was sold south and died of typhoid fever on a Louisiana cotton plantation in 1858. The Garner tragedy continued to surface in the debate over slavery during and after the Civil War, but after one final, vague mention in Frances E.W. Harper's novel *Iola Leroy* in 1892, the event disappeared from the American consciousness, to resurface only in the 1980s with the publication of *Beloved* (Weisenburger 286). Thus Morrison's Gothic novel—extensively reviewed, almost universally praised, popularized by Oprah Winfrey on her television talk show, and finally made into a "major motion picture" starring Winfrey herself—has done the work Gothic is said to do: resurrect those suppressed elements of human and national experience that we would like to forget. *Beloved* not only calls attention in a general way to certain forgotten aspects of slavery, such as the breaking of the bonds uniting mothers and daughters and the terrors of the Middle Passage; it also brings to light once again the specific case of Margaret Garner, whose story is now recorded in *Modern Medea* (1998), the first and only book-length account of the woman's infanticide. As the study's author, Steven Weisenburger, acknowledges, reading *Beloved* piqued his interest in the Garner case and resulted, after nearly ten years of research, in the publication of his book.

Critics have recently begun acknowledging the strong ties between Gothic and African-American literature. Louis S. Gross observes in *Redefining the American Gothic* that African-American authors have often felt compelled to write in forms "acceptable within culturally determined norms of literariness" (65)—forms that did not usually include the Gothic. According to Gross, these "safe," accepted forms, while perhaps promoting access to the white-controlled publishing industry, "could restrict authentic minority discourse, a view of American society that confronts life as based on fear and repression" (65). The Gothic, however, is well suited to such discourse and, despite its pitfalls, has been used by black writers from the time of slave narrators such as Frederick Douglass and Harriet Jacobs.

In *Gothic America,* Teresa Goddu begins her chapter on the Gothic and African-American history and literature by reminding us what Richard Wright asserted in his preface to *Native Son* more than fifty years ago: the African-American experience provides us with so many real horrors that America needed no Hawthorne or Poe to invent any new ones; furthermore, the black experience in this country reads like a Gothic tale (131). Goddu argues, however, that the Gothic tends to be "exempt from the forces of history" (132). (Mark Edmundson and other recent critics would argue that this is decidedly not true of American Gothic, which, they assert, is inextricably tied to the nation's history.) Goddu insists that the Gothic threatens to "dematerialize and displace the source of its effect even while representing it" (134). Thus African-American writers who use Gothic characters, settings, and situations may, even when taking as their subject matter actual events from history (as slave narratives do), inadvertently achieve an unintended result: these conventions could distance their readers from the dreadful reality of slavery rather than engaging them and moving them to action. The first readers of slave narratives would have been familiar with Gothic conventions and might have been impressed, even unconsciously, more by the narratives' recognizably fictive elements than by their claims of strict truthfulness. Additionally, if the writer were to overdo the descriptions of slavery's horrors, the emphasis might end up on the reader's shocked emotions and not on the plight of the slaves themselves. Should that happen, the sensitive reader, tormented by what he or she had read, would ironically become "the tortured victim of the slavery system" (Goddu 135).

Goddu analyzes a scene from Frederick Douglass's *Narrative* to demonstrate how Douglass skillfully skirts these dangers and turns the Gothic scene of his Aunt Hester's brutal whipping into a description that serves his own purpose, which is to use "the gothic's narrative power to represent slavery and to create a strong effect while insisting on the difference between event and effect" (139). He is equally successful in describing the death of a slave fleeing a whipping. Demby goes into a creek and refuses to come out despite the overseer's repeated demands. The overseer, Austin Gore (note the singularly appropriate last name), then shoots Demby in the head, spilling his brains, and the body sinks beneath the water. "A thrill of horror flashed through every soul upon the plantation" (52), writes Douglass in true Gothic style. Gore alone shows no feeling, and he suffers no punishment for murdering an "unmanageable" slave. To return the reader's attention away from the killing itself and the emotions associated with it, Douglass ends his account of Demby's death by noting that for all he knows, Gore is still alive and "as highly esteemed and as much respected as though his guilty soul had not been stained with his brother's blood" (52). The reader is led from the horror of the crime itself and is invited to reflect upon the ongoing injustices of the slave system.

The dangers and opportunities the Gothic presented to Frederick Douglass, Harriet Jacobs, and others still confront African-American writers today. They recognize the genre's "typical association with the 'unreal' and the sensational" (Goddu 139), which threatens to undermine their determination, even in their fiction, to write about the realities of African-American life and history. Alice Walker dislikes the Gothic label being applied to her work because she "feels what she writes has 'something to do with real life' " (Goddu 140). But her distaste for the genre has not prevented Walker from writing one full-fledged Gothic novel, *Possessing the Secret of Joy*. The book centers on the unlikely subject of female circumcision, treating it as a long-suppressed horror of African women's lives, a "secret" Walker sets out to expose and combat. Walker even produced a nonfiction film on the subject and stipulated that part of the proceeds from the sale of *Possessing the Secret of Joy* go toward programs to inform and alert the public about the practice.

Toni Morrison also dislikes the association of her novels with the Gothic (Goddu 140), but she uses the genre superbly in *Beloved*, her only novel to date dealing specifically with slavery, American Gothic's ideal subject. Despite her disavowal, Morrison must feel some attraction toward the Gothic, for she has stated that she began writing so that she could read the kind of novels she wanted to read. An even deeper necessity, apparently, compelled the writing of *Beloved*. Morrison expresses it this way:

There is no place you or I can go, to think about or not think about, to summon the presences of, or recollect the absences of slaves; nothing that reminds us of the ones who made the journey and of those who did not make it. There is no suitable memorial or plaque or wreath or wall or park or skyscraper lobby. There's no 300 foot tower. There's no small bench by the road. There is not even a tree scored, an initial that I can visit or you can visit in Charleston or Savannah or New York or Providence or, better still, on the banks of the Mississippi. And because such a place does not exist (that I know of), the book had to. (Andrews and McKay 3)

The book, Morrison asserts, had to exist. But when a novelist comes to feel that she must confront slavery, how does she proceed? Where does she begin, and what aspect of that vast and terrible subject does she choose for her story? As early as 1974, Morrison was acquainted with the Margaret Garner case, having learned of it through her work on *The Black Book*, a collection of source materials about black life (Matus 15). But Morrison has insisted that the Garner episode, which she did not research extensively, gave her only the "seed" for *Beloved* (Weisenburger 10). Why Morrison did not choose to write a novel using the characters and specifics of the actual historical events is perhaps easily explained: she simply did not feel inspired to move in that direction. One thing is certain: because Morrison did not write a historical novel, she avoided the criticism sometimes aimed at authors whose interpretations of events and characterizations of actual people do not square with the views of historians and critics. William Styron learned this truth well when *The Confessions of Nat Turner*, his decidedly Gothic novel (replete with apocalyptic visions, portents, and mass slaughter), was greeted with an outraged response from critics, most of them black, who felt that he had grossly misrepresented the character and motives of the book's protagonist.

No such criticism of *Beloved* has been forthcoming. Indeed, with one notable exception, Stanley Crouch's review "Aunt Medea" (Solomon 64–71), praise for the novel has been wide and lavish. Critics have noted from the first that the novel is full of Gothic elements. Wesley Britton, for example, traces the similarities between *Beloved* and Hawthorne's *House of the Seven Gables*. Besides sharing Gothic elements such as spooky houses and their "haunted" inhabitants, both novels deal with pervasive Gothic themes such as guilt, the hold of the past on the present, human pride, and expiation for old family sins. Britton suggests that Morrison borrows from the white Gothic tradition to remind us that its traditional preoccupations apply to African-American history as well and that we have a "cultural responsibility to remember a shared past too significant to be forgotten" (11).

The dominant Gothic element in *Beloved* is the ghost-girl of its title. Most critics agree that Beloved actually is the incarnated ghost of the child Sethe killed out of loving determination to protect her from a life of slavery. Deborah Horvitz expands this view by asserting that Beloved is also the ghost of Sethe's mother and thus the tangible reminder of how slavery tore apart generations of mothers and daughters (94). Pamela Barnett sees in the girl Beloved both succubus and vampire; like a succubus, she seduces Paul D, draining him of his masculine life force and reducing him to a powerless, drunken drifter. Like a vampire, the insatiable Beloved feeds on Sethe, demanding the love she believed her mother denied her when she cut her throat. By emphasizing the sexual nature of Beloved's predations, Barnett calls attention to how the novel exposes a truth about the place of rape within a racist society. Rather than being limited to an assault by men upon women, rape, as treated in *Beloved* (which also describes how the white prison guards perpetrated homosexual rape upon Paul D and the other victims of the black chain gang), becomes a locus for "a discourse for the rape of black women and men that has been largely absent in twentieth-century America" (84). Thus Morrison's novel uses and refashions Gothic materials to uncover buried truths of the African-American experience.

Gothic compels us to look at a past we wish to forget. Everyone agrees that this same dynamic lies at the heart of *Beloved*. Toni Morrison says, "There is a necessity for remembering the horror, but of course there's a necessity for remembering it in a manner in which it can be digested, in a manner in which the memory is not destructive. The act of writing the book, in a way, is a way of confronting it and making it possible to remember" (Plasa 33). Morrison's character Sethe has tried for years to suppress the memory of how she killed her own daughter, but because she has not dealt with her own past in a way that makes it possible for her to live productively in the present, Sethe is literally haunted and nearly loses Paul D, the man who can love her; Denver, her one remaining child; and, indeed, her own life. According to *Beloved*, the past must be remembered and acknowledged, but not permitted to destroy the present. The end of the novel suggests that this can be achieved, if only precariously. Beloved is exorcised by the gathering of women who rally around Sethe and accept her back into the community. Paul D returns, and Denver ventures successfully into the world. But although Beloved disappears, evidence of her presence remains; the novel, which has told Beloved's story in detail, paradoxically asserts that "this is not a story to pass on" (275). Thus Morrison expresses the dilemma: the past is so painful that we naturally avoid it, but the past threatens to over-whelm the present if we do not approach it correctly. Even when we do face the past, there are no guarantees that the confrontation will be successful. Beloved disappears, but her footprints "come and go," as if the insatiable spirit of the past is only waiting to reassert its claim on those who, like Sethe, Paul D, and Denver, want a present and future for themselves.

Two critics have directly addressed *Beloved* as the Gothic novel it is. Interestingly, they agree on its agenda. Comparing it to Harriet Jacobs's *Incidents in the Life of a Slave Girl*, Teresa Goddu asserts that *Beloved* "insists on speaking the unspeakable" (154). She continues, "For Morrison as for Jacobs, the gothic serves as a mode of resistance. By writing their own gothic tales, these authors combat the master's version of their history; by breaking the silence, they reclaim their history instead of being controlled by it" (155). In *Nightmare on Main Street*, Mark Edmundson writes that *Beloved* shifts the blame for slavery from the black slaves themselves onto the white masters, where blame belongs, and so rewrites the distorted view of history proffered by the dominant social group. Just as the Germans have had to face the Nazi Holocaust, so now must white America face its past: "It's the white community, authors of the Holocaust, that's now to be haunted. This book, a work of genius, seeks to effect a transference; from black to white, the guilt of slavery must go" (176). Both Goddu and Edmundson acknowledge the limitations of Morrison's Gothic view. Goddu reiterates what we have already noted: the past can be only partly reclaimed, and the past, once remembered, "may refuse to be exorcized and subsume both the present and the future" (155). The novel suggests that the black community is the solution for African Americans dealing with their past, but offers no suggestions for healing the racial divide. Edmundson notes that the black community in *Beloved* begins to heal when Sethe strikes out at the white man she believes has come to take Beloved away (176). Fighting back against whites brings the possibility of healing to blacks, but, asserts Edmundson, the novel ultimately "reaffirms the division of the races" (177). The Gothic vision, it seems, is better at exposing the dark secrets of individuals and nations than it is at promoting an agenda for healing the wounds that come with either repressing or remembering the past. But given the great critical and popular success of *Beloved*, one must agree that Morrison's Gothic novel has encouraged America's painful but necessary discourse on race, even if it has not, or cannot, heal the hurts and solve the problems.

SELECTED CRITICISM

Andrews, William L., and Nellie Y. McKay. *Toni Morrison's Beloved: A Casebook.* New York: Oxford University Press, 1999. Includes nine critical essays and a discussion of Morrison's work by three prominent critics of African-American literature.

Barnett, Pamela. "Figurations of Rape and the Supernatural in *Beloved*." In *Toni Morrison: Beloved.* Ed. Carl Plasa. New York: Columbia University Press, 1998: 73–85. Treats the character Beloved as both succubus and vampire who highlights the novel's theme of the sexual violation of both black women and men by an oppressive white, racist society. One of the strongest critical treatments of Beloved as a demonic figure.

Britton, Wesley. "The Puritan Past and Black Gothic: The Haunting of Toni Morrison's *Beloved* in Light of Hawthorne's *The House of the Seven Gables*." *Nathaniel Hawthorne Review* 21:2 (1995): 7–23. Notes many similarities between the two novels and suggests that Morrison consciously uses elements of the Gothic to show how its themes of the power of the past, guilt, and expiation apply to black Americans as well as whites, and that the white and black literary traditions share much in common.

Douglass, Frederick. *Narrative of the Life of Frederick Douglass, an American Slave.* Ed. David W. Blight. Boston: Bedford Books of St. Martin's Press, 1993.

Edmundson, Mark. *Nightmare on Main Street: Angels, Sadomasochism, and the Culture of Gothic.* Cambridge, MA: Harvard University Press, 1997. Discusses the pervasive presence of Gothic in American culture at the end of the twentieth century. Briefly treats *Beloved* as a Gothic text intent on making America face the holocaust of slavery and removing the guilt of slavery from blacks and placing it on its white perpetrators.

Goddu, Teresa. *Gothic America: Narrative, History, and Nation.* New York: Columbia University Press, 1997. Devotes a full chapter to the connection between Gothic and African-American literature, highlighting works of Frederick Douglass and Harriet Jacobs. In her concluding chapter, Goddu briefly discusses *Beloved*, noting how it reclaims the truth of African-American history from distortion by the dominant white society, but remarks that the novel does not offer a solution to the ongoing racial divide in America.

Gross, Louis S. *Redefining the American Gothic: From Wieland to Day of the Dead.* Ann Arbor: UMI Research Press, 1989. In the chapter "Unseen Objects, Observed Subjects," Gross discusses African-American literature and the Gothic. He offers detailed readings of two works, Pauline Hopkins's novel *Of One Blood; or, The Hidden Self* and Amiri Baraka's *System of Dante's Hell.*

Harris, Trudier. "*Beloved*: Woman, Thy Name Is Demon." In *Toni Morrison's Beloved: A Casebook.* Ed. William L. Andrews and Nellie Y. McKay. New York: Oxford University Press, 1999: 127–157. Examines the character of Beloved within the scope of Morrison's novels, which, according to Harris, progressively treat women and the female body as "other"—dangerous, evil, even demonic.

Horvitz, Deborah. "Nameless Ghosts: Possession and Dispossession in *Beloved*." In *Critical Essays on Toni Morrison's Beloved.* Ed. Barbara Solomon. New York: G.K. Hall, 1998: 93–103. One of the first and most persuasive essays on the novel to argue that the girl Beloved is definitely a ghost, but not only the ghost of Sethe's killed daughter but also of her own mother, and by extension, of many mothers and daughters torn from each other by slavery.

House, Elizabeth B. "Toni Morrison's Ghost: The Beloved Who Is Not Beloved." In *Critical Essays on Toni Morrison's Beloved.* Ed. Barbara Solomon. New York: G.K. Hall, 1998: 117–126. House stands nearly alone among critics in arguing (unconvincingly, I believe) that the girl Beloved is simply a flesh-and-blood young woman who has found her way to Sethe's house and mistakenly believes that Sethe is her mother, just as Sethe comes to believe that the girl is the ghost of her daughter. Worth reading for House's careful attention to some difficult passages in the novel.

Krumholz, Linda. "The Ghosts of Slavery: Historical Recovery in Toni Morrison's *Be-loved*." In *Toni Morrison's Beloved: A Casebook*. Ed. William L. Andrews and Nellie Y. McKay. New York: Oxford University Press, 1999: 107–125. Krumholz highlights the novel's emphasis on the importance of African Americans' recla-mation of their history and its use in a process of healing. Although the chapter does not specifically discuss *Beloved* as Gothic, it does highlight the Gothic theme of remembering and facing the past in order to effect healing.

Matus, Jill. *Toni Morrison*. Manchester: Manchester University Press, 1998. Useful, brief introduction to Morrison's work within cultural and historical contexts, with dis-cussion of all the novels through *Paradise*.

Morrison, Toni. *Playing in the Dark: Whiteness and the Literary Imagination*. New York: Vintage Books, 1993. Critical essays frequently relevant to the American Gothic.

Plasa, Carl, ed. *Toni Morrison: Beloved*. New York: Columbia University Press, 1998. Extremely useful collection of essays on the novel with excellent introductions. The essays are very well chosen to highlight varying critical perspectives.

Solomon, Barbara H., ed. *Critical Essays on Toni Morrison's Beloved*. New York: G.K. Hall, 1998. Collects reviews and essays on the novel and includes four new essays written for this collection. Includes some of the most highly regarded essays on *Beloved*.

Weisenburger, Steven. *Modern Medea*. New York: Hill and Wang, 1998. Excellent his-torical account of the Margaret Garner case, which was the inspiration for Mor-rison's *Beloved*. Weisenburger's research reveals much about the characters, black and white, who had a part in the Garner tragedy and recounts how the case figured into American life and thought in the second half of the nineteenth century.

JOYCE CAROL OATES
(1938–   )
Susan Allen Ford

PRINCIPAL GOTHIC WORKS

Expensive People. New York: Vanguard, 1968; Princeton: Ontario Review Press, 1990.

them. New York: Vanguard, 1969; Fawcett, 1996; Random House [Modern Library], 2000.

The Wheel of Love and Other Stories. New York: Vanguard, 1970. (Significant Gothic dimensions in "Where Are You Going, Where Have You Been?" "Unmailed, Unwritten Letters," "Accomplished Desires," "How I Contemplated the World from the Detroit House of Correction and Began My Life Over Again," "Demons," "Bodies," "The Assailant," "The Heavy Sorrow of the Body," "Matter and Energy," and "What Is the Connection between Men and Women?")

Wonderland. New York: Vanguard, 1971; Greenwich, CT: Fawcett, 1971; Princeton: Ontario Review Press, 1992. (Oates changed the ending after the book's publication by Vanguard.)

Marriages and Infidelities: Short Stories. New York: Vanguard, 1972.

Do with Me What You Will. New York: Vanguard, 1973.

The Goddess and Other Women. New York: Vanguard, 1974. (Story collection.)

Where are You Going, Where Have You Been? Stories of Young America. Greenwich, CT: Fawcett, 1974.

The Assassins: A Book of Hours. New York: Vanguard, 1975.

The Poisoned Kiss and Other Stories from the Portuguese. "Translations" from Fernandes by Joyce Carol Oates. New York: Vanguard, 1975.

The Seduction and Other Stories. Los Angeles: Black Sparrow, 1975.

Childwold. New York: Vanguard, 1976.

The Triumph of the Spider Monkey. Santa Barbara, CA: Black Sparrow, 1976.

Night-Side: Eighteen Tales. New York: Vanguard, 1977.

A Sentimental Education: Stories. Los Angeles: Sylvester & Orphanos, 1978; New York: Dutton, 1980. (Includes "Queen of the Night," "The Precipice," "The Tryst," "A Middle-Class Education," "In the Autumn of the Year," and "A Sentimental Education.")

Son of the Morning. New York: Vanguard, 1978.

All the Good People I've Left Behind. Santa Barbara, CA: Black Sparrow; 1979.

Bellefleur. New York: Dutton, 1980.
A Bloodsmoor Romance. New York: Dutton, 1982.
Last Days. New York: Dutton, 1984. (Story Collection.)
Mysteries of Winterthurn. New York: Dutton, 1984.
Raven's Wing. New York: Dutton, 1986.
Lives of the Twins. New York: Simon and Schuster, 1987. (As Rosamond Smith.)
The Assignation. New York: Ecco, 1988.
American Appetites. New York: Dutton, 1989.
Soul/Mate. New York: Dutton, 1989. (As Rosamond Smith.)
Nemesis. New York: Dutton, 1990. (As Rosamond Smith.)
Oates in Exile. Toronto: Exile, 1990.
Heat and Other Stories. New York: Dutton, 1991.
The Rise of Life on Earth. New York: New Directions, 1991.
Black Water. New York: Dutton, 1992.
Snake Eyes. New York: Dutton, 1992. (As Rosamond Smith.)
Where Is Here? Hopewell, NJ: Ecco, 1992.
Where Are You Going, Where Have You Been? Selected Early Stories. Princeton: Ontario
    Review Press, 1993.
Haunted: Tales of the Grotesque. New York: Dutton, 1994.
You Can't Catch Me. New York: Dutton, 1995. (As Rosamond Smith.)
Zombie. New York: Dutton, 1995.
Demon and Other Tales. West Warwick, RI: Necronomicon, 1996.
First Love: A Gothic Tale. Hopewell, NJ: Ecco, 1996.
Will You Always Love Me? and Other Stories. New York: Dutton, 1996.
Double Delight. New York: Dutton, 1997. (As Rosamond Smith.)
Man Crazy. New York: Dutton, 1997.
The Collector of Hearts: New Tales of the Grotesque. New York: Dutton, 1998.
My Heart Laid Bare. New York: Dutton, 1998.
Starr Bright Will Be with You Soon. New York: Dutton, 1999. (As Rosamond Smith.)
Blonde. New York: Echo Press, 1999.

Since the early 1960s, Joyce Carol Oates has published in a variety of genres: at this writing, forty novels or novellas (including seven under the pseudonym Rosamond Smith), twenty-five collections of short stories, eight books of poetry, five collections of plays, and nine works of nonfiction, as well as introductions to thirteen anthologies and a variety of as-yet-uncollected work. Much of this work, particularly her fiction, has been Gothic in nature, and even more, though apparently realistic, has provided glimpses of Gothic worlds as she explores the claustral structures of the self and of America. Like the books that the troubled and dangerous Bruno Sokolov describes to the narrator of "Hostage," Oates's fiction is "[s]tuff that scares you into thinking" (*Heat* 289). Oates charts the terrors of the self under threat from a dehumanizing and disintegrating world. Her work constitutes a history of the shaping of the American self, imprisoned by its geographies both external and internal as well as by the structures that should provide sustenance or challenge to these restrictions.

Oates's nonfiction writing on the Gothic provides a way into her obsessive renderings. In "Wonderlands," she defines the appeal of the Gothic as the temptation of the interior abyss (89): " 'wonderful regions'—ruined castles, accursed houses, the poisoned garden of a Rappaccini—are dimensions of the psyche given a luridly tangible form, in which unacknowledged (or rigorously suppressed) wishes are granted freedom" (89). As she argues in *Haunted*, "We [inhabit] the material . . . we can see no way out except to go forward" (307). Although Oates returns frequently to the notion that *we* are *they*, made "active accomplices" by evil (306), she locates the essential mystery of the Gothic not in identity but in separation: "Though we each exist subjectively, and know the world only through the prism of self, this 'subjectivity' is inaccessible, thus unreal, and mysterious to others" (304).

The Gothic's "kinship with the religious imagination," then, stems from this desire for "meld[ing] the sacred and profane" (Introduction to *American Gothic Tales* 7), the physical and the spiritual, self and other. Responding to the terrors of these estrangements and the correlative vastness of the American landscape, the American Gothic writer is engaged in an "obsessive" struggle to define self and world. For Oates, the American Gothic is a record of the depiction of "assaults upon individual autonomy and identity" (3). What Oates says of Kafka is true also of her own fiction: "Only the imagery of Kafka's surfaces is dreamlike; what lies beneath is history" ("Wonderlands" 105).

Oates charts American history by exploring five Gothic geographies: the mythical Eden County, New York (often compared to Faulkner's Yoknapatawpha); Detroit, the monstrous and entangling city; the sterile suburban-intellectual worlds of the upper-middle-class northeastern corridor; and the microcosms of home and body. Eden County, a transformed version of the region in upstate New York in which she grew up, is perhaps her most visited territory. Worn and abandoned rural buildings inhabited by ghosts or dead souls bracing themselves against poverty are scattered through Oates's fiction like gravestones: "Always there were stories behind the abandoned houses and always the stories were sad" (*Haunted* 7). The slightly seedy town with water surging under bridges that provide only tenuous support to those crossing them defines stories such as "Why Don't You Come Live With Me It's Time" (*Heat*), in which an adolescent girl makes her way by night to her grandmother's kitchen, or Man Crazy, in which a girl and her mother cross and recross the evocatively named Tintern Falls Bridge, vulnerable to time and memory and men. These images obsessively draw characters and readers alike to the intersection of past and present and to the mysteries of the self.

Oates's use of Detroit places her in the tradition of writers for whom the city is an ambivalent and powerful force. Detroit was her "great subject" between 1963 and 1976, from the gritty and dangerous streets of her National Book Award–winning novel *them* to the sterile suburban world of *Expensive People* and stories like "How I Contemplated the World from the Detroit House of Correction and Began My Life Over Again." It was "[t]he quintessential American city. That fast-beating stubborn heart . . . , a brooding presence, a force, larger and more significant than the sum of its parts" ("Visions of Detroit" 348–349). Oates's fiction explores its dangers and seductions, its racial and class tensions, mapping the disintegrations of community and self assaulted by the fears of urban violence.

The suburban landscape of New Jersey and the Northeast generally is less specifically rendered, perhaps because of its very familiarity. As in stories like "The Knife" or "The Hair" or in *Lives of the Twins*, it is a world characterized by comfortable houses in clearly defined lots; by dinner parties and jobs in which people are paid to think while growing distant from their bodies; by surfaces without history, revealing the mechanisms through which people struggle to control their lives; and by sudden eruptions of violence, which shatter these surfaces just as the glass walls of the McCulloughs' house in *American Appetites* are shattered.

The microcosmic spaces central to the Gothic world are reenvisioned in Oates's fiction as part of a seemingly naturalistic domestic landscape. The house in Oates's fiction, like the castle in the classic Gothic novel, also stands for the female body. For Oates's male characters, the house operates as isolating and entrapping feminine space, which they strive to understand, to define, to control. The power of this image is articulated in *Wonderland*, where the young Jesse Vogel studies a drawing on a lavatory wall:

a woman's body seen from the bottom up, the legs muscular and very long, spread apart, the head at the far end of the body small as a pea, with eyes and eyelashes nevertheless drawn in very carefully so that they look real. Someone has added to the drawing with another, blunter pencil, making the body boxlike, the space between the legs shaded in to a hard black rectangle like a door. The arms have also been changed to walls and even the suggestion of brick added to them. . . . It is a mysterious drawing, two mysterious drawings, one on top of the other like a dream that fades into another dream, a nightmare conquered by another! . . . A house or a barn or a warehouse. It is something you could walk into and lose yourself in, all that empty blackness. (30–31)

For Oates's female characters, the house also figures the body, operating as a space frequently invaded, a labyrinth protecting and obscuring the mysteries of the physical and emotional self. "Haunted" and "The Doll" use houses as portals through which the female protagonists are chastened for their desires, for the selves that would transgress the limits and controls of the rational, public self. In *First Love*, the Reverend's house, "weatherworn and shabby, with a look of anger, resentment" (7), becomes a correlative for the darkness of the knowledge into which the incest plot draws young Josie.

These Gothic geographies allow Oates to chart the terrors of family structure and its assaults on the autonomy of the self. Mother/child relationships are often defined by neglect, by violence, or by an unhealthy desire for identity. The figure of the threatening father is central in much of Oates's fiction: in *Wonderland* and *Zombie* or stories such as "By the River" in *Marriages and Infidelities*, the father is a tyrant who makes his children in his own image, attempting to erase, or kill, those who disappoint him. These forces of parental violence and repression can lead to rebellion. In "Demons," a daughter eliminates her retarded sister, her competitor for parental love, then brings home a man who kills her possessive father and frees her to say "in a voice of wonder" of her mother, "Oh, let her die!" (*The Wheel of Love* 222). Oates's postapocalyptic story "Family" indicates the nightmarish direction of family history: the family unit, isolated from any larger community, becomes a tyrannical structure of replaceable members in which parents kill children and children consume parents. With no memory of individual relationships, only the hierarchical and gendered powers inherent in the roles of mother, father, sister, brother remain in the struggle for survival.

A pervasive theme in Oates's fiction is the construction by the self of a personality—or at least a persona—to control the chaos within. From *them*'s Maureen Wendall to *Blonde*'s Norma Jeane, Oates's protagonists systematically harden themselves to deal with the assaults of the world on their naked selves. Sometimes, as in the case of *Man Crazy*'s Ingrid Boone, that hardening is so deadening that bodily pain, literal bleeding, is the only sign of life. The anxieties of that loss of control empower some of Oates's most compelling fiction. "Naked," the story of a woman attacked by children while hiking and left without clothes or keys, charts the disintegration of all the structures of her civilized self: from professional woman, cheerful mother of stepchildren, liberal in her racial attitudes, she is redefined not as person but as body, at the story's end crouching naked like an animal outside the house, "until such time as it would become known to her why she was waiting" (*Heat* 138).

But freedom from the structures of the self is also alluring, as Oates's biography makes clear. In an essay entitled "Pseudonymous Selves," she speculates that "our instinct for anonymity [may be] as powerful as that for identity; or, more precisely, for an erasure of the primary self in that another (hitherto undiscovered?) self may be released" (385). Indeed, that "perversity, the instinct for freedom and newness in the human psyche" (387), can lead to the charting of new fictional territory. In 1987, Oates produced *Lives of the Twins*, the first of her novels written under the pseudonym "Rosamond Smith." These novels explore, within the conventions of genre fiction, issues of identity through the trope of twins.

Another kind of redefinition is represented by Oates's experimentation with the narratives of other writers, including her revisions of classic Gothic texts. Her exploration of the Gothic spaces of Henry James's fiction reinscribes his structure with her own designs, creating new Gothic spaces. *Marriages and Infidelities* is a collection defined by both Oates's allegiance to and departure from her predecessors. "As a dialogic daughter, Oates herself 'honors' the fathers—James, Joyce, or Chekhov—but asserts her own right to create, her right to claim cultural authority" (Daly, *Lavish* 74). She transforms Poe's "The Man of the Crowd" into "Stalking," in which a teenage girl follows her "Invisible

Adversary" through the mazes of the shopping mall and into her suburban home. "The Turn of the Screw" is a two-column narrative in which the older Henry James observes the young Patrick Quarles II, misunderstanding him and missing the murder he contemplates but finding nonetheless the source of his own story. In *Haunted*, Oates reworks Poe's "Black Cat," which she has defined as "Poe at his most brilliant, presenting a madman's voice with such mounting plausibility that the reader almost—*almost*—identifies with his unmotivated and seemingly unresisted acts of insane violence" (Introduction to *American Gothic Tales* 4). Oates's version, "The White Cat," is reworked as the narrator's desire for possession and absolute power of life and death over both cat and wife. Here, however, the narrator's wife Alissa and the cat Miranda not only are mysteriously identical but overcome the narrator, ironically subduing him to a life of powerless gratitude. Similarly, James's *Turn of the Screw* is revised as "Accursed Inhabitants of the House of Bly," a story of the love of Miss Jessel and Peter Quint for each other as well as for the children Miles and Flora, a triumph of a reconstructed family against the conventional moralities of James's governess and her employer.

But Oates's most complex exploration and reinvention of the Gothic comes in her quartet of experimental novels characterized by their nineteenth-century shapes and themes: *Bellefleur, A Bloodsmoor Romance, Mysteries of Winterthurn*, and *My Heart Laid Bare*. These novels form what Oates has described as "an immense design: America as viewed through the lens of its most popular genres" ("Five Prefaces" 373). Oates explains her fascination with genre, demonstrating why these novels epitomize not only her Gothic vision but her entire fictional project:

[T]he formal discipline of *genre*—that it forces us inevitably to a radical re-visioning of the world and of the craft of fiction—was the reason I found the project so intriguing. To choose idiosyncratic but not distracting "narrators" to recite the histories; to organize the voluminous materials in patterns alien to my customary way of thinking and writing; to "see" the world in terms of heredity and family destiny and the vicissitudes of Time (for all four of the novels are secretly fables of the American family); to explore historically authentic crimes against women, children, and the poor, in the guise of entertainment; to create, and to identify with, heroes and heroines whose existence would be problematic in the clinical, unkind, and one might almost say, flourescent-lit atmosphere of present-day fiction—these factors proved irresistible. (372–373)

Bellefleur is a family saga spread across seven generations of the Bellefleur family and the building and progressive disintegration of its empire and castle. The novel is also "organized" across Germaine Bellefleur's life, from the night of her conception until her fourth birthday, on which her father destroys Bellefleur by crashing a dynamite-filled airplane into it. *Bellefleur*'s rich style is one of its most appealing features. Sentences are capacious but swiftly moving, narratives that are interrupted to limn out past or future narratives, mirroring the complexities of relationships and possible multiple interpretations. Oates's warning in her "Author's Note" to the novel acknowledges that "time twists and coils and is, now, obliterated, and then again powerfully present." Time elapses differently, for example, for the twins Bromwell and Christabel and their younger sister Germaine: Germaine develops slowly and idiosyncratically while Bromwell and Christabel age more quickly; Christabel marries, leaves home, and then elopes with her former tutor before her twin Bromwell is eleven and a half years old. *Bellefleur* is also populated by characters who shift shape, changed into bears, dogs, vampires, or ponds, from one or both genders to another, from dead to living, from good to evil.

Bellefleur's Gothic landscape suggests both mythic resonances and political realities. Bellefleur Manor, designed as English Gothic with Moorish influences for a family descended from French *ancien régime* nobility, is located in a region of New York State bounded by Lake Noir and Mount Blanc. When the original Bellefleur was banished from France for his interest in individual rights, "the past simply ceased to exist. 'We are all Americans now' " (4). But another part of the family history reveals that Louis Bellefleur's intention was to take the three million acres of land he had amassed, secede from the state and the country, and found his own empire to control the waterways and trade with Canada. The family's control of the region—established through power, violence, and marriage—operates as a critique of the aspirations that define nineteenth-century capitalism. While *Bellefleur* exposes the American will to dominate space, time, and the creatures (natural or supernatural) with whom we share them, it is essentially comic in structure. Its critique of America "is in the service of a vision of America that stresses, for all its pessimism, the ultimate freedom of the individual. One by one the Bellefleur children free themselves of their family's curse (or blessing). . . . The castle is destroyed, the Bellefleur children live. Theirs is the privilege of youth; and the 'America' of my imagination despite the incursions of recent decades, is a nation still characterized by youth" ("*Five Prefaces*" 371).

A Bloodsmoor Romance is a romance distorted into Gothic proportions, a parodic version of *Little Women*. The narrator is a Victorian maiden lady, unacquainted with the facts of biology and certain of the absolute truth of Episcopal doctrine. The novel chronicles the fortunes of the five Zinn sisters, daughters of an inventor and his heiress wife, whose lives are changed when the adopted Dierdre is abducted by "an outlaw balloon of sinister black-silken hue, manned by an unidentified pilot" (3–4). The narrator's resistance to the adventures presented in her history (she denies any control over her plight) highlights the restrictions that confine these women no less than the corsets and layers of ruffles they must wear. The eldest daughter, Constance Philippa, flees the Baron von Mainz on their wedding night, leaving her dressmaker's form in her place, a substitution discovered only after consummation. Going out west, she becomes (somehow) a man, returning to rescue from domestic imprisonment the woman she has always loved before lighting out for Alaska, Mexico, or

Argentina. Malvinia, the most beautiful of the sisters and in love with her own performance, runs off to become an actress. She has relationships with men, including Samuel Clemens, but these relationships and her career are ended by the appearance in her of "The Beast" (an excessive desire for alcohol and an active sexuality) when lights are out. Octavia, the narrator's exemplar of Christian ladyhood, conforms to feminine and Christian precepts while accidentally killing her abusive husband by, at his direction, tightening a cord around his neck during sexual intercourse, failing to rescue her demonic child, and ultimately marrying the coachman's-son-turned-congressman, to whom she has always been attracted. Samantha, the brainy one, works for her inventor father but eventually elopes with his assistant, breaking with her father when he accepts a commission from Congress to invent a means of execution (the electric chair); instead, her inventions are domestic, practical. Finally, Dierdre, whose true parentage the novel discovers, spends years as a medium, repressing the physical, until finally she suffers a breakdown and "cannot bring herself to reject" (580) the magnetic and sensual Hassan Agha. All these women, consciously or not, are in search of freedom from the restrictions of socially constructed femininity; all find a measure of that freedom, however restricted.

In chronicling the romance of these little women, Oates simultaneously charts the romance of the United States. Her narrative is peopled with historical figures such as Samuel Clemens and Charles Guiteau (James Garfield's assassin). She establishes a literary context that includes both the mystical aspirations of the transcendentalists and the conformist fictions of conduct-book writers, a conjunction that accounts for the Gothic excesses of her characters. The inventions of John Quincy Zinn seem similarly caught by these forces: from early ideas that delightfully predict both Thomas Edison's discoveries and later twentieth-century technologies, he moves to machines of death, finally inventing the atomic bomb. Indeed, the United States itself is seen as a living invention, characterized by its impulse to break through barriers and to dream up new structures of imprisonment.

Mysteries of Winterthurn is Oates's homage to the nineteenth-century detective novel, a set of three novels featuring the detective Xavier Kilgarvan introduced by an editor with firm opinions about morality and hierarchy. Portrayed at sixteen, twenty-eight, and forty, Xavier is the type of the detective whose belief in empirical evidence and the powers of ratiocination and intuition will lead him to the truth; he might also be, as the editor claims, "the very emblem of our souls, a sort of mortal savior, not only espying but isolating, and conquering Evil; in his triumph is our triumph" (341). Such confidence, however, is misplaced; neither the detective nor the narratives constructed by or around him can solve mysteries or ensure justice. "The Virgin in the Rose-Bower; or, The Tragedy of Glen Mawr Manor," a locked-room mystery, is the story of an infant bitten to death and partially eaten and a mother driven mad. Although Xavier's investigation reveals the crimes of incest, child murder, and revenge of those spirits on the living, this truth is not explainable by recourse to the rational; indeed, it is "too loathsome" (145) even to write down, and the editor himself misses it. "Devil's Half Acre; or, The Mystery of the Cruel Suitor" pits Xavier against Valentine Westergaard, son of the oldest family in Winterthurn, who seduces mill girls with gifts, music, and charm before repeatedly stabbing them. Although Valentine is finally brought to trial (after the Jewish Isaac Rosenwald is lynched by the KKK-like Brethren of Jericho for the crime), he is acquitted when he claims to have been possessed by the spirit of a legendary local religious fanatic and murderer. "The Bloodstained Bridal Gown; or, Xavier Kilgarvan's Last Case" represents Xavier's most troubling venture, an investigation that determinedly overlooks the guilt of Perdita, a possible victim of both incest and spousal abuse, the woman with whom he has been in love since the first case. Xavier not only hounds and kills an innocent man but goes mad himself. Indeed, the real mysteries of Winterthurn seem to ask how human pride and blindness to truth can be so general, how the evils of power and prejudice can inhabit not only the institutions but the souls of almost all in the community.

Mysteries of Winterthurn celebrates the efforts of the detective to create order even while it exposes the limitations of these attempts. These limitations are central to Winterthurn's American identity. At Winterthurn, mysteries are never solved, patterns of crime remain unremarked, and crimes are not recognized as such. Winterthurn is a society complacent in its racism, its anti-Semitism, and its class divisions; its women are either marginalized or victims of violence and abuse. Institutional powers and mob violence work together to enforce the will of the dominant. But although—perhaps because—the mysteries escape solution, the shape of the novel is comic. Free and triumphant, the image of a new beginning, Perdita rides back into the narrative on a bicycle and dressed in bloomers. The marriage of Xavier and Perdita, whether it is a marriage between detective and murderer or a marriage between accomplices, suggests a plot beyond the closures and conventions of genre.

My Heart Laid Bare combines family saga, picaresque structure, and the transforming energies of the Oatesian Gothic. The prologue tells the story of Sarah, an eighteenth-century confidence woman and shape-shifter, whose self seems to be defined by acquisition and winning, whose body seems to be buried in the Muirkirk swamp, and whose spirit seems now to inhabit Abraham Licht, patriarch of a family of tricksters. The novel tracks the fortunes of this family through The Game, a Darwinian strategy of dealing with the world, of dealing with all others. In this novel, Oates's family saga again becomes an American saga. But more than in her other Gothic novels, Oates in *My Heart Laid Bare* explores the issue of race in America. It is as if the myth of the American Eden were retold here in racial terms. The most talented of Abraham's children is Elisha, found in a ditch, trained to perform as Jim Crow and play other stereotypically "black" roles, but nonetheless told that he is one of the family because they all "stand outside the white race" (138). His separation from Abraham, however, begins when he sees the disgust the white world feels for him because of his blackness and the way that Abraham Licht both exploits and helps create that disgust. The final clarification—and the beginning of the family's disintegration—comes when Elisha and Abraham's daughter Millie fall in love and Abraham casts out Elisha, calling him "Nigger." Elisha's story, involving resurrections and transformations, takes him into the black nationalist movement and allows Oates to examine racial pride, racial hatred, and the disintegration of self that results from the messages encoded in American law and culture. Millie's story, as she obeys the father's law and repudiates her love, explores the habit of defining racial categories in terms of the separation of self and other and the corrupting effect of internalizing the systems of American racial prejudice. For God's chosen people, a wandering nation of immigrants, racial prejudice is a destructive force, separation and genocide a kind of cultural suicide. In *My Heart Laid Bare*, Oates again uses the expansive definition of genre to suggest the American desire for exploration and aspiration as well as its contradictory urge for exclusion and restriction.

In a 1972 interview with Joe David Bellamy, Oates mentioned the process of her writing as "transcribing dreams, giving them a certain civilized, extended shape" (Milazzo 26). A decade and a half later she defined herself to David Germain as "of the school of the writer as witness. Witness to history and society" (Milazzo 177). That intersection of dream and reality is at the heart of the Gothic, capturing both its exhilarations and its terrors. Joyce Carol Oates's exploration of these American Gothic forms suggests that the confines of genre are not finally imprisoning. Rather, they are labyrinths that Oates penetrates in order to confront the nature of the tales we tell, have told, will tell. As she writes in the Preface to *Bellefleur*, "Our past may weigh heavily upon us but it cannot contain us, let alone shape our future. America is a tale still being told—in many voices—and nowhere near its conclusion" ("Five Prefaces" 371).

SELECTED CRITICISM

Bender, Eileen-Teper. *Joyce Carol Oates: Artist in Residence*. Bloomington: Indiana University Press, 1987. An elegant analysis of Oates's search for forms as her novels represent her continuing experimentation with narrative conventions.

———. "History as Woman's Game: *Bellefleur* as *Texte de Jouissance*." *Soundings* 76 (1993): 369–381. Reads *Bellefleur* as an explosion of American masculine models of historical fiction.

Chell, Cara. "Un-Tricking the Eye: Joyce Carol Oates and the Feminist Ghost Story." *Arizona Quarterly* 41 (1985): 5–23. Analyzes *Mysteries of Winterthurn* as a feminist novel that highlights violence toward women while parodying nineteenth-century models.

Coale, Samuel Chase. "Joyce Carol Oates: Contending Spirits." In *In Hawthorne's Shadow: American Romance from Melville to Mailer*. Lexington: University Press of Kentucky, 1985. Rpt. in *Joyce Carol Oates*. Ed. Harold Bloom. Modern Critical Views. New York: Chelsea House, 1987: 119–136. Analyzes Oates's fiction through *Bellefleur* as Hawthornian romance.

Creighton, Joanne V. *Joyce Carol Oates*. Boston: Twayne, 1979. A study of Oates's increasingly visionary fiction from 1963 to 1976. Argues that "the realistic novel is too clumsy a vehicle for her modernist formulation and assessment of the problems of selfhood and for the private vision she posits."

————. *Joyce Carol Oates: Novels of the Middle Years.* New York: Twayne, 1992. Argues that "Oates remains deeply if somewhat ironically subscribed to the traditions of American romanticism."

Daly, Brenda. *Lavish Self-Divisions: The Novels of Joyce Carol Oates.* Jackson: University Press of Mississippi, 1996. A Bakhtinian feminist approach to the multivocal novels of the mid-1960s through the mid-1980s, underscoring her complex relationship to genre and her struggle to be free of the constraints of gender.

————. "Where Is She Going, Where Are We Going, at Century's End? The Girl as Site of Cultural Conflict in Joyce Carol Oates's 'The Model.' " In *The Girl: Constructions of the Girl in Contemporary Fiction by Women.* Ed. Ruth O. Saxton. New York: St. Martin's Press, 1998: 1–19. Examines the transformation of "Where Are You Going, Where Have You Been?" into "The Model" as a cultural shift from the 1960s to the 1990s.

Egan, James. " 'Romance of a Darksome Type': Versions of the Fantastic in the Novels of Joyce Carol Oates." *Studies in Weird Fiction* 7 (1990): 12–21. Argues that Oates combines a contemporary and an "antiquarian" form of the Gothic to delineate the American dream and its workings in *Wonderland, Son of the Morning, Bellefleur, A Bloodsmoor Romance,* and *Mysteries of Winterthurn.*

Gardner, John. "The Strange Real World." *New York Times Book Review* 20 July 1980. Rpt. in *Joyce Carol Oates.* Ed. Harold Bloom. Modern Critical Views. New York: Chelsea House, 1987: 99–104. Reads *Bellefleur* as the "symbolic summation" of Oates's fiction.

Goodman, Charlotte. "Women and Madness in the Fiction of Joyce Carol Oates." *Women and Literature* 5:2 (1977): 17–28. Focuses on the Gothic world into which Oates's female characters are born and their consequent powerlessness, despair, and psychological disintegration.

Jeannotte, M. Sharon. "The Horror Within: The Short Stories of Joyce Carol Oates." *Sphinx* 2:4 (1977): 25–36. Analyzes the Gothic merging of victim and villain "into a moral blankness."

Johnson, Greg. *Joyce Carol Oates: A Study of the Short Fiction.* New York: Twayne, 1994. Includes a section by Johnson on Oates's use of the Gothic, an extensive selection of her writing on the short story, and a collection of essays by other critics.

————. *Invisible Writer: A Biography of Joyce Carol Oates.* New York: Dutton, 1998; Plume, 1999. A comprehensive and thoughtful study of Oates's life and work.

Lercangée, Francine. *Joyce Carol Oates: An Annotated Bibliography.* Preface and annotations Bruce F. Michelson. New York: Garland, 1986.

Manske, Eva. "The Nightmare of Reality: Gothic Fantasies and Psychological Realism in the Fiction of Joyce Carol Oates." In *Neo-Realism in Contemporary American Fiction.* Ed. Kristiaan Versluys. Amsterdam: Rodopi, 1992: 131–143. Views Oates's fiction as "gothic with a small-letter g" in its violence, presentation of extreme emotional states, and exploration of female fears.

Milazzo, Lee, ed. *Conversations with Joyce Carol Oates.* Jackson: University Press of Mississippi, 1989.

Nodelman, Perry. "The Sense of Unending: Joyce Carol Oates's *Bellefleur* as an Experiment in Feminine Storytelling." In *Breaking the Sequence: Women's Experimental Fiction*. Ed. Ellen Friedman and Miriam Fuchs. Princeton: Princeton University Press, 1989: 250–264. Defines Oates's liberating "feminine innovation" as a "means of transcending the limitations of both conventional and conventionally innovative forms of fiction."

Oates, Joyce Carol. "Wonderlands." *Georgia Review* 38 (1984): 487–506. Rpt. in *(Woman) Writer: Occasions and Opportunities*. New York: Dutton, 1988. 79–105. "Frequently in Gothic fiction the innocent are not only victimized but are co-opted by the wicked: the wonderland is a marvelous place where *we* are *they*— our shadow selves given both substance and potency."

———. "Visions of Detroit." *Michigan Quarterly Review* 25 (1986): 308–311. Rpt. in *(Woman) Writer: Occasions and Opportunities*. New York: Dutton, 1988: 346–351.

———. "Pseudonymous Selves." *New York Times Book Review* 6 December 1987: 12+. Rpt. in *(Woman) Writer: Occasions and Opportunities*. New York: Dutton, 1988: 383–397. On the erasure of identity through the assumption of a pseudonym— or any narrative voice.

———. "Five Prefaces." Rpt. in *(Woman) Writer: Occasions and Opportunities*. New York: Dutton, 1988: 365–382. Includes prefaces to *them, Bellefleur*, and *Mysteries of Winterthurn*.

———. Introduction to *American Gothic Tales*. Ed. Joyce Carol Oates. New York: Plume, 1996: 1–9. American Gothic is characterized by "assaults upon individual autonomy and identity," a theme reflected in the anthology's selections.

———. "The Aesthetics of Fear." *Salmagundi* Fall 1998: 176–185. Rpt. in *Where I've Been, and Where I'm Going: Essays, Reviews, and Prose*. New York: Plume, 1999: 26–35. Oates's views on the Gothic pleasure principle.

Showalter, Elaine. "Where Are You Going, Where Have You Been?/ Joyce Carol Oates." In *Women Writers: Texts and Contexts*. New Brunswick, NJ: Rutgers University Press, 1994. The text and twelve excellent essays on Oates's most anthologized story, including Oates's own response to the film version, *Smooth Talk*.

Souther, Randy. *Celestial Timepiece*. ⟨http://storm.usfca.edu/~southerr/jco.html⟩. A Web site devoted to Oates's works, particularly useful for bibliographic information.

Waller, G.F. *Dreaming America: Obsession and Transcendence in the Fiction of Joyce Carol Oates*. Baton Rouge: Louisiana State University Press, 1979. Studies Oates as an American Gothic writer who obsessively "attempts to dramatize the mystery of the human spirit struggling amongst our personal and shared nightmares."

FLANNERY O'CONNOR
(1925–1964)
Douglass H. Thomson

PRINCIPAL GOTHIC WORKS

Wise Blood. New York: Farrar, Straus, 1952.

A Good Man Is Hard To Find, and Other Stories. New York: Harcourt, Brace, 1955. (Contains the short stories "Good Country People," "A Good Man Is Hard to Find," "A Stroke of Good Fortune," "The Displaced Person," "A Late Encounter with the Enemy," and "A Circle in the Fire.")

The Violent Bear It Away. New York: Farrar, Straus, & Cudahy, 1960.

Everything That Rises Must Converge. New York: Farrar, Straus, & Giroux, 1965. (Contains the short stories "Everything That Rises Must Converge," "The Lame Shall Enter First," "Revelation," and "Parker's Back.")

MODERN REPRINTS AND EDITIONS

The Complete Short Stories. New York: Farrar, Straus, & Giroux, 1960. (This edition is cited in the text.)

Three (By Flannery O'Connor). Intro. by Sally Fitzgerald. New York: New American Library, 1962. (The "3" are *Wise Blood*, "A Good Man Is Hard to Find," and *The Violent Bear It Away.*)

Wise Blood. New York: Noonday Press, 1990.

The term "Southern Gothic" perhaps defines too conveniently or, worse, too condescendingly a region's cultural psychosis. Usually it means the presence of something perverse, rotten, and nightmarish in a world allegedly governed by strict piety, family values, and a proud past. This emergence of the abject carries with it an easy poetic and moral justice: because, as the story goes, Southern religious fundamentalism is too reductive, it breeds fascination with the forbidden and the charlatan. Beneath its facade of "good country people" and lingering nostalgia for the way things were, one finds an enormous potential for hypocrisy and cruelty. It is as if this return of the abject upon the normal, of darkness upon whiteness, serves as a fitting revenge upon the legacy of Southern racism and bigotry. Flannery O'Connor hated the term "Southern Gothic" because she found such an understanding of her homeland too reductive and dismissive. Certainly, her fiction reveals a devastatingly keen eye for her region's hypocrisy and racial injustice. Who can forget the "revelation" of the sanctimonious Mrs. Turpin in her hog pen as she has a vision of blacks, white trash, and whole "battalions of freaks and lunatics" ("Revelation" 508) preceding her in their joyous ascent to heaven? But O'Connor's use of freaks and lunatics—what is often referred to as the "grotesque" in her writing—to indict Southern hypocrisy and, worse, racism only characterizes one aspect of her Gothic vision. She just as frequently relies upon the traditional Gothic imagery of sinners in the hands of an angry God to chastise modern skeptics, including those inclined to dismiss the backwardness of the South. On a more profound level, one that completely unsettles the dismissive logic usually associated with the term "Southern Gothic," one finds in her two completed novels, *Wise Blood* and *The Violent Bear It Away*, alleged freaks and lunatics who earn a terrible wisdom and disturbingly insist upon their kinship with us. In these novels, O'Connor transforms the abject into the anagogic and discovers within the grotesque and the Gothic a startling and, she insists, redemptive view of the soul hungering for God.

Many critics consider O'Connor's Gothicism primarily in terms of her use of the "grotesque," meaning her frequent and often-startling juxtaposition of the comic and tragic, the banal and violent, and especially the religious and profane. Joy Hopewell's purloined artificial leg in "Good Country People," the bruised image of a tattooed Byzantine Christ on Parker's back in "Parker's Back," Enoch's shriveled homunculus as the "new Jesus," the corpse of General Sash after his dubious epiphany waiting "in the long line at the Coca-Cola machine" (144) in "A Late Encounter with the Enemy"—a gallery of her grotesqueries would include these profiles and many more. But O'Connor's pervasive use of the grotesque does not so much suggest a dispiriting worldview of the kind one finds in many of her modernist contemporaries; instead, it is primarily strategic, a means to a higher end. One of these ends is to offer a primarily Catholic, sacramental criticism of the Southern fundamentalist tendency to "crucify Christ with the head downward," to quote from William Blake. In addition to the finely comic unraveling of Mrs. Turpin's smug piety, we have the poor Mrs. Shortley in "The Displaced Person," who, convinced of the "advanced" stage of her "reformed" religion, suspects the Displaced Person and his sponsoring priest of a vast popish conspiracy threatening the integrity of her South Georgia farming life. Another example is the famous grandmother of "A Good Man Is Hard to Find," whose too-strategic righteousness is abruptly terminated by the Misfit. Also prominent among the grotesque portraits of waywardly religious people are Parker's "idolatrous" tattoo of Christ and his wife's equally questionable excommunication of him and it—the list could go on. Perhaps O'Connor's most decisive response to self-serving religion can be found in the severely sincere

Hazel Mote of *Wise Blood* running over the quack preacher who has been imitating and mocking him.

O'Connor tactically uses the grotesque to characterize the more extreme and often brutal strains of Southern fundamentalism or even to take theological revenge upon its heresies. But often even these misguided good country people have their moments of revelation, especially if they are children, and O'Connor reserves her more severe punishment, as is uncomfortably known in academic circles, for the intellectual who would existentially deny God. The genuine horrors that await these unbelievers have great resonance in the Gothic tradition: countless Gothic novels enact the revenge of the supernatural and irrational realm upon the rationalist who denies its existence. In "Good Country People," Joy Hopewell, a Ph.D. in philosophy, receives sexual degradation and the loss of her artificial leg as the price for her condescending ways. The skeptic Julian—another character infected by college education—in "Everything That Rises Must Converge" learns too late the quality of forbearance as he sees his mother crumple before him. Sheppard, an atheist and too-self-satisfied doer of good works, loses his son because he fails to understand that "the lame shall enter first." So too does George Rayber, the schoolteacher of *The Violent Bear It Away*, who serves as a vehicle for everything O'Connor believes is misguided about modern social sciences. One can add the quasi-existentialist nonsense preached by Hazel that screens his desperate search for spiritual truth. All of these intellectually assured characters meet, in good Gothic fashion, terrible and utterly unexpected retribution as they learn that there are more things in heaven and earth than dreamt of in their philosophies.

And more things in hell as well. O'Connor is one of the few serious modern writers to include the demonic in her fiction, not as a mere symbol or psychic analog, but as a force of biblical evil. As Preston Browning argues, "The devil seems not only an essential feature of her technique but also an integral part of her theology" (30). A list of her lesser satanic characters includes the huckster Onnie Jay Holy in *Wise Blood*, who delights in perverting Scripture and exploiting Hazel; Mr. Shortley of "The Displaced Person," whose sacrifice of Mr. Guizac invites significant allegorical reading; and the malevolent Misfit of "A Good Man Is Hard to Find." But all these pale next to O'Connor's brilliant evocation of the demonic in the figure of the Stranger who tries to lure Tarwater from his chosen path in *The Violent Bear It Away*. Initiating and then accompanying every one of Tarwater's doubts, the Stranger appears climatically at the end as a spectrally "sibilant shifting of air dropped like a sigh into his ear" to tempt Tarwater to relinquish, finally, his spiritual calling: "The presence was as pervasive as an odor, a warm sweet body of air encircling him, a violent shadow hanging over his shoulders" (264). O'Connor never personifies the Stranger, yet he is clearly something dreadfully more than the figment of Tarwater's tortured thoughts. Few devils in the Gothic tradition can match the power of her creation.

O'Connor's most harrowing moments are finally reserved for those characters who must struggle with the devil and persevere in their quest for some terrible revelation. Seemingly haunted by God or (to put it in terms more akin to O'Connor's theology) selected by grace, these characters refuse the easy answers provided by modern religion and embark upon a nightmare journey of the soul. Genuinely horrific events, matching the worst the Gothic can offer, accompany the arduous spiritual pilgrimages of Hazel Oates and the younger Tarwater. Oates brutally blinds himself, in part as a penitence that is continued with his barbed-wire version of the hair shirt and walking on broken glass and in part as an indication of his desperate longing for an inner illumination. Tarwater's murderous baptism of Rayber's son, then his own homosexual rape, precede his fiery return to his ancestral home and to his rightful place in a line of thundering Old Testament prophets. Just about every reader is disturbed by these violently Gothic journeys as evidence of God's grace, no matter how clearly orthodox they may be on the allegorical and anagogic levels. As O'Connor reveals in "The Fiction Writer and His Country" (1957), this unsettling of the reader is precisely her aim: "The novelist with Christian concerns will find in modern life distortions which are repugnant to him, and his problem will be to make these appear as distortions to an audience which is used to seeing them as natural; and he may very well be forced to take ever more violent means to get his vision across to this hostile audience" (33–34). Part of that strategy also includes "embu[ing] this action with an awe and terror" which "will suggest its awful mystery. I have to distort the look of the things to represent as I see them both the mystery and the fact" (qtd. in Fitzgerald's Intro. to *Three*, xxi). O'Connor's comments make perfectly clear her use of grotesque and Gothic elements to convey a higher spiritual truth. In doing so, she most nearly shares kinship with that first and most powerful of writers in the Gothic tradition, the Dante of *The Inferno*.

SELECTED CRITICISM

Andreas, James. " 'If It's a Symbol, the Hell with It': The Medieval Gothic Style of Flannery O'Connor in 'Everything That Rises Must Converge.' " *Christianity and Literature* 38:2 (1989): 23–41. O'Connor's fiction draws its power not from the "pseudo-Gothics of Radcliffe and Poe" but from the medieval Gothic, which eschewed the symbolic in favor of concrete, "realistic" treatment of damnation and salvation.

Baumgaertner, Jill P. *Flannery O'Connor: A Proper Scaring*. Wheaton, IL: Harold Shaw, 1988. Studies O'Connor's use of "awe and terror" as essential parts of her artistic vision.

Browning, Preston M. "Flannery O'Connor and the Demonic." *Modern Fiction Studies* 19 (1973): 29–41. The genuinely demonic presences in O'Connor's fiction, which are closely related to modern skepticism, function as a direct inversion of her sacred themes. More than symbol, the satanic appears as an integral part of her understanding of religious conflict.

Burns, Margie. "A Good Rose Is Hard to Find: 'Southern Gothic' as Social Dislocation in Faulkner and O'Connor." *Works and Days: Essays in the Socio-historical Dimensions of Literature and the Arts* 6 (1988): 185–201. Rpt. in *Image and Ideology in Modern/Postmodern Discourse*. Albany: State University of New York Press, 1991: 105–23. Includes discussion of how Gothic conventions inform the dynamics of psychosocial dislocation in "A Good Man Is Hard to Find."

Di Renzo, Anthony. "Gargoyles, Grotesques, and Marginalia: The Hideously Beautiful, Beautifully Hideous Art of Flannery O'Connor." In *American Gargoyles: Flannery O'Connor and the Medieval Grotesque*, Carbondale: Southern Illinois University Press, 1993: 1–17. Studies O'Connor's use of medieval symbolism on the allegorical and anagogic level of her tales, especially her recurrent saint and martyr figures.

Kahane, Claire. "The Maternal Legacy: The Grotesque Tradition in Flannery O'Connor's Female Gothic." In *The Female Gothic*. Ed. Juliann E. Fleenor. Montreal: Eden Press, 1983: 242–256. Within the context of the female Gothic and aided by some sophisticated Freudian analysis, argues that O'Connor's "grotesque-Gothic" presentation of "vulnerable and impaired" female bodies provides images "of both [women's] revolt against the cultural order and their sense of helplessness within it."

Martin, Carter W. "The Gothic Impulse." In *The True Country: Themes in the Fiction of Flannery O'Connor*. Nashville, TN: Vanderbilt University Press, 1969: 152–188. Good on the various uses of the Gothic in O'Connor's fiction. Her Gothicism enables her depiction of a fallen world, yet in its presentation of dire situations, it also presents man with choices that can define his moral character in a positive way.

Nisly, Paul W. "The Mystery of Evil: Flannery O'Connor's Gothic Power." *Flannery O'Connor Bulletin* 11 (1982): 25–35. "As a devout Christian, O'Connor surely believed in the ultimate triumph of good over evil; as a Gothic fictionist, she left the outcome in doubt. . . . It is her triumph as an artist that religious polemic never overwhelms her Gothic power."

O'Connor, Flannery. "The Fiction Writer and His Country." In *Mystery and Manners: Occasional Prose*. Ed. Sally Fitzgerald and Robert Fitzgerald. New York: Farrar, Straus, & Giroux, 1969: 24–39. Argues against reductive views of the term "Southern school," suggesting that it wrongly "conjures up an image of Gothic monstrosities and the idea of a preoccupation with everything deformed and grotesque," but goes on to explain her own use of "awe and terror" in fiction and its Christian aims.

Palmer, Louis H., III. "Southern Gothic and Appalachian Gothic: A Comparative Look at Flannery O'Connor and Cormac McCarthy." *Journal of the Appalachian Studies Association* 3 (1991): 166–176. Compares Gothic elements in *Wise Blood* with McCarthy's *Suttree* (1979).

Schleifer, Ronald. "Rural Gothic: The Stories of Flannery O'Connor." *Modern Fiction Studies* 28 (1982): 475–485. Revised as "Rural Gothic: The Sublime Rhetoric of Flannery O'Connor" for *Frontier Gothic: Terror and Wonder at the Frontier in American Literature*. Ed. David Mogen, Scott P. Sanders, and Joanne B. Karpinski. Rutherford, NJ: Fairleigh Dickinson University Press, 1993: 175–186. Discusses the Americanizing or regionalizing of traditional Gothic crises and haunting in O'Connor's fiction; while O'Connor defines terror in terms of crises in family and cultural heritage, she maintains the traditional Gothic evocation of the genuinely supernatural.

Snow, Ollye Tine. "The Functional Gothic of Flannery O'Connor." *Southwest Review* 50 (1965): 286–299. Point-by-point analysis of conventions O'Connor borrows from the mainline Gothic tradition.

VLADIMIR FYODOROVICH ODOEVSKY
(1804–1869)

Frederick S. Frank

PRINCIPAL GOTHIC WORKS

Pestrye skazki s krasyym sloytsom [Variegated Tales], St. Petersberg, 1833; Facsimile-Rpt. *Pestrye Skazki*. Edited with an introduction and notes by Neil Cornwell. Durham Modern Languages Series; ST2. [Durham]: University of Durham, 1988.
Russkie nochi [Russian Nights], 1844.

MODERN REPRINTS AND EDITIONS

Das Gespenst Und Andere Spukgeschichten [The Ghost and Other Spook Stories] von V.F. Odoeskii. Trans. into German by Werner Creutziger, Charlotte Kossuth, und Dieter Pommerenke. Berlin: Aufbau Verlag, 1974. (Contains "The Dead Man's Sneer" [Das Hohnlachen des Toten], "Imbroglio," "Die Sylphide" [The Sylph], "Das Gespenst" [The Ghost], "The Live Corpse" [Der Lebende Leichnam].)
Russian Nights (1965). Ed. and trans. Olga Koshansky-Olienikov and Ralph E. Matlaw. Afterword by Neil Cornwell. Evanston, IL: Northwestern University Press, 1997. (Contains the tales "The Dead Man's Sneer," "The Ball," and "The Last Suicide.")
Russian Romantic Prose: An Anthology. Ed. Carl R. Proffer. Trans. David Lowe. Ann Arbor: Translation Press, 1979. (Has an English translation of "The Live Corpse.")
Russkie Nochi. Ed. B.F. Egorov, E.A. Maimin, M.I. Medovoi. Leningrad: Nauka, 1975.
The Salamander and Other Gothic Tales. Ed. Neil Cornwell. (Modern Edition in Russian) Evanston, IL: Northwestern University Press, 1992. (English translations of eight stories: "New Year," "The Tale of a Dead Body, Belonging to No One Knows Whom," "The Story of a Cock, a Cat, and a Frog," "The Sylph," "Letter IV [To Countess Ye. P. Rostopchina]," "The Live Corpse," "The Cosmorama," and "The Salamander." Most of the tales are taken from *Russian Nights*. "The Tale of a Dead Body" is taken from *Variegated Tales*. "The Salamander" is a novella. Among these stories, "The Tale of a Dead Body," "The Live Corpse," "The Cosmorama," and "The Salamander" contain the most purely Gothic elements and moods. This edition is cited in the text.)

Readers of Poe, Hawthorne, Hoffmann, Le Fanu, and Maupassant will recognize many connections with the master of the Russian Gothic short story, Prince Vladimir Odoevsky. His two collections of short stories, *Russian Nights* and *Variegated Tales*, are grounded in the ghostly, the grotesque, and the supernatural, synthesizing these Gothic features with the peculiar intellectual distresses and dreary cultural insularities of Russian life in the mid-nineteenth century. Not translated until very recently, Odoevsky's Gothic work is now coming to the forefront of a vigorous Russian Gothic tradition that includes Pushkin, Lermontov, and Dostoevsky, three writers whose own Gothicism may have profited by their intellectual contacts with Odoevsky by way of exchanges within the salon. Although Odoevsky was of noble birth (his title is "Prince"), he led a highly bourgeois existence in pursuit of his several careers as civil servant and journal editor, combining these mundane vocations with the more intellectual ventures of museum directorship, the founding of the St. Petersburg and Moscow conservatories, and the maintenance of his own salon dedicated to fostering the progress of Russian literature and arguing the rival philosophies of the era. Drawn to Plato, Shakespeare, Swedenborg, Saint Germain, Byron, and the Romantic writers of the West, Odoevsky was also fascinated by pragmatic or activist thinkers who advocated action over thought.

In evaluating Odoevsky's personality and his standing in Russian literature, Neil Cornwell has judged him to be the most prominent advocate of the Romantic awakening in Russian letters, "one of the most extraordinarily versatile figures of nineteenth-century Russia . . . a romantic writer, children's writer, musicologist, educationist, philanthropist, amateur scientist, and general 'Renaissance man' " (Introduction, *The Salamander and Other Gothic Tales*, 1). Although his Gothic tales are clearly indebted to the German fantasist E.T.A. Hoffmann and display at frequent points an affinity with Edgar Allan Poe, his work is a unique example of the fusion of the Western Gothic spirit, mood, and tone with the special hopes and fears of Russian intellectual life at midcentury. His primary subject is spiritual incarceration or, more accurately, self-incarceration as he adapts the Gothic's mandatory predicament of horrifying confinement to the symbolic prisons that his characters erect around themselves. The unnatural and the supernatural are nearly always extensions of Odoevsky's characters' misperception, distortion, or avoidance of self, their terror of assertion or immersion in a half-beckoning, half-menacing world that seems a tangle of the mysterious and ridiculous somewhat in the vein of a Kafka nightmare. The crimes they commit are usually crimes against the self perpetrated in the perverse hope of some kind of bizarre self-punishment, a motivational chain of cause and effect later developed by Dostoevsky. The Gothic drive for guilt is as thematically central to Odoevsky's tales as it is to Charles Robert Maturin's *Melmoth the Wanderer* and Poe's homicidal and suicidal fantasies involving crime and punishment. The compulsive act of a crime committed to obtain punishment is sometimes taken to apocalyptic limits in Odoevsky's envisioning of the violent end of the world. Three Poe stories, each involving self-violation and self-rejection, are particularly relevant to Odoevsky's Gothic sensibility in this respect: "The Man of the Crowd," "The Black Cat," and "The Tell-Tale Heart." Just as there is a doubling or bonding between criminal and victim in the Poe tales, so the relationship of Odoevsky's characters to their spectral or demonic revenants is rooted in the theme of confrontation with the double.

Of the ten tales in Odoevsky's *Russian Nights*, the majority are heavily or moderately inlaid with Gothic details and decor, their climaxes and crises often transmogrified by Odoevsky's insertion of absurd effects that will remind readers of Nikolai Gogol's comic technique in his grotesque anatomical and sartorial fantasies "The Nose" and "The Overcoat." Odoevsky's similar devotion to physiological distortion or disorientation as well as to extrasensory out-of-body experience receives close-up treatment in "The Live Corpse," a half-comic tale of involuntary disembodiment terminating in permanent imprisonment of the self by the self. The main character, the gluttonous, lecherous, self-centered Vasily Kuzmich, awakens from one nightmare to an even more terrifying nightmare when he finds himself displaced from his own dead body and thrust into the role of helpless posthumous observer forced to witness the sordid fate that awaits him. Keeping vigil over his own dead body, he discovers that he is completely unloved, unmourned, and unmissed by his family, who now compete like vultures for his estate as he looks on. In a highly cynical dénouement worthy of Ambrose Bierce, Vasily Kuzmich awakens from his nightmare within the nightmare to the cold facts of his domestic insignificance. In the eyes of the world, he is simply an inconvenient corpse, but dismissing this truth as a bad dream, he rejects his impending fate and resumes his smug and crass self-delusions totally unchanged by the dream vision. This pattern of possession and relinquishment is the crux and core of Odoevskian Gothic. " 'What a stupid dream!' he said finally. 'What a fever I've broken out in. What horrors I dreamed and how vivid they were; exactly like reality. . . . They don't even allow a decent man to get to sleep peacefully' " (88). Thus he slips lethargically back into the Gothic prison of the body, quite oblivious to his missed moment of enlightenment.

Several other tales make use of the villainy of the body and how its chamber of horrors functions as a metaphysical prison. "The Dead Man's Sneer" is a chilling piece of visionary necromantic horror in which a hyperconscious cadaver observes the material futilities and the pointlessness of all human endeavor. The tale cleverly adapts a regular feature of the horror story, the corpse smile or ghastly grin, to its cynical purposes. The corpse's smirk of wisdom is a last laugh at the reality that is no reality but mere vain delusion. Another unsettling tale of grim finalities is "The Last Suicide," one of Odoevsky's most effective Gothic apocalypses, presenting a Malthusian nightmare of the last survivor who witnesses the death of civilization, a theme reminiscent of such antiutopian fantasies as Mary Shelley's *The Last Man*.

"The Tale of a Dead Body, Belonging to No One Knows Whom" is a macabre piece of Gothic drollery, a sketch somewhat in the Irvingesque mode of sportive

Gothic that toys with the stock Gothic event of cadaverous encounter or meeting with the ghostly double. The corrupt, carnal, and drunken village clerk Sevastyanich is charged with the responsibility of identifying "a body belonging to no one knows whom" (17), a bureaucratic plum that the boozy clerk welcomes since he has made a bit of money off such unclaimed remains lying about his village on several previous occasions. "Feathering his nest" with such cases has brought Sevastyanich a petty sense of power that he often indulges in his sadistic daydreams. "How great it would be if he could grab someone by the hand— and the hand would be off—or someone by the head—and the head would be off!" (20). In the midst of one of these daydreams, the clerk is confronted by an insistent visitor from the other side, Odoevsky's brilliant inversion of the restless body seeking reunion with the soul, for it is the soul that wants a reunion with the body. While Sevastyanich is processing the burial documents for the unidentified corpse, a voice addresses him, "humbly requesting that my body be returned to me, as its lawful owner," then materializes into "a formless face; first appearing, then lost, like a young man arriving at a ball for the first time" (22). The revenant is clearly the ghost of the brutish Sevastyanich's better self, human, vibrant, and imaginative, the romantic self within him that he is too stupid and carnally driven to recognize. The interview with the lost self ends abruptly when Sevastyanich awakens amid the alcoholic rubble of his latest binge, "looking at the empty liquor flask standing in front of him" (24). Paper-pushing bureaucrat that he is, he duly records his supernatural experience (described euphemistically as "the nocturnal happening") in his postmortem report, to the dismay of his superiors, who advise him to "sober up." There is no grand Gothic climax and, most significantly, utterly no evolution in Sevastyanich's view of self as a result of his encounter with the potentially revitalizing double. He cannot understand that he himself is a dead body as well as a dead soul and therefore deserves the mockery of the legend that now springs up in the village about his "nocturnal happening" (25). They say that when the district physician lanced the anonymous body to verify that it was dead, "the body got up and ran off, and that Sevastyanich chased after it for ages round the village for all he was worth shouting for all he was worth, 'Catch him, catch that deceased' " (25). His futile pursuit comprises a sort of droll rerendition of Melmoth the Wanderer's cycle of despair or the Wandering Jew's futile pursuit of death.

The hollowness of self endured by Odoevsky's characters indicates an inertia of soul that inevitably leads to a denial of their own humanity or a refusal to be human. In "The Sylph," a character who finds his way upward into the transcendent world of higher being is wrenched back to earth by well-meaning but boorish companions who demean the value of his supernatural liaison with the celestial being. Bearing some resemblance to Maupassant's "Horla" and Fitz-James O'Brien's "Diamond Lens," the tale is narrated prismatically through three points of view. From the failed quester, Mikhail Platonovich, we get seven letters and a journal fragment. A pragmatic and highly rational man, he has gone to the country to settle his uncle's estate, inherit his fortune, and live in sluggish

comfort forever after. Bored and restless, he is plagued by vague guilts over a
wasted life and begins to read the books in his uncle's secret library that consists
mainly of cabalistic volumes full of incantations, charms, and alchemical lore.
Inspired by his reading with the desire to "see a sylph," he dabbles in alchemy
and concocts a solar potion wherein "reposed an amazing, indescribable, un-
believable creature: in short, a woman barely visible to the eye" (51). The closing document of the story, fragments from Platonovich's journal, contains the
sylph's monologue and a summons to Platonovich to "follow me, follow me.
. . . There is another world, a new world" (54). The higher world that the sylph
reveals rivals the poetic heaven of Poe's angel Israfel and the imagination's
miraculous realm of "rare device" of Coleridge's Xanadu in "Kubla Khan." The
sylph offers a paradise where "dead elements are transformed by the spiritual
essence. Here, everything merges into delightful harmony; here your speck of
dust is no suffering world, but a mellifluous instrument, whose harmonious
sounds gently pulsate the ethereal waves" (55). Placed between Platonovich's
letters and his journal extracts is a single letter by his father-in-law-to-be, Gavril
Sofronovich Rezhensky, complaining of Platonovich's indolence, solitariness,
and possible madness, which he blames on Platonovich's "dabbling in the black
books" (52). This document is followed by a concerned note headed "My Account" and written by Platonovich's unnamed correspondent to the effect that
he now finds it his moral duty to save Platonovich from psychotic fantasies.
Platonovich's particular type of dementia is diagnosed as "demonomania," or
hallucinative contact with demons brought on by self-isolation and intellectual
idleness "in the country and alone, without any amusements, engrossed in reading of all kinds of rubbish" (53). Accompanied by the doctor who has rendered
the diagnosis, the correspondent goes down to the country to join Platonovich's
future father-in-law in undertaking to cure the maniac, marry him off, and restore
to him the worldly bliss of "rosy cheeks and a respectable paunch" (59). In
short, these friends set out to slay the demon of imagination that has taken
possession of Mikhail Platonovich. When he is asked if he is now happy, Platonovich turns on these destroyers of romance. "In a word you gave me a
happiness, but not mine. You are very pleased that you have, what you call,
cured me; that is to say, blunted my perceptions, covered them with some impenetrable shell, made them dead to any world except your box" (58). But
pathetically, after this brief flight of spiritual vitality, Platonovich falls back into
the condition of special deadness perpetrated by cronies who deny his vision.
This is not sensational Gothic villainy in the shrill manner of Monk Lewis or
Maturin, nor is the climate of evil heavy with the tenebrous intensity of a typical
Gothic tale involving the terrors of isolation. Nevertheless, its evil stems from
the sort of benign malice that deprives the sensitive man of his poetic soul and
vision. Like other Odoevsky villains, the unnamed narrator fails to comprehend
his own role in the "murder" of his friend's higher being or expulsion of the
sylph within. "I must confess," reads the narrator's statement in the final sentence of the tale, "that I have understood nothing in this narrative; will its readers

be a little luckier?" (59). The Gothic must always take place, either literally or metaphorically, within some horrifying space or place that continually closes in. In Poe's "Pit and the Pendulum," the horrifying place is a contracting dungeon. In George Orwell's *1984*, the place is Room 101, the room that contains the worst thing in the world, which will vary from individual to individual. The infernal place in Jean-Paul Sartre's play *No Exit* is a plain room containing ordinary people. The chamber of horrors in "The Sylph" is nothing less than normality itself, presided over by dull, well-meaning friends and family.

Most students of Odoevsky's Gothicism agree that the long story "The Cosmorama" is his Gothic masterwork. It offers "as full a gamut of occult and Gothic paraphernalia as may be encountered in any work of Russian romanticism: the walking dead, crime and torture, amorous intrigue, second sight, supernatural arson, and spontaneous human combustion" (Cornwell Introduction, *The Salamander and Other Gothic Tales*, 5), with the most shockingly sensational of these, supernatural incineration, reserved for the tale's final pages. To the inventory of Gothic contraptions and effects can be added Odoevsky's ironic use of one of the first and most durable of Gothic ploys, the mysterious or arcane manuscript, as well as the fall of a house atop the victim-lovers following the return of the house's master from the tomb. The reliability as well as the sanity of the writer of the manuscript remains unresolved at the tale's end, with all lines of demarcation between waking reality and an equally vivid and equally real dream life permanently blurred. An inset story midway through the narrative turns out to be a version of Plato's famous allegory of the cave (concerning the deception of the senses and the epistemological dilemmas of appearance versus reality) and perhaps holds the clue to the entrapment of the main character between two worlds, his soul as much lost in the dark labyrinths of the spirit as Maturin's Melmoth is lost in the corridors of time.

The manuscript containing the "incomprehensible, marvellous adventures" (90) of Vladimir Petrovich (called Valodia as a child) is prefaced by "A Warning from the Publisher," who now offers these papers to the public without elucidation or commentary of any kind. The manuscript contains the biography of a Byronic young man whose passion to transcend mortality and to live on some higher plane of existence is alternately fulfilled and thwarted by his play with a mysterious box. The shifting lenses of the cosmorama offer him phantasmagoric glimpses of his future self enjoying the highest degree of love in that other world where fleshly and spiritual pleasure are totally fused. Using the cosmorama also concentrates this vision to various focal points of beauty, allowing Vladimir Petrovich to envision Blake's "heaven in a wild flower" or to behold "the world in a grain of sand." "Oh, you ill-starred fortunate!" warns his friend, Doctor Bin. "You—you can see everything—everything without the covering, without the astral shroud" (96). But like a monkey's paw or a bottle imp or a golden touch, the cosmorama exacts a terrible price for its ecstasies. "That miraculous door within you had opened equally for good and evil, for bliss and for perdition . . . and it will never more close," warns the doctor. Vladimir Petrovich's manipulation of the cosmorama leads to passionate affairs with two opposite women, his intellectual cousin Sophia and the sensual Countess Eliza B. Deriving from two Gothic character prototypes, the persecuted maiden and the femme fatale, each woman signifies the lighter and darker aspects of the cosmorama. As the dark lady, somewhat in the manner of Poe's Ligeia, asserts control, he feels growing within himself "the presence of several independent beings who were struggling fiercely and could not overcome one another" (108). His savage sexual desires apparently cause in some mysterious way the death of Eliza B.'s dissolute husband, the Count, this event foreshadowed by the cosmorama, whose evil capacities can apparently be activated by the selfish will of the user/viewer. Attending the Count's funeral, Vladimir Petrovich cannot silence an inner voice as it exults that "the corpse of your enemy always smells sweet!" (111). At this point, the story accelerates toward a chain of Gothic circumstances of the type that one might expect to find on the closing pages of a chapbook, bluebook, or penny dreadful. The Countess reports a graphic nightmare during which she feels the Count's dead hand stroking her face as he vows to return to take vengeance on the couple for willing his death. "I shall return to your embraces, my loyal spouse!" (113), he whispers melodramatically. When this necromantic promise is fulfilled, Vladimir Petrovich realizes by way of his cosmoramic insight that there is a "living link" that binds him to the Count, that the "dark and secret deeds" and "hellish power" of Eliza's husband are mirror images of his own evil self, and that "this whole monstrous concatenation was interlinked back to him, the semi-corpse, and he had brought the whole of it with him into this world. My being was, as it were, fragmented" (115). With such guilty knowledge in hand, one might suppose that self-salvation is still within the narrator's grasp, or, to put it in Gothic terms, that escape from the mazes of the dark self might still be possible. But just as there is no egress from the castle of self in a Charles Brockden Brown novel or in one of Poe's tales of premature burial, so Odoevsky opts to doom his hero to everlasting anguish.

   To complete the fatal enclosure, Odoevsky combines the spectacular stock Gothic occurrences of spontaneous combustion and architectural collapse, catastrophic events employed by Brown and Poe to generate horror in *Wieland* and "The Fall of the House of Usher." The cadaverous Count, now fully recognizable as Vladimir Petrovich's evil double, first interrupts a liaison of the two lovers at the opera, the Count's "penetrating glance," "thin lips," and "odour of the grave" (124) all suggestive of the physiognomy of John Polidori's vampire, Lord Ruthven, Odoevsky's possible source for the episode of the return of the vampire. When he appears to them again, he interrupts their assignation by self-destructing in their astonished presence, apparently by self-induced spontaneous combustion. "Eliza screamed . . . the furniture started smoking . . . a blue flame ran over all the dead man's limbs . . . amid the sanguinary brilliance were revealed the white features of his bones. I could hear, as though in a dream, the howls of people and the crash of the house which was collapsing around me. . . . I do not know how my hand was extricated from that of the dead man"

(127). Yet the Count's cadaverous clutch remains unbroken in the final sense, as Vladimir Petrovich suffers the fate of many Odoevsky characters when he misuses the meaning of this Gothic encounter by rejecting his bond with the Count. Dying the sort of spiritual death that befalls many Odoevsky characters, he consigns himself to "a state of inexpressible horror, tormented every minute, and fear[ing] to think, fear[ing] to feel, fear[ing] to love and to hate" (131). Now exiled from the cosmoramic world of imagination, passion, and grandeur of soul, he becomes yet another of Odoevsky's spiritual corpses. How appropriate then that the inert soul of Vladimir Petrovich should choose to express his stagnant condition of nonbeing by means of the Gothic metaphor of live burial. "I have buried myself alive, in a small remote village in the depths of an impenetrable forest, not known to anyone" (132). The magic lens of the cosmorama darkens and closes forever, stranding the romantic dreamer in a hellish desolation of his own making.

Like Dostoevsky later in the century, Odoevsky adapted the Gothic spirit as well as the entire range of Gothic devices and effects to the themes of spiritual failure, debased and misdirected romantic energy, artistic disappointment and inertia, self-isolation, self-possession, and self-entrapment. The result was a unique type of Russian Gothic tale that reflected Western Gothic conventions, but spoke very eloquently and very personally to the distressing conditions of Russian intellectual and spiritual life. In Odoevsky's hands, European and American Gothic props and plots were applied subjectively to express the terrors of an inner darkness that drives the Russian soul to its peculiar spiritual suicides.

SELECTED CRITICISM

Cornwell, Neil. *The Life, Times, and Milieu of V.F. Odoevsky, 1984–1869*. London: Athlone Press, 1986. Authoritative modern biography and critical study.
————. Introduction to *The Salamander and Other Gothic Tales*. Evanston, IL: Northwestern University Press, 1992: 1–8. Comments on the "Gothic detail and thematic content" of the eight pieces. Comparisons can be made not only with Hoffmann, but also with Charles Brockden Brown and, of course, Poe, and with Mary Shelley, Maturin, and Odoevsky's near contemporary, Sheridan Le Fanu.
————. "Gothic and Its Origins in East and West: Vladimir Odoevsky and Fitz-James O'Brien." In *Exhibited by Candlelight: Sources and Developments in the Gothic Tradition*. Ed. Valeria Tinkler-Villani, Peter Davidson, and Jane Stevenson. Amsterdam: Rodopi, 1995: 117–128. Compares the Russian and Irish Gothic story writers, finding many structural similarities. Among the stories discussed are Odoevsky's "Sylph" and Fitz-James O'Brien's "Diamond Lens."
————. "Russian Gothic." In *The Handbook to Gothic Literature*. Ed. Marie Mulvey-Roberts. New York: New York University Press, 1998: 199–204. "Odoevsky's tales collectively run the full gamut of the occult and Gothic paraphernalia."
————. "Vladimir Fedorovich Odoevskii: Prose Writer and Cultural Dignitary." In *Reference Guide to Russian Literature* Ed. Neil Cornwell and Nicole Christian. London and Chicago: Fitzroy Dearborn, 1998: 586–591. Notes and discusses

Odoevsky's connections with Western Gothicism and his "Gothic leanings" even in his philosophical fiction.

————. *Vladimir Odoevsky and Romantic Poetics: Collected Essays. Studies in Slavic Literature, Culture, and Society, vol. 1.* Providence: Berghahn Books, 1998. Interpretive essays discussing both Odoevsky's Gothicism and his ties with western romantic writers.

Karlinsky, Simon. " 'A Hollow Shape': The Philosophical Tales of Prince Vladimir Odoevsky." *Studies in Romanticism* 5 (1966): 169–182. The philosophic tales often turn to Gothic devices to highlight the horrors of mental inertia and creative failure. Plato, Swedenborg, and other Western mystics influenced Odoevsky's philosophic ideals.

Kiely, Timothy John. "The Professionalization of Russian Literature: A Case Study of Vladimir Odoevsky and Osip Senkovsky." Doctoral dissertation, University of Michigan, 1998. [*DAI* 59:508–509]. On the emergence of Odoevsky as an important voice of Russian Romanticism.

Mersereau, John, Jr. *Russian Romantic Fiction.* Ann Arbor: Ardis, 1983. Places Odoevsky in the history of Russian Romanticism.

Passage, Charles. *The Russian Hoffmannists.* The Hague: Mouton, 1963. Explains Odoevsky's debt to E.T.A. Hoffmann's style and sense of the fantastic.

EDGAR ALLAN POE
(1809–1849)
Frederick S. Frank

PRINCIPAL GOTHIC WORKS

Some of Poe's best Gothic tales had only periodical publication during his lifetime.

"Bon-Bon." *Southern Literary Messenger*, August 1835.

The Narrative of Arthur Gordon Pym of Nantucket. New York: Harper, 1838.

Tales of the Grotesque and Arabesque. Philadelphia: Lea & Blanchard, 1840. (Contains these tales: "Metzengerstein," "Morella," "Berenice," "Ligeia," "The Fall of the House of Usher," "William Wilson," "The Black Cat," "The Facts in the Case of M. Valdemar," "The Duc de L'Omelette," "MS. Found in a Bottle," "The Devil in the Belfry," "King Pest," and "The Assignation.")

"The Oval Portrait." *Graham's Magazine*, April 1842.

"The Masque [Mask] of the Red Death." *Graham's Magazine*, May 1842.

"The Pit and the Pendulum." *The Gift*, 1843.

"The Tell-Tale Heart." *The Pioneer*, January 1843.

"The Premature Burial." *Philadelphia Dollar Newspaper*, July 1844.

"The Oblong Box." *Godey's Lady's Book*, September 1844.

"The Angel of the Odd." *Columbian Magazine*, October 1844.

Tales by Edgar A. Poe. New York: Wiley & Putnam, 1845. (Contains these tales: "The Gold-Bug," "The Black Cat," "Mesmeric Revelation," "Lionizing," "The Fall of the House of Usher," A Descent into the Maelström," "The Colloquy of Monos and Una," "The Conversation of Eiros and Charmion," "The Murders in the Rue Morgue," "The Mystery of Marie Roget," "The Purloined Letter," and "The Man of the Crowd.")

"The Imp of the Perverse." *Graham's Magazine*, July 1845.

"A Predicament." *Broadway Journal*, July 1845.

"Never Bet the Devil Your Head." *Broadway Journal*, August 1845.

"The Thousand-and-Second Tale of Scheherazade." *Broadway Journal*, October 1845.

"The System of Doctor Tarr and Professor Fether." *Graham's Magazine*, November 1845.

"The Cask of Amontillado." *Godey's Lady's Book*, November 1846.
"Hop-Frog." *The Flag of Our Union*, March 1849.

MODERN REPRINTS AND EDITIONS

Collected Works of Edgar Allan Poe. Ed. Thomas Ollive Mabbott, Eleanor D. Kewer,
     and Maureen C. Mabbott. 3 vols. Cambridge, MA: Belknap Press of Harvard
     University Press, 1969.
Collected Writings of Edgar Allan Poe. 4 vols. Ed. Burton R. Pollin. Boston: Twayne,
     1981; New York: Gordian Press, 1985.
The Complete Tales and Poems of Edgar Allan Poe. New York: Vintage/Ballantine,
     1975.
The Complete Works of Edgar Allan Poe. Ed. James A. Harrison. 17 vols. New York:
     Thomas Y. Crowell, 1902. Rpt. New York: AMS Press, 1965.
The Narrative of Arthur Gordon Pym of Nantucket. Ed. Harold Beaver. Baltimore: Pen-
     guin Books, 1975.
Selected Writings of Edgar Allan Poe: Poems, Essays, and Reviews. Ed. David Galloway.
     Baltimore: Penguin Books, 1975. (This edition is cited in the text.)

The relationship of Poe's work to the Gothic tradition has been the subject of
much critical debate and disagreement since the appearance of Marie Bonaparte's psychoanalytic interpretation of the tales in *The Life and Works of Edgar
Allan Poe: A Psychoanalytic Interpretation.* Without direct reference to the
Gothic, Bonaparte's study nevertheless provided the framework for explaining
its recurrent use in both satiric and serious modes throughout his fiction. For
Poe, both the stylistics and the thematics of Gothic fiction became a major
aesthetic imperative, partly because he found in the Gothic a means of giving
objective expression to the subjective demons at large in his short, sad life and
partly because he recognized in the Gothic a medium well suited for the presentation of what a recent critical reader has called "moments of ambiguity,
linguistic, hermeneutic, and ontological uncertainty" (Hustis 3).

Except for the lighter pieces among the seventy-plus stories, the Gothic is a
major aspect and frequently the dominant element of their tone, structure, and
substance. Critics after Bonaparte have often detected in Poe's Gothicism a
satiric or ironic undercutting behind his Gothic practices, but the purity of the
Gothicism itself has seldom been questioned. Two modern critics, G.R. Thompson and Daniel Hoffman, have extended this position by arguing that Poe's
writings are ironic, deceptive, and satiric, and that Poe himself is a master of
the literary hoax. It is certainly true that Poe's Gothic cannot be grasped without
granting his penchant for deception and black comedy, but it may not follow
that generations of readers have been duped by Poe's mock seriousness. According to G.R. Thompson, Poe "deceptively intrudes the comic into the tragic,
the satiric into the demonic," and by so doing, "achieves a liberating transcendental perception of the dark paradox of human existence" (18).

Less contrarian views of Poe's Gothicism accept the premise that Poe's work owes its artistic success to the example of the Gothic tradition. Donald Ringe has drawn a distinction between writers such as Charles Brockden Brown and Nathaniel Hawthorne, who avoided Gothic extremes, and Poe, whose aesthetic goals were similar to the supernatural audacity of early Gothic writers such as Horace Walpole and William Beckford. According to Ringe, "Poe freed the Gothic tale from the constricting limits imposed on it. He was much too serious a thinker to make his stories merely the source of meaningless titillation. In his best work the Gothic devices, though effective in themselves, are also necessary elements in the exposition of theme. Until Poe's time, no American writer had managed to forge so organic a bond between Gothic device and symbolic meaning" (151). In "Poe and the Gothic Tradition," Maurice Lévy builds a strong case for Poe as a generic and highly conventional Gothicist who is "incontestably following a precise literary tradition. Without abandoning the images of the Gothic castle, the subterranean passages, the labyrinth, and the prisons of the Inquisition, he gives these locations the new dimensions of prisons projected by anguish in dream" (Lévy 19).

Like the critics, Poe's biographers have often disagreed about the interconnections between his life and his art, but most have concurred that the interaction of the two is the basis for understanding Poe's Gothicism, that "the fever called 'Living,' " as Poe himself described it in his poem "For Annie," imbues and informs the tales. Certainly the melancholy, violent, and traumatic events of Poe's life contained enough Gothic incident to fill several Gothic novels. The distressing events of his parentless infancy, romantic boyhood, and troubled manhood left their imprint on a body of work that moved Freud to call Poe "a greater writer with pathologic trends." The affection that Poe missed when his actress mother, Elizabeth Poe, died when he was two years old, the paternal guidance that he was denied when his biological father, David Poe, mysteriously vanished, never to reappear, the life-and-death struggle with his austere and authoritarian foster father, John Allan, the slow tubercular demise of his wife, Virginia, and his own progressive alcohol dependency are but a few of the abjections that worked upon Poe's imagination. Had he known Emily Dickinson's poem "One Need Not Be a Chamber to Be Haunted," he would have readily subscribed to the terrifying relevance to his own life of her insight that "One need not be a chamber to be haunted / the brain has corridors surpassing material place." The tribute paid to Poe by H.P. Lovecraft recognized his aptitude for transposing private torments into "a master's vision of the terror that stalks about and within us. He penetrated to every festering horror in the gaily painted mockery called existence, and the solemn masquerade called human thought and feeling" (54). Driven by the subjective demons and monsters stalking the corridors of memory, he rendered them into universal tropes of fear and, in so doing, placed his readers in the uncomfortable position of experiencing a strange bond with both the victim and the victimizer. With his life always looming in the foreground, the transformation of personal abjection into Gothic parables of the soul's terror seems to lie at the heart of Poe's Gothic method. This is not to say that his personalized Gothic is unrelated to the society in which he lived and worked. His Gothic questions not only the scientific absolutes of a comfortable Newtonian universe and the mind's stability, but also the aggressive pragmatism of nineteenth-century American culture as well as the assumed beneficence of Christianity and other religious systems. Perhaps this is why Poe's Gothic retains the power to disturb and terrify by undermining our assumptions about the logical structure of the self and the cosmos. Part of the Americanness of Poe's Gothic lies in the fact that he "is the first American author to use and surpass the machinery of the Gothic for the expression of discontent with a society being shaped so unqualifiedly by empiricist thought and industrial capitalism" (Voller 225).

Although Poe's Gothic tales are never straight autobiographical analogues, in most of the suicidal and homicidal fantasies as well as in the love stories (which should more properly be called love/hate stories) and his tales of the final or fatal voyage, the biographical resonances are too numerous to ignore. The anonymous murderers of "The Tell-Tale Heart" and "The Black Cat" act out Poe's own fantasies of domestic violence, particularly the clashes with John Allan, his foster father. The situation of the nameless victim of the Inquisition in "The Pit and the Pendulum" contains overtones of the strained Poe–John Allan relationship in the paternal threat from the "dark fathers" above and the maternal void yawning below the immobilized victim. The mad and bereaved lovers and psychologically unstable narrators of "Ligeia" and "Berenice" image Poe's own sexual fears and desires. The aggressive intellects of Montresor in "The Cask of Amontillado" and Monsieur Dupin in the detective stories reflect the sane and controlled side of Poe's character, a persona he exercised almost daily as a journalist, reviewer, and puzzle solver. But while we recognize parallels between Poe's personality and those of his characters, such as the doomed artist Roderick Usher or the posthumous narrator of "Ms. Found in a Bottle" who has gone over the edge or the cynical logician in "The Imp of the Perverse," Poe contrives to separate life from art by depersonalizing and objectifying the undercurrents of private and public failure and unresolved antagonisms that flowed through his career.

Poe formulated his artistic objectives in a series of reviews and essays in which he theorized exactly how horror, terror, and beauty might be synergized into one aesthetic whole. In his review of Hawthorne's *Twice-told Tales*, he set down the guidelines for the successful horror story by requiring that the tale writer adopt a strategy of brevity and "preconceived effect" to bring the reader totally under the writer's control. In "The Philosophy of Composition," he evolved a working principle for achieving an aesthetic unity of horror, terror, and sublimity stating that "a close circumscription of space is absolutely necessary to the effect of insulated incident" (*Selected Writings* 488). "Insulated incident" and "close circumscription" are the structural absolutes of Poe's Gothic pieces. By concentrating the action of the tale and isolating the characters, Poe converted the physical spaces used by previous Gothic writers into constrictive mental spaces using such common Gothic templates as the dark descent or the mad monologue to achieve a "preconceived effect." Explaining his method to Thomas W. White, editor of the *Southern Literary Messenger*, Poe stressed the metamorphic nature of the creative process by declaiming that his aim was to render "the ludicrous heightened into the grotesque, the fearful coloured into the horrible, the witty exaggerated into the burlesque, the singular wrought out into the strange and mystical" (letter to Thomas W. White, 30 April 1835; see *The Letters of Edgar Allan Poe*, Ed. John Ward Ostrom [New York: Gordian Press, 1966].) One function of the transformational process, as Roy Male has suggested, was "to kill or bury the destructive aspects of his own psyche" (9). Elsewhere in his criticism, Poe explored and analyzed the central paradox of horror and terror—the fact that it was attractive at the same time that it was repulsive. In the preface to *Tales of the Grotesque and Arabesque*, Poe set forth a famous axiom for the type of Gothic tale he had in mind: "If in many of my productions terror has been the thesis, I maintain that terror is not of Germany, but of the soul,—that I have deduced this terror only from its legitimate sources, and urged it only to its legitimate results." (*Collected Works*, vol. 2, 473.) The application of this thesis of horror results in "a psychosomatic theory of hell" (Stableford 453) in the best Gothic work whereby damnation precedes death. Hell then becomes not a place but a psychic state for his entrapped characters. The most unnerving quality of Poe's Gothic is its psychosomatic circumscription of mental space, that is, the mind closing in upon itself.

Nearly all of Poe's horror tales were first published in popular household journals and magazines such as *Graham's Magazine, Godey's Lady's Book, Burton's Gentleman's Magazine*, and the *Broadway Journal*. Many exist in several versions, since he revised extensively and often made significant changes when he included his work in collections such as *Tales of the Grotesque and Arabesque*. "Ligeia," for example, was first published in the *American Museum* for September 1838 and did not contain the poem "The Conqueror Worm" that later became a crucial part of the story's text when "Ligeia" appeared again in the *New York World* on 15 February 1845 and then again in the *Broadway Journal* on 27 September 1845. After appearing in *Graham's Magazine* for May 1842, "The Masque of the Red Death" was retitled "The Mask of the Red Death" when it was republished in the *Literary Souvenir* of 4 June 1842. Poe combined short-story writing with book reviewing in his numerous journalistic positions, churning out copy at an astonishing rate and acquiring a reputation as a savage but fair-minded reviewer. His experiences in the rough arena of journalism are registered in several of the comic tales, including "The Literary Life of Thingum Bob, Esq., Late Editor of the 'Goosetherumfoodle' by Himself," "How to Write a Blackwood Article," and "Lionizing." These tales are outstanding examples of Poe's ability to transmogrify the daily drudgery of the magazine trade into biting burlesques of acerbic journalism and unrestricted literary warfare.

Gothic comedy depicting absurd deaths, ridiculous punishments, odd revenges, and demonic chicanery forms a significant portion of Poe's output.

These comic tales are often tinged with a sarcastic and gruesome wit of the brutal sort later to be found in the work of Ambrose Bierce. In "A Predicament" (first titled "The Scythe of Time"), Poe mocked the magazine Gothic stock-in-trade crisis of lethal entrapment and extravagant victimization by locating the main character under the gradual guillotine of a slowly descending clock hand. Throughout her ordeal, the Signora Psyche Zenobia analyzes her gradual decapitation in great detail in a mock-up of the same situation played out in a serious key in "The Pit and the Pendulum." Horror and hilarity are also synthesized in "The Man That Was Used Up," a tale showing Poe's contempt for the democratic masses and their repeated duping by great men of the people who actually amount to nothing. Satanic encounter, another standard event in Gothic fiction, is treated with morbid gusto in "Never Bet the Devil Your Head," a tale that brings a loudmouth to his deserved doom. Satan's culinary skill as a roaster of souls is on display in "Bon-Bon," a delightfully fiendish play on the Faustian bargain. When Pierre Bon-Bon offers the devil his soul, Satan turns him down because hell is overcrowded at present. Several narrators' overeating and overdrinking lead to satanic encounters and comic damnations and punishments in "The Duc de L'Omelette" and "The Angel of the Odd," two tales of gastronomic and alcoholic distress in which Poe draws upon his own private or "psychosomatic" hells to obtain the preconceived effect by reversing his own dictum through debasing the grotesque into the ludicrous.

The serious Gothic tales can be thematically categorized to show Poe's prowess at manipulating all of the high Gothic plot formulas and machinery to his own ends. These Gothic types and subtypes are as follows: homicidal and suicidal monologues told from the insider's point of view; the madman's monodrama, a type overlapping with the homicidal/suicidal fantasy; sagas of the last survivor or final participant in a drama of cosmic end; tales of infernal descent involving vertical expeditions of the Gothic sort into an underground of no return; tales of the fatal voyage; love stories featuring cadaverous rendezvous and resurrections; incarceration and enclosure stories in both the natural and supernatural mode; Gothified science fiction involving hypnosis and metempsychosis; dangerous predicament stories involving live burial, nightmares of time, or the menace of the clock; fantasies of revenge; tales of the double or secret sharer ("William Wilson"); and Gothic fairy tales ("Hop-Frog") that give a dark twist to the happily-ever-after formula. Far less Gothic in tone and theme are the three tales starring the superdetective C. Auguste Dupin, "The Murders in the Rue Morgue," "The Purloined Letter," and "The Mystery of Marie Roget." The detective stories contain Gothic elements but offer a world where reason is always in control. Landscape sketches and topographical rhapsodies and reveries such as "The Domain of Arnheim" and "The Island of the Fay" have occasional Gothic tonalities but are mainly prose poems celebrating eerie beauty. Grotesque tall tales such as "King Pest," with its pestilential array of animated rotten bodies, and "The System of Doctor Tarr and Professor Fether," with the lunatics in control of the madhouse, are too droll for the high Gothic category. This is

also true of the scientific hoaxes and fake big stories such as the hot-air extravaganzas of balloons and ballooning, "The Unparalleled Adventure of One Hans
Pfaall," "Mellonta Tauta," and "The Balloon Hoax," lampoons of the voyage of
discovery. In "The Gold-Bug," Poe momentarily put aside horror and terror to
indulge his fascination for cryptography, codes, and ingenious puzzle solving.

Poe's earliest attempts to write Gothic tales that might appeal to the tastes of
the magazine readership can be seen in the supershocker "Metzengerstein," the
whirlpool story "MS. Found in a Bottle," and the gruesome "Berenice," a tale
of oral mutilation of the beloved that might have been written specifically with
the lurid appetites of *The Monk*'s audience in view. In "Metzengerstein," Poe
imitated and perhaps mocked outrageous Germanic supernaturalism in a tale of
grotesque revenge and equine metempsychosis, since the tale features a trans-
migration from human into horse. The wronged and murdered Baron Berlifitz-
ing, whose stables have been burned by the wicked Baron Metzengerstein,
returns as a steed to exact doom by bearing Metzengerstein to a fiery death.

"MS. Found in a Bottle" is the first in a trilogy of sea tales that also includes
"A Descent into the Maelström" and the novel *The Narrative of Arthur Gordon
Pym*. Told in the first person (a posthumous narrator who reports from the other
side), the narrative is an account of a shipwreck and subsequent voyage of
discovery aboard a second ship named *The Discovery*, a nautical version of the
haunted castle gone afloat and manned by a spectral crew. The narrator is the
first of several Poe narrators to choose death over life in return for ultimate
cosmic insight when he submits to the force of the whirlpool and experiences
an elevation of perception and expanded insight into life once he has opted for
death. *The Narrative of Arthur Gordon Pym* offers a similar moment of destructive enlightenment at its abortive climax. As Pym "descends" to the South Pole,
he experiences most varieties of Gothic awe, wonder, and terror as Poe glob-
alizes the Gothic castle by turning the traditional underworld into a southern
hemisphere replete with monsters, gruesome deaths, threats of premature burial,
cannibalism, butchery, and finally an absurd rescue for the hero as he sails
"beyond the veil" and into the embrace of a huge figure of whiteness at the
South Pole itself. The dream currents that convey Pym to this bizarre nirvana
are taken one step further in the finest of the saltwater-trilogy tales in which
Poe moves the landlocked and earthbound Gothic romance to the open sea. "A
Descent into the Maelström" completes the trio of vertical journeys of discovery
begun by the "MS. Found in a Bottle" narrator and *Pym*. The narrator has
successfully made a fatal voyage into one of nature's deadliest places, the whirlpool, and come back to the surface with a deeper knowledge of the universe
and its mysterious ways. The Gothic's live-burial motif takes a submarine rather
than a subterranean form in a tale of creative self-annihilation. Submitting totally
to the beauty inherent in the horrible vortex, he is able to transcend the terror
and see profoundly for the first time. With particular brilliance, Poe converts
the Gothic's chamber of horrors or deadly enclosure into a seemingly deadly

natural chamber of horrors, then transforms the watery spiral from tomb into womb in the eye of the voyager.

The three "love/hate" stories, "Berenice," "Morella," and "Ligeia," also draw extensively upon traditional Gothic practices and characterization. Together, they form a triad in Poe's work that might be called his "marriage group," each demonstrating the progress of Poe's Gothic from physical horror and dread to metaphysical horror and awe. Underlying each story are powerful erotic tensions that manifest themselves in warped sexual frustration, marital violence, and postmortem visitations.

The first tale in the triad, "Berenice," is also the most repulsive in its treatment of the narrator's strained love affair. Affection, desire, and the need to possess the woman assume a grisly shape as the narrator's compulsive drive to extract Berenice's teeth climaxes in an act of oral mutilation that constitutes one of Poe's most emetic *coups de gothique*. Because of the dental idée fixe, modern criticism has neutered the tale by seeing it as a caricature of Gothic gore as well as Poe's mockery of the mandatory incident of maidenly assault, contending that the narrator's dental fetish ("In the multiplied objects of the external world I had no thoughts but for her teeth. For these I longed with a frenzied desire") is so overdone that it is nothing more than a mordant satire of Gothic violence in general and of Monk Lewis and the Marquis de Sade in particular.

Less repulsive in its disfigurement of the love object, although no less obsessive in its concentration on postmortem beauty, the second tale in the marriage group, "Morella," takes up the theme of psychic survival. The self-deceived narrator cannot love Morella while she is alive, detesting the mortal Morella and longing for her death. Vowing to return, Morella predicts that he will embrace her as passionately in death as he had spurned her in life, a promise that is kept when the narrator visits the dead Morella's empty crypt.

Morella's reanimation and posthumous return are restaged in the third love/hate story, "Ligeia." Here Poe piles complexities and ambiguities upon a stock and elementary Gothic plot, the supernatural return of a dark and mysterious lady who may or may not be a femme fatale, as recounted in a memoir of her return composed by a narrator who may or may not be madly hallucinating all that he recalls. In "Morella" and "Berenice," the narrator would seem to be the dominant member of the connubial relationship, but in "Ligeia," the amnesiac narrator, who cannot even recall his own name, venerates Ligeia while she is alive and submits to her colossal intellect with childlike devotion. When she succumbs to a vague but fatal illness, she proclaims that her will is stronger than death. The narrator marries Ligeia's physical and mental opposite, Lady Rowena, then immediately grows sick of her to the point where many readers have implicated him in Rowena's strange illness and death. The Gothic mystery here might involve nothing less than postmortem bigamy, since the marital bond forged by Ligeia through her will remains in force from beyond the grave. As Rowena pales, wastes away, and dies, Ligeia wills her return by apparently

inhabiting, then displacing, Rowena's corpse in a "hideous drama of revivifi-
cation" (124). The grisly finale is a brilliant revival of a stock Gothic exposure
scene when the specter draws aside the cloak or the mask or the cowl falls away
from the monk's head to reveal the smiling skull. Not abject terror, but delight
seems to be the narrator's mood as he watches in fascination while the grave
clothes fall away, revealing Ligeia's form. In cruder versions of this stock Gothic
legend of the dead beloved's return, the condition of the narrator is inconse-
quential, but in Poe's reworking of these materials, the condition of the narrator
will not permit a reading at a single level. Instead, as is typical of Poe's Gothic
usages in general, a phalanx of questions confronts the reader, who is forced to
think through the evidence of the deceased beloved's conquest of death. Has
Poe rewritten an orthodox *schauerromantik* thriller in which the terrors are of
Germany rather than the soul? Is the dark lady of the narrator's life a demonic
or ethereal presence, and is her second coming an objective or subjective occurrence? Does the narrator's final mental condition reflect a frenzied farewell
to sanity or a bereaved lover's rapture? Who or what killed Rowena and why?
Does vampirism play some strange part in Ligeia's miraculous return through
the bodily host of Rowena? The fact that all of these questions of meaning and
intent are valid suggests that no other horror tale by Poe combines such simplicity of plot and character with such complexity of meaning and mood.

Among the tales in the high Gothic category, five stories deserve special place
as preeminently successful in their intensification of older Gothic energy into
new channels of artistic power. "The Fall of the House of Usher," "The Cask
of Amontillado," "The Pit and the Pendulum," "The Masque of the Red Death,"
and "The Tell-Tale Heart" all duplicate on their surfaces well-worn Gothic settings, ordeals, characters, and deeds, but each tale leaves the impression of
managing the equipment of the Gothic romance to provoke a degree and quality
of horror not attained by any Gothic writer before Poe. Without overlooking the
value of physical anguish to the Gothic milieu, Poe adds a dimension of metaphysical anxiety and crisis. "Poe's subject is the precariously logical human
mind which is capable of gross misperception, unreal construction, and instant
irrationality" (Thompson 22).

When the narrative elements of "The Fall of the House of Usher" are simply
cataloged, the story would appear to be little more than an ingenious condensation of a typical English Gothic novel. A decaying house, an accursed family,
an atmosphere of lurking horror, dark secrets, live burial, cadaverous return,
luridly illuminated vaults, copper-sheathed coffins, psychotic paintings, preternatural movement of architecture, mysterious sounds and subterranean noises,
and the spectacular collapse of the doomed building during a howling tempest
are among the reusable parts that Poe reconstructs into a new Gothic gestalt.
Because the entire tale is the recollection of the escaped narrator, it is fair to
say that the story is "about" the narrator and his understanding or misunderstanding of his adventure, since the narrator is the re-creator of these strange
events. What then is the deeper horror that emerges from such an emphasis on

a flawed narrator or an obtuse "central intelligence," to apply Henry James's term to the teller of the tale? Is there a mental fall involved that is infinitely more appalling than the fall of the house or the fall of the dead-and-risen sister collapsing atop her dying brother? Poe's Gothic introduces such perplexities and raises such ambiguities by posing doubts about how much we know—or ever can know—about ourselves and the universe.

Equally adept in its deepening and extending the possibilities of the Gothic, "The Cask of Amontillado" is a comedy of revenge and odd justice that reads like one episode or subplot of a longer Gothic work in its reuse of the subterranean journey. The Gothic decor of the underground with its foul-smelling nitrous passageways narrowing down to a coffinlike niche is the stuff of a thousand Gothic cellars, but in Poe's hands, these overworked materials take on a new allure. The tale is both a dramatic monologue and a reminiscence. Although a superficial reading might attach a confessional moral to Montresor's memoir, it is clear that after fifty years he can still savor the memory point by point like a well-aged wine in his ritualized reenactment of his foolish rival's "immmolation." Alert readers must have smiled at the double entendre of the Latin epitaph, "In Pace Requiescat," for it is not Fortunato, but Montresor who has been able to "rest in peace" for the fifty years since the elimination of an annoying fool from his life.

Poe demonstrates his command of a similar stock Gothic ordeal in "The Pit and the Pendulum," in which the sluggish horrors of dozens of Inquisition Gothics are compacted into one of the great horror stories of the world, told from the point of view of the anonymous victim. The richness of the tale's Gothicism is confirmed by the varieties of interpretation it has evoked. Reductive readings see the story as Poe's brilliant condensation of a highly popular subtype of Gothic novel, the monastic shocker or narrative of Inquisition fiendishness, resembling "The Spaniard's Tale" in Charles Robert Maturin's *Melmoth the Wanderer*. But the voice from the pit, at once hysterical and analytic, suggests that Poe is seeking a response beyond mere shudder in his concentration on political, psychological, metaphysical, or even existential distress in the victim's double lethal predicament from above and below. The agonized consciousness faced with the nothingness of the pit below and the descending menace of time from above touches upon universal fears of an unknown world whose shape and direction can never be ascertained. From the story's opening metronomic sentence, "I was sick—sick unto the death with that long agony" (261), to the absurd, yet timely, salvation of the heretic-victim by the godlike hand of General Lasalle, Poe elevates one of the Gothic's most familiar situations into a parable of the helpless human condition suspended in space and time.

Even though Poe rules out the didactic as a legitimate preconceived effect, "The Masque of the Red Death" seems to contain an austere moral warning for the artist who would create a private imaginative kingdom immune from the ravages of reality. Poe's reading of Beckford's *Vathek* may have been the inspiration for the highly Vathekian Prince Prospero, a wealthy, powerful, hedonistic ruler who thinks that he has found safety from the red plague by secluding himself with "his thousand hale and light-hearted friends" within his abbey. "All these and security were within. Without was the 'Red Death.' The external world could take care of itself" (254). This exclusive world of private pleasure is more than a modification of Beckfordian hedonism, for, as in "The Fall of the House of Usher" and "The Pit and the Pendulum," Poe extends his Gothic sources of the tale's setting and conflict into an apocalyptic vision of the end of the world. In a reversal of the usual Gothic pattern of flight and pursuit, Prince Prospero stalks, then confronts a masked figure, only to be felled when the phantom turns upon him. Might the Red Death, the uninvited guest who has crashed Prospero's party, also be the first-person voice that proclaims "dominion over all" in the tale's closing sentence?

The bleak, squalid, unadorned setting of "The Tell-Tale Heart" stands in contrast to the plush decadence of the setting in "The Masque of the Red Death." A dilapidated house, a recumbent old man, a nameless narrator who may be either male or female, lanterns, tubs, creaky floor planks, and other fixtures of poverty and proletarian gloom comprise one of Poe's starkest settings. The narrator recalls precisely when and how he/she murdered his/her fellow lodger by tipping the bed over on him, then smothering him, meticulously dismembering the body, and concealing the pieces beneath the floor planking. The motive for the murder, however, despite the narrator's protestations of sanity, remains shrouded in mystery. To expose the blackness of the human mind, Poe turned to a pair of well-worn Gothic utilities, the terrible optic or the eye that can maim or slay and the hideous noise in the night, transferring these to the irksome body of the geriatric victim. Having put out the annoying eye, the narrator is assailed by the deafening pulsations of the body's clock, the beating heart of a dead and mutilated old man, as Poe raises the temperature of Gothic horror by showing matter depriving mind of choice or control. Without summoning specters to achieve his climax or resorting to any supernatural chicanery, Poe produced a Gothic story in the disturbingly modern mode. Forced to "scream or die" (282), the narrator is caught inside a cerebral maze of confused motive and is confined permanently to the dungeon of the self, certainly the blackest of Gothic prisons.

Retaining literally all of the secondhand mechanisms of Gothic fiction, Poe forged a higher Gothic by internalizing horror and terror to a point of no return. Amid every hideous circumstance or supernatural effusion in Poe's work, the reader is constantly called upon to respond intellectually as well as emotionally. Whether his Gothic art can, or ought, to be separated from his personal hells remains moot. The large and growing body of critical literature on Poe's Gothic has still not produced a final satisfactory answer to the issue of where and how Poe's Gothic vision fits into the American Gothic mosaic, although critics such as Richard Benton and Paul Lewis are certainly on the right track when they insist that Poe is the kind of Gothic writer who makes us think as well as cringe and quiver and the kind of Gothic writer who is eager to test the Gothic's capacity for ideas. Benton's statement "The principal appeal of the high Gothic lies in its epistemological and moral ambiguity. It makes us think" seems particularly relevant to Poe's adaptations of the form. His horror art is tempered by irony and detachment; his characters are "psychological archetypes dredged out of the depths of human experience" (Benton 8). Although Poe's American-ness has often been dismissed or denied, his Gothic raises fundamental questions about who we are and what we might become, both nationally and individually. By entertaining through fear, Poe's Gothic puts us in touch with ourselves, or, to revert to the Poe-Dickinson connection, "ourselves behind ourselves concealed."

SELECTED CRITICISM

Benton, Richard P. "The Problems of Literary Gothicism," *ESQ: A Journal of the American Renaissance* 18 (1972): 5–9.

Bonaparte, Marie. *The Life and Works of Edgar Allan Poe: A Psychoanalytic Interpretation*. Trans. John Rodker. London: Imago, 1949. First published in 1933. French as *Edgar Poe, étude psychoanalytique. Avant-Propo de Sigmund Freud*. Paris: Denoël et Steele.

Budick, E. Miller. "Poe's Gothic Idea: The Cosmic Geniture of Horror." *Essays in Literature* 3 (1976): 73–85. "Gothicism in Poe is the natural human response to the implications of idealism."

Engel, Leonard W. "Claustrophobia, the Gothic Enclosure, and Poe." *Clues: A Journal of Detection* 10: 2 (1989): 107–117. Enclosure tales such as "MS. Found in a Bottle" and "The Premature Burial" have positive resolutions because they end in liberation.

Fiedler, Leslie. "The Blackness of Darkness: E.A. Poe and the Development of the Gothic." In *Love and Death in the American Novel*. New York: Criterion, 1960: 370–382. Reads *The Narrative of Arthur Gordon Pym* as a Gothic racial fantasy. "Poe's novel is surely the first which uses Gothicism to express a peculiarly American dilemma identifying the symbolic blackness of terror with the blackness of the Negro and the white guilts he embodies."

Garrison, Joseph M., Jr. "The Function of Terror in the Work of Edgar Allan Poe." *American Quarterly* 18 (1966): 136–150. Argues that the Gothic in Poe's writings produces "the possibility that terror and horror, if rightly understood, can and should yield pleasure."

Ginsberg, Lesley. "Slavery and the Gothic Horror of Poe's 'The Black Cat.' " In *American Gothic: New Interventions in a National Narrative*. Ed. Robert K. Martin and Eric Savoy. Iowa City: University of Iowa Press, 1998: 99–128. A revisionist reading that sees the story as Poe's "investigation into the peculiar psychopolitics of the master/slave relationship." "The disjunction between Poe's proslavery pronouncements and the writer who produced fiction which plays out the proslavery agenda to its most horrifying conclusions might allow us to imagine a Poe whose relation to race was far more complex than it might first appear."

Griffith, Clark. "Poe and the Gothic." In *Papers on Poe: Essays in Honor of John Ward Ostrom*. Ed. Richard Veler. Springfield, OH: Chantry Music Press at Wittenberg University, 1972: 21–27. Poe changed the emphasis of the Gothic from external phenomena to the internal mind.

Hoffman, Daniel. *Poe Poe Poe Poe Poe Poe Poe*. Garden City, NY: Doubleday, 1972. Controversial reading of Poe that portrays him as the master hoaxer and sardonic comedian throughout his works.

Hustis, Harriet. " 'Reading Encrypted But Persistent': The Gothic of Reading and Poe's 'The Fall of the House of Usher.' " *Studies in American Fiction* 27 (1999): 3–20. Concentrates on the function of the reader in "creating" a Gothic text. "The dual critique and enactment of the Gothic in 'The Fall of the House of Usher' represent an exploration of the very nature of Gothic textuality itself."

Lévy, Maurice. "Edgar Poe et la tradition 'gothique.' " *Caliban* 5 (1968): 35–51. Translated as "Poe and the Gothic Tradition." *ESQ: A Journal of the American Renaissance* 18 (1972): 19–28. Rejects Freudian approaches to Poe's Gothic and discusses his resourceful adaptations of the Gothic tradition. No psychoanalytic theory is needed to understand his Gothic.

Lewis, Paul. "The Intellectual Functions of Gothic Fiction: Poe's 'Ligeia' and Tieck's 'Wake Not the Dead.' " *Comparative Literature Studies* 16 (1979): 207–221. Sees Poe's Gothic as a medium for ideas as well as sensational thrills. Poe's Gothic addresses "important questions about man, society, and the universe."

Lovecraft, H.P. "Edgar Allan Poe." In *Supernatural Horror in Literature*. New York: Dover, 1973: 52–59. "Poe himself . . . certainly possessed much of the depression, sensitiveness, mad inspiration, loneliness, and extravagant freakishness which he attributes to his haughty and solitary victims of Fate." Lovecraft's monograph was originally published in 1927.

Magistrale, Tony, and Sidney Poger. "Poe's Children: The Conjunction of Detective and Gothic Tales." In *Poe's Children: Connections between Tales of Terror and Detection*. New York: Peter Lang, 1999: 29–44. "The conservative nature of the detective tale parallels the essential dynamic found in the horror tale. Both horror and detection analyze, challenge, and sometimes subvert the value systems of any given cultural epoch; they ask us to pay close attention to repressed communal insecurities."

Mainville, Stephen. "Language and the Void: Gothic Landscapes in the Frontiers of Edgar Allan Poe." In *Frontier Gothic: Terror and Wonder at the Frontier in American Literature*. Ed. David Mogen, Scott Sanders, and Joanne Karpinski. Rutherford, NJ: Fairleigh Dickinson University Press, 1993: 187–202. Analyzes the significance of frontiers in *The Narrative of Arthur Gordon Pym*. "Poe's frontier is the frontier of the unconscious."

Male Roy R. "Edgar Allan Poe," In *American Literary Masters*, Ed. Charles R. Anderson, New York: Holt, Rinehart, and Winston, 1965.

Mooney, Stephen L. "Poe's Gothic Wasteland." *Sewanee Review* 70 (1962): 261–283. Poe's Gothic projects "ironic images of man in the nineteenth-century age of anxiety. Poe's typical theme is alienation; his plot, survival; and his characters, anxiety personified."

Ringe, Donald. *American Gothic: Imagination and Reason in Nineteenth-Century Fiction* Lexington: University Press of Kentucky, 1982.

Shelden, Pamela J. " 'True Originality': Poe's Manipulation of the Gothic Tradition." *American Transcendental Quarterly* 29 (1976): 75–80. Poe manipulates the Gothic to expose the torments of the inner life.

Stableford, Brian. "Poe, Edgar Allan." In *St. James Guide to Horror, Ghost, and Gothic Writers*. Ed. David Pringle. Detroit: St. James Press, 1998: 453–455. Perhaps more than any other American writer, Poe "extended the stylistic and thematic boundaries of the genre."

Thompson, G.R. *Poe's Fiction: Romantic Irony in the Gothic Tales*. Madison: University of Wisconsin Press, 1973. Theorizes that Poe's Gothic is used to suggest "the deceptive perversity of the universe." His Gothicism "intrudes the comic into the tragic, the satiric into the demonic to achieve a liberating transcendental perception of the dark paradox of human existence."

Voller, Jack G. "Allegory and Fantasy: The Short Fiction of Hawthorne and Poe." In *The Supernatural Sublime: The Metaphysics of Terror in Anglo-American Romanticism*. De Kalb: Northern Illinois University Press, 1994: 209–239. Poe's Gothic is a cerebral and thoughtful Gothic. "One of the most horrific aspects of Poe's work is the implied failure of sense perception and intellection in apprehending the totality of human existence; horror emerges as Poe reveals the inadequacy of that which we have long believed adequate."

JOHN POLIDORI
(1795–1821)
Douglass H. Thomson

PRINCIPAL GOTHIC WORKS

Ernestus Berchtold; or, The Modern Oedipus: A Tale. London: Longman, Hurst, Rees, Orme, & Brown, 1819.
The Vampyre. New Monthly Magazine, April 1819.
The Vampyre: A Tale. London: Sherwood, Neely, & Jones, 1819.
The Vampyre: A Tale by the Right Honorable Lord Byron. Paris: Galignani, 1819.

Translations and Adaptations

Nodier, Charles. "Lord Ruthwen, ou les Vampires." Paris: Chez Ladrocat, 1820.
Planché, J.R. *The Vampire; or, The Bride of the Isles: A Romantic Melodrama in Two Acts.* London: John Lowndes, 1820.
Lord Ruthwen; o, I Vampiri. Napoles: Presso R. Marotta e Vanspandoch, 1826.

MODERN REPRINTS AND EDITIONS

The Diary of Dr. John William Polidori, 1816. Ed. William Michael Rossetti. London: E. Matthews, 1911.
"The Ghost-Story Contest." Appendix C in *Frankenstein; or, The Modern Prometheus.* Ed. James Rieger. Indianapolis: Bobbs-Merrill, 1974. (Contains *The Vampyre* and Byron's fragment of the tale. This edition is cited in the text.)
Three Gothic Novels, and a Fragment of a Novel by Lord Byron. Ed. by E.F. Bleiler. New York: Dover, 1966. (One of the three is Polidori's *Vampyre.*)
The Vampyre: A Tale. In *The Evil Image: Two Centuries of Gothic Short Fiction and Poetry.* Ed. Patricia Skarda and Nora Crow Jaffe. New York: New American Library, 1981.
The Vampyre. Ed. Jonathan Wordsworth. Oxford: Woodstock, 1990.
The Vampyre; and, Ernestus Berchtold, or, The Modern Oedipus: Collected Fiction of

John William Polidori. Ed. D.L. MacDonald and Kathleen Scherf. Toronto: University of Toronto Press, 1993.
The Vampire. Adapted by Les Martin; illustrated by Paul Van Munching. New York: Random House, 1994.

"A star in the halo of a moon" is how John Polidori described himself in relation to Byron (*Diary* 150). He was certainly a lesser light in the constellation of writers who gathered for the ghost-story-telling contest that fateful June evening in 1816, but his slender contribution, *The Vampyre*, has had a decisive impact on this special subgenre of Gothic literature. (See the Mary Wollstonecraft Shelley entry for information on this contest, which involved Mary and Percy Shelley, Byron, and Polidori.) Arising out of Polidori's own complex relationship with Byron (part longing, part loathing, and also part self-loathing), the tale can be seen as a *roman à clef* with a vengeance, casting Byron as the ruthless, spirit-sapping Lord Ruthven and Polidori himself as the virtuous but hopelessly mismatched Aubrey. Polidori's treatment of the vampire legend is one of the first to acknowledge the author's fascination with this dark seducer in sexual and psychological terms. From this lesser luminary of the Romantic writers, and, in part, because of his anxiety about being a lesser presence, came a treatment of the vampire legend that would have great resonance in the bloodthirsty tradition to come.

Polidori accompanied Byron to Europe ostensibly as his personal physician, having recently completed his medical thesis, *De morbo oneirodynia dicto*, a study of sleep disorders, nightmares, and hallucinations prefaced by an epigraph from the sleepwalking scene in *Macbeth*. We now know that he also was offered 500 pounds by the publisher John Murray to keep a diary recording the infamous goings-on of the Byron-Shelley circle. Young, handsome, and vain, and with more than a touch of anxiety and paranoia, "Polly Dolly," as Byron nicknamed him, must have proved an irresistible target for the elder poet's acerbic wit. The homosexual portion of Polidori's being must have felt enormous attraction to the sexually potent and ambiguous figure of Byron, while the Catholic in him must have felt guilt about such desires. As an aspiring writer, he also must have felt compelled to compete with Byron and the Shelleys, a daunting task for an untried twenty-year-old. Polidori, in fact, borrowed the idea of his vampire tale from a fragment Byron had begun as his contribution to the ghost-story contest. He turned the tale against its creator, using the vampire legend to characterize the demonic hold Byron had on him and his own sense of an acutely paralyzed will, one desiring but terrified of desire, one wishing to free itself but unable to do so.

In a tale packed with literary borrowings and personal allusions, Polidori steals his name for the vampire, Lord Ruthven, from another character assault on Byron in Lady Caroline Lamb's Gothicky novel *Glenarvon*. Lamb, whose highly public affair with Byron proved shocking even by Regency standards, also has a cameo role in the tale as the brazenly adulterous Lady Mercer. Ruthven appears as a striking and mysterious figure amid the usual "dissipations attendant upon a London winter" (266), haughty and reserved yet possessing "irresistible powers of seduction" for both the virtuous and "impudent" ladies of the salon world, although he prefers ruining the former. He immediately attracts the notice of a rather vain, handsome young aristocrat, Aubrey, who, with his fair share of romantic proclivities, instantly converts Ruthven into "the hero of a romance," this despite "his deadly hue" and "dead grey eye" (267–268). Eagerly joining his hero on a tour of the Continent, Aubrey receives hints about the vicious character of Ruthven but cannot resist his mysterious appeal, "which to [Aubrey's] exalted imagination began to assume the appearance of the supernatural" (270). Finally alerted by his concerned guardians and thus able to frustrate Ruthven's designs to ruin a young Roman maid, Aubrey quits the company of the dark lord, heads to Greece for antiquarian research, falls in love with Ianthe (a Shelleyan dream maiden), and blithely dismisses the warnings of her parents that this is a land where vampires are known to conduct their "nocturnal reveries" (274).

But the will of this vampire cannot be resisted. Ruthven returns and, unknown to Aubrey at the time, vampirizes the delicate Ianthe; brazenly attends upon the sick and distraught Aubrey and wins back his trust; secretly returns from the dead after his apparent murder by banditti; and astounds Aubrey by reemerging in London society with the seduction of Aubrey's own sister as his next dark design. Finally fully aware of Ruthven's sinister nature, Aubrey is yet helpless to avert the tragic events, as Ruthven had earlier extracted from him a vow of silence, a detail Polidori lifts from Byron's fragment but one that also recalls a similar occurrence in Coleridge's vampirish "Christabel," a poem very much in circulation among the ghost story contestants at the Villa Diodati. Reduced, as so many exasperatingly ineffectual Gothic heroes are, to delirium and sickbed—one recalls Goethe's remark "Romanticism I call sickness"—Aubrey pops a blood vessel from the excruciating pressure of his oath and dies. The last sentence of this briskly moving tale reveals the inevitable: "Lord Ruthven had disappeared, and Aubrey's sister had glutted the thirst of a VAMPYRE!"

The unmistakably sexual nature of Polidori's predator had a lasting impact on the tradition of vampiric literature. Equally influential is the psychology of possession Polidori explores: as Frank suggests, it appears that our erstwhile hero is "vampirized without being aware of it" (286). Ruthven's mastery of Aubrey's will underscores the power of all vampiric literature: the inability to resist the allure and power of an evil that yet appears so monstrous and potent. In the unqualified triumph of evil, an ending unusual for early Gothics, Polidori offers a dark counterpoint to the "exalted imagination" characteristic of his fellow ghost-story contestants. Perhaps in the figures of the too-romantically inclined and self-absorbed Aubrey and the utterly idealized Ianthe Polidori takes direct aim at the poetic flights of Byron and Shelley. Yet Aubrey's doomed fascination is also surely Polidori's, as the vampiric trope allows him to express his own tortured relationship with Byron. In his tale's oblique expression of longing and loathing, of power and powerlessness, Polidori unwittingly provided the essential ingredients for a literature of horror that still thrives today.

Polidori's less regarded novel *Ernestus Berchtold* picks up on another Diodati theme, one of special importance to Mary Shelley and her father William Godwin: the destruction of domestic harmony by an egotistical and overreaching male. Polidori's version of Godwin's St. Leon and Mary Shelley's Victor Frankenstein is the ruthless patriarch Count Filiberto Doni, who travels to Asia in pursuit of wealth and gains it from the "hideous form" of a "spirit" who demands in return some unspecified "domestic affliction" (138). This affliction becomes apparent when the Count much later recognizes to his horror that Ernestus, the man who has married his daughter Louisa, is none other than his son from a previous marriage. Although the novel is spiced with such Gothic elements as supernatural intervention and incest, it wallows in the prolonged despair of Ernestus, recognizable again as a sad alter ego of Polidori in his isolation and helplessness. Unable to contend with psychic conflicts coming to a head, Polidori, author of *The Vampyre* and physician to the stars, returned to his father's house in 1821 and took his own life at the age of twenty-five.

SELECTED CRITICISM

Astle, Richard S. "Ontological Ambiguity and Historical Pessimism in Polidori's 'The Vampyre.' " *Sphinx: A Magazine of Literature and Society* 8 (1977): 8–16. Credits Polidori with a serious philosophical perspective. His understanding of the "ontological ambiguity" of life is reflected in the triumph of the foreign and irrational over the domestic and rational. Emphasizes that this is one of the first Gothics where evil prevails.

Barbour, Judith. "Dr. John William Polidori, Author of *The Vampyre*." In *Imagining Romanticism: Essays on English and Australian Romanticisms*. Ed. Deirdre Coleman and Peter Otto. West Cornwall, CT: Locust Hill, 1992: 85–110. Contextual study of the story in terms of Polidori's futile attempts to enter the Byron-Shelley circle. Polidori "willfully misrepresents" himself into a part Byron designed for Shelley (Aubrey), and Byron's *Giaour* and Henry Fuseli's *Nightmare* provide important references.

Boone, Troy. "Mark of the Vampire: Arnod Paole, Sade, Polidori." *Nineteenth-Century Contexts* 18 (1995): 349–366. Uses Sade's *Justine* as a bridge between the infamous Medregia vampire case of Paole in the 1730s and Polidori's novel to chart a shift in the treatment of vampirism from "a well-contained menace to society" to a way of analyzing "the relations of sexuality and individualism, law and power. The violent combatants of Polidori's novel display the vampire's victorious mastery of homosocial relations and [the victim's] failure to dodge homoerotic desire."

Cass, Jeffrey. "The Contestatory Gothic in Mary Shelley's *Frankenstein* and J.W. Polidori's *Ernestus Berchtold*: The Spectre of a Colonialist Paradigm." *JAISA: The Journal of the Association for the Interdisciplinary Study of the Arts* 11:2 (1996):

33–41. "Gothic fiction, while opening up a narrative space in which Shelley and Polidori might . . . build a personal and cultural identity, also forces them to conjure up the spectre of a colonialist paradigm."

Foust, Ronald. "Rite of Passage: The Vampire Tale as Cosmogonic Myth." In *Aspects of Fantasy: Selected Essays from the Second International Conference on the Fantastic in Literature and Film.* Ed. William Coyle. Westport, CT: Greenwood Press, 1986: 73–84. Places the tale within the tradition of vampire literature and emphasizes the psychological aspects of Polidori's depiction.

Frank, Frederick S. "The Vampyre." In *The First Gothics: A Critical Guide to the English Gothic Novel.* New York: Garland, 1987: 285–286.

MacDonald, D.L. *Poor Polidori: A Critical Biography of the Author of The Vampire* Toronto: University of Toronto Press, 1991. The only book-length biography, and a good one. Divided into three Byronic sections: before, during, and after Polidori's acquaintance. Argues for the centrality of Byron in his life, both psychoanalytically and metaphorically.

McFarland, Ronald E. "The Vampire on Stage: A Study in Adaptations." *Comparative Drama* 21 (1987): 19–33. A study of the many stage adaptations of the vampire, including early ones based on Polidori's tale.

Morrill, David F. " 'Twilight Is Not Good for Maidens': Uncle Polidori and the Psychodynamics of Vampirism in 'Goblin Market.' " *Victorian Poetry* 28 (1990): 1–16. Identifies her uncle Polidori's *Vampyre* as a source for the Gothic atmospherics and conventions in Christina Rossetti's "Goblin Market."

Rieger, James. "Dr. Polidori and the Genesis of *Frankenstein*." *SEL: Studies in English Literature, 1500–1900* 3 (1963): 461–472. Offers a defense of Polidori, regarding both the "far from contemptible" *Vampyre* and his role in suggesting some of the key scientific details for *Frankenstein*. Casts doubt on Viet's thesis that Polidori's death was not suicide.

Skarda, Patricia L. "Vampirism and Plagiarism: Byron's Influence and Polidori's Practice." *Studies in Romanticism* 28 (1989): 249–269. Poor Polidori, indeed: "Polidori's plunder of Byron the man and Byron the artist goes beyond plagiarism to the bloodless vampirism" of vainly trying to capture the essence of Byron's genius.

Switzer, Richard. "Lord Ruthven and the Vampires." *French Review* 29 (1955): 107–112. Traces the influence of Polidori's version on French vampiric literature.

Waller, Gregory A. *The Living and the Undead: From Stoker's Dracula to Romero's Dawn of the Dead.* Urbana: University of Illinois Press, 1986. Lord Ruthven represents a nightmare of the middle class, which can find no hope in an older order nor faith in "new life."

ANN RADCLIFFE
(1764–1823)
Frederick S. Frank

PRINCIPAL GOTHIC WORKS

The Castles of Athlin and Dunbayne: A Highland Story, London: T. Hookham, 1789.

A Sicilian Romance. London: T. Hookham, 1790.

The Romance of the Forest, Interspersed with Some Pieces of Poetry. London: T. Hookham & J. Carpenter, 1791.

The Mysteries of Udolpho: A Romance Interspersed with Some Pieces of Poetry. London: G.G. & J. Robinson, 1794.

The Italian; or, The Confessional of the Black Penitents. London: T. Cadell, Jr., & W. Davies, 1797.

Gaston de Blondeville; or, The Court of Henry III Keeping Festival in Ardenne: A Romance; St. Albans Abbey: A Metrical Tale. London: Henry Colburn, 1826. (Prefixed by a memoir of Radcliffe by Thomas Noon Serjeant Talfourd accompanied by extracts from her journals.)

"On the Supernatural in Poetry." *New Monthly Magazine* 16 (1826): 145–152.

MODERN REPRINTS AND EDITIONS

The Castles of Athlin and Dunbayne. Ed. Frederick Shroyer. New York: Arno Press, 1972. (The introduction stresses the ways in which Radcliffe's first Gothic uses "the terrible forces of nature to reflect the dark passions of men.")

The Castles of Athlin and Dunbayne. Ed. Devendra P. Varma. London: Folio Society, 1987. (The introduction sees her first Gothic "as an essay, a first step. It contains in embryo all the notable elements of Radcliffe's romances.")

The Castles of Athlin and Dunbayne. Ed. Alison Milbank. New York: Oxford University Press, 1995. (The introduction discusses Radcliffe's first novel in light of the two Jacobite rebellions of 1715 and 1745, Samuel Johnson's *Preface to Shakespeare*, and Scottish nationalism. The novel "situates itself in a particularly eighteenth-century mode of writing about the Highlands as a melancholy site, a fallen nation, yet one with privileged access to the past.")

Gaston de Blondeville; or, The Court of Henry III Keeping Festival in Arden. Ed. Devendra P. Varma. New York: Arno Press, 1972. (Series edition and modern reprinting.)

Gaston de Blondeville; or, The Court of Henry III Keeping Festival in Arden. Ed. Devendra P. Varma. London: Folio Society, 1987. (In this posthumous novel, Radcliffe finally broke with her standard method of explained supernatural by "introducing a spectre which is not explained away, but stalks unabashed through Kenilworth Castle.")

The Italian; or, The Confessional of the Black Penitents. Ed. Frederick Garber. London: Oxford University Press, 1968. (The best modern edition of the novel. "*The Monk* inspired her to produce a better book than any she had written." The result was *The Italian*. This edition is cited in the text.)

The Italian; or, The Confessional of the Black Penitents. Ed. Devendra P. Varma. London: Folio Society, 1987. (*The Italian* is Radcliffe's realization of her Gothic ideals, "the highwatermark of Radcliffe's achievement.")

The Mysteries of Udolpho. Ed. Bonamy Dobrée; explanatory notes by Frederick Garber. London: Oxford University Press, 1970; Rpt. 1998 with a new introduction and notes by Terry Castle. (This edition is cited in the text.)

The Mysteries of Udolpho. Ed. Devendra P. Varma. London: Folio Society, 1987. (The castle attains its highest development in *Udolpho*, in which "the architectural element in her landscape acquires a personality and motivates the plot.")

The Romance of the Forest. Ed. Devendra P. Varma; foreword by Frederick Garber. New York: Arno Press, 1974. (Regards Radcliffe's third novel as a model Gothic achievement in its presentation of "dark dungeons, shattered abbeys, and closeted skeletons.")

The Romance of the Forest. Ed. Chloe Chard. New York: Oxford University Press, 1986. (The introduction cites Michel Foucault's "language of infinity" as a principal stimulus to terror in the novel.)

The Romance of the Forest. Ed. Devendra P. Varma. London: Folio Society, 1987. (The introduction comments on the novel as "the first dawn of Radcliffe's mature powers.")

A Sicilian Romance. Ed. Devendra P. Varma. New York: Arno Press, 1972. (The novel demonstrates Radcliffe's willingness to experiment with castles and landscapes as vehicles of soul-expanding terror.)

A Sicilian Romance. Ed. Devendra P. Varma. London: Folio Society, 1987. (The introduction discusses Radcliffe's second novel as an "endeavor to establish a kind of organic relationship between scenery and character.")

A Sicilian Romance. Ed. Alison Milbank. New York: Oxford University Press, 1993. (The introduction discusses Radcliffe's evolution of a Gothic style in her first two novels and relates the novel to "a tradition of writings by women novelists about imprisonment. Most notably, it shows strong similarities to Sophia Lee's *The Recess; or, A Tale of Other Times*.")

Ann Radcliffe rose to national prominence in the 1790s with the publication of five Gothic romances, each book registering the progress of her Gothic toward the realization of an artistic ideal of a terror that pleases and attracts even as it frightens and repels. While she was widely known and respected in the world of letters in her own time, Radcliffe was by choice a shadowy figure, an almost spectral presence among the Gothic novelists. The essential details of her life come down to us from a single source, a reminiscence written by Sir Thomas Noon [Serjeant] Talfourd, a companion of William Radcliffe, prefixed to her final novel, *Gaston de Blondeville*. Talfourd's memoir attempted to "draw aside the veil from the personal course of this celebrated lady," but details were scanty. Talfourd lamented that "her biographer cannot exhibit any of the amusing varieties, which usually chequer the lives of successful authors. Even the great events of Radcliffe's life, the successive appearance of her novels, extend over a small part only of its duration" (qtd. in Rogers, *Bio-Bibliography* 5). Still, his portrait of Radcliffe remains factually valuable. Christina Rossetti later experienced similar frustration when she projected a biography of Radcliffe, then abandoned the work when it became clear that Radcliffe's life was too much the ectoplasmic silhouette to provide a biographer with ample material.

The "mother of a female Gothic," (Rogers, *Ann Radcliffe: A Bio-Bibliography, 2*) as Radcliffe has been called by one modern biographer, Deborah Rogers, countered the notoriety and public fame of her novels with a desire for privacy, seclusion, and the studied self-effacement of an anchorite. The facts of her life recorded by Talfourd are filtered through the memory of William Radcliffe, and although they are reliable, they tell us almost nothing about the Gothic predilections of Ann Ward Radcliffe. She was born into the middle-class family of the Wards in London in 1764. Educated in Bath, she became acquainted with Sophia Lee, author of *The Recess*. In her teens, she read Shakespeare and the Graveyard poets and pondered Edmund Burke's theoretical writings on the sublime. In January 1787, she married the London lawyer William Radcliffe, barrister of the Inner Temple and later the editor of the newspaper the *English Chronicle*. Two years later, her first novel appeared, followed rapidly by four Gothic romances and a travelogue, *A Journey Made in the Summer of 1794 through Holland and the Western Frontier of Germany with a Return down the Rhine* (1795). By 1797, her meteoric literary career was over, and, scorning the fame that might have been hers, she receded into absolute privacy. Her final years up until her death in 1823 were marred by ill health and respiratory ailments. Radcliffe died on 7 February 1823 and was buried in the Chapel of Ease in Bayswater. Of her fifty-nine years, a mere eight had been devoted to the writing of Gothic fiction. Some of the mysteries of Radcliffe's veiled life have been dispelled by Rictor Norton in *Mistress of Udolpho: The Life of Ann Radcliffe*. This biography not only unearths new information about such gray areas as her reclusiveness, mental illness, and breakdown, but also relocates Radcliffe by associating her with other radical women writers of the 1790s, thus reversing the standard critical view of Radcliffe as a conservative Gothicist in a revolutionary age. "Contrary to the received image of Ann Radcliffe as a privileged, well-educated, refined gentlewoman, she emerged from a radical Unitarian, rather than a conventional Anglican, background. She fully merits consideration as part of that circle of radical Dissenters that included Anna Laetitia Barbauld, Elizabeth Inchbald, Mary Hays, and Mary Wollstonecraft. She was indeed one of the 'unsex'd revolutionaries' of her time" (xi).

Yet biographical criticism can throw little light on Radcliffe's Gothic art or her attitudes toward that art. Because she shunned all contact with the public that read her books and eschewed the fame that could have been hers, her life came to be regarded as another typical case of introverted authorship, like the later self-sequestered careers of Emily Dickinson or the Brontë sisters. Her reticence gave the impression that writing was a pastime, not a profession or a serious endeavor. It was once fashionable, especially among nineteenth-century literary historians, to categorize her Gothic novel writing as the diversionary scribblings of a recluse who filled her lonely hours with Gothic fantasy while her husband, William Radcliffe, managed the weighty affairs of the *English Chronicle*.

In his "Prefatory Memoir" to the Ballantyne Library's edition of Radcliffe's works (1824), Sir Walter Scott ranked her as "the first poetess of romantic fiction." Her mastery of landscape and the infusion of that dark landscape with sublime imaginative energy revealed to Scott "the eye of a painter, with the spirit of a poet. Radcliffe, as an author, has the most decided claim to take her place among the favoured few, who have been distinguished as the founders of a class or school. She led the way in a peculiar style of composition." But despite Scott's praise and the accolades paid to her by Byron, Keats, Hazlitt, and the Shelleys, she remained throughout the nineteenth century a stereotypical closet author, a timid female novelist whose Gothicism was defaced by her tendency to explain and rationalize away the supernatural world in the final chapters of her novels.

Studies of Radcliffe in the twentieth century have reaffirmed the validity of Scott's recognition of her "peculiar style of composition." Her early-twentieth-century advocates, Clara McIntyre, Edith Birkhead, Eino Railo, and Montague Summers, placed her work at the epicenter of the Gothic movement in the eighteenth century. In *Ann Radcliffe in Relation to her Time*, McIntyre assigned Radcliffe a major place in the rise of the novel, while Summers hailed her as "a landmark and a power in English literature" (29) in his 1917 monograph "A Great Mistress of Romance: Ann Radcliffe, 1764–1823." More analytic appraisals of the value of Radcliffean Gothicism followed the close reading of her novels by Devendra P. Varma in *The Gothic Flame* (1957). When a full-length study of Radcliffe by E.B. Murray was included in Twayne's English Author Series in 1972, Radcliffe became the subject of heated critical debate over the nature, depth, seriousness, and artistic integrity of Gothic fiction. The 1980s witnessed an outpouring of doctoral dissertations on Radcliffe's fiction, particularly by students anxious to install her as a pioneering practitioner of "female Gothic." Although feminist criticism of "the Radcliffean Gothic model" may not be said to have abated in the 1990s, less restrictive and more eclectic interpretations of her Gothicism by Robert Miles, Fred Botting, and Deborah Rogers have done much to restore Ann Radcliffe to her original status as a Gothic writer for all classes and both sexes. Arguing that "Radcliffe is once again making contact with the larger reading public" (6), Robert Miles demonstrates that "her texts possess aesthetic depth, that they develop in interesting 'intentional' ways, and that she is properly seen in the context of her social origins" (3). Botting echoes this view of Radcliffe's restored relationship with twentieth-century readers as an author whose themes, settings, and characters communicate social and psychological crises and conflicts: "These heroines journey through a mysteriously threatening world composed of an unholy mixture of social corruption, natural decay, and imagined supernatural power. Invoking poetic power, Radcliffe's texts also set out to contain it within orders of reason, morality and domesticity" (64).

With the exception of the posthumously published *Gaston de Blondeville*, a novel with a real phantom but almost no other significant Gothic content, Radcliffe's novels established a standard for Gothic fiction and a formula for Gothic romance that extends down to the present day. She made her debut with the short but overplotted *Castles of Athlin and Dunbayne*, a tale of clan revenge, intrigue, usurpation, domestic tyranny, and genealogical suspense set in the medieval Scottish highlands. The two castles of the title refer to the two feuding families, as Radcliffe began to use the haunted castle as the main generator of terror. She continued her apprenticeship to the craft of terror in her second novel, *A Sicilian Romance*, a work longer than *The Castles of Athlin and Dunbayne* but less cumbersome in plot. Set in the 1580s at the castle of the Mazzini family on the north coast of Sicily, it marks Radcliffe's first use of an Italianate milieu to evoke suspense and terror. While the two heroines, Julia and Emilia, are little more than props for the villainy of their nasty father and stepmother, they foreshadow a full commitment of the maiden's imagination to the kind of pleasure that only the fearful or painful can incite.

Following these two experimental romances, Radcliffe advanced and refined her Gothic ideal with the three works that in some ways mark the zenith of Gothic romance in the eighteenth century. *The Romance of the Forest* brings into high focus the primary elements of Radcliffean Gothic romance that had been loosely displayed in the first two novels: the menaced maiden, the mysterious castle, and internecine family villainy. The plot turns on what will become the classic Radcliffean crisis and dénouement, the villain's discovery that the maiden he preys upon is a blood relative. Adeline's ordeal at the hands of her uncle, the Marquis de Montalt, alternates with the "supernatural" experiences of her abbey confinement. Radcliffe refined her formula for terror by locating the maiden between the authentic natural evil of the villain and the imagined supernatural evil of a dark building crammed with audiovisual surprises. The novel's twenty-six chapters are headed by poetic epigraphs, including several from her adored Graveyard poet, William Collins. The epigraph to chapter 2 is taken from Walpole's drama *The Mysterious Mother* and underscores the fulcrum of pleasurable fear at the heart of Radcliffean Gothic, the fear that elates even as it deepens the appreciation of a sinister beauty: "How these antique towers and suspended courts chill the suspended soul! Till expectation wears the face of fear, and fear, half ready to become devotion, mutters a kind of mental orison" (Walpole, *Mysterious Mother*, act I, scene 1).

The Mysteries of Udolpho is a kind of inspired rewriting of *The Romance of the Forest*. It has sometimes been called a bildungsroman in Gothic shape that traces the wayward progress of the maiden from excessive sensibility to proper sense, with many self-induced supernatural adventures intervening between the two stages of development. The heroine, Emily St. Aubert, is so heavily victimized by her own emotional profligacy that she misapprehends the real horrors stalking abroad in a world controlled by wicked relatives and aggressive noblemen like her aunt Madame Cheron and her evil host at Castle di Udolpho, Signor Montoni. As the tale's narrator repeatedly warns, "To a warm imagination, the dubious forms that float half-veiled in darkness afford a higher delight, than the most distinct scenery, the sun can show" (598). While Emily St. Aubert is a prisoner within Montoni's castle deep in the Apennines, she is propelled along corridors of ecstatic fright by her own unchecked sensibility until she arrives at the chamber that holds the black veil. In her famous confrontation with the black-veiled portrait, the "explained supernatural" is given its fullest expression in the coaxing and then the hoaxing of both maiden and reader. In a modern edition of *The Mysteries of Udolpho* (Oxford University Press, 1970), Emily peers behind the veil on page 248, then faints. The cause of her stupefaction is not disclosed or even mentioned until page 662, when her panic is explained by the revelation of a worm-clotted corpse behind the veil that turns out to be "no human, but formed of wax."

The titillating usage of an illusory supernatural to induce hysteria can also be seen in the heroine's reaction to her first view of Castle di Udolpho in all of its "Gothic magnificence." The approach to the castle and the entranced pause and prolonged shudder before its animate facade afford the heroine the chance to convert the morbid data of her senses into something supernaturally thrilling. Her gaze climaxes in the imagination's hedonistic transformation of the castle into a massive stone face glaring back at her:

Emily gazed with melancholy awe upon the Castle, which she understood to be Montoni's; for, though it was now lighted up by the setting sun, the gothic greatness of its features, and its mouldering walls of dark grey stone, rendered it a gloomy and sublime object. Silent, lonely, and sublime, it seemed to stand the sovereign of the scene, and to frown defiance on all, who dared to invade its solitary reign. As the twilight deepened, its features became more awful in obscurity, and Emily continued to gaze, till its clustering towers were alone seen, rising over the tops of the woods, beneath whose thick shade the carriages soon after began to ascend. (226–227)

Although *The Mysteries of Udolpho* is full of suspenseful ambience, it is a static Gothic compared with the accelerating melodrama of Radcliffe's last novel, *The Italian*. Without abandoning those elements that had brought so much success to her earlier romances, Radcliffe now chose to work in the "male Gothic" mode for the first time, shifting from a maiden-centered to a villain-centered format of fear. Aware of the horrific extremes and genuine supernatural excitement of "monastic shockers" such as Matthew Lewis's *Monk*, she resolved to write a monastic shocker of her own that gained its effect by momentum of incident and dramatic closure rather than by still-life portraiture, creepy background, and gloomy panorama. The poetics of terror give way to the dramatics of horror in *The Italian*, from the titling of the book for the evil monk who controls the action (he is not *an* Italian, but *the* Italian) to the pseudotragic fall of the villain as he raises his dagger over the sleeping body of his niece, Ellena di Rosalba, in a concession to sexual violence not previously found in her work. Readers accustomed to the genteel thrills and moral reserve of her first four Gothics must have quickly sensed a fundamental shift in Radcliffe's attitudes toward fear for fear's sake in *The Italian*. The characters, particularly the omnipresent and omnicompetent Father Schedoni, are no longer subordinate to the scenery and the mood. Sublimity itself no longer resides in shadowy innuendoes and atmospheric forebodings of terror conveyed through landscapes and buildings. Terror more than once verges on horror and in several instances crosses over into the genuinely horrific if not quite revolting.

Chief among her departures from her own previous Gothic methods is her rendition of the mystery of evil in the novel's concentration on Father Schedoni. "Unlike Montoni [in *The Mysteries of Udolpho*] or the Marquis de Montalt [in *The Romance of the Forest*], Schedoni is no luxuriant, self-indulgent nobleman. The other villains one can understand; their horrors are clear. His are not because they are more within himself than in what he does to other people. With a difference of this sort *The Italian* could not help but diverge from the patterns of the other novels" (Garber xiv). It is as if Radcliffe had decided to merge the fearfully sublime qualities of the landscape and the castle facade and other gruesome perspectives into the profile of Schedoni, whose face and figure are, according to the epigraph to the novel, "wrapt in clouds of mystery and silence" and whose motives are "unheard, unknown, unsearchable." Even when he is absent from the action, he permeates the lives of the other characters with his inscrutable malice. His dedication to evil exceeds a lust for the heroine's property or virginity and extends to perverse pride, hatred of goodness, and infernal grandeur. Where the penumbral villains of *The Romance of the Forest* and *The Mysteries of Udolpho* had limited their malevolence to sneers and lurkings ("You speak like a heroine. We shall see if you can suffer like one" [381], Montoni snarls at Emily), Schedoni's dominance outpaces the machinations of the earlier vile male schemers. A collage of Miltonic and Shakespearean villainy, Schedoni also exhibits the melancholy guilt of Walpole's Manfred and the evil-eyed sadism of Beckford's Vathek. In "the livid paleness of his face" are redrawn the "pale ire, envy, and despair" of Milton's Satan. His "large melancholy eyes which approached to horror . . . were so piercing that they seemed to penetrate, at a single glance, into the hearts of men and to read their secret thoughts; few persons could support their scrutiny or even endure to meet them twice" (35). Schedoni's face is the Gothic template for the glare of cosmic defiance mixed with secret regret to be found in the countenances of the villains of

Charles Brockden Brown and Nathaniel Hawthorne, Carwin and Roger Chillingworth, and the half-evil men of Emily and Charlotte Brontë, Heathcliffe and Rochester. Radcliffe's Father Schedoni provides the link between Miltonic and Byronic hero-villainy that would furnish the major Romantics with a heroic conception of evil. The impact of the character on the Romantic imagination can be seen in a variety of nineteenth-century works from Charles Robert Maturin's Melmoth to Herman Melville's Captain Ahab in *Moby-Dick* and Claggart in *Billy Budd*. Melville's descriptions of heroic evil seem written with Schedoni's personality specifically in mind. Ishmael calls Ahab "a grand, godless, godlike man," equally applicable to Radcliffe's colossal villain. In Melville's *Billy Budd*, both Claggart's physiognomy and psychology seem based on Radcliffe's Schedoni, a tormented tormentor who, like the master-at-arms, can "apprehend the good, but is powerless to be it."

Through her novels, Radcliffe contributed to the emergent debate concerning the sublime in the arts and its legitimacy as a catalyst of beauty. Edmund Burke in *A Philosophical Enquiry into the Origin of Our Ideas of the Sublime and Beautiful*, Hugh Blair in *Lectures on Rhetoric and Belles Lettres*, and John Baillie in *An Essay on the Sublime* had written philosophic treatises theorizing on the paradoxical nature of the sublime. Radcliffe's novels converted their theories to practice by exposing her characters to the imaginative compensations of what Burke called "the great power . . . [that] hurries us on by an irresistible force" (*Enquiry* Part 2 Sec. 1, 57), Burke had theorized that "Whatever therefore is terrible . . . is sublime too" (57) an aesthetic equation that Radcliffe brought into perfect balance in *Udolpho* and *The Italian*. In her own excursus into sublime theory in a philosophical essay published in the *New Monthly Magazine* three years after her death, "On the Supernatural in Poetry," Radcliffe identified the theoretical basis for her notions of Gothic beauty. With five Gothic novels behind her, she now dichotomized terror and horror as oppositional and mutually incompatible responses in a Gothic work. Terror, an aesthetically positive quality, is always subliminal, psychological, and proleptic and should result in artistic compensations for the imagination; horror, an aesthetically negative quality, is always physiological, repulsive, and deprivational and inevitably leads to inartistic impasse for the imagination. Choosing examples from *Hamlet* and *Macbeth*, Mr. Willoughton, the dialogue's spokesman for the sublimity of terror, states the Radcliffean aesthetic premise: "Terror and horror are so far opposite, that the first expands the soul and awakens the faculties to a high degree of life; the other contracts, freezes and nearly annihilates them. I apprehend, that neither Shakespeare nor Milton by their fictions, nor Mr. Burke by his reasoning, anywhere looked to positive horror as a source of the sublime."

After her triumph with *The Italian*, Radcliffe withdrew totally from the literary scene, but her Gothic spirit continued to preside over the growth of Gothic fiction in England, eastern and western Europe, America, and eventually the third world. The Gothic's survival as a genre in the 1790s, its proliferation in the nineteenth century, and its currency and popularity today are due in no small measure to her aptitude for what the essayist William Hazlitt called "the harrowing up the soul with imaginary horrors, and making the flesh creep and the nerves thrill." (Hazlitt, "On the English Novelists." *Works*, Vol. 16, 165)

SELECTED CRITICISM

Benedict, Barbara M. "Pictures of Conformity: Sentiment and Structure in Ann Radcliffe's Style." *Philological Quarterly* 68 (1989): 363–377. Concentrating on *The Mysteries of Udolpho*, investigates the "relationship between Radcliffe's explicit ideology lauding reason and order, and her practice of minutely describing the vacillations of doubt, fear, and imagination."

Botting, Fred. *Gothic*. London and New York: Routledge, 1996.

Broadwell, Elizabeth P. "The Veil Image in Ann Radcliffe's *The Italian*." *South Atlantic Bulletin* 40:4 (1975): 76–87. Veil imagery charges the language of *The Italian*, "where it appears in the form of words such as 'reveal,' 'obscure,' 'shroud,' and 'conceal' " and as a disguiser of identity in the form of a "social veil."

Burke, Edmund. *A Philosophical Enquiry into the Origin of Our Ideas of the Sublime and Beautiful*, Ed. James T. Boulton. Notre Dame, In: University of Notre Dame Press, 1968.

Castle, Terry. "The Spectralization of the Other in *The Mysteries of Udolpho*." In *The New Eighteenth Century: Theory, Politics, and English Literature*. Ed. Felicity Nussbaum and Laura Brown. New York and London: Methuen, 1987: 231–253. Attributes the success of *The Mysteries of Udolpho* to "a new obsession with the internalized images of other people" that "resulted in the spectralization of the other."

Conger, Syndy M. "Sensibility Restored: Radcliffe's Answer to Lewis's *The Monk*." In *Gothic Fictions: Prohibition/Transgression*. Ed. Kenneth W. Graham, New York: AMS Press, 1989: 113–149. *The Italian* is "the first significant literary protest against *The Monk*." Radcliffe regarded Lewis's unsuspenseful horror and ugly sensationalism as "a trangression against her own notion of sensibility as heightened consciousness."

Cottom, Daniel. "Ann Radcliffe: The Figure in the Landscape"; "Ann Radcliffe: The Labyrinth of Decorum." In *The Civilized Imagination: A Study of Ann Radcliffe, Jane Austen, and Sir Walter Scott*. Cambridge: Cambridge University Press, 1985: 35–67. Landscapes in Radcliffe's novels are "cultural topographies in which characters often seem nothing but reflections of those landscapes." Within the "labyrinth of decorum," various heroines are threatened with loss of self-control "even when they are not paralyzed, unconscious, or physically abducted and confined by others."

Durant, David S. *Ann Radcliffe's Novels: Experiments in Setting*. New York: Arno Press, 1980. A careful reading of the novels reveals a conscious shift in style and changing "fictional strategies." Not content with a single Gothic style, she experimented freely.

Fawcett, Mary Laughlin. "*Udolpho*'s Primal Mystery." *Studies in English Literature, 1500–1900* 23 (1983): 481–494. Radical textual analysis of *The Mysteries of Udolpho* asserting that the primal mystery involves "the child's vision of the sexual act between the parents."

Graham, Kenneth W. "Emily's Demon-Lover: The Gothic Revolution and *The Mysteries of Udolpho*." In *Gothic Fictions: Prohibition/Transgression*. New York: AMS Press, 1989: 163–171. Examines the grounds for terror and suspense as generated by the presence of the demon-lover, Montoni. Emily's demon-lover is almost wholly a creation of her imagination, "a figure of Burkean sublimity that both attracts and repels her."

Greenfield, Susan C. "Veiled Desire: Mother-Daughter Love and Sexual Imagery in Ann Radcliffe's *The Italian*." *The Eighteenth Century: Theory and Interpretation* 33 (1992): 73–89. Discusses the sexual repressions of the heroine Ellena di Rosalba.

Hazlitt, William. *The Complete Works of William Hazlitt*. 21 vols. Ed. P.P. Howe after the edition of A.R. Waller and Arnold Glover. London and Toronto: J.M. Dent, 1930–34.

Hushahn, Helga. "Sturm und Drang in Radcliffe and Lewis." In *Exhibited by Candlelight: Sources and Developments in the Gothic Tradition*. Ed. Valeria Tinkler-Villani, Peter Davidson, and Jane Stevenson. Amsterdam: Rodopi, 1995: 89–98. On the considerable influence of such German plays as Goethe's *Götz von Berlichingen* and Schiller's *Die Räuber* on the two English Gothic novelists.

London, April. "Ann Radcliffe in Context: Marking the Boundaries of *The Mysteries of Udolpho*." *Eighteenth-Century Life* 10:1 (1986): 35–47. *The Mysteries of Udolpho* contains a pattern of "harmony disrupted and then restored suggesting Radcliffe's unequivocal commitment to the triumph of conservative principles."

McIntyre, Clara F. *Ann Radcliffe in Relation to Her Time*. Yale Studies in English Number 62. New Haven: Yale University Press; 1920. Rpt. Hamden, CT: Archon, 1970. A key critical text in Radcliffe studies. Collects early reviews, comments on translations and continental influence, and delineates Radcliffe's role in the establishment of the Gothic genre.

Medlin, Dorothy. "Ann Radcliffe's *Italian* in French: Translations by Mary Gay, André Morellet, and Narcisse Fournier." *Annales du Monde Anglophone* 8 (1998): 11–32. Demonstrates the immediate popularity of Radcliffe's Gothics with French translators and readers. "1797 was a boom year for Ann Radcliffe in France, with the publication of six translations of her works, including two versions of *The Italian*."

Miles, Robert. *Ann Radcliffe: The Great Enchantress*. Manchester and New York: Manchester University Press; New York: St. Martin's Press, 1995. An astute and corrective rereading of Radcliffe's Gothic and her place in the tradition. Rebuts the view of various critics who have insisted on Radcliffe's conservatism in a revolutionary literary movement and returns to the original assertions of Montague Summers that Radcliffe was and remains a great mistress of romance. The eight chapters are 1. "The Great Enchantress"; 2. "The Gentlewoman and the Authoress"; 3. "The Aesthetic Context"; 4. "The Historical Context"; 5. "The Early Works: *The Castles of Athlin and Dunbayne* and *The Sicilian Romance*"; 6. "In the Realm of the Figural: *The Romance of the Forest*"; 7. "The Hermeneutics of Reading: *The Mysteries of Udolpho*"; and 8. "Radcliffe's Politics: *The Italian*."

Murray, E.B. *Ann Radcliffe*. TEAS 149. New York: Twayne, 1972. Rudimentary but sound introduction to Radcliffe's Gothic writings. Has critical chapters on all the novels with the exception of *Gaston de Blondeville*. The conclusion refers to her as "one of the most influential mediocre writers that English literature has produced."

Norton, Rictor. *Mistress of Udolpho: The Life of Ann Radcliffe*. London and New York: Leicester University Press, 1999. A full-scale critical biography that contains new information about Radcliffe's life.

Rogers, Deborah. "Ann Radcliffe in the 1980s: An Annotated Bibliography of Criticism." *Extrapolation* 32 (1991): 343–349. Consists of sixty-two annotated entries under the categories "Bibliographies," "Journals," "Books," "Dissertations," and "Unexamined."

———, ed. *The Critical Response to Ann Radcliffe*. Westport, CT: Greenwood Press, 1994. An assemblage of contemporary reviews, letters, diary extracts, and critical appraisals showing shifts in critical attitudes toward her work from the eighteenth to the twentieth centuries.

———. *Ann Radcliffe: A Bio-bibliography*. Westport, CT: Greenwood Press, 1996. Excellent bibliographical portrait of the leading Gothic novelist of the 1790s. The entries in each section are by year, with critical entries current to 1994. The eight bibliographical sections are preceded by 1. "The Life of Ann Radcliffe, 1764–1823." Chapters are organized as follows: 2. "Primary Bibliography: Editions and Translations (P)"; 3. "Early Reviews and Notices, 1789–1826 (E)"; 4. "Criticism, 1827–1899 (C)"; 5. "Twentieth-Century Criticism, Part I: 1900–1949 (T)"; 6. "Twentieth-Century Criticism, Part II: 1950–Present (TC)"; 7. "Full-Length Works (F)"; 8. "Dissertations (D)"; 9. "Bibliographies (B)". There are three appendixes: "Appendix I: Adaptations and Abridgments"; "Appendix II: Parodies and Imitations"; "Appendix III: Spurious Attributions."

Russett, Margaret. "Narrative as Enchantment in *The Mysteries of Udolpho*." *ELH* 65:1 (1998): 159–186. A Foucaultian analysis of Radcliffe as one of the "imitators of discursive practices who produce not only their own work" but also the formation of other texts. The enchantment of the Gothic "lies in the way that its most conventional motifs articulate a commentary on the psychodynamics of narrative form."

Schmitt, Cannon. "Techniques of Terror, Technologies of Nationality: Ann Radcliffe's *The Italian*." *ELH* 61:4 (1994): 853–876. By placing readers in "imaginative dilemmas of victimization," Radcliffe's novel investigates the superiority of English over Italian. "Like a conduct book, *The Italian* teaches young women how to behave; in the heroine it models proper behavior, in the villain improper and un-English behavior."

Sedgwick, Eve Kosofsky. "The Character of the Veil: Imagery of the Surface in the Gothic Novel." *PMLA* 96 (1981): 255–270. Discusses the "sexual function" of veils in *The Mysteries of Udolpho* and *The Italian*. "The attributes of the veil, and of the surface generally, are contagious metonymically, by touch. A related thematic strain depicts veils, like flesh, as suffused or marked with blood."

Smith, Nelson. "Sense, Sensibility, and Ann Radcliffe." *Studies in English Literature, 1500–1900* 13 (1973): 577–590. Interprets the novels to be intentional critiques of too much sensibility. Radcliffe is "far from being an advocate of sensibility, for she, like Jane Austen two decades later, shows its weaknesses and flaws."

Summers, Montague. "A Great Mistress of Romance: Ann Radcliffe, 1764–1823." *Transactions of the Royal Society of Literature* 35 (1917): 39–78. Rpt. in *Essays in*

Petto. Freeport, NY: Books for Libraries Press, 1967. A major monograph in Radcliffe studies and a piece of critical heresy when it appeared in 1917.

Todd, Janet. " 'The Great Enchantress: Ann Radcliffe." In *The Sign of Angellica: Women, Writing, and Fiction, 1660–1800*. New York: Columbia University Press, 1989: 253–272. Radcliffe invariably "insists on moral clarity" while maintaining "the conventional image of the woman writer, the genteel domestic lady who happens to write and whose writing could serve as an extension of her domestic social role."

Varma, Devendra P. *The Gothic Flame*. New York: Russell and Russell, 1966.

Voller, Jack. "Didacticism and Romantic Error: Reeve, Radcliffe, and the Conservative Supernatural." In *The Supernatural Sublime: The Metaphysics of Terror in Anglo-American Romanticism*. De Kalb: Northern Illinois University Press, 1994: 43–60. *The Mysteries of Udolpho* is "the representative text for the conservative nonsupernatural mode of the supernatural sublime. The conservative Gothic asserts the validity of received intellectual traditions."

Wolff, Cynthia G. "The Radcliffean Gothic Model: A Form for Feminine Sexuality." *Modern Language Studies* 9:3 (1979): 98–113. Sees the feminism of Gothic fiction as a product of "the Radcliffean Gothic model. The achievement of Ann Radcliffe is quite remarkable, for she invented a fictional language and a set of conventions with which 'respectable' female sexuality might find expression."

CLARA REEVE
(1729–1807)
Jack G. Voller

PRINCIPAL GOTHIC WORKS

The Champion of Virtue. Colchester: W. Keymer, 1777.

The Old English Baron: A Gothic Story. London: E. & C. Dilly, 1778.

The Progress of Romance, through Times, Countries, and Manners. Colchester: Printed
      for the author by W. Keymer, 1785; London: G.G.J. & J. Robinson, 1785; Dublin:
      Price, Exshaw, 1785.

The Old English Baron. Dublin: M'Kenzie, 1790.

The Old English Baron. Philadelphia: Stewart & Cochran, 1797. (First American edition.)

*Edmond, Orphan of the Castle: A Tragedy in Five Acts, Founded on the "Old English
      Baron," a Gothic Story.* Adapted by John Broster. London: R. Faulder & T. Hurst,
      1799.

The Old English Baron. The British Novelists series, vol. 22. London: F.C. & J. Riving-
      ton, 1810.

MODERN REPRINTS AND EDITIONS

The Old English Baron: A Gothic Story. In *Seven Masterpieces of Gothic Horror.* Ed.
      Robert D. Spector. New York: Bantam, 1963.

The Old English Baron: A Gothic Story. Ed. James Trainer. London and New York:
      Oxford University Press, 1967. (Oxford English Novels series. Reissued in pa-
      perback in 1977.)

The Progress of Romance and the History of Charoba, Queen of Aegypt. New York:
      Facsimile Text Society, 1930.

The Progress of Romance. New York: Garland, 1970; Plan de la Tour, Var, France:
      Editions d'Aujourd'hui, 1980; New York.

The daughter and granddaughter of clergymen, Clara Reeve brought the strict
moral and religious propriety of her upbringing to bear on the nascent Gothic
tradition, represented in her time primarily by one work, Walpole's *Castle of*

Otranto. She thereby secured for herself a much more prominent place in literary history than she otherwise would have achieved. Reeve's accomplishment, more specifically, was to modulate the supernatural excesses of Walpole's first Gothic novel while taking a more aggressively didactic and moral stance, thereby preparing the way for the more sophisticated proto-Gothics of Charlotte Smith and the fully realized and nuanced moral Gothics of Ann Radcliffe. A hugely popular novel—by the end of the nineteenth century it had gone through thirteen editions—*The Old English Baron* was Reeve's only Gothic work (aside from the lost manuscript of *Castle Connor: An Irish Story*), yet it forever influenced the evolution of the Gothic.

Reeve's primary objection to Walpole's famous tale is straightforward in its simplicity: *The Castle of Otranto*, she writes in the preface to her novel, "palls upon the mind (though it does not upon the ear); and the reason is obvious, the machinery is so violent, that it destroys the effect it is intended to excite. Had the story been kept within the utmost *verge* of probability, the effect had been preserved, without losing the least circumstance that excites or detains the attention." This concern with probability, derived perhaps from the writings of the aesthetician Hugh Blair and prefiguring Hawthorne's musings on the same issue, is at the heart of Reeve's revisionary Gothic. As she wrote in her own manifesto of literary theory and practice, *The Progress of Romance*:

The Romance is an heroic fable, which treats of fabulous persons and things. The Novel is a picture of real life and manners, and of the times in which it is written. The Romance in lofty and elevated language, describes what never happened nor is likely to happen. The Novel gives a familiar relation of such things, as pass every day before our eyes, such as may happen to our friend, or to ourselves. (1930, 1.111)

In *The Old English Baron*, Reeve subtitles her romance *A Gothic Story*, thus establishing a generic positioning that allows her the leeway necessary for the inclusion of the genuine, if restrained, supernatural. Yet her limited use of the supernatural became an important model for later Gothic writers. The peasant lad, young Edmund Twyford, performs a night vigil within the forbidden eastern apartment of Lovel Castle in an episode that would be duplicated in countless Gothics to come. Reeve was the first to install the haunted and forbidden chamber, although the scene's potential terror is muted by the didactic ghost who appears to Edmund.

This taming of the romance came at high literary cost for Reeve, who sacrificed character complexity and narrative energy and suspense, along with historical accuracy, a deficiency evident in her other historical romance, *Memoirs of Sir Roger de Clarendon* (1793). Nor was Reeve, unlike her followers, much interested in the realism that can be generated by careful descriptions of setting. Even her description of the castle's haunted suite of rooms, vaunted by James Trainer in his edition of *The Old English Baron* as setting the course for subsequent generations of writers, is so brief and so limited in scope that it really does nothing more than hint at the atmospherics yet to come in Gothic fiction. Compelling characters and narrative momentum would enter the Gothic in the early works of Charlotte Smith and most notably in the mature novels of Ann Radcliffe, but they were outside Reeve's interest, perhaps beyond her literary range. Reeve sought to ensure probability not for the sake, as one might readily suppose, of psychological verisimilitude, but for the sake of didacticism. A restrained supernatural left her an emotionally uncluttered narrative stage on which to enact the morality play that is the main concern of her fiction. In *The Old English Baron*, morally good characters are unruffled by their encounters with evidence of the supernatural, which is always under the aegis of a providential Divine, and it is that self-possession that declares their moral superiority; wicked characters are terrified and undone by the supernatural, and such physical cowardice is the token of their evil and corrupt motives. This black-and-white map of the moral universe is followed confidently and unflinchingly by Reeve, and her novel's validation of moral righteousness is as assured as the groveling and ultimate self-abasement of the work's wicked Lord Lovel and his accomplices.

Hand in hand with this celebration of pious morality is the novel's vindication of class, a characteristic the work shares with *The Castle of Otranto* and with dozens if not hundreds of later Gothics: the peasant lad of noble bearing and high integrity is eventually revealed to be the rightful possessor of the contested property, and in the end he acquires his true name and place in society. The popularity of Reeve's novels and those of Radcliffe—who did much the same thing, only with greater literary artistry and a distaff twist—confirms the depth and power of the need in the British reading public of the 1780s and 1790s for works of reassurance and affirmation. It is no accident that Reeve first published her novel under a much more accurate if less marketable title, *The Champion of Virtue*. The not-especially-germane *Old English Baron* was added, she tells us, at the instigation and encouragement of "friends," chief among whom was Samuel Richardson's daughter.

Yet despite these limitations, Reeve's contribution to the Gothic is a real one, for her highly successful novel demonstrated unequivocally that there was great demand for tales of "terror" that reaffirmed a British Christian worldview (as indeed Walpole's novel did) without the distracting histrionics and egregious supernaturalism of *The Castle of Otranto*. Reeve helped prepare the way for Charlotte Smith and for Ann Radcliffe, who, taking the next step, would distill the supernaturalism even further, attenuating its agency to the point of nonexistence while expanding the study of its effects, introducing the suspense and drama that Reeve could not attain, and that a later generation of Romantic readers would see as reflecting their own pursuit of stability in an age of ferment and revolution.

SELECTED CRITICISM

Bardin, Barbara. "Clara Reeve." In *Eighteenth-Century Anglo-American Women Novelists: A Critical Reference Guide*. Ed. Doreen Alvarez Saar and Mary Anne Schofield. New York: G.K. Hall, 1996. Discusses Reeve's life and works and accounts for her conservative reaction to and revision of Walpole's Gothic extremes.

Clery, E.J. "Clara Reeve and Sophia Lee." In *Women's Gothic: From Clara Reeve to Mary Shelley*. Horndon, Tavistock, Devon, UK: Northcote House Publishers, 2000: 25–50. Reeve "sought to engage readers on multiple levels, through the marvellous, the probable, and the sentimental. The interaction of these three levels—the narrative economy of *The Old English Baron*—can provide a model or benchmark for further investigation of the strategies of much female Gothic writing."

Ehlers, Leigh. " 'A Striking Lesson to Posterity': Providence and Character in Clara Reeve's *The Old English Baron*." *Enlightenment Essays* 9 (1978): 62–76. Devoted mostly to the inheritance/identity element of Reeve's novel as it correlates with the work's pronounced moral element.

Finan, Eileen. "Clara Reeve." In *An Encyclopedia of British Women Writers*. Ed. Paul Schlueter and June Schlueter. New York: Garland, 1988: 377–378. Reeve "introduced the conventions of the haunted suite, the portentous dream, and the identifying token of jewelry while curbing the supernatural power that Walpole had unleashed in full."

Spector, Robert D. "The Beginnings: Horace Walpole and Clara Reeve." In *The English Gothic: A Bibliographic Guide from Horace Walpole to Mary Shelley*. Westport, CT: Greenwood Press, 1984: 98–109. "[*The Old English Baron*] remains a footnote to literary history." The accompanying bibliography lists twenty-nine primary and secondary items.

Trainer, James. Introduction to *The Old English Baron* by Clara Reeve. London and New York: Oxford University Press, 1967: vii–xv. A biographical overview and critical essay, devoted largely to Reeve's place in the Gothic canon and her impact on its development.

COUNT DONATIEN ALPHONSE FRANÇOIS SADE [THE MARQUIS DE SADE] (1740–1814)

Douglass H. Thomson

PRINCIPAL GOTHIC WORKS

Justine; ou, Les Malheurs de la vertu. [Justine; or, The Misfortunes of Virtue]. 2 vols. Paris: Girouard, 1791.

La Philosophie dans le boudoir [Philosophy in the Bedroom]. 2 vols. London, 1795.

La Nouvelle Justine; ou, Les Malheurs de la vertu. 4 vols. London, 1797.

La Nouvelle Justine; ou, Les Malheurs de la vertu, suivie de L. Historic de Juliette; ou, Les Prospérités des vice [The History of Juliette, or the Fortunes of Vice]. 10 vols. Holland: Chez les Libraries Associés, 1797.

Les Crimes de l'amour: Nouvelles héroïques et tragiques; précédés d'une Idée sur les romans [The Crimes of Love]. Paris: Chez Masse, 1800.

Les 120 Journées de Sodome; ou, L'Ecole du libertinage [The 120 Days of Sodom; or, The School of Libertinage]. 3 vols. Paris: S. and C. by subscription, 1931–1935. From the original autograph by Maurice Heine.

MODERN REPRINTS AND EDITIONS

The Gothic Tales. Trans. with an introduction by Margaret Crosland. London: Picador, 1992. (Contains "Eugénie de Franval" and "Florville et Courval.")

Juliette. Trans. Austryn Wainhouse. New York: Grove Press, 1968.

Justine, Philosophy in the Bedroom, and Other Writings. Trans. Richard Seaver and Austryn Wainhouse, with introductions by Jean Paulhan and Maurice Blanchot. New York: Grove Weidenfeld, 1990.

The Misfortunes of Virtue, and Other Early Tales. Ed. and trans. David Coward. Oxford: Oxford University Press, 1992.

The 120 Days of Sodom, and Other Writings. Trans. Austryn Wainhouse and Richard Seaver; with introductions by Simone de Beauvoir and Pierre Klossowski. New York: Grove Press, 1966.

In a scene whose general contours are terribly familiar to Gothic readers, the corrupt Abbess Delbène brings her fellow debauchees and the heroine of the novel *Juliette* to a dark subterranean vault beneath a convent, where lie moldering the corpses of nuns she has murdered. In a centrally Sadeian way, what follows exceeds anything even darkly dreamt of in the tradition of the first English Gothic tales, including its most obvious parallel in the grotto passages of Matthew Lewis' *Monk*, a novel, not surprisingly, greatly admired by Sade. For Delbène has brought her band of revelers—and Juliette, far from being some heroine in distress, is a very willing member of the band—to the tumuli so that she might receive "five or six thumping fuckings upon [one of] her victim's corpses" (96). In another way, however, the scene stops short of the Gothic. As Delbène's debauchees quite literally reach their climax, it seems, but only seems, that a genuine moment of Gothic horror awaits them: "A dreadful shrill screech was heard, all the candles snuffing out that very instant" (97). Juliette faints away in terror, and all are struck deaf and dumb. Have our voluptuaries met their moment of divine retribution or infernal apotheosis? No, the unflustered Delbène assures them: it was only the sound of a wood owl, whose startled flight caused the lights to go out. "In supernatural occurrences," she serenely asserts, "I have no belief at all" (97).

Aside from its wicked little parody of Ann Radcliffe's "explained supernatural," the scene in Delbène's dark pleasure dome reveals some important facts about Sade's relationship to the Gothic tradition. First, of course, the scene indicates that he is willing to take the usually nervous Gothic fascination with the profane and the taboo to its point of extreme fulfillment and satiety; every threshold of painful and forbidden pleasure must be crossed, from mutilation to "stricturing" to incest to the murder of one's own children, all in the name of increasing sexual gratification. His fiction provides graphic realization of the libidinal content often found sublimated and deferred in mainstream Gothic literature. Thus "sadism" and its closely related offspring, masochism, have proved useful conceptual tools to explore the dark psychological terrains of Gothic literature. The sadistic character, after all, of an Ambrosio in *The Monk* or of a character like Charlotte Dacre's Victoria di Loredani in *Zofloya* differs not so much in kind as in degree from Sade's gallery of insatiable perverts. Sade's denial of the supernatural, indeed, his fierce contempt for any traditional moral framework, also reflects tellingly on the Gothic tradition from which it emphatically, on this point, departs. After all, what is it from Sade's atheist perspective that haunts and terrorizes countless Gothic heroes and heroines? Is it not their "nursing" of unacted desires—which, as William Blake says, breeds pestilence—their fear of moral retribution, their guilt engendered by a hypocritical and cruelly arbitrary societal superego? Sade's frontal assault on all hegemonic structures provides a provocative way of reading the Gothic and has endeared him to postmodern criticism, but the actual experience of reading his fiction yields a strange irony. His long novels, marked by what Pierre Klossowski calls "apathetic reiteration" (30), are devoid of conflict and laboriously thesis-driven; indeed, they are more apt to bore than to scandalize a reader. It is only in some of his shorter works, less ridden by the dictates of his renegade

philosophy and more in line with familiar Gothic patterns of deferral and revelation, that Sade succeeds as a writer of Gothic horror fiction.

Let us first briefly review this fiction in relation to the Gothic tradition before
considering the relationship of sadism to Gothicism. *Justine; or, The Misfortunes
of Virtue* bears the most striking affinities to the Gothic, but Sade so carries to
the extreme every feature this laboriously developed novel shares with the tradition that it reads like a parody of the female Gothic. Justine appears to be a
caricature of the Radcliffean heroine, doggedly clinging to her cherished notions
of virtue while physically losing her virtue in the most varied and outrageous
ways. A poor and vulnerable outcast, she becomes the plaything of, among
others, the philosopher-villain Bressac and his always-eager band of sodomites;
the pedophile-surgeon Rodin, who brands her; the gourmand-bloodletter, Ger-
nade; and the vicious recluse Saint-Florent, who enjoys sex best when he is
aroused by near hanging. Many of the castles and corrupt convents where Justine
suffers multiple rapes and worse provide distinctly Gothic settings, especially
the corpse-filled catacombs of Saint-Florent, where Justine must undergo premature burial and witness the crucifixion of a nude, sexually mutilated *jeune
fille*. Whereas in most Gothic fiction these dark settings evince a sense of supernatural awe and fear, in Sade's fiction they provide repeated occasion for
ferocious sacrilege as his freethinking villain-heroes ransack every religious
scruple and mock every appeal to the supernatural in making their case that
monstrous crimes are in perfect accord with natural law. *Justine* parodies the
Gothic not just in its perverse delight in outraging virtue, as poor Justine can
repeatedly attest, but in suggesting that pursuing such a chimera as virtue leads
to suffering and persecution. In a final, grim parody of divine retribution, the
much-abused but finally delivered Justine meets death by lightning bolt, while
the sadists who have used her and killed thousands of other peasants for their
amusement find their power and financial resources "mysteriously" augmented.
Vice, not virtue, is its own reward.

As E.J. Clery has perceptively noted, one encounters a paradox in the triumph
of Sade's aristocratic philosopher-villains: from an advocate (albeit a latecomer)
of the French Revolution and a man who spent the better portion of his life in
prison, "The libertinism he advocated [would seem] cognate with 'liberty,' yet
sexual freedom as he portrays it is invariably decked out in the Gothic trappings
of incarceration and tyranny" (1998, 205). Here is another related paradox: while
one might expect from Sade, given his heretical program and the official censure
of his books, some kind of radical new fiction, some breaking of boundaries,
his novels provide only the most perfunctory reading. Take, for example, the
sequel to *Justine*, the sister novel *Juliette*. Its thesis, "the prosperities of vice,"
already amply demonstrated by the previous novel, *Juliette* quickly lapses into
the numbingly familiar Sadeian pattern of "apathetic reiteration": graphic sexual
scene followed by philosophical justification, then more pornography, followed
by more philosophy, and so on. Strangely, despite the contrast promised by the
change in central characters, Juliette, as vice-loving as her sister was virtuous,

occupies a role almost identical to that of her sibling: she serves as subject (albeit now willing) for a variety of more experienced sadists, then must listen to their interminable natural philosophies (essentially Enlightenment arguments for reasoned self-interest and against "superstition" taken to their reductio ad absurdum). The same pattern is found in the less Gothic *The 120 Days of Sodom* (a kind of sexual *Decameron* plus 20) and *Philosophy in the Bedroom* (a Sadeian *Kama sutra* of sorts). Perhaps this is the central paradox inherent in pornographic literature: while such literature's entire claim to excitement is built on the premise of ever more virtuosic variation on its sexual content, it more likely will lapse into metonymy, that most masturbatory of tropes, offering, instead, only the possibility of repetition and substitution. Despite its often-tendentious moralizing and other timidities, the Gothic knew better. Its typically disguised and sublimated libidinal energies allow the reader room for fantasy; the reader of Sade's longer fiction, in a way strangely consistent with his sexual philosophy, must be more passive, more a consumer of fantasy than a producer of it.

Margaret Crosland, translator of some of Sade's shorter works of fiction from *Les Crimes de l'amour*, justifies entitling them *Gothic Tales* because they possess the one thing lacking in his previous fiction: "suspense" (8). Prefaced by "Idée sur le roman," an essay in which Sade directly acknowledges the English Gothic tradition, *Les Crimes* offers at least two tales that can qualify as high Gothic. "Eugénie de Franval," with its story of a father's incestuous relationship with his daughter Eugénie, replete with his philosophical defenses of incest and attacks on the institution of marriage, may at first seem just one more variation on themes from *La Philosophie dans le boudoir*. But the suspense that drives the short novel concerns whether or not the two lovers will be caught. With an unmistakable allusion to the woman who first had him imprisoned for his outrageous sexual behavior, Sade introduces a powerful mother-in-law, Madame de Farneille, who threatens prosecution. Driven to flee Paris and to encourage his daughter to poison her mother, Franval eventually relents and repents. As he returns home through a gloomy Gothic forest, having been ravaged by banditti, he hears bells tolling that finally turn his thoughts to the Deity. But too late: Eugénie has poisoned Madame de Franval and, in a paroxysm awakened by a very late dawning conscience, has died of grief herself. There is nothing left for Franval except to stab himself and throw himself into the coffin of his lately deceased wife. Intrigue and melodrama replace the more typically Sadeian graphic content, and the moralistic closure—"great peril always dogs those who do as they wish in order to satisfy their desires" (11)—places "Eugénie de Franval" in the company of other early Gothics. More tightly woven is the story of "Florville and Courval." Florville is indeed the unwitting victim of the "fatality of destiny" (138). At age fifteen she has an affair with a man who, it turns out, is her brother; accidentally kills a would-be rapist who, it turns out, is their son; supplies testimony against a murderess who, it turns out, is her mother; and has married the generous Courval, who, it turns out, is her father. None of these revelations occur until the very end of the story, after Florville has had a very Gothic dream of mysterious bodies beckoning to her from their coffins and right after she has been reading "an English novel of incredible grimness" (131). The heroine's extreme suffering and the multiple incests are pure Sade, but there is an undeniable virtuosity in the way he pulls together the various plot strands at the end. One suspects that in many of the stories from *Les Crimes de l'amour*, Sade adapted his usual sexual themes to the Gothic form to produce a fiction that, while still daring, would be publishable.

The argument that a reading of Sade's fiction requires a tendency toward masochism attests to the conceptual power and pliability of the two pathologies that are his legacy. The nineteenth-century psychologist Richard von Krafft-Ebing first coined the term *sadism* to refer to the obtaining of sexual pleasure through degradation of others and later, in reference to the Austrian author Leopold von Sacher-Masoch, defined its opposite, masochism, in which pleasure depends upon being the tormented and humiliated victim. Freud importantly saw the two as active and passive manifestations of a single instinctual complex of fantasy and behavior, with masochism becoming a kind of internalized sadism.

As a psychological interpretation of personal and political relationships—for sadism and masochism are all about power and mastery—the terms have a special resonance in the Gothic tradition. Walpole's Manfred, Radcliffe's Mediterranean counts, Lewis's Monk, William Godwin's demonic Gines, James Hogg's Gil-Martin—all these and many other characters in the Gothic canon define themselves through and take considerable pleasure in the suffering they cause others. They all provide terrifying depictions of the id unleashed, insatiate, ever seeking more refined variations on the pleasure to be derived from cruelty. But they also all serve as indications of tyranny, the sadistic extension of the politics of self-interest and aggrandizement. In his important essay "Idée sur le roman," Sade himself perceives the Gothic novel as "the inevitable product of the revolutionary shocks with which the whole of Europe resounded." Because in this "iron age" there "was nobody left who had not experienced more misfortunes" than the most gifted novelist could depict, it became "necessary to call upon hell for aid" in conveying "the ills that are brought upon men by the wicked" and the mighty (Sage, *Casebook*, 22). Although, as Clery notes, his own fiction equivocates on the issue, Sade clearly saw the familiar Gothic pattern of demonic persecution and extreme victimization as tortured reflections upon the political upheavals of the day, an insight that has since been thoroughly developed by recent critics of the Gothic in their historicist treatment of the genre's sadistic tyrants.

Elisabeth Bronfen argues that while the sadistic impulse in Gothic fantasy involves "intersubjective conflict," that is, a conflict between subjects or classes, the domination-submission complex "can also be found manifested in the register of intrasubjective conflict, where characters enact the struggle between a sadistic super-ego as representative of the law and a masochistic ego as representative of forbidden pleasures, by suffering from guilt, self-punishment, or self-purging" (207). One thinks immediately of such characters as Godwin's Caleb Williams, who worships his persecutor, the criminal Falkland; Charles Brockden Brown's Edgar Huntly, who might be a sleepwalking murderer, Coleridge's Christabel; Hogg's Wringham; and even Melville's reclusive Bartleby and suicidal Pierre Glendinning. These masochists function as an even more dramatic indication of a cruelly arbitrary power, for they are so conditioned by the laws and morality of the ruling ideology that they willingly submit to, even revel in, suffering for some real or imagined wrong.

It is interesting to speculate about what Sade would have made of a character like Christabel. One shudders to think of her in the hands of one of Sade's own sadistic tyrants. As in many ways she is a martyr to her own repressed sexuality, Christabel is exactly the kind of subject the Sadeian philosopher-villain most enjoys outraging. But perhaps Sade would have read Geraldine as a necessarily sadistic counterpart to Christabel's masochism—a Juliette to a Justine—and thanks in part to Sade's interpreters, we can now read both as an indictment of the gloomy, life-denying, patriarchal world of Sir Leoline. Perhaps his own fiction is negligible, but in providing a vocabulary that explores the complexly sexual dimensions of power, Sade and his critical legacy will continue to illumine many dark regions of the Gothic world, a world where power frequently expresses itself in terms of sexual domination and submission—and where sex always speaks of power.

SELECTED CRITICISM

Berman, Lorna. "The Marquis de Sade and His Critics." *Mosaic: A Journal for the Interdisciplinary Study of Literature* 1:2 (1968): 57–73. Covers reactions to and attitudes toward Sade over two centuries.

Bronfen, Elisabeth. "Sado-Masochism." In *The Handbook to Gothic Literature*. Ed. Marie Mulvey-Roberts. New York: New York University Press, 1998: 206–207. Concisely relates this "domination-submission" complex to the Gothic tradition in general and Sade in particular.

Carter, Angela. *The Sadeian Woman and the Ideology of Pornography*. New York: Pantheon, 1978. Carter controversially appropriates and radically rethinks Sade as part of her project to reimagine from a feminist perspective the power relationships of pornography.

Chanover, E. Pierre. *The Marquis de Sade: A Bibliography*, Metuchen, NJ: Scarecrow Press, 1973. Charts Sade's rise from the forbidden lists to his postmodern canonization.

Clery, E.J. "Ann Radcliffe and D.A.F. de Sade: Thoughts on Heroinism." *Women's Writing: The Elizabethan to Victorian Period* 1 (1994): 203–214. On parallels and departures in the handling (or possibly mishandling) of the persecuted maiden in the writings of Radcliffe and Sade.

———. "Sade." In *The Handbook to Gothic Literature*. Ed. Marie Mulvey-Roberts. New York: New York University Press, 1998: 204–205. Links and intelligently contrasts Sade's fiction with the Gothic.

Grayson, Susan B. "Gothic Sexuality and Social Decay in Diderot and Sade." In *The French Revolution in Culture and Society*. Ed. David G. Troyansky, Alfred Cismaru, and Norwood Andrews, Jr. Westport: Greenwood Press, 1991: 81–90. "Gothic decay in the settings of both [Diderot's] *La Religieuse* and *Justine* signifies the disintegration of the Enlightenment and of religious orders."

Klossowski, Pierre. *Sade My Neighbor*. Trans. and intro. Alphonso Lingis. Evanston, IL: Northwestern University Press, 1991. Reprint of the 1947 text. Contains the prefatory essay "The Philosopher-Villain," added in 1967. Sade's outrage perversely acknowledges the divine law it transgresses. Although it is not specifically concerned with the Gothic, this study of the dialectics of transgression ("in outrage what is outraged is maintained") provides an illuminating context to study similar patterns in the Gothic.

Le Brun, Annie. "Un Rêve de pierre." In *Les Châteaux de la subversion*. Paris: J.J. Pauvert aux Éditions Garnier Frères, 1982: 103–110. Places Sade directly in the mainstream of Gothic fiction.

McAllister, Harold S. "Apology for Bad Dreams: A Study of Characterization and the Use of Fantasy in *Clarissa, Justine*, and *The Monk*." Doctoral dissertation, University of New Mexico, 1971. [*DAI* 32:6383A]. Relates *Justine* to the sadomasochistic motifs of the Gothic tradition.

Senelick, Laurence. *The Prestige of Evil: The Murderer as Romantic Hero from Sade to Lacenaire*, New York: Garland, 1987. Notes resemblances between Sade's philosophic villains and their Gothic counterparts in the 1790s.

Werner, S. "Diderot, Sade, and the Gothic Novel." *Studies on Voltaire and the Eighteenth Century* 114 (1973): 273–290. In revealing the necessity for the monstrous, Sade elevated the philosophic value of evil.

FRIEDRICH VON SCHILLER
(1759–1805)
Tom Lloyd

PRINCIPAL GOTHIC WORKS

Die Raüber [The Robbers]. Frankfurt and Leipzig: I.B. Metzler, 1781. (Published at
   Schiller's expense; first performed at the Mannheim Theater in 1782.)
Der Geisterseher: Eine Gesichte aus den Memoires des Graf en von O. [The Ghost-Seer:
   A Story from the Memoirs of Count von O.]. First published serially in five issues
   of the periodical *Thalia*, 1787–1789; Leipzig: G.J. Goschen, 1789; revised edi-
   tions in 1797 and 1798. (Schiller never completed this fragmentary novel.)

MODERN REPRINTS AND EDITIONS

Five Plays. Trans. David MacDonald, intro. Nicholas Dromgoole and Tom Sutcliffe.
   London: Absolute Classics, 1998; New York: Consortium Book Sales, 1998. (In-
   cludes a commissioned translation of *The Robbers* used for a production at the
   Gate Theatre, London, in 1995 that captures the spirit of the original.)
The Ghost-Seer or the Apparitionist. In *Gothic Tales of Terror: Classic Horror Stories
   from Great Britain, Europe, and the United States, 1765–1840*. Ed. Peter Haining.
   New York: Taplinger, 1972.
The Ghost-Seer. Trans. Henry G. Bohn, intro. Jeffrey L. Sammons. Columbia, SC: Cam-
   den House, 1992. (The 1849 Bohn translation is the best available. Modern
   German editions follow the 1798 edition, but this version is closer to Schiller's
   1789 edition. This edition is cited in the text.)
Sämtliche Werke [Collected Works]. Intro. Benno von Wiese. 5 vols. Munich: Winkler-
   Verlag, 1968.

Friedrich Schiller is not usually associated with the Gothic, and for good reason.
Although he was interested in themes of criminality, in his mature phase the
German writer pursued the ideal and, even in his ideas about the tragical sublimity, eschewed the material sublimity often associated with Gothic horrors for
sudden transcendences and freedom from life's fetters. This is evident in plays

like *Maria Stuart* and *Die Jungfrau von Orleans* [The Maid of Orleans], as well as in his philosophical works influenced by Kant. In "Über das Erhabene" [On the Sublime], his theories of the sublime (*das Erhabenheit*) are tied to the pursuit of the ideal and decoupled from the terrors, pleasurable or not, traditionally associated with the sublime. Yet ironically, the two works that achieved the greatest popularity in his lifetime were strongly influenced by the Gothic. Schiller's first play, *Die Räuber* [The Robbers], and his unfinished novel *Der Geisterseher* [The Ghost-Seer] are products of the tension between repression and rage, mystery and reason, that roiled Schiller's personality and ultimately led him to embrace idealism.

The opening-night audience's reaction to *The Robbers* at the Mannheim Theater in 1782 suggested less the stately tragic sublimity aimed at in the mature works than the effects of grisly visitations by the spirit world. To one observer, the audience seemed like inmates in a madhouse, with rolling eyes, balled fists, stamping feet, and so on (Leidner 57). As late as 1826, Thomas Carlyle felt impelled to defend the play against charges of immorality, noting in Schiller's passions and emotions something like "the volcanic fire that smoulders and fuses in secret . . . till [its] force grew irresistible" (13).

The play is the effusion of a young man of twenty-one subjected to an incredibly strict academic discipline at the Karlsschule, the notorious academy founded by Karl Eugen, duke of Württemberg. Schiller literally fled his duty as regimental surgeon to pursue his art. The rebellion against repression the play exemplifies is evident in its wild plot and its questioning of all assumptions about materialism and the soul. Its descent into neo-Gothic terrors is linked above all to the influences of Schwabian pietism and baroque apocalyptic teachings that focus more on a God of punishment than on the merciful Christ. As in *The Ghost-Seer*, Schiller, who did not believe in hell, nonetheless seemed fascinated by the conjunction of freethinking and damnation.

Franz von Moor manipulates his feeble old father to disinherit his other son Karl, who is driven into a life of increasingly terrible crimes as the head of an outlaw band. But Karl remains tenuously connected to the moral order he accepts at the play's end, when he turns himself over to the authorities and certain execution after perversely keeping his oath to his fellow robbers by killing his beloved Amalia von Edelreich. He dies of his own free will for justice, seeing to it that a poor worker with eleven children will collect the reward. But if Karl is the noble outlaw redeemed, Franz is the pre-Nietzschean Superman manqué. He peers fully over the abyss, yet, like the Prince in the *Ghost-Seer*, he is unable to escape the lingering horrors of his traditional religious upbringing with its stress on damnation for malefactors, above all, freethinking sinners.

Schiller became uncomfortable with the implications here. Although Karl learns to listen to his conscience, his tragic end points to the absence of a synthesis that might lead him from irrational despair to transfiguration. Schiller had not yet studied Immanuel Kant's transcendental ideas; the play remains stuck in a dialectic of rebellion and damnation, that is, within the parameters associated with Gothic horrors and nightmares. More radical writers like William Godwin and some of the English Romantic poets continued to be attracted to the play's questioning of a traditional moral order and, ostensibly at least, its sympathy for the robber/outcast figure. Schiller himself developed a more conservative bent as he rejected the violence associated with the French Revolution and turned toward classicism. He replaced political and individual revolution with aesthetic education as an effective agent of change.

In his self-dramatized monstrosity, and seemingly part Richard III and part Iago, Franz von Moor tries to live beyond moral categories within a materialistic ethos, but this merely intensifies the Gothic and apocalyptic horrors to come. Like his brother, he rejects his father and in so doing rebels against the Father. But Franz goes far beyond Karl, who clings to a perverse morality in his oath of loyalty to the robber band. Refusing to be bound by the iron yoke of material laws, Franz repudiates loyalties of blood and sentiment and, having rejected the bond between father and son, employs terror to drive his father to an early death. Having convinced the Count that Karl has died in battle, and that he is responsible for the desperation that led to this, Franz succeeds in awakening in him the guilt-induced terrors of hell. Franz fakes his father's death and secretly imprisons him in a Gothic tower suggestive of the paternal, from which he emerges in act 4, appearing before Karl as a shrunken, wraithlike man on the brink of death. Indeed, Karl at first mistakes him for a ghost who will explain the riddle of eternity that eludes him.

But for Karl, the horror of damnation remains an external threat, unlike the case with Franz, whose nightmare and confrontation with the brimstone pastor Moser in act 5 reflect his rejected and mutilated but not entirely eradicated conscience. As Arthur McCardle suggests, Karl retains a pietist's conscience enlightened by idealism, while Franz, who embraces materialism, is visited by " 'Gespenstermärchen' [ghost stories] of judgment . . . the sole remnants of a childhood faith his perverted reason had rejected" (172). Karl's reawakened moral conscience contrasts with the horror with which Franz is consumed. The nightmare he recounts to Daniel in act 5, scene 1, with its references to the books of Ezekiel and Revelation, reflects the remnants of a conscience tortured by the suspicion that parricide is the one unforgivable sin, an idea confirmed by Moser. Franz dreams about a day of judgment in which truth is victorious, and he himself is forever cast out. An old man, evidently his own father, casts a lock of his silver hair into the scale of Franz's sins as it sinks into the pit, forever separating him from atonement.

Franz's acrimonious debate with Moser contrasts with Karl's denunciation of the priest in act 2, where apocalyptic guilt remains externalized and thus relatively manageable. Franz can only associate religion with empty horror stories; to renounce materialism and pursue Christianity now would be to surrender to apocalyptic horror alone. Hence he abuses Moser and insists that the soul dies with the body. Yet soon thereafter he demands that Daniel pray for him: "God damn it, pray!" (179). But Franz cannot pray and, unlike Karl in act 4 commits suicide by strangling himself.

Schiller's most influential experiment in Gothic literature is *The Ghost-Seer*, which achieved considerable popularity within his lifetime and for a period beyond despite its fragmentary, unfinished state. As Jeffrey Sammons points out, it is less a Gothic novel than a commentary on its atmosphere (vii). With a complicated publication history, it stands as testimony to Schiller's inability to spend long periods of time developing a difficult subject. He encountered some of the same problems with the play *Don Carlos* about the same time, but at least completed it. Whether he would not or could not bring closure to the novel is the subject of some debate, but its fragmentary state is oddly appropriate, for we are forced to join Count von O., the Prince, and other characters in exploring complex mysteries that become more puzzling the more we think we have understood them. *The Ghost-Seer* is a complex exploration of the "explained supernatural" associated especially with British Gothic tales and Ann Radcliffe's romances. At the same time, its relative lack of Gothic chills was dissatisfying for some readers. The novel influenced later writers who explored Gothic themes, for instance, E.T.A. Hoffmann in "Das Majorat" ['The Entail'], where the narrator's very mention of reading it during Daniel's horrifying visitation undermines otherworldly explanations for terror. This is because in 1817 Hoffmann's readership would associate Schiller's popular tale with the explained supernatural, not with the Gothic clichés of popular German *Triviallliteratur* [trivial literature].

Schiller put the novel through several changes after its appearance in 1787–1789 in five issues of his journal *Thalia*. A 1789 book version included a philosophical dialogue but omitted a "Departure" published in *Thalia*. A 1797 edition cut the dialogue in half but included some additions; a 1798 version cut the philosophical dialogue still further and reinserted the "Departure" (Sammons v–vi). Attempts to finish and translate the novel into English reveal the dissatisfaction some readers felt for *The Ghost-Seer*, which lacked the requisite thrill of Gothic horror they expected. One who finished it, Emmanuel Friedrich Follenius (1796), added the requisite "Germanico-terrific" (Menhennet 27–47) Gothic horrors. Yet the novel's fall from grace later in the nineteenth century is evident in the fact that the translation of Henry Bohn (1849) is the most readily available one in English. *The Robbers* and *The Ghost-Seer* were the first two works by Schiller translated in the United States, but the latter work almost dropped out of sight by the late nineteenth century, especially after Schiller's dismissal of it became known. It has been all but ignored by the critical community in recent years (Treder 30).

Yet as an admired and influential precursor to the Gothic tales of Hoffmann, Mary Shelley, Byron, and Edgar Allan Poe, *The Ghost-Seer* is of considerable interest. There are, for instance, experiments with narrative perspective one associates with Gothic mysteries. The story begins with a reference to "a certain political event" (1) whose solution will be found in the following account. Schiller lived in a time of political turmoil whose culmination was the French Revolution of 1789, that historical event that overturned categories and introduced the irrational into an apparently orderly world. Count von O. and the Prince stay at the Moor Hotel, perhaps a reference to the Gothic castle in the earlier play, where likewise violent aberrations introduce a hope for radical revaluations and solutions. Schiller completed his work on *The Ghost-Seer* during the period of the French Revolution. By the time he published his second edition in 1797, his disillusionment with it was well under way. Thus the novel straddles Schiller's growing discomfort with his youthful "Storm and Stress" excesses and his discovery of the aesthetic as a synthesis between form and matter that can make social change possible. He linked the Gothic with unbridled impulses and revolutionary destructiveness and hence was never comfortable with a work that continued to attract more radical writers. Ironically, as impractical as Schiller's aesthetic synthesis may appear, its influence on Hegel and, through him, Karl Marx have led many to call him the first Marxist.

In *The Ghost-Seer*, the deceased frame narrator, Count von O., tells the story of a German Prince residing in Venice, who is initially able to explain apparently supernatural events as impostures, yet paradoxically is drawn to irrational power as a result of his success. Assured of his rational abilities, he falls prey to the deeper mysteries of the Freemasons and the Jesuits. In the fragmentary and incomplete final letters he is seduced into converting to Catholicism by the mysterious Armenian, who, like the Grand Inquisitor in the play *Don Carlos*, is a master manipulator and parodic deity.

A key to the Prince's eventual downfall is clear at the start of "Book the Second," not long before the Count is replaced as principal narrator by the even more marginal Baron von F. His less informed letters force us to demystify the web that is carefully being woven around the Prince as he pursues a life of debt and gambling and becomes obsessed by a beautiful "Grecian" (really a German) who may be an agent of the Armenian. Like Franz in *The Robbers*, he is the product of a strict religious upbringing that avenges itself on him to the degree that he becomes comfortable with the rational. Having come to regard religious matters as "like an enchanted castle, into which one does not set one's foot without horror" (46), he is defeated by the conflict between too-rational Enlightenment and narrow religious approaches to life. A bigoted Protestant upbringing has transformed religion from a source of comfort into a source of Gothic terrors. This creates a hyperskepticism toward even the most sacred objects, which in turn ironically makes him subject to the more subtle mysteries engineered by the Armenian.

At least this subjection appears to be Schiller's intent. The question he did not fully resolve in his narrative was the process by which skepticism gives way to a deeper credulousness. This is a problem Mary Shelley explores more fully in *Frankenstein*, in which Victor's faith in reason leads him to embrace fairy tales of science—with disastrous consequences. Schiller seems aware that the

Enlightenment combined credulousness with reason in its faith that we can solve the mysteries of life and death through intellectual investigation.

Thus the Prince's ability to solve the ghostly visitations and the Sicilian's dishonest narrative about Jeronymo paradoxically ensnare him in further mysteries that lie beyond his grasp. Tempted toward self-assurance and into a life of sensual gratification that enables him to escape the irrational parts of his psyche beyond the grasp of reason, he is set up for the ultimate emotional dilemma that leads him to violence, atonement, and Jesuit-tinged Catholicism. The Armenian, who appears in many disguises in *The Ghost-Seer* and has ties with the Inquisition, presents himself as a mysterious person who can predict the future. Soon he leads the Prince toward a séance presided over by his accomplice, the Sicilian, which the Prince can readily solve. The appearance of two ghosts when the Prince asks to see the Marquis de Lanoy, a friend killed in battle, represents a set-piece example of the "explained supernatural." When the officers of the Inquisition arrest the Sicilian and follow the orders of the "Russian" (really the Armenian), it is easy for the Prince to explain the machinery behind supposedly supernatural visitations. But other mysteries evade and provoke him, above all, the Armenian's identity. As Count von O. points out, "a fondness for the marvellous had ever been his prevailing weakness" (10). That is, he is drawn to the very thing his reason rejects as a mere fiction or imposture. The Prince has faith in his reason at the same time that he enjoys the frisson of realizing that there is something inexplicable at the heart of it all. Exercise of the mind becomes an addiction whose inverse, sensual gratification and gambling, enable him to evade those mysteries that supposedly do not really exist in a materialistic universe. Or, as Count von O. puts it, "He had entered this labyrinth as a credulous enthusiast, had left it as a sceptic, and at length became a perfect freethinker" (48). Yet the ghosts of irrational belief become all the more powerful when they are denied and repressed.

The next stage in the Prince's rational self-assurance comes when he questions the Sicilian at the lead roofs, the most terrible prisons in Venice. He successfully sees through the Sicilian's attempts to convince him that the Armenian can transcend time and place, except for the midnight hour when he must return to hell. But the narrative fallacies, also evident in the Sicilian's story about Lorenzo del M., who murders his brother Jeronymo—the subplot used by Hoffmann in "The Entail"—are too obvious. Jeronymo appears in proper Gothic fashion, "with a deep wound in his neck" (33). The Sicilian and Loreno have created the specter to convince Antonia C. to marry him. Afterwards the Armenian appears in the guise of a Franciscan monk, bringing a more horrible, accusatory specter who reveals that he was killed by Lorenzo del M. The evidence of the ring, combined with other narrative lacunae, allows the Prince to solve yet another mystery revolving around dual ghostly visitations, but this seems to result from the Armenian's plotting rather than the Sicilian's incompetence. The Prince's realization that the Sicilian and the Armenian must have conspired with the younger brother in murdering Jeronymo is what he is supposed to conclude.

Schiller points to the mysteries of narrative, in which fragments must be joined together to explain mysteries that still elude complete explanation. He is thus an originator of the modern detective story, which has its origins in the Gothic. In this sense he foreshadows Edgar Allan Poe's detective fiction.

In conclusion, Schiller's encounters with the Gothic are tied to a youthful spirit of rebellion he eventually abandoned. Under the influence of Kant and Goethe, he embraced idealism in thought and art. The key turning point came in 1792 when, disillusioned with the Terror unleashed by the French Revolution, he studied Kant and developed the third way (or synthesis) that enabled him to move beyond the solipsistic enclosure he associated with Gothic sensibilities. His later works, such as *The Maid of Orleans*, may contain ghostly visitations, but they are at the service of the ideal and provoke no Gothic horrors. Schiller decisively turned against the Gothic in his pursuit of the ideal, but his experiments with Gothic themes in *The Robbers* and *The Ghost-Seer* created a reputation for innovative art that, even after he embraced classicism, continued to attract both the average reader and radical thinkers like William Godwin.

SELECTED CRITICISM

Carlyle, Thomas. *The Life of Friedrich Schiller*. Vol. 25 of *The Works of Thomas Carlyle*. Ed. H.D. Traill. 30 vols. New York: AMS Press, 1969. Excellent general account of the life and works intended to introduce Schiller to the British reader. Carlyle defends him against accusations of wildness and immorality.

Conger, Syndy M. "A German Ancestor for Mary Shelley's Monster: Kahlert, Schiller, and the Buried Treasure of *Northanger Abbey*." *Philological Quarterly* 59 (1980): 216–232. Schiller's *Verbrecher aus verlorener Ehre* [The Criminal of Lost Honor] was an important source for Mary Shelley in the creation of Victor Frankenstein's character in *Frankenstein*.

———. "Another Secret of the Rue Morgue: Poe's Transformation of the Geisterseher Motif." *Studies in Short Fiction* 24 (1987): 9–14. Another example of Schiller's influence beyond his actual productions (or intentions) on Gothic literature via another influential admirer who used *The Ghost-Seer* as a subtext in one of his most popular and influential short stories.

Dromgoole, Nicholas. "Schiller and Romanticism." In *Five Plays*. Trans. David MacDonald. London: Absolute Classics, 1998: 9–52. Places Schiller within his cultural contexts, including the Gothic and the melancholy, a "precursor of romanticism."

Hanson, James Carl. "Style and Structure in Schiller's *Der Geisterseher*." Doctoral dissertation, University of Michigan, 1968. [*DAI* 28:3183A]. Useful discussion of *The Ghost-Seer*. Schiller's style is "highly contrastive, often terse, and even asyndetic."

Leidner, Alan C. " 'Fremde Menschen fielen einander schluchzend in die Arme': *Die Räuber* and the Communal Response." *Goethe Yearbook: Publications of the Goethe Society of North America* 3 (1986): 57–71. Contains an interesting discussion about Schiller's original audiences' wild identification with the "dialectic of salvation and damnation" in *The Robbers*. Leidner analyzes the influences of pietism and baroque "apocalyptic resonances" that enable the "unfettered terror" of the first four acts to liberate the audience.

McCardle, Arthur W. *Friedrich Schiller and Swabian Pietism*. New York: Peter Lang, 1986. Useful chapter on *The Robbers* in which he discusses the tension between Schwabian pietism and Leibniz's rationalistic idealism.

Menhennet, Alan. "Schiller and the 'Germanico-terrific' Romance." *Publications of the English Goethe Society* 51 (1981): 27–47. Wide-ranging account of the relationship between nineteenth-century theories of the sublime and Gothic literature. Menhennet offers an informative account of Schiller's discomfort with the "cockpit of popularity" aroused by *The Ghost-Seer* and *Der Verbrecher aus verlorener Ehre* [The Criminal of Lost honor], which "risked loss of contact with ideality."

Negus, Kenneth. "The Allusions to Schiller's *Der Geisterseher* in E.T.A. Hoffmann's *Das Majorat*: Meaning and Background." *German Quarterly* 32 (1959): 341–355. Recounts the complex ways Hoffmann incorporates the Jeronymo story into "The Entail." Notes that Hoffmann's intertextuality is also personal: he associated the young Schiller with things "he prefers to forget, but cannot."

Sammons, Jeffrey L. "Schiller's *Der Geisterseher* [The Ghost-Seer]." In *The Ghost-Seer*. Trans. Henry G. Bohn. Columbia, SC: Camden House, 1992: v–xv. The introduction is particularly good for its account of the genesis, publication history, and translations of Schiller's work. There is also an interpretive overview of *The Ghost-Seer*.

Thiergard, Ulrich. "Schiller und Walpole: Ein Beitrag zur Schillers Verhältnis zur Schauerliteratur." *Jahrbuch der deutschen Schiller-Gesellschaft* 3 (1959): 102–117. Links Schiller to Walpole and the Gothic tradition.

Treder, Uta. "Wundermann oder Scharlatan? Die Figur Cagliostros bei Schiller und Goethe." *Monatshefte* 79 (1987): 30–43. Informative study of the influence of the notorious pre–French Revolution con artist Cagliostro on Schiller's Sicilian and Armenian.

SIR WALTER SCOTT
(1771–1832)

Michael Gamer

PRINCIPAL GOTHIC WORKS

The Chase and William and Helen: Two Ballads, from the German of Gottfried Augustus Bürger. Edinburgh: Manners and Miller, 1796.

Goetz of Berlichingen with the Iron Hand: A Tragedy, Translated from the German of Goethe by Walter Scott, Esq., Advocate, Edinburgh. London: J. Bell, 1799.

"The Eve of St. John," "The Fire King," "Frederick and Alice," "Glenfinlas, or Lord Ronald's Coronach," and "The Wild Huntsmen." Printed in *Tales of Wonder: Written and Collected by M.G. Lewis, Esq, M.P.* 2 vols. London: J. Bell, 1801.

Minstrelsy of the Scottish Border: Consisting of Historical and Romantic Ballads, Collected in the Southern Counties of Scotland; with a Few of Modern Date. 3 vols. Kelso: James Ballantyne, 1802–1803.

The Lay of the Last Minstrel: A Poem. London: Longman, 1805.

Marmion: A Tale of Flodden Field. Edinburgh: A. Constable, 1808.

Rokeby: A Poem. Edinburgh: J. Ballantyne, 1813.

Waverley; or, 'Tis Sixty Years Since. Edinburgh: A. Constable, 1814.

The Antiquary. 3 vols. Edinburgh: A. Constable, 1816.

The Black Dwarf. Edinburgh: William Blackwood, 1816.

Old Mortality. 3 vols. Edinburgh: William Blackwood; London: John Murray, 1816. (Published as vols. 2–4 of *Tales of My Landlord Collected and Arranged by Jedediah Cleishbotham.*)

The Heart of Mid-Lothian. 4 vols. Edinburgh: A. Constable, 1818. (Published as *Tales of My Landlord, Second Series, Collected and Arranged by Jedediah Cleishbotham.*)

The Bride of Lammermoor. Edinburgh: A. Constable, 1819.

Ivanhoe. 3 vols. Edinburgh: A. Constable, 1820. (Actually published 1819.)

The House of Aspen. In *The Keepsake.* Vol. 3 Ed. Frederic Mansel Reynolds. London: Thomas Davidson, 1830: 1–66. (Composed 1798.)

The Doom of Devorgoil: A Melo-drama. Edinburgh: Cadell; London: Simpkin and Marshall, 1830. (Composed 1817–1818.)

MODERN REPRINTS AND EDITIONS

Most of Scott's novels are available in paperback from Oxford University Press and Penguin Books. The Oxford editions are based on Scott's revised "Magnum Opus" collected edition of 1830, while the Penguin editions take their text and notes from the new Edinburgh Edition of the Waverley Novels, which work from first editions and Scott's own manuscripts.

The Antiquary. Ed. David Hewitt. Edinburgh: Edinburgh University Press, 1995.
The Antiquary. Ed. David Hewitt. London: Penguin, 1998.
The Chase, and, William and Helen, 1796, Oxford: Woodstock, 1989.
The Heart of Midlothian. Ed. Claire Lamont. Oxford: Oxford University Press, 1982.
The Heart of Mid-Lothian. Ed. Tony Inglis. London: Penguin, 1994.
Ivanhoe. Ed. Ian Duncan. Oxford: Oxford University Press, 1996.
Ivanhoe. Ed. Graham Tulloch. Edinburgh: Edinburgh University Press, 1998.
Ivanhoe. Ed. Graham Tulloch. London: Penguin, 2000.
The Lay of the Last Minstrel, 1805, Oxford: Woodstock, 1992.
The Letters of Sir Walter Scott. 12 vols. Ed. Herbert Grierson. London: Constable and
    Co., 1932.
Old Mortality. Ed. Jane Stevenson and Peter Davidson. Oxford and New York: Oxford
    University Press, 1993.
The Poetical Works of Sir Walter Scott, with the author's introduction and notes. Ed. J.
    Logie Robertson, London: Oxford University Press, 1904.
Selected Poems. Ed. James Reed. Manchester: Fyfield, 1992.
The Supernatural Short Stories of Sir Walter Scott. Ed. Michael Hayes. London: J. Cal-
    der, 1977. (Contains "The Tapestried Chamber," "My Aunt Margaret's Mirror,"
    "Wandering Willie's Tale," "The Two Drovers," and "The Highland Widow.")
The Tale of Old Mortality. Ed. Douglas Mack. Edinburgh: Edinburgh University Press,
    1993.
The Tale of Old Mortality. Ed. Douglas Mack. London: Penguin, 1999.
Waverley; or, 'Tis Sixty Years Since, Ed. Claire Lamont. Oxford: Oxford University
    Press, 1986.
The Works of Sir Walter Scott. Ware: Wordsworth Poetry Library, 1995.

Walter Scott's reputation has revived strongly in the last two decades, thanks largely to the critical and editorial work of scholars like J.H. Alexander, Ian Duncan, Ina Ferris, Peter Garside, Nancy Moore Goslee, David Hewitt, James Kerr, Claire Lamont, Jane Millgate, Peter T. Murphy, Fiona Robertson, John Sutherland, and Judith Wilt. These primarily historicist accounts have helped to reanchor Scott squarely within Romantic-period writing and within the political, economic, and cultural contexts in which he moved. As might be expected, this recent work usually has treated Scott as a writer of fiction, focusing most often upon issues of authorship and his handling of historical materials and the conventions of metrical and prose romance. It is easy to see why. Beginning with *Waverley* in 1814 and extending through over two dozen works by his death in

1832, Scott's career as a writer of fiction is one of the great stories of nineteenth-century literature. Peter T. Murphy puts the matter succinctly: "His success remains, I think, almost unparalleled, even in our era of smash hits and giant blockbusters" (136). Appearing anonymously, Scott's novels broke all existing sales records and influenced everything from the content to the price of British fiction. They also created cottage industries among printmakers and dramatists, who found lucrative trades in representing scenes from the novels and in transferring their stories to the stage. Ironically, the person to upstage the dominance and fame of the "author of *Waverley*" in 1826 was Scott himself. The financial crisis of 1825–1826 brought on a series of business failures that finally enveloped the two firms in which Scott was a silent partner, publishers Archibald Constable and Company and printers James Ballantyne and Company. Their bankruptcies brought on Scott's financial ruin, leaving him £126,000 in debt and forcing him to make a formal, public avowal of authorship of the *Waverley* Novels. For nineteenth-century literary historians, Scott's dogged determination to repay the debt through increased literary production rather than declaring bankruptcy created a tale as romantic as any of those he penned, one that came with a fitting tragicomic ending. While the strain of Scott's prodigious output surely hastened his death in 1832 from a series of strokes, the sale of his copyrights in 1833 not only erased the outstanding balance but also allowed Scott's children to keep Abbotsford, the estate that for over two decades Scott had determinedly transformed into an ancestral extravaganza reminiscent of, but grander than, Horace Walpole's Strawberry Hill.

Waverley's opening chapter may famously reject Gothic fiction as a model for itself, but Abbotsford's conical turrets and rooms of heraldry, its suits of armor and commissioned paintings of ancient ancestors, tell another story. Like Scott's very readable letters and *The Doom of Devorgoil* (1830), the play he penned for actor Daniel Terry on the stipulation that Terry claim authorship for it, Scott's house displays his fondness for the Gothic more plainly and intimately than his published poetry and fiction. His purchase of the estate in 1811, largely with profits derived from his poetry, should also remind us that when Scott published *Waverley*, he was forty-three years old and a successful and experienced man of letters. By the end of 1814, Scott already had published two works of antiquarian scholarship (*Minstrelsy of the Scottish Border* and *Sir Tristrem*); edited the works of Dryden and Swift; translated Gottfried Augustus Bürger's *Lenore* and Goethe's *Götz von Berlichingen*; and coconspired in the launching of the *Quarterly Review*. He also was, with Byron, the most celebrated and commercially successful poet of his day. Beginning with *The Lay of the Last Minstrel* in 1805, Scott had published a series of wildly popular metrical romances, each six cantos long and similar in style and scope to one another. *Marmion* followed *The Lay* in 1808 and in turn was succeeded by the even more popular *Lady of the Lake* in 1810 and *Rokeby* in 1813. Compared to the sensation caused by *Waverley* and its successor *Guy Mannering* (1815), the disappointing sales of Scott's next poems, *The Lord of the Isles* (1815) and

Harold the Dauntless (1817), most likely confirmed Scott in his decision to move from poetry into prose fiction.

It is only when we examine these metrical romances and the poems and plays of the 1790s that we can begin to see the degree to which Scott in his early career figured himself primarily as a disciple of Matthew Lewis and of William Taylor of Norwich. Taylor's translation of Bürger's *Lenore*, first circulated in manuscript before appearing in the *Monthly Magazine* in March 1796, spurred four subsequent imitations by other writers in less than two years. Scott first heard Taylor read the poem aloud late in 1794; his own version, "William and Helen," was his first publication and followed translations already published by J.H. Spencer, W.T. Stanley, and Poet Laureate Henry James Pye. While Henry Mackenzie had introduced Edinburgh to Schiller as early as 1788 in his "Account of the German Drama," it was the success of Taylor's poem and Lewis's 1796 novel *The Monk* (which contained a number of ballads imitating Bürger) that really created a popular market for "German" writing in Britain. The success of Taylor's translation and Lewis's imitations led Scott to produce a number of supernatural poems and to name his mare 'Lenore' in 1795 to commemorate the midnight gallop of Bürger's poem.

With the London stage successes of the German playwright August von Kotzebue and of Lewis's *Castle Spectre* at Drury Lane Theatre in 1798, Scott moved from poetry to dramatic translation and adaptation. *The Castle Spectre*'s popular success showed Scott, first and foremost, Gothic drama's remunerative potential, and Scott responded by accelerating the production of his own translations and original compositions. By 1799, Scott had translated or imitated no fewer than five German dramas, and in March 1799, thanks to Lewis's ministrations with publisher John Bell, he received fifty pounds for his translation of Goethe's *Götz von Berlichingen*. While Scott was in London celebrating the publication of his *Götz*, he composed the full-length Gothic tragedy *The House of Aspen*, cultivated his friendship with Lewis in hopes that Lewis would help him in getting his play produced, and agreed to contribute several poems to Lewis's collected edition, *Tales of Wonder* (1801). Drury Lane's rejection of Scott's play in 1799 led him thereafter to refuse all requests that he write for the theater; still, the quantity and seriousness of Scott's dramatic work at the end of the eighteenth century suggest that the considered himself as late as 1799 principally a Gothic dramatist and a poet of the supernatural, holding an additional interest in collecting, imitating, and translating English and German ballads.

We further may wish to consider Scott a pupil of Lewis, then, not only because he wrote in the same genres but also because he displayed a lifelong sensitivity to the very issues of genre and reception that plagued Lewis during these last years of the eighteenth century. Given this similarity of taste, the hostility accorded to Lewis by reviewers between 1798 and 1802 led Scott after 1800 to avoid the literary and political associations that had brought Lewis public scandal and dishonor. These years also saw Scott cultivating the friendship of several eminent antiquarians, among them Kenneth Curry, Richard Heber, Robert Surtees (author of the *History of Durham*), and original *Anti-Jacobin* contributor George Ellis, who in turn introduced Scott to fellow *Anti-Jacobin*s George Canning, John Hookham Frere, and William Gifford. When Scott's "Eve of St. John," "The Fire King," "Frederick and Alice," "Glenfinlas," and "The Wild Huntsmen" finally appeared in Lewis's *Tales of Wonder* in 1801, these same friends criticized the publication as "injudicious" (*Letters*, ed. Grierson 1: 103n). Their uneasiness no doubt increased when *Tales of Wonder* itself became the object of numerous attacks and parodies. Whether in response to such warnings or simply because of changes in his own interests, Scott's own attitudes appear to have changed at this time as well. As John Sutherland puts it in his biography of Scott, "From this point on in his literary life, Scott became a witheringly sarcastic commentator on his early 'German mad' productions" (74). In his correspondence, he began to observe that "ghosts . . . have of late been put out of fashion by a promiscuous & ill-judged introduction of tales relating to them" and vowed never again to produce "Germanized brats" for the stage or press: "Should I ever again attempt dramatic composition, I would endeavour after the genuine old English model" (*Letters* 1:118n, 1:124).

The extent to which Scott's move from "fashion" and "the German" to a "genuine old English model" involved distancing himself from the tradition of Gothic writing embodied by Lewis is best captured in Scott's next production, *Minstrelsy of the Scottish Border*. Presented as a respectably national work of antiquarian research, the three-volume ballad collection claimed not Lewis as its main influence but Bishop Thomas Percy, author and editor of the foundational ballad collection *Reliques of Ancient English Poetry* (1765). Published in 1802, the *Minstrelsy*'s first two volumes contained scholarly essays and "ancient" ballads. Its positive reception inspired Scott to publish in 1803 a scholarly edition of *Sir Tristrem* and a third volume of the *Minstrelsy*, this time featuring modern "Imitations of the Ancient Ballad" by antiquarians Robert Jamieson, John Leyden, and Charles Kirkpatrick Sharpe. In addition, Scott included his own "Thomas the Rymer" and a single, decidedly unsupernatural ballad of Lewis's (likely as a gesture of thanks), as well as republishing his own "Glenfinlas" and "The Eve of St. John." As a cultural document, the third volume of Scott's *Minstrelsy* is a wonderful testimony to the power of repackaging textual materials. While many of the tales resemble those published in *Tales of Wonder*, to compare the two is to marvel at their differences in presentation. Impressively printed by Ballantyne, Scott's volume provided each poem with an introduction and elaborate scholarly notes usually longer than the poem itself. Leyden's 264-line "Lord Soulis," for example, carried with it a nine-page introduction and seventeen pages of closely printed notes. As they do in Scott's later poetry and fiction, scholarly footnote and "national" (as opposed to "foreign") subject matter in the *Minstrelsy* feed off of one another, legitimizing the other's enterprise. Transplanted from *Tales of Wonder* into such a setting and next to such company, the heavily introduced and footnoted "Glenfinlas" and "The Eve of St.

John" take on a very different significance and cultural status, becoming respectful homages "after the genuine old English model." The same can be said, needless to say, of the *Minstrelsy*'s effect on Scott's literary reputation and authority.

When we consider the metrical romances Scott published between 1805 and 1817, then, we see similar issues at work. Scott's *Lay of the Last Minstrel*, for example, employs a series of motifs familiar to students of the Gothic: a "withered" monk guarding a magic book both he and William of Deloraine are forbidden to open, the undecaying corpse of a wizard, halls that echo with "Loud sobs, and laughter louder . . . / And voices unlike the voice of man" (Canto 2.58, 192, 258–259). These textual moments, interestingly, also see Scott's scholarly notes at their lengthiest and most historical. Of Michael Scott, the wizard in the poem who raises both evil secrets from the crypts of abbeys and embodies ancestral *virtu*, he writes, "He appears to have been addicted to the abstruse studies of judicial astrology, alchemy, physiognomy, and chiromancy. Hence he passed among his contemporaries for a skilful magician" (*Poetical Works* 517). As with the third volume of the *Minstrelsy*, the effect is to bestow upon the text a historicized and enlightened distance and to inscribe a degree of irony into its formal features. Readers are free within the text of the poem to indulge in a host of supernatural effects, from shape-shifting to raising spirits from the grave, and these readerly fantasies in turn are safely encased within a scholarly apparatus of enlightened antiquarianism.

As *The Lay* and its successors make clear, Scott's recurrence to Gothic motifs in his work does not stem merely from their commercial attractiveness; these same moments perform ideological functions as well. The Scottish-English conflict dramatized in *The Lay*, for example, depends entirely on the device of Lord Cranstoun's goblin page, who steals the magic book procured by William of Deloraine and uses a spell within it to lure the young heir of Branksome Tower away from his home until an army of English soldiers captures him. With the young boy as hostage, the army then marches to Branksome to demand William of Deloraine in exchange, and the threatened battle is only broken up when Cranstoun uses the same spell to assume the form of Deloraine and win a single combat. Canto 5's dramatization of the two armies passing the time until the single combat at brotherly play confirms Scott's tendency to locate Scottish-English strife in the machinations of power-hungry individuals rather than in any real or lasting cultural differences. Here the suggestion is that without a magic book and a goblin page to create mischief with it, no English-Scottish conflict would occur.

Similar issues govern the plots of the later metrical romances as well. While all dramatize military episodes of internal strife—whether the Battle of Flodden Field in *Marmion* or the English Civil War in *Rokeby*—these poems repeatedly direct our focus to the attempts of petty nobles and warlords to manipulate moments of crisis for selfish ends. Like the villain Oswald in *Rokeby* who attempts to profit from the chaos caused by the Battle of Marston Moor, Scott's

Gothic hero-villain Marmion freely subverts the institutions of chivalric warfare and courtship: he seduces a nun, spurns her for the betrothed woman of another knight, accuses that knight of treachery, and defeats him in single combat. For Scott, Marmion is a double traitor—both for his betrayal of a fellow countryman and for his exploitation of the chivalric codes of honor and courtship for his own ends. Before Scott published *Waverley*, then, he already had made a career out of deftly appropriating Gothic conventions by relocating them in a historical, national past and by bringing the language of antiquarian scholarship to bear upon them.

Scott's fiction features these practices even more strongly. As the wealth of recent critical work approaching Scott from Bakhtinian perspectives suggests, Scott's careful and usually ironic handling of the Gothic in his fiction stems less from a change of attitude toward the Gothic than from the dialogic potential offered to him by the novel—its formal ability to balance competing discourses against one another within a single textual arena. Much of this work has taken its cue from James Kerr's *Fiction against History* (1989), which argues that Scott's novels manage discursively to oppose themselves to their Gothic predecessors by first appropriating, then defamiliarizing, and finally historicizing their conventions (Kerr 5–6). One sees such oppositional practices even in the opening chapter of Scott's first novel, *Waverley*, which explicitly rejects both "A Tale of Other Days" and "A Romance from the German" as subtitles for the book because they will cause readers to associate it with Gothic fiction. As Ina Ferris has noted, Scott's reviewers engage in similar acts of generic demarcation, praising his historical and factual facility as a healthy antidote to the distortions and excesses perpetrated by women novelists. Kerr's suggestion that we view the *Waverley* Novels as "counterfictions" to Gothic has in turn been persuasively questioned by Fiona Robertson, who instead has suggested that "the discomfort created in critical circles by the notion of a Gothic Scott" has caused commentators to construct a "legitimate history" with "its own unformulated agenda, which at its most simple is the denial of significant influence from earlier fiction" (51). Such critical accounts, she finds, ignore both "the inbuilt identity of the 'Author of *Waverley*' " and the ways in which that author simultaneously invokes the Gothic while associating it with femininity, adolescence, Germanness, and naïveté. Such a critical approach to Scott's writing requires that we recognize his narrative practice to be as shifting and duplicitous as his authorial practice. We should not be surprised, for instance, when Scott asks his readers to connect Edward Waverley's early reading of romances both to his "romantic" decision to support the Pretender and to his representation of the Scotch magistrate who questions him as having "tortured" him "on the racks of the Inquisition" (*Waverley*, Lamont ed., 170). In *The Antiquary*, it is hardly accidental that Lovel's nightmare is explained by the mature antiquary Oldbuck, that the German "Fortunes of Martin Waldeck" is translated by Miss Waldour, or that the supernatural sham that dupes Sir Arthur is imposed upon him by the German quack Dousterswivel. Scott's relationship to his Gothic predecessors is ongoing and at times even dissembling. Where he utilizes the Gothic most strongly, he also always takes care to package it with care—either by locating it within a naïve and disordered subjectivity or, more often, by exporting, ironizing, and historicizing it.

SELECTED CRITICISM

Alexander, J.H., and David Hewitt, eds. *Scott in Carnival: Selected Papers from the Fourth International Scott Conference, Edinburgh, 1991*, Aberdeen: Association for Scottish Literary Studies, 1993. An excellent collection of several dozen essays, many engaging in Bakhtinian approaches to Scott's work.

Cottom, Daniel. *The Civilized Imagination: A Study of Ann Radcliffe, Jane Austen, and Sir Walter Scott*. Cambridge: Cambridge University Press, 1985. Focusing on Scott's wielding of romance conventions, this book concentrates especially upon the ideological use of enchantment in Scott's fiction.

Duncan, Ian. *Modern Romance and Transformations of the Novel: The Gothic, Scott, Dickens*. Cambridge: Cambridge University Press, 1992. An influential study that locates the narrative practices of Scott and Dickens in Gothic fiction's handling of character. Scott transforms romance, according to Duncan, by dramatizing the interaction between public and private, thereby providing a more complex representation of historical change.

———. "Walter Scott, James Hogg, and Scottish Gothic." In *A Companion to the Gothic*. Ed. David Punter. Oxford, UK, and Malden, MA: Blackwell, 2000: 70–80. "The thematic core of Scottish Gothic consists of an association between the national and the uncanny or supernatural. Scottish Gothic represents the uncanny recursion of an ancestral identity alienated from modern life." Discusses *Waverley; or, 'Tis Sixty Years Since, Guy Mannering; or, The Astrologer, Redgauntlet, The Antiquary*, and *Ivanhoe*.

Ferris, Ina. *The Achievement of Literary Authority: Gender, History, and the Waverley Novels*. Ithaca, NY: Cornell University Press, 1991. Perhaps the best study of Scott's relationship to Maria Edgeworth and an excellent exploration of how reception shapes authorial careers and processes of canonization.

Freye, Walter. *The Influence of "Gothic" Literature on Sir Walter Scott*. Rostock, Germany: H. Winterberg, 1902. Early-twentieth-century study of Scott's Gothic connections. Has material on *The Bridal of Triermain* (1813).

Gamer, Michael C. "Marketing a Masculine Romance: Scott, Antiquarianism, and the Gothic." *Studies in Romanticism* 32 (1993): 523–549. The Gothic romance offers Romantic poets a means of tapping the popular readership that both attracts and repels them. By including Walpole, Reeve, and Radcliffe in an edition of standard British novels in the Ballantyne Novelists' Library, Scott attempts both to construct the genealogy of the Gothic novel and to canonize it by placing it with the belles lettres of British prose fiction in such works as *Rokeby, Marmion*, and *Lady of the Lake*.

Goslee, Nancy Moore. *Scott the Rhymer*. Lexington: University Press of Kentucky, 1988. Likely the best full-length study of Scott's poetry, this book seeks to recall Scott the poet for modern audiences and to highlight his ties to medieval romance and to oral tradition. Its treatment of gender in the poems is illuminating.

Hayden, John O., ed. *Walter Scott: The Critical Heritage*. London: Routledge, 1995. Originally published in 1970 as *Scott: The Critical Heritage*. An essential anthology of contemporary reviews of Scott, as well as important nineteenth- and twentieth-century essays on him.

Kerr, James. *Fiction against History: Scott as Storyteller*. Cambridge: Cambridge University Press, 1989. Locating the complexity of Scott's novels in the ways in which he pits "fiction" and "history" against one another, this study argues that the *Waverley* Novels must be understood "as a dialectical response to Gothic romance . . . a counter-genre," and that "Scott defined his position as a novelist within and against the Gothic mode."

Kropf, David Glenn. *Authorship as Alchemy: Subversive Writing in Pushkin, Scott, Hoffmann*. Stanford, CA: Stanford University Press, 1994. An ambitious study exploring the relation between Scott's various authorial constructs and his creative practice.

Le Tellier, Robert Ignatius. *Sir Walter Scott and the Gothic Novel*. Lewiston, NY: Edwin Mellen Press, 1995. A book-length study of Scott's relationship to his Gothic predecessors.

Mayo, Robert D. "The Waverley Novels in Their Relations to Gothic Fiction." Doctoral dissertation, Princeton University, 1938.

Millgate, Jane. *Walter Scott: The Making of the Novelist*. Edinburgh: Edinburgh University Press, 1984. This book combines a compelling account of the origins of Scott's narrative practice with very good readings of individual novels.

Murphy, Peter T. *Poetry as an Occupation and an Art in Britain, 1760–1830*. Cambridge: Cambridge University Press, 1993. Fine study of Scott's success story.

Orr, Marilyn. "Repetition, Reversal, and the Gothic: *The Pirate* and *St. Ronan's Well*." *English Studies in Canada* 16 (1990): 187–199. In these novels and others, Scott allows "the Gothic anti-hero to replace duality with a triad by which he can multiply himself without being threatened."

Robertson, Fiona. *Legitimate Histories: Scott, Gothic, and the Authorities of Fiction*. Oxford: Clarendon Press, 1994. Explores the relationship between Scott's various authorial identities and the ways each wields Gothic conventions. It remains one of the best accounts of how the construction of a canonical, historical Scott depends upon either ignoring or trivializing his Gothic predilections.

Shaw, Harry E. *Narrating Reality: Austen, Scott, Eliot*. Ithaca, NY: Cornell University Press, 1999. Seeks to reread Scott and other novelists within current debates concerning the nature of realism and should be read ultimately as a defense both of Scott and of realism.

Sutherland, John. *The Life of Walter Scott*. Oxford: Blackwell, 1995. A perceptive and dark account of Scott's life, focusing especially on his dealings with printers and publishers.

Wilt, Judith. *Secret Leaves: The Novels of Walter Scott*. Chicago: University of Chicago Press, 1985. One of the best sustained readings of Scott's fiction, one that also provides an account of Scott's novels as the "enabling environment" within which Victorian fiction functioned.

MARY WOLLSTONECRAFT SHELLEY
(1797–1851)

Marie Mulvey-Roberts

PRINCIPAL GOTHIC WORKS

Frankenstein; or, The Modern Prometheus. 3 vols. London: Lackington, Hughes, Harding, Mavor, & Jones, 1818.

Frankenstein; or, The Modern Prometheus. The Standard Novels Series. London: Henry Colburn & Richard Bentley, 1831. (For a discussion of the significant differences between the 1818 and 1831 texts, see Macdonald and Scherf's edition of *Frankenstein* [38–41] and Mellor [165–180].)

Mathilda. (Written in 1819–1820, the novel was not published during Mary Shelley's lifetime.)

Valperga; or, The Life and Adventures of Castruccio, Prince of Lucca. 3 vols. London: G. & W.B. Whittaker, 1823.

"On Ghosts." *London Magazine*, March 1824: 253–256.

The Last Man. London: Henry Colburn, 1826.

"The Evil Eye." *The Keepsake for MDCCCXXX* (1830): 150–175.

"Transformation." *The Keepsake for MDCCCXXXI* (1831): 18–39.

"The Mortal Immortal: A Tale." *The Keepsake for MDCCCXXXIV* (1834): 71–87.

"Roger Dodsworth: The Reanimated Englishman." In *Yesterday and To-Day*. London: T. Cautley Newby, 1863:2, 150–165.

"Valerius: The Reanimated Roman." (Short story not published in Mary Shelley's lifetime. See *Collected Tales and Stories*. Ed. Charles E. Robinson.)

MODERN REPRINTS AND EDITIONS

The Annotated Frankenstein. Ed. Leonard Wolf. New York: C.N. Potter (Distributed by Crown Publishers), 1977. Reissued as *The Essential Frankenstein: including the complete novel by Mary Shelley*. Ed. Leonard Wolf. New York: Plume, 1993.

Collected Tales and Stories. Ed. Charles E. Robinson. Baltimore: Johns Hopkins University Press, 1976. (Contains "The Evil Eye," "Transformation," "The Mortal Immortal," "Roger Dodsworth: The Reanimated Englishman," and "Valerius: The

Reanimated Roman." Two other tales have pronounced Gothic content: "The Heir of Mondolfo" and "The Dream.")

Frankenstein; or, The Modern Prometheus. Ed. James Rieger. Indianapolis: Bobbs-Merrill, 1974. (First printing of the 1818 text. Has an appendix on "The Ghost-Story Contest" of 1816.)

Frankenstein; or, The Modern Prometheus. The 1818 version. Ed. D.L. Macdonald and Kathleen Scherf, Petersborough, Ontario: Broadview Press, 1994.

The Frankenstein Notebooks: A Facsimile Edition of Mary Shelley's Manuscript Novel, 1816–17 (with Alterations in the Hand of Percy Bysshe Shelley) As It Survives in Draft and Fair Copy. Ed. Charles E. Robinson. 2 vols. The Manuscripts of the Younger Romantics. New York and London: Garland Publishing, 1996.

The Journals of Mary Shelley, 1814–1844. Ed. Paula R. Feldman and Diana Scott-Kilvert. 2 vols. Oxford: Clarendon Press, 1987.

The Last Man. Ed. Anne McWhir. Peterborough, Ontario: Broadview Press, 1997.

Mary Shelley, Frankenstein. Case Studies in Contemporary Criticism. Ed. Johanna Smith. Boston: Bedford Books of St. Martin's Press, 1992. (Text accompanied by a casebook of critical approaches to the novel.)

The Mary Shelley Reader. Ed. Betty T. Bennett and Charles E. Robinson. New York and Oxford: Oxford University Press, 1990. (Contains "Roger Dodsworth: The Reanimated Englishman," "Transformation," "The Dream," and "The Mortal Immortal.")

Masterpieces of Science Fiction. Ed. Sam Moskowitz. Cleveland: World Publishing, 1966. (Contains "The Mortal Immortal.")

Matilda. Ed. Janet Todd. London and New York: Penguin Books, 1991. (The volume also contains *Mary* and *Maria* by Mary Wollstonecraft.)

The Novels and Selected Works of Mary Shelley. Ed. Nora Crook with Pamela Clemit, intro. Betty T. Bennett. 8 vols. London: William Pickering, 1996; Brookfield, VT: Pickering & Chatto, 1996. (Volume 1, *Frankenstein*, has the 1818 text with collations, ed. Nora Crook; volume 2, *Matilda*, ed. Pamela Clemit; volume 3, *Valperga*, ed. Nora Crook; volume 4, *The Last Man*, ed. Jane Blumberg; volume 5, *Perkin Warbeck*, ed. Doucet Devin Fischer; volume 6, *Lodore*, ed. Fiona Stafford; volume 7, *Falkner*, ed. Pamela Clemit; volume 8, *Travel Writing*, containing *History of a Six Weeks Tour* and *Rambles in Germany and Italy in 1840, 1842, and 1843*, ed. Jeanne Moskal.)

Valperga; or, The Life and Adventures of Castruccio, Prince of Lucca. Ed. Tilottama Rajan. Peterborough, Ontario: Broadview Press, 1998.

Although few writers have been more markedly associated with the Gothic than Mary Shelley, recognition of her contribution tends to be limited to her best-known novel, *Frankenstein; on, The Modern Prometheus*. Yet Gothicism creeps over the boundaries between her life and work. It is encrypted within such writings as the novella *Mathilda*, which dates from 9 November 1819 but was not published until 1959; the novels *Valperga*, *Falkner* (1837), and *The Last Man*; the travelogue *Rambles in Germany and Italy* (1844); and the essay "On Ghosts" (1824). In addition, she wrote a number of short stories with Gothic themes, most of which were published in the literary annual *The Keepsake*. These include "Valerius: The Reanimated Roman," "Roger Dodsworth: The

Reanimated Englishman," "The Evil Eye," "Transformation," and "The Mortal Immortal: A Tale."

Shelley came from Gothic stock. Her mother, Mary Wollstonecraft, was the author of the unfinished novel *Maria* (1798), which is set in a madhouse, while her pedagogical treatise, *Thoughts on the Education of Daughters* (1787), is a blueprint for *Frankenstein* as a bildungsroman. Shelley's masterpiece, written when she was nineteen, is dedicated to her father, William Godwin, whom Thomas De Quincey described as provoking in most people he met "the same alienation and horror" as does "the monster created by Frankenstein" (3.25). Godwin's interest in supernatural means of overcoming death is apparent from his Gothic novel *St. Leon*. He also produced a biographical *Lives of the Necromancers* (1834), a taxonomy of magicians that includes Cornelius Agrippa and Albertus Magnus.

Mary's husband, Percy Bysshe Shelley, commenced his literary career with two potboiler Gothic novellas, *Zastrozzi* (1810) and *St. Irvyne; or, The Rosicrucian* (1811), which were inspired by the vogue for the Germanic Sturm und Drang. Mary expressed strong reservations about her husband's early dabblings with the Gothic, commenting in a footnote to her edition of Shelley's *Queen Mab*:

He was a lover of the wonderful and wild in literature, but had not fostered these tastes at their genuine sources—the romances and chivalry of the middle ages—but in the perusal of such German works as were current in those days. Under the influence of these he, at the age of fifteen, wrote two short prose romances of slender merit. The sentiments and language were exaggerated, the composition imitative and poor.

The Rosicrucian hero in *St. Irvyne*, who pursues the secret of the elixir of life from the philosopher's stone, is an alchemist equivalent of Victor. Percy Shelley's own nefarious activities, which included visiting graveyards in the hope of resurrecting the dead and carrying out scientific experiments for the purpose of raising the devil, provided Mary Shelley with a model for her scientist hero Victor. In *Frankenstein*, a novel ripe for psychobiographical readings, her own monster was constructed literally from parts of dead bodies.

Shelley's literary lineage conditioned the darkness in her writing, much of which may be classified as "family Gothic." *Frankenstein* depicts dysfunctional families, while *Mathilda* toys with the imagined incestuous relationship between a father and daughter. As Shelley's mother died in 1797, a mere ten days after giving birth to her, it may be significant that much of her fiction concerns motherless or fatherless children. When Godwin married Mary Jane Clairmont in 1801, he began to spend less time with Mary, at one point sending her to spend nearly two years with friends in Scotland, creating in his daughter a sense of neglect and laying the groundwork for familial anxiety. Victor's abandonment of the creature in *Frankenstein* (he "fathers" the monstrous child but rejects it) sharply reflects her anxiety. In this picture of paternal irresponsibility, Mary

Shelley may well have been influenced by the behavior of Percy Shelley, whose negligence in his role as father was egregious. After separating from his first wife, he had no communication with the children from this first family until he fought and lost a battle for custody following the suicide of their mother.

In Mary Shelley's novels, images of dead mothers occur with telling frequency. *Falkner* opens with the sinister image of a child whose mother has recently died, defending her grave against a stranger. Later, there is an exhumation of another mother's remains, a skull, wrapped in her long dark hair, and discolored bones. In *Frankenstein*, Victor has a nightmare about his fiancée Elizabeth Lavenza turning into the decaying cadaver of his dead mother. Gothic terror in *Frankenstein* is generated by Victor's privileging of his scientific brainchild over mother nature. The novel warns of the dangers of solitary male propagation and the perversity of bringing a child into the world without maternal nurturing.

According to the preface for the 1831 edition, *Frankenstein* was conceived during a cold and rainy night in 1816 at Villa Diodati on Lake Leman in Geneva, where she was staying with Shelley, Lord Byron, and his physician Dr. John Polidori. She explains how the effect of reading some German ghost stories translated into French, *Fantasmagoriana; ou, Recueil d'histoires d'apparitions de spectres, revenans, fantômes, etc.; traduit de l'allemand, par un amateur* (1812), "excited in us a playful desire of imitation." Two tales, "The Death-Bride" (about a spectral lover) and "The Family Portraits" (in which a portrait comes to life), are credited by her with influencing the writing of *Frankenstein*, although it also owes much to a dream she had as she suffered through her inability to produce a ghost story in response to the challenge of the group's game of ghost-story writing. After a horrifying dream of a young student who creates a living being, she set out to write a story that would frighten others just as her dream had frightened her. The novel she produced is, however, much more than a mere horror thriller.

The monster and its trail of destruction have provoked various readings, from autobiographical analyses to political interpretations in the light of the French Revolution. Shelley's contemporary, Edmund Burke, employed a Gothic horror metaphor for the revolutionary forces in his *Reflections on the Revolution in France* (1790) similar to Victor's creature, who arose indirectly from the charnel houses of Geneva. "[O]ut of the tomb of the murdered monarchy in France has arisen a vast, tremendous, unformed spectre, in a far more terrific guise than any which ever yet have overpowered the imagination" (qtd. in Levine and Knoepflmacher 143). Mary Shelley's political Gothic also owes much to the work of her father, whose radical treatise *Political Justice* (1793), informs her presentation of a creature who, fundamentally good, becomes an agent of violence because of his ill-treatment.

Frankenstein tells the story of a Genevan student who discovers the secret of imbuing inanimate matter with life. He builds a nameless giant of supernatural strength whose appearance is so hideous that it alienates all who see it. In its misery, the creature parallels the career of the Wandering Jew, who had been condemned to roam the earth until the Second Coming of Christ. Postcolonial readings exploring racism and Marx's theory of alienation in regard to class have been applied to the monster's ostracization. Deserted by its creator, the creature, desperate for human company, spies on the De Lacey family, even managing to acquire an education by eavesdropping on these cottagers while they read aloud Constantin-François Volney's *Ruins of Empires*. Beset with loneliness and despair, the created turns against the creator in a reenactment of the Fall. Victor at first complies with its plea to create a mate of similar kind, but he later reneges by destroying the female monster he has created. Enraged, the creature wreaks revenge by murdering Victor's best friend Henry Clerval and Victor's bride Elizabeth. Bent on revenge—and thus becoming much like the creature—Victor pursues his creation to the Arctic but dies before he is able to carry out his intention, though not before he has narrated his story to Captain Robert Walton, who has rescued him from the sea. The creature declares Victor to be the final victim of this reign of terror and departs to end its own life.

The 1818 edition was followed by a two-volume second edition in 1823 that had been highly corrected, almost certainly by Percy alone, who had made the creature slightly more menacing. For the third edition, published in 1831, Mary made extensive revisions and produced a longer introduction. Compared to the first edition, it is considered by some critics to be less radical and more sentimental and deterministic, with greater emphasis on fate and the occult. The novel was first published anonymously, and reviewers assumed the author to be male. The critical reception of the novel was not inordinately hostile, although fellow Gothic novelist William Beckford was less charitable in a private note he wrote on the fly-leaf of his own copy of the first edition, in which he referred to it as "perhaps, the foulest Toadstool that has yet sprung up from the reeking dunghill of the present times."

The title of the book may have been taken from Schloss Frankenstein, the home of Johann Konrad Dippel, who, like Victor, signed his name "Frankenstein" and robbed graves for his experiments. The Shelleys would have passed the castle on their voyage down the Rhine in 1814, although it is not known whether or not they ever visited it. Another possible source is the fusion of the German word *stein* (stone) with "Frank" in Benjamin Franklin, who was celebrated as a "modern Prometheus" for his experiments with electricity and lightning. Percy Shelley was the author of the poem *Prometheus Unbound* (1820), while the hero of *St. Irvyne* is named Wolfstein. *Frankenstein*'s subtitle, *The Modern Prometheus*, signals that Mary was constructing a new birth myth by reconfiguring the story of the creation told in Genesis, as well as the ancient Greek myths of Prometheus as the maker of man and the bringer of fire from heaven. The horror of miscreation is implicit in the response of one contemporary reviewer who deemed the book a "monstrous literary abortion" (qtd. in Botting 5).

The narratives of Victor and the creature are contained within a frame story of letters from Captain Robert Walton to his sister Margaret Walton Saville (Mary's initials M.W.S.). The creature comes into being in December 1796, the month in which *Frankenstein* begins following a realistic chronology that can be deduced from the frame narrative. The outer narrative structure of the novel spans a gestation period of nine months from the first letter to the last. Victor dies on 11 September 1797, one day after Shelley's mother died from puerperal fever ten days after childbirth. In a mirroring of this maternal loss, Mary's daughter expired also eleven days after she was born in 1815. In her journal for 19 March, Mary records a "dream that my little baby came to life again that it had only been cold and that we rubbed it before the fire and it lived" (*Journals* 11:170).

Frankenstein is finally a novel about atonement. Victor is punished for his overreaching by the deaths of his loved ones. Among these are Justine Moritz, a family servant who is put to death for the murder of Victor's youngest brother William, who was actually killed by the creature, a fact that Victor knows but chooses to keep silent. William's death strangely appears to foretell that of Mary's baby son William, who was to die at the age of three, along with Mary's half brother of that name, who died of cholera as a young man in 1831. From the author's point of view, the creation of the monster can be interpreted as a textual resurrection of some of the dead members within her family circle.

The novel marks a turning point in the representation of Gothic convention by redefining the machinery of Gothic terror. The stock setting of the ruined castle has been transmogrified into a laboratory in which Victor is immured rather like a cloistered monk. The graveyard scenes are no longer sites of diabolical conjuring. Rather, they are scavenging territory for the body snatcher intent on dissection. The Oedipal conflict between father and son, the Hegelian master-and-servant dialectic, the pursuit of a damsel by a villain, and the biblical revolt of the created against the Creator are reconfigured as Mary Shelley offers as a Gothic climax the final battle between mad scientist and his monstrous living mutant against the backdrop of the arctic sublime.

Shelley's other works also provide distinctive variations on time-honored Gothic themes. The ice that figures prominently in the chilling frame of *Frankenstein* also serves to preserve the body of the eponymous hero of Shelley's short story "Roger Dodsworth: The Reanimated Englishman." Based on a hoax surrounding the alleged revival of a seventeenth-century Englishman, the tale is not only a comic variation on the monster, but also on ghost-story conventions. Another departure from archetypal Gothic is in the way in which she employs female Gothic in *Valperga*, transforming the gloomy castle perched on top of a craggy mountain, inhabited by a tyrannical father figure, into the female abode of the wise Euthanasia, who is betrothed to the titular hero. Set in early-fourteenth-century Italy, *Valperga*'s Gothic machinery includes secret passages, cavernous mountains, a witch of the forest named Fior di Mandragola, a Wandering Jew figure, and an albino dwarf. "Transformation" is a Gothic fairy tale that focuses upon an exchange of bodies between a dwarf and a handsome and dissolute young man, Guido. In "The Evil Eye," Shelley extends the optical power of the villain through the Albanian, Dmitri, a variation on the Wandering Jew, who instills terror in all who meet his glance. Defying death and immortal youth are the subjects of "The Mortal Immortal," in which the whimsical hero Winzy takes the elixir of life and acquires perpetual life while those around him age and die. Living death is found again in her final novel, the futuristic *The Last Man*, in which the human race is wiped out by plague at the turn of the twenty-second century with the exception of one solitary individual, Lionel Verney.

By the time Mary Shelley had produced the revised edition of *Frankenstein* in 1831, Percy Shelley, Byron, and Polidori were all dead. Mindful of this, she records in her *Rambles in Germany and Italy* (1844) her reaction on seeing Villa Diodati from a steamer on the lake many years later: "Was I the same person who had lived there, the companion of the dead? . . . I looked on the inanimate objects that had surrounded me, which survived, the same in aspect as then, to feel that all my life since was but an unreal phantasmagoria—the shades that gathered round that scene were the realities" (*Novels and Selected Works* 148). Like her hero in *The Last Man*, she too had survived the death of those around her, yet in common with her own Frankenstein monster, Mary Shelley was doomed to live in isolation from love and companionship in a kind of living death. She might have identified with the hero of her story "Valerius: The Reanimated Roman," whose "semblance was that of life, yet he belonged to the dead." In her essay "On Ghosts," she invokes an image that resonates for the creator of a creature composed of human cadavers: "I thought:—the earth is a tomb, the gaudy sky a vault, we but walking corpses" (*Mary Shelley Reader* 336). By projecting herself as a living corpse, Mary Shelley was able to enter her own narratives in a deathlike embrace of their multivalanced Gothic parts.

SELECTED CRITICISM

Baldick, Chris. *In Frankenstein's Shadow: Myth, Monstrosity, and Nineteenth-Century Writing*, Oxford: Clarendon Press, 1987. Surveys the far-reaching influence of the novel and sees it as the progenitor of "an authentic new myth" because her book confronts "the most pressing problems of modern history."

Banerji, Krishna. "Enlightenment and Romanticism in the Gothic: A Study of Mary Shelley's *Frankenstein*." In *The Romantic Tradition*. Ed. Visvanath Chatterjee. Calcutta: Jadavpur University Press, 1984: 95–105. Weighs the Gothic properties and evaluates the novel's position in a waning Gothic tradition.

———. "Mary Shelley, *Frankenstein*, and the Woman Writer's Fate." In *Romantic Women Writers: Voices and Countervoices*. Ed. Paula R. Feldman and Theresa M. Kelley. Hanover, NH: University Press of New England, 1995: 69–87. On Mary Shelley's feminist voice in the novel.

Bloom, Harold. "*Frankenstein, or the New Prometheus*." *Partisan Review* 32 (1965): 611–618. Important and influential article that treats the novel "as one of the most vivid versions of the Romantic mythology of the self."

Botting, Fred. *Making Monstrous: Frankenstein, Criticism, Theory.* Manchester and Manchester University Press, 1991. The eleven chapters study "the metaphor of monstrosity and the monstrosity of metaphor which inhabits and anticipates the texts of *Frankenstein*'s critics. Throughout its long, popular and controversial history Frankenstein's monster has been associated with cultural anxieties and deployed as a signifier of a variety of dangerous and uncontrollable others that threaten the limits and unity of established positions."

The Collected Works of Thomas DeQuincey. 16 vols. Ed. David Masson. Edinburgh: A. and C. Black, 1880. De Quincey draws a parallel between Godwin and the monster.

Conger, Syndy McMillen. "Mary Shelley's Women in Prison." In *Iconoclastic Departures: Mary Shelley after Frankenstein: Essays in Honor of the Bicentenary of Mary Shelley's Birth.* Ed. Syndy M. Conger, Frederick S. Frank, and Gregory O'Dea. Madison, NJ: Fairleigh Dickinson University Press, 1997: 81–97. "Investigates the early fictional solutions that Mary Shelley offers to . . . Mary Wollstonecraft's most frequently restated problem: women's metaphoric imprisonment." Mary Shelley endorses and acknowledges Mary Wollstonecraft's profeminist views, and in doing so, acts as "chief executor of her mother's intellectual estate."

Crook, Nora. "Mary Shelley, Author of *Frankenstein.*" In *A Companion to the Gothic.* Ed. David Punter. Oxford, UK, and Malden, MA: Blackwell, 2000: 58–69. Asks and answers the question "What kind of Gothic is *Frankenstein?*" In its use of a Germanic title, the props of Gothic terror fiction such as suspense, persecution, and panic, and the flight-and-pursuit motif of the arctic climax, *Frankenstein* is a hybrid of the German shudder novel or *Schauerroman.* Also discusses *Valperga* and *Rambles in Germany and Italy* as generically Gothic works.

Fisch, Audrey A., Anne K. Mellor, and Esther Schor, eds. *The Other Mary Shelley.* Oxford: Oxford University Press, 1993. A collection of fourteen essays dealing with the post-*Frankenstein* fiction. According to the editors, "By bringing Mary Shelley to the center of Romantic studies the essays progress beyond a simple recognition of masculinism at the heart of canonical romanticism."

Florescu, Radu. *In Search of Frankenstein.* Boston: New York Graphic Society, 1975. Travelogue and tour guide of the *Frankenstein* territory near Darmstadt, Germany. Has a chapter titled "Mary Shelley and the Gothic Novel."

Frank, Frederick S. "Mary Shelley's Other Fiction: A Bibliographical Census." In *Iconoclastic Departures: Mary Shelley after Frankenstein: Essays in Honor of the Bicentenary of Mary Shelley's Birth.* Ed. Syndy M. Conger, Frederick S. Frank, and Gregory O'Dea. Madison, NJ: Fairleigh Dickinson University Press, 1997: 295–349. Provides annotated coverage of scholarship and criticism on Mary Shelley's other novels and short fiction. "Her many unique fictional contributions to the annuals and her intelligent activity as a novelist reveal not a reclusive Victorian scribbler but a working author who thought of herself as a career writer rather than the creator of a single sensational book."

Gigante, Denise. "Facing the Ugly: The Case of *Frankenstein.*" *ELH* 67 (2000): 565–587. With frequent references to Burke's *Enquiry*, examines the role of ugliness in *Frankenstein.* "Ugliness in *Frankenstein* is less of an aesthetic experience than a question of survival. The ugly ultimately bursts forth to consume whatever it confronts."

Hale, Terry, ed. *Tales of the Dead: The Ghost Stories of the Villa Diodati* (1816). Trans. Sarah Elizabeth Brown Utterson. Chislehurst: Gothic Society, Gargoyle's Head Press, 1992. On the ghost-story-writing game that produced *Frankenstein*.

Harpold, Terrence. " 'Did You Get *Mathilda* from Papa?: Seduction Fantasy and the Circulation of Mary Shelley's *Mathilda*." *Studies in Romanticism* 28 (1989): 49–67. A psychobiographical interpretation. In *Mathilda*, "Mary Shelley rehearses the problematic scene of her origin and foregrounds the oedipalization of the primal scene of seduction between father and daughter."

Hill-Miller, Katherine. *"My Hideous Progeny": Mary Shelley, William Godwin, and the Father-Daughter Relationship.* Newark: University of Delaware Press, 1995. Explores Godwin's unsettling psychological legacy and his generous intellectual gifts to his daughter. Godwin brought up Mary Shelley to be a thinker and writer. Yet as Mary Wollstonecraft Godwin grew into womanhood, her once-supportive father rejected her, perhaps because of the incestuous feelings her developing womanhood called up. "If Mary Wollstonecraft cast a long shadow over her daughter from the grave, William Godwin cast an even longer one from his home in Skinner Street."

Hoeveler, Diane Long. "Mary Shelley and Gothic Feminism: The Case of 'The Mortal Immortal.' " In *Iconoclastic Departures: Mary Shelley after Frankenstein: Essays in Honor of the Bicentenary of Mary Shelley's Birth.* Ed. Syndy M. Conger, Frederick S. Frank, and Gregory O'Dea. Madison, NJ: Fairleigh Dickinson University Press, 1997: 150–163. This Wandering Jew story "plays in its oxymoronic title with ambiguity and impossibility, suggesting that there may be a way to make mortals immortal, just as Mary desperately wanted to believe that there may be a way to equalize women and men." The story also "plays with variations of beating fantasies, with sometimes the male protagonist as victim, sometimes the female."

Levine, George, and U.C. Knoepflmacher. eds. *The Endurance of Frankenstein.* Berkeley: University of California Press, 1979. The twelve essays indicate in various ways "the inexhaustibility of interpretation" that the novel provokes. Reprints Ellen Moers's "Female Gothic: The Monster's Mother."

Marshall, Tim. "*Frankenstein* and the 1832 Anatomy Act." In *Gothick Origins and Innovations.* Ed. Allan Lloyd Smith and Victor Sage. Amsterdam and Atlanta, GA: Rodopi, 1994: 57–64. Relates the cadaverous themes of the novel and Victor Frankenstein's research interests to the 1832 Anatomy Act, which legalized the use of bodies for professional dissection and medical research. The three editions of the novel prior to 1832 (1818, 1823, 1831) "are a prolepsis, a script which anticipates the legislative intervention in the anatomy contest."

Mellor, Anne K. *Mary Shelley: Her Life, Her Fiction, Her Monsters.* New York and London: Routledge, 1988. A biocritical study of the life and achievement of Mary Shelley. Devotes six chapters to *Frankenstein* and the remainder to her other novels. *Frankenstein* is in part her reaction to Percy Shelley's "Prometheanism."

Moers, Ellen. "Female Gothic: The Monster's Mother." *New York Review of Books* 21 March 1974: 24–28. An explication of the novel's maternal themes. "What Mary Shelley actually did in *Frankenstein* was to transform the standard Romantic matter of incest, infanticide, and patricide into a phantasmagoria of the nursery." Mary Shelley's monster novel became the model for the term "female" Gothic, now widely used to describe a dominant strain of Gothic fiction.

Paley, Morton D. "Mary Shelley's *The Last Man*: Apocalypse without Millennium."
    Keats-Shelley Review 4 (1989): 1–25. Details negative reaction to the novel and
    discusses Mary Shelley's "ambivalence toward millenarianism, denying the link-
    age of apocalypse and millennium that had previously been celebrated in some
    of the great works of the Romantic epoch."
Scott, Sir Walter. "Remarks on *Frankenstein*." *Blackwood's Edinburgh Magazine* 2
    (1818). Rpt. in *Frankenstein; or, The Modern Prometheus*. Ed. D.L. MacDonald
    and Kathleen Scherf. Peterborough, Ontario, Canada: Broadview Press, 1994:
    303–309.
Smith, Johanna M, ed. *Mary Shelley, Frankenstein*. Case Studies in Contemporary Crit-
    icism. Boston: Bedford Books of St. Martin's Press, 1992. Contains the 1831 text
    of the novel as well as various critical essays intended to provide students "with
    an entrée into the curious critical and theoretical ferment" that the novel has
    provoked. The book's final essay, Lee E. Heller's "*Frankenstein* and the Cultural
    Uses of Gothic," discusses Mary Shelley's modifications of the Gothic tradition.
Veeder, William. *Mary Shelley and Frankenstein: The Fate of Androgyny*. Chicago:
    University of Chicago Press, 1986. Approaches *Frankenstein* and her other fiction
    "in light of the psychological model she and Percy looked upon as ideal, the
    androgyne." In the writing of *Frankenstein*, "Mary seeks to compensate Godwin
    for not being the son he wanted, to provide Percy with the 'antitype' he craves,
    and to convince Byron she is the intellectual he can never really take her for."

PERCY BYSSHE SHELLEY
(1792–1822)

Jack G. Voller and Douglass H. Thomson

PRINCIPAL GOTHIC WORKS

"Ghasta; or, The Avenging Demon!!!" In *Original Poetry by Victor and Cazire*. London: J.J. Stockdale, 1810. (Gothic poetry written in coilaboration with Elizabeth Shelley.)

"The Spectral Horseman." In *Posthumous Fragments of Margaret Nicholson*, London: J. Munday, 1810. (Gothic poetry.)

"The Wandering Jew." 1810? (Published from Shelley's manuscripts in the *Edinburgh Literary Journal*, 1829.)

Zastrozzi: A Romance. London: G. Wilkie & J. Robinson, 1810.

St. Irvyne; or, The Rosicrucian. London: J.J. Stockdale, 1811.

"The Wandering Jew's Soliloquy." 1811? (In the *Esdaile Notebook: A Volume of Early Poems*. Ed. Kenneth Neill Cameron. New York: Alfred A. Knopf, 1964.)

Queen Mab. London: privately printed, 1813.

The Cenci: A Tragedy in Five Acts, Italy: for C. and J. Ollier, London, 1819.

Hellas: A Lyrical Drama. London: Charles & James Ollier, 1822.

MODERN REPRINTS AND EDITIONS

The Complete Works of Percy Bysshe Shelley. Ed. Roger Ingpen and Walter E. Peck. 10 vols. London: Gordian Press; Ernest Benn, 1965.

Zastrozzi. London: Golden Cockerel Press, 1955.

Zastrozzi: A Romance, and St. Irvyne; or, The Rosicrucian: A Romance. Ed. Frederick S. Frank. New York: Arno Press, 1977.

Zastrozzi: A Romance and *St. Irvyne; or, The Rosicrucian* (combined editions). Ed. Stephen C. Behrendt. Oxford: Oxford University Press, 1986. (This edition is cited in the text.)

Of all the major Romantic poets and their many interesting entanglements with the Gothic tradition, critics generally single out Percy Bysshe Shelley as the one

writer most attracted to the Gothic flame. His youthful pursuit of darkly transcendental experience led him to many of the most powerful and notorious of
the first Gothics. Thomas Love Peacock asserted that "nothing so blended itself
with the structure of his interior mind as the creations of [Charles Brockden]
Brown" (*Memoirs*, ed. Mills 43); Thomas Medwin reported how Radcliffe's
novels "pleased him most" but Dacre's *Zofloya* simply "enraptured him" (*Life*
25); Mary Shelley lamented that "he was a lover of the wonderful and wild in
literature, but had not fostered these tastes at their genuine sources—the romances and chivalry of the middle ages—but in the perusal of such German
works as were current in those days" (note 9 to *Queen Mab*); and all critics
today agree in stressing the seminal influence of William Godwin's *Caleb Williams* and *St. Leon* and the work of Monk Lewis upon Shelley's imagination.
Perhaps the most delightful detail is Peck's recovery from the Shelley estate of
a copy of the *Tales of Terror*, "which bears evidence of hard use, and is marked
throughout by childish characters, perhaps in the hand of Shelley" (305).

Although there is no denying Shelley's youthful engagement with the Gothic,
critics have been unsure what to make of it, some (following Mary's lead)
lamenting the influence and glad to see him leave it behind as he embarks upon
his mature, "Romantic" career, others stressing how a certain Gothic fatalism
and diseased idealism haunt his writing right up until the end. Neither view is
quite right. Shelley's later works, it is true, still employ Gothic tropes and characters, none more powerful than "his old friend" (to quote Mary), the Wandering
Jew. But these mature works leave behind the superficial gloom and melodrama
that characterize his early Gothic novels and poetry to discover the energies and
impulses of transcendence. Inherently a language of the extranatural, the Gothic
became for Shelley an alternative language of transcendence, a valuable reser-
voir of imagery and rhetoric that could speak of the power of human passion
and desire.

Shelley's notorious early experiments in Gothic fiction, *Zastrozzi* (1810) and
St. Irvyne; or, The Rosicrucian (1811), are rather unremarkable as Gothic novels,
although they do reveal a rhetorical and intellectual capacity that would come
to fruition in the later poetry. *Zastrozzi*, with its convoluted psychosocial dynamics of revenge, desire, and pursuit, dimly presages *The Cenci*, although it
lacks the intellectual coherence and artistic control of the latter; it is, to a considerable extent, a study of emotional intensity, of superhuman will grafted to
human desire. Matilda's maniacal and obsessive devotion to Verezzi is mirrored
by Zastrozzi's lifelong hatred of him, and the novel traces a trajectory of betrayal
and revenge that culminates in a troubled conclusion. Driven to madness by the
discovery that his beloved Julia was not dead, as he had been manipulated into
believing, Verezzi commits suicide; Matilda, to whom Verezzi had been married, then murders Julia. Brought before an Inquisition-like tribunal, Zastrozzi,
"towering as a demi-god" (101), reveals the purpose of his machinations and
deceits: revenge. His mother having been seduced and abandoned by Verezzi's
father, Zastrozzi devotes the rest of his life to revenge, and he exults, even as

he expires on the rack, in the completion of his life's single purpose. As with the more accomplished *St. Irvyne*, this novel is ultimately at odds with itself—or, more accurately, Shelley's desire to write commercially successful fiction is at odds with his Prometheanism. Conventional pieties litter the roadway of these novels, but the high valorizations of personal will and emotional intensity provide a discordant and incongruent counterpoint.

The conventional element in *St. Irvyne* is simple and superficial, resident mostly in the pious platitudes and conventional Christian gestures at the novel's conclusion and indicative of nothing more than a calculated attempt by the eighteen-year-old Percy to sell books and cultivate an audience (Behrendt viii). Indeed, the conventionality of the novel's moral element seems to have put off Shelley himself, for it is drastically undermined by the hasty, patchwork conclusion with which he ended the novel when he tired of it.

Those elements more indicative of Shelley's idealist and reformer principles, however, are more carefully integrated into *St. Irvyne*, despite the novel's problematic coordination of its two narrative lines and its tacked-on final paragraph of explanation and conventional moral posturing. Most obvious is the use of the image of the "terrific precipice" (182), which occurs repeatedly in dreams of the principal characters. What this image ultimately suggests, with its associations of annihilation and consumption, is the fragile coherence of the phenomenal world. In both the Ginotti/Wolfstein and Nempere/Eloise narrative threads, the demonic intensity of Ginotti/Nempere and his lengthy manipulations of Wolfstein and Eloise are reminiscent of Zastrozzi's single-minded pursuit and destruction of Verezzi and Matilda and accomplish a similar purpose of facilitating both the physical and moral destruction of his victims. Yet unlike the earlier novel, *St. Irvyne* takes care to offer a more complex vision of destructive will: Ginotti is the outlaw facilitator of Wolfstein's crimes; as Nempere, he is the polished, sophistical destroyer of Eloise's virtue. The enigmatic Ginotti/ Nempere, the obsessed pursuer of Wolfstein and seducer of Eloise, sells his soul rather than face the terror of the abyss, a terror that destroys the hapless Wolfstein; for the innocent and naïve Eloise, the yawning gulf (appearing in her dream about an apparently helpful stranger, but in reality the malevolent Ginotti/ Nempere) opens at her feet at a moment of supposed fulfillment, thereby revealing the true nature of *St. Irvyne*'s moral universe: one in which the overpowering natural landscape speaks not of transcendence, but of annihilation and dread. In a close parallel to Matthew Lewis's *Monk, St. Irvyne* subverts its own token gestures toward traditional piety by repeatedly suggesting fundamental challenges to traditional assumptions about divinity, will, and morality.

No single figure in Shelley's canon better represents these challenges than Ahasuerus, the Wandering Jew, the man who denies Christ only to be blasted by the curse of immortality and the damning knowledge of his sinfulness. Wandering Jew figures occupy an important place in the Gothic tradition, appearing most memorably in Lewis's *Monk*, Godwin's novels, and, later, Charles Robert Maturin's *Melmoth the Wanderer*. Rieger and Porte argue that the Jew is an archetypal figure of the Gothic imagination in his crystallizing the recurrent Gothic pattern of outrage and retribution. It is tempting but ultimately misguided to see Shelley's preoccupation with Ahasuerus as a reflection of his own heresies and their at-times-tragic aftermath. Tracing the evolution of the Wandering Jew in his poetry instead provides a perfect illustration of how he discovers, within the psychology of a Gothic archetype, a new language of transcendence and political prophecy.

Shelley's earliest incarnations of Ahasuerus seem mainly indebted to Lewis and are clumsily Gothic. A Wandering Jew figure, with signature "burning Cross on his forehead," first appears in "Ghasta; or, The Avenging Demon!!!" from the not-always *Original Poetry by Victor and Cazire* ("not always" because Shelley's early poetic collaboration with his sister includes a plagiarized version of Lewis's "Black Canon of Elmham; or, St. Edmond's Eve"). This brooding "Stranger" appears on the scene to liberate the demon-plagued knight Rodolph. He does so by summoning the hellhound Ghasta to "drag . . . to the depths below" (178) the specter of Theresa, a *belle dame sans merci* who has been haunting Rodolph. Nothing more than a Gothic prop in a very derivatively Gothic poem, this Jew simply functions as supernatural agent and exorciser, exactly as he did for the Bleeding Nun of *The Monk*. Paolo, from the fairly long poem "The Wandering Jew," and Ginotti/Nempere, from *St. Irvyne*, provide more traditionally religious but still quite conventional versions of Ahasuerus figures: with both, divine retribution figures uppermost, although before consigning himself to hell flames, Paolo invites some sympathy for his sufferings, having quite Gothically lost his soul mate Rosa to accidental poisoning by his lone companion and friend, Victorio. "The Wandering Jew" and other youthful poems, such as "Revenge" and "The Spectral Horseman," share with his early novels a thorough immersion in conventional Gothicism and offer few hints about how the later Shelley would transform its practice.

One transformation, hardly surprising from the author of *The Necessity of Atheism*, is the use of Ahasuerus as a vehicle for attacking the injustice and cruelty of God. In "The Wandering Jew's Soliloquy" (1811?), a new Ahasuerus emerges, outraged at his punishment and accusing "the Eternal Triune" of violent crimes against humanity throughout history. Shelley's earlier versions of the damned wanderer, much like Maturin's, had tempered anguished cries of torment with supplication ("To him [the God of Mercy] would I lift my suppliant moan / That power should hear my harrowing groan") ("The Wandering Jew" 1434–1435). The Jew of the "Soliloquy" remains completely defiant, railing against the "Tyrant of Earth! pale Misery's jackal" (11). His virulent attack on the Deity anticipates Shelley's portrait of God as "Profuse of poisons" (676) in "Alastor" during a passage in which he summons the precedent of the Wandering Jew, sad "Vessel of deathless wrath" (680), as an analogue to the Poet's fate. In *Queen Mab*, Shelley assigns to yet another Ahasuerus figure his fullest early exposition of God's tyranny as he teaches Ianthe of "The massacres and misery which [God's] name / Had sanctioned in my country" and throughout world history (VII.176–177).

Shelley's Wandering Jew thus parts company from his Gothic brethren in rejecting the guilt normally assigned to him. Whereas all tormented Jews in the Gothic tradition serve as spectacular demonstrations of divine retribution upon sinning mortals, Shelley's serve as an indictment of the very act of divine retribution; indeed, the Godwinian Ahasuerus of *Queen Mab* has even found a kind of peace in a way that prefigures Shelley's later Prometheus:

> Reason may claim our gratitude, who now
> Establishing the imperishable throne
> Of truth, and stubborn virtue, maketh vain
> The unprevailing malice of my foe. (VII.245–248)

Yet the breakthrough moment, both politically and artistically, in *Queen Mab* is Shelley's depiction of this wanderer as a symbol, "a phantasmal portraiture / Of wandering human thought (7:274–275)," "the matter of which dreams are made" (7:272). Ahasuerus, despite his philosophic consolation, still represents the mind-forged manacles doing battle with the God of the old Dispensation and exists, to quote Reiman, as an "aberrant human idea" (*Norton Shelley* 58 n. 9) What the spirit of Ianthe learns from this "idea" is that the Jew is yet another victim of tyranny, not only of his own dark imaginings but of the political tyranny that goes forward in God's name in this, "religion's iron age" (7:43). She must liberate herself from the guilt and trepidations that typically plague Gothic heroines and oppose those "priests [who] dare babble of a God of peace / Even whilst their hands are red with guiltless blood" (44–45).

Shelley's most famous re-working of the psychology of the Gothic heroine appears in his complex portrait of Beatrice Cenci. The play continues his fascination with the dark themes of guilt and retribution that he explores in his depictions of the Wandering Jew, even as it provides another striking example of how he transforms Gothic conventions. As Michasiw and Murphy have noted, "*The Cenci* abounds with Gothic trappings: the Cenci castle, a world full of dark intrigue and unspeakably dark desires; an absolutely virulent anti-Catholicism in its depiction of corrupt church officials; the villainous Count Cenci in whom Shelley unblinkingly explores the nature of depravity with a skill and power that outdo any Gothic treatment of the subject; the incest theme now not hinted at but horridly driving the plot—the list could go on. Yet now we have a great poet exploring the familiar Gothic terrain of tortured and tempestuous passion." Witness Beatrice's imagining the place of her father's death, a passage that also acutely reflects her own nightmarish state of mind (she is the rock brooding over the abyss):

> the road
> Crosses a deep ravine; 'tis rough and narrow,

And winds with short turns down the precipice;
And in its depth there is a mighty rock
Which has, from unimaginable years,
Sustained itself with terror and with toil
Over a gulph, and with the agony
With which it clings seems slowly coming down;
Even as a wretched soul hour after hour,
Clings to the mass of life; yet clinging leans;
And leaning, makes more dark the dread abyss
In which it fears to fall: beneath this crag,
Huge as despair, as if in weariness,
The melancholy mountain yawns . . .
You hear but see not an impetuous torrent
Raging among the caverns . . .
. . . At noon day here
'Tis twilight, and at sunset blackest night. (*The Cenci* 3.1.245–265)

This passage, modeled on a description of Hell by the Spanish playwright Pedro Calderón de la Barca certainly reads like Gothic poetry, but it outstrips any of its predecessors in psychological depth and poetic power. While reflecting Shelley's love of Ann Radcliffe's sublime landscape painting, Beatrice's description surely takes us beyond earlier Gothic landscape painting in its journey into a tortured soul. It may be tempting to see Beatrice's murder of the Count as the ultimate revenge of the Gothic heroine upon the cruel father and also as another of Shelley's Gothic borrowings, this time from his youthful reading of Charlotte Dacre's *Zofloya*, with its transgressive heroine Vittoria di Loredani. But Shelley's revision of the Gothic is far more important than his borrowings from it. Shelley's aim, as he writes in the "Preface" to the play, is to expose the "casuistry with which men seek the justification of Beatrice, yet feel that she has done what needs justification; it is in the superstitious horror with which they contemplate alike her wrongs and their revenge" (Reiman *Shelley* 240). Her wrongs, the reader's *revenge*: Shelley here re-reroutes the entire logic governing that simple and enduring Gothic moral formula: bad person does wrong; the reader awaits and enjoys his punishment. Only specious reasoning ("casuistry") can excuse Beatrice's act of murder, even if she is the most unequivocally wronged of Gothic heroines. Shelley's fundamental pacifism lies beneath this Jacobean and Gothic infused revenge tragedy: one act of violence, no matter how extreme, cannot justify another.

The political imperative that underlies this message and that informs Shelley's poetry as a whole finds its most pointed expression in *Hellas*, in which he summons again his "old friend" Ahasuerus, who has always been in a privileged position to speak on the empty process of guilt, retribution, and violence. Shelley's final incarnation of the Wandering Jew is both "aberrant human idea" (largely a figment of the despot Mahmud's guilty conscience) and a vehicle for one of Shelley's most powerful indictments of tyranny. He is summoned to help interpret the King's nightmare, a gloomy vision of eventual Turkish defeat that haunts him "from sleep into the troubled day" (129). What makes this Ahasuerus so effective is Shelley's sharp realization of an integral feature of this archetype, a feature, aside from Maturin's treatment of it, rarely fully explored in the Gothic tradition: the Wandering Jew is a witness to human history, not just a victim but an observer who can powerfully address the vicissitudes of political change. From his now-visionary perspective of "the One,—/ The unborn and the un-dying" (769–770), "that which cannot change" (768), Ahasuerus places the im-mediate Turkish victory over Hellas in its true place in history, for history has taught him that no victories of tyranny last, that all tyrants eventually overreach themselves in their material devotion to power here and now and in their denial of the "One." Where in other places in his poetry Shelley's idealism may seem otherworldly, even Gothically so, Ahasuerus's ideal vision of human potential is grounded in history. What ultimately issues from Shelley's early experiments with this most Gothic of wanderers is one of the most successful unions of his idealism and his call for political action.

It is in this union that Shelley vindicates his own Gothic visions, finding a redeeming purpose for the imagery and language that had long attracted him for its ability to articulate energies and desires beyond the range of normal human experience. Moving beyond the uncongenial Gothic gestures of the early novels and poetry—although even these show his desire to exploit the emotional and thematic power of Gothic tropes—Shelley eventually discovers in the language of this dark genre an arresting new way of voicing some of his brightest ideals.

SELECTED CRITICISM

Antippas, Andy. "The Structure of Shelley's *St. Irvyne* and the Gothic Mode of Evil." *Tulane Studies in English* 18 (1970): 59–71. Examines the relationship between the two narrative lines, the Wolfstein-Ginotti story and the Eloise-Ginotti story, and suggests that Shelley mirrors these plots to enhance the Gothic presentation of evil.

Behrendt, Stephen C. Introduction to *Zastrozzi: A Romance* and *St. Irvyne; or, The Rosicrucian*. Oxford: Oxford University Press, 1986: vii–xxiii. An effective over-view of the novels and their place in Shelley's poetic development.

Chesser, Eustace. *Shelley and Zastrozzi: Self-Revelation of a Neurotic*. London: Gregg, 1965. A psychiatric reading that includes the text of Shelley's first Gothic novel.

Frank, Frederick S. Introduction to *Zastrozzi: A Romance, and St. Irvyne; or, The Rosicrucian: A Romance*. New York: Arno Press, 1977: ix–xxv. The discussion focuses on the role novel writing had in developing Shelley's rhetorical and lit-erary skills and how this early practice contributed to his later poetic achieve-ments.

Halliburton, David G. "Shelley's 'Gothic' Novels." *Keats-Shelley Journal* 16 (1967): 39–49. Treats the Gothic novels as studies of Shelley's uncertainties regarding faith and Christianity.

Hogle, Jerrold E. "Early Attachments: From the 'Gothic Sensibility' to 'Natural Piety' and *Alastor*." In *Shelley's Process: Radical Transference and the Development of His Major Works*. New York: Oxford University Press, 1988: 28–58. Discusses Shelley's youthful attraction to the Gothic and shows how his juvenile Gothicism contributes to the greatness of poems such as "The Hymn to Intellectual Beauty."

Michasiw, Kim Ian. "Haunting the Unremembered World: Shelley's Gothic Practice." *Gothic Fictions: Prohibition/Transgression*. Ed. Kenneth W. Graham. New York: AMS Press, 1989: 199–225. Finds the real Gothic horror of *The Cenci* lies in Beatrice's agonizing realization that she is no longer the person she once thought she was. Shelley transfers "the locus of terror from epistemology to ontology, from knowledge to being."

Murphy, John V. *The Dark Angel: Gothic Elements in Shelley's Works*. Lewisburg, PA: Bucknell University Press, 1975. An important study of Shelley's Gothicism and its enduring influence on his poetry. Devotes a chapter to *Zastrozzi* and *St. Irvyne*.

Peacock, Thomas Love. "Memoirs of Percy Bysshe Shelley." In *Memoirs of Shelley, and Other Essays, and Reviews*. Ed. Howard Mills. New York: New York University Press, 1970. Valuable for its record of influences upon Percy Bysshe Shelley. "[Charles Brockden] Brown's four novels, Schiller's *Robbers*, and Goethe's *Faust* were, of all the works with which he was familiar, those which took the deepest root in his mind, and had the strongest influence on his character. . . . He devotedly admired Wordsworth and Coleridge, and in a minor degree Southey . . . but admiration is one thing and assimilation is another; and nothing so blended itself with the structure of his interior mind as the creations of Brown" (43).

Peck, Walter E. "Appendix A: Shelley's Indebtedness in *Zastrozzi* to Previous Romances." In *Shelley: His Life and Work*, Boston: Houghton, Mifflin, 1927:1:305–309. An early discussion of sources and influences.

Porte, Joel. "In the Hands of an Angry God: Religious Terror in Gothic Fiction." In *The Gothic Imagination: Essays in Dark Romanticism*. Ed. G.R. Thompson. Pullman: Washington State University Press, 1974: 42–64. Drawing from James Rieger's *The Mutiny Within: The Heresies of Percy Bysshe Shelley*, Porte discusses the Godwin-Shelley Gothic connection in his exploration of the Wandering Jew motif.

Rajan, Tilottama. "Promethean Narrative: Overdetermined Form in Shelley's Gothic Fiction." In *Shelley: Poet and Legislator of the World*. Ed. Betty T. Bennett and Stuart Curran. Baltimore: Johns Hopkins University Press, 1996: 240–252. Focusing on the problematic ending of *St. Irvyne* and its complex relation to Shelley's first novel, Rajan argues that "Shelley's Gothic novels begin an experiment with the pretexts and leitmotifs of prometheanism that is intertextually replayed in *Prometheus Unbound*."

Reiman, Donald H. and Sharon B. Powers, Ed. *Shelley's Poetry and Prose*. New York and London: W. W. Norton, 1977. This Norton Critical Edition includes a textual introduction and helpful annotations as well as a selection of scholarly essays.

Rieger, James. *The Mutiny Within: The Heresies of Percy Bysshe Shelley*. New York: G. Braziller, 1967. Studies how the Wandering Jew figures as a symbol chastizing the Godwinian freethinkers of the day; those who would deny the Father of the old dispensation in their political agendas find his terrifying return in their fictional representations of Ahasuerus.

Seed, David. "Shelley's 'Gothick' in *St. Irvyne* and After." In *Essays on Shelley*. Ed. Miriam Allott. Totowa, NJ: Barnes & Noble, 1982: 39–70. Finds in the early

Gothics the source of a lifelong interest in Gothic imagery and the symbolic value thereof.

————. "Mystery and Monodrama in Shelley's *Zastrozzi*." *Dutch Quarterly Review of Anglo-American Letters* 14 (1984): 1–17. A discussion of what Seed argues are the fairly conventional depictions of Gothic sexual innuendo and Gothic fear in Shelley's first and less sophisticated novel.

Whatley, John. "Romantic and Enlightened Eyes in the Gothic Novels of Percy Bysshe Shelley." *Gothic Studies* 1 (1999): 201–221. Both novels "work against Gothic supernaturalism" and present villains who "hold progressive ideals that invert the usual values of the genre and imbed an uncertainty of vision in the novels' themes."

CHARLOTTE TURNER SMITH
(1749–1806)
Jack G. Voller

PRINCIPAL GOTHIC WORKS

Emmeline, the Orphan of the Castle. London: T. Cadell, 1788; London: Minerva Press, 1816.

Ethelinde; or, The Recluse of the Lake. London: T. Cadell, 1789; Dublin: H. Chamberlaine, 1790; London: A.K. Newman, Minerva Press, 1814.

Celestina. London: T. Cadell, 1791; Dublin: R. Cross, P. Wogan, 1791.

The Old Manor House. London: J. Bell, 1793; London: B. Crosby, 1810.

Rayland Hall; or, The Remarkable Adventures of Orlando Somerville: An Original Story. London: John Arliss, 1810. (A forty-page chapbook abridgement of *The Old Manor House*; note "Somerville" for Smith's "Somerive.")

MODERN REPRINTS AND EDITIONS

Emmeline, the Orphan of the Castle. Ed. Anne Henry Ehrenpreis. Oxford English Novels. London and New York: Oxford University Press, 1971.

Emmeline, the Orphan of the Castle. Ed. Zoe Fairbairns. Mothers of the Novel. London and New York: Pandora, 1988.

The Old Manor House. Ed. Anne Henry Ehrenpreis. London and New York: Oxford University Press, 1969; Rpt. 1989 in The World's Classics series with introduction by Judith Stanton.

The Old Manor House. The Feminist Controversy in England, 1788–1810. New York: Garland, 1974.

The Old Manor House. Mothers of the Novel. London and New York: Pandora, 1987.

Although she never wrote a work that could be called high Gothic, Charlotte Smith is a keystone figure in any study of the development of the Gothic, for some of her fiction—particularly the early novels *Emmeline, Celestina*, and *Ethelinde*, and later *The Old Manor House*—serves as a bridge between the clunky Gothicism and egregious emotionalism of Horace Walpole and Clara Reeve and the more nuanced Gothic ventures of Ann Radcliffe. Certainly some later Gothic novelists such as Matthew Lewis and Charles Robert Maturin owed little to Smith directly, but the considerable popularity of her early novels, their careful incorporation of aesthetic concerns (particularly the sublime and the picturesque, thanks to Smith's awareness of Edmund Burke, William Gilpin, and other theoreticians), their extending of the sentimental mode via the inclusion of dramatically heightened situations, and their mediate position between neoclassicism and Romanticism mean that Smith's "Gothic" fictions helped, in a very real sense, to create the genre in which all later Gothic writers worked.

Her importance in the field is rather ironic given Smith's disdain for the sensationalism of the Gothic and her own preference for writing poetry. Indeed, writing novels was something of a final resort for Smith, who turned to fiction out of financial desperation. Born in 1749 to a prosperous family, Smith was married to the profligate and irresponsible Benjamin Smith when she was sixteen and soon found herself with a large family (eventually having twelve children in twenty years) and a husband in debtor's prison, where she briefly joined him. Although her volume *Elegiac Sonnets* (1784) enjoyed some success and went through a number of editions, Smith's financial situation remained grim, for a substantial inheritance from her father-in-law, who recognized his son's shortcomings, was tied up in legal proceedings that were not to be resolved until after Smith's death. She turned to writing fiction, and her first novel, *Emmeline, the Orphan of the Castle*, met with considerable success. She followed this with one novel a year for the next nine years.

Emmeline, although in many ways a novel very much in the well-established sentimental mode, was groundbreaking in its careful incorporation of those sublime and picturesque backgrounds that would become scenographic clichés of the Gothic within a decade. As J.M.S. Tompkins notes, *Emmeline* was the first novel to feature a young heroine pursued through a ruined castle (though there is in fact a similar episode in *The Castle of Otranto*), even if the scene is ultimately of little narrative consequence. "It is impossible not to see in the young beauty of Emmeline, set in its Gothic frame, the prototype of [Radcliffe's] Adeline and Emily" (375). Pursuit and tribulation against a scenic and emotionally powerful natural backdrop, often including picturesque or half-ruined buildings, is in fact Smith's major contribution to the Gothic. As Carrol Fry has shown, Radcliffe's aesthetics were largely influenced by Smith; her dislike of the sensational led her to include no supernaturalism in her works, and even suggestions of the supernatural are resolved quickly. The startling glimpse of a mysterious face in *The Old Manor House*, leading to suggestions of a possible ghostly presence, is explained away just a few pages later. Ethelinde's belief that she sees the beckoning ghost of her father is also quickly dispelled. Subsequent users of the explained supernatural, such as Radcliffe, would come to exploit such episodes and prolong their suspenseful potential for a couple of volumes.

Strongly interested throughout her life in landscape, painting, and botany,

Smith quickly learned the power of natural description in furthering the emotional reach of her narratives. *Ethelinde* and *Celestina* continue in the same vein as *Emmeline*, adding powerful and often-Burkean descriptions of "wild" nature (the Lake Country in *Ethelinde*, the Hebrides and Pyrenees in *Celestina*) and picturesque renderings of secluded cottages inhabited by virtuous rustics or nobility fleeing persecution or infamy. Wordsworth, thinking primarily of her poetry, recognized the considerable influence of Smith, but much the same could be said of her fiction, which helped to define and create a taste for recognizably "Romantic" tropes and conventions.

In her middle and later novels, Smith moved even further away from the sentimental quasi-Gothic and the fairly conventional eighteenth-century didacticism she used it to support. Her support for the French Revolution and sympathy for those displaced by it came to take precedence in her work, and her minimal interest in the Gothic faded as her interest in the psychology of displacement and social and political questions increased. Yet her novels continued to record the suffering of the virtuous—both male and female—at the hands of indifferent or war-mongering governments, venal lawyers, and greedy nobility. These social and human concerns were, finally, of greater moment to Smith than were the emotional or literary exercises of her early sentimental Gothicism. Yet the explosive emergence of Gothic fiction in the 1790s was made possible in significant part by Smith, whose sensitive depictions of virtuous heroines and heroes against the background of dramatic landscapes and decaying buildings helped, by adding Gothic energy to the sentimental novel, simultaneously to stimulate a public appetite for works that, using these tropes, could address the emerging concerns of social and cultural change, of stability and revolution, of new understandings of human psychological and emotional capacities in a world experiencing dramatic and lasting change. The residual Gothicism of her final works brings her closer to William Godwin's adaptation of the novel of terror to arouse the social conscience.

SELECTED CRITICISM

Bartolomeo, Joseph. "Subversion of Romance in *The Old Manor House*." *Studies in English Literature, 1500–1900* 33 (1993): 645–657. Treatment of political and sexual ideologies in the novel.

Burgess, Miranda J. "Charlotte Smith, *The Old Manor House*." In *A Companion to Romanticism*. Ed. Duncan Wu. Oxford: Blackwell, 1998: 122–130. Discussion of the novel's pre-Romantic features.

Ellis, Katherine. "Charlotte Smith's Subversive Gothic." *Feminist Studies* 3 (1976): 51–55. A study of how Smith's use of Gothic elements is part of a larger critique of patriarchal authority.

Fletcher, Loraine. "Charlotte Smith's Emblematic Castles." *Critical Survey* 4 (1992): 3–8. Discusses, with an eye toward Burke's theories of the sublime, the political symbolism of landed estates in Smith's novels.

————. *Charlotte Smith: A Critical Biography*. New York: St. Martin's Press, 1998. Full-length study of Smith's life and works with comments on her relationship to the Gothic fiction of the 1790s.

Foster, James R. "Charlotte Smith: Pre-Romantic Novelist." *Publications of the Modern Language Association* 43 (1928): 463–475. An early but useful study of Smith as an influence on Ann Radcliffe.

Fry, Carrol L. *Charlotte Smith: Popular Novelist*. New York: Arno, 1980. Studies the influence of Smith on early Gothic fiction.

————. *Charlotte Smith*. New York: Twayne, 1996. Excellent introduction to Smith's life and works.

Hilbish, Florence May Anna. *Charlotte Smith, Poet and Novelist (1749–1806)*. Gettysburg, PA: Times and News Publishing, 1941. A largely biographical study that also recognizes Smith as one of the founders of Gothic fiction and an important influence on Radcliffe and other Gothicists.

Hoeveler, Diane Long. "Gendering the Civilizing Process: The Case of Charlotte Smith's *Emmeline, the Orphan of the Castle*." In *Gothic Feminism: The Professionalization of Gender from Charlotte Smith to the Brontës*. University Park: Pennsylvania State University Press, 1998: 27–50. Smith's first novel "clearly stands as the forgotten urtext for the female Gothic novel tradition and deserves to be recognized as such."

Imig, Barbara L. "Shooting Folly As It Flies: A Dialogic Approach to Four Novels by Charlotte Smith." Doctoral Dissertation, University of Nebraska, 1991. *DAI* 52: 548A. Examines Smith's use of Gothic elements, among other devices, as a tool for social critique.

Morgan, Rebecca. "Radical Gothic: A Study of a Literary Genre and Its Purpose in the Novels of Charlotte Smith." Ph.D Thesis, University of Newcastle upon Tyne, 1996. A full consideration of Smith's place as a bonafide Gothic novelist.

Rogers, Katharine M. "Romantic Aspirations, Restricted Possibilities: The Novels of Charlotte Smith." In *Re-Visioning Romanticism: British Women Writers, 1776–1837*. Ed. Carol Shiner Wilson and Joel Haefner. Philadelphia: University of Pennsylvania Press, 1994: 72–88. A study of Smith's relationship to Romanticism.

Stanton, Judith Philips. Introduction to *The Old Manor House* by Charlotte Smith. Ed. Anne Henry Ehrenpreis. New York: Oxford University Press, 1989. Provides biographical and critical background.

Tompkins, J.M.S. "Appendix III: Radcliffe's Sources." In *The Popular Novel in England, 1770–1800*. London: Constable, 1932. Rpt. London: Methuen, 1969: 375–377. Tompkins also notes the influence of "the momentary supernatural suggestion of *The Old Manor House*" and "the Pyrenean scenes of *Celestina*" on Radcliffe's *The Mysteries of Udolpho*.

ROBERT LOUIS STEVENSON
(1850–1894)
Douglass H. Thomson

PRINCIPAL GOTHIC WORKS

"The Body-Snatcher." *Pall Mall Christmas Extra*, 1884.
"Olalla." *Court and Society Review*, Christmas Number 1885.
Dr. Jekyll and Mr. Hyde, and An Inland Voyage. Leipzig: B. Tauchnitz, 1886.
"Markheim." *Unwin's Annual*, 1886: 27–40.
The Strange Case of Dr. Jekyll and Mr. Hyde. London: Longmans, Green, 1886.
The Strange Case of Dr. Jekyll and Mr. Hyde. New York: Charles Scribner's Sons, 1886.
"Thrawn Janet." In *The Merry Men and Other Tales and Fables*. London: Chatto & Windus, 1887.
"The Bottle Imp." In *Island Nights' Entertainments*. London: Cassell, 1893.
The Body-Snatcher. New York: Merriam, 1895.
"The House of Eld." In *Fables. McClure's Magazine*, October 1895: 455–458.

MODERN REPRINTS AND EDITIONS

The Annotated Dr. Jekyll and Mr. Hyde. Ed. Richard Dury. Milan: Guerini, 1993.
The Body Snatcher and Other Stories. Ed. Jeffrey Meyer. New York: New American Library, 1988.
"The Body-Snatcher." In *Victorian Ghost Stories: An Oxford Anthology*. Ed. Michael Cox and R.A. Gilbert. Oxford and New York: Oxford University Press, 1991.
The Complete Short Stories. Ed. Ian Bell. New York: Henry Holt, 1994.
Dr. Jekyll and Mr. Hyde. Intro. Abraham Rothberg. New York: Bantam Books, 1967.
Dr. Jekyll and Mr. Hyde. Intro. Vladimir Nabokov. New York: Penguin, 1987.
Dr. Jekyll and Mr. Hyde. New York: Penguin Books, 1995.
The Essential Dr. Jekyll and Mr. Hyde. Ed. Leonard Wolf. New York: Plume, 1995.
"Markheim." In *The Evil Image: Two Centuries of Gothic Short Fiction and Poetry*. Ed. Patricia L. Skarda and Nora Crow Jaffe. New York: New American Library, 1981.
"Olalla." In *The Oxford Book of Gothic Tales*. Ed. Chris Baldick. Oxford and New York: Oxford University Press, 1992.

The Strange Case of Dr. Jekyll and Mr. Hyde and Other Stories. Ed. Jenni Calder. New
     York: Penguin Books, 1979.
The Strange Case of Dr. Jekyll and Mr. Hyde. Intro. Joyce Carol Oates. New York:
     Vintage Books, 1991.
The Supernatural Short Stories of Robert Louis Stevenson. Ed. Michael Hayes. London:
     Calder, 1976. (Contains "The Bottle Imp," "Thrawn Janet," and other supernatural
     fiction.)

Robert Louis Stevenson's *Strange Case of Dr. Jekyll and Mr. Hyde* provides a
paradigm or central metaphor for many Gothic concerns. Its famous treatment
of the doppelgänger or double personality epitomizes the Gothic obsession with
the dual nature of man's existence; its emphatic allegory of good versus evil
reformulates, even crystallizes, the primary moral concern of Gothic fiction; its
parable of the overreacher and of the dangers of the scientific imagination inevitably recalls *Frankenstein* and other Gothic Prometheans; its highly visible
Freudian presentations of id and superego recall the psychological dynamics of
countless Gothic tales. Its very title is arguably the most famous of all Gothic
titles, having passed into the popular lexicon as a generic synonym for the split
personality. Stevenson half-fondly, half-ashamedly referred to the tale as my
"penny (12 penny) dreadful," a mere "Gothic gnome" (*letters*, vol. 5: 128, 163).
His acknowledgment of its popular appeal underscores the tale's deliberate exploitation of Gothic conventions, but raises another important issue as well, for
the story of the critical reception of *The Strange Case of Dr. Jekyll and Mr.
Hyde*—its fall and rise among academic readers while maintaining its hold on
the popular imagination—tellingly reflects historical attitudes toward and reap-
praisals of the Gothic as a whole.

   The son of an engineer who oversaw the improvement of lighthouses throughout England and nurtured in his childhood sickbed by a kindly but strictly Calvinist nanny who distrusted novels and their readers, Robert Louis Stevenson
went on to strike a singular presence in late Victorian Great Britain, in part
because the dichotomies that characterize his life and fiction reflect those of the
age. His picaresque career set the bohemian against the heroic artist writing in
the face of lifelong illnesses and the freethinker against the Scottish Presbyterian
nature of his upbringing. Following the lead of his father, Stevenson became
conversant with the latest scientific advancements, yet he achieved renown as a
writer of childhood verse who often expressed skepticism about science. His
voluminous literary output includes such diverse personas as the Scottish ver-
nacularist and the South Seas adventurer, voices that indicate his dual allegiance
to the nationalistic and the exotic.

   Many critics have focused on the conflict within Stevenson's fiction between
romance and realism and between his uncertain reaction to being an immensely
popular author and his desire to be accepted as a serious writer of "high" literature. On these scores it is worth stressing that he burned the first draft of
Jekyll and Hyde, having written it in "white-hot haste" at the promptings of the

"Brownies of his dream world" ("A Chapter on Dreams" 263). As unbeckoned emissaries of his dream world, the brownies supplied the "central idea of a voluntary change becoming involuntary" and left it to his waking self to supply the moral because "my Brownies have not the rudiment of what we call a conscience" ("A Chapter on Dreams" 264). His wife complained that in the first draft he treated the narrative "simply as a story, whereas it was in reality an allegory" (Brantlinger and Boyle 267). He rewrote "the bogy tale" (Calder 220) to supply it with a higher literary purpose. As William Veeder's excellent textual study (in Veeder and Hirsch) has shown, in surviving drafts of the novel Stevenson toned down indications of an immoral side to Dr. Jekyll before the appearance of Mr. Hyde, thus better setting up an allegory between good and evil and placating Fanny Stevenson's concern about the sexual nature of Jekyll's improprieties. These tensions between psychological revelation and moral purpose, between the dreaming and the waking world, reflect those found in the novel and help explain its hold on the reader's imagination.

Stevenson's attempt to supply the tale with the high literary sanction of moral allegory, however, has not pleased all of his critics. Keith complained: "Had not the book a moral? (Oh, but a blatant one!) If you weren't careful, the evil in you would swallow up the good, as the wicked Hyde does to Dr. Jekyll. And you'd be lost. So be careful! Nearly as crude as that. But with the subtler psychologists of today, *Dr. Jekyll* has faded out. And you'll turn with relief to Scott's novels" (qtd. in Veeder and Hirsch x). This reading of *Jekyll and Hyde* places the novel in the undistinguished company of many eighteenth-century Gothics, with their emphatic and often-shrill moral resolutions. Add to the "subtler psychologists" of the 1950s the New Critics, who found *Jekyll and Hyde* (and virtually all Gothics) to lack complication, indirection, and irony, and one can see why the reputation, if not the popularity, of Stevenson's novel experienced such a sharp decline. But succeeding these dismissals of *Jekyll and Hyde*, there have come more subtle and historically minded readers who have revolutionized our thinking about the old classic and have reawakened the power of its mystery in the years after its hundredth anniversary.

Indeed, the publication of Veeder and Hirsch's *Dr. Jekyll and Mr. Hyde after One Hundred Years* represents the culmination of this reappraisal of Stevenson begun by critics such as Jenni Calder, with her biography and Penguin edition of the tale, and Roger Swearingen, with his important bibliography. This collection of essays remains an obligatory read for those interested in the novel and in the larger issue of new approaches to Gothic fiction. In addition to providing a fine selected bibliography of its own and important manuscript drafts of *Jekyll and Hyde*, Veeder and Hirsch's centennial appraisal offers essays that acknowledge and affirm its popular appeal—included are an illustrator's interpretations and analysis of stage and screen portrayals—while opening up fascinating new directions for criticism (see individual titles under "Selected Criticism"). The first target of this criticism is the facile kind of dialectical understanding exhibited by Keith's dismissal of the novel. The essays of Peter

Garrett and Ronald Thomas deconstruct "the conservative, ordering force of its moral oppositions" (70) through close attention to its radically plural and often-subversive form and syntax. They call attention to such aspects as the curious layering of Utterson's narrative, Enfield's report and then his disappearance, Lanyon's deathbed confession, Jekyll's posthumous narrative, and, most important, the notoriously slippery pronouns or interchangeable "voices" of the novel, for example, Dr. Jekyll's exasperated but telling "He, I say—I cannot say I." Veeder and Hogle address the curiously neglected issue that most seems to set *Jekyll and Hyde* apart from traditional Gothics: the absence of the feminine in the novel. Both make this absence a telling presence: Veeder argues that the novel goes beyond traditional readings that see Stevenson as attacking Victorian moral rigidity and hypocrisy to confront patriarchy itself; Hogle employs Kristevan poetics to unearth and complicate Oedipal motifs.

These four essays provide especially effective case studies of how poststructuralist approaches can reopen and invigorate the Gothic text, yet it is left to Hirsch and Lawler to address directly *Jekyll and Hyde* in relation to the Gothic as a genre. Hirsch neatly argues that the novel's "volatile, Gothic elements" undermine "the too easy reassurances" of its seeming participation in detective fiction: "The rationalist, bourgeoisie assumptions of the [detective] genre are challenged by the Romantic Gothic attitudes that are inscribed in its origins" (241). Donald Lawler treats the novel as a "strange case of Gothic science fiction" whose darker and more malevolent strains call into question the ruling paradigms of late-nineteenth-century science. From this view, Stevenson's novel provides a vital link between Mary Shelley's *Frankenstein* and many twentieth-century examples of Gothicized science fiction. Patrick Brantlinger and Richard Boyle study *Jekyll and Hyde* in its contemporary context, tracing Stevenson's ambiguous reaction to writing a popular novel for Matthew Arnold's philistine audience and linking the threat of Hyde to "the shadowy, demonic double of the artist" (280) and to the anarchic forces of the new readership. Finally, Virginia Wright Wexman studies popular stage adaptations of the play and its numerous patterns of victimization and stigmatization. All in all, *Dr. Jekyll and Mr. Hyde after One Hundred Years* offers compelling new directions for approaching the Gothic's most famous double and provides a kind of paradigm for what one can call New Gothic studies.

Stevenson wrote a number of other short tales of terror or "crawlers," as he referred to them. "The House of Eld" reminds us of Stevenson's admiration for Hawthorne's "romances," as it charts the quest of young Jack to free his village from a crippling puritanical morality, symbolized by its inhabitants wearing fetters on their right legs. To do so, he is told to kill a weird sorcerer, and wielding a magic sword, he does so, even though the magician apparently assumes the forms of his father and mother. Upon returning to the village, Jack is dismayed to find that the townspeople have swapped one ridiculous morality for another, as they now wear the fetters on their left legs, and is horrified to find his parents murdered. "The Body-Snatcher" employs the grisly profession of corpse stealing to weave a tale in which two grave robbers are horrified to find in their latest disinterred coffin the body of a man they had previously killed and served up to the medical profession. "Markheim" provides a psychological study of a murderer and thief with a conscience who, in danger of being caught, resists the easy way out provided to him by the devil and surrenders to the police. "Thrawn Janet" ("thrawn" from the Scot "thraw" as in "death throes") is a tale comprised in large part of Scottish dialect that perfectly catches the cadences and superstitions of a folk ghost story. A too-bookish and too-English minister learns the darker ways of the Scotch "bogle" in his terrifying confrontations with a distorted ("thrawn") and devil-possessed woman and with the devil himself, who appears as a black man. The tale also reminds us of Stevenson's kinship with his countryman, James Hogg, who in his *Confessions of a Justified Sinner* and other fiction offers significant dialect features as well as a powerful anticipation of the schizophrenic Jekyll/Hyde dynamic. "The Bottle Imp" is a South Seas tale that rewrites the genie-in-the-bottle tale with a darker twist. The imp will grant the bottle's possessor any number of wishes, but damnation awaits if the owner has not sold the bottle at a price less than he paid for it to another before his or her death. The catch: the owner must sell the bottle for less than the purchased price, and as it works its way through the centuries, the inevitable temptation—and deflation—confront its latest (last?) owner, a loving Hawaiian husband and wife. "Olalla" recounts a rendezvous with superhuman beauty in a desolate Spanish residencia and has been included by Chris Baldick in his anthology of Gothic tales. The story makes use of the sinister painting and is an inspired rewriting of Poe's "The Oval Portrait."

There are other "crawlers" as well, most walking the taut line between fantasy and realism that critics have noted in Stevenson's major fiction and surely deserving greater critical attention. But it seems certain that among both readers of the Gothic and scholars of the form, Robert Louis Stevenson's name will always be associated with that famous work he dubbed his "Gothic gnome," *The Strange Case of Dr. Jekyll and Mr. Hyde.*

SELECTED CRITICISM

Bell, Ian. *Dreams of Exile: Robert Louis Stevenson, a Biography.* New York: H. Holt, 1995. An important new biography from one of Stevenson's most accomplished scholars.

Block, Edwin F, Jr. *Rituals of Dis-integration: Romance and Madness in the Victorian Psychomythic Tale.* New York: Garland, 1993. Reads *Jekyll and Hyde* in terms of the "psychomythic tale," defined as a form that "deals more overtly and in more modern fashion with those kinds of psychological tensions that Gothic romance had treated a century earlier."

Booth, Bradford A., and Ernest Mehew, eds. *The Letters of Robert Louis Stevenson.* 8 vols. New Haven: Yale University Press, 1994–1995.

Brantlinger, Patrick, and Richard Boyle. "The Education of Edward Hyde: Stevenson's 'Gothic Gnome' and the Mass Readership of Late Victorian England." In *Dr.*

Jekyll and Mr. Hyde after One Hundred Years. Ed. William Veeder and Gordon Hirsch. Chicago: University of Chicago Press, 1988: 265–282. Reads the subtext of the novella as "an unconscious 'allegory' about the commercialization of literature and the emergence of a mass consumer society."

Brennan, Matthew C. "Robert Louis Stevenson's *Dr. Jekyll and Mr. Hyde*." In *The Gothic Psyche: Disintegration and Growth in Nineteenth-Century English Literature*. Columbia, SC: Camden House, 1997: 97–112. "Like other novelists in the Gothic tradition who paid close attention to the workings of their unconscious and used this intuitive knowledge to construct their plots, Stevenson drew heavily on his dream life."

Calder, Jenni. *Robert Louis Stevenson: A Life Study*. New York: Oxford University Press, 1980. A solid biography that canvasses the many rich contradictions in Stevenson's upbringing and character.

Doane, Janice and Devon Hodges. "Demonic Disturbances of Sexual Identity: *The Strange Case of Dr. Jekyll and Mr/s Hyde*." *Novel: A Forum on Fiction* 23 (1989): 63–74. Examines gender confusion in the tale as one source of the demonic.

Eigner, Edwin M. *Robert Louis Stevenson and Romantic Tradition*. Princeton: Princeton University Press, 1966. Places Stevenson in the tradition of the "intellectualized romance" of Hugo; seeks to rehabilitate the "popular" Stevenson through extensive comparative study with Conrad, James, and Guy de Maupassant.

Geduld, Harry M., ed. *The Definitive Dr. Jekyll and Mr. Hyde Companion*. New York: Garland, *Publishing* 1983. Presents materials from various critical perspectives suitable for a case study of the novella.

Jefford, Andrew. "Dr. Jekyll and Professor Nabokov: Reading a Reading." In *Robert Louis Stevenson*. Ed. Andrew Noble. New York: Barnes & Noble, 1983. 47–72. Studies Nabokov's Cornell lecture notes on the novel; Nabokov considered the most "difficult artistic problem" of the story to be the general problem of rendering the Gothic plausible.

Kiely, Robert. "Robert Louis Stevenson." In *Victorian Fiction: A Second Guide to Research*. Ed. George H. Ford. New York: Modern Language Association, 1978: 333–347. Stevenson appears in the *Guide* for the first time. Kiely provides an overview of critical developments.

Lawler, Donald. "Reframing Jekyll and Hyde: Robert Louis Stevenson and the Strange Case of Gothic Science Fiction." In *Dr. Jekyll and Mr. Hyde after One Hundred Years*. Ed. William Veeder and Gordon Hirsch. Chicago: University of Chicago Press, 1988: 247–261. "The Gothic contributes a psychosexual force generated by forbidden, repressed desire which operates on both the structural and psychological levels."

Maixner, Paul. *Robert Louis Stevenson; The Critical Heritage*. London: Routledge & Kegan Paul, 1981. Contains a useful critical history of comments on Stevenson's fiction from the 1880s to the date of publication, including many contemporary reviews.

McGuire, Karen E. "The Artist as Demon in Mary Shelley, Stevenson, Walpole, Stoker, and King." *Gothic*, n.s. 1 (1986): 1–5. An interesting phenomenological study that interprets the claustrophobic spaces and schizoid characters of Gothic fiction as metaphoric commentary on the relationship of the artist to his work.

McLynn, Frank. *Robert Louis Stevenson: A Biography*. New York: Random House, 1994.

Presents Stevenson as a radically divided man, torn between his Scottish Calvinist inheritance and his "Jacobite" romantic longings for escape.

Mulholland, Honor. "Robert Louis Stevenson and the Romance Form." In *Robert Louis Stevenson*. Ed. Andrew Noble. Totowa, NJ: Barnes & Noble, 1983: 96–117. Follows Eigner in studying Stevenson's tales in the romance tradition, with special attention to affinities with Hawthorne.

Oates, Joyce Carol. Introduction to *The Strange Case of Dr. Jekyll and Mr. Hyde*. New York: Vintage Books, 1990: vii–xiv. A lively and perceptive short essay from a postmodern master of the (post)macabre exploring the various meanings of Hyde, among them sin and the Freudian id. Conjectures that "had Dickens lived to complete *The Mystery of Edwin Drood*, with its schizophrenic Jasper, it would have made *The Strange Case of Dr. Jekyll and Mr. Hyde* redundant."

Saposnik, Irving S. "The Anatomy of *Dr. Jekyll and Mr. Hyde*." *Studies in English Literature, 1500–1900* 11 (1971): 715–731. Treats the novel as a social criticism of Victorian class and moral rigidity and treats the novella as "a fable of Victorian anxieties."

Seed, David. "Behind Closed Doors: The Management of Mystery in *The Strange Case of Dr. Jekyll and Mr. Hyde*." In *Gothick Origins and Innovations*. Ed. Allan Lloyd Smith and Victor Sage. Costerus New Series 91. Amsterdam and Atlanta, GA: Rodopi, 1994: 180–189. Stevenson generates and intensifies mystery by "building the action around figures of concealment and then of exclusion. A central part of the novella consists of a series of entries into Jekyll's house and these entries constitute the gradual uncovering of his secret."

Spehner, Norbert. *Jekyll and Hyde, Opus 600: Guide chrono-bibliographique des éditions internationales du roman de Robert Louis Stevenson 1818–1997* (1818 sic); Roberral, [Jekyll and Hyde, Opus 600: Chrono-bibliographic Guide to Editions, Versions, and International Adaptations of Robert Louis Stevenson's Novel] Quebec: Ashem Fictions, 1997.

Stevenson, Robert Louis. "A Chapter on Dreams." *Scribner's Magazine* December 1887. Rpt. in *The Travels and Essays of Robert Louis Stevenson*. New York: Charles Scribner's Sons, 1895: 263–265. Details the genesis of *The Strange Case of Dr. Jekyll and Mr. Hyde* and another story of "man's double being," "The Travelling Companion," burned by Stevenson because "*Jekyll* had supplanted it."

Swearingen, Roger G. *The Prose Writings of Robert Louis Stevenson: A Guide*. Hamden, CT: Archon Books, 1980. An important and much-needed bibliographic guide of both primary and secondary materials.

Veeder, William, and Gordon Hirsch, eds. *Dr. Jekyll and Mr. Hyde after One Hundred Years*. Chicago: University of Chicago Press, 1988. A critical anthology of ten essays organized topically under "Questions of Text," "Questions of Voice," "Questions of Repression," "Questions of Genre," and "Questions of Context." The editors claim that "Gothic conventions and transformations can symbolize that deconstruction of the ruling Newtonian paradigms which was effected by the implications of recessive Darwinism, entropy, and molecular randomness." For focus on the novella's Gothicism, see the essays by Brantlinger and Boyle and by Lawler. Other essays bearing on the Gothicism of the novel are William Veeder, "Collated Fractions of the Manuscript Drafts of *Strange Case of Dr. Jekyll and Mr. Hyde*"; Peter K. Garrett, "Cries and Voices: Reading *Jekyll and Hyde*"; Ronald R. Thomas, "The Strange Voices in the Strange Case: Dr. Jekyll,

Mr. Hyde, and the Voices of Modern Fiction"; William Veeder, "Children of the Night: Stevenson and Patriarchy"; Jerrold E. Hogle, "The Struggle for a Dichotomy: Abjection in Jekyll and His Interpreters"; Gordon Hirsch, "*Frankenstein, Detective Fiction, and Jekyll and Hyde*"; and Virginia Wright Wexman, "Horrors of the Body: Hollywood's Discourse on Beauty and Rouben Mamoulian's *Dr. Jekyll and Mr. Hyde.*"

BRAM STOKER
(1847–1912)
Jack G. Voller

PRINCIPAL GOTHIC WORKS

"The Crystal Cup." *London Society*, September 1872.

"The Chain of Destiny." *Shamrock*, 1–22 May 1875.

Under the Sunset. London: Sampson, Low, Maiston, Searle and Rivington, 1882. (Contains the stories "Under the Sunset," "The Rose Prince," "The Invisible Giant," "The Shadow Builder," "The Castle of the King," "How 7 Went Mad," and "The Wondrous Child.")

"The Burial of the Rats." *Holly Leaves*, 5 December 1891.

"The Judge's House." *Holly Leaves*, 5 December 1891.

"The Secret of the Growing Gold." *Black and White*, 23 January 1892.

"The Squaw." *Holly Leaves*, 2 December 1892.

"A Dream of Red Hands." *Sketch*, 11 July 1894.

"Crooken Sands." *Holly Leaves*, 1 December 1894.

Dracula. London: Constable, 1897; New York: Doubleday, 1899; London: Constable, 1900 (abridged edition).

The Jewel of Seven Stars. London: Heinemann, 1903; New York: Harper, 1904.

The Lady of the Shroud. London: Heinemann, 1909.

The Lair of the White Worm. London: Rider, 1911.

Dracula's Guest and Other Weird Stories. London: Routledge, 1914.

MODERN REPRINTS AND EDITIONS

Dracula has been continuously in print since its initial publication, existing like its titular figure in too many incarnations and forms to be cataloged here. The editions listed here are among the best known and respected as well as widely used in both the classroom and by general readers.

Best Ghost and Horror Stories. Ed. Richard Dalby, Stefan Dziemianowicz, and S.T. Joshi. Mineola, NY: Dover, 1997. (Contains "The Crystal Cup," "The Chain of

Destiny," "The Castle of the King," "The Dualitists," "The Burial of the Rats,"
"The Judge's House," "The Secret of the Growing Gold," "The Coming of Abel
Behenna," "The Squaw," "A Dream of Red Hands," "Crooken Sands," "Dracula's
Guest," "A Star Trap," and "A Gipsy Prophecy.")

Bram Stoker's Dracula Omnibus. London: Orion, 1992; Edison, NJ: Chartwell Books,
1992. (Contains *Dracula,* "Dracula's Guest," and *The Lair of the White Worm.*)

Dracula. Ed. A.N. Wilson. New York: Oxford University Press, 1983.

Dracula. Ed. Maurice Hindle. New York: Penguin, 1993.

Dracula. Ed. Maud Ellmann. New York: Oxford University Press, 1998.

Dracula. Ed. Glennis Byron. New York: St. Martin's Press, 1999.

Dracula: The Rare Text of 1901. Ed. Robert Eighteen-Bisang. Intro. Raymond McNally.
White Rock, BC: Transylvania Press, 1994. (A casebook edition featuring essays
exploring the novel from a variety of theoretical perspectives, this edition reprints
Stoker's abridged version published in 1900. Has an introduction by Raymond
McNally.)

The Essential Dracula. Ed. Leonard Wolf. New York: Penguin, 1993. (Overall, a helpful
volume that includes extensive notes.)

The Jewel of Seven Stars. New York: Carroll & Graf, 1989.

The Jewel of Seven Stars. New York: Oxford University Press, 1996.

The Jewel of Seven Stars. Westcliff-on-Sea, Essex, UK: Desert Island Books, 1996.

The Jewel of Seven Stars. Ed. Clive Leatherdale. New York: Tor, 1999.

The Jewel of Seven Stars. Stroud: Alan Sutton, 1996.

The Lady of the Shroud. Mattituck, NY: Amereon, 1989.

The Lady of the Shroud. Stroud: Alan Sutton, 1994.

The Lady of the Shroud. Ed. William Hughes. Westcliff-on-Sea, Essex, UK: Desert Island, 2000.

The Lair of the White Worm. Dingle, Ireland: Brandon, 1991.

The Lair of the White Worm. Polegate, East Sussex: Pulp Publications, 1998.

Bram Stoker was a lucky man. Blessed with only a modicum of literary talent,
Stoker made up in sheer energy, will, and drive what he lacked in artistic skill
and with a heroic diligence and work ethic found time amid the pressures of a
demanding career and a problematic homelife to create *Dracula,* one of the most
enduring literary myths the Gothic has ever known.

His most famous novel powerfully articulates what is in fact an overriding
concern in much if not all of Stoker's fiction: boundaries and their transgression.
Most obviously this involves the life/death boundary and its violation by the
vampire in *Dracula,* the mummy or its spirit, anyway, as in *The Jewel of Seven
Stars,* the visionary seeker in "The Castle of the King," or the ghost in "The
Judge's House," most famously. Often this life/death transgression is intimately
connected to another of Stoker's "boundary" concerns: those boundaries and
barriers that define and delimit acceptable female sexuality and female cultural
power. The female vampires in Dracula's castle are the expression of unrestrained female sexuality, unleashed libido, a suggestion also evident in the
"Dracula's Guest" section of the novel, excised for reasons of length but published separately. This sexuality is consuming and destructive, as we see even

more dramatically in the transformation of Lucy Westenra, "the light of the West," into a creature of Eastern darkness, a suddenly dark-haired vampire whose egregious sexual invitations powerfully invert the living Lucy's delicacy and restraint. A similar transformation threatens Margaret in *The Jewel of Seven Stars*, in which another "Eastern" influence, the mummy-spirit of Queen Tera, begins to take over the spirit and consciousness of Margaret, transforming her from the meek and lovable Victorian woman into a creature of threatening energy and dark vitality. Yet, like Lucy staked in her coffin and Mina freed from Dracula's power, Margaret is rescued by a band of intrepid men who love her, and thus the threat is destroyed, a fact Stoker emphasized in the revised version of the novel. While it strikes many readers that the concluding sentences of *Dracula* are reductive, turning the entire novel and its adventures into a chivalric love parable, that ending in fact—like the ending of *Jewel* and *Lair of the White Worm*—is the only ending Stoker, could provide, for his horror novels are, in one very real sense, rants against the darkness, assertions of the supremacy of reason and Victorian propriety over the monstrous, libidinal forces from the East, the place of human origins.

Are these endings expressions of Stoker's personal demons? Perhaps. His own early childhood was problematic in its physicality; Stoker himself records that a mysterious childhood illness (some now believe it to be psychosomatic) kept him so bedridden that until he was seven years old he did not know what it was to stand upright, and in those years he was cared for by a hovering mother who helped pass the time with tales of banshees and cholera epidemics. Yet in college he distinguished himself as an athlete, and every report of him notes his powerful physical presence, his large size, and his considerable strength and energy. There has even been some suggestion, although the evidence is slender in the extreme, that Stoker's marriage to the beautiful and somewhat self-absorbed Florence turned sour, and that his wife, after the birth of their son Noel, became frigid, . forcing Stoker to a celibacy that may have lasted for years until, finally succumbing, he eventually contracted the syphilis that killed him.

The Lair of the White Worm, Stoker's last novel, is often mentioned in connection with this possible if not highly likely cause of Stoker's death. Unquestionably ill during the writing of that novel, Stoker created a messy book, its plotting and characterization incoherent at best, its literary qualities almost nonexistent. Yet, characteristically for Stoker, he manages to push the action along almost by force of will, and it is "action" that tells a powerful subliminal tale. The characterization (such as it is) of Lady Arabella Marsh insistently and repeatedly emphasizes her sexuality—her tight-fitting clothes and "lithe figure." Yet she is a figure of evil, as is Edgar Caswell, the patrician and mysterious landholder in this backwater corner of Mercia. Fittingly, Caswell is undone by his own lordly arrogance, and Arabella Marsh/The White Worm is destroyed by the resolute and pragmatic Adam Salton, who relies not on magic or superstition but on dynamite to destroy the Worm in a famous scene of loathsome putridity, as Poe might say. If, as some believe, Stoker was suffering the final stages of syphilis, both the incoherence and the vitriol of this antisexual parable become quite understandable, though we hardly need to have recourse to such a physiological basis to locate in Stoker a deep ambivalence and anxiety about sexuality in a time of such profound sociocultural change.

Less graphic but equally instructive is the essentially unexplained instantaneous decay of the mummy and spirit of Queen Tera in *The Jewel of Seven Stars*, and we might here remind ourselves of *The Lady of the Shroud*, whose heroine only pretends to be a vampire; revelation of her true, human nature ends the threat of sexual aggression. Repeatedly, then, and in various ways, Stoker insists on closing off female or violative sexuality. Much of his oeuvre thus constitutes an action of repression or denial, perhaps reflective not only of Stoker's ambivalence regarding the channelings and expressions of sexual energy but even of Stoker's personal situation. Such denial may help explain Stoker's incredible dedication to his work as manager of the Lyceum Theatre and as Henry Irving's theatrical manager; his legendary commitment and management of such a large undertaking, with his characteristically indefatigable enthusiasm, diligence, and care, may well represent a sublimation of libidinal and psychological energies.

Tellingly, those works of Stoker in which the life/death boundary is "successfully" violated involve little sexuality. Widely and correctly regarded as his best short work, "The Judge's House," a story strongly influenced by Joseph Sheridan Le Fanu's "Mr. Justice Harbottle," emphasizes a "successful" return from the dead, a haunting by the spirit of a malevolent judge that so effectively terrorizes young Malcolm Malcolmson—despite a powerful commitment to rationalism indicated by Malcolmson's devotion to mathematical studies—that he commits suicide, hanging himself by the rope frequently employed by the judge as his favorite means of execution.

Interestingly, both "The Judge's House" and "The Burial of the Rats" (to say nothing of *Dracula*) make significant use of rats, the stereotypically unclean "vermin" that in these tales effectively signal the corruption and uncleanliness that oppose the daylight world of rationalism and restraint. "Burial" is literally set in a Parisian dump, chronicling with great attention to atmospheric detail the hero, who, we are carefully told, is engaged to be married, much as Stoker himself was at the time he was writing the tale, and his escape from the violent vagrants who inhabit the dump and seek to murder him for his jewelry. Having strayed into the dump, thus violating social rules of decorum and safety, the hero must rely on himself, on his cunning, strength, and speed to outwit and outrun those who seek to kill him. That Stoker would write such a validation of physicality and resourceful cunning while planning his marriage tells us much of the man and his mind-set, with its confrontational dynamic of resoluteness and voluptuousness, cunning and sexuality, reason and libido. Yet interestingly, Stoker's tales often keep that balance in check, as though he himself realized the necessity of a dynamic counterpoise between the rational and intuitional elements of the psyche. We need only consider *Dracula*, with its "Crew of Light," as Christopher Craft terms them, embodying both American pragmatism (Quincey Morris) and rational science (the law of Harker and the medicine of Seward and Van Helsing) as well as the intuitive and the mystical (Van Helsing's knowledge of folklore and superstition).

This issue of balance and of imbalances redressed can be taken another step. Stoker was familiar with America, having arranged and overseen tours of the Lyceum Theatre company to the United States, and in a couple of tales included American characters. Yet these representatives of the world of pragmatic frontier values keep dying. Most famously there is Quincey Morris with his Bowie knife, valiant fighter and man of action who dies in the Carpathian mountains near Dracula's castle, as though by having traveled so far east, so far into the world that gave birth to the antirational forces of dread, magic, and superstition, he has moved into an element so foreign that he cannot survive. Such is also the case with Elias P. Hutcheson in "The Squaw," a story whose very title alludes to the Americanness that Hutcheson embodies. But Hutcheson is on the other side of "the big drink," as he so quaintly puts it; he is in fact in Nuremberg, like Quincey heading too far east for his own good. His desire to experience "the Iron Virgin of Nurnberg"—this "iron maiden" is a virgin—leads Hutcheson to his death, for the cat whose kitten Hutcheson had inadvertently killed attacks the caretaker of the Iron Virgin while Hutcheson is standing inside. The caretaker recoils from the cat's attack, releasing the rope he had been holding and thus allowing the door to slam shut and impale Hutcheson. There is a place, these "American" tales imply, for frontier pragmatism, but the murky torture chambers and superstition-filled mountains of eastern Europe are not that place; there, different rules apply, different forces are at work, and those not tuned into them pay with their lives.

Stoker's struggles to keep the balance of this dynamic are evident also in the various sentimental romances he authored (such as the nonsupernatural novel *The Man*, which flirts with convention-defying gender roles only to conclude by reasserting them, "taming" the boundary-testing woman) and in the "fairy tales" he wrote for his only child, *Under the Sunset*. Many of these pieces feature the dark violence of the Grimm fairy tales, though Stoker often merges that violence with the Dunsany-like atmospherics of dream and portentousness. "The Invisible Giant," an allegory of cholera, and "The Castle of the King," a retelling of the Orpheus and Eurydice myth, are representative examples, with their mood of dark horror proving triumphant in the end.

Yet ultimately this was not Stoker's view of the world, for all his major literary productions validate the triumph of reason and rationalism, modernity and masculinity. Any shadows Stoker may have held at bay in his own mind are likewise banished from the daylight world that triumphs at the end of his major fictions.

SELECTED CRITICISM

Arata, S.D. "The Occidental Tourist: *Dracula* and the Anxiety of Reverse Colonization."
    Victorian Studies 33 (1990): 621–645. A "cultural studies" look at the novel and
    its delineation of a dynamics of decay of British cultural and empirical hegemony.

Belford, Barbara. *Bram Stoker: A Biography of the Author of Dracula.* New York: Knopf,
    1996. The best biography of Stoker available, Belford's work is a careful and
    detailed analysis of Stoker's life and the "double meanings and double identities"
    that so permeated it that she likens him to a Russian nesting doll that disappears
    as one peels away the layers. Belford argues that *Dracula* "celebrates Stoker's
    final quest to safeguard embattled Victorian values from modernism, to preserve
    the romance of the family." One especially valuable feature of this book is Bel-
    ford's access to sources never before used by Stoker researchers.

Bentley, C.F. "The Monster in the Bedroom: Sexual Symbolism in Bram Stoker's *Dra-
    cula.*" *Literature and Psychology* 22 (1972): 27–34. An early examination of the
    sexual symbolism and dynamics of the novel that, in light of recent theoretically
    informed analyses of the novel, seems almost mundane, this remains a useful
    study that helped point the way for later, more nuanced psychologically informed
    analysis of the novel. This article is included in Margaret Carter's *Dracula: The
    Vampire and the Critics*, 25–34.

Bierman, Joseph S. "Dracula: Prolonged Childhood Illness and the Oral Triad." *American
    Imago* 29 (1972): 186–198. Looks perhaps too dogmatically at the role played
    by Stoker's lengthy and mysterious childhood invalidism and other early psy-
    chosexual experiences in their influence on the novel's fascination with con-
    sumption.

Bignell, Jonathan. "A Taste of the Gothic: Film and Television Versions of Dracula." In
    The Classic Novel: From Page to Screen. Ed. Robert Giddings and Erica Sheen.
    New York: St. Martin's Press, 2000: 114–130. Surveys the transformations of
    Stoker's Count from ink and paper to celluloid and tube.

Carter, Margaret, ed. *Dracula: The Vampire and the Critics.* Ann Arbor MI: UMI Re-
    search Press, 1988. An important collection of critical essays all originally pub-
    lished elsewhere, this is one of the premier volumes of research that any student
    of the novel must consult.

Clemens, Valdine. "The Reptilian Brain at the Fin de Siècle: *Dracula.*" In *The Return
    of the Repressed: Gothic Horror from The Castle of Otranto to Alien.* Albany:
    State University of New York Press, 1999: 153–183. Finds that the novel dram-
    atizes the "conflict between the modern world and Dracula's ancient one" and
    the psychological and political complexities that follow. This essay appeared in
    Elizabeth Miller's *Dracula: The Shade and the Shadow.*

Craft, Christopher. " 'Kiss Me with Those Red Lips': Gender and Inversion in Bram
    Stoker's *Dracula.*" *Representations* 8 (1984): 107–133. A powerful and still-
    compelling study of the novel's complex sexuality and its culturally constructed
    context. This article is included in Margaret Carter's *Dracula: The Vampire and
    the Critics*, 167–194.

Daniels, Les. "Bram Stoker." In *Supernatural Fiction Writers*, Ed. E.F. Bleiler. New
    York: Scribner's, 1985: 375–381. A serviceable overview of Stoker's life and
    Gothic works, with a great deal of interest in the place of *Dracula* in the Gothic

tradition and in its dark sexual dynamics. Daniels finds the Count to be an "aristocrat of the id."

Farson, Daniel. *The Man Who Wrote Dracula*. New York: St. Martin's Press, 1975. Farson, a great-grandnephew of Stoker, presents a somewhat sensationalist overview of Stoker's life and works and is one of the main sources for the suggestion that Stoker died of complications from syphilis.

Griffin, Gail B. " 'Your Girls That You All Love Are Mine': *Dracula* and Victorian Male Sexual Imagination." *International Journal of Women's Studies* 3 (1980): 454–465. A study of the novel's psychosexual dynamics, primarily in terms of aggressiveness and passivity. This article is included in Margaret Carter's *Dracula: The Vampire and the Critics*, 137–148.

Halberstam, Judith. "Technologies of Monstrosity: Bram Stoker's *Dracula*." *Victorian Studies* 36 (1993): 333–352. Beginning with a recognition of an anti-Semitic dimension to the novel, Halberstam goes on to argue that the Gothic itself is a "technology of monstrosity" that can fuse elements of class, race, and gender into deviant Others that, ultimately, reflect our own anxieties and obsessions. This article is included in Halberstam's *Skin Shows: Gothic Horror and the Technology of Monsters* (Durham, NC: Duke University Press, 1995).

Howes, Marjorie. "The Mediation of the Feminine: Bisexuality, Homoerotic Desire, and Self-Expression in Bram Stoker's *Dracula*." *Texas Studies in Literature and Language* 30 (1988): 104–119. Another important study of sexual desire and its various channelings and expressions in Stoker's novel.

Hughes, William, and Andrew Smith, eds. *Bram Stoker: History, Psychoanalysis, and the Gothic*. New York: St. Martin's Press, 1998. This volume contains a number of new essays on Stoker's major fictions: "Introduction: Bram Stoker, the Gothic, and the Development of Cultural Studies" by William Hughes and Andrew Smith; "Powers Old and New: Stoker's Alliances with Anglo-Irish Gothic" by Alison Milbank; "Fables of Continuity: Bram Stoker and Medievalism" by Clare A. Simmons; "Vampire Arts: Bram Stoker's Defence of Poetry" by Maggie Kilgour; "Sex, History, and the Vampire" by R. Mighall; "Dracula and the Doctors: Bad Blood, Menstrual Taboo, and the New Woman" by Marie Mulvey-Roberts; "The Alien and the Familiar in *The Jewel of Seven Stars* and *Dracula*" by R. Edwards; "Exchanging Fantasies: Sex and the Serbian Crisis in *The Lady of the Shroud*" by Victor Sage; "Crowning the King, Mourning His Mother: *The Jewel of Seven Stars* and *The Lady of the Shroud*" by L. Hopkins; "A Crucial Stage in the Writing of *Dracula*" by J.S. Bierman; "Echoes in the Animal House: *The Lair of the White Worm*" by David Punter; "Eruptions of the Primitive into the Present: *The Jewel of Seven Stars* and *The Lair of the White Worm*" by David Seed; and "Stoker's Counterfeit Gothic: *Dracula* and Theatricality at the Dawn of Simulation" by Jerrold E. Hogle.

McNally, Raymond and Radu Florescu. *In Search of Dracula: A True History of Dracula and Vampire Legends*. Greenwich, CT: New York Graphic Society, 1972. One of the best known of the many source studies for *Dracula*.

Miller, Elizabeth, ed. *Dracula: The Shade and the Shadow*. Westcliff-on-Sea, Essex, UK: Desert Island Books, 1998. This volume collects twenty essays of varying quality and scholarly value from the "Dracula 97" conference. Those most pertinent to Gothic studies are Nina Auerbach's "Dracula Keeps Rising from the Grave," which discusses the continuing appeal of the novel; Amanda Fernbach's study of gender inversion in "Dracula's Decadent Fetish"; and Pericles Lewis's "*Dracula and the Epistemology of the Victorian Gothic Novel*," which examines the way the novel's pastiche textuality problematizes belief and credibility. There are, as well, source and historical studies and discussions of the novel's personal references and internal errors and inconsistencies.

Nandris, Grigore. "The Historical Dracula: The Theme of His Legend in the Western and in the Eastern Literatures of Europe." *Comparative Literature Studies* 3 (1966): 367–396. An excellent source study of the historical basis for *Dracula*. Links Stoker's character with the Wallachian ruler Vlad V, called "the Impaler." Attributes the novel's success to "memories of Londoners at the time of the novel's gestation [that] were haunted by the horror of the undetected murders of women by the criminal sex maniac, Jack the Ripper."

Roth, Phyllis. *Bram Stoker*. Boston: Twayne, 1982. An excellent overview of Stoker's life and work, with particular attention paid to the Gothic works. Particularly good on the psychosexual aspects of *Dracula* and on the complexities of Stoker's psychological life, especially the way his "fascination with boundaries" and "blurring of identities" is expressed in much of his life and fiction and nonfiction, as in Stoker's exposé *Famous Imposters*. For Roth, "The appeal of *Dracula* derives, not only from its masterful sustaining of suspense and its nightmarish depiction of landscape, castle, and cemetery, but from its portrait of a seemingly universal horror—the horror of the human mind faced with its own desires for sexual fusion and violence."

Seed, David. "The Narrative Method of *Dracula*." *Nineteenth-Century Fiction* 40 (1986): 61–75. Seed's article offers a thoughtful corrective to the common view of Stoker's narrative as disjointed, a deliberate fragmentation designed to mask his weak command of narrative organization. While not entirely persuasive, Seed's analysis of Stoker's planning and the structure of the novel is valuable reading. This article is included in Margaret Carter's *Dracula: The Vampire and the Critics*, 195–206.

Senf, Carol. "*Dracula*: The Unseen Face in the Mirror." *Journal of Narrative Technique* 9 (1979): 160–170. A consideration of the novel and its vampirism from the standpoint of identity and individuality. This article is included in Margaret Carter's *Dracula: The Vampire and the Critics*, 93–103.

———. "*Dracula*: Stoker's Response to the New Woman." *Victorian Studies* 26 (1982): 33–49. Stoker's inclusion of references to the Victorian "New Woman" is an oft-remarked aspect of this novel. Senf finds this element of *Dracula* to be evidence of Stoker's ambivalence toward changing cultural constructions of femaleness.

———. *The Critical Response to Bram Stoker*. Westport, CT: Greenwood Press, 1993. A collection of contemporaneous reviews of each of Stoker's major works, along with a few recent scholarly essays.

Spear, Jeffrey L. "Gender and Sexual Dis-ease in *Dracula*." In *Virginal Sexuality and Textuality in Victorian Literature*. Ed. Lloyd Davis. Albany: State University of New York Press, 1993: 179–192. A text preoccupied with dualities, *Dracula* is a novel that seeks to control what cannot be acknowledged, to articulate what polite society does not discuss.

Stableford, Brian. "Bram Stoker." In *St. James Guide to Horror, Ghost, and Gothic Writers*. Ed. David Pringle. Detroit: St. James Press, 1998, 573–575. A brief overview of Stoker's main Gothic works, with no punches pulled in highlighting the many weaknesses in Stoker's writing. Of *The Lair of the White Worm* Stableford writes that it "is one of the most spectacularly incoherent novels ever to reach print."

Stevenson, John Allen. "A Vampire in the Mirror: The Sexuality of *Dracula*." *PMLA* 103 (1988): 139–149. An analysis of the complex sexual dynamics of the novel that stresses the competitive nature of sexuality.

Weissman, Judith. "Women and Vampires: *Dracula* as a Victorian Novel." *Midwest Quarterly* 18 (1977): 392–405. After briefly examining some prior literary depictions of sexually active women, Weissman argues that Stoker's novel dramatizes a psychosexual dynamic of anxiety and power, one in which the prize is power and the battlefield is the sexual female body, which the men seek to dominate in what is finally "a fight for control over women." This article is included in Margaret Carter's *Dracula: The Vampire and the Critics*, 69–77.

LUDWIG TIECK
(1773–1853)
Tom Lloyd

PRINCIPAL GOTHIC WORKS

Abdallah, oder das furchtbare Opfer [Abdallah, or the Horrible Sacrifice]. Berlin and
　　Leipzig: Carl August Nicolai, 1795.
William Lovell. Berlin and Leipzig: C.A. Nicolai, 1795.
"Der blonde Eckbert" [Blond Eckbert]. In *Volksmärchen*. Ed. Peter Leberrecht. Berlin
　　and Leipzig: C.A. Nicolai, 1797. (Later included in *Phantasus*.)
"Der getreue Eckart und der Tannenhäuser" [Trusty Eckart and Tannhaeuser]. In *Ro-
　　mantische Dichtungen*. Jena: Frommann, 1799. (Later included in *Phantasus*.)
"Der Runenberg" [The Runenberg]. In *Taschenbuch für Kunst und Laune*. Köln: Haas
　　& Sohn, 1804.
Phantasus: Eine Sammlung von Märchen, Erzählungen, Schauspielen, und Novellen.
　　[*Phantasus*: A Collection of Fairy Tales, Stories, Dramas, and Novellas] 3 vols.
　　Berlin: Realschulbuchhandlung, 1812–1816. (Contains "Die Elfen" [The Elves]
　　and "Die Pokal" [The Goblet].)
Tales from the Phantasus. Trans. Julius C. Hare, James Anthony Froude, et al. London:
　　J. Burns, 1845.

MODERN REPRINTS AND EDITIONS

Four Romantic Tales from Nineteenth Century German. Ed. and trans. Helene Scher.
　　New York: Ungar, 1975. (Contains "Der blonde Eckbert." [Blonde Eckbert])
German Literary Fairy Tales. Ed. Frank G. Ryder and Robert M. Browning. The German
　　Library, volume 30. New York: Continuum, 1983. (Contains "The Runenberg.")
German Romance Vol. 21 of *Centenary Edition of the Works of Thomas Carlyle*. New
　　York: AMS Press, 1969. (Contains English translations of the art fairy tales dis-
　　cussed here.)
*Gothic Tales of Terror: Classic Horror Stories from Great Britain, Europe, and the
　　United States, 1765–1840*. Ed. Peter Haining. New York: Taplinger, 1972. (Con-
　　tains "The Bride of the Grave.")

Outpourings of an Art-loving Friar. Trans. Edward Mornin. New York: Ungar, 1975.
    (Coauthored with Wilhelm Wackenroder.)
Romantic Gothic Tales, 1790–1840. Ed. G.R. Thompson. New York: Harper, 1979. (Con-
    tains "Der blonde Eckbert." [Blond Eckbert])
Werke in vier Bänden. Ed. Marianne Thalmann. 4 vols. Munich: Winkler, 1963–1966.
    (Tieck's works in four volumes in German.)

Ludwig Tieck was not primarily a Gothic writer, though like many Romantics
he displayed a youthful interest in Gothic "trivial literature" and indeed continued to employ Gothic devices in such Romantic works as *Franz Sternbalds
Wanderungen* [The Wanderings of Franz Sternbald]. Two patterns are worth
consideration: like Friedrich Schiller, Tieck saw aspects of his own mental turmoil reflected in the Gothic novels he voraciously read as a youth, and, looking
forward, the Gothic, with its emphasis on the supernatural, the medieval, and
the irrational, had key aspects in common with Tieck's brighter, sunnier Romanticism, where the horrible ghosts of the abyss are transformed into the re-
generative visitations of Raphael, and horror rooted in youthful insecurity
matures into artistic idealism in *Franz Sternbalds Wanderungen* and *Herzensergiessungeneines kunstliebenden Klosterbruders* [Heart-Outpourings of an Art-
loving Friar], but also remains evident in Romantic art fairy tales in which the
supernatural and madness intermingle.

    Tieck's juvenalia include an over-the-top Gothic novel, *Abdallah, oder das
furchtbare Opfer*, in which, as Roger Paulin puts it, he "out-Gothicked any other
representatives of that mode" (59). Like Schiller's *Die Räuber* [The Robbers]
or Goethe's *Die Leiden des jungen Werthers* [The Sufferings of Young
Werther], the 250-page novel was a means of distancing himself from thoughts
that, if we can believe some 1792 letters to his friend and collaborator Wilhelm
Wackenroder, very nearly drove him insane. Fascinated by English Gothic literature, above all William Beckford's *Vathek*, and influenced by his teacher and
sometime collaborator Friedrich Rambach, Tieck identified too closely with the
darkest descriptions of death, terror, and ghostly visitations, the "Grauen" (terror) that contrasts with the "explained supernatural" advocated by Clara Reeve
and Ann Radcliffe. As a schoolboy and at the University of Halle, he experienced alienation and emotional fear that led him to internalize the horrors of
Gothic literature as real yet inexplicable phenomena.

    James Trainer places *Abdallah* in the context of Tieck's emotional and literary
development toward Romanticism. He points out that its nihilism, like that of
William Lovell (1795), represents a place of departure, not arrival, for the young
writer. Central to what Roger Paulin in *Ludwig Tieck: A Literary Biography*
calls an oriental Gothic tale of "moral seduction and nihilistic despair" (51) is
the decision of Abdallah, under the influence of the diabolical Omar, to betray
his father Selim so that he can possess the daughter of Selim's mortal enemy,
Ali. Also important is his failed attempt to defeat the powers of darkness by
confronting their supernatural powers directly. Tricked by Omar, ally of Mondal,

the monster of destruction, into a descent into nihilistic despair for which he is neither morally nor mentally prepared, Abdallah is overwhelmed by the fiendish apparitions that haunt him. There is finally no escape, no "explained supernatural," that will lead him to clarity or emotional reassurance. Finally, rejected by Zulma, for whom he has sacrificed his own father, Abdallah goes mad and dies wretchedly. Like Schiller's Franz von Moor, he cannot escape the abyss to which he has subjected himself.

Even in his interest in Shakespeare, Tieck, like other Romantic writers, was drawn to terror and the supernatural, seeking in literature, whether in trashy novels or in sublimely great plays, those aspects that addressed his inner turmoil. Hence in his preface to *Abdallah*, he cites the pervasive "Grauen" (terror) in *Macbeth* and *Hamlet*. In 1796, he wrote an essay on "Shakespeares Behandlungen des Wunderbaren" [Shakespeare's Handling of the Wondrous], focusing on the supernatural elements that stimulated his feverish imagination.

It was his friendship with the Sturm und Drang writer Wilhelm Wackenroder (1773–1798) that tempered Tieck's absorption with "Grauen," leading him in the direction of a Romantic Middle Ages and causing him to turn from demonic hallucinations toward transformative artistic visions. The major product, *Herzensergiessungen*, while hardly Gothic and mainly the work of Wackenroder, points to Tieck's stepping back from the dangerous mental encounters that, like Abdallah's with grotesque horror, threatened to overwhelm his being. Horror gives way to the Jakob Boehme–inspired medieval "Catholicism" whose aesthetic visitations provide thrills yet reassurance. It is replaced by artistic visions, a pattern Tieck revisited on purely his terms in *Franz Sternbalds Wanderungen*. Instead of Abdallah's terrifying apparitions, we have Raphael's spirit, a "delightful vision" in which "there before my very eyes, standing hand in hand apart from all the others, were Raphael and Albrecht Dürer, looking calmly and in amicable silence at their paintings hanging together" (*German Romance* 57). Horror threatened to extinguish his being, but art offers a direct connection with God.

Yet Tieck hardly abandoned his interest in themes associated with Gothic literature. His most influential short stories, which influenced E.T.A. Hoffmann and perhaps Edgar Allan Poe, illustrate this. Thomas Carlyle's early interest in Tieck's art fairy tales, some of which he translated for *German Romance* (1827), reveals an attraction to natural supernaturalism that, like Tieck's, remained after he outgrew earlier bouts with nihilism and Gothic horror. Two of them, "The Blond Eckbert" and "The Runenberg," are the best known and most often analyzed and anthologized of Tieck's shorter works. Carlyle writes that "the ordinary lovers of witch and fairy matter will mark a deficiency of specters and enchantments here" (266). But the ghosts of these Romantic tales are psychological; the characters inhabit a world dominated by supernatural agencies, fragmentation, and confusion where ultimate meaning is just out of reach and insanity and obsession always threaten. No longer merely a part of the Gothic machinery, nature participates in the good or evil that mysteriously surrounds the human consciousness. In his *Fragments*, Friedrich Schlegel describes a Romantic irony that enables us to transcend enclosure, confusion, and fragmentation. Tieck's characters, like many of Hoffmann's and Poe's, are unable to do so, and the result is psychological entrapment.

"The Blond Eckbert" is a disturbing tale of escape, guilt, murder, incest, and madness whose hidden ghosts are in the repressed mind of its protagonist Eckbert, who cannot solve the "riddle" of his past and so dies insane, repeating the pattern of confrontation and defeat Tieck presented in *Abdallah*. Eckbert, a middle-aged knight, has his wife tell her strange life's story to Philip Walther, a visitor. She left her impoverished home where she was unwanted and traveled over mountains, whose "sound" had been a terror to her. She experiences *Waldeinsamkeit* (forest loneliness), the alienation accompanied by soon-buried terror that besets many of Tieck's characters. She steps from this "hell" to a "paradise" associated with the old woman who takes her in and teaches her to read and use the spinning wheel. Yet peace never comes, for she feels as if she is merely falling from one dream into another. Events now seem disjointed in memory (she cannot recall the dog's name), and she is pursued by guilt, her soul split between discordant and confusing forces. What is real and what is fiction? Bertha's "fable" points to the solipsism experienced by anyone who lives the inner life too intensely, especially the artist. Her discomfort impels her to leave the "straight path" where, paradoxically, mental peace is possible. Departing from the old woman while she is away, she leaves the dog (she supposes) to starve, but steals the mysterious bird, with its song of *Waldeinsamkeit*. Returning to the village where she was born and uncomfortable with its singing, she chokes the bird, buries it, and proceeds to embark on a bourgeois married life that evidently allows her to bury the past. But in inducing her to tell her story, Eckbert disinters it, and Walther, it turns out, knows that the bird's name was Strohmian. Eckbert, "at variance with himself" (*German Romance* 284), kills the knight while hunting, but his ultimate fragmentation is evident when Walther reappears as a young knight, Hugo, and again as the old woman who taught Bertha how to read and spin. Her story, it turns out, was Eckbert's. He has become an unquiet spirit, both ghostly and haunted alike. He has married his own sister Bertha (an ultimate sign of solipsistic confusion) and, far from being able to view the supernatural via the natural, lives in a nether state where nothing is explained. Memory, meaning, and identity collapse as the "marvelous" is mingled with the "common" and existence itself seems an unsolvable riddle.

"The Runenberg" similarly displays the thrills if not all the stage machinery of a Gothic story. It too centers on a protagonist, a hunter, who is unable to escape from the circle of his past, however much he alters the superficial aspects of his life. Having pulled a root from the earth and having experienced "a horrid universe of putrefaction" (337), he is drawn to nature as a destructive organism, one that yet is likewise integral to his identity. As in E.T.A. Hoffmann's "The Mines at Falun," which Tieck's story influenced, the main character is drawn to a mysterious woman, the ever-shifting Woodwoman, who finally lures him to the depths of the earth through an old ruined shaft. The hunter first encounters her one night on the vertiginous heights of the Runenberg (Rune Mountain), where he experiences an abyss, wild imaginings, a ruined castle, and within it a naked woman who, like the old man who led him there, is a manifestation of the Woodwoman. She presents him with a magic tablet of stones, a symbolic link with the magic stones of the mine shaft, which he loses. In this story, landscapes alter from flatlands to sublimely dizzying heights, to the plain country, and back as the hunter moves through the stages of life. But the inner dissonance remains, and the mysterious truth represented by the elusive lost tablet torments his memory. Like Eckbert, he cannot escape and is overcome by madness. Though he marries the fair-haired Elizabeth and seems to find a prosperous, Edenic life, the restlessness returns, and he revisits the earlier scenes of his haunting. The mountain and the mysterious Woodwoman symbolize the obsessiveness at the center of his being, which marriage to Elizabeth has not stilled. He finds his father and momentarily leaves these steep shapes and horrid chasms, returning home to find a modicum of happiness until a mysterious stranger leaves a sum of gold, an accursed metal that ultimately brings madness to him ("I know myself no more!" [*German Romance* 334]) and infertility to nature itself, once he enters the ruined shaft and withdraws entirely from humanity. Years later Elizabeth meets her husband once again before he disappears permanently with the hideous Woodwoman. The Romantic demonism evident in "The Runenberg" presupposes a mysterious otherworldly realm that cannot be explained or fully understood, but recognition of which educes connection both with an essential self and with insanity. The result is an inability to distinguish dream from reality, self from other. Neither a purely Gothic story nor entirely a fairy tale, but containing strong elements of both, "The Runenberg," like "Blond Eckbert," presents a world whose realities are never secure from those disintegrating visitations that emanate from within as well as (perhaps, but it is never clear) from external sources.

Other stories collected in *Phantasus* bear mentioning for their intermittent Gothicism. "The Elves," "The Trusty Eckart," and "The Goblet" also concern protagonists who are enticed from time, change, and life into mysterious places where they lose themselves. In the first story, Mary forgets time in her sojourn with Zerina and the elves; the gold and the metal-prince symbolize the alternate realm beyond this world and the solipsistic desire for aloneness that, years later, characterizes Mary's daughter Elfrida, who befriends Zerina and receives her own piece of gold. By revealing the forbidden fairy world to her husband Andres, Mary causes them to leave the fertile countryside, which becomes a blighted wasteland. Once more, Tieck, like Hoffmann some years later, treats the connection with the mysterious as the source of inspiration and insanity, ultimate truth and unreality. It is the dilemma of the artist, who must experience the abyss, the mysterious tablet or here the fairy realm, but may lose his understanding in trying to reveal or understand it.

"The Goblet," also interpretable as an art parable, centers around Ferdinand's attempt to grasp his beloved in the vision that his friend Albert raises in a magic goblet. But the head and body break away "as in a thousand lines" (*German Romance* 371), and Ferdinand, whose nearly religious worship of her makes him unable to reach out, loses her. Only years later do they communicate and find each other when, as a spectral conjuror and gold maker, he visits her house to be present at her daughter's wedding, not knowing initially where he is.

In "The Trusty Eckart," the Venusberg, the mountain associated with the Tannhäuser legend, symbolizes, like the metal in other stories, the fixations of people who are unable to forget the past and cope with life. It is haunted by hellish hosts of worldly Lusts that represent what is repressed in the world above, the path to which, as Tannhäuser puts it in the story's second half, is "now as in a subterraneous mine" (315). As Tannhäuser indicates to Friedrich, the longing for the Venusberg arises from his need for annihilation as well as ravishment. He too goes mad, murdering his past beloved and Friedrich's wife Emma. As the story concludes, he is pursued by Friedrich into the Venusberg, unable to withstand the "magic force" of the "subterraneous chasm" (318). As in others of Tieck's art fairy tales, he has failed to reconcile the divisions in his being so that he can cope with life: the ghosts of his inner self have overcome him.

Tieck's most significant contribution to the Gothic tale may well lie in his rejection of "happily-ever-after" endings in his stories. With their pronounced element of the supernatural grotesque, these pieces sometimes depict the triumph of the irrational and malign, a high Gothic effect. "The Blond Eckbert" ends with the fair-haired hero "distracted and dying on the ground" (*Romantic Gothic Tales* 74). For other Romantic writers, the nature world often offers an avenue for personal and spiritual wholeness, but Tieck's protagonists struggle to create such redemptive views of order.

SELECTED CRITICISM

Bidney, Martin. "Beneficent Birds and Crossbow Crimes: The Nightmare-Confessions of Coleridge and Ludwig Tieck." *Papers on Language and Literature* 25 (1989): 44–58. The focus is on "The Rime of the Ancient Mariner" and "The Blond Eckbert." Studies parallel themes but makes no case for direct influences either way in these 1797 works.

Carlyle, Thomas. "Ludwig Tieck." In *Centenerary Edition of the Works of Thomas Carlyle*. vol 21. New York: AMS Press, 1969: 257–267. Carlyle's introduction to his translations of Tieck's stories contains inaccuracies and lacunae, but is useful as an early British response to German literature in general and Tieck in particular.

Ewton, Ralph W. "Childhood without End: Tieck's *Der blonde Eckbert*." *German Quarterly* 46 (1973): 410–427. "One of the story's most perplexing motifs is incest, which modern depth psychology views as a characteristically childish wish."

Haase, Donald P. "Ludwig Tieck." In *Supernatural Fiction Writers*. Ed. E.F. Bleiler. New York: Scribner's, 1985: 83–89. "Out of a heteromorphic background of

Gothic horror and enlightened satire," Tieck emerges as one of the most innovative of the German Romantics.

Hagedorn, Jutta Angelika. "Der gotische Roman als sozialer Roman des spätens achtzehnten Jahrhunderts: Eine vergleichende Studie englischer und deutscher gotischer und sozialer Romane." Doctoral dissertation, University of Georgia, 1987 [*DAI* 48:2057A]. Discusses Tieck's *Abdallah*, maintaining that the Gothic novel should be "redefined as a type of social novel."

Klett, Dwight A. *Ludwig Tieck: An Annotated Guide to Research*. New York: Garland, 1993. Indispensable and exhaustive, this is a good starting point for any research on Tieck. There are useful cross-references among the thematic divisions (e.g., "Landscape, Nature") into which he divides research on Tieck. There is no section on Gothic themes, but there are related ones on "The Demonic, Fateful, Supernatural" and "Incest."

Lewis, Paul. "The Intellectual Functions of Gothic Fiction: Poe's 'Ligeia' and Tieck's 'Wake Not the Dead.' " *Comparative Literature Studies* 16 (1979): 207–221. Compares Poe's tale with Tieck's story as media for ideas as well as sensational thrills.

Liedke, Otto K. "Tieck's *Der Blonde Eckbert*: Das Märchen von Verarmung und Untergang." *German Quarterly* 44 (1971): 311–316. Focuses on characters' inabilities to sustain happiness in Tieck's fairy tale, which is dominated by guilt, anxiety, and violence. Characters are unable to overcome the evil forces that beset them. "Der Blonde Eckbert" becomes an "Antimärchen."

Lillyman, William J. *Reality's Dark Dream: The Narrative Fiction of Ludwig Tieck*. Berlin and New York: Walter de Gruyter, 1979. Highly useful critical study with bibliographies.

Otto, Linda. "A Study of Evil and Insanity in Tieck's Early Works." Doctoral dissertation, Northwestern University, 1974. [*DAI* 34:4277A]. Discusses *Abdallah* and "Der Blonde Eckbert" as fantasies of guilt. Also discovers links between "the question of the origin of evil, the phenomenon of insanity, and the supernatural, especially with respect to ecstatic or mystical experience."

Paulin, Roger. *Ludwig Tieck: A Literary Biography*. Oxford: Clarendon Press, 1985. The fact that the definitive biography of Tieck was written in English is a testament to his popularity in the English-speaking world, where his stature may be higher than in Germany. Paulin covers all aspects of his intellectual and literary development, including his eventual rejection of Romanticism as too decadent.

Schlaffer, Heinz. "Roman und Märchen: Ein formtheoretischer Versuch über Tiecks 'Blonden Eckbert.' " In *Gestaltungsgeschichte und Gesellschaftsgeschichte Literatur-, Kunst- und muikwissenschaftliche Studieu*. Ed. Helmut Kreuzer and Käte Hamburger. Stuttgart: Metzler, 1969: 224–241. Analyzes the influence of trivial literature and the Gothic novel on Tieck's art fairy tales.

Trainer, James. "The Incest-Theme in the Works of Tieck." *Modern Language Notes* 76 (1961): 819–824. Explores incest across Tieck's canon. Useful for an understanding of the incest and solipsism evident in his earlier works.

———. *Ludwig Tieck: From Gothic to Romantic*. The Hague: Mouton, 1964. An informative study of Tieck's Gothic influences, with a chapter on *Abdallah*. Traces Tieck's wide reading of "trivial literature," especially English works. Also provides a background chapter on the English Gothic writers.

Tymms, Ralph. "Ludwig Tieck." In *German Romantic Literature*. London: Methuen,

1955: 52–120. Explores Tieck's influence on the *Märchen* or fairy tale and his influence on E.T.A. Hoffmann. "He was most successful in evoking in his *Märchen* the atmosphere of mystery and terror, for these were sensations with which he was familiar—menacing natural forces which might take possession of man's mind like a malignant fiend."

Wells, Larry D. "Sacred and Profane: A Spatial Archetype in the Early Tales of Ludwig Tieck." *Monatshefte* 70 (1978): 29–44. Applying Cassirer's "spatial archetype" and "notion of mythic consciousness" to "Blond Eckbert" and "The Runenberg," discusses sacred and profane spaces in Tieck's art fairy tales. Eckbert and Christian are unable to maintain paradisiacal childhood or aesthetic states as they traverse radically different spaces throughout their lives. Their restless souls eventually find oracular meaning in madness.

HORACE WALPOLE
(1717–1797)

Frederick S. Frank

PRINCIPAL GOTHIC WORKS

The Castle of Otranto: A Story. Translated by William Marshal, Gent., From the Original Italian of Onuphrio Muralto, Canon of the Church of St. Nicholas at Otranto. London: Tho. Lownds, 1765. (The first edition was published on 24 December 1764. Later editions printed the novel's subtitle as *A Gothic Story*.)

The Mysterious Mother. Printed privately by Walpole at Strawberry Hill in 1768. London: Dodsley, 1781.

MODERN REPRINTS AND EDITIONS

The Castle of Otranto: A Gothic Story. Ed. W.S. Lewis with a new introduction and notes by E.J. Clery. Oxford & New York: Oxford University Press, 1996.

The Castle of Otranto and Hieroglyphic Tales. Ed. Robert Mack. London: Everyman/ J.M. Dent, 1993; Rutland, VT: Charles E. Tuttle, 1993.

The Castle of Otranto and The Mysterious Mother. Ed. Montague Summers. Chiswick: Printed at the Chiswick Press for Houghton, Mifflin & Constable, 1925.

"Horace Walpole's *The Mysterious Mother*: A Critical Edition." Ed. Janet A. Dolan. Doctoral dissertation, University of Arizona, 1970. [*DAI* 31:4115A–4116A].

Three Gothic Novels: The Castle of Otranto, Vathek, The Vampyre. Ed. E.F. Bleiler. New York: Dover, 1966.

Three Gothic Novels: Walpole/The Castle of Otranto, Beckford/Vathek, Mary Shelley/ Frankenstein. Ed. Mario Praz and Peter Fairclough. Baltimore: Penguin Books, 1968. (This edition is cited in the text.)

The Works of Horatio Walpole, Earl of Orford, Ed. Peter Sabor. 5 vols. London: Pickering & Chatto, 1998.

The first Gothic novel and the first Gothic drama were the inventions of Horace Walpole, dilettante, socialite, and enthusiastic patron of the medieval revival that permeated the arts of painting, architecture, and literature in the 1750s.

Reacting to the rigidities of the rule-bound aesthetics fostered by neoclassicism, Walpole's Gothicism expressed the new romantic impulse to indulge the strange, the exotic, the savage, the improbable, the mysterious, the supernatural, the surreal, and the unreal. These corridors to a forbidden sublime were made accessible again through Walpole's exploratory Gothic. Although Walpole never mentions Edmund Burke's treatise on the aesthetics of horror, *A Philosophical Enquiry into the Origin of Our Ideas of the Sublime and Beautiful* (1757), *The Castle of Otranto* and *The Mysterious Mother* applied Burke's theory of pleasurable fear to create the prototypical Gothic novel and Gothic drama. Optimal pleasure in the horrid, Burke posited, arose out of a confrontation with objects and events with which the mind could not rationally cope. "The mind is so entirely filled with its object that it cannot entertain any other, nor by consequence reason on that object which employs it. Hence arises the great power of the sublime that hurries us on by an irresistible force" (*Enquiry* II 1 57). Walpole's first Gothic novel and drama were filled with suprarational Burkean moments and objects.

From the descent of the enormous helmet, the novel's initial spectacular event, to the shattering of the castle walls by the immense and reinvigorated supernatural anatomy of Alfonso, Walpole crafted his Gothic so as to achieve a suspension of reason within enclosed settings, where readers might feel as lost and disoriented as the characters entrapped by the Gothic world and find pleasure in such sequestration and helplessness. Referring to terror as the "principal engine" or driving force of his story, Walpole designed a plot consisting of an inlaid system of architectural contraptions, fantastic acoustical effects, and supernatural props installed throughout a Gothic castle where normal laws of motion and gravity gave way to the "extraordinary positions" (44) that were soon to become the hallmarks of the Gothic world, where characters were enmeshed in "a constant vicissitude of interesting passions" (40). Confronted by portraits that come alive and walk, statues that bleed, walls that seem tumescent with some gigantic body seeking egress, and similar objects of Burkean sublimity, the characters are given repeated opportunities to test Burke's idea that the gruesome and dreadfully supernatural could be necessary aspects of an object's beauty, and furthermore that an object's sublimity was often heightened and intensified by its very gruesomeness and fearfulness.

When *The Castle of Otranto* was published at his private printing press at Strawberry Hill on Christmas Eve 1764, Walpole somewhat self-consciously concealed his authorship behind two pseudonyms. Uneasy over the novel's public reception, Walpole counterfeited his authorship in the fake preface to the first edition, in which readers were told that the book had been recovered from an Italian manuscript set down by the monastic chronicler Onuphrio Muralto, Canon of the Church of St. Nicholas at Otranto, and later rendered into English by that scholarly gentleman William Marshal, whose antiquarian zeal closely resembled Walpole's own exuberance for antiquarian and Gothic lore. In the preface to the second edition, Walpole abandoned these poses, declared his authorship, invoked the invulnerable examples of Shakespeare and Voltaire to justify his methods of characterization, and affixed the adjective "Gothic" to the subtitle of the novel. Because of its offensive connotations for the eighteenth-century mind, Walpole's description of his novel as "Gothic" was a bold choice, for it both enticed the curious reader and captured the essence of the form in a single word. The bogus authorship of the first edition was a favorite game of eighteenth-century writers, but in Walpole's case, the double pseudonym was protective as well as diverting. By giving free vent to the Gothic impulse in the composition of his novel, Walpole had risked his reputation as a man of taste, refinement, and neoclassic virtue.

These same notions of the repressed pleasures of the imagination arising from fear had frequently surfaced in the morbid lines of the poets of the Graveyard school. Walpole's lifelong friend, Thomas Gray, a leading writer of Graveyard verse, influenced Walpole's visions of morbid delight. The Graveyard poets' passion for Gothic settings and dark, subterranean places, as well as lonesome landscapes haunted by spectral figures, also had an impact on Walpole's architectural fantasizing. The Gothic revival of the 1750s had seen the construction of ruins and medieval villas as a new rage in the arts began to displace the taste for neat, symmetrical building styles. Gothic fashions and fads in mortuarial landscaping and private castle building appealed strongly to Walpole's antiquarian instincts. The foundations of *The Castle of Otranto* were laid in 1749 when Walpole began to rebuild his newly purchased Strawberry Hill estate, designing it into a fully equipped medieval architectural fantasy. His "little Gothic castle" at Strawberry Hill on the Thames became the imaginative catalyst for the bizarre tale of aviating helmets, mobile portraits, subterranean flights and pursuits, and supernatural alarms and diversions. With a head "full of Gothic story," he enthusiastically began the conversion of the Georgian-style house he had purchased at Strawberry Hill on the upper Thames into a Gothic villa. Thus the novel's "long labyrinth of darkness" (61) was an architectural fact before Walpole transmuted his surroundings into a first Gothic fiction. While musing over his architectural plaything, Walpole experienced what might be called a Burkean nightmare in which he saw a gigantic hand in armor above the banister of a staircase inside his little Gothic castle. The beckoning hand became the inspirational spark for the novel, as Walpole reported in a letter to his friend William Cole: "I waked one morning in the beginning of last June, from a dream, of which, all I could recover was, that I had thought myself in an ancient castle (a very natural dream for a head filled like mine with Gothic story) and that on the uppermost banister of a great staircase I saw a gigantic hand in armour" (letter to Cole, 9 March 1765 in *Horace Walpole's Correspondence* 1:88).

Reassured by the success of the hoaxing first edition, Walpole emerged from behind the fake pen names to acknowledge his authorship. The meanings currently attached to the adjective "Gothic" were changing as the aesthetic zeitgeist itself changed, and Walpole, keenly aware of the word's new connotations, exploited its value as a descriptor. Gothic now implied not just something medieval, barbaric, superstitious, and formless, but something mysterious and strangely attractive, a password to an alternative universe to which entry had been forestalled by Newtonian science and neoclassical rules of taste. Walpole's usage stuck as the unofficial rubric or generic signifier for the horror and terror novels and tales of his innumerable successors. Adhering to convenient formulas of *The Castle of Otranto*, Gothic space would invariably depict claustrophobic victimization within "a vault totally dark" (64). Gothic emotions, as one modern editor of the novel has pointed out, would invariably disclose a "consuming and overwhelming concern with the threats of sexuality and desire" (Mack xvi). Walpole's stage dramatized to the full the mandatory conditions of Gothic conflict and crisis, as signified by the narrative's collapsing structures, evil enclosures, supernatural hyperactivity, strangely pleasing disorder, and attractively packaged anxieties of genealogy, fate, and identity. To Walpole the tradition would owe not just its generous array of props and properties but also its central, most persistent psychological asset as a fable of identity.

Although the haunted castle is not already a ruin at the outset of the story, as would be the case with many Gothic works to follow, its stability is illusory, just as its legitimate ownership is in doubt. Marked for disintegration, the castle would become Gothic literature's first unstable and unsafe world in which supernatural forces disrupt and eventually displace natural law. The novel's resolution in favor of the supernatural presents the spectral colossus of Alfonso the Good as the living statue bursts through the castle's foundation and, in so doing, obliterates the rational security of the reader. The first Gothic ruin created by gathering supernatural forces suggests the shift from reason to feeling, from unity to fragmentation, from stability to collapse, and from natural to supernatural occurring in the period as classic order began to give way to romantic agitation. The paradoxical construction of devastation, whether in architecture or in literary narrative, evoked a spontaneous overflow of powerful feeling and challenged the norms of the Enlightenment.

Like much Romantic art to follow, the novel is also an intense personal expression of the artist's buried emotional life, a psychological register of secret and ambivalent sexual tensions. Recent readings of *The Castle of Otranto* and *The Mysterious Mother* stress Walpole's need to Gothicize as a means of confronting his secretly obsessive homosexuality and filial inadequacies. The text of the novel has been closely psychoanalyzed (see Betsy Perteit Harfst, *Horace Walpole and the Unconscious*), while other critics have found it to reveal "a psychobiographic record of parricidal guilts and fears, homosexual longings and drives, castration phobias, and Oedipal desires. Manfred's sexual frenzy and violent self-assertion are in some significant ways connected to Walpole's own suppressed or misdirected anger and contempt" (Haggerty 342). The harsh contrasts of the novel's various Gothic objects and effects, for example, the puniness of the crushed son and heir, Conrad, versus the huge and overwhelming form of Alfonso, and the peculiar affection of Manfred for one child as against his indifference for the other, are among the alluringly psychoanalytic data that seem to support such readings. The gadgetry of shock, hectic plotting, and melodramatic dialogue further invite autobiographical approaches to the novel and the play. For a readership accustomed to the neat couplets and graceful closures of the Augustan writers, Walpole's statement in the second preface to the novel must have held special meaning. His reference to emotional blockage, that "the great resources of fancy have been dammed up by a strict adherence to common life" (43), reverberates with Walpole's own emotional containment and artistic frustration.

Walpole's proposal for the liberation of fancy appears in the pair of informative prefaces to the first two editions of *The Castle of Otranto*. In both, he sets forth the behavioral laws of the Gothic world and suggests a technology and psychology of future tales of terror. Both prefaces offer useful criteria for the construction of catastrophic narrative. In an aptly chosen metaphor, Walpole refers to terror as "the author's principal engine" (40), thus anticipating the driving mechanisms of Gothic fiction, the machinery of interworking preternatural and supernatural devices that would come to characterize countless Gothic works. The operation of such infernal machinery installed throughout the castle would ensure a level of terror capable of placing the inmates of the castle in "extraordinary positions" (44), such as the one occupied by the mangled and crushed Conrad beneath the fallen helmet on the first page of the novel. When the apparatus of anguish was skillfully manipulated, it would have the additional effect of keeping the emotional lives of the entrapped characters in "a constant vicissitude of interesting passions" (40). Walpole did not provide specific examples of "extraordinary positions," just as he did not state precisely what was to be inferred by "interesting passions," but clearly at the top of the list of interesting passions is the characters' sexual consternation. As the Gothic grew from Walpole's prototype, an "extraordinary position" for residents of the castle might be either physical or psychological or both. Conrad's lethal predicament in the landing zone of an enormous flying helmet is entirely physical, but the extraordinary position of the anonymous victim in Poe's "The Pit and the Pendulum" is both physical and psychological, with both mind and body menaced by contracting space and descending time.

As would be the case with all true Gothic novels to follow from Walpole's model, the most potent and determined personality in *The Castle of Otranto* is the sentient castle itself. More than simply a receptacle for the absurd or an atmospheric framework for the containment of the villain's persecution of the maiden, the castle has a weird biology and a willful intelligence of its own. It responds to Manfred's erotic villainy and concealment of paternal crime with all the vigor of a revitalized human body. The symbolic layout of the castle with its own heaven and hell and its interior networked with secret corridors spiraling inward and downward to various secret compartments are features that suggest the structure of the human brain. Commenting on the symbolic properties of the haunted castle, Elizabeth MacAndrew is one of numerous critics to draw an analogy between the interior of the castle and the interior of the mind under stress: "A dire and threatening place, it remains more than a dwelling. It starts out as a stone representation of the dark, tortured windings in the mind of those eminently civilized, and therefore unnatural, vices, ambition and cruelty; it bears the whole weight of the ages of man's drift away from an ideal state; and it becomes a lasting representation of the torments of the subconscious pressing upon the conscious mind and making a prison of the self" (48). The subterranean sectors of the castle then equate symbolically with the subconscious aspects of the self. To the idea of the castle as emblematic of the imprisoned self may be added the historical view that sees the castle as a configuration of a doomed social structure, seemingly solid but approaching collapse.

Next in importance to the personality of the castle in Walpole's Gothic cast is his sinister superman, Manfred, a Gothic hero with no face described at this stage in the character's development. A figure of great potential virtue, he has a warped spiritual magnificence corrupted by dark passions and half-understood motives. His lust for power and perverted moral energy are similar in stature to Milton's Satan, while his domestic savagery carries reminders of many of the sexually driven hero-villains of the Elizabethan and Jacobean blood tragedies. Never absolutely repulsive or totally degenerate, Manfred seems to have inherited his evil tendencies through a corrupt family line, and his maliciousness seems to be a result of a divided nature continually at war with itself; he is, like Goethe's Faust, a tormented man within whom "two souls in one breast contend." Although Manfred lacks the contorted brow and diabolic glance of later Gothic villains, he exhibits most of the psychological traits of the Gothic's half-evil protagonists. Walpole endeavored to give his tormented tormentor a morally ambivalent status when he "explained" Manfred as a man who was "naturally humane when his passions did not obscure his reason" (66–67). Throughout the story, Manfred is driven by base passions, making him the ancestor of the Byronic hero, whose vices are often virtues in reverse and whose defiance of fate and commitment to crime have heroic overtones. When Manfred refers to himself as "a man of many sorrows" (102), he forecasts the angst, weltschmerz, and metaphysical exasperation later to be noted in the half-evil heroes of the Romantic period. Almost never delighting in his evil, Manfred is the progenitor of Gothic literature's strangely fascinating race of fallen creatures whose bondage to a moldering feudal building signifies both their twisted inner conditions and their enslavement to exhausted ideals of power. Although Manfred may appear to possess the Kingdom of Otranto and to control its interior affairs, it is really the castle that owns and torments him.

Manfred's villainy is directed against the two Gothic maidens condemned to reside in perpetual suspense in the gloomy chambers of Otranto. Isabella and Matilda are the forerunners of the menaced maidens of countless Gothic thrillers who spend most of their lives as subterranean sufferers in the Gothic underworld. One of the two, Manfred's daughter, Matilda, is Gothic literature's first victim of a homicidal father. The other persecuted maiden, Isabella, is little more than a focal point for Manfred's erotic urges and tyrannical scheming, her principal function being to give Manfred the opportunity to fulfill his legacy of evil by sadistic pursuit of the maiden through "the long labyrinth of darkness" (61). Flight and pursuit in an underground setting is a repeated pattern of emergency for Isabella, but the rhetoric used in describing her Gothic panics sometimes spills over into a sardonic sense of the ridiculous. As she descends through a series of trapdoors and screams on cue, Isabella's hysterics during her flight from Manfred debase crisis into comedy: " 'Oh, heavens!' cried Isabella, 'it is the voice of Manfred! Make haste, or we are ruined! And shut the trap-door after you' " (64). Yet this scene becomes mandatory in what will later be called "the female Gothic." Nonetheless, to Walpole goes the credit for originating the collision of villain and maiden, while Isabella's desperate series of subterranean adventures as she seeks egress from the hell of the castle to a domestic Eden outside its walls remains a fixture of Gothic romance throughout the history of the form.

The natural encounter of villain and maiden in the castle's depths is paralleled by the supernatural encounter between Manfred and the forces of retribution that oppose his criminal ownership of the castle. All later disastrous events at Otranto are foreshadowed by the tale's initial spectacular event: the arrival from the sky of Alfonso's Brobdingnagian helmet that crushes Manfred's son Conrad. Walpole's strategy of immediate shock at the outset of the novel was calculated to shatter his reader's faith in a controllable universe of empirical cause and effect and to stimulate irrational expectations. If the reader can get past the odd compound of the lurid and the ludicrous found in the unidentified-flying-helmet episode of the novel's opening pages, he is then in a position to enjoy the unremitting series of Gothic shudders and marvels to come. Future Gothics will owe much to Walpole's first law of Gothic motion as demonstrated by the page-one arrival of the huge helmet: this law states that the deader or more inanimate an object is, the more likely it is to move, to feel, to think, and to exert its own peculiar supernatural jurisdiction over events in the natural world. Statues that bleed, pictures that desert their frames to converse with the denizens of the castle, mirrors whose reflections yield macabre images of the past or future, and chambers that change their shape without warning all derive from the incident of the helmet and establish the total aliveness and material ghostliness of the Gothic world.

The durability of the novel's hardware of horror is also to be seen in Walpole's ingenious designing of several type-scenes that would prove almost indispensable to a successful Gothic work. A sterling example of such a type-scene is Frederic of Vicenza's transforming encounter with the hooded monk in Isabella's chapel. The scene demonstrates in a high style that moment of transition from terror to horror or from the mysterious to the baleful when a character is moved from something dreaded to the appalling realization that the horrid thing confronting him is real. Exploring the forbidden chambers of Otranto in search of the missing Hippolita, Frederic comes upon a robed figure kneeling before an altar. The meeting that follows becomes a modular moment in Gothic fiction as the figure slowly turns to reveal a skeletal face. A famous cinematic version of the terrible turn occurs in *The Phantom of the Opera* (1925) with the unmasked phantom at the organ. Walpole's introduction of this jolt-scene lacks the horrific effect it would have in later adaptations, yet the scene itself is fully finished and ready for future use:

The marquis was about to return, when the figure rising, stood some moments fixed in meditation, without regarding him. The marquis, expecting the holy person to come forth, and meaning to excuse his uncivil interruption, said, "Reverend Father, I sought the Lady Hippolita."—"Hippolita!" replied a hollow voice, "camest thou to this castle to seek Hippolita?" And then the figure, turning slowly round, discovered to Frederic the fleshless jaws and empty sockets of a skeleton, wrapt in a hermit's cowl. (139)

It is easy to understand why *The Castle of Otranto*, filled with these sorts of contraptions, became the dynamo to which later Gothic writers found it convenient to connect their own plots to electrify the reader. From its prominence in the Gothics of Radcliffe, Lewis, and Maturin to its continued presence in H.P. Lovecraft and Stephen King in the twentieth century, Walpole's power source remains a steady producer of Gothic energy. Although Lovecraft thought *The Castle of Otranto* "flat, stilted, and altogether devoid of true cosmic horror," he did not dismiss Walpole's achievement in providing the Gothic with its basics: "All this paraphernalia appears with amusing sameness, yet sometimes with tremendous effect, throughout the history of the Gothic novel; and is by no means extinct even today, though subtler technique now forces it to assume a less naive and obvious form" (26). But it would be a disservice to see Walpole's innovations as merely mechanical or technical. His Gothic also acknowledged some disturbing psychic realities that the Enlightenment did not wish to face, most particularly, the fact that we are not always in control or fully aware of who and what we are. In the fall of the House of Otranto at the climax of the first Gothic novel there can be heard the reverberations of what a later and greater master of the Gothic, Edgar Allan Poe, would call the "terrors of the soul."

Written four years after *The Castle of Otranto, The Mysterious Mother* was published in a private limited edition of fifty copies at Walpole's Strawberry Hill Press. Because its subject was incest, Walpole suppressed publication and circulated the play privately among close friends, never intending to allow it to be performed except in closet performances as readers' theater. It was included in the 1798 collected edition of *The Works of Horatio Walpole*, but was not edited until the twentieth century. The play has both scenic and dramatic appeal as well as a certain psychological depth of character lacking in *The Castle of Otranto*. Its stageworthiness was recognized by its first editor, Montague Summers, while later students of the play have been struck by its bonding of the Gothic and the tragic in both diction and form. "Its intense portrayal of family trauma, its fascination with verbal power, and its intertextual fusion of Greek and French dramatic material in a new Gothic form" (Baines 288) show a movement away from the superficial Gothic of *The Castle of Otranto* to the deeper horrors of the soul.

Set within the Castle of Narbonne, wherein "antique towers and vacant courts chill the suspended soul, / Till expectation wears the cast of fear" (the play's opening speech), the plot relates the last days and suicide of the Countess of Narbonne, the mysterious and incestuous mother of the title. Profound in both mood and style, the drama differs sharply in these respects from *The Castle of Otranto* and shows a serious effort to probe the "Oedipal dynamics of sex and power" (Baines 289) within a marked and fated family. Like an earlier domestic tragedy, *Hamlet*, the play's plot has a starkness revolving around a sexual mystery at its center. Having given in to sexual passion, the Countess has deceived her son, Edmund, into sleeping with her and remains fully conscious of her incestuous deed. Edmund remains unaware that his partner was his mother and that her beautiful ward and Edmund's destined bride, Adeliza, is both his sister and the daughter of their union. This tragic situation is compounded by the connivances of the sinister confessor, Father Benedict, a monastic Machiavel who plots to gain power over the Countess by prying her secret from her during the confession. His quest for power over a helpless female gives to Father Benedict the sinister role of monastic tyrant or villainous priest whose austere Catholicism is a guise for evil and lecherous desires. While the castle has lost none of its power of entrapment, there is no Manfred character operating within, nor are there any strolling portraits or animated armor inhabiting the walls and towers. The Gothic drama focuses instead on the guilty suffering provoked by the Countess's concealed sexual crime and its gruesome aftermath. It is interesting to note the introspective maturation of Walpole's Gothic vision from the half-risible composition of *The Castle of Otranto* to the serious and dignified presentation of a family destroyed by one moment of forbidden incestuous pleasure. It is Gothic naturalism rather than Gothic supernaturalism that gives the play its tragic power and psychodramatic amplitude, as Walpole dispenses with all ghostly gadgetry and allows no comic relief to intrude upon an atmosphere of gloom, intrigue, and death. *The Mysterious Mother* is a solemn and painful spectacle that points the way toward a higher Gothic or a deeper Gothic that concerns itself with the darkness of the human heart, Hawthorne's primary subject in his grim sagas of family guilt and moral decay. Walpole's somber purpose in *The Mysterious Mother* is expressed in the drama's closing speech by Edmund when he refers to these awful events as "this theatre of monstrous guilt," for unlike the first Gothic novel, the first Gothic drama consigns its characters permanently to the outer darkness. *See also* **Gothic Drama**.

SELECTED CRITICISM

Baines, Paul. " 'This Theatre of Monstrous Guilt': Horace Walpole and the Drama of Incest." *Studies in Eighteenth-Century Culture* 28 (1999): 287–309. Discusses the psychoanalytic criticism of the play and refers to it as "an extreme version of the incest narrative, even in literary terms. Presents a reading of the play's (Oedipal dynamics of sex and power which does not depend on a direct identification of the play with Walpole's personal sexuality."

Bentman, Raymond. "Horace Walpole's Forbidden Passion." In *Queer Representations: Reading Lives, Reading Cultures*. Ed. and intro. Martin Duberman. New York: New York University Press, 1997: 276–289. On homophobic and homoerotic themes and textual undercurrents in *The Castle of Otranto*. Links Walpole's homosexuality to the dream imagery of the novel.

Burke, Edmund. *A Philosophical Enquiry into the Origin of Our Ideas of the Sublime and Beautiful*. Ed. and intro. James T. Boulton. Notre Dame, IN: University of Notre Dame Press, 1968.

Campbell, Jill. " 'I Am No Giant': Horace Walpole, Heterosexual Incest, and Love among Men." *The Eighteenth Century: Theory and Interpretation* 39 (1998): 238–260. On the heterosexual-homosexual tensions visible in the incident and style of the novel.

Clery, Emma. "Against Gothic." In *Gothick Origins and Innovations*. Ed. Allan Lloyd Smith and Victor Sage. Costerus New Series 91. Amsterdam and Atlanta, GA: Rodopi, 1994: 34–43. On the reception of *The Castle of Otranto* by early reviewers. Also deals with Walpole's two prefaces to the two first editions. "*The Castle of Otranto* interprets its own project in material terms, most specifically with reference to class hierarchy and the development of a consumer society."

Conger, Syndy M. "Faith and Doubt in *The Castle of Otranto*." *Gothic: The Review of Supernatural Horror Fiction* 1 (1979): 51–59. Studies the novel's subversive theological outlook. The skepticism of the novel causes the reader to contemplate "Descartes's unthinkable: that the world may be in the hands of a demon."

Dole, Carol M. "Three Tyrants in *The Castle of Otranto*." *English Language Notes* 26: (1988): 26–35. The tyrannical models for Manfred, "the powerful, passion-ridden villain," are George III, Henry VIII, and Leontes in Shakespeare's *Winter's Tale*.

Ehlers, Leigh A. "The Gothic World as Stage: Providence and Character in *The Castle of Otranto*." *Wascana Review* 14:2 (1980): 17–30. Although it is a Gothic novel, the work is best understood as "a Gothic drama revealing the means by which providence resolves chaos into order."

Haggerty, George. "Literature and Homosexuality in the Late Eighteenth Century: Walpole, Beckford, and Lewis." In *Homosexual Themes in Literary Studies*. Ed. Wayne R. Dynes and Stephen Donaldson. New York: Garland, 1992: 167–178. Essay reprinted from *Studies in the Novel* 18 (1986): 341–352. The homosexuality of Walpole, Beckford, and Lewis is reflected in "their private obsessions [and] urgency of private meaning" that give their Gothics "their peculiar and at times unsettling power in their gruesome picture of human experience and deep sense of unresolved emotional feeling."

Harfst, Betsy Perteit. *Horace Walpole and the Unconscious: An Experiment in Freudian Analysis*. New York: Arno Press, 1980. Important psychoanalytic interpretation of Walpole's Gothic writings. Decodes *The Mysterious Mother* as a "punishment dream" through which Walpole confronts unresolved Oedipal conflicts. Similarly, *The Castle of Otranto* is a psychobiographic record of parricidal guilts and fears, homosexual longings and drives, castration phobias, and Oedipal desires.

Lewis, Wilmarth S., Ed. *Horace Walpole's Correspondence*. 44 vols. New Haven: Yale University Press, 1937–1983.

Lovecraft, H.P. "The Early Gothic Novel." In *Supernatural Horror in Literature*. New York: Ben Abramson, 1945: 23–29. Lovecraft's monograph was originally published in 1927 with "Mansfield" used for "Manfred."

MacAndrew, Elizabeth. *The Gothic Tradition in Fiction*. New York: Columbia University Press, 1979.

Mack, Robert. Introduction *The Castle of Otranto and Hieroglyphic Tales* by Horace Walpole. London: J.M. Dent; Rutland, VT: Charles E. Tuttle, 1993: xi–xxvii. Makes some interesting points about the autobiographical content of the novel. "*Otranto* was produced within a crucible of passion that was both political and personal."

McKinney, David. " 'The Castle of My Ancestors': Horace Walpole and Strawberry Hill." *British Journal for Eighteenth-Century Studies* 13 (1990): 199–214. On the relationships between the building of Strawberry Hill and the novel that followed.

Mowl, Timothy. *Horace Walpole: The Great Outsider*. London: John Murray, 1996. "*Otranto* has survived because not only does it pack all the horrors and clichés of the Gothic novel into a hundred pages, but it adds a subtext of laughter which ridicules the entire convention."

Stevenson, John Allen. "*The Castle of Otranto*: Political Supernaturalism." In *The British Novel, Defoe to Austen: A Critical History*. Boston: Twayne, 1990: 90–109. Sees many of the supernatural events and characters as reflective of political tensions.

Watt, Ian P. "Time and the Family in the Gothic Novel: *The Castle of Otranto*." *Eighteenth-Century Life* 10:3 (1986): 159–171. Studies the retributive force of time in *Otranto*. "The very word 'Gothic' suggests that the genre has got something to do with time."

Watt, James. "Origins: Horace Walpole and *The Castle of Otranto*." In *Contesting the Gothic: Fiction, Genre, and Cultural Conflict, 1764–1832*. Cambridge: Cambridge University Press, 1999: 12–41. Argues that Walpole constructed the Gothic "as a form of private and recreational class property, to which he was able to lay claim because of the status he had forged for himself as a licensed risk-taker."

Wein, Toni. "Tangled Webs: Horace Walpole and the Practice of History in *The Castle of Otranto*." *English Language Notes* 35:4 (1998): 12–22. Explores the "aestheticized feudalism" and other pseudohistorical features of *The Castle of Otranto* to test the success of Walpole's theory of blending the two kinds of romance.

TIMELINE OF GOTHIC AUTHORS AND WORKS
(1762–1999)

1762   *Longsword, Earl of Salisbury: An Historical Romance* (Thomas Leland)

1763   *The Countess of Salisbury* (Hall Hartson)

1764   *Les Amans malheureux; ou, le Comte de Comminge* [The Unfortunate Lovers; or, The Count of Comminge] (François Thomas Marie de Baculard d'Arnaud)

        The Castle of Otranto: A Story (Horace Walpole)

1768   *Euphémie; ou, Le Triomphe de la réligion* [Euphémie; or, The Triumph of Religion] (François Thomas Marie de Baculard d'Arnaud)

        The Mysterious Mother (Horace Walpole)

1771   *The Grecian Daughter* (Arthur Murphy)

1773   "On the Pleasure Derived from Objects of Terror; with Sir Bertrand, a Fragment" (John Aikin and Anna Laetitia Aikin Barbauld)

1776   *Kinko Kidan Ugetsu monogatari* [Tales of Moonlight and Rain] (Ueda Akinari)

1777   *The Champion of Virtue* (Clara Reeve)

1778   *The Old English Baron: A Gothic Story* (Clara Reeve)

1781   *The Count of Narbonne* (Robert Jephson)

1781   *Die Räuber* [The Robbers] (Friedrich Schiller)

1783   *The Recess; or, A Tale of Other Times* (Sophia Lee)

1784   *Imogen: A Pastoral Romance* (William Godwin)

1786   *Vathek: An Arabian Tale* (William Beckford)

1787   *Der Geisterseher* [The Ghost-Seer] (Friedrich Schiller)

        Vimonda: A Tragedy (Andrew McDonald)

1788   *Emmeline, the Orphan of the Castle* (Charlotte Turner Smith)

1789   *Alexis; ou, La Maisonnette dans les bois* [Alexis; or, The Cottage in the Woods] (François Guillaume Ducray-Duminil)

       The Castles of Athlin and Dunbayne: A Highland Story (Ann Radcliffe)

1790   *Ethelinde; or, The Recluse of the Lake* (Charlotte Turner Smith)

       A Sicilian Romance (Ann Radcliffe)

1791   *Justine; ou, Les Malheurs de la vertu* [Justine, or the Misfortunes of Virtue] (Marquis de Sade)

       The Kentish Barons (Francis North)

       The Romance of the Forest, Interspersed with Some Pieces of Poetry (Ann Radcliffe)

1793   *Castle of Wolfenbach: A German Story* (Eliza Parsons)

       The Old Manor House (Charlotte Turner Smith)

1794   *Fontainville Forest* (James Boaden)

       The Mysteries of Udolpho: A Romance Interspersed with Some Pieces of Poetry (Ann Radcliffe)

       The Necromancer; or, The Tale of the Black Forest (Lawrence Flammenberg/ Karl Friedrich Kahlert)

       Things As They Are; or, The Adventures of Caleb Williams (William Godwin)

1795   *Abdallah, oder das furchtbare Opfer* [Abdallah, or the Horrible Sacrifice] (Ludwig Tieck)

1796   *Horrid Mysteries* (Carl Grosse)

       The Iron Chest (George Colman the younger)

       The Monk (Matthew Gregory Lewis)

       The Mysterious Warning: A German Tale (Eliza Parsons)

       Victor; ou, L'Enfant de la forêt [Victor; or, The Child of the Forest] (François Guillaume Ducray-Duminil)

1797   *Azemia* (William Beckford/Jacquetta Jenks)

       L'Histoire de Juliette; ou, Les Prospérités du vice [The History of Juliette, or the Fortunes of Vice] (Marquis de Sade)

       The Italian Monk (James Boaden)

       The Italian; or, The Confessional of the Black Penitents (Ann Radcliffe)

1798   *Canterbury Tales* (Sophia Lee)

       The Castle Spectre (Matthew Gregory Lewis)

Clermont: A Tale (Regina Maria Roche)

Coelina; ou, L'Enfant du mystère [Coelina; or, The Mysterious Child] (François Guillaume Ducray-Duminil)

The Inquisitor (Thomas Holcroft)

The Midnight Bell: A German Story Founded on Incidents of Real Life (Francis Lathom)

The Orphan of the Rhine (Eleanor Sleath)

Wieland; or, The Transformation (Charles Brockden Brown)

1799 *Arthur Mervyn; or, Memoirs of the Year 1793* (Charles Brockden Brown)

  Edgar Huntly; or, The Memoirs of a Sleepwalker (Charles Brockden Brown)

  Ormond; or, The Secret Witness (Charles Brockden Brown)

  St. Leon: A Tale of the Sixteenth Century (William Godwin)

1800 *De Monfort* (Joanna Baillie)

1802 *A Tale of Mystery* (Thomas Holcroft)

1805 *Confessions of the Nun of St. Omer* (Charlotte Dacre/Rosa Matilda)

  The Towers of Urbandine (George Charles Carr)

1806 *Zofloya; or, The Moor: A Romance of the Fifteenth Century* (Charlotte Dacre/Rosa Matilda)

1807 *Fatal Revenge; or, The Family of Montorio* (Charles Robert Maturin)

  The Libertine (Charlotte Dacre/Rosa Matilda)

  The Wood Daemon; or, The Clock Has Struck (Matthew Gregory Lewis)

1809 *Venoni; or, The Novice of St. Mark's* (Matthew Gregory Lewis)

1810 *Zastrozzi: A Romance* (Percy Bysshe Shelley)

1811 *The Passions* (Charlotte Dacre/Rosa Matilda)

  St. Irvyne; or, The Rosicrucian (Percy Bysshe Shelley)

1812 *Phantasus: Eine Sammlung von Märchen Erzählungen, Schauspielen und Novellen* [Phantasus: A Collection of Fairy Tales] (Ludwig Tieck)

1814 *Fantasiestücke in Callots Manier* [Fantasy Pieces] (E.T.A. Hoffmann)

1815 *Die Elixiere des Teufels: Nachgelassene Papiere des Bruders Medardus* [The Devil's Elixirs: Posthumous Papers of Brother Medardus] (E.T.A. Hoffmann)

1816 *The Antiquary* (Sir Walter Scott)

  Bertram; or, The Castle of St. Aldobrand (Charles Robert Maturin)

The Black Dwarf (Sir Walter Scott)

1817   *The Doom of Devorgoil: A Melo-drama* (Sir Walter Scott)

      Manfred: A Dramatic Poem (Lord Byron)

      Nachtstücke [Night Pieces] (E.T.A. Hoffmann)

1818   *The Brownie of Bodsbeck* (James Hogg)

      Frankenstein; or, The Modern Prometheus (Mary Shelley)

      The Heart of Mid-Lothian (Sir Walter Scott)

      Northanger Abbey (Jane Austen)

1819   *The Bride of Lammermoor* (Sir Walter Scott)

      The Sketch Book of Geoffrey Crayon, Gent. (Washington Irving)

      The Vampyre (John Polidori)

1820   *The Cenci* (Percy Bysshe Shelley)

      Melmoth the Wanderer: A Tale (Charles Robert Maturin)

      The Vampire; or *The Bride of the Isles: A Romantic Melodrama in Two Acts* (J. R. Planché)

1822   *The Three Perils of Man*; or *War, Women, and Witchcraft: A Border Romance* (James Hogg)

1823   *Presumption; or, The Fate of Frankenstein* (Richard Brinsley Peake)

      The Three Perils of Woman; or, Love, Leasing, and Jealousy: A Series of Domestic Scottish Tales (James Hogg)

1824   *The Private Memoirs and Confessions of a Justified Sinner, Written by Himself; with a Detail of Curious Traditionary Facts, and Other Evidence, by the Editor* (James Hogg)

      Tales of a Traveller (Washington Irving)

1826   *Frankenstein; or, The Man and the Monster! or, The Fate of Frankenstein: A Peculiar Romantic Melo-dramatic Pantomimic Spectacle* (Henry M. Milner)

1827   *Falkland* (Edward Bulwer-Lytton)

1832   *The Alhambra: A Series of Tales and Sketches of the Moors and Spaniards* (Washington Irving)

1833   *Pestrye skazki s krasyym slovtsom* [Variegated Tales] (Vladimir Fyodorovich Odoevsky)

1834   *The Last Days of Pompeii* (Edward Bulwer-Lytton)

      Rookwood (William Harrison Ainsworth)

1837 "The Bagman's Story" (Charles Dickens)

"A Madman's Manuscript" (Charles Dickens)

"The Story of the Goblins Who Stole a Sexton" (Charles Dickens)

Twice-told Tales (Nathaniel Hawthorne)

1838 "The Ghost and the Bone-Setter" (Joseph Sheridan Le Fanu)

The Narrative of Arthur Gordon Pym of Nantucket (Edgar Allan Poe)

1839 "The Baron of Grogzwig" (Charles Dickens)

1840 *Tales of the Grotesque and Arabesque* (Edgar Allan Poe)

The Tower of London: An Historical Romance (William Harrison Ainsworth)

1842 "The Masque of the Red Death" (Edgar Allan Poe)

Zanoni (Edward Bulwer-Lytton)

1843 "The Tell-Tale Heart" (Edgar Allan Poe)

1844 *The Ladye Annabel; or, The Doom of the Poisoner* (George Lippard)

Russkie nochi [Russian Nights] (Vladimir Fyodorovich Odoevsky)

The Quaker City; or, The Monks of Monk Hall (George Lippard)

1845 *Tales by Edgar A. Poe* (Edgar Allan Poe)

1846 "The Cask of Amontillado" (Edgar Allan Poe)

Lucretia; or, The Children of Night (Edward Bulwer-Lytton)

Mosses from an Old Manse (Nathaniel Hawthorne)

1847 *Jane Eyre* (Charlotte Brontë/Currer Bell)

Wuthering Heights (Emily Brontë/Ellis Bell)

1848 *The Haunted Man and the Ghost's Bargain* (Charles Dickens)

The Lancashire Witches: A Romance of Pendle Forest (William Harrison Ainsworth)

1850 *The Killers: A Narrative of Real Life in Philadelphia* (George Lippard)

The Scarlet Letter (Nathaniel Hawthorne)

1851 *Ghost Stories and Tales of Mystery* (Joseph Sheridan Le Fanu)

The House of the Seven Gables (Nathaniel Hawthorne)

Moby-Dick; or, The Whale (Herman Melville)

The Snow-Image, and Other Tales (Nathaniel Hawthorne)

1852 *Pierre; or, The Ambiguities* (Herman Melville)

1853 *Villette* (Charlotte Brontë)

1856 *After Dark* (Wilkie Collins)

   The Piazza Tales (Herman Melville)

1857 "The Ghost in the Bride's Chamber" (Charles Dickens)

1859 "The Haunted and the Haunters" (Edward Bulwer-Lytton)

   "The Haunted House" (Charles Dickens)

   The Queen of Hearts (Wilkie Collins)

1860 *The Woman in White* (Wilkie Collins)

1861 *A Strange Story* (Edward Bulwer-Lytton)

1862 "An Authentic Narrative of a Haunted House" (Joseph Sheridan Le Fanu)

1864 *Uncle Silas* (Joseph Sheridan Le Fanu)

1865 *Our Mutual Friend* (Charles Dickens)

1866 *Armadale* (Wilkie Collins)

   "No. 1 Branch Line: The Signalman" (Charles Dickens)

1868 "De Grey: A Romance" (Henry James)

   The Moonstone (Wilkie Collins)

   "The Romance of Certain Old Clothes" (Henry James)

1869 "Green Tea" (Joseph Sheridan Le Fanu)

1870 *The Mystery of Edwin Drood* (Charles Dickens)

1871 "Carmilla" (Joseph Sheridan Le Fanu)

1872 *In a Glass Darkly* (Joseph Sheridan Le Fanu)

1878 *The Haunted Hotel: A Mystery of Modern Venice* (Wilkie Collins)

1882 *The Portrait of a Lady* (Henry James)

1883 "A Symphony in Lavender" (Mary Wilkins Freeman)

1884 *The Body-Snatcher* (Robert Louis Stevenson)

1886 *The Strange Case of Dr. Jekyll and Mr. Hyde* (Robert Louis Stevenson)

1889 "A Gentle Ghost" (Mary Wilkins Freeman)

1891 *A New England Nun and Other Stories* (Mary Wilkins Freeman)

   Tales of Soldiers and Civilians (Ambrose Bierce)

1892 "Death and the Woman" (Gertrude Atherton)

   In the Midst of Life (Ambrose Bierce)

1893   *Can Such Things Be?* (Ambrose Bierce)

1894   *The Great God Pan and The Inmost Light* (Arthur Machen)

1895   "The Altar of the Dead" (Henry James)

       "Gekashitsu" [The Surgery Room] (Izumi Kyoka)

1897   *Dracula* (Bram Stoker)

1898   "The Turn of the Screw" (Henry James)

1900   "Koya Hijiri" [The Holy Man of Mount Koya] (Izumi Kyoka)

1901   *The Sacred Fount* (Henry James)

1902   "Luella Miller" (Mary Wilkins Freeman)

       "The Vacant Lot" (Mary Wilkins Freeman)

       "The Wind in the Rose-Bush" (Mary Wilkins Freeman)

1903   "The Beast in the Jungle" (Henry James)

       The Jewel of Seven Stars (Bram Stoker)

       "The Southwest Chamber" (Mary Wilkins Freeman)

1905   *The Bell in the Fog and Other Stories* (Gertrude Atherton)

1908   "The Jolly Corner" (Henry James)

1911   *The Lair of the White Worm* (Bram Stoker)

1915   *The Rainbow* (D.H. Lawrence)

1917   *Tenshu monogatari* [The Castle Tower] (Izumi Kyoka)

       The Terror: A Fantasy (Arthur Machen)

1920   "Baishoku kamonanban" [Osen and Sokichi] (Izumi Kyoka)

1923   "The Fox" (D.H. Lawrence)

       "The Rats in the Walls" (H.P. Lovecraft)

1927   *The Case of Charles Dexter Ward: A Novel of Terror* (H.P. Lovecraft)

1928   "The Dunwich Horror" (H.P. Lovecraft)

       The Shunned House (H.P. Lovecraft)

       The Woman Who Rode Away and Other Stories (D.H. Lawrence)

1936   *The Shadow over Innsmouth* (H.P. Lovecraft)

1955   *Wise Blood* (Flannery O'Connor)

       A Good Man Is Hard to Find, and Other Stories (Flannery O'Connor)

1960   *The Violent Bear It Away* (Flannery O'Connor)

1965   *Everything That Rises Must Converge* (Flannery O'Connor)

1968   "Speeches for Dr. Frankenstein" (Margaret Atwood)

1969   *them* (Joyce Carol Oates)

1970   *The Wheel of Love and Other Stories* (Joyce Carol Oates)

1972   *Surfacing* (Margaret Atwood)

1974   *Carrie* (Stephen King)

       Where Are You Going, Where Have You Been? Stories of Young America (Joyce Carol Oates)

1975   *'Salem's Lot* (Stephen King)

1976   *Lady Oracle* (Margaret Atwood)

1977   *Night-Side* (Joyce Carol Oates)

       The Shining (Stephen King)

1978   *Night Shift* (Stephen King)

1979   *The Dead Zone* (Stephen King)

1980   *Bellefleur* (Joyce Carol Oates)

       Firestarter (Stephen King)

1981   *Cujo* (Stephen King)

1982   *A Bloodsmoor Romance* (Joyce Carol Oates)

       Different Seasons (Stephen King)

1983   *Pet Sematary* (Stephen King)

1984   *Mysteries of Winterthurn* (Joyce Carol Oates)

1985   *Skeleton Crew* (Stephen King)

1987   *Beloved* (Toni Morrison)

       IT (Stephen King)

1992   *Gerald's Game* (Stephen King)

1994   *Insomnia* (Stephen King)

1995   *Zombie* (Joyce Carol Oates)

1996   *First Love: A Gothic Tale* (Joyce Carol Oates)

       The Green Mile (Stephen King)

1998   *Bag of Bones* (Stephen King)

1999   *Blonde* (Joyce Carol Oates)

       Hearts in Atlantis (Stephen King)

GENERAL BIBLIOGRAPHY OF CRITICAL SOURCES AND RESOURCES

PRIMARY BIBLIOGRAPHIES OF THE GOTHIC

Brauchli, Jakob. *Der englische Schauer-roman um 1800: Unter Berücksichtigung der unbekannten Bücher: Ein Beitrag zur Geschichte der Volksliteratur.* Weida: Thomas & Hubert, 1928.

Christopher, Joe R. "A Gothic and Dark Fantasy Checklist." *NIEKAS 45: Essays on Dark Fantasy.* Ed. Joe Redt. Center Harbor, NH: Niekas Publications, 1998: 113–117.

Frank, Frederick S. "The Gothic Romance, 1762–1820." In *Horror Literature: A Core Collection and Reference Guide.* Ed. Marshall B. Tymn. New York: R.R. Bowker, 1981: 3–175.

———. *The First Gothics: A Critical Guide to the English Gothic Novel.* New York: Garland, 1987.

———. "The Early Gothic, 1762–1824." In *Horror Literature: A Reader's Guide.* Ed. Neil Barron. New York: Garland, 1990: 3–57.

———. *Through the Pale Door: A Guide to and through the American Gothic.* Westport, CT: Greenwood Press, 1990.

———. "The Early and Later Gothic Traditions, 1762–1896." In *Fantasy and Horror: A Critical and Historical Guide to Literature, Illustration, Film, TV, Radio, and the Internet.* Ed. Neil Barron. Lanham, MD: Scarecrow Press, 1999: 5–44.

Lévy, Maurice. "Bibliographie chronologique du roman 'gothique,' 1764–1824." In *Le Roman "gothique" anglais, 1764–1824.* Toulouse: Association des Publications de la Faculté des Lettres et Sciences Humaines de Toulouse, 1968: 684–708.

———. "English Gothic and the French Imagination: A Calendar of Translations, 1767–1828." In *The Gothic Imagination: Essays in Dark Romanticism.* Ed. G.R. Thompson. Pullman: Washington State University Press, 1974: 150–176.

Radcliffe, Elsa J. *Gothic Novels of the Twentieth Century: An Annotated Bibliography.* Metuchen, NJ: Scarecrow Press, 1979.

Redden, Sister Mary Maurita. *The Gothic Fiction in the American Magazines (1765–1800).* Washington, DC: Catholic University of America Press, 1939.

Stableford, Brian. "The Later Gothic Tradition, 1825–1896." In *Horror Literature: A Reader's Guide.* Ed. Neil Barron. New York: Garland, 1990: 58–92.

———. "Early Modern Horror Fiction, 1897–1949." In *Fantasy and Horror: A Critical*

     and Historical Guide to Literature, Illustration, Film, TV, Radio, and the Internet.
     Ed. Neil Barron. Lanham, MD: Scarecrow Press, 1999: 103–138.

Summers, Montague. *A Gothic Bibliography* (1941). New York: Russell & Russell, 1964.

Tracy, Ann B. *The Gothic Novel, 1790–1830: Plot Summaries and Index to Motifs.*
     Lexington: University Press of Kentucky, 1981.

SECONDARY BIBLIOGRAPHIES OF THE GOTHIC

Barron, Neil, and Michael E. Stamm. "Reference Sources and Online Resources." In
     Fantasy and Horror: A Critical and Historical Guide to Literature, Illustration,
     Film, TV, Radio, and the Internet. Ed. Neil Barron. Lanham, MD: Scarecrow
     Press, 1999: 435–451.

Benton, Richard P. "The Problems of Literary Gothicism." *ESQ: A Journal of the Amer-*
     ican Renaissance 18 (1972): 5–9.

Crawford, Gary W., Benjamin Franklin Fisher IV, and Frederick S. Frank. "The 1978
     Bibliography of Gothic Studies." *Gothic: The Review of Supernatural Horror*
     Fiction 1 (1979): 65–67.

————. "The 1979 Bibliography of Gothic Studies" *Gothic: The Review of Supernatural*
     Horror Fiction 2 (1980): 48–52.

————. *The 1980 Bibliography of Gothic Studies.* Baton Rouge: Gothic Press, 1983.

Fisher, Benjamin F., IV. "Ancilla to the Gothic Tradition: A Supplementary Bibliogra-
     phy." *American Transcendental Quarterly* 30:2 (1976): 22–36.

————. "The Residual Gothic Impulse, 1824–1873." In *Horror Literature: A Core Col-*
     lection and Reference Guide. Ed. Marshall B. Tymn. New York: R.R. Bowker,
     1981: 176–220.

————. *The Gothic's Gothic: Study Aids to the Tradition of the Tale of Terror.* New
     York: Garland, 1988.

Frank, Frederick S. "The Gothic Novel: A Checklist of Modern Criticism." *Bulletin of*
     Bibliography 30 (1973): 45–54.

————. "The Gothic Novel: A Second Bibliography of Criticism." *Bulletin of Bibliog-*
     raphy 35 (1978): 1–14, 52.

————. *Guide to the Gothic: An Annotated Bibliography of Criticism.* Metuchen, NJ:
     Scarecrow Press, 1984.

————. *Gothic Fiction: A Master List of Twentieth Century Criticism and Research.*
     Westport, CT: Meckler, 1988.

————. "Gothic Studies and Horror Literature." In *Montague Summers: A Bibliograph-*
     ical Portrait. Great Bibliographers Series, no. 7. Metuchen, NJ: Scarecrow Press,
     1988: 159–172.

————. "Montague Summers: A Bibliographical Portrait." *Bulletin of Bibliography* 45
     (1988): 167–178.

————. *Guide to the Gothic II: An Annotated Bibliography of Criticism, 1983–1993.*
     Lanham, MD: Scarecrow Press, 1995.

Garside, Peter. "Romantic Gothic." In *Literature of the Romantic Period: A Bibliograph-*
     ical Guide. Ed. Michael O'Neill. Oxford: Clarendon Press; New York: Oxford
     University Press, 1998: 315–340.

Le Tellier, Robert Ignatius. "The Gothic Novel." In *A Bibliography of the English Novel*
     from the Restoration to the French Revolution: A Checklist of Sources and Crit-

ical Materials, with Particular Reference to the Period 1660 to 1740. Salzburg, Austria: Institut für Anglistik und Amerikanistik, Universität Salzburg, 1994: 97–110.

McNutt, Dan J. *The Eighteenth-Century Gothic Novel: An Annotated Bibliography of Criticism, and Selected Texts.* Foreword Devendra Varma and Maurice Lévy. New York: Garland, 1975.

Morrison, Michael A. "History and Criticism." In *Horror Literature: A Reader's Guide.* Ed. Neil Barron. New York: Garland, 1990: 347–384.

Richter, David. "The Gothic Impulse: Recent Studies." *Dickens Studies Annual* 11 (1983): 279–311.

Spector, Robert D. *The English Gothic: A Bibliographic Guide to Writers from Horace Walpole to Mary Shelley.* Westport, CT: Greenwood Press, 1983.

Spehner, Norbert. *Écrits sur le fantastique: Bibliographie analytique des études et essais sur le fantastique publiés entre 1900 et 1985 (littérature/cinema/art fantastique).* Longueuil, Quebec: Le Préambule, 1986.

Wolfe, Gary K. "History and Criticism." In *Fantasy and Horror: A Critical and Historical Guide to Literature, Illustration, Film, TV, Radio, and the Internet.* Ed. Neil Barron. Lanham, MD: Scarecrow Press, 1999: 453–470.

THE TERM "GOTHIC" IN HISTORY AND LITERATURE

Baldick, Chris, and Robert Mighall. "Gothic Criticism." In *A Companion to the Gothic.* Ed. David Punter. Oxford, UK, and Malden, MA: Blackwell, 2000: 210–228.

Fry, Carrol. "The Concept of the Sublime in Eighteenth-Century Gothic Fiction." *Mankato State College Studies* 1 (1966): 31–34.

Holbrook, William C. "The Adjective 'Gothique' in the Eighteenth Century." *Modern Language Notes* 56 (1941): 498–503.

Kliger, Samuel. "The Goths in England: An Introduction to the Gothic Vogue in Eighteenth-Century Aesthetic Discussion." *Modern Philology* 43 (1945): 107–117.

———. *The Goths in England: A Study in Seventeenth and Eighteenth Century Thought.* Cambridge, MA: Harvard University Press, 1952.

Lévy, Maurice. " 'Gothic and the Critical Idiom." In *Gothick Origins and Innovations.* Ed. Allan Lloyd Smith and Victor Sage. Costerus New Series 91. Amsterdam and Atlanta, GA: Rodopi, 1994: 1–15.

Longueil, Alfred E. "The Word 'Gothic' in Eighteenth Century Criticism." *Modern Language Notes* 38 (1923): 453–460.

McIntyre, Clara. "Were the Gothic Novels Gothic?" *PMLA* 36 (1921): 644–667.

Sowerby, Robin. "The Goths in History and Pre-Gothic Gothic." In *Companion to the Gothic.* Ed. David Punter. Oxford, UK, and Malden, MA: Blackwell, 2000: 15–26.

REFERENCE WORKS: HANDBOOKS, CASEBOOKS, SOURCEBOOKS, GUIDES, ENCYCLOPEDIAS

Abensour, Liliane, and Françoise Charras. *Romantisme noir.* Paris: Herne, 1978.

Barron, Neil, ed. *Horror Literature: A Reader's Guide.* New York: Garland, 1990.

————, ed. *Fantasy and Horror: A Critical and Historical Guide to Literature, Illustration, Film, TV, Radio, and the Internet.* Lanham, MD: Scarecrow Press, 1999.

Bleiler, E.F., ed. *The Guide to Supernatural Fiction: A Full Description of 1,775 Books from 1750 to 1960,* Kent, OH: Kent State University Press, 1983.

————, ed. *Supernatural Fiction Writers.* 2 vols. New York: Charles Scribner's Sons, 1985.

Bloom, Clive, ed. *Gothic Horror: A Reader's Guide from Poe to King and Beyond.* New York: St. Martin's Press, 1998.

Burgess, Michael. *Reference Guide to Science Fiction, Fantasy, and Horror.* Englewood, CO: Libraries Unlimited, 1992.

Clery, E.J., and Robert Miles, eds. *Gothic Documents: A Sourcebook, 1700–1820.* Manchester and New York: Manchester University Press, 2000.

Harwell, Thomas Meade, ed. *The English Gothic Novel: A Miscellany,* 4 vols. Salzburg: Universität Salzburg, 1986.

Magill, Frank N., ed. *Survey of Modern Fantasy Literature.* 5 vols. Englewood Cliffs, NJ: Salem Press, 1983.

Mulvey-Roberts, Marie, ed. *The Handbook to Gothic Literature.* New York: New York University Press, 1998.

Mussell, Kay. *Women's Gothic and Romantic Fiction: A Reference Guide.* Westport, CT: Greenwood Press, 1983.

————. "Gothic Novels." In *Handbook of American Popular Literature.* Ed. M. Thomas Inge. Westport, CT: Greenwood Press, 1988: 157–173.

Norton, Rictor, ed. *Gothic Readings: The First Wave, 1764–1840.* London and New York: Leicester University Press, 2000.

Pringle, David, ed. *St. James Guide to Horror, Ghost, and Gothic Writers.* Preface Dennis Etchison. Detroit: St. James Press, 1998.

Sage, Victor, ed. *The Gothick Novel: A Casebook.* Basingstoke, UK: Macmillan, 1990.

Sage, Victor, and Allan Lloyd Smith, eds. *Modern Gothic: A Reader.* Manchester and New York: Manchester University Press, 1996.

Stevens, David. *The Gothic Tradition* Cambridge Contexts in Literature Series, ed. Adrian Barlow. Cambridge: Cambridge University Press, 2000.

Sullivan, Jack, ed. *The Penguin Encyclopedia of Horror and the Supernatural.* Intro. Jacques Barzun. New York and Harmondsworth, Middlesex, UK: Viking/Penguin, 1986.

Tymn, Marshall, ed. *Horror Literature: A Core Collection and Reference Guide.* New York: R.R. Bowker, 1981.

Vinson, James, and D.L. Kirkpatrick, eds. *Twentieth-Century Romance and Gothic Writers.* Detroit: Gale, 1982.

GENERAL HISTORIES AND STUDIES IN DEFINITION AND THEORY

Aguirre, Manuel. *The Closed Space: Horror Literature and Western Symbolism.* Manchester and New York: Manchester University Press, 1990.

Andriano, Joseph. *Our Ladies of Darkness: Feminine Daemonology in Male Gothic Fiction,* University Park: Pennsylvania State University Press, 1993.

Atwood, Margaret. *Strange Things: The Malevolent North in Canadian Literature*. Oxford: Clarendon Press; New York: Oxford University Press, 1995.

Backus, Margot Gayle. *The Gothic Family Romance: Heterosexuality, Child Sacrifice, and the Anglo-Irish Colonial Order*. Durham, NC: Duke University Press, 1999.

Baldick, Chris. *In Frankenstein's Shadow: Myth, Monstrosity, and Nineteenth-Century Writing*. Oxford: Clarendon Press, 1987.

Bayer-Berenbaum, Linda. *The Gothic Imagination: Expansion in Gothic Literature and Art*. Rutherford, NJ: Fairleigh Dickinson University Press, 1982.

Becker, Susanne. *Gothic Forms of Feminine Fictions*. Manchester and New York: Manchester University Press, 1999.

Bhalla, Alok. *The Cartographers of Hell: Essays on the Gothic Novel and the Social History of England*. New Delhi: Sterling Publishers Private, 1991: New York: APT Books, 1991.

Birkhead, Edith. *The Tale of Terror: A Study of the Gothic Romance* (1921). New York: Russell & Russell, 1963.

Botting, Fred. *Gothic*. London: Routledge, 1996.

Bozzetto, Roger. *Territoires des fantastiques: Des romans gothiques aux récits d'horreur moderne*. Aix-en-Provence: Publications de la Université de Provence, 1998.

Brennan, Matthew C. *The Gothic Psyche: Disintegration and Growth in Nineteenth-Century English Literature*. Columbia, SC: Camden House, 1997.

Breton, André. "Limites non Frontières du Surréalisme." *Nouvelle Revue Française* 48: 1 (1937): 210–211. Rpt. As "Limits Not Frontiers of Surrealism" in *Surrealism* ed. Herbert Read. London: Faber and Faber, 1936: 106–111. University of Pennsylvania Press, 1994.

Briggs, Julia. *Night Visitors: The Rise and Fall of the English Ghost Story*. London: Faber, 1977.

Brissenden, Robert F. *Virtue in Distress: Studies in the Novel of Sentiment from Richardson to Sade*. London: Macmillan, 1974.

Bronfen, Elisabeth. *Over Her Dead Body: Death, Femininity, and the Aesthetic*. Manchester: Manchester University Press, 1992.

Bruhm, Steven. *Gothic Bodies: The Politics of Pain in Romantic Fiction*. Philadelphia: University of Pennsylvania Press, 1994.

Büssing, Sabine. *Aliens in the Home: The Child in Horror Fiction*. New York: Greenwood Press, 1987.

Carnochan, W.B. *Confinement and Flight: An Essay on English Literature of the Eighteenth Century*. Berkeley: University of California Press, 1977.

Carroll, Noel. *The Philosophy of Horror; or, Paradoxes of the Heart*. New York and London: Routledge, 1990.

Carson, James P. "Enlightenment, Popular Culture, and Gothic Fiction." In *The Cambridge Companion to the Eighteenth-Century Novel*. Ed. John Richetti. Cambridge: Cambridge University Press, 1996: 255–276.

Carter, Margaret L. *Specter or Delusion? The Supernatural in Gothic Fiction*. Ann Arbor: UMI Research Press, 1987.

Castle, Terry. *The Female Thermometer: Eighteenth-Century Culture and the Invention of the Uncanny*. New York: Oxford University Press, 1995.

Cavaliero, Glen. *The Supernatural and English Fiction*, New York: Oxford University Press, 1995.

Clemens, Valdine. *The Return of the Repressed: Gothic Horror from The Castle of Otranto to Alien.* Albany: State University of New York Press, 1999.

Clery, E.J. *The Rise of Supernatural Fiction, 1762–1800.* Cambridge and New York: Cambridge University Press, 1995.

———. *Women's Gothic: From Clara Reeve to Mary Shelley.* Horndon, Tavistock, Devon, UK: Northcote House in Association with the British Council, 2000.

Cooke, Arthur. "Some Side-lights on the Theory of Gothic Romance." *Modern Language Quarterly* 12 (1951): 429–436.

Cornwell, Neil. *The Literary Fantastic: From Gothic to Postmodernism.* London: Harvester Wheatsheaf, 1990.

———, ed. *The Gothic-Fantastic in Nineteenth-Century Russian Literature.* Amsterdam and Atlanta, GA: Rodopi, 1999.

Cummiskey, Gary. *The Changing Face of Horror: A Study of the Nineteenth Century French Fantastic Short Story.* New York: Peter Lang, 1992.

Davenport-Hines, Richard. *Gothic: Four Hundred Years of Excess, Horror, Evil, and Ruin.* London: Fourth Estate, 1998.

Day, William Patrick. *In the Circles of Fear and Desire: A Study of Gothic Fantasy.* Chicago: University of Chicago University Press, 1985.

DeLamotte, Eugenia. *Perils of the Night: A Feminist Study of Nineteenth-Century Gothic.* New York: Oxford University Press, 1989.

Edmundson, Mark. *Nightmare on Main Street: Angels, Sadomasochism, and the Culture of Gothic.* Cambridge, MA: Harvard University Press, 1997.

Ellis, Kate Ferguson. *The Contested Castle: Gothic Novels and the Subversion of Domestic Ideology.* Urbana: University of Illinois Press, 1989.

Ellis, Markman. *The History of Gothic Fiction.* Edinburgh: Edinburgh University Press, 2000.

Fiedler, Leslie A. *Love and Death in the American Novel* New York: Criterion, 1960.

Foster, James R. *History of the Pre-Romantic Novel in England.* New York: Modern Language Association of America, 1949.

Fowler, Douglas. "The Pleasures of Terror." *Extrapolation* 28 (1987): 75–86.

Garber, Frederick. "Meaning and Mode in Gothic Fiction." In *Racism in the Eighteenth Century.* Ed. Harold E. Pagliaro. Cleveland: Press of Case Western Reserve University, 1973: 155–169.

Garrett, John. "The Eternal Appeal of the Gothic." *Sphinx: A Magazine of Literature and Society* 2:4 (1977): 1–7.

Gaull, Marilyn. *English Romanticism: The Human Context.* New York: Norton, 1988.

———. "The Profession of Romanticism: The Caverns Measureless and the Sunless Sea." *The Wordsworth Circle* 27 (1996): 51–53.

Geary, Robert F. *The Supernatural in Gothic Fiction: Horror, Belief, and Literary Change.* Lampeter, Dyfed, Wales: Edwin Mellen Press, 1992.

Goddu, Teresa A. *Gothic America: Narrative, History, and Nation.* New York: Columbia University Press, 1997.

Gross, Louis S. *Redefining the American Gothic: From Wieland to Day of the Dead.* Ann Arbor: UMI Research Press, 1989.

Grudin, Peter D. *The Demon Lover: The Theme of Demoniality in English and Continental Fiction of the Late Eighteen and Early Nineteenth Centuries.* New York: Garland, 1987.

Hadley, Michael. *The Undiscovered Genre: A Search for the German Gothic Novel*. Berne and Las Vegas: Peter Lang, 1978.

Haggerty, George E. *Gothic Fiction/Gothic Form*. University Park: Pennsylvania State University Press, 1989.

———. "The Gothic Novel, 1764–1824." In *The Columbia History of the British Novel*. Ed. John Richetti. New York: Columbia University Press, 1994: 200–246.

Halttunen, Karen. *Murder Most Foul: The Killer and the American Gothic Imagination*. Cambridge, MA: Harvard University Press, 1998.

Hart, Francis R. "The Experience of Character in the English Gothic Novel." In *Experience in the Novel*. Ed. Roy Harvey Pearce. New York: Columbia University Press, 1968: 83–105.

Harwell, Thomas Meade. "Toward a Gothic Metaphysic: Gothic Parts." *Publications of the Arkansas Philological Association* 12:2 (1986): 33–43.

Heiland, Donna. *Gothic Novels: A Feminist Introduction*. Oxford: Blackwell, 2000.

Heller, Terry. *The Delights of Terror: An Aesthetics of the Tale of Terror*. Urbana: University of Illinois Press, 1987.

Hendershot, Cyndy. *The Animal Within: Masculinity and the Gothic*. Ann Arbor: University of Michigan Press, 1998.

Hennessy, Brendan. *The Gothic Novel*. Harlow: Longman for the British Council, 1978.

Hoeveler, Diane L. *Gothic Feminism: The Professionalization of Gender from Charlotte Smith to the Brontës*. University Park: Pennsylvania State University Press, 1998.

Hogle, Jerrold E. "The Restless Labyrinth: Cryptonomy in the Gothic Novel." *Arizona Quarterly* 36 (1980): 330–358.

Howard, Jacqueline. *Reading Gothic Fiction: A Bakhtinian Approach*. Oxford: Clarendon Press; New York: Oxford University Press 1994.

Howells, Coral Ann. *Love, Mystery, and Misery: Feeling in Gothic Fiction* London: Athlone Press, 1978; Atlantic Highlands, NJ: Humanities Press, 1978.

———. "The Gothic Way of Death in English Fiction, 1790–1820." *British Journal for Eighteenth-Century Studies* 5 (1982): 207–215.

Hume, Robert D. "Gothic versus Romantic: A Revaluation of the Gothic Novel." *Publications of the Modern Language Association* 84 (1969): 282–290.

Hurley, Kelly. *The Gothic Body: Sexuality, Materialism, and Degeneration at the Fin de Siècle*. New York: Cambridge University Press, 1996.

Ingebretsen, Edward J. *Maps of Heaven, Maps of Hell: Religious Terror as Memory from the Puritans to Stephen King*. Armonk, NY: M.E. Sharpe, 1996.

Jarrett, David. *The Gothic Form in Fiction and Its Relation to History*. Winchester Research Papers in the Humanities, no. 5. Winchester: King Alfred's College, 1980.

Just, Martin-Christoph. *Visions of Evil: Origins of Violence in the English Gothic Novel*. Frankfurt am Main and New York: Peter Lang, 1997.

Karl, Frederick R. "Gothic, Gothicism, Gothicists." In *The Adversary Literature: The English Novel in the Eighteenth Century: A Study in Genre*. New York: Farrar, Straus, & Giroux, 1974: 235–274.

Keech, James M. "The Survival of the Gothic Response." *Studies in the Novel* 6 (1974): 130–144.

Kiely, Robert. *The Romantic Novel in England*. Cambridge, MA: Harvard University Press, 1972.

Kilgour, Maggie. *The Rise of the Gothic Novel*. London and New York: Routledge, 1995.

Klein, Jürgen. *Der gotische Roman und die Ästhetik des Bösen.* Darmstadt: Wissenschaftliche Buchgesellschaft, 1975.

Kristeva, Julia. *Powers of Horror: An Essay on Abjection.* Trans. Leon S. Roudiez. New York: Columbia University Press, 1982.

Le Brun, Annie. *Les Châteaux de la subversion.* Paris: J.-J. Pauvert aux Éditions Garnier Frères, 1982.

Le Tellier, Robert Ignatius. *An Intensifying Vision of Evil: The Gothic Novel (1764–1820) as a Self-contained Literary Cycle.* Salzburg: Institut für Anglistik und Amerikanistik, Universität Salzburg, 1980.

Lévy, Maurice. *Le Roman "gothique" anglais, 1764–1824.* Toulouse: Association des Publications de la Faculté des Lettres et Sciences Humaines de Toulouse, 1968.

———. *Images du roman noir.* Paris: Eric Losfeld, 1973.

———. "Le Roman gothique: Genre anglais." *Europe: Revue Littéraire Mensuelle* 659 (March 1984): 5–13.

Lewis, Paul. "Fearful Lessons: The Didacticism of the Early Gothic Novel." *College Language Association Journal* 23 (1980): 470–484.

———. "Mysterious Laughter: Humor and Fear in Gothic Fiction." *Genre* 14 (1981): 309–327.

Lloyd Smith, Allan Gardner. *Uncanny American Fiction: Medusa's Face.* New York: St. Martin's Press, 1989.

Lord, Michel. *En quête du roman gothique québécois, 1837–1860: Tradition littéraire et imaginaire romanesque.* Quebec: Centre de Recherche en Littérature Québécoise, Université Laval, 1985.

Lovecraft, H.P. *Supernatural Horror in Literature* (1945). New York: Dover Publications, 1973.

Lyndenberg, Robin. "Gothic Architecture and Fiction: A Survey of Critical Responses." *Centennial Review* 22 (1978): 95–109.

MacAndrew, Elizabeth. *The Gothic Tradition in Fiction.* New York: Columbia University Press, 1979.

Malchow, Howard L. *Gothic Images of Race in Nineteenth-Century Britain.* Stanford, CA: Stanford University Press, 1996.

Malin, Irving. *New American Gothic.* Preface Harry T. Moore. Carbondale: Southern Illinois University Press, 1962.

Massé, Michelle A. *In the Name of Love: Women, Masochism, and the Gothic.* Ithaca, NY: Cornell University Press, 1992.

May, Leland C. *Parodies of the Gothic Novel.* New York: Arno Press, 1980.

McGuire, Karen. "Gothicism." In *Encyclopedia of Romanticism: Culture in Britain, 1780s–1830s.* Ed. Laura Dabundo. New York: Garland, 1992: 239–243.

Meindl, Dieter. *American Fiction and the Metaphysics of the Grotesque.* Columbia: University of Missouri Press, 1996.

Milbank, Alison. *Daughters of the House: Modes of the Gothic in Victorian Fiction.* New York: St. Martin's Press, 1992.

Miles, Robert. *Gothic Writing, 1750–1820: A Genealogy.* London and New York: Routledge, 1993.

Mishra, Vijay C. *The Gothic Sublime.* Albany: SUNY Press, 1994.

Moers, Ellen. *Literary Women.* Garden City, NY: Doubleday, 1976.

Morgan, Jack. "Toward an Organic Theory of the Gothic: Conceptualizing Horror." *Journal of Popular Culture* 32:3 (1998): 59–80.

Morse, David B. "Gothic Sublimity." *New Literary History* 16 (1985): 299–319.

Murphy, Agnes Genevieve. *Banditry, Chivalry, and Terror in German Fiction, 1790–1830*. Chicago: University of Chicago Libraries, 1935.

Mussell, Kay. *Fantasy and Reconciliation: Contemporary Formulas of Women's Romance Writing*. Westport, CT: Greenwood Press, 1984.

Napier, Elizabeth R. *The Failure of Gothic: Problems of Disjunction in an Eighteenth-Century Literary Form*. New York: Oxford University Press, 1986.

Nelson, Lowry, Jr. "Night Thoughts on the Gothic Novel." *Yale Review* 52 (1963): 236–257.

Nochimson, Martha. "Gothic Novel." In *Critical Survey of Long Fiction*. Ed. Frank Magill. Englewood Cliffs, NJ: Salem Press, 1983: 8: 3121–3131.

Northey, Margot Elizabeth. *The Haunted Wilderness: The Gothic and Grotesque in Canadian Fiction*. Toronto: University of Toronto Press, 1976.

Novak, Maximillian E. "Gothic Fiction and the Grotesque." *Novel: A Forum on Fiction* 13 (1979): 50–67.

Paizis, George. *Love and the Novel: The Poetics and Politics of Romantic Fiction*, New York: St. Martin's Press, 1998.

Palmer, Paulina. *Lesbian Gothic: Transgressive Fictions*. London and New York: Cassell, 1999.

Paragon Summaries: The Gothic Novel. Leeds, UK: Paragon Press, 1999.

Paulson, Ronald. "Gothic Fiction and the French Revolution." *ELH* 48 (1981): 532–554.

Penzoldt, Peter. *The Supernatural in Fiction* (1952). New York: Humanities Press, 1965.

Platzner, Robert L. *The Metaphysical Novel in England*. New York: Arno Press, 1980.

Porte, Joel. "In the Hands of an Angry God: Religious Terror in Gothic Fiction." In *The Gothic Imagination: Essays in Dark Romanticism*. Ed. G.R. Thompson. Pullman: Washington State University Press, 1974: 42–64.

Praz, Mario. *The Romantic Agony* (1933). Trans. Angus Davidson. New York: Meridian, 1960.

Prungnaud, Joëlle. *Gothique et décadence: Recherches sur la continuité d'un mythe et d'un genre au XIXe siècle en Grande-Bretagne et en France*. Paris: Honoré Champion, 1997.

Punter, David. *The Literature of Terror: A History of Gothic Fictions from 1765 to the Present Day*. London and New York: Longman, 1980. Rpt. in 2 vols. London and New York: Longman, 1996.

Railo, Eino. *The Haunted Castle: A Study of the Elements of English Romanticism* (1927). New York: Humanities Press, 1964.

Rajan, Tilottama. *Dark Interpreter: The Discourse of Romanticism*. Ithaca: Cornell University Press, 1986.

Rieger, James. *The Mutiny Within: The Heresies of* Percy Bysshe Shelley. New York: George Braziller, 1967.

Ringe, Donald A. *American Gothic: Imagination and Reason in Nineteenth-Century Fiction*. Lexington: University Press of Kentucky, 1982.

Ringel, Faye. *New England's Gothic Literature: History and Folklore of the Supernatural from the Seventeenth through the Twentieth Centuries*. Lewiston, NY: Edwin Mellen Press, 1995.

Roberts, Bette B. *The Gothic Romance: Its Appeal to Women Writers and Readers in Late Eighteenth-Century England*. New York: Arno Press, 1980.

Robillard, Douglas, ed. *American Supernatural Fiction: From Edith Wharton to the*

Weird Tales Writers. Garland Studies in Nineteenth-Century American Literature, no. 6. New York: Garland, 1996.

Ruddick, William. "The Gothic Novel." In *A Handbook to English Romanticism*: Ed. Jean Raimond and J.R. Watson New York: St. Martin's Press, 1992: 184–193.

Sage, Victor. *Horror Fiction in the Protestant Tradition*. New York: St. Martin's Press, 1988.

———. "Gothic Novel." In *Encyclopedia of the Novel*. Ed. Paul Schellinger. Chicago and London: Fitzroy Dearborn, 1998: 1: 497–501.

Scarborough, Dorothy. *The Supernatural in Modern English Fiction* (1917). New York: Octagon, 1967.

Schmitt, Cannon. *Alien Nation: Nineteenth-Century Gothic Fictions and English Nationality*. Philadelphia: University of Pennsylvania Press, 1997.

Sedgwick, Eve Kosofsky. *The Coherence of Gothic Conventions*. New York: Arno Press, 1980.

Showalter, Elaine. "American Female Gothic." In *Sister's Choice: Tradition and Change in American Women's Writing*. Oxford: Clarendon Press, 1991: 127–144.

Simpson, Mark S. *The Russian Gothic Novel and Its British Antecedents*. Columbus, OH: Slavica Publishers, 1986.

Smith, Andrew. *Gothic Radicalism: Literature, Philosophy, and Psychoanalysis in the Nineteenth Century*. New York: St. Martin's Press, 2000, Houndmills, Basingstoke, Hampshire, UK: Macmillan, 2000.

Sousa, Maria Leonor Machado de. *A Literatura "negra" ou "de terror" en Portugal (seculos XVIII e XIX)*. Lisbon: Editorial Novaera, 1978.

Stevens, David. *The Gothic Tradition*. Cambridge: Cambridge University Press, 2000.

Sullivan, Jack. *Elegant Nightmares: The English Ghost Story from Le Fanu to Blackwood*. Athens: Ohio University Press, 1978.

Summers, Montague. *The Gothic Quest: A History of the Gothic Novel* (1938). New York: Russell & Russell, 1964.

Tarr, Sister Mary Muriel. *Catholicism in Gothic Fiction in England: A Study of the Nature and Function of Catholic Materials in Gothic Fiction in England (1762–1820)*. Washington, DC: Catholic University of America Press, 1946; Rpt. Ann Arbor: University Microfilms International, 1980.

"The Terrorist System of Novel, Writing." *Monthly Magazine* 4 (August 1797): 102–104.

Thompson, G.R. "Introduction: Gothic Fiction of the Romantic Age: Context and Mode." In *Romantic Gothic Tales, 1790–1840*. New York: Harper & Row, 1979: 1–54.

Thorslev, Peter, Jr. *The Byronic Hero: Types and Prototypes*. Minneapolis: University of Minnesota Press, 1962.

Todorov, Tzvetan. *The Fantastic: A Structural Approach to a Literary Genre*. Trans. Richard Howard. Ithaca: Cornell University Press, 1973.

Tompkins, J.M.S. "The Gothic Romance." In *The Popular Novel in England, 1770–1800* (1932). London: Methuen, 1969: 243–295.

Tracy, Ann B. *Patterns of Fear in the Gothic Novel, 1790–1830*. New York: Arno Press, 1980.

Tropp, Martin. *Images of Fear: How Horror Stories Helped Shape Modern Culture, 1818–1918*. Jefferson, NC: McFarland, 1990.

Twitchell, James B. *Dreadful Pleasures: An Anatomy of Modern Horror*. New York: Oxford University Press, 1985.

Varma, Devendra P. *The Gothic Flame: Being a History of the Gothic Novel in England: Its Origins, Efflorescence, Disintegration, and Residuary Influences* (1957). Foreword Herbert Read, intro. J.M.S. Tompkins. New York: Russell & Russell, 1966.

Varnado, S.L. *Haunted Presence: The Numinous in Gothic Fiction*. Tuscaloosa: University of Alabama Press, 1987.

Voller, Jack G. *The Supernatural Sublime: The Metaphysics of Terror in Anglo-American Romanticism*. De Kalb: Northern Illinois University Press, 1994.

Watt, James. *Contesting the Gothic: Fiction, Genre, and Cultural Conflict, 1764–1832*. Cambridge, and New York: Cambridge University Press, 1999.

Weiss, Fredric. *The Antic Spectre: Satire in Early Gothic Novels*. New York: Arno Press, 1980.

Wiesenfarth, Joseph. *Gothic Manners and the Classic English Novel*. Madison: University of Wisconsin Press, 1988.

Wilczynski, Marek. *The Phantom and the Abyss: Gothic Fiction in America and Aesthetics of the Sublime 1798–1856*. Frankfort and New York: Peter Lang, 1999.

Williams, Anne. *Art of Darkness: A Poetics of Gothic*. Chicago: University of Chicago Press, 1995.

Winter, Kari J. *Subjects of Slavery, Agents of Change: Women and Power in Gothic Novels and Slave Narratives 1790–1865*. Athens: University of Georgia Press, 1992.

Wolstenholme, Susan. *Gothic (Re)visions: Writing Women as Readers*. Albany: State University of New York Press, 1993.

ESSAY COLLECTIONS DEDICATED TO THE GOTHIC

Byron, Glennis, and David Punter, eds. *Spectral Readings: Towards a Gothic Geography*. New York: St. Martin's Press, 1999.

Docherty, Brian, ed. *American Horror Fiction from Brockden Brown to Stephen King*. New York: St. Martin's Press, 1990.

Duperray, Max, ed. *Le Roman noir anglais dit gothique*. Paris: Ellipses, 2000.

Fleenor, Juliann, ed. *The Female Gothic*. Montreal: Eden Press, 1983.

Graham, Kenneth W., ed. *Gothic Fictions: Prohibition/Transgression*. New York: AMS Press, 1989.

Grunenberg, Christoph, ed. *Gothic: Transmutations of Horror in Late Twentieth Century Art*. Cambridge, MA: MIT Press, 1997.

Kerr, Howard, John W. Crowley, and Charles L. Crow, eds. *The Haunted Dusk: American Supernatural Fiction, 1820–1920*. Athens: University of Georgia Press, 1983.

Lloyd Smith, Allan, and Victor Sage, eds. *Gothick Origins and Innovations*. Costerus New Series 91. Amsterdam and Atlanta, GA: Rodopi, 1994.

Magistrale, Tony, and Michael A. Morrison, eds. *A Dark Night's Dreaming: Contemporary American Horror Fiction*. Columbia: University of South Carolina Press, 1996.

Martin, Robert K, and Eric Savoy, eds. *American Gothic: New Interventions in a National Narrative*. Iowa City: University of Iowa Press, 1998.

Mogen, David, Scott P. Sanders, and Joanne B. Karpinski, eds. *Frontier Gothic: Terror*

and Wonder at the Frontier in American Literature. Rutherford, NJ: Fairleigh
    Dickinson University Press, 1993.
Punter, David, ed. *A Companion to the Gothic.* Blackwell Companions to Literature and
    Culture. Oxford and Malden, MA: Blackwell, 2000.
Redt, Joe, ed. *Niekas: Dark Fantasy; Essays on Gothic and Modern Horror Fiction.*
    Center Harbor, NH: Niekas Publications, 1998.
Thompson, G.R., ed. *The Gothic Imagination: Essays in Dark Romanticism.* Pullman:
    Washington State University Press, 1974.
Tinkler-Villani, Valeria, Peter Davidson, and Jane Stevenson, eds. *Exhibited by Candle-
    light: Sources and Developments in the Gothic Tradition.* DQR Studies in Lit-
    erature 16. Amsterdam and Atlanta, GA: Rodopi, 1995.

JOURNALS AND SPECIAL JOURNAL ISSUES ON THE GOTHIC

ESQ: A Journal of the American Renaissance 18:1–2 (1972). "The Gothic Tradition in
    Nineteenth-Century American Literature." Ed. Richard P. Benton.
Europe: Revue Littéraire Mensuelle 659 (March 1984).
Gothic Studies. Published by Manchester University Press for the International Gothic
    Association. Editor-in-Chief, Robert Miles. Editor, William Hughes.
Gothic: The Review of Supernatural Horror Fiction. Publisher, Gary W. Crawford. Baton
    Rouge: Gothic Press. First issued in June 1979. Suspended publication after two
    numbers, Replaced by a chapbook series appearing irregularly.
Modern Fiction Studies 46:3 (Fall 2000). "The Gothic and Modernism." Ed. John Paul
    Riquelme.

WEB SITES AND INTERNET RESOURCES

Gothic Literature. ⟨http://www2.gasou.edu/facstaff/dougt/gothic.html⟩. Maintained by
    Douglass Thomson.
The Gothic Literature Page. ⟨http://members.aol.com/iamudolpho/basic.html⟩. Main-
    tained by Franz Potter.
The Gothic Press. ⟨http://www.gothicpress.com/⟩. Maintained by Gary W. Crawford.
The International Gothic Association. ⟨http://www-sul.stanford.edu/mirrors/romnet/iga/⟩.
The Literary Gothic. ⟨http://www.Litgothic.com/⟩. Maintained by Jack G. Voller.
Materials for Gothic Studies. ⟨http://www.engl.virginia.edu/~enec981/Group/Title.html⟩.
    Maintained by The University of Virginia.
Romanticism on the Net. ⟨http://users.ox.ac.uk/~scat0385/⟩. Maintained by Michael
    Eberle-Sinatra.
The Sickly Taper: Dedicated to Gothic Bibliography. ⟨http://www.toolcity.net/~ffrank/
    Index.html⟩. Maintained by Fred Frank.

INDEX OF AUTHORS AND TITLES

Page numbers in **bold type** refer to author entries.

The Abbess of St. Hilda: A Dismal, Dreadful, Horrid Story! (unsigned), 135

The Abbot (Scott), 134

Abdallah, oder das furchtbare Opfer [Abdallah, or the Horrible Sacrifice] (Tieck), 429, 430, 431, 432, 435

Abellino der grosse Bandit (Zschokke), 254

"Die Abenteuer der Silvester-Nacht" [The Adventures of New Year's Eve] (Hoffmann), 177, 180

Absalom, Absalom! (Faulkner), 176

"Accomplished Desires" (Oates), 303

"Account of German Drama" (Schiller), 383

"Account of Some Strange Disturbances in Aungier Street" (LeFanu), 248

"The Accursed Inhabitants of the House of Bly" (Oates), 308

Adelgitha; or, The Fruits of a Single Error. A Tragedy in Five Acts (Lewis), 254

Adelmorn, the Outlaw: A Romantic Drama in Five Acts (Lewis), 149, 254, 256

"An Adventure at Brownville" (Bierce), 65

"The Advenure of My Aunt" (Irving), 195

"The Adventure of My Uncle" (Irving), 195

"The Adventure of the German Student" (Irving), 195, 197, 200, 201

"The Adventure of the Mason" (Irving), 195

"The Adventure of the Mysterious Picture" (Irving), 195

"The Adventure of the Mysterious Stranger" (Irving), 195

Adventures of a Novelist (Atherton), 21

The Affecting History of Louisa, the Wandering Maniac; or, "The Lady of the Hay-Stack." (unsigned), 135

After Dark (Collins), 90, 94

Aikin, Dr. John, **1–6**

Ainsworth, William Harrison, **7–11**, 95, 250, 268

"Ai to kon' in" [Love and Marriage] (Kyoka), 228

Akinari, Ueda, **12–19**, 225, 226

"Alastor, or The Spirit of Solitude" (Shelley), 402, 406

Albina, Countess of Raimond (Crowley), 148, 156

Alcott, Louisa May, 175

Alexis; ou, La Maisonnette dans les bois
    [Alexis; or, The Cottage in the Woods]
    (Ducray-Duminil), 116, 117, 118, 119
Alfonso, King of Castile (Lewis), 254
*The Alhambra: A Series of Tales of
    Sketches of the Moors and Spaniards*
    (Irving), 195, 200
"Alice Doane's Appeal" (Hawthorne),
    175
All the Good People I've Left Behind
    (Oates), 303
*Almagro and Claude; or, Monastic
    Murder Exemplified in the Dreadful
    Doom of an Unfortunate Nun*
    (unsigned), 135, 144
"The Altar of the Dead" (James), 202,
    206, 209
"Alternate Thoughts from Underground"
    (Atwood), 28
*Les Amans malheureux; ou, Les Comte
    de Comminge* [The Unfortunate Lovers;
    or, The Count of Comminge] (Baculard
    d'Arnaud), 48, 50, 51
*Ambrose Bierce and the Queen of
    Spades*, 61
Ambrosio; or The Monk: a romance
    (Lewis), 254
American Appetites (Oates), 304, 306
*The Ancestral Footstep: Outlines of an
    English Romance* (Hawthorne), 165,
    167, 175
Andrews, Miles Peter, 147, 164
Angelina; or, Wolcot Castle (Goldsmith),
    148, 158
"The Angel of the Odd" (Poe), 330, 335
*The Angels of Mons, the Bowmen, and
    Other Legends of the War* (Machen),
    278
The Antiquary (Scott), 380, 381, 386, 387
"Apt Pupil" (King), 212, 221
*Arabian Nights. See The Thousand and
    One Arabian Nights*
*An Arabian Tale, from an Unpublished
    Manuscript, with notes Critical and
    Explanatory* [*Vathek*] (Beckford), 53
"Arasmanes, The Seeker" (Bulwer-
    Lytton), 83

Armadale (Collins), 90, 92, 98
Arnold, Matthew, 280, 415
*Arthur Mervyn; or, Memoirs of the Year
    1793* (Brown), 76,79, 80, 173, 263
"The Assailant" (Oates), 303
The Assassins: A Book of Hours (Oates),
    303
The Assignation (Oates), 304
"The Assignation" (Poe), 330
"The Astrologer's Prediction; or, The
    Maniac's Fate" (unsigned), 139
The Atheist's Tragedy (Tourneur), 163
At the Mountains of Madness (Lovecraft),
    275
Atherton, Gertrude, **20–23**
Atwood, Margaret, **24–32**
Auriol; or, The Elixir of Life (Ainsworth),
    7
Austen, Jane, 21, 30, 32, **33–47**, 69, 75,
    247, 357, 359, 387, 388, 447
"The Authentic Narrative of a Haunted
    House" (LeFanu), 248
Die Automata [Automatons] (Hoffmann),
    177, 179
*The Avenger; or, Sicilian Vespers, A
    Romance of the Thirteenth Century,
    Not Inapplicable to the Nineteenth*
    (unsigned), 135
Azemia (Beckford as "Jaquetta Jenks"),
    53, 55, 59

The Bachman Books: Four Early Novels
    (King), 213
Bacon, Sir Francis, 226
Baculard d'Arnaud, François Thomas
    Marie de, **48–52**, 116, 117, 242, 246
Bag of Bones (King), 213, 215
"The Bagman's Story" ["The Queer
    Chair"] ["Why Haunt the Inns?"]
    (Dickens), 104
Baillie, Joanna, 147, 151, 152, 158, 162,
    164
Baillie, John, 356
"The Ball" (Odoevsky), 321
"The Balloon Hoax" (Poe), 336
*The Banditti of the Forest: or, The
    Mysterious Dagger* (signed "C."), 135

Banditti; or, Love in a Labyrinth (O'Keefe), 150

Baraka, Amiri, 301

Barbauld, Anna Laetitia Aikin, **1–6**, 136, 138, 351

"The Barber of Duncow" (Hogg), 194

Barker, Clive, 221

Barnaby Rudge: A Tale of the Riots of 'Eighty' (Dickens), 104, 105

Barnett, C. Z., 147

Baron Fitzallan (Legge), 134

"The Baron of Grogzwig" (Dickens), 104, 107

Barrett, C. F., 144, 145

Barrington, George, 133

"Bartleby the Scrivener: A Story of Wall Street" (Melville), 290, 292, 294

Batilde; ou, L'Héroisme de l'amour, anecdote historique [Batilde; or, The Heroism of Love, Historical Anecdote] (Baculard d'Arnaud), 48

Baudelaire, Charles, 226, 230, 286

"The Beast in the Jungle" (James), 202, 207, 209

Beautiful Losers (Cohen), 25

Beckford, William, **53–59**, 131, 140, 153, 169, 291, 332, 339, 355, 393, 430, 437, 446

Behn, Aphra, 247

The Bell and the Fog and Other Stories (Atherton), 20, 21, 22, 23

"The Bell Tower" (Melville), 290, 291, 294

Bellamy, Thomas, 138

Bellefleur (Oates), 304, 308, 309, 312, 313

Beloved (Morrison), 295, 298, 299, 300, 301, 302

"Benito Cereno" (Melville), 290, 291, 292, 294

"Berenice" (Poe), 272, 330, 333, 336, 337

"Die Bergwerke zu Falun" [The Mines at Falun] (Hoffmann), 177, 182, 432

Bertram; or, The Castle of St. Aldobrand (Maturin), 149, 151, 152, 158, 159, 160, 162, 283, 284, 285, 286, 288, 289

Bethlem Gabor, Lord of Transylvania; or, The Man Hating Palatine: An Historical Drama in Three Acts (Burk), 125

The Better Sort (James), 202

"Beyond the Wall" (Bierce), 64

Bierce, Ambrose Gwinett, 22, **60–68**, 174, 210, 264, 268, 271, 323, 335

Billy Budd, Foretopman (Melville), 290, 291, 356

Biographical Memoirs of Extraordinary Painters (Beckford), 57

Birch, Samuel, 147

"Bird of Paradise" (Akinari), 12

Birney, Earle, 25

"The Birthmark" (Hawthorne), 165, 172, 279

"The Biter Bit" (Collins), 90, 91

The Black Band (Braddon), 91

The Black Book (Harris), 298

"The Black Canon of Elmham; or, St. Edmond's Eve" (Lewis), 402

The Black Castle; or, The Spectre of the Forest (unsigned), 135

"The Black Cat" (Poe), 308, 323, 330, 333, 341

The Black Dwarf (Scott), 380

The Black Forest (Birch), 147

The Black Forest; or, The Cavern of Horrors (unsigned), 135

"The Black Spider" (M'Kenny), 139

The Black Valley; or, The Castle of Rosenberg (unsigned), 144

Black Water (Oates), 304

Blackwood, Algernon, 271

Blair, Hugh, 356, 362

Blake, William, 263, 316, 326, 366

Blavatsky, Madame Elena Petrovna, 89

Bleak House (Dickens), 92, 104, 105, 106, 109, 113, 114

The Bleeding Nun; or, Raymond and Agnes (unsigned), 159, 254

A Blighted Life (Rosina Bulwer-Lytton), 85, 88

The Blithedale Romance (Hawthorne), 175

Blonde (Oates), 304, 307

"Der Blonde Eckbert" [Blond Eckbert]
  (Tieck), 429, 430, 431, 432, 434, 435,
  436
A Bloodsmoor Romance (Oates), 304,
  308, 309, 313, 314
"The Bloodstained Bridal Gown; or
  Xavier Kilgarvan's Last Case" (Oates),
  311
"The Bloodstained Robe" (Akinari), 12
The Bloody Hand; or, The Fatal Cup, A
  Tale of Horror (unsigned), 135, 144
"Blow Up the Brig!" (Collins), 91, 96
"The Blue Hood" (Akinari), 12, 16
Boaden, James, 147, 151, 157, 164
Boccaccio, Giovanni, 368
"Bodies" (Oates), 303
Bodily Harm (Atwood), 31
The Body-Snatcher (Stevenson), 412, 415
Boehme, Jacob, 431
"The Bold Dragoon" (Irving), 195
"Bon Bon" (Poe), 330
The Bond (Gore), 152
The Book of Common Prayer, 62
"The Border-Line" (Lawrence), 233, 238,
  239
"Borrhomeo the Astrologer" (LeFanu),
  248
Bosch, Hieronymus, 259
"The Bottle Imp" (Stevenson), 412, 413,
  416
Boutet de Monvel, Jacques-Marie, 50,
  254
Bowers, Hans Heinz, 271
"The Bowmen" (Machen), 281
Bracebridge Hall, or the Humorists
  (Irving), 195, 199
Braddon, Mary Elizabeth, 88, 91
The Bravo of Venice, a Romance:
  Translated from the German (Lewis),
  254
The Bridal of Triermain (Scott), 387
The Bride of Lammermoor (Scott), 380
"The Bride of the Grave" (Tieck), 429
"The Bride of the Isles: A Tale Founded
  on the Popular Legend of the
  Vampire" (unsigned), 139
Brontë, Anne, 73
Brontë, Charlotte, 69–75, 352, 356, 411

Brontë, Emily, 69–75, 352, 356, 411
Broster, John, 361
Brown, Charles Brockden, 76–82, 118,
  126, 130, 173, 174, 222, 263, 266,
  268, 269, 327, 328, 332, 356, 370,
  400, 406
The Brownie of Bodsbeck, and Other
  Tales (Hogg), 185, 189, 190, 192
"The Brownie of the Black Haggs"
  (Hogg), 189
Bulwer-Lytton, Edward, 83–89, 91, 106,
  250
Bürger, Gottfried Augustus, 2, 382, 383
"The Burial of the Rats" (Stoker), 420,
  421, 423
Burk, John, 125, 129
Burke, Edmund, 2, 65, 130, 253, 351,
  356, 357, 392, 396, 409, 410, 438
Burke, Miss, 152
Burning Your Boats (Carter), 30
Burns, Robert, 186, 193
"A Bus Along St. Clair: December"
  (Atwood), 28
Byron, George Gordon Lord, 55, 70, 100,
  102, 103, 148, 149, 154, 159, 160,
  256, 284, 285, 322, 344, 345, 346,
  347, 348, 352, 375, 382, 392, 395, 398
"By the River" (Oates), 306

C. (initial), 135
Calderón De La Barca, Pedro, 404
Caleb Williams [Things As They Are; or,
  The Adventures of Caleb Williams]
  (Godwin), 81, 125, 126, 127, 129, 130,
  131, 132, 148, 166, 400
Caleb Williams; with a Life of the Author
  by Mrs. Shelley (Godwin), 125
"The Call of Cthulhu" (Lovecraft), 274
"Can. Lit." (Birney), 25
Canning, George, 384
Can Such Things Be? (Bierce), 60, 66
The Canterbury Tales (Lee), 241, 245,
  246
"The Captain's Doll" (Lawrence), 233
"The Captain's Last Love" (Collins), 90
The Captive: A Monodrama or Tragic
  Scene (Lewis), 149, 152
Captive of the Banditti; A Terrific Tale

Concluded (Drake and "A. N. Other"),
139

Carlyle, Thomas, 113, 373, 429, 431

The Carmelite (Cumberland), 148

"Carmilla" (LeFanu), 249, 251, 253

"The Carp That Came In from My
Dream" (Akinari), 12

Carr, George Charles, 148

Carrie (King), 212, 213, 222, 223

Carter, Angela, 30

The Case of Charles Dexter Ward, 270,
273, 274, 275

"The Cask of Amontillado" (Poe), 331,
333, 338, 339

Castle Connor: An Irish Story (Reeve),
362

The Castle De Warrenne: A Romance
(unsigned), 139, 142

The Castle of Constanzo (unsigned), 138

The Castle of Indolence (Thomson), 199

*The Castle of Lydenberg; or, The History
of Raymond and Agnes, with the Story
of the Bleeding Nun; And the Method
by which the Wandering Jew Quieted
the Nun's Troubled Spirit* (unsigned),
135

*The Castle of Montabino; or, The
Orphan Sisters* (Wilkinson), 144, 145

*The Castle of Montreuil and Barre; or,
The Histories of the Marquis La Brun
and the Baron La Marche, the Late
Inhabitants and Proprietors of the Two
Castles: A Gothic Story* (unsigned),
135

The Castle of Ollada (Lathom), 40

The Castle of Otranto (Kemble), 149

The Castle of Otranto: A Gothic Story
(Walpole), 18, 51, 118, 132, 135, 137,
149, 151, 152, 154, 155, 156, 162,
163, 173, 181, 186, 246, 361, 362,
363, 409, 437, 438, 439, 440, 441,
444, 445, 446, 447

The Castle of St. Gerald (unsigned), 135

"The Castle of the King" (Stoker), 420,
421, 424

The Castle of Wolfenbach (Parsons), 33,
38, 44, 46

*The Castles of Athlin and Dunbayne: A
Highland Story* (Radcliffe), 135, 349,
353, 358

*The Castle Spectre. A Drama in Five
Acts* (Lewis), 143, 149, 151, 152, 157,
158, 162, 254, 256, 258, 383

The Castle Spectre; or, Family Horrors
(Wilkinson), 144

The Castle Tower [Tenshu monogatari]
(Kyoka), 225, 230

"The Cauldron of Kibitsu" (Akinari), 12,
15

Caunter, John Hobart, 125

The Cave of St. Sidwell: A Romance
(signed "E. F."), 138, 142

*The Cavern of Horrors; or, Miseries of
Miranda: A Neapolitan Tale*
(unsigned), 135

Celestina (Smith), 408, 410, 411

The Cenci (Shelley), 150, 151, 159, 160,
161, 399, 400, 406

"The Chain of Destiny" (Stoker), 420

Chamberlain, Frederick, 133

Chamisso, Adelbert von, 180

Chapman, M., 133

"A Chapter in the History of a Tyrone
Family" (LeFanu), 248

"A Chapter on Dreams" (Stevenson),
414, 418

"Charivari" (Atwood), 27

*The Chase and William and Helen: Two
Ballads, from the German of Gottfried
Augustus Bürger* (Scott), 380, 381

*La Château des Appenins; ou Le
Fantôme vivant* (Pixierecourt), 117

Chekhov, Anton, 307

Chesnutt, Charles, 294

Chetwynd Calverlly (Ainsworth), 8

"Chickamauga" (Bierce), 63

The Children of the Abbey (Roche), 46

"The Children of the Corn" (King), 212,
223

The Children of the Pool (Machen), 281

"The Child That Went with the Fairies"
(LeFanu), 248

Childwold (Oates), 303

"Chimera" [Kecho] (Kyoka), 225, 228

Les choses comme elles sont; ou, Les aventures de Caleb Williams [Things As They Are; or, The Adventures of Caleb Williams] (Godwin), 125
"Christabel" (Coleridge), 346
Christine (King), 212
A Christmas Carol" (Dickens), 106, 107
"A Christmas Witch" (Atherton), 20, 21, 22, 23
The Chronicle of Clemendy (Machen), 278
The Chronicles of Golden Friars (LeFanu), 249
The Circle Game (Atwood), 32
"A Circle in the Fire" (O'Connor), 315
Clairville Castle; or, The History of Albert and Emma (unsigned), 135
Clarissa; The History of a Young Lady (Richardson), 48, 371
Clary; ou, Le retour a la vertu récompensé [Clary; or, The Return to virtue rewarded] (Baculard d'Arnaud), 48
"The Clergyman's Confession" (Collins), 90
"The Clergyman's Tale; or Pembroke" (Lee), 241, 245, 246
Clermont (Roche), 34, 44, 46, 47
Cleveland (Prévost), 242
The Clock Has Struck!!! (Farrow), 138
Clough, Arthur Hugh, 280
Cobb, Irvin S., 271
Cobb, James, 148, 156, 157
Cocksure (Richler), 25
Coelina; ou, L'Enfant du mystère [Coelina; or, The Child of Mystery] (Ducray-Duminil), 116, 117, 119
Coelina; ou, L'Enfant du mystère [Coelina; or, The Child of Mystery] (Pixérécourt), 148
Cohen, Leonard, 25
Cole, William, 439
Coleridge, Samuel Taylor, 4, 45, 162, 256, 285, 289, 325, 346, 370, 406, 434
Coligny; ou, La Saint Barthelemi (Baculard d'Arnaud), 48, 50
The Collected Works of Ambrose Bierce, 60

The Collector of Hearts: New Tales of the Grotesque (Oates), 304
Collins, Wilkie, 88, **90–98**, 105, 106, 112, 114, 249, 250
Collins, William, 3, 187, 353
"The Colloquy of Monos and Una" (Poe), 330
Colman, George the Younger, 125, 148, 164
"The Color Out of Space" (Lovecraft), 273, 276
"The Coming of Abel Behenna" (Stoker), 421
The Coming Race (Bulwer-Lytton), 83, 87
Comus (Milton), 127
Confessions of Nat Turner (Styron), 298
Confessions of the Nun of St. Omer (Dacre), 99, 100, 101, 102
Congreve, William, 154
"The Conqueror Worm" (Poe), 334
Conrad, Joseph, 417
Contemplations on the Night (Hervey), 50
Contemporary California Short Stories (Atherton), 20
The Convent of St. Ursula; or, Incidents at Ottagro (unsigned), 136
The Convent Spectre; or, The Unfortunate Daughter (unsigned), 136
"The Conversation of Eiros and Charmion" (Poe), 330
"The Cosmorama" (Odoevsky), 321, 326
The Count of Narbonne (Jephson), 149, 152, 156, 157, 164
The Countess of Salisbury (Hartson), 148, 155
Crane, Stephen, 268
Crawford, F. Marion, 18
"Creative Writers and Daydreaming" (Freud), 63
Creepshow (King), 212
Crichton (Ainsworth), 10
Les Crimes de l'amour [The Crimes of Love] (Sade), 365, 368, 369
Cronstadt Castle; or, The Mysterious Visitor (unsigned), 136

Crookenden, Isaac, 133, 142, 143, 144, 145, 146
"Crooken Sands" (Stoker), 420, 421
Cross, John Cartwright, 152, 164
Crowe, Catherine, 104, 107
Crowley, Aleister, 281
Crowley, Hannah, 148, 156
"Crowned Yazaemon" [Kanmuri Yazaemon] (Kyoka), 225
"Crysanthemum Tryst" (Akinari), 12
"The Crystal Cup" (Stoker), 420
Cujo (King), 212, 221, 223
Cumberland, Richard, 148
Curry, Kenneth, 384
Cycle of the Werewolf (King), 212
Cymbeline (Shakespeare), 242

D., (initial), 139
Dacre, Charlotte [Rosa Matilda], 50, 70, **99–103**, 134, 139, 156, 230, 366, 400, 404
Dacre of the South (Gore), 152
D'Alamanzi, anecdote française (Baculard d'Arnaud), 49
"The Damned Thing" (Bierce), 63, 64, 67
Damon and Delia (Godwin), 127
Danse Macabre (King), 212, 213, 217
Dante [Allighieri], 318
The Dark Half (King), 213, 215
The Dark Tower: The Gunslinger (King), 212, 214, 221
The Dark Tower II: The Drawing of the Three (King), 213
The Dark Tower III: The Waste Lands (King), 213
The Dark Tower IV: Wizard and Glass (King), 213
Darwin, Charles, 272
David Copperfield (Dickens), 92
Dawn of the Dead (Romero), 348
"The Dead and the Countess" (Atherton), 20, 22, 23
"The Dead Hand" (Collins), 90, 91, 94, 95, 98
"The Dead Man's Sneer" (Odoevsky), 321, 323
The Dead Secret (Collins), 90

"The Dead Sexton" (LeFanu), 249, 251
The Dead Zone (King), 212, 214, 221
"Death and the Woman" (Atherton), 20, 22
"The Death Bride" (unsigned), 392
"The Death of Halpin Frayser" (Bierce), 62, 65, 67
"The Deaths of the Other Children" (Atwood), 28
The Decameron (Boccaccio), 368
"Dedicatory Verses to Lady Anne Scott" (Hogg), 192
DeFoe, Daniel, 447
"De Grey: A Romance" (James), 202, 205, 210
De La Mark and Constantia; or, Ancient Heroism, A Gothic Tale (unsigned), 136, 144
Demon and Other Tales (Oates), 304
De Monfort (Baillie), 147, 151, 152, 158, 164
The Demon of Venice; An Original Romance (signed "by a lady"), 99, 139
"Demons" (Oates), 303, 307
De morbo oneirodynia dicto (Polidori), 345
"Departure" (Schiller), 375
De Quincey, Thomas, 198, 391, 396
Descartes, René, 437
"A Descent into the Maelström" (Poe), 330, 336
Desperation (King), 213
"The Devil and Tom Walker" (Irving), 195
"The Devil in Manuscript" (Hawthorne), 165
"The Devil in the Belfry" (Poe), 330
The Devil's Dictionary (Bierce), 62, 63, 66
The Devil's Elixir (Fitzball), 151
"The Devil's Spectacles" (Collins), 90, 96
"Devil's Half Acre; or the Mystery of the Cruel Suitor" (Oates), 311
"The Diamond Lens" (O'Brien), 324, 328
"The Diary of Anne Rodway" (Collins), 90

The Diary of Dr. John William Polidori (Rossetti), 344

Dibdin, Thomas John, 148, 163

Dickens, Charles, 10, 84, 86, 87, 88, 92, 94, 95, 97, **104–15**, 249, 250, 387

Dickinson, Emily, 332, 341, 352

"Dickon the Devil" (LeFanu), 249

Diderot, Denis, 133, 288, 371

Different Seasons (King), 212

"The Displaced Person" (O'Connor), 315, 316, 317

Doctor Faustus (Marlowe), 154, 171

Der Dolch [The Dagger] (Grosse), 45

"The Doll" (Oates), 306

The Dolliver Romance (Hawthorne), 165, 167, 175

Dolores Claiborne (King), 213, 215, 219, 220, 221

"Dolph Heyliger" (Irving), 195, 199, 201

"The Domain of Arnheim" (Poe), 335

Dombey and Son (Dickens), 104, 105, 109, 114

Domestic Manners of Sir Walter Scott (Hogg), 187

Domestic Misery; or, The Victim of Seduction (unsigned), 136

Don Algonah; or, The Sorceress of Montillo (unsigned), 136

Don Carlos (Schiller), 375, 376

Don Raymond; or, The Castle of Lindenberg (unsigned), 151, 159

The Doom of Devorgoil, a Melo-drama (Scott), 380, 382

Dos Passos, John, 268

Dostoevsky, Feodor, 322, 328

"The Double-bedded Room" (Collins), 95

Double Delight (Oates as Rosamund Smith), 304

Douglas (Home), 155

Douglas Castle; or, The Cell of Mystery: A Scottish Tale (Barrett), 144

Douglass, Frederick, 296, 297, 301

Do with Me What You Will (Oates), 303

Doyle, Sir Arthur Conan, 280

Dracula (Stoker), 216, 222, 251, 348, 420, 421, 422, 423, 425, 426, 427, 428

"Dracula's Guest" (Stoker), 421

Dracula's Guest and Other Weird Stories (Stoker), 420

Drake, H. B., 271

Drake, Nathan, 138

"The Dream" (Shelley), 390

"Dreamland" (Poe), 228

The Dream of Eugene Aram (Hood), 88

"A Dream of Red Hands" (Stoker), 420, 421

"The Dreams in the Witch-House" (Lovecraft), 273, 274

Dreams, Waking Thoughts, and Visions (Beckford), 53, 55

"The Dream-Woman" (Collins), 90, 91, 95

Dreiser, Theodore, 264, 268

Dr. Jekyll and Mr. Hyde (Mamoulian), 419

Dr. Jekyll and Mr. Hyde, and an Inland Voyage (Stevenson), 412

"The Drunkard's Dream" ["The Vision of Tom Chuff"], 248, 249

Dryden, John, 382

"The Dualitists" (Stoker), 421

"The Duc de L'Omelette" (Poe), 330, 335

The Duchess of Malfi (Webster), 154

Ducray-Duminil, François Guillaume, **116–19**

Dunsany, Lord, 271, 424

"The Dunwich Horror" (Lovecraft), 273, 274

Dürer, Albrecht, 431

Durston Castle; or, The Ghost of Eleonora: A Gothic Story (unsigned), 144

The Earls of Hammersmith; or, The Cellar Spectre (Lawler), 149, 159

"Earth's Holocaust" (Hawthorne), 165

Edeliza: A Gothic Tale (signed "E.W."), 138

Edgar Huntly; or, Memoirs of a Sleepwalker (Brown), 76, 78, 80, 81, 82, 173

Edgar; or, Northern Feuds (Manners), 149

Edgeworth, Maria, 387

Edmond, Orphan of the Castle a Tragedy in Five Acts, Founded on the "Old English Baron," a Gothic Story (Broster), 361

Edmund and Albina; or, Gothic Times (unsigned), 136

"Edward Randolph's Portrait" (Hawthorne), 165, 170

Edwards, Jonathan, 267

Edwy and Edilda: A Gothic Tale in Five Parts (Whalley), 134, 144

"Egotism; or, The Bosom Serpent" (Hawthorne), 16, 165, 172

Einstein, Albert, 271, 273

Elegiac Sonnets (Smith), 409

"Die Elfen" [The Elves] (Tieck), 429, 433

Eliot, George [Mary Ann Evans], 74, 91, 388

Die Elixiere des Teufels: Nachgelassene Paperes des bruders Medardus [The Devil's Elixirs: Posthumous Papers of Brother Medardus] (Hoffmann), 177, 178, 179, 180, 183, 184, 193

Eliza; or, The Unhappy Nun (Barrington), 133

Ellis, George, 384

Emerson, Ralph Waldo, 263

Emmeline, the Orphan of the Castle (Smith), 408, 409, 410, 411

The Empire City; or, New York by Night and Day (Lippard), 261

The Enchanted Castle (Andrews), 147, 164

The Enchanted Castle; A Fragment (unsigned), 144

"The English Earl; or, The History of Fitzwalter" (unsigned), 136

An Enquiry Concerning Political Justice (Godwin), 100, 126, 127, 129, 392

The Entertainer (unsigned), 136

The Entranced; or, The Wanderer of Eighteen Centuries (Lippard), 261

The Episodes of Vathek (Beckford), 53, 55, 57

Les Époux malheureux; ou Histoire de Monsieur et Madame de la Bédoyère

[The Wicked Husband; or History of Mr. and Mrs. Bédoyère] (Baculard d'Arnaud), 48, 51

Les Épreuves du sentiment [The Trials of Feeling] (Baculard d'Arnaud), 50

Ernestus Berchtold; or, The Modern Oedipus: A Tale (Polidori), 344, 347

L'Esplendente (Beckford), 57

An Essay on the Sublime (Baillie), 356

"The Eternal Now" (Atherton), 22

"Ethan Brand" (Hawthorne), 165, 171

Ethelbert; or, The Phantom of the Castle (unsigned), 144

Ethelinde; or, The Recluse of the Lake (Smith), 408, 410

"Eugénie de Franval" (Sade), 365, 368

Euphémie; ou, Le Triomphe de la Réligion [Euphemie; or, The Triumph of Religion] (Baculard d'Arnaud), 48, 50

Evadne; or, The Statue (Sheil), 150

"The Eve of St. Agnes" (Keats), 198

"The Eve of St. John" (Scott), 380, 384

"Everything That Rises Must Converge" (O'Connor), 315, 317, 318

"The Evil Eye" (Shelley), 389, 391, 395

The Exiles; or, The Memoirs of the Count de Cronstadt (Reeve), 49

Expensive People (Oates), 303, 305

The Eyes of the Dragon (King), 213, 214, 221

Ezekiel, Book of, 374

F., E., (initials), 138

"The Facts in the Case of M. Valdemar" (Poe), 330

Falkland (Bulwer-Lytton), 83, 84

Falkner (Shelley), 390, 392

"The Fall of the House of Usher" (Poe), 127, 181, 272, 327, 330, 338, 340, 342

"The Familiar" (LeFanu), 249

"Family" (Oates), 307

"The Family Portraits" (unsigned), 392

Famous Impostors (Stoker), 427

Fanni, ou la nouvelle Paméla [Fanny, or the new Pamela] (Baculard d'Arnaud), 48

Fanshawe (Hawthorne), 165, 167, 175
Fantasiestücke [Fantasy pieces]
  (Hoffmann), 179
*Fantasmagoriana, ou Recueil d'Histoires
  d'Apparitions de Spectres, Revenants,
  Fantômes, etc.; traduit de l'allemand,
  par un Amateur* (signed "un
  Amateur"), 392
Fantastic Fables (Bierce), 60
"A Far-Away Melody" (Freeman), 120,
  122
Farrow, William, 138
The Fatal Discovery (Home), 148, 156
The Fatal Marriage (Southerne), 155
*Fatal Revenge; or, The Family of
  Montorio* (Maturin), 283, 285
Fatal Secrets; or, Etherlinda de Salmoni
  (Crookenden), 133
*Fatal Vows; or, The False Monk: A
  Romance* (unsigned), 136
Faulkner, William, 176, 214, 305, 319
"Fauntleroy" (Collins), 91
Faust (Goethe), 84, 406
Fayel (Baculard d'Arnaud), 48, 50
"The Festival" (Lovecraft), 273
"The Fiction Writer and His Country"
  (O'Connor), 318
"The Fire King" (Scott), 380, 384
Firestarter (King), 212, 215
"Fire Worship" (Hawthorne), 165, 172
First Love: A Gothic Tale (Oates), 304,
  306
Fitzball, Edward, 151
Five Hundred Years Hence! (signed "D"),
  139
Flammenberg, Lawrence [pseud. Karl
  Friedrich Kahlert], **33–47**, 378
*The Flitch of Bacon; or, The Custom of
  Dunmow: A Tale of English Home*
  (Ainsworth), 8
Florian, Jean-Pierre Claris de, 117
"Florville et Courval" (Sade), 365, 368
The Flying Dutchman (Fitzball), 151
"The Foghorn" (Atherton), 20, 22, 23
The Foghorn Stories (Atherton), 20
Folenius, Emmanuel Friedrich, 375
Fontainville Forest (Boaden), 147, 157

"For Annie" (Poe), 332
Ford, John, 154, 161
*The Forest of Hermanstadt; or, A
  Princess and No Princess* (Dibdin),
  148
"The Fortunes of Sir Robert Ardagh"
  ["The Haunted Baronet] ["Sir
  Dominick's Bargain"] (LeFanu), 248,
  249
Fournier, Narcisse, 358
Four Past Midnight (King), 213
"The Fox" (Lawrence), 233
"A Fragment of Life" (Machen), 278
Fragments (Schlegel), 432
*Fragments of Ancient Poetry Collected in
  the Highlands of Scotland*
  (Macpherson), 187
*Frankenstein; or, The Man and the
  Monster! or the Fate of Frankenstein:
  A Peculiar Romantic Melo-Dramatic
  Pantomimic Spectacle, in Two Acts
  Founded Principally on Mrs. Shelley's
  Singular Work* (Milner), 150, 151, 160,
  163
*Frankenstein; or, The Modern
  Prometheus* (Shelley), 30, 81, 84, 85,
  127, 130, 143, 159, 160, 162, 163,
  172, 186, 187, 194, 216, 222, 279,
  344, 347, 348, 376, 378, 389, 390,
  391, 392, 393, 394, 395, 396, 397,
  398, 413, 415, 437
Franz Sternbalds Wanderungen [The
  Wanderings of Franz Sternbald]
  (Tieck), 430, 431
"Frederick and Alice" (Scott), 380, 384
Fredolfo: A Tragedy in Five Acts
  (Maturin), 149, 283
Freeman, Mary Wilkins, **120–24**
Frere, John Hookham, 384
Freud, Sigmund, 63, 178, 181, 259, 271,
  279, 287, 332, 369
The Friar's Tale (Seward), 138, 139
"The Friend of the Friends" ["The Way it
  Came"] (James), 202, 206, 207
"From Beyond" (Lovecraft), 274
Fuentes, Carlos, 61
Fuseli, Henry, 347

Galland, Antoine, 54
Galt, John, 187
Gargoyles and Grotesques (King), 213
Garner, Margaret, 298
Gaskell, Elizabeth, 10
Gaston de Blondeville; or, The Court of Henry III Keeping Festival in Ardennes: A Romance: St. Albans Abbey: A Metrical Romance (Radcliffe), 349, 350, 351, 353, 358
Gay, Mary, 358
Der Geisterbanner: Eine Wundergeschichte aus mündlichen und schriftlichen traditionen gesammelt [The Ghostly Banner: A Wondrous Tale Collected from Oral and Written Traditions] (unsigned), 33
Der Geisterseher: Eine Geschichte aus den memoires des Graffen von O. [The Ghost Seer: Story from the Memoirs of the Count of O.] (Schiller), 181, 183, 372, 373, 375, 376, 377, 378, 379
Genlis, Felicité de Saint-Aubin Madame de, 50, 117
"A Gentle Ghost" (Freeman), 120
"George Dobson's Expedition to Hell" (Hogg), 188
Gerald's Game (King), 213, 215, 219, 220, 221
German Romance (Carlyle), 431, 432, 433, 434
"Der getreue Eckart und der Tannenhäuser" [Trusty Eckart and Tannhaeuser] (Tieck), 429, 433
"Ghasta; or, The Avenging Demon!!!" (Shelley), 399, 402
"The Ghost" (Odoevsky), 321
"The Ghost and the Bone-Setter" (LeFanu), 248, 249
"The Ghost in Master B's Room" (Dickens), 104, 112
"The Ghost in the Bride's Chamber" (Dickens), 104, 107, 108, 114
"The Ghostly Rental" (James), 202, 204, 205
"Ghosts and Ghost-seers" (Dickens), 104
"Ghost Stories and Tales of Mystery" (LeFanu), 248

"Ghost Stories of the Chapelizod" (LeFanu), 248
The Giaour (Byron), 347
Giberne, Charles, 134
Gifford, William, 384
Gilpin, William, 409
"A Gipsy Prophecy" (Stoker), 421
The Girl Who Loved Tom Gordon (King), 213, 214, 221
"Glad Ghosts" (Lawrence), 238
Glenarvon (Lamb), 345
"Glenfinlas, or Lord Ronald's Coronach" (Scott), 380, 384
"Goblin Market" (Rossetti), 348
The Goddess and Other Women (Oates), 303
Godolphin (Bulwer-Lytton), 85
Godwin, William, 81, 84, 89, 100, 102, **125–32**, 148, 166, 176, 264, 347, 369, 370, 374, 378, 391, 396, 397, 398, 400, 401, 406, 410
Goethe, Johann Wolfgang von, 84, 178, 179, 358, 378, 379, 382, 383, 406, 442
Goetz of Berlichingen with the Iron Hand: A Tragedy. Translated from the German of Goethe by Walter Scott, Esq., Advocate (Scott), 380
Gogol, Nikolai, 323
"The Gold-Bug" (Poe), 330, 336
The Golden Dog (Kirby), 25
Goldsmith, Mary, 148, 158
Gombrowicz, Witold, 209
"Good Country People" (O'Connor), 315, 316
"A Good Man Is Hard To Find" (O'Connor), 315, 316, 317, 319
A Good Man Is Hard To Find, and Other Stories (O'Connor), 315
Gore, Catherine, 152
Gothic stories: "The Enchanted Castle; A Fragment"; "Ethelbert; or, The Phantom of the Castle"; "The Mysterious Vision; or, Perfidy Punished" (unsigned), 144
Gothic Stories: Sir Bertrand by Mrs. Barbauld (Aikin), 1
Gothic Stories: Sir Bertrand's Adventures in a Ruinous Castle (unsigned), 1, 136

The Gothic Story of Courville Castle; or, The Illegitimate Son, A Victim of Prejudice and Passion (unsigned), 136, 144

Götz von Berlichingen (Goethe), 358, 382, 383

"Governor Manco and the Soldier" (Irving), 195

"The Grass Labyrinth" (Kyoka), 230

"The Grave of Miyagi" (Akinari), 17

"The Gray Champion" (Hawthorne), 165, 169

Gray, Thomas, 439

Great Expectations (Dickens), 104, 106, 113

"The Great God Pan" (Machen), 278, 279, 280, 282

The Great God Pan and the Inmost Light (Machen), 278

"The Great Good Place" (James), 203

"The Greatest Good of the Greatest Number" (Atherton), 22

The Grecian Daughter (Murphy), 150, 156

The Green Mile (King), 213

The Green Round (Machen), 278, 281

"Green Tea" (LeFanu), 248, 250, 252, 253

"The Grey Owl Syndrome" (Atwood), 26

Grosett, Emilia, 134

Grosette, Henry William, 148

Grosse, Carl, **33–47**, 179

Guy Fawkes; or, The Gunpowder Treason: A Historical Romance (Ainsworth), 7

Guy Mannering; or, The Astrologer (Scott), 382, 387

Haggard, H. Rider, 24

"The Hair" (Oates), 306

"The Hall Bedroom" (Freeman), 120, 121

Hall, Oakley, 61

Hamlet (Shakespeare), 154, 356, 431, 445

The Handmaid's Tale (Atwood), 31

Harold the Dauntless (Scott), 383

Harper, Frances E. W., 296

The Harper's Daughter (Lewis), 254

Harris, Middleton, 298

Hartson, Hall, 148, 155

Harvey, Margaret, 152

"Haunted" (Oates), 306

"The Haunted and the Haunters" ["The House and the Brain"] (Bulwer-Lytton), 83, 85, 86, 88

"The Haunted Baronet" (LeFanu), 249, 250, 251

The Haunted Hotel: A Mystery of Modern Venice to Which Is Added My Lady's Money (Collins), 90, 92

"The Haunted House" (Dickens), 104

The Haunted Man and the Ghost's Bargain: A Fancy for Christmas-time (Dickens), 104, 105, 106, 107, 108, 109, 111

"The Haunted Mind" (Hawthorne), 165, 170, 171, 176

The Haunted Omnibus (Atherton), 20

Haunted: Tales of the Grotesque (Oates), 304, 305, 308

The Haunted Tower (Cobb), 148, 156, 157

Haunted Tower; or, The Adventures of Sir Egbert Rothsay (Giberne), 134

Hawthorne, Nathaniel, 16, 79, 82, 89, 129, **165–76**, 178, 221, 223, 227, 240, 264, 266, 268, 272, 279, 284, 296, 298, 301, 312, 322, 332, 333, 343, 356, 362, 415, 418, 445

Hays, Mary, 5, 351

Hazlitt, William, 158, 162, 352, 357

Hearn, Lafcadio, 12, 13

The Heart-Broken (Lippard), 261, 263

The Heart of Mid-Lothian [Tales of My Landlord, Second Series, Collected and Arranged by Jedediah Cleishbotham] (Scott), 380, 381

Hearts in Atlantis (King), 213

Heat and Other Stories (Oates), 304, 305, 307

"The Heavy Sorrow of the Body" (Oates), 303

Heber, Richard, 384

Hegel, Georg Wilhelm Friedrich, 376

Heidegger, Martin, 236

"The Heir of Mondolfo" (Shelley), 390

Hellas: A Lyrical Drama (Shelley), 399, 404

Helvétius, Claude Adrien, 101

Henley, Samuel, 53, 55, 58

Henry Fitzowen [Sir Gawen] (Drake), 138

Henry the Second; or, The Fall of Rosamund (Hull), 149, 156

Herne the Hunter: A Romantic Drama in Three Acts (Tom Taylor), 7

The Heroine of the Cave (Hiffernan), 148

Hervey, James, 49

Herzensergiessungeneines künstliebenden Klosterbruders [Heart-Outpourings of an Art-loving Friar] (Tieck), 430, 431

Hieroglyphic Tales (Walpole), 447

Hiffernan, Paul, 148

Higgie, Thomas H., 7

"The Highland Widow" (Scott), 381

The Hill of Dreams (Machen), 278, 280

History of a Six Weeks Tour and Rambles in Germany and Italy in 1840, 1842, and 1843 (Shelley), 390, 395, 396

History of Durham (Surtees), 384

Hoffmann, E.[rnst] T.[eodor] A.[madeus], **177–84**, 193, 230, 322, 328, 329, 375, 379, 388, 431, 432, 433

Hogg, James, 93, 110, 183, **185–94**, 369, 370, 387, 416

Holcroft, Thomas, 148, 151, 158

"The Hollow of the Three Hills" (Hawthorne), 165, 170

"The Holy Man of Mount Koya" [Koya hijiri] (Kyoka), 18, 225, 229, 230, 231

Home, John, 148, 155, 156

Hood, Thomas, 88

"Hop-Frog" (Poe), 331, 335

Hopkins, Pauline, 301

Horatio and Camilla; or, The Nuns of St. Mary (unsigned), 136

"The Horla" (Maupassant), 16, 324

The Horrible Revenge; or, The Assassin of the Solitary Castle (unsigned), 136

Horrible Revenge; or, The Monster of Italy! (Crookenden), 134, 144

Horrid Mysteries (Grosse), 33, 37, 41, 42, 44, 137, 179

The Horrors of the Secluded Castle; or, Virtue Triumphant (unsigned), 136

Hosea, Book of, 128

"Hostage" (Oates), 304

"The Hound" (Lovecraft), 275

Hours of Solitude: A Collection of Original Poems Now First published by Charlotte Dacre (Dacre), 99

"The House Amid the Thickets" (Akinari), 12

"*The House of Aspen* (Scott), 380, 383

"The House of Eld" (Stevenson), 412, 415

The House of Souls (Machen), 278

The House of the Seven Gables (Hawthorne), 165, 166, 173, 175, 176, 272, 298, 301

Howard, Edward, 113

Howells, William Dean, 210

"Howe's Masquerade" (Hawthorne), 165

"How I Contemplated the World from the Detroit House of Correction and Began My Life Over Again" (Oates), 303, 305

"How 7 Went Mad" (Stoker), 420

"How to Write a Blackwood Article" (Poe), 334

Hugo, Victor, 417

Hull, Henry, 149, 156

A Humble Romance and Other Stories (Freeman), 120

Hume, David, 242

"The Hunt of Eildon" (Hogg), 194

Huysmans, J. K., 230

"The Hymn to Intellectual Beauty" (Shelley), 406

"Hypnos" (Lovecraft), 274

"Idée sur le roman" [Idea of the Novel] (Sade), 368, 369

"Ignaz Denner" (Hoffmann), 177, 179

Ildefonzo and Alberoni; or, Tales of Horror (unsigned), 145

"Imbroglio" (Odoevsky), 321

"The Immigrants" (Atwood), 27

Imogen: A Pastoral Romance (Godwin), 125, 126, 127, 132
"The Imp of the Perverse" (Poe), 330, 333
In a Glass Darkly (LeFanu), 249, 253
Inchbald, Elizabeth, 351
Incidents in the Life of a Slave Girl (Jacobs), 300
The Inferno (Dante), 318
"An Inhabitant of Carcosa" (Bierce), 62
"The Inmost Light" (Machen), 278
The Inquisitor (Holcroft), 148
"Insanity: A Fragment" (Brown), 76
Insomnia (King), 213
"In the Autumn of the Year" (Oates), 303
In the Midst of Life (Bierce), 60, 63
"The Invisible Giant" (Stoker), 420, 424
Iola Leroy (Harper), 296
The Iron Chest (Colman), 125, 148, 164
Irving, Henry, 423
Irving, Washington, 79, **195–201**
"The Island of the Fay" (Poe), 335
"The Isle of Devils" (Lewis), 257
"Israfel" (Poe), 228
IT (King), 213, 214, 215, 217, 218, 220
Italian Letters (Godwin), 127
The Italian Monk (Boaden), 148, 157, 164
The Italian; or, The Confessional of the Black Penitents (Radcliffe), 103, 113, 133, 140, 142, 148, 171, 349, 350, 354, 357, 358, 359
Italy, with Sketches of Spain and Portugal (Beckford), 54
Ivanhoe (Scott), 380, 381, 387

Jack Sheppard: A Romance (Ainsworth), 7, 10
Jacobs, Harriet, 296, 297, 300
"The Jade Bracelet" (Freeman), 120
James, Henry, 21, 91, 123, 168, 174, 197, 200, **202–11**, 268, 307, 308, 339, 417
James, M.[ontague] R.[hodes], 271
James, William, 203
Jamieson, Robert, 384

Jane Eyre (C. Brontë), 69, 70, 71, 72, 73, 74
Jaspers, Karl, 236
Jephson, Robert, 149, 151, 156, 157, 163, 164
The Jew of Malta (Marlowe), 154
The Jewel of Seven Stars (Stoker), 420, 421, 422, 423, 426
"John Jago's Ghost" (Collins), 90
Johnson, Dr. Samuel, 154, 349
"The Jolly Corner" (James), 202, 203, 208, 210
Journal of a West India Proprietor (Lewis), 257
The Journal of William Beckford in Portugal and Spain, 1787–88; Italy, with Sketches of Spain and Portugal (Beckford), 53–54, 55
The Journals of Susanna Moodie (Atwood), 24, 26, 32
A Journey Made in the Summer of 1794 Through Holland and the Western Frontier of Germany with a Return Down the Rhine (Radcliffe), 351
Joyce, James, 286, 288, 307
"The Judge's House" (Stoker), 420, 421, 423
Julia of Louvain; or, Monkish Cruelty (Cross), 152
Juliette (Sade), 103
Die Jungfrau von Orleans [The Maid of Orleans] (Schiller), 373, 378
The Jungle (Sinclair), 268
Justine, ou les Malheurs de la Vertue [Justine, or the Misfortunes of Virtue] (Sade), 103, 266, 347, 365, 367, 371
Juvenis, 138

Kabale und Liebe (Schiller), 254
Kafka, Franz, 286, 305, 322
"Kanmuri Yazaemon" (Kyoka), 225
Kant, Immanuel, 4, 178, 179, 373, 378
Keats, John, 198, 352
"Kecho" [Chimera] (Kyoka), 225, 228, 232
Kemble, Stephen, 149
Kenilworth (Scott), 243
The Kentish Barons (North), 150, 152

Kerr, John Atkinson, 149, 151, 160

The Killers: A Narrative of Real Life in Philadelphia . . . by a Member of the Philadelphia Bar (Lippard), 261

King Lear (Shakespeare), 154

"King Pest" (Poe), 330, 335

King, Stephen, **212–24**, 264, 276, 277, 417, 444

Kipling, Rudyard, 93

Kirby, William, 25

"The Knife" (Oates), 306

The Knights of Calatrava; or, The Days of Chivalry (Wilkinson), 134

Koenigsmark the Robber; or, The Terror of Bohemia (Sarret), 139

Kotzebue, August von, 254, 383

Kraft Ebing, Richard von, 369

"Kubla Khan" (Coleridge), 325

Kyd, Thomas, 154, 161

Kyoka, Izumi, 18, 19, **225–32**

Kyoka zenshu (Kyoka), 225

Lacenaire, Pierre François, 371

Lacy, Thomas H., 7

Lady Audley's Secret (Braddon), 91

"The Ladybird" (Lawrence), 233, 238, 239, 240

"Lady Eleanor's Mantle" (Hawthorne), 165

"The Lady of Glenwith Grange" (Collins), 90, 91

The Lady of the Lake (Scott), 382, 387

The Lady of the Shroud (Stoker), 420, 421, 423, 426

Lady Oracle (Atwood), 24, 29, 30, 31, 32

The Ladye Annabel: A Romance of the Alembic, the Altar, and the Throne (Lippard), 261

The Ladye Annabel; or, The Doom of the Poisoner (Lippard), 261, 264, 265, 269

The Lair of the White Worm (Stoker), 420, 421, 422, 426, 427

Lamb, Lady Caroline, 345

"The Lame Shall Enter First" (O'Connor), 315

The Lancashire Witches: A Romance of Pendle Forest (Ainsworth), 8

Lang, Andrew, 280

Last Days (Oates), 304

The Last Days of Pompeii (Bulwer-Lytton), 83, 88, 89

"The Last Laugh" (Lawrence), 238

The Last Man (Shelley), 323, 389, 390, 395, 398

"The Last of the Valerii" (James), 202, 205, 209

"The Last Suicide" (Odoevsky), 321, 323

"A Late Encounter with the Enemy" (O'Connor), 315, 316

Lathom, Francis, **33–47**, 137

"Laura Silver Bell" (LeFanu), 249

Lawler, Dennis, 149, 159

Lawrence, D. H., **233–40**

The Lay of the Last Minstrel: A Poem (Scott), 380, 381, 382, 385

Lectures on Rhetoric and Belles Lettres (Blair), 356

"The Ledge" (King), 212

Lee, Harriet, 5, 152, 241

Lee, Nathaniel, 155

Lee, Sophia, 49, 52, 119, **241–47**, 351, 364

LeFanu, Joseph Sheridan, 91, 97, 105, 197, 200, **248–53**, 279, 284, 322, 328, 423

"The Legend of Don Munio Sancho de Hinojosa" (Irving), 195

"The Legend of Prince Ahmed al Kamel" (Irving), 195

"The Legend of Sleepy Hollow" (Irving), 195, 199

"The Legend of the Arabian Astrologer" (Irving), 195

"The Legend of the Enchanted Soldier" (Irving), 195

"The Legend of the Midnight Death, a Story of the Wissahikon" (Lippard), 261

"The Legend of the Moor's Legacy" (Irving), 195

"The Legend of the Rose of the Alhambra" (Irving), 195

"The Legend of the Two Discreet Statues" (Irving), 195

"Legends of the Province House" (Hawthorne), 165

Legge, F., 134
Leibnitz, Gottfried Wilhelm von, 379
Die Leiden des jungen Werthers [The Sufferings of Young Werther] (Goethe), 430
"Leixlip Castle" (Maturin), 283, 286
Leland, Thomas, 148, 155
"Lenore" (Bürger), 2, 382, 383
Lermontov, Michael, 322
Leroux, Gaston, 444
Le Tourneur, Pierre Prime Félicien, 49
"Letter IV [To Countess Ye. P. Rostopchina]" (Odoevsky), 321
Lewis, Matthew Gregory "Monk," 17, 44, 46, 47, 50, 54, 58, 75, 81, 93, 96, 100, 103, 106, 110, 114, 118, 129, 133, 134, 136, 140, 141, 142, 143, 149, 151, 152, 153, 156, 157, 158, 161, 162, 163, 164, 166, 170, 179, 184, 230, **254–60**, 268, 287, 294, 325, 337, 355, 357, 358, 366, 369, 383, 384, 400, 401, 402, 409, 444, 446
Lewis Tyrell; or, The Depraved Count (unsigned), 144
Leyden, John, 384
The Libertine (Dacre), 99, 101
The Life and Adventures of Martin Chuzzlewit (Dickens), 104, 105,
The Life and Adventures of Nicholas Nickleby (Dickens), 104, 105, 107
The Life and Horrid Adventures of the Celebrated Doctor Faustus (unsigned), 139
"The Lifted Veil" (Eliot), 91
"Ligeia" (Poe), 96, 227, 330, 333, 334, 337, 342, 435
"The Lightning-Rod Man (Melville), 290, 292
"Lionizing" (Poe), 330, 334
Lippard, George, **261–69**
"The Literary Life of Thingum Bob, Esq., Late Editor of the 'Goosetherumfoodle' by Himself" (Poe), 334
Little Dorrit (Dickens), 104, 113
"The Little Maid at the Door" (Freeman), 120
Little Novels (Collins), 90
Little Women (Alcott), 309

"The Live Corpse" (Odoevsky), 321, 323
Lives of the Necromancers; or, An account of the most eminent persons in successive ages, who have claimed for themselves, or to whom has been imputed by others, the exercise of magical power (Godwin), 125, 126, 391
Lives of the Twins (Oates as Rosamund Smith), 304, 306, 307
Lodore (Shelley), 390
"London" (Blake), 263
London, Jack, 268
"The Long Arm" (Freeman), 124
"The Long Story" ["The Vision"] (Beckford), 56
Longsword, Earl of Salisbury (Leland), 148, 155
The Long Walk (King as Richard Bachman), 212
Longinus, 3
"Looking in the Mirror" (Atwood), 27
Lord of the Castle (unsigned), 151
Lord of the Isles (Scott), 382
Lord of the Rings (Tolkien), 215
"Lord Ruthwen, ou les Vampires" (Nodier), 344
Lord Ruthwen; o I Vampiri (unsigned), 344
"Lord Soulis" (Leyden), 384
"The Lost Ghost" (Freeman), 120, 121, 122
"Love and Marriage" [Ai to Kon'in] (Kyoka), 228
Lovecraft, H.[oward] P.[hillips], 229, **270–77**, 332, 342, 444
Lovel Castle; or, The Rightful Heir Restored, A Gothic Tale (unsigned), 136, 144
Lucretia; or, The Children of the Night (Bulwer-Lytton), 83, 85
Lucretia; or, The Robbers of the Hyrcanean Forest (Chamberlain), 133
"Luella Miller" (Freeman), 120, 121, 122, 124
Luke, Book of, 128
The Lunatic and His Turkey: A Tale of Witchcraft (unsigned), 139

"The Lurking Fear" (Lovecraft), 275
"The Lust of the White Serpent"
    (Akinari), 12, 16
The Lyrical Ballads (Wordsworth and
    Coleridge), 140

Macbeth (Shakespeare), 154, 345, 356,
    431
Machen, Arthur, 271, **278–82**
Mackenzie, Henry, 383
Macpherson, James, 187
"A Mad Man's Manuscript" (Dickens),
    104, 108
"Mad Monkton" (Collins), 90, 91, 94
"Madam Crowl's Ghost" (LeFanu), 249,
    250
*The Magician; or, The Mystical
    Adventures of Seraphina* (unsigned),
    136
"Der Magnetiseur" [The Magnetizer or
    Mesmerist] (Hoffmann), 177, 179
"The Maidenhair" (Kyoka), 230
Mailer, Norman, 264, 268, 312
"Das Majorat" [The Entail or Estate]
    (Hoffmann), 177, 180, 181, 375, 377,
    379
Mamoulian, Rouben, 419
The Man (Stoker), 424
"The Man and the Snake" (Bierce), 66
Man Crazy (Oates), 304, 305
"The Mangler" (King), 212
"The Man of Adamant: An Apologue"
    (Hawthorne), 165, 172
"The Man of the Crowd" (Poe), 307,
    323, 330
"The Man That Was Used Up" (Poe),
    335
Manfred: A Dramatic Poem (Byron),
    148, 149, 159
Manfredi; or, The Mysterious Hermit
    (unsigned), 136
Manfroné; or, The One-Handed Monk
    (Mary-Anne Radcliffe), 46
Manners, George, 149
Manuel: A Tragedy (Maturin), 149, 283
"A Manuscript Found in a Mad-House"
    (Bulwer-Lytton), 83, 85
The Marble Faun; or, The Romance of

Monte Beni (Hawthorne), 165, 166,
    173
Märchen [Tales] (Tieck), 179
Maria (Wollstonecraft), 390, 391
Maria Stuart (Schiller), 373
"Markheim" (Stevenson), 412, 416
*Marleton Abbey; or, The Mystic Tomb of
    St. Angelo* (Chapman), 133
Marlowe, Christopher, 154, 171
Marmion: A Tale of Flodden Field
    (Scott), 380, 382, 385, 387
Marmontel, Jean François, 117
Marriages and Infidelities: Short Stories
    (Oates), 303, 306, 307
Martin Chuzzlewit (Dickens), 92
Marx, Karl, 376, 393
Mary (Wollstonecraft), 390
"Mary Burnet" (Hogg), 189
"The Masque of the Red Death" (Poe),
    22, 94, 272, 330, 334, 338, 339, 340
"Masters" (Blavatsky), 89
Mather, Cotton, 199
Matheson, Richard, 277
Mathilda (Shelley), 389, 390, 391, 397
"Matter and Energy" (Oates), 303
Maturin, Charles Robert, 44, 50, 84, 91,
    106, 126, 129, 149, 151, 152, 153,
    158, 159, 160, 161, 162, 166, 167,
    171, 172, 176, 191, 192, 253, 271, **283–
    89**, 294, 322, 325, 326, 339, 356, 401,
    402, 405, 409, 444
"Maud-Evelyn" (James), 202
Maupassant, Guy de, 16, 230, 322, 324,
    417
*Maximilian and Selina; or, The
    Mysterious Abbot: A Flemish Tale*
    (unsigned), 145
McCarthy, Cormac, 319
McDonald, Andrew, 149, 156, 157, 162,
    164
McTeague: A Story of San Francisco
    (Norris), 268
Meditations Among the Tombs (Hervey),
    50
Medwin, Thomas, 400
Meeke, Mary, 116
"Mellonta Tauta" (Poe), 336
Melmoth the Wanderer (Maturin), 50, 84,

91, 129, 153, 154, 162, 167, 171, 186, 191, 192, 271, 283, 284, 285, 286, 287, 288, 322, 339, 401

Melmoth the Wanderer: A Melo-dramatic Romance in Three Acts (West), 150, 283

Melville, Herman, 79, 89, 167, 223, 235, 240, 264, 266, 268, 284, **290–94**, 312, 356, 370

Memoires de comte de Comminge (Tencin), 48

The Memoirs of a Preacher, a Revelation of the Church and the Home (Lippard), 261

Memoirs of Sir Roger de Clarendon (Reeve), 362

Mencken, H. L., 61, 66

The Merry Men and Other Tales and Fables (Stevenson), 412

"Mesmeric Revelation" (Poe), 330

"Metzengerstein" (Poe), 330, 336

"A Middle-Class Education" (Oates), 303

"The Middle Toe of the Right Foot" (Bierce), 64

The Midnight Assassin; or, The Confessions of the Monk Rinaldi (unsigned), 142, 145

Midnight Bell: A German Story (Lathom), 33, 40, 44, 46, 137

The Midnight Groan; or, The Spectre of the Chapel, Involving and Exposure of the Horrible Secrets of the Nocturnal Assembly: A Gothic Romance (unsigned), 136, 139, 144

Midnight Horrors; or, The Bandit's Daughter (unsigned), 137

The Midnight Monitor; or, Solemn Warnings from the Invisible World (unsigned), 137, 144

The Milesian Chief (Maturin), 285, 287

Milner, Henry M., 150, 151, 160, 163

Milton, John, 3, 127, 171, 355, 356, 442

The Minister: A Tragedy in Five Acts (Lewis), 254

"The Minister's Black Veil" (Hawthorne), 165, 166, 170, 175

The Minstrelsy of the Scottish Border: Consisting of Historical and Romantic

Ballads, Collected in Southern Counties of Scotland; with a Few of Modern Dates (Scott), 186, 380, 382, 384, 385

Miscellaneous Pieces in Prose (Aikin), 1

Misery (King), 213, 215, 216, 219, 221, 222, 223

Mishima, Yukio, 13, 230, 231

"Miss Bertha and the Yankee" (Collins), 91

"Miss Jéromette and the Clergyman" (Collins), 90

"The Mist" (King), 213

Mistrust; or, Blanche and Osbright: A Feudal Romance (Lewis), 255

M'Kenny, William, 139

Moby-Dick; or, The Whale (Melville), 290, 293, 294, 356

"The Model" (Oates), 313

Modern Medea (Garner)

Modern Novel Writing (Beckford), 59

The Monastery (Scott), 134

The Monastery of St. Mary; or, The White Maid of Avenel (Grosett), 134

"The Money-Diggers" (Irving), 195

The Monk (Lewis), 17, 35, 46, 50, 51, 54, 75, 81, 96, 101, 103, 110, 118, 129, 133, 134, 135, 136, 140, 141, 151, 153, 157, 163, 166, 179, 180, 184, 254, 255, 256, 257, 258, 259, 260, 266, 336, 355, 357, 366, 371, 383, 401, 402

The Monk: A Romance: In Which Is Depicted the Wonderful Adventures of Ambrosio, Friar of the Order of Capuchins, Who Was Diverted from the Track of Virtue by the Artifices of a Female Demon (unsigned), 137

Monkcliffe Abbey: A Tale of the Fifteenth Century (Wilkinson), 145

"The Monkey" (King), 213

"The Monk of Horror; or, The Conclave of Corpses" (unsigned), 139

The Monk; or, Father Innocent, Abbot of Capuchins (unsigned), 137

The Monks of Cluny; or, Castle-Acre Monastery (unsigned), 137

"Monos and Daimonos--A Legend"
(Bulwer-Lytton), 83, 86, 89

"Monsieur du Miroir" (Hawthorne), 165,
171

"The Monster" (Crane), 268

*The Monster and the Magician; or, The
Fate of Frankenstein* (Kerr), 149, 151,
160

*The Monster Made by Man; or, The
Punishment of Presumption* (unsigned),
146

"The Monster with Three Names"
(Lippard), 261

"The Moonlit Road" (Bierce), 62, 64

The Moonstone (Collins), 90, 92, 93, 98

More, Hannah, 135, 150, 156

"Morella" (Poe), 330, 337

Morellet, André, 358

Morgan, Lady [Sydney Owenson], 287,
288

Morrison, Toni, 294, **295–302**

"The Mortal Immortal: A Tale"
(Shelley), 389, 390, 391, 395, 397

"The Mortals in the House" (Dickens),
104, 107

Mosses from an Old Manse (Hawthorne),
165, 167, 168, 171, 172

The Mourning Bride (Congreve), 154

"Moxon's Master" (Bierce), 66

"Mr. Adamson of Laverhope" (Hogg),
188

"Mr. Justice Harbottle" (LeFanu), 423

"Mr. Lepel and the Housekeeper"
(Collins), 91

"Mr. Policeman and the Cook" (Collins),
91

"Mrs. Zant and the Ghost" (Collins), 90,
96

"MS. Found in a Bottle" (Poe), 330, 333,
336, 341

"The Murders in the Rue Morgue" (Poe),
330, 335

Murphy, Arthur, 150, 156

"My Aunt Margaret's Mirror" (Scott),
381

Myddleton Pomfret (Ainsworth), 8

My Heart Laid Bare (Oates), 304, 308,
311, 312

"My Kinsman, Major Molineux"
(Hawthorne), 165, 168

Les Mystères de Paris [The Mysteries of
Paris] (Sue), 268

The Mysteries of the Castle (Andrews),
147

*The Mysteries of Udolpho: A Romance
Interspersed with Some Pieces of
Poetry* (Radcliffe), 30, 36, 37, 43, 44,
45, 46, 98, 117, 140, 147, 150, 152,
154, 162, 166, 170, 349, 350, 354,
355, 357, 358, 359, 411

The Mysteries of Winterthurn (Oates),
304, 308, 310, 311, 312, 313, 314

"The Mysterious Bride" (Hogg), 187

*The Mysterious Bride; or, The Statue
Spectre* (unsigned), 137

"The Mysterious Lodger" (LeFanu), 248

The Mysterious Marriage (Lee), 152

The Mysterious Mother (Walpole), 150,
151, 153, 155, 156, 160, 161, 162,
353, 437, 438, 440, 444, 446

*The Mysterious Murder; or, The Usurper
of Naples. An Original Romance, To
Which Is Prefixed the Nocturnal
Assassin or Spanish Jealousy*
(Crookenden), 133, 134

*The Mysterious Novice; or, The Convent
of the Grey Penitents* (Wilkinson), 139

*The Mysterious Omen; or, Awful
Retribution* (unsigned), 137

*The Mysterious Vision; or, Perfidy
Punished* (unsigned), 144

The Mysterious Warning (Parsons), 33,
38, 44, 46

The Mystery of Edwin Drood (Dickens),
92, 105, 110, 111, 418

"The Mystery of Marie Roget" (Poe),
330, 335

*The Mystery of the Black Convent; An
Interesting Spanish Tale of the
Eleventh Century* (unsigned), 137

The Mystic Cavern (unsigned), 151

The Mystic Tower; or, Villainy Punished
(unsigned), 137, 144

Nabokov, Vladimir, 417

Nachtstücke [Night pieces] (Hoffmann),
180

"Naked" (Oates), 307

Nanboku, Tsuruya, 208

"Narenor" (Bulwer-Lytton), 87

The Narrative of Arthur Gordon Pym of Nantucket (Poe), 330, 336, 341, 342

Narrative of the Life of Frederick Douglass, An American Slave (Douglass), 297, 301

Native Son (Wright), 296

Neal, John, 174

The Necessity of Atheism (Shelley), 402

The Necromancer; or, The Tale of the Black Forest (Flammenberg), 33, 40, 41, 44

Needful Things (King), 213, 214, 215, 218

Nemesis (Oates as Rosamund Smith), 304

"Never Bet the Devil Your Head" (Poe), 330, 335

A New England Nun and Other Stories (Freeman), 120, 123

The New Knebworth Edition of the Novels and Romances of the Right Hon. Lord Lytton, 83

The New Monk (R. S.), 35

New Tales for Lamplight, 14

"New Year" (Odoevsky), 321

Night and Morning (Bulwer-Lytton), 87

"Night Bear Which Frightened Cattle" (Atwood), 27

"The Night Bell Tolls" (Kyoka), 230

"Night-Doings at 'Deadman's'" (Bierce), 64

The Nightmare (Fuseli), 347

Nightmares and Dreamscapes (King), 213

Nightmares in the Sky: Gargoyles and Grotesques (King), 212, 213

"The Night Patrol" (Kyoka), 230

Night Shift (King), 212

Night-Side: Eighteen Tales (Oates), 303

The Nightside of Nature; or, Ghosts and Ghost-Seers (Crowe), 104, 107

Night Thoughts [*The Complaint; or Night Thoughts on Life, Death, and Immortality*] (Young), 49

1984 (Orwell), 326

Nodier, Charles, 344

No Exit (Sartre), 326

"Nona Vincent" (James), 203, 209

No Name (Collins), 98

"No. 1 Branch Line: The Signalman" (Dickens), 105, 107, 108, 113

Norris, Frank, 264, 268

North, Francis, 150, 152

Northanger Abbey (Austen), 21, 30, 32, 33, 34, 35, 37, 42, 43, 44, 378

"The Nose" (Gogol), 323

"Notes on Writing Weird Fiction" (Lovecraft), 270, 274

La Nouvelle Justine, ou les Malheurs de la Vertue, suivie de l'Histoire de Juliette, sa soeur, ou les Prospérités du vice [The New Justine, or the Misfortunes of Virtue, followed by the History of Juliette, her sister, or the Prosperities of vice] (Sade), 365, 366, 367

Novalis [pseud. Leopold Friedrich Von Hardenburg], 178

"The Novel of the Black Seal" (Machen), 280

The Novels and Tales of Henry James, 202

Les Nuits d'Young (Le Tourneur), 49

The Nun (signed "S. P."), 138

Oates, Joyce Carol, 24, 264, **303–14**

Oates in Exile (Oates), 304

"The Oblong Box" (Poe), 330

O'Brien, Fitz-James, 324, 328

"An Occurrence at Owl Creek Bridge" (Bierce), 60, 62, 66

O'Connor, Flannery, **315–20**

"An Ode on the Popular Superstitions of the Highlands of Scotland" (Collins), 187

"Ode to Fear" (Collins), 3

Odoevsky, Vladimir, **321–29**

"Of a Dragon in the Deep" (Kyoka), 230

Of One Blood; or, the Hidden Self (Hopkins), 301

"Of the Mathematically Sublime" (Kant), 4

"Ogus and Cara Khan; or, The Force of Love" (unsigned), 136

O'Keefe, John, 150

"Olalla" (Stevenson), 412, 416

The Old Curiosity Shop (Dickens), 92, 104, 105, 109, 113

The Old English Baron: A Gothic Story [*The Champion of Virtue*] (Reeve), 49, 95, 136, 137, 156, 361, 362, 363, 364

"Old Esther Dudley" (Hawthorne), 165

Old Gringo (Fuentes), 61

The Old Manor House (Smith), 408, 409, 410, 411

Old Mortality [*Tales of My Landlord, Collected and Arranged by Jedidiah Cleishbotham*] (Scott), 189, 380, 381

The Old Oak Chest (Scott), 152

The Old Tower of Frankenstein (unsigned), 139, 143

Oliver Twist; or, The Parish Boy's Progress (Dickens), 92, 104, 105, 109, 110, 113, 115

The Omen (Galt), 187

"One Day in Spring" [Shunshu gokoku] (Kyoka), 18, 225, 230

Les 120 Journées de Sodome; ou, L'Ecole du libertinage [The 120 Days of Sodom; or, The School of Libertinage] (Sade), 365, 368

One O'Clock! or, The Knight and the Wood Daemon: A Grand Musical Romance in Three Acts (Lewis), 254

"One of the Missing" (Bierce), 62

"On Ghosts" (Shelley), 389, 390, 395

"On the Knocking at the Gate in Macbeth" (De Quincey), 198

"On the Pleasure Derived from Objects of Terror; with Sir Bertrand, a Fragment" (Aikin) 1

"On the Sublime" (Longinus), 3

"On the Supernatural in Poetry" (Radcliffe), 4, 349, 356

Original Poetry by Victor and Cazire (Shelley), 399, 402

Ormond; or, The Secret Witness (Brown), 76, 79

The Orphan of the Rhine (Sleath), 34, 37, 41, 44, 47

Orwell, George, 326

"Osen and Sokichi" [Baishoku kamonanban] (Kyoka), 18, 225, 230

"The Ostler" (Collins), 90, 95

Oswick, The Bold Outlaw (unsigned), 136

Othello, 154

Otway, Thomas, 155

Our Mutual Friend (Dickens), 92, 105, 110

"The Outsider" (Lovecraft), 272

The Outsider and Others (Lovecraft), 270

"The Oval Portrait" (Poe), 330, 416

"The Overcoat" (Gogol), 323

"Owen Wingrave" (James), 202, 205

P., S., (initials), 138

Pamela; or, Virtue Rewarded (Richardson), 48

Paradise (Morrison), 302

Paradise Lost (Milton), 171

Parental Murder; or, The Brothers: An Interesting Romance in Which Virtue and Villainy Are Contrasted, and Followed by Reward and Retribution (unsigned), 137

"Parker's Back" (O'Connor), 315, 316

"The Parricide Punished" (unsigned), 139

Parsons, Eliza, **33–47**

The Passions (Dacre), 99, 100, 101

Paul; ou, La Ferme abandonée [Paul; or, The Abandoned Farmhouse] (Ducray-Duminil), 116

Peacock, Thomas Love, 400

Peake, Richard Brinsley, 150, 151, 152, 160

Pelham; or, The Adventures of a Gentleman (Bulwer-Lytton), 83, 85

Percy (More), 150, 156

Percy, Bishop Thomas, 384

Perkin Warbeck (Shelley), 390

Pet Sematary (King), 212, 215, 221, 223

Phantasus, Eine Sammlung von Märchen, Erzählungen, Schauspiel und Novellen [Phantasus, A Collection of Tales, Stories, Plays and Novels] (Tieck), 429, 433

The Phantom Bride; or, The Castilian Bandit (Barnett), 147

The Phantom of the Opera (Leroux), 444

The Phantom; or, Montoni (Sheil), 150

A Philosophical Enquiry into the Origin of Our Ideas of the Sublime and Beautiful (Burke), 2, 5, 65, 356, 396, 438

La Philosophie dans le boudoir

[Philosophy in the Bedroom] (Sade), 365, 368

"The Philosophy of Composition" (Poe), 333

The Piazza Tales (Melville), 290

"The Picture in the House" (Lovecraft), 272, 273

Pierre; or, The Ambiguities (Melville), 290, 292, 293, 294

Pilgrims of the Rhine (Bulwer-Lytton), 83, 88

The Pirate (Scott), 388

"The Pit and the Pendulum" (Poe), 94, 326, 330, 333, 335, 338, 339, 340, 441

Pixérécourt, Réne-Charles Guilbert de, 117, 119, 148

Planché, James Robinson, 151, 344

Planck, Max, 273

"The Planters" (Atwood), 27

Plato, 322, 326, 329

Poe, Edgar Allan, 18, 19, 22, 58, 62, 64, 79, 82, 86, 89, 94, 95, 96, 97, 108, 168, 170, 174, 176, 178, 181, 183, 184, 197, 200, 225, 226, 227, 228, 230, 240, 250, 262, 265, 269, 271, 272, 286, 296, 307, 308, 318, 322, 325, 326, 327, 328, **330–43**, 375, 378, 416, 423, 431, 432, 435, 441, 444

Poems (Bürger), 2

The Poisoned Kiss and Other Stories from the Portuguese (Oates), 303

"Die Pokal" [The Goblet] (Tieck), 429, 433

Polack, Elizabeth, 152

Polidori, John, 327, **344–48**, 392, 395

Pope, Alexander, 36

The Portrait of a Lady (James), 202, 203, 209

A Portrait of the Artist as a Young Man (Joyce), 288

Possessing the Secret of Joy (Walker), 297, 298

Posthumous Fragments of Margaret Nicholson (Shelley), 399

The Posthumous Papers of the Pickwick Club (Dickens), 104, 105, 107, 108

Power Politics (Atwood), 32

"The Precipice" (Oates), 303

"A Predicament" [The Scythe of Time] (Poe), 330, 335

Preface to Shakespeare (Johnson), 349

"The Premature Burial" (Poe), 22, 330, 341

Prest, Thomas Peckett, 113

Presumption; or, The Fate of Frankenstein (Peake), 150, 151, 152, 160

Prévost, Abbe, 50, 117, 242

The Principles of Psychology (W. James), 203

"The Prisoner; or, The Fortress of Holwitz: A German Tale" (unsigned), 138

"The Private Life" (James), 202, 207, 209

The Private Memoirs and Confessions of a Justified Sinner, Written by Himself; with a Detail of Curious Traditionary Facts, and Other Evidence, by the Editor (Hogg), 93, 110, 183, 185, 186, 190, 191, 192, 193, 194, 416

The Progress of Romance and the History of Charoba, Queen of Aegypt (Reeve), 361

The Progress of Romance, through Times, Countries and Manners (Reeve), 361, 362

Prometheus Unbound (Shelley), 149, 393, 406

"The Prophetic Pictures" (Hawthorne), 165, 170

The Prophetic Warning; or, The Castle of Lindendorff (unsigned), 137, 144

"Pseudonymous Selves" (Oates), 307

The Purcell Papers (Le Fanu), 249

"The Purloined Letter" (Poe), 330, 335

Pushkin, Alexander, 322, 388

Pye, Henry James, 383

The Quaker City: A Romance of the Rich and Poor (Lippard), 261

The Quaker City; or, The Monks of Monk Hall (Lippard), 261, 262, 263, 265, 266, 268, 269

Queen Mab (Shelley), 391, 399, 400, 402, 403

The Queen of Hearts (Collins), 90, 94
"Queen of the Night" (Oates), 303

Radcliffe, Ann, 4, 29, 34, 36, 37, 38, 39,
    41, 44, 46, 47, 49, 52, 70, 74, 78, 85,
    86, 93, 95, 98, 103, 106, 110, 112,
    113, 114, 116, 117, 119, 126, 127,
    130, 131, 133, 134, 135, 136, 140,
    142, 147, 148, 150, 152, 153, 156,
    157, 158, 162, 164, 166, 171, 176,
    197, 198, 204, 242, 243, 244, 247,
    291, 293, 294, 318, **349–60**, 362, 363,
    366, 369, 370, 375, 387, 400, 404,
    409, 411,430, 444
Radcliffe, Mary-Anne, 46
"The Raft" (King), 213
Rage (King as Richard Bachman), 212
The Rainbow (Lawrence), 233, 234, 236,
    240
Rambach, Friedrich, 430
Raphael [Raffaello Santi], 431
"Rappaccini's Daughter" (Hawthorne),
    165, 171, 279
"The Rapping Spirits" (Dickens), 104,
    107
"The Rats in the Walls" (Lovecraft), 272,
    277
Rattlin the Reefer (Howard), 113
Die Räuber [The Robbers] (Schiller),
    133, 159, 182, 285, 358, 372, 373,
    375, 378, 379, 406, 430
Raven's Wing (Oates), 304
*Rayland Hall; or, The Remarkable
    Adventures of Orlando Somerville, an
    original story* (unsigned), 408
"Raymond: A Fragment" (signed
    "Juvenis"), 138, 139, 146
*Raymond and Agnes; or, The Bleeding
    Nun* (unsigned), 151
*Raymond and Agnes; or, The Bleeding
    Nun of Lindenburg* (Grosette), 148
Raymond de Percy (Harvey), 152
Reade, Charles, 106, 114
"The Real Right Thing" (James), 202,
    206
The Recess; or, A Tale of Other Times
    (Lee), 49, 241, 242, 244, 245, 246,
    247, 351

*The Recluse of the Woods; or, The
    Generous Warrior, A Gothic Romance*
    (unsigned), 137, 144
*Recollections of an Excursion to the
    Monasteries of Alcobaça and Batalha*
    (Beckford), 54, 55
Redgauntlet (Scott), 387
"The Red Hand" (Machen), 278, 280
Reeve, Clara, 4, 38, 49, 52, 78, 95, 136,
    137, 140, 156, 246, 247, 360, **361–64**,
    387, 408, 430
Reflections on the French Revolution
    (Burke), 392
The Regulators (King), 213
La Réligieuse [The Nun] (Diderot), 133,
    288, 371
Reliques of Ancient English Poetry
    (Percy), 384
Retribution: A Tale Founded on Facts
    (Bellamy), 138
"Revelation" (O'Connor), 315, 316
Revelation, Book of, 374
"Revenge" (Shelley), 402
The Revenger's Tragedy (Tourneur), 154
Reynolds, G.W.M., 114, 268
Rhymer, John Malcolm, 113
Riccoboni, Marie Jeanne de Heurlcs
    Laboras de Mézières, Madame, 117
Rice, Anne, 221
Richardson, John, 25
Richardson, Samuel, 48, 363
Richler, Mordecai, 25
*Right and Might; or, The Castle of
    Ellangowan* (unsigned), 151
"The Rime of the Ancient Mariner"
    (Coleridge), 45, 434
*Rinaldo and Adeline; or, The Ghost of St.
    Cyril* (signed), 137
"Rip Van Winkle" (Irving), 195, 198,
    201
The Rise of Life on Earth (Oates), 304
The Rival Queens (Lee), 155
Roadwork (King as Richard Bachman),
    212
Robertson, William, 242
Robinson, Mary, 102
Roche, Regina Maria, **33–47**

"The Rocking Horse Winner"
    (Lawrence), 240
Rodriguez and Isabella, or the Terrors of
    Conscience: a Tale (unsigned), 138
"Roger Dodsworth: The Reanimated
    Englishman" (Shelley), 389, 390, 394
"Roger Malvin's Burial" (Hawthorne),
    165, 172
Rokeby: A Poem (Scott), 285, 380, 382,
    385, 387
Rolla; or, The Peruvian Hero: A Tragedy
    in Five Acts (Lewis), 254
"The Romance of Certain Old Clothes"
    (James), 91, 202, 203, 204
The Romance of the Forest, interspersed
    with some pieces of poetry (Radcliffe),
    116, 119, 135, 147, 157, 247, 349,
    350, 353, 354, 355, 358
Romano Castle; or, The Horrors of the
    Forest (Watkins), 144, 145
Romantic Tales (Lewis), 166, 254
Romantic Tales: "The Revengeful Turk;
    or, Mystic Cavern"; "The Distressed
    Nun; or, Sufferings of Herselia di
    Brindoli of Florence"; "The Vindictive
    Monk; or, The Fatal Ring"
    (Crookenden), 134
Romantische Dichtungen (Tieck), 429
Romero, George, 348
Rookwood (Ainsworth), 7, 8, 9
Rookwood: A Romantic Drama in Two
    Acts (Ainsworth), 7
A Room of One's Own (Woolf), 70
The Rose and the Key (LeFanu), 250
Rose Madder (King), 213, 215, 220, 221
"The Rose Prince" (Stoker), 420
Rossetti, Christina, 348, 351
Rossetti, William Michael, 344
Roughing It in the Bush (Atwood), 26
The Round Tower; or, The Mysterious
    Witness: An Irish Legendary Tale of
    the Sixth Century (Barrett), 144, 145
Rousseau, Jean-Jacques, 50, 101, 102
The Ruffian Boy; or, The Castle of
    Waldemar: A Venetian Tale, on Which
    Is Founded the Interesting Popular
    Melodrama Now Performing at the
    Surrey Theatre, Taken from Mrs.

Opie's Celebrated Tale of That Name
    (Wilkinson), 134
Rugantino; or, The Bravo of Venice: A
    Grand Romantic Melodrama in Two
    Acts (Lewis), 149, 254
The Ruins of Empires (Volney), 393
"The Ruins of the Abbey of Fitzmartin"
    (unsigned), 139
"Der Runenberg" [The Runenberg]
    (Tieck), 182, 429, 431, 432, 433, 436
The Running Man (King as Richard
    Bachman), 212
Ruskin, John, 240
Russell, Bertrand, 271
Russian Nights [Russkie Nochi]
    (Odoevsky), 321, 322, 323

S., R., 35, 36
Sacher-Masoch, Leopold von, 369
The Sacred Fount (James), 202, 203, 210
Sade, Marquis de, 50, 52, 102, 337, 347,
    365–71
"The Salamander" (Odoevsky), 321
'Salem's Lot (King), 212, 215, 216, 217,
    218, 222
"Der Sandmann" [The Sandman]
    (Hoffmann), 177, 178, 180, 182
Sarret, Victor Jules, 139
Sartre, Jean-Paul, 326
The Scarlet Letter (Hawthorne), 165, 166,
    173, 175
Shabraco, a Romance (unsigned), 139
Schiller, Friedrich, 45, 126, 133, 159,
    181, 182, 183, 186, 254, 285, 358, 372–
    79, 383, 406, 430, 431
Schlegel, Friedrich, 178, 432
"The School-Teacher's Story" (Freeman),
    120
Scott, Jane, 152
Scott, Sir Walter, 9, 134, 159, 164, 166,
    167, 176, 178, 186, 188, 189, 191,
    192, 193, 243, 253, 256, 284, 285,
    287, 352, 357, 380–88, 414
The Secret Castle; or, Henry and Edwy
    (unsigned), 151
The Secret Glory (Machen), 278
The Secret Oath; or, The Blood-Stained
    Dagger (unsigned), 137

"The Secret of Macarger's Gulch" (Bierce), 64

"The Secret of the Growing Gold" (Stoker), 420, 421

The Secret Tribunal (Boaden), 147, 157

The Secret Tribunal; or, The Court of Wencelaus (unsigned), 145

The Seduction and Other Stories (Oates), 303

Senkovsky, Osip, 329

"A Sentimental Education" (Oates), 303

A Sentimental Education: Stories (Oates), 303

Die Serapionsbrüder [The Serapion Brothers] (Hoffmann), 182

A Series of Lay Sermons (Hogg), 191

Seven Tales of My Native Land (Hawthorne), 167

The Severed Arm; or, The Wehr-wolf of Limousin (unsigned), 139

Seward, Anna, 138

"The Shadow Builder" (Stoker), 420

The Shadow of Ashlydyat (Wood), 91

"The Shadow Out of Time" (Lovecraft), 275

"The Shadow Over Innsmouth" (Lovecraft), 270, 273, 276

Shadowy Thing (Drake), 271

"Shakespeares Behandlungen des Wunderbaren" (Tieck), 431

Shakespeare, William, 3, 154, 161, 199, 280, 322, 351, 356, 431, 446

Sharpe, Charles Kirkpatrick, 384

Shaw, George Bernard, 110

Sheil, R. L., 150

Shelley, Elizabeth, 399

Shelley, Mary Wollstonecraft, 26, 45, 70, 79, 81, 84, 85, 95, 126, 130, 131, 138, 143, 151, 159, 160, 162, 172, 255, 279, 287, 328, 345, 347, 348, 352, 364, 375, 376, 378, **389–98**, 400, 415, 417, 437

Shelley, Percy Bysshe, 57, 79, 100, 103, 126, 129, 131, 138, 149, 150, 159, 160, 345, 346, 347, 352, 391, 392, 393, 395, 397, 398, **399–407**

The Shepherd's Calendar (Hogg), 185, 186, 188, 189, 193

The Shining (King), 212, 215, 216, 217, 218, 221, 222

Shrewtzer Castle; or, The Perfidious Brother: A German Romance Including the Pathetic Tale of Edmund's Ghost, 137, 144

The Shunned House (Lovecraft), 270, 272

A Sicilian Romance (Radcliffe), 52, 133, 349, 350, 353, 358

The Sicilian Romance; or, The Apparition of the Cliff (Siddons), 150

Siddons, Henry, 150

Silence and Other Stories (Freeman), 120

Sinclair, Upton, 268

"Sinners in the Hands of an Angry God" (Edwards), 267

"Sir Bertrand, a Fragment" (Aikin), 5, 6

"Sir Dominick Ferrand" (James), 203

"Sir Edmund Orme" (James), 202, 205

Sir John Chiverton: A Romance (Ainsworth), 7, 9

Sir Rohan's Ghost (Spofford), 91

Sir Tristrem (Scott), 382, 384

Skeleton Crew (King), 213

The Skeleton; or, Mysterious Discovery: A Gothic Romance (Crookenden), 144, 145

The Sketch Book of Geoffrey Crayon, Gent. (Irving), 195, 199

Sleath, Eleanor, **33–47**

"The Smiling Death's Head" (Akinari), 12, 17

Smith, Charlotte, 46, 70, 362, 363, **408–11**

Smollett, Tobias, 247

Snake Eyes (Oates as Rosamund Smith), 304

The Snow-Image, and Other Tales (Hawthorne), 165, 171, 172

The Soft Side (James), 202

Somerset Castle; or, The Father and Daughter (unsigned), 144

"Sometimes They Come Back" (King), 212

Son of the Morning (Oates), 303, 313

Sophonisba (Lee), 155

The Sorcerer's Palace; or, The Princess of Sinadone (Wilkinson), 134

Soul/Mate (Oates as Rosamund Smith), 304

The Southern Tower; or, Conjugal Sacrifice and Retribution (unsigned), 144

Southerne, Thomas, 155

Southey, Robert, 406

"The Southwest Chamber" (Freeman), 120, 122

"Spalatro, from the Notes of Fra Giacomo" (LeFanu), 248

Die Spanier in Peru oder Rollas Tod [The Spaniards in Peru or Rolla's Death] (Kotzebue), 254

The Spanish Tragedy (Kyd), 154

"The Spectral Horseman" (Shelley), 399, 402

"The Spectre Bride" (Ainsworth), 10

"The Spectre Bridegroom" (Irving), 195, 198

The Spectre Chief; or, The Blood-Stained Banner: An Ancient Romance (Legge), 134, 144

The Spectre Mother; or, The Haunted Tower (unsigned), 139, 144

The Spectre of the Turret; or, Guolto Castle (Crookenden), 144, 145

The Spectres; or, Lord Oswald and Lady Rosa. Including an Account of the Marchioness of Cevetti Who Was Basely Consigned to a Dungeon beneath Her Castle by her Eldest Son, Whose Cruel Avarice Plunged Him into the Commission of the Worst of Crimes. That Stain the Annals of the Human Race: An Original Romantic Tale (Wilkinson), 134

"Speeches for Dr. Frankenstein" (Atwood), 24, 26

Spencer, J. H., 383

Spenser, Edmund, 229

"The Spider" (Bowers), 271

Spofford, Harriet Elizabeth, 91

"Eine Spukgeschichte" [A Ghost Story] (Hoffmann), 177, 182

"The Squaw" (Stoker), 420, 421, 424

"Squire Toby's Will" (LeFanu), 248

"Stalking" (Oates), 307

The Stand (King), 212, 214, 215, 217, 218, 220

Stanley, W. T., 383

St. Clair of the Isles (Polack), 152

St. Germain, Comte de, 322

St. Irvyne; or, The Rosicrucian (Shelley), 100, 103, 129, 138, 391, 393, 399, 400, 401, 405, 406

St. Leon: A Drama, in Three Acts (Caunter), 125

St. Leon: A Tale of the Sixteenth Century (Godwin), 125, 126, 130, 131, 391, 400

St. Margaret's Cave (Carr), 148

St. Ronan's Well (Scott), 388

Stanley Brereton (Ainsworth), 8

Starr Bright Will Be with You Soon (Oates as Rosamund Smith), 304

"A Star Trap" (Stoker), 421

Stevenson, Robert Louis, 193, 279, **412–19**

Stoker, Bram, 251, 279, 348, 417, **420–28**

"A Stolen Letter" (Collins), 90, 91

"Stories of Lough Guir" (LeFanu), 249, 250

"The Story of a Cock, a Cat, and a Frog" (Odoevsky), 321

The Story of Morella De Alto; or, The Crimes of Scorpino Developed (Crookenden), 133

"The Story of the Bagman's Uncle" [The Ghosts of the Mail] (Dickens), 104

"The Story of the Goblins Who Stole a Sexton" (Dickens), 104, 107

"The Story of the Young Italian" (Irving), 195

Stowe, Harriet Beecher, 268

The Strange Case of Dr. Jekyll and Mr. Hyde (Stevenson), 216, 279, 280, 412, 413,414, 415, 416, 417, 418, 419

"Strange Event in the Life of Schalken the Painter" (LeFanu), 248, 249

"The Stranger" (Bierce), 62

"Strange Stories by a Nervous Gentleman" (Irving), 195, 197, 201

A Strange Story (Bulwer-Lytton), 83, 86, 87, 89, 91

Straub, Peter, 212

"The Striding Place" ["The Twins"](Atherton), 22

"A Stroke of Good Fortune" (O'Connor), 315

"The Student of Salamanca" (Irving), 195

Styron, William, 298

The Subterraneous Passage; or Gothic Cell (Wilkinson), 134

Sue, Eugène, 268

The Sufferings of Young Werther (Goethe), 179

"The Suitable Surroundings" (Bierce), 65

Supernatural Horror in Literature (Lovecraft), 271

Surfacing (Atwood), 24, 25, 27, 28, 29, 32

"The Surgery Room" [Gekashitsu] (Kyoka), 18, 225, 226, 227, 228

Surtees, Robert, 384

Survival: A Thematic Guide to Canadian Literature (Atwood), 24, 25, 26, 32

"Survivor Type" (King), 213

Suttree (McCarthy), 319

Swedenborg. Emanuel, 253, 322, 329

Swift, Jonathan, 382

"The Sylph" (Odoevsky), 321, 324, 326, 328

"A Symphony in Lavender" (Freeman), 120, 122

The System of Dante's Hell (Baraka), 301

"The System of Doctor Tarr and Professor Fether" (Poe), 330, 335

"The Tale of a Dead Body, Belonging to No One Knows Whom" (Odoevsky), 321, 323

"The Tale of Guzman's Family" (Maturin), 286

"The Tale of Kosem Kesamin the Magician" (Bulwer-Lytton), 83

A Tale of Mystery (Holcroft), 148, 151, 158

A Tale of Mystery; or Celina (Meeke), 116

A Tale of Mystery; or, The Castle of Solitude. Containing the Dreadful Imprisonment of Count L. and the

Countess Harmina, His Lady (unsigned), 137, 140

A Tale of Terror (Siddons), 150

"The Tale of the Indians" (Maturin), 286

"The Tale of the Lovers" (Maturin), 286

"The Tale of the Parricide" (Maturin), 286

"The Tale of the Spaniard" (Maturin), 288

"A Tale of Three Who Were Blind" (Kyoka), 225

A Tale of Two Cities (Dickens), 86

Tales by Edgar A. Poe (Poe), 330

Tales from the Phantasus (Tieck), 429

Tales of a Traveller (Irving), 195, 197

Tales of Moonlight and Rain (Akinari), 12, 13, 14, 15, 17, 18, 19

Tales of Soldiers and Civilians (Bierce), 60, 62

Tales of Terror (Lewis), 400

Tales of the Crypt—in the Style of the Monk (unsigned), 139

Tales of the Grotesque and Arabesque (Poe), 330, 334

Tales of the Spring Rain (Akinari), 14, 17, 18, 19

Tales of Wonder: Written and Collected by M. G. Lewis, Esq., M. P. (Lewis), 254, 380, 383, 384

Talfourd, Thomas Noon [Serjeant], 349, 351

The Talisman (King and Straub), 212, 215, 220

Tamberlaine (Marlowe), 154

"The Tapestried Chamber" (Scott), 381

Taschenbuch für Kunst und Laune [Notebook for Art and Mood] (Tieck), 429

Taylor, Tom, 7

Taylor, William, 2, 383

"The Tell-Tale Heart" (Poe), 89, 95, 323, 330, 333, 338, 340

The Tenant of Wildfell Hall (A. Brontë), 73

Tencin, Madame de [Claudine Alexandrine Guérin], 48, 49, 50, 52

Tenshu monogatari [The Castle Tower] (Kyoka), 225, 230, 232

"A Terribly Strange Bed" (Collins), 90, 91, 94, 98

The Terror: A Fantasy (Machen), 278

"The Terrorist System of Novel Writing" (A Jacobin Novelist), 34, 35

Terry, Daniel, 382

them (Oates), 305, 307, 314

Theodore and Emma; or, The Italian Bandit, in Which the Fatal Effects of Revenge Are Portrayed in the Character of Marquis De Rovigno, Who, Disappointed at the Preference Given to the Count De Valenza by the Daughter of the Duke of Parma, Enrolls Himself in the Company of Daring Banditti, in Order to Accomplish His Diabolical Scheme of Assassinating the Count, Waldemar, Who, in the Engagement with Theodore, Accidentally Kills His Own Father! Also, the Melancholy Catastrophe Which Attends the Counts De Valenza and Ravenna, in the Deaths of Theodore and Emma (signed "an Etonian"), 137

"The Thing on the Doorstep" (Lovecraft), 273, 274, 275

Thinner (King as Richard Bachman), 213

"The Third Person" (James), 202, 207

"Thomas the Rymer" (Scott), 384

Thompson, Alexander, 144

Thomson, James, 199

Thoreau, Henry David, 263

Thoughts on the Education of Daughters (Wollstonecraft), 391

The Thousand and One Arabian Nights (Galland), 54, 59

"The Thousand-and-Second Tale of Scheherazade" (Poe), 330

"Thrawn Jane" (Stevenson), 412, 413, 416

The Three Ghosts of the Forest, A Tale of Horror: An Original Romance (Thompson), 138, 146

The Three Impostors (Machen), 278, 281

The Three Perils of Man, War, Women, and Witchcraft: A Border Romance (Hogg), 185, 186, 187, 190, 193

The Three Perils of Woman; or, Love, Leasing, and Jealousy: A Series of Domestic Scottish Tales (Hogg), 185, 190, 193

Tieck, Ludwig, 179, 181, 182, 183, 184, 342, **429–36**

Timour the Tartar (Lewis), 149

'Tis Pity She's a Whore (Ford), 154

Titus Andronicus (Shakespeare), 154

"To Be Read at Dusk" (Dickens), 104

Tolkien, J.R.R., 215

"The Tomb" (Lovecraft), 272, 275

The Tomb of Aurora; or, The Mysterious Summons (unsigned), 138

The Tommyknockers (King), 213, 214, 215, 276

Torbolton Abbey; A Gothic Tale (Wilkinson), 134

Tourneur, Cyril, 154

The Tower of London: A Historical Romance (Ainsworth), 7, 10

The Tower of London; or, Queen Mary, an Historical Drama in Three Acts (Taylor), 7

The Tower of London; or, The Death Omen and the Fate of Lady Jane Grey, a Drama in Three Acts (Higgie and Lacy), 7

The Towers of Urbandine (Carr), 148

"Transformation" (Shelley), 389, 390, 391, 394

"The Trial for Murder: To be Taken with a Grain of Salt" (Dickens), 105, 108, 113

The Triumph of the Spider Monkey (Oates), 303

Trollope, Anthony, 37

"Trucks" (King), 212

"The Tryst" (Oates), 303

The Turn of the Screw (James), 21, 202, 203, 204, 206, 209, 210, 211, 308

Turpin's Ride to York (Ainsworth), 7

Twain, Mark, 174

"The Twelfth Guest" (Freeman), 120, 122

Twice-Told Tales (Hawthorne), 165, 168, 169, 170, 333

"The Twins" (Atherton), 20
"The Two Drovers" (Scott), 381

"Über das Erhabene" [On the Sublime] (Kant), 373
"Ultor de Lacy" (LeFanu), 248, 250
"The Unbroken Chain" (Cobb), 271
"Uncle Otto's Truck" (King), 213
Uncle Silas: A Tale of Bartram Haugh (LeFanu), 91, 250, 253
Under the Sunset (Stoker), 420, 424
"Under the Sunset" (Stoker), 420
Undine (Hoffmann), 178
"Unmailed, Unwritten Letters" (Oates), 303
"The Unparalleled Adventure of One Hans Pfaall" (Poe), 336

"The Vacant Lot" (Freeman), 120
"The Vale of Esthwaite" (Wordsworth), 5
"Valerius: The Reanimated Roman" (Shelley), 389, 390, 395
Valperga; or, The Life and Adventures of Castruccio, Prince of Lucca (Shelley), 389, 390, 394, 396
"Vampirismus" [Vampirism] (Hoffmann), 177, 182
The Vampire (Planché), 151
The Vampyre: A Tale (Polidori), 344, 345, 347, 348, 437
The Vampyre: A Tale by the Right Honourable Lord Byron (Polidori), 344, 347, 348
The Vampyre; or the Bride of the Isles: A Romantic Melodrama in Two Acts (Planché), 344
Vandover and the Brute (Norris), 268
Varbeck (Baculard d'Arnaud), 242
Variegated Tales [Pestrye Skazki s krasyym slovtsom pyostryye skazki] (Odoevsky), 321, 322
The Varieties of Religious Experience (W. James), 203
Varney the Vampyre (Prest or Rhymer), 113
Vathek; An Arabian Tale from an Unpublished Manuscript (Beckford), 53, 55, 56, 57, 58, 59, 339, 430, 437

Venice Preserved (Otway), 155
Venoni; or, The Novice of St. Mark's (Lewis), 149, 254
Der Verbrecher aus verlorener Ehre [The Criminal of Lost Honor] (Schiller), 378, 379
Les Victimes de cloîtrées (Boutet de Monvel), 50, 254
Victor; ou, L'Enfant de la forêt [Victor; or, The Child of the Forest] (Ducray-Duminil), 116, 117, 118, 119
Villette (C. Brontë), 69, 71, 72, 74, 75
Vimonda, A Tragedy (McDonald), 149, • 156, 157, 162, 164
A Vindication of the Rights of Woman (Wollstonecraft), 122
"The Vindictive Monk; or, The Fatal Ring" (Crookenden), 139
"The Violent Bear It Away" (O'Connor), 315, 316, 317
"The Virgin in the Rose-Bower; or, the Tragedy of Glen Mawr Manor" (Oates), 310
"Visions of the Night" (Bierce), 63
Volksmärchen herausgegeben von Peter Leberrecht [Folk Tales Published by Peter Leberrecht) (Tieck), 429
Volney, Constantin-François de Chasseboeuf, Count, 393
Voltaire [François Marie Arouet], 50, 59, 117

W., E. (initials), 138
Wackenroder, Wilhelm, 430, 431
Wacousta; or, The Prophecy: A Tale of the Canadas (Richardson), 25
Wagner, the Wehr-wolf (Reynolds), 268
"Wakefield" (Hawthorne), 165
"Wake Not the Dead" (Tieck), 342, 435
Walker, Alice, 297
Walker, C. E., 150
Walpole, Horace, 3, 18, 51, 59, 84, 85, 93, 106, 116, 118, 126, 127, 131, 135, 136, 137, 140, 149, 150, 151, 152, 153, 154, 155, 158, 160, 161, 162, 163, 164, 173, 181, 247, 287, 291, 294, 332, 353, 355, 361, 362, 363,

364, 369, 379, 382, 387, 408, 417, **437–47**

The Wandering Boys; or, The Castle of Olival (Kerr), 149

"The Wandering Jew" (Shelley), 399, 402

"The Wandering Jew's Soliloquy" (Shelley), 399, 402

The Wandering Spirit; or, The Memoirs of the House of Morno (unsigned), 138, 144

"Wandering Willie's Tale" (Scott), 381

The Ward of the Castle (Burke), 152

The Warlock of the Glen (Walker), 150

"The Watcher" ["The Familiar"] (LeFanu), 248, 249, 250, 251

The Watcher and Other Weird Stories (LeFanu), 249

"A Watcher by the Dead" (Bierce), 65

The Water Spectre; or, An Bratach (Wilkinson), 134

Watkins, Lucy, 144, 145

Waverley; or, 'Tis Sixty Years Since (Scott), 380, 381, 382, 386, 387

"Wealth and Poverty" (Akinari), 12

Webster, John, 154, 161

"The Wedding Knell" (Hawthorne), 165, 169

"Wereman" (Atwood), 27

West, B., 283

West, Benjamin, 150

Weymyss, Francis C., 269

Whalley, Thomas Sedgwick, 134, 144

Wharton, Edith, 123

"What Is the Connection between Men and Women?" (Oates), 303

The Wheel of Love and Other Stories (Oates), 303, 307

"Where Are You Going, Where Have You Been?" (Oates), 303, 313, 314

Where Are You Going, Where Have You Been? Selected Early Stories (Oates), 304

Where Are You Going, Where Have You Been? Stories of Young America (Oates), 303

Where Is Here? (Oates), 304

"The Whisperer in Darkness" (Lovecraft), 273, 274

"The White Cat" (Oates), 308

"The White Cat of Drumgunniol" (LeFanu), 249, 250

"The White Old Maid" (Hawthorne), 165, 167, 170

"White Peak" (Akinari), 12, 15

"The White People" (Machen), 278, 280

"The White Witch's Tale" (Kyoka), 230

"Who Killed Zebedee?" (Collins), 90

"Why Don't You Come Live with Me It's Time" (Oates), 305

"Wicked Captain Walshawe of Wauling" (LeFanu), 248

Wieland; or, The Transformation (Brown), 76, 78, 79, 80, 118, 173, 327

Wilde, Oscar, 209

Wild Geese (Ostenso), 32

"The Wild Huntsmen" (Scott), 380, 384

The Wild Irish Boy (Maturin), 285, 288

Wilkinson, Sarah, 134, 142, 143, 144, 145, 146

"William and Helen" (Scott), 383

William Lovell (Tieck), 429, 430

"William Wilson" (Poe), 330, 335

Will You Always Love Me? and Other Stories (Oates), 304

Wilson, John, 191

"The Wind in the Rose-Bush" (Freeman), 120

The Wind in the Rose-Bush and Other Stories of the Supernatural (Freeman), 120

Windsor Castle (Ainsworth), 7

The Winter's Tale (Shakespeare), 199, 446

Wise Blood (O'Connor), 315, 316, 317

"The Witches of Traquair" (Hogg), 188

"The Witch's Daughter" (Freeman), 120, 121

"The Wives of the Dead" (Hawthorne), 165, 172

"Wolfert's Roost" (Irving), 195

Wolfert's Roost and Other Papers (Irving), 195

"Wolfert Webber" (Irving), 195, 198

Wolfstein; or, The Mysterious Bandit: A Terrific Romance to which Is Added the Bronze Statue, A Pathetic Tale (unsigned), 138, 144

Wollstonecraft, Mary, 43, 100, 102, 122, 130, 351, 390, 391, 397

The Woman in White (Collins), 90, 92, 93, 97, 98

The Woman Who Rode Away and Other Stories (Lawrence), 233

Women in Love (Lawrence), 233, 234,236, 240

Women; or Pour et Contre (Maturin), 285

Wonderland (Oates), 303, 306, 313

The Wonders of the Invisible World (Mather), 199

"The Wondrous Child" (Stoker), 420

The Wood Daemon; or, "The Clock Has Struck" (Lewis), 149, 158, 163, 254

Wood, Mrs. Henry, 91

Woolf, Virginia, 69, 122

Woolfert's Roost and Other Papers, Now First Collected (Irving), 195

"The Wool-Gatherer" (Hogg), 194

Wordsworth, William, 140, 158, 193, 406, 410

The Works of Anna Laetitia Barbauld, with a Memoir (Aikin), 5

The Works of Horatio Walpole (Walpole), 437, 444

Worldly Apes with a Smattering of Various Arts (Akinari), 13

Wright, Richard, 296

Wuthering Heights (E. Brontë), 69, 71, 73, 74, 287

Wylder's Hand: A Novel (LeFanu), 248

The Wyvern Mystery (LeFanu), 248

Yeats, William Butler, 281

"The Yellow Mask" (Collins), 90, 94

You Can't Catch Me (Oates as Rosamund Smith), 304

Young, Edward, 49

"Young Goodman Brown" (Hawthorne), 129, 165, 168

"The Young Lady's Tale: The Two Emilys" (Lee), 241, 245

Zanoni (Bulwer-Lytton), 83, 86, 87, 89

Zastrozzi: A Romance (P. B. Shelley), 100, 103, 138, 391, 399, 400, 405, 406, 407

Zicci (Bulwer-Lytton), 83, 86

Zittaw the Cruel; or, The Woodsman's Daughter: A Polish Romance (Wilkinson), 145

Zofloya; or The Moor: A Romance of the Fifteenth Century (Dacre), 50, 99, 100, 102, 103, 139, 366, 400, 404

Zombie (Oates), 304, 306

Zschokke, Heinrich, 254

INDEX OF CRITICS, EDITORS, AND TRANSLATORS

Abensour, Liliane, 51
Achilles, Jochen, 252
Ackley, Katherine Anne, 222
Adams, Robert M., 185
Adelsperger, Walter Charles, 161
Akiyama, Masayuki, 208
Alexander, Boyd, 57, 59
Alexander, Christine, 70, 72
Alexander, J. H., 164, 381, 387
Allen, Michael, 252
Allen, M. L., 175
Allen, Paul M., 84
Alliston, April, 241, 242, 246
Allott, Miriam, 406
Anderson, Charles, 342
Anderson, Howard, 255, 258
Anderson, Quentin, 203
Anderson, Walter E., 42
Andreas, James, 318
Andrew, R. V., 96
Andrews, Malcolm, 105
Andrews, Norwood, Jr., 371
Andrews, William L., 298, 300, 302
Anthony, M. Susan, 161
Antippas, Andy, 405
Araki, James T., 18
Arata, S. D., 425
Arvin, Newton, 293
Ashley, Mike, 252, 258
Astle, Richard S., 347

Atwood, Margaret, 31
Auerbach, Nina, 42, 426
Axton, William F., 283, 286
Aziz, Maqbool, 203

Backscheider, Paula R., 153, 161
Badley, Linda, 219, 221
Baines, Paul, 151, 445
Baker, Christine, 105
Baker, Ernest A., 125
Baker, Houston, 295
Baldick, Chris, 1, 139, 143, 395, 412, 416
Ballinger, Leonora M., 208
Banerji, Krishna, 395
Banta, Martha, 209
Barbour, Judith, 347
Bardin, Barbara, 363
Baridon, Michel, 58
Barnett, Pamela, 299, 300
Barron-Wilson, Mrs. Cornwall, 258
Bartolomeo, Joseph, 410
Baumgaertner, Jill P., 318
Baym, Nina, 82, 175
Beahm, George, 221
Beauvoir, Simone de, 365
Beaver, Harold, 331
Becker, Susanne, 31
Beckett, Juliet, 126
Behrendt, Stephen C., 399, 401, 405

Beidler, Peter G., 203, 206, 209
Belford, Barbara, 425
Bell, Ian, 412, 416
Bell, Michael Davitt, 77, 80, 197, 198, 200
Bender, Eileen-Teper, 312
Bendixen, Alfred, 20, 121, 123
Benedict, Barbara M., 357
Bennett, Betty T., 390, 406
Benrahhal-Serghini, El-Habib, 57
Bentley, C. F., 425
Bentman, Raymond, 446
Benton, Richard, 340, 341
Berman, Lorna, 370
Bernard-Griffiths, Simone, 119
Bernstein, Stephen, 97
Berryman, John, 255
Berthoff, Warner, 76
Berthold, Dennis, 80
Bidney, Martin, 434
Bierman, Joseph S., 425, 426
Bignell, Jonathan, 425
Birkhead, Edith, 352
Black, Robert Kerr, 42
Blakemore, Steven, 258
Blakey, Dorothy, 43
Blanchot, Maurice, 365
Bleiler, E.[verett] F., 11, 23, 53, 59, 60, 63, 66, 68, 90, 97, 177, 179, 182, 183, 194, 201, 221, 249, 252, 260, 266, 286, 344, 425, 434
Bleiler, Richard, 221
Blight, David W., 301
Bloch, Robert, 270
Block, Edwin F., Jr., 416
Bloede, Barbara, 193
Blondel, Jacques, 193
Bloom, Harold, 221, 312, 313, 395
Blumberg, Jane, 390
Bohn, Henry G., 372, 379
Bonaparte, Marie, 331, 341
Boone, Troy, 347
Booth, Bradford E., 97, 416
Botting, Fred, 93, 97, 352, 357, 393, 396
Boudreau, Gordon V., 293
Boulton, James T., 357, 446
Bowden, Mary Weatherspoon, 200
Boyle, Richard, 414, 415, 416, 418

Bradbury, Malcolm, 196
Bradley, Sculley, 166
Brancaccio, Patrick, 77, 80
Brandenberg, Alice S., 161
Brantlinger, Patrick, 91, 97, 98, 414, 415, 416, 418
Brennan, Matthew C., 73, 417
Briggs, Julia, 281
Britton, Wesley, 298, 299, 301
Broadwell, Elisabeth P., 357
Bronfen, Elisabeth, 370
Brooks, Peter, 258
Brown, Julie, 124
Brown, Laura, 357
Brown, Margaret, 105
Browne, Nelson, 252
Browne, Ray B., 221, 240
Browning, Preston M., 317, 318
Browning, Robert M., 429
Budick, E. Miller, 341
Bullough, Geoffrey, 59
Burgess, Miranda J., 410
Burke, Edmund, 5
Burleson, Donald R., 276
Burns, Edward, 151
Burns, Gail, 222
Burns, Margie, 318
Butler, Marilyn, 130
Butterfield, Roger, 268
Byron, Glennis, 210, 421

Cady, Edwin H., 209
Calder, Angus, 105
Calder, Jenni, 413, 414, 417
Calhoun, Thomas O., 175
Cameron, Kenneth Neill, 161, 399
Campbell, Ann, 258
Campbell, James, 252
Campbell, Jill, 446
Cannon, Peter, 276
Carey, John, 185
Carlyle, Thomas, 378, 434
Carpenter, Juliet, 231
Carpenter, Lynette, 123
Carpi, Daniela, 161
Carter, Angela, 370
Carter, Margaret, 425, 426, 428
Casebeer, Edwin F., 222

Cass, Jeffrey, 347
Castle, Terry, 350, 357
Castro, Jan Garden, 32
Chandler, Wayne A., 66
Chanover, E. Pierre, 370
Chapman, Guy, 53, 57
Chapman, Mary, 76
Chard, Chloe, 350
Charlton, William, 282
Charras, Françoise, 51
Charvat, P. E., 166
Charvat, William, 116, 166
Chase, Richard, 81, 290, 291
Chatterjee, Visvanath, 395
Chell, Cara, 312
Chesser, Eustace, 405
Chisholm, Richard M., 175
Christensen, Allan Conrad, 89
Christensen, Merten A., 45
Christian, Nicole, 328
Christophersen, Bill, 80
Cismaru, Alfred, 371
Claésson, Dick, 57
Clemens, Valdine, 425
Clemit, Pamela, 126, 130, 390
Clendenning, John, 200
Clery, E.[mma] J., 364, 367, 370, 437, 446
Coale, Samuel Chase, 312
Cobb, Palmer, 183
Cockroft, T. G. L., 276
Cohan, Stephen, 5, 151, 157, 161
Cohen, Steven, 151
Coleman, Deirdre, 347
Collings, Michael R., 222
Conger, Syndy M., 45, 71, 73, 258, 357, 378, 396, 397, 446
Coolidge, Archibald, 112
Cordery, Gareth, 112
Cordner, Michael, 151
Cornwell, Neil, 321, 326, 328, 329
Cornyetz, Nina, 231
Cottom, Daniel, 357, 387
Coughlan, Patricia, 252
Coward, David, 365
Cowie, Alexander, 76
Cowley, Julian, 283
Cox, Arthur J., 105

Cox, Jeffrey N., 149, 152, 153, 158, 160, 161, 255
Cox, Michael, 412
Coyle, William, 348
Craciun, Adriana, 99, 101, 102, 139
Craft, Christopher, 424, 425
Crawford, Gary William, 252
Creighton, Joanne V., 312
Creutziger, Werner, 321
Crook, Nora, 390, 396
Crosby, Christina, 73
Crosland, Margaret, 365, 368
Crouch, Stanley, 298
Crow, Charles L., 67, 201, 261
Crowley, John W., 67, 201
Cuddon, J. A., 177
Cunliffe, Marcus, 60
Curran, Ronald T., 173, 175
Curran, Stuart, 406
Curtis, Julia, 268
Cvetkovich, Ann, 98

Dabundo, Laura, 288
Dahl, Curtis, 89
Dalby, Richard, 283, 420
Daly, Brenda, 307, 313
D'Amico, Diane, 287
Daniels, Les, 425
Dansky, Richard, 287
David, Deirdre, 98
Davidson, Arnold E., 32
Davidson, Cathy N., 32
Davidson, Peter, 43, 143, 164, 287, 328, 358, 381
Davis, Jonathan P., 222
Davis, Lloyd, 427
Dawson, Leven M., 287
Dawson, Robert L., 51, 52
Day, Leon, 67
DeCamp, L. Sprague, 276
DeGrazia, Emilio, 269
Deleuze, Gilles, 258
Delon, Michel, 49, 52
DePiaggi, Giorgio, 117, 118
Derleth, August, 249, 270
Dickerson, Vanessa, 73
DiRenzo, Anthony, 319
Doane, Janice, 417

Dobrée, Bonamy, 350
Docherty, Brian, 222
Doe, Donald Bartlett, 162
Dolan, Janet A., 437
Dole, Carol, 446
Donaldson, Norman, 96, 97
Donaldson, Stephen, 58, 446
Doubleday, Neal F., 168, 175
Douglass, Frederick, 296, 297, 301
Doyle, Barry, 258
Dromgoole, Nicholas, 372, 378
Duberman, Martin, 446
Duerksen, Roland A., 151
Duncan, Ian, 193, 381, 387
Dunn, James A., 103
Dunn, Richard J., 69
Durant, David S., Jr., 357
Dury, Richard, 412
Dynes, Wayne R., 58, 446
Dziemianowicz, Stefan, 277, 420

Easson, Angus, 105
Eckhardt, Jacob C., 277
Edel, Leon, 202, 203, 210
Edge, Charles, 259
Edmundson, Mark, 295, 296, 300, 301
Edwards, R., 426
Egan, James, 222, 313
Egorov, B. F., 321
Ehlers, Leigh A., 364, 446
Ehrenpreis, Anne Henry, 34, 43, 408, 411
Ehrlich, Heyward, 266, 267, 269
Eighteen-Bisang, Robert, 421
Eigner, Edwin M., 89, 417
Eliot, T.[homas] S.[arns], 97
Elliott, Emory, 77
Ellis, Kate Ferguson, 246
Ellis, Katherine, 410
Ellis, S. M., 97
Ellmann, Maud, 10, 421
Emden, Cecil S., 43
Emmons, Winfred S., Jr., 276
Engel, Leonard W., 341
Ernle, Lord, 141
Euridge, Gareth M., 258
Evans, Bertrand, 147, 149, 153, 154, 155, 156, 157, 159, 160, 162
Ewton, Ralph W., 434

Fairbairns, Zoe, 408
Fairclough, Peter, 105, 437
Farmer, Steve, 91
Farson, Daniel, 426
Fawbert, Libby, 73
Fawcett, Mary Laughlin, 357
Feldman, Paula R., 390, 395
Fernbach, Amanda, 426
Ferris, Ina, 381, 386, 387
Fiedler, Leslie, 81, 262, 269, 341
Figliola, Samantha, 217, 222
Finan, Eileen, 364
Fisch, Audrey A., 396
Fischer, Doucet Devin, 390
Fisher, Benjamin F., IV, 123, 201, 293
Fishwick, Marshall W., 240
Fisken, Beth Wynne, 123
Fitzgerald, Robert, 319
Fitzgerald, Sally, 315, 319
Flanders, Wallace, 131
Fleenor, Juliann E., 32, 73, 74, 319
Fletcher, Loraine, 410, 411
Fliegelman, Jay, 76, 80
Florescu, Radu, 396, 426
Fogle, Richard, 259
Ford, George H., 417
Forry, Steven Earl, 151, 162
Fortenberry, George E., 67
Foster, Edward, 123
Foster, James R., 51, 52, 246, 411
Fothergill, Brian, 57, 58
Foucault, Michel, 258, 350
Foust, Ronald, 348
Fowler, Kathleen, 287
Fradin, Joseph, 89
Francechina, John, 152
Frank, Frederick S., 43, 57, 58, 144, 145, 259, 346, 348, 396, 397, 399, 405
Franklin, Michael, 57
Frenz, Horst, 161
Freye, Walter, 387
Friedman, Ellen, 314
Froude, James Anthony, 429
Fry, Carrol L., 66, 409, 411
Frye, Northrup, 24
Fuchs, Miriam, 314
Furbank, P. N., 105

Gale, Robert L., 66
Galloway, David, 331
Gamer, Michael C., 162, 387
Garber, Frederick, 350, 355
Gardner, John, 313
Garrett, John, 57
Garrett, Peter K., 414, 418
Garrison, Joseph M., Jr., 341
Garside, Peter, 381
Gaspard, Claire, 119
Gasson, Andrew, 97
Gates, Barbara, 252
Geduld, Harry M., 417
Geismar, Maxwell, 166
Gemmett, Robert James, 56, 58
Getz, John R., 201
Giddings, Robert, 425
Gide, André, 185
Gifford, Douglas, 185, 187, 191
Gigante, Denise, 396
Gilbert, Harriet, 241
Gilbert, R. A., 412
Gilbert, Sandra M., 70, 73
Gill, R. B., 58
Gill, Stephen, 105
Gillespie, Tracey, 31
Gillet, Jean, 119
Ginsberg, Lesley, 341
Glasser, Leah Blatt, 122, 123
Glock, Waldo, 43
Glover, Arnold, 358
Goard, Robert R., 52
Goddu, Teresa A., 80, 175, 297, 300, 301
Goldner, Ellen J., 294
Goldstone, Adrian, 281
Goodman, Charlotte, 313
Gordon, Jan B., 73
Goslee, Nancy Moore, 381, 387
Grabo, Norman S., 76, 77, 78, 80
Grace, Sherrill, 31
Graham, Kenneth W., 44, 55, 57, 131,
    132, 144, 294, 357, 358, 406
Graham, Wendy, 175
Grant, Douglas, 283
Grayson, Susan B., 371
Greenfield, Susan C., 358
Greenman, David J., 113
Grenander, Mary Elizabeth, 66

Grieder, Josephine, 52
Grierson, Herbert, 381
Griffin, Gail B., 426
Griffith, Clark, 341
Griffith, Kelly, Jr., 201
Grogan, Claire, 34
Gross, Louis, 296, 301
Gross, Seymour L., 166
Grove, Allen Whitlock, 5, 46
Groves, David, 186
Gruner, Elisabeth Rose, 98
Guattari, Felix, 258

Haase, Donald P., 434
Haefner, Joel, 411
Hagedorn, Julia Angelica, 435
Haggerty, George E., 58, 59, 73, 440,
    446
Haining, Peter, 1, 105, 139, 143, 145,
    283, 372, 429
Halberstam, Judith, 426
Hale, Terry, 52, 117, 119, 397
Hall, Daniel, 145
Halliburton, David G., 405
Hammond, Karla, 31
Handwerk, Gary, 126, 131
Hanson, Clare, 222
Hanson, James Carl, 378
Harding, Anthony, 59
Hare, Julius C., 429
Harfst, Betsy Perteit, 440, 446
Harper, Howard M., Jr., 259
Harpold, Terrence, 397
Harris, John Bernhard, 287
Harris, Trudier, 301
Harrison, James A., 331
Haslam, Richard, 287
Hasler, Antony, 186, 191, 193
Hatlen, Burton, 214, 215, 222
Hayden, John O., 388
Hayes, Elizabeth, 23
Hayes, Michael, 381, 413
Hayford, Harrison, 290, 293
Hayter, Alethea, 162, 283
Hazlitt, William, 80, 158, 162, 357, 358
Hearn, Lafcadio, 12, 13
Heilman, Robert, 73
Heine, Maurice, 365

Heinritz, Reinhard, 183, 193
Heller, Lee E., 398
Heller, Terry, 81
Heller, Wendy Tamar, 73, 97, 98
Hendershot, Cyndy, 97
Henley, Samuel, 53, 55
Hennelly, Mark M., Jr., 98, 259
Hewitt, David, 164, 381, 387
Hicks, James, 222
Hilbish, Florence May Anna, 411
Hill-Miller, Katherine, 397
Hindle, Maurice, 126, 421
Hinds, Elizabeth Jane Wall, 81
Hirsch, David H., 123
Hirsch, Gordon, 414, 415, 417, 418, 419
Hitchens, Gordon, 162
Hodgell, Pat, 109, 113
Hodges, Devon, 417
Hoeveler, Diane Long, 43, 74, 103, 397,
    411
Hoffman, Daniel, 331, 341
Hogle, Jerrold E., 259, 405, 415, 419,
    426
Hohne, Karen A., 218, 222
Holland, Peter, 151
Hollier, Denis, 116
Hollingdale, R. J., 177
Holloway, John, 105
Holt, Marilyn J., 23
Holzknecht, Karl J., 162
Homans, Margaret, 74
Hopkins, Ernest Jerome, 60
Hopkins, L., 426
Hoppenstand, Gary, 61, 66, 221
Horvitz, Deborah, 299, 301
House, Elizabeth B., 301
Howard, Richard, 210
Howe, P. P., 81, 358
Howells, Coral Ann, 31, 46
Howes, Marjorie, 253, 426
Hughes, Henry J., 18, 231
Hughes, William, 421, 426
Hull, Ramona E., 175
Humbertclaude, Pierre, 18
Hume, Robert D., 244, 246
Humma, John, 240
Humphrey, George, 119
Hurley, Kelly, 281

Hushahn, Helga, 358
Hustis, Harriet, 331, 342
Hutter, A. D., 98
Hyland, Peter, 58

Imig, Barbara L., 411
Indick, Ben, 276
Ingersoll, Earl G., 31
Inglis, Tony, 381
Ingpen, Roger, 399
Inklaar, D., 52
Inouye, Charles Shiro, 18, 225, 226, 229,
    231
Inverso, Mary Beth, 162
Irwin, Joseph James, 255, 259
Issac, Megan Lyn, 246

Jack, Ian, 69
Jack, Malcolm, 53
Jackman, Barry, 12, 19
Jackson, Joseph, 269
Jackson, Rosemary, 112, 113
Jacobs, Edward, 145
Jaffe, Nora Crow, 1, 344, 412
James, Henry, 175
Jansohn, Christa, 233, 240
Jarrett, David, 109, 113
Jasper, David, 253
Jeannotte, M. Sharon, 313
Jefford, Andrew, 417
Jerenic, Maria, 43
Jewel, Mark, 231
Johnson, Anthony, 287
Johnson, Greg, 313
Jones, Ann H., 103
Jones, Douglas, 193
Jones, Linda B., 287
Jones, Robert, 67
Jones, Wendy, 259
Joshi, S. T., 60, 61, 66, 67, 270, 276,
    277, 279, 282, 420

Kahane, Claire, 319
Kamla, Thomas, 183
Kanner, Melinda, 222
Karlinsky, Simon, 329
Karpinski, Joanne P., 81, 319, 342
Kaufman, Pamela J., 163

Kawakami, Chiyoko, 231
Keene, Donald, 232
Kelley, Theresa M., 395
Kelly, Gary, 191, 193
Kelly, Richard, 89
Kendrick, Walter M., 97, 98
Kent, Brian, 222
Kent, Charles, 89
Kent, Leonard J., 177
Kerr, Howard, 67, 201
Kerr, James, 381, 386, 388
Kewer, Eleanor D., 331
Kiely, Robert, 417
Kiely, Timothy John, 329
Kilgour, Maggie, 426
Killen, Alice, 116
Kimbrough, Robert, 203, 206
Kirkpatrick, Larry, 109, 113
Klein, Jürgen, 58
Kleinfeld, Herbert L., 196
Klett, Dwight A., 435
Klossowski, Pierre, 365, 366, 371
Knight, Elizabeth C., 177
Knight, G. Wilson, 99
Knoepflmacher, U. C., 98, 392, 397
Kolmar, Wendy K, 123
Koshansky-Olienikov, Olga, 321
Kosok, Heinz, 294
Kossuth, Charlotte, 321
Kramer, Dale, 287
Krause, Sydney J., 76, 79, 81
Kreuzer, Helmut, 435
Kron, Wolfgang, 177
Kropf, David Glenn, 388
Krumholz, Linda, 302
Kullmann, Thomas, 287

Lackey, Kris, 294
Lamont, Claire, 43, 381
Lang, Alexander, 20
Lang, Cecil Y., 103
Lanier, Henry W., 121
Lant, Kathleen Margaret, 223
Lau, Beth, 74
Lawler, Donald, 415, 417, 418
Lawrence, D. H., 81, 234, 240
Lawrence, William, 83, 86
Leatherdale, Clive, 421

LeBrun, Annie, 371
Lee, Harriet, 214, 246
Leerssen, J. Th., 287
Leiber, Fritz, 276
Leider, Emily Wortis, 23
Leidner, Alan C., 373, 378
Lercangée, Francine, 313
Le Tellier, Robert Ignatius, 45, 388
Levine, George, 43, 392, 397
Levine, Paul, 77, 81
Lévy, Ellen, 131
Levy, Henry Mittle, Jr., 53
Lévy, Maurice, 52, 117, 119, 277, 283,
    332, 342
Lew, Joseph, 288
Lewis, Hanna B., 240
Lewis, Jayne Elizabeth, 247
Lewis, Paul, 154, 163, 173, 175, 340,
    342, 435
Lewis, Pericles, 427
Lewis, Roger, 185
Lewis, Wilmarth S., 437, 447
Liedke, Otto K., 435
Ligocki, Llewllyn, 10
Liljegren, S. B., 89
Lillyman, William J., 435
Lingus, Alphonso, 371
Lloyd Smith, Allan, 97, 175, 201, 252,
    287, 294, 397, 418, 446
Loe, Thomas, 113
London, April, 358
Lonsdale, Roger, 53
Loomis, Emerson R., 163
Looser, Devoney, 43
Lougy, Robert, 288
Lovecraft, H. P., 342, 447
Loveridge, Mark, 43
Low, Lisa, 59
Lowe, David, 321
Lozes, Jean, 288
Lundblad, Jane, 173, 176
Lupack, Barbara Tepa, 201
Lustig, T. J., 209

Mabbott, Maureen C., 331
Mabbott, Thomas Ollive, 331
MacAndrew, Elizabeth, 441, 447

MacDonald, D. L., 194, 259, 345, 348, 389, 390
MacDonald, David, 372, 378
Mack, Douglas S., 185, 186, 188, 189, 193, 381
Mack, Robert, 437, 440, 447
MacLachlan, Christopher, 255
MacMillan, Dougald, 163
MacPherson, Jay, 294
Maertz, Gregory, 131
Magill, Frank N., 57, 81
Magistrale, Tony, 216, 222, 223, 294, 342
Mahmoud, Fatma Moussa, 59
Maimin, E. A., 321
Mainville, Stephen, 342
Maixner, Paul, 417
Male, Roy, 334, 342
Mandel, Eli, 24, 32
Manning, Susan, 196
Manske, Eva, 313
Manzalaoui, Mahmoud, 59
Marchand, Ernest, 76
Margolyes, Miriam, 73
Mariconda, Steven J., 277
Marken, Jack W., 126
Markley, Arnold A., 126
Marshall, Peter H., 126, 131
Marshall, Tim, 397
Martin, Angus, 52
Martin, Carter W., 319
Martin, John, 81
Martin, Les, 345
Martin, Robert K., 176, 341
Marzials, Frank, 53
Massé, Michelle, 10
Masson, David, 396
Matheson, Neill, 209
Matlaw, Ralph E., 321
Matus, Jill, 298, 302
Maxwell, Richard, 113
Maynard, Temple James, 58, 151, 163
Mayo, Robert D., 117, 119, 145, 388
McAllister, Harold S., 371
McCardle, Arthur W., 374, 379
McClure, Charlotte S., 23
McCombs, Judith, 32
McConnochie, Arthur, 46

McCormack, W. J., 253
McCracken, David, 125
McElderry, Bruce R., Jr., 21, 23
McEvoy, Emma, 255
McFarland, Ronald E., 348
McGann, Jerome J., 84
McGlathery, James T., 178, 183
McGuire, Karen E., 288, 417
McIntyre, Clara F., 154, 163, 352, 358
McKay, Nellie Y., 298, 300, 302
McKillop, Alan D., 37, 45
McKinney, David, 44, 447
McLean, Robert C., 67
McLynn, Frank, 417
McMaster, R. D., 113
McMillan, Ann, 32
McNally, Raymond, 421, 426
McWhir, Anne, 390
Medlin, Dorothy, 358
Medovoi, M. I., 321
Mehew, Ernest, 416
Mehl, Dieter, 233, 240
Melada, Ivan, 253
Mellor, Anne K., 389, 396, 397
Menhennet, Alan, 375, 379
Mergenthal, Silvia, 183, 193
Merivale, Patricia, 209
Mersereau, John, Jr., 329
Meyer, Jeffrey, 412
Meyer, Michel, 259
Michasiw, Kim Ian, 99, 103, 403, 406
Michelson, Bruce F., 313
Mighall, Robert, 109, 113, 426
Milazzo, Lee, 312, 313
Milbank, Alison, 74, 97, 113, 253, 349, 350, 426
Milder, Robert, 290
Miles, Robert, 103, 294, 352, 358
Miller, Chuck, 217, 221, 222, 223, 224
Miller, D. A., 98
Miller, Elizabeth, 425, 426
Miller, J. Hillis, 105
Millgate, Jane, 381, 388
Mills, Howard, 406
Mishima, Yukio, 13
Moers, Ellen, 397
Mogen, David, 81, 319, 342
Monaghan, David, 42

Monroe, Judson T., 288
Mooney, Stephen L., 342
Moorman, Mary, 5
Morgan, Chris, 288
Morgan, Rebecca, 411
Mornin, Edward, 430
Morrill, David F., 348
Morris, Roy, 61, 67
Morrison, Michael A., 222
Morrison, Toni, 302
Moskal, Jeanne, 390
Moskowitz, Sam, 390
Mowl, Timothy, 447
Mudrick, Marvin, 44
Muller, C. H., 98
Müller-Seidel, Walter, 177
Mulholland, Honor, 418
Mulman, Lisa Naomi, 259
Mulvey-Roberts, Marie, 52, 58, 88, 89,
    119, 328, 370
Murphy, John V., 403, 406
Murphy, Peter T., 381, 382, 388
Murray, E. B., 352, 358
Myers, Mitzi, 131

Nabokov, Vladimir, 412
Nadel, Ira B., 90
Nandris, Grigore, 427
Napier, Elizabeth, 79, 103
Negus, Kenneth, 183, 379
Nehring, Wolfgang, 183
Neider, Charles, 196
Nettles, Elsa, 209
Neufeld, Mary Diana, 163
Newlin, Paul A., 176
Newman, Beth, 69
Nichols, Nina da Vinci, 74
Nikolopoulou, Anastasia, 288
Nisly, Paul W., 319
Nitchie, Elizabeth, 163
Noble, Andrew, 417, 418
Nodelman, Perry, 313
Northey, Margot, 25, 32
Norton, Rictor, 1, 8, 34, 44, 53, 139,
    151, 241, 247, 351, 359
Null, Jack, 288
Nussbaum, Felicity, 357

Oakes, David A., 277
Oaks, Susan, 123
Oates, Joyce Carol, 24, 31, 270, 314,
    413, 418
O'Connor, Flannery, 318, 319
O'Dea, Gregory, 396, 397
Oost, Regina B., 288
Orr, Marilyn, 388
Ostrom, John Ward, 334
Otto, Linda, 435
Otto, Peter, 347

Page, Norman, 90, 105
Paley, Morton D., 398
Palmer, Louis H., III, 319
Palombo, Donald, 294
Parker, Patricia, 81
Parreaux, André, 59, 259
Parrington, Vernon, 81
Partin, Bruce Lynn, 163
Passage, Charles, 329
Patell, Cyrus R. K., 290
Patrick, Barbara, 124
Pattee, Fred Lewis, 76, 77, 81, 124
Patten, Robert L., 105
Paulhan, Jean, 365
Paulin, Roger, 430, 435
Pearce, Roy Harvey, 166
Pearsall, Anthony B., 277
Pearson, Norman Holmes, 166
Peacock, Thomas Love, 406
Peck, Louis F., 158, 163, 255, 259
Peck, Walter E., 103, 399, 406
Pennell, Melissa McFarland, 23
Penzoldt, Peter, 270, 271, 277
Perry, Ruth, 5
Peters, Catherine, 90
Peterson, Linda H., 69
Pharr, Mary, 218, 223
Phillips, Walter, 114
Philp, Mark, 126
Pires, Maria Laura Bettencourt, 58
Pitcher, E. W., 5, 146
Plasa, Carl, 299, 300, 302
Pochmann, Henry A., 196
Poger, Sidney, 342
Pollin, Burton R., 89, 131, 331
Pollitt, Irene, 8

Pommerenke, Dieter, 321
Pope, Bertha Clark, 62, 67
Pope, Rebecca A., 193
Porte, Joel, 128, 129, 131, 401, 406
Poston, Lawrence, 89
Poulton, Cody, 228, 229, 232
Powers, Sharon B., 406
Praz, Mario, 437
Price, Kenneth M., 66
Price, L. M., 52
Pringle, David, 59, 252, 258, 282, 288,
   342, 427
Pritchard, Allan, 109, 114
Proffer, Carl R., 321
Punter, David, 114, 164, 193, 210, 247,
   253, 259, 387, 396, 426
Pykett, Lyn, 74, 98

Railo, Eino, 352
Rajan, Tilottama, 390, 406
Rance, Nick, 98
Ranger, Paul, 163
Rao, Eleonora, 32
Rathburn, Robert C., 73
Redden, Sister Mary Maurita, 146
Redekop, Magdalene, 193
Reed, James, 381
Reichardt, Mary R., 121, 124
Reid, S. W., 76
Reierstad, Keith Brown, 98
Reiman, Donald H., 99, 403, 404, 406
Reino, Joseph, 223
Reynolds, Aidan, 282
Reynolds, David S., 262, 263, 264, 265,
   267, 269
Reynolds, Frederic Mansel, 380
Richter, David H., 5, 74
Ridgely, J. V., 269
Rieger, James, 128, 129, 131, 344, 348,
   390, 401, 406
Ringe, Donald A., 81, 174, 176, 201,
   210, 332, 342
Rizzo, Betty, 131
Roberts, Adam, 59
Roberts, Bette B., 37, 44, 46, 247
Roberts, Marilyn, 44
Robertson, Eric, 59
Robertson, Fiona, 164, 381, 386, 388

Robertson, J. Logie, 381
Robillard, Douglas, 123
Robinson, Charles E., 389, 390
Rogers, Deborah, 351, 352, 359
Rogers, Katharine M., 411
Rombes, Nicholas, Jr., 81
Romero, Christiane Zehl, 184
Ronald, Ann, 74, 110, 114
Rosengarten, Herbert, 69
Rosenthal, Bernard, 82
Rosowski, Susan J., 32
Rossetti, William Michael, 344
Roth, Phyllis, 427
Rothberg, Abraham, 412
Rubens, Phillip M., 67
Russell, Sharon A., 223
Russett, Margaret, 359
Rust, Richard Dilworth, 196
Ryan, Steven T., 294
Ryder, Frank G., 429

Saar, Doreen Alvarez, 363
Sabor, Peter, 437
Sadleir, Michael, 37, 38, 40, 42, 43, 44,
   45, 47, 143
Sage, Victor, 97, 114, 201, 252, 253,
   287, 294, 369, 397, 418, 426, 446
Saintsbury, George, 37, 44
Sale, William R., Jr., 69
Sammons, Jeffrey L., 372, 375, 379
Sanders, Andrew, 10
Sanders, Joe, 259
Sanders, Scott P., 81, 319, 342
Saposnik, Irving S., 418
Savoy, Eric, 176, 210, 341
Saxton, Ruth O., 313
Sayers, Dorothy L., 91
Scher, Helene, 429
Scherf, Kathleen, 194, 345, 389, 390
Schlaffer, Heinz, 435
Schleifer, Ronald, 319
Schlueter, June, 364
Schlueter, Paul, 364
Schmitt, Cannon, 359
Schofield, Mary Anne, 363
Scholten, Willem, 288
Schor, Esther, 396
Schroeder, Natalie E., 11, 46, 47

Schultz, David E., 61, 67, 277
Scott, Sir Walter, 194, 398
Scott-Kilvert, Diana, 390
Seaver, Richard, 365
Sedgwick, Eve Kosofsky, 194, 359
Seed, David, 406, 407, 418, 426, 427
Segebrecht, Wulf, 177
Seidensticker, Edward, 225
Seneleck, Lawrence, 371
Senf, Carol, 427
Sgard, Jean, 119
Shaffer, E. S., 59
Shaw, Harry E., 388
Shaw, S. Bradley, 124
Sheen, Erica, 425
Shelden, Pamela Jacobs, 210, 342
Sherburn, George, 125
Shetty, Nalini V., 294
Showalter, Elaine, 74, 314
Shroyer, Frederick, 249, 349
Siegel, Adrienne, 269
Simmons, Clare A., 426
Skarda, Patricia L, 1, 344, 348, 412
Sklepowich, E. A., 210
Slater, Michael, 105
Small, Helen, 89
Smith, Amy Elizabeth, 288
Smith, Andrew, 426
Smith, Johanna M., 390, 398
Smith, Margaret, 69
Smith, Nelson C., 194, 359
Smith, Susan Belasco, 66
Snow, Ollye Tine, 320
Sohmapp, Friedrich, 177
Solomon, Barbara H., 301, 302
Souther, Randy, 314
Spear, Jeffrey L., 427
Spector, Robert D., 1, 138, 139, 142,
    153, 249, 255, 361, 364
Spehner, Norbert, 418
Spence, G. W., 105
Spencer, Jane, 247
Spiller, Robert E., 262
Springer, Haskell S., 196
Stableford, Brian, 59, 280, 281, 282, 334,
    342, 427
Stafford, Fiona, 390
Stafford, William T., 290

Staines, David, 31
Stanton, Judith Philips, 408, 411
Stark, Cruce, 67
Stark, Susanne, 145
St. Armand, Barton Levi, 176, 277
Stein, William Bysshe, 67, 176
Steinmann, Martin Jr., 73
Stern, Philip Van Doren, 278, 282
Stevenson, Jane, 43, 143, 164, 287, 328,
    358, 381
Stevenson, John Allen, 428, 447
Stevenson, Robert Louis, 418
Stewart, Randall, 166, 176
Stoddart, Helen, 253
Stone, Harry, 114
Stoneman, Patsy, 69, 74
Storey, Graham, 105
Stout, Janis, 269
Stroupe, John H., 240
Sucksmith, Harvey P., 91, 114
Sullivan, Garrett A. Jr., 132
Sultana, Donald, 162
Summers, Montague, 34, 37, 45, 49, 52,
    100, 103, 116, 119, 140, 142, 146,
    151, 153, 352, 358, 359, 437, 444
Sutcliffe, Tom, 372
Sutherland, John, 381, 384, 388
Svilpis, J. E., 58
Swearingen, Roger G., 414, 418
Sweeney, Gerard M., 210
Sweetser, Wesley D., 281, 282
Swinburne, Algernon Charles, 103
Switzer, Richard, 348

Takada, Mamoru, 19
Taylor, Jenny Bourne, 98
Taylor, Ronald, 177
Thacker, Christopher, 5
Thalmann, Marianne, 430
Thiergard, Ulrich, 379
Thomas, Ronald R., 415, 418
Thomas, William, 260
Thoms, Peter, 98
Thompson, G. R., 131, 201, 331, 338,
    343, 406, 430
Thompson, James, 132
Thompson, Teresa, 223
Thomson, Douglass H., 5

Thorburg, Raymond, 210
Thorp, Willard, 164, 262
Tienhooven, Marie-José, 260
Tilby, Michael, 119
Tillotson, Kathleen, 105
Tinkler-Villani, Valeria, 43, 143, 164, 287, 328, 358
Todd, Janet, 360, 390
Todorov, Tzvetan, 64, 204, 210
Tofanelli, John, 74
Tompkins, J.M.S., 119, 241, 409, 411
Touitou, Béatrice, 52
Tournebize, Casilde, 74
Tracy, Ann B., 5, 45, 146, 260
Tracy, Robert, 114, 249, 253
Traill, H. D., 378
Trainer, James, 361, 362, 364, 430, 435
Treder, Uta, 375, 379
Trimpi, Helen, 294
Troyansky, David G., 371
Tuite, Clara, 260
Tulloch, Graham, 381
Twitchell, James B., 75
Tymms, Ralph, 184, 435
Tymn, Marshall B., 435, 436

Underwood, Tim, 217, 221, 222, 223, 224
Utterson, Sarah Elizabeth Brown, 397

Vaid, Krishna B., 203, 210
Valentine, Mark, 282
Van Munching, Paul, 345
Van Spanckeren, Kathryn, 32
Van Thal, Herbert, 83, 91
Varma, Devendra P., 34, 45, 46, 47, 58, 59, 99, 126, 153, 241, 249, 260, 279, 349, 350, 352, 360
Vaughan, David K., 222
Veeder, William, 201, 210, 398, 414, 415, 417, 418, 419
Veler, Richard, 341
Verhoeven, W. M., 164
Versluys, Kristiaan, 313
Vincent, Sybil Korff, 30, 32
Voller, Jack G., 176, 333, 343, 360
Voloshin, Beverly R., 77, 82
Von der Lippe, George B., 184

von Frank, Albert, 175
von Wiese, Benno, 372

Wagenknecht, Edward, 60, 121, 196
Wahba, Magdi, 59
Wainhouse, Austryn, 365
Wallace, Tara Ghoshal, 44
Waller, A. R., 358
Waller, G. F., 314
Waller, Gregory A., 348
Wandrei, Donald, 270
Ward, Lynd, 20
Warfel, Harry R., 82
Watkins, Daniel, 260, 289
Watt, Ian P., 447
Watt, James, 132, 447
Watt, William Whyte, 141, 142, 146
Watts, Steven, 82
Waugh, Robert, 277
Wegelin, Christof, 203
Wein, Toni, 75, 447
Weisenburger, Steven, 296, 298, 302
Weissman, Judith, 428
Wellek, Rene, 177
Wells, Larry P., 436
Werner, S., 371
Wescott, W. W., 89
Westbrook, Perry, 124
Wexman, Virginia Wright, 415, 419
Whatley, John, 407
Whitlark, James, 260
Wiggins, Martin, 151
Wiggins, Robert A., 67
Wilcox, Angela, 252
Willen, Gerald, 202, 206
Williams, Raymond, 105
Willson, A. Leslie, 184
Wilson, A. N., 421
Wilson, Angus, 105
Wilson, Carol Shiner, 411
Wilson, Lisa M., 260
Wilt, Judith, 240, 381, 388
Winter, Douglas E., 223
Wischhusen, Stephen, 151, 255
Witherington, Paul, 82
Wolf, Leonard, 249, 389, 412, 421
Wolff, Cynthia G., 360

Wolff, Robert Lee, 88, 89
Wolfreys, Julian, 83
Woolf, Virginia, 75, 205, 210
Wordsworth, Jonathan, 151, 344
Worrall, David, 164
Worth, George J., 11
Wright, Elizabeth, 184
Wright, T. R., 253

Wu, Duncan, 410
Wymer, Thomas L., 68

Yarbro, Chelsea Quinn, 218, 223

Zablotny, Elaine, 211
Zolbrod, Leon M., 12, 13, 19
Zytaruk, George J., 240

ABOUT THE EDITORS AND CONTRIBUTORS

CAROL MARGARET DAVISON is Assistant Professor of English at the University of Windsor, Ontario. She is the editor of *Bram Stoker's Dracula: Sucking through the Century, 1897–1997*. Her book *Anti-Semitism and British Gothic Fiction* will be published in 2002.

DAVID DUDLEY is Associate Professor, Department of Literature and Philosophy, Georgia Southern University, Statesboro, Georgia. He is the author of *My Father's Shadow: Intergenerational Conflict in African American Men's Autobiography* and essays on African-American fiction.

SUSAN ALLEN FORD is Professor of English, Division of Languages and Literature, Delta State University, Cleveland, Mississippi. She has published articles on Jane Austen and detective fiction.

FREDERICK S. FRANK is Professor Emeritus of English, Allegheny College, Meadville, Pennsylvania. He is the author of two other books published by Greenwood Press, *The Poe Encyclopedia* (with Tony Magistrale) and *Through the Pale Door: A Guide to and through the American Gothic*.

MICHAEL GAMER is Assistant Professor of English, University of Pennsylvania, Philadelphia. He is the author of *Romanticism and the Gothic: Genre, Reception, and Canon Formation* (2000), as well as articles published in *PMLA*, *ELH*, *Studies in Romanticism*, and *Novel: A Forum on Fiction*.

JOHN HUMMA is Professor of English, Department of Literature and Philosophy, Georgia Southern University, Statesboro, Georgia. He is the author of *Metaphor and Meaning in D.H. Lawrence's Later Novels* and articles on Hardy, Fowles, James, and Lawrence.

S.T. JOSHI is an independent scholar in New York City. His books on H.P. Lovecraft include *H.P. Lovecraft: Four Decades of Criticism* and *H.P. Lovecraft: A Life*. For Greenwood Press, he has written *Ambrose Bierce: An Annotated Bibliography of Primary Sources* (with David E. Schultz) and has forthcoming *The H.P. Lovecraft Encyclopedia* (also with David E. Schultz).

TOM LLOYD is Professor of English, Department of Literature and Philosophy, Georgia Southern University, Statesboro, Georgia. He is the author of a book on the British novel, *Crises of Realism*, and articles on Dickens, Carlyle, and Schiller.

TONY MAGISTRALE is Professor of English, University of Vermont, Burlington. He is the author (with Sidney Poger) of *Poe's Children: Connections between Tales of Terror and Detection* and the editor of *The Dark Descent: Essays Defining Stephen King's Horrorscape* (Greenwood Press).

MARIE MULVEY-ROBERTS is Senior Lecturer in Literary Studies, the University of the West of England, Bristol. She is the author of *Gothic Immortals: The Fiction of the Brotherhood of the Rosy Cross* and the editor of *The Handbook to Gothic Literature*.

DOUGLASS H. THOMSON is Associate Professor of English, Department of Literature and Philosophy, Georgia Southern University, Statesboro, Georgia. He is the author of articles on English Romanticism and the novel and of the forthcoming critical and bibliographical entry on "American Gothic Fiction" in *The Handbook of American Popular Culture* (Greenwood Press).

JACK G. VOLLER is Associate Professor of English, Southern Illinois University at Edwardsville. He is the author of *The Supernatural Sublime: The Metaphysics of Terror in Anglo-American Romanticism*. He maintains an important Web site on Gothic studies, *The Literary Gothic*.